TWO TOWNS GO TO WAR

Irlam and Cadishead's Part in the Second World War 1939-1945

Volume 2

Pete Thomas and Neil Drum

Published in the United Kingdom by Thomas-Drum Publications

First printed March 2014

ISBN: 978-0-9564489-1-0

CONTENTS

MARCH 1944 continued

The following members of D Company, 42nd Battalion, Home Guard passed their proficiency badge tests to earn the right to wear the red diamond and bar: Corporals Leonard Tupling and Arthur Barnshaw; Lance Corporal Albert White; Privates C. Farrington, D. Blundell, John Phillips, Sidney Hampson and Sydney Mann.

The Rixton-with-Glazebrook Victory Fund Committee held its first meeting on Tuesday, 21st March at the day school. Reverend Harold Firth was elected chairman, Mr J. Farrington, treasurer and Mr B. Eaves, secretary. During the meeting Mr H. Lewis asked for a definition of 'members of HM Forces' to whom the fund was to be applied, and was informed that this was intended to include only those serving in the Navy, Army and Air Force. George Wright was appointed to organise a household goods sale, which was to be held shortly at the social club room. Other schemes planned included a field day during the coming summer, and a house-to-house collection.

The largest Fire Guard exercise to be held in the district (at least up to this date) took place at Cadishead on Wednesday evening, 22nd March. The four sectors concerned, numbers 922, 923, 924 and 925, all operated from one sector point at the Cadishead Co-operative Hall. In all, 21 incidents were staged, 11 for fire guard reinforcements and ten for NFS assistance. The fire guard reinforcing times were excellent and the ten incidents involving the NFS were dealt with promptly and capably, and co-operation between the Fire Guard and NFS was excellent. At the inquest that followed the exercise, great praise was heard from all the incident and sector umpires and, for the first time during these types of exercise, NFS personnel were present and took an active part in the inquest. Mr J.C. Booth (fire guard area captain) and Section Leader Jamieson (NFS) were singled out for praise by the fire guard officer. Exercises under the Fire Guard Plan had previously taken place at the three sectors in the Higher Irlam area, operating from Arthur Lowe's hut on Ferryhill Road, and the two sectors operating from the Higher Irlam Co-operative Hall. Harry Crawford and Harold Roberts, and other senior officers of the Fire Guard, were pleased with the efficiency of all taking part. Throughout the whole of the district, Fire Guard Plan exercises had been completed for both residential and business premises. The next exercise would be the regional test exercise which was to be staged within the next three or four weeks.

No. 147 unit of the WJAC, commanded by Unit Commander M.J. Martin and Unit Adjutant Jean Patterson, was visited by three members of the Royal Canadian Air Force (RCAF): Flying Officers Parkinson, Marcott, DFC and Moroney, DFM. The WJAC cadets listened to talks on flying duties and life in Canada. As a result of the close ties which were developed from this meeting, officers of the RCAF regularly visited the unit on the cadets' parade days (Fridays and Sundays) at Irlam Council School. WJAC cadets received instruction in Morse code and navigation from

Canadian experts, and other fields covered included drill and first aid. An appeal was made for volunteers in late March for girls between the ages of 14 and 20, who were invited to enrol on either of the parade nights.

On the night of 24th/25th March 200 Allied prisoners of war escaped from Stalag Luft III, in Germany. The escape plan, which had taken a year to complete, and involved the digging of three escape tunnels, Tom, Dick and Harry, would become famous as the Great Escape and was immortalised in a film of the same name. Pilot Officer Billy Dean had been placed in the camp only one month before the breakout. Although he wasn't among those chosen to escape (the escapees had been identified many months before) he was involved in the preparations, helping create the fake passes for the airmen selected for the escape. Billy described his involvement during an interview with the authors: *So with that they sent me to the Great Escape Camp, Stalag Luft III and I was in there. I think I'm the last survivor of the Great Escape Camp, I think there might be just one more person alive. There I had a really wonderful time, it wasn't long after I'd been there when the escape happened and the last of the troops that had got out were murdered. Fifty were murdered by being shot in the head and a few were returned. The commandant was a very nice man, the commandant and me got on very well, strangely enough because I wasn't a very senior rank but he liked what I was interested in, in fact Shakespeare and poetry. He liked Pope and Dryden and the great poets, Cowper and Shelley and we used to discuss Shakespearean plays, you know King Lear and the other plays and he was a lovely man. I made use of that time in prisoner of war camp, I studied, I used to sit by the fire pool and study the various small creatures that lived in the fire pool, and at that time I could mention 30 or 40 different types of beetle and amoeba and various things, and so I divorced myself in that respect from the war. I helped Bertie Barrett who was a chappie in the escape who was going blind, I helped him with making the colours because having a degree in botany I knew the colours that plants could give, for instance white colours, blue colours, red colours, because he was making the Hausreise passes.* Billy, along with other surviving men from Stalag Luft III, was invited to the London film premiere of *The Great Escape* on 20th June 1963.

Sixty cadets of 292 (Eccles) Squadron, ATC, including ten cadets from the Irlam detached flight, visited a northern aerodrome on Saturday, 25th March. They inspected aircraft in various stages of construction and later in flight.

Irlam's £100,000 target set for Salute the Soldier week (planned for 17th to 24th June), was based on the cost of transporting a division from Irlam to Berlin. At a meeting at Irlam Central School on Monday, 27th March Councillor Albert J. Keal, chairman of the local Savings Committee, stressed the importance of additional vigour during the week in order to reach the target. Councillor Owen, chairman of the Council, praised the efforts already made, but reminded attendees that they should be compared with the efforts made by the soldiers at the front, which extended from the coastline of England to the defences of Africa, Italy and the Far East. He urged that giving or lending during Salute the Soldier week would only be a sacrifice when it involved money which was required for one's own needs. The honorary publicity officer, Mr T. Goddard, outlined the arrangements for the week. A grand parade was planned and the opening speech would take place on the Sunday, followed by a display of battle tactics by the local companies of the 42nd County of Lancaster Battalion, Home Guard. Mr H. Wilde, assistant commissioner, made an appeal to group secretaries, and urged them to work harder than they had ever done before to make the week a success. He knew from his service during the First World War and the present war just what it meant to the soldier to have efficient and sufficient material with which to fight. During the course of the meeting it was decided that group secretaries should fix individual street targets.

Another group of Home Guard men from D Company were successful with their examinations for proficiency in all sections of Home Guard training, including general knowledge, rifle, 36M grenade, submachine-gun, battle craft and map reading: Lance Corporal Henry Jackman, Corporal Ernest Lacey, Privates John A. Howarth, Frederick W. Thornton, William Henry Smith, John Dixon, Harold Whalley, David Henry Hurst, W. Kennedy, John Bird, F. Thomas (Frederick or Francis) and S. Deakin. Many of these candidates were the wrong side of middle-aged, for example, Private Deakin passed through his various subjects with first class honours at the age of 58. One of these Home Guard men, Henry Jackman, had served in the Royal Engineers in 1940. Henry was born in 1918 and resided with his wife, Mrs Jackman at 5 Dixon Street, Irlam. Following his discharge from the Army he joined the Home Guard on 22nd January 1941 and served in 1 Platoon of D Company.

On Wednesday, 29th March the male members of the Centenary Methodist Church, Glazebrook, staged a variety concert at Cadishead Senior School. The concert, given by the Bolton Civil Defence Variety Company, was in aid of two funds: the Rixton-with-Glazebrook Forces Canteen Fund and the War Comforts Fund.

On Thursday, 30th March Corporal Gerald Bannister of the Reconnaissance Regiment married Gladys Brown, the only daughter of Catherine Brown (nee Coward) and the late Tom Brown of Adswood, New Moss Road, Cadishead. The ceremony took place at St Mary's Church, Cadishead, and Gerald's brother, Harry, who was serving with the Royal Marine Commandos, was the best man. Gladys' brother, Tom Brown, had been seriously wounded in the fighting for the Mareth Line, Tunisia in 1943 and, at the time of the wedding, was recovering in a Liverpool hospital. After the reception Gerald and Gladys went to visit Tom in hospital and Gladys distributed wedding cake to her brother's comrades in hospital.

Examinations for the St John preliminary first aid certificates were held for WJAC members, at Irlam Council School on Friday, 31st March. Certificates were awarded to Sergeant J. Hodge, Corporal Y. Micklewright and volunteers M.J. Holt, G. Motley, D. Barrow, F.M. Kerslake, M.E. Wrigley, J.P. Cragg, J.M. Borrino, J. Alldred, J. Sharpe, I. Jones, I.A. Dawson, H.M. Longbottom, M. Hindley and O. Shaw.

Private Henry Jackman, Royal Engineers, and later, Home Guard

Local men found themselves in far flung parts of the World. One such man was Leading Aircraftman Frank Barrow. Frank was a wireless operator in the Royal Air Force, who was stationed in Sierra Leone in West Africa. He also spent some time in the RAF Regiment. Frank was born in Cadishead and resided at 79 Victory Road, Cadishead. After the war, on 29th June 1946 at St Mary's Church, Cadishead, he married Elizabeth Simpson. Elizabeth was a native of Bolton who had served in the Women's Auxiliary Air Force (WAAF) as an officer's batwoman.

Sergeant James Henry 'Harry' Behenna, Royal Air Force Volunteer Reserve, suffered frostbite during a bombing raid on Nuremburg on the night of 31st March. Harry was the rear gunner on a Lancaster bomber of 115 Squadron, Bomber Group No.3, based at RAF Witchford, Cambridgeshire, and this was his first operational flight. During the flight, the bomber was attacked by German fighters, which caused a fire in the bomb bay and the rear turret, putting the turret's heating and oxygen systems out of action. The skipper gave the order for the crew to don their parachutes. At the time the aircraft was at 19,000 feet and the temperature was 3°C. Harry left the turret and went to the escape hatch. The aircraft was corkscrewing violently to lose the enemy fighters, which made it difficult for him to clip on his portable oxygen supply. He passed out several times, but eventually he managed to get the oxygen supply working and returned to his turret, where he clipped back onto the main oxygen supply. He noticed his fingers turning numb after he got back into the turret, but continued to man the guns until the aircraft touched down at Witchford, nearly five hours later. His turret was white with frost. He reported to sick bay and was treated for frostbite for five days before being cleared to fly.

On 19th April he went on his second sortie to bomb the railway yards at Rouen in France. While over the target the electrics failed in his turret and he lost all heating. The aircraft was at 13,300 feet and the temperature was -10°C. He was treated for frostbite at RAF Hospital, Ely and, although he was keen to return to flying duties he would not be cleared for them until the war had ended. He was given ground duties and was later promoted to station warrant officer.

Harry was born in Manchester on 18th July 1906 and was raised in Hollins Green. At some point he moved into the district, where, in June 1933, he married Esther Annie Stephenson and they resided on Liverpool Road, Cadishead, before moving to 10 Green Lane, Cadishead. Before the war Harry worked as a crane driver. He joined the local Home Guard on 5th June 1940, serving in 5 Platoon, D Company and later with H Company. He enlisted into the Royal Air Force Volunteer Reserve on 19th April 1943, but, next day, he was transferred to reserve. He was called up for service on 26th July 1943.

Leading Aircraftman Frank Barrow, Royal Air Force

Leading Aircraftman Frank Barrow, Royal Air Force
Sierra Leone

Leading Aircraftman Frank Barrow, Royal Air Force
Sierra Leone

Elizabeth Simpson (later Barrow), Women's Auxiliary Air Force

Sergeant Harry Behenna, RAFVR

The separation of the Fire Guard from the ARP service resulted in the Fire Prevention Committee paying increased charges for the Fire Guard organisation. When the rate was levied 12 months earlier the County Council had included in the county rate provision for Fire Guard expenditure in the county districts. The County Council had repaid the provision they made to the county districts, on the basis of 0.66 of a penny. *You will be aware that during the past year there has been a considerable extension of the activities of the Fire Guard organisation, and to provide these facilities it is, of course, necessary to incur certain expenditure. Actually, the Fire Prevention Committee have required from us less than was anticipated, as the Council's contribution to the exchequer in respect of the fire service is £176 less than was estimated.*

Corporal James N. Howes wrote to the *Guardian: India calling again with more ideas of post-war planning of Irlam and Cadishead. Maybe I'm shouting into thin air or maybe I'm not, but I feel that I must have a little say in the planning of the town I was born in. Here is the idea I have in mind, knowing I have the backing of a number of the boys out here, whom I am sure must be thinking on the same lines as I am. How about a column in the Guardian for suggestions from the boys on their ideas of what they would like to see done after we have finished with this little argument? I am sure there are numbers of them who would like to air their views if only they had the lead. After all, we are the people who are going to help in the re-building of the country and I really think we should have a say in these things. Perhaps the idea has been in your mind before now or maybe you haven't the space in your paper – I don't know, but I should like to see the answer to this if it is at all possible, please, so here's hoping the idea cottons on like I should like to see it.*

In reply the editor of the *Guardian* stated: *In the March 11th issue of the Guardian, Onlooker asked men and women serving in the Forces to send in their views on post-war planning. This issue of the Guardian has, naturally, not yet reached India.*

Private Francis Norman Lennie, Royal Army Service Corps, serving in North Africa, wrote to his friends at home to describe a visit to a casbah in Algiers: *This letter I am about to write will most certainly be of interest to you if you have already seen the film Algiers. I think most people will have, as it is quite an old film now. Well, I have actually seen the buildings and roofs where that film was taken – but, to begin at the beginning! Bill and myself went on an organised tour of the casbah last weekend, on our half-day off. Under normal circumstances, the casbah is strictly out of bounds to all American and British military personnel, and I can tell you, I wouldn't wish to go alone, anyhow! We arrived at the appointed place in town, to find a party of about 30 people, so we joined in. The crowd was chiefly composed of WACs, American and British soldiers and RAF men, our guide being an English-speaking Frenchman. We started off in a trolley-bus, the first stop being the Roman Catholic cathedral, a magnificent building. We went inside and it was very beautiful, but not like any other I have been in at home. There was a service on, so really I did not have a fair chance to look around as much as I should have liked to do. From there we mounted the trolley bus again, and off we went to visit two old palaces, but don't be misled when I say palaces, for they were not what I guess you would imagine them to be. It was the history that to me was the most intriguing. Some horrible crimes were committed in them in the old slave trading* days. Both places were built by the Turkish Pashas, heads of the slave trade in those days. The palaces are closed in on every side by houses almost touching each other. The squalor outside is unbelievable, though one gets used to that sort of thing here. Inside there is the usual courtyard open to the sky, but let me explain – all the old houses, built before the French invaded, get their light from the inside, not the outside, like at home. There are two windows outside, and all the doors to the room face the courtyard, in the centre of which is a fountain, encircled by a tiled floor. The first floor of the palace was for the men, the second floor was the harem, where all the wives of the Pasha were, and on the top floor was transacted all the Pasha's business of state, etc. The women were then, as they are now, veiled to everyone except their husband, but these days they seem to be relaxing that idea somewhat, for they take their veils off at the cinema, for instance. After leaving here, we went in the bus right to the top of the casbah, which, by the way, means fort. I believe we went through the fort itself, still inhabited by soldiers. Then we had a look through the military museum, all swords, daggers and the usual things one expects to see there. Our next stop was at the mosque, but before I describe this, I will tell you a little about the religion. All the people are believers in Mohammed, as you know, and there are five times every day when the people can worship – sunrise, mid-morning, mid-day, afternoon and sunset, and a good Mohammedan goes at least once a day. The only women who are allowed to worship in the main part of the mosque are those who have been to Mecca, and there are only about 12 in the whole of this city. Inside the mosque it is absolutely bare, except for a plain altar, which faces Mecca. The people come in, go to a fountain at the other end of the mosque, wash their hands, face and feet, and then take off their footwear (I say that because they wear anything from army boots to an old sack) and go on to the mats facing the altar. Here they kneel, and begin to worship with head down to the mat, and arms outstretched – up again, down again, and so they go on. Mohammed, it is understood, states that the prayer must be more physical than anything else, and believe me, do they carry it out! From there, we came into real contact with the casbah. The people who live within its walls are Berbers. People downcast by Mohammed, must never prosper; therefore, being believers, they don't try, and believe me, it is quite right and true to their religion to live in such a way. The women are like all Arab women, veiled, but they are branded with a blue mark on the forehead, between the eyes, that is done when they become women. We were warned by our guide that we must keep together, even these days, for people have been known to disappear into the casbah, and leave no trace whatsoever. I can quite believe it too! The film Algiers doesn't even give a true conception of it, and it's bad enough, I believe, although I haven't seen the film myself. Walking behind us was a couple of Military Police, so being well escorted we started off, walking downhill the whole of the time. Steps, steps and more steps. Streets so narrow that you could touch both walls with your hands. The stench is horrible. Small, low doors, peeping faces. You pass an open door – it's a haircutter cum dentist! He's cutting hair, and on the floor are teeth. You look up, heads bob back from the flat roof. A beggar sits cross-legged on the floor, you almost tread on him. You pass a dingy café, you look through the door, down the steps, thick smoke, and dim shapes sat drinking wine. A chatter of Arabic, a recess in the wall, a box of dates, and Arabs sat cross-legged. Such filth is truly unbelievable, but then anything, yes anything, can be believed when you see it. Murders can easily be a matter of course to these people, it all seems so possible and natural when you are there. Then, round the corner and into civilisation again in

an instant, trams people and air. Such was my afternoon out. I hope you like it – I did!!
Francis was born in the district in 1918, the son of Albert E. and Hilda Lennie (nee Atherton) of 82 Liverpool Road, Cadishead. He joined the Home Guard on 6th June 1940, serving as Private 306 in 3 Platoon of D Company, before being called up into the Army on 5th March 1941. His father, Albert, was the chief steward of Zone 3 (Cadishead Central) of the Irlam and Cadishead Traders' Salvage Scheme.

APRIL

The massive preparations for the Normandy landings, planned for June, required the Allies to gather together the necessary ships required to transport the infantry across the English Channel. Landing Craft 180 was one of the ships called back from operations in the Mediterranean to take part in the invasion. Lawrie Cottam, on board Landing Craft 180, described the journey and preparations: *Whilst in Gibraltar, thinking we would be home in a few days, we all bought oranges and very green bananas. We set sail from Gibraltar and headed west, miles and miles out to sea. I thought we were going back to America. What we were really doing was making a great detour of the Bay of Biscay, to avoid the U-boats and torpedo boats that were based on the French coast. Finally we turned and headed for the English Channel. But a terrific storm broke out. We were low on fuel and water. We had no ballast whatsoever as we were a flat-bottomed vessel. We were all struggling to even keep on course. After a while, the leading craft flashed a signal for us to alter course and head for Milfordhaven, for shelter. As soon as we got in the lee of the Welsh mainland, things quietened down and we limped into Milfordhaven. We were all glad to tie up and get a night's sleep. The next day we discussed what we could do with all the oranges and bananas as they had started to ripen in the heat of our mess deck. So we decided to go ashore and give them to the children on the streets. Some of the children had never seen a banana or an orange, but they were highly delighted to have them. After sheltering in Milfordhaven until the weather improved, we set sail. Our next port of call was up the River Humber, into King George's dock in Hull. Two ladies came aboard; a mother and her daughter called Alice. They were gun fitters. We, as gunners, were instructed to help them with the heavier parts of the guns. Alice asked me when I had last washed my dirty overalls and I explained that they had never been washed. We did not have the facilities on board the 'sardine tin'. Her mother then invited me to their home, so that I could have a bath and they could wash my clothes. There was no funny business, they were very kind, friendly, decent people. The people in Hull were as kind as any we ever met in our travels. We repaid them by obtaining some rations; things that they just could not get hold of. We were sad when we had to leave Hull. Our next port of call was a small fishing jetty at a place called Invergordon on the Murray Firth, up in the highlands of Scotland. To be honest, we all thought it was a dump. It did nothing but drizzle that kind of small rain that soaks you through in no time, but we were soon to get more water than we bargained for. After we had been in Invergordon about two weeks, the engineer went ashore one night and didn't come back. At least that's what we all thought, but he did come back about midnight. He was blind drunk. He went down to the engine room and opened the sea cocks before getting into his bunk fully dressed. All of a sudden there was such a hullabaloo. One of the lads shouted that we were sinking. Soon there was several feet of water in our quarters. We all scrambled to salvage the clothing that was in the top half of our lockers, clothing that was still dry. Then we all made our way to the wheel house and the galley. These two areas, along with the skipper's cabin were all dry, being above decks. The craft filled with water and soon settled on the bottom, alongside the fish jetty. Fortunately, it was not very deep. The military police came and took the engineer away. We all made our way to the recreation back room of the shore canteen, which had a pot-bellied stove. We were in a real mess. It was a freezing cold night. The skipper sent for the Inverness Fire Brigade, then he ordered Lofty and I to go down to the engine room and dive down and keep taking turns at the two wheels, in order to close the skittle valves. The firemen from Inverness thought it a huge joke that the English had scuttled their own ship. The skipper assembled us all in the back room of the canteen and told us there was only one thing we could do. He intended to split the crew into two halves. Half the men were to go home on 14 days' leave, then when they returned the other half would go on leave. The six men left on the ship would have to manage in the wheel house, the Captain's cabin and the galley. You see all the electrics had to be stripped out and sent down to England to be cleaned and reconditioned. This is the only thing they could do. The steering gear, tiller flat equipment and engine room all had American fittings. We were the joke of the flotilla and constantly ribbed. 'What men will do to get out of the next invasion!' We didn't think it funny at all, but that's exactly what took place.*

Another man training for landing craft operations in Scotland was John T. Rushton, son of Mr and Mrs Bryn Rushton of Irlam. John had been employed in the accounts department at the Council Offices until he joined the Navy. He wrote an article for the BBC's People's War in 2004, part of which is reproduced below: *I joined the Royal Navy in October 1943, my call-up having been deferred so that I might sit the London Matriculation examination. The importance of this lay in the weight it attached to my educational claims, and in the chronology of the war, for I was commissioned in June 1944, a few days before D-Day. Otherwise, had I been viewed as an ordinary recruit, I would have later served as a DEMS gunner aboard a merchant ship, quite a hazardous occupation to follow, though the U-boat war, by this time, was being won. But, on joining HMS Glendower, whether on the strength of the matriculation qualification, or on the evidence from the battery of psychological tests to which we were subjected, I was selected as a CW candidate. Thence forward I was trained as a prospective officer, and subjected to an incessant winnowing process, until I was commissioned, in early June 1944. There was then an assumption, taking the Dieppe raid as a precedent, that there would be many casualties amongst landing craft personnel, so that many people on my course found themselves directed into Combined Operations as replacements, but in the event, were not rushed into the hazards of the war. The CW course, unlike that held at Lochailort, was not intended to prepare officers solely for Combined Operations. Thus from HMS King Alfred one might go on to serve in many types of naval vessel, from the largest to the smallest. Thus we were all trained in seamanship, ship-handling, navigation, signals, gunnery, power-of command, anchors and cables, ship and aircraft-recognition, pilotage and much more. It was a very varied and intensive diet for young men, who, six months earlier, would have been ignorant in all these fields. It was also a measure of the country's desperate need, that the command of naval vessels could be put into the hands of such people. In large ships, it was unlikely to occur, but not so in minor vessels. Irony and factual accuracy are beautifully combined in the classification 'Men dressed as seamen.' What was true of the men was equally true of the ships. At the time of Dunkirk, there was no such thing as a major landing craft. By June 1944, there were hundreds of landing craft, large and small. Well established naval officers, at that time, were unused to the idea of running ships ashore, other than in an emergency. To run vessels ashore repeatedly would have seemed like an invitation to commit professional suicide. With conventional ocean-going vessels, such it probably would have been, and so the new landing craft had to have some radically different characteristics from ocean-going vessels. Firstly, they were flat-bottomed, to enable them to slide up a beach, and to remain upright if they dried-out there. Secondly, they had to be of shallow draught, so that troops did not have to swim for the shore. This, in turn, meant that the landing craft's grip on the water was superficial. This could be a comfort, in that they were unlikely to be torpedoed, the conventional torpedo running some 9 feet below the surface. The bad news was that landing craft were very responsive to wind and tidal currents, so that ship-handling was always interesting, if not positively exciting. Troon harbour, for instance, had a tidal stream running across the harbour entrance, and a stone, light-bearing bollard within the harbour's mouth. A speedy approach was therefore needful, but if the angle of approach was wrong, or insufficient allowance had been made for the wind, the landing craft would enter the harbour in-off the stone bollard, and if way was not taken off her pretty smartly, she might proceed to inflict damage on newly-built frigates fitting out against an adjacent harbour wall (a tank landing craft, her great steel door poised at a deadly angle, would be a prime vessel for this task). There was indeed an apocryphal story that a frigate had been launched by a tank landing craft under these circumstances. Increasingly, as the war progressed, the Germans became anxious to identify where any sea-borne attack upon them might be mounted. Would it be the Pas de Calais, or Normandy, or perhaps even Norway, or even the south of France? The whole coast of Europe was vulnerable and, accordingly, needed to be defended. The raid on Dieppe, in 1942, gave some indication of intent, but the capture of tank landing craft in that adventure gave the Germans some logistics to work on. They would then calculate that a tank landing craft had a range of about 3,000 miles before it required refuelling. Some potential allied targets might then suggest themselves, given known Allied bases. Such speculations were aided by Allied intelligence units. The 3,000 mile range of the tank landing craft depended on two five-hundred horsepower engines, which gave a maximum speed of ten knots. They were presided over by a petty-officer motor mechanic, two stokers and a wireman. This team were responsible for everything mechanical and electrical on board, including the capstan and the door winches. At sea, their place of work was located just forward of a bulkhead separating the messdeck from the engine-room There the sea-sick mechanic could sit between his two noisy engines, being sick into a bucket between his knees, whilst he awaited any change in orders from the bridge. However, given that the Allies were going to land on open beaches, not all beaches were equally suitable. There were quick-sands, beaches in which runnels featured, largely rock covered beaches, or beaches which sloped at inhospitable angles. There were British beaches enough which shared these and other unfortunate characteristics, some of which tank landing craft discovered for themselves.*

Sub-Lieutenant John Rushton, Royal Navy

In April Sergeant Thomas Edwin Southern, RAF, of Irlam, married Margery Pollard, the fifth daughter of Mr and Mrs H. Pollard of Red House Cottage, Dunham Massey. The wedding took place at St Mark's Church in Dunham Massey and the best man was Flight Sergeant C.F. Shepperd, an RAF pilot, and the groomsman was Craftsman J. Pollard, REME, brother of the bride.

The chairman of the War Comforts Fund, Albert J. Keal, responded to calls for a Welcome Home Fund to be set up: *Sir, at a meeting of the Irlam and Cadishead War Comfort Fund on Monday evening last* (27th *March), the committee interviewed a deputation of ladies from the canteen staff of the Lancashire Steel Corporation Ltd, who were desirous of forming a fund to give the local men and women serving in the Forces a welcome home at the conclusion of hostilities. After hearing the ladies, the committee was unanimously of the opinion that there should not be a separate fund created for the purpose of giving a welcome home, but that it was desirable that the energies of everyone in the district should be co-ordinated to swell the War Comforts Fund. From the inception of the fund, it has been the policy of the committee to maintain a balance in hand, and it is the intention to distribute any balance among the men and women when they return home. The War Comforts Fund Committee make the point that the war is not yet won, and that it is the primary duty of the people of this district to see that gifts are sent to those who are still serving, and may be serving even after the conclusion of hostilities, as it is very evident that there must be a considerable time lag before all men and women now engaged in the Forces can be returned to their civilian employment. The committee feels that if another fund is set up there will be considerable confusion in the public mind. In the members' opinion, it is better to have one fund for the whole of the district operating from the War Comforts Fund Committee, and that every effort should be made to swell the income of the Comforts Fund so that a substantial balance will be available for distribution to returned servicemen and women. The committee has built up, over a period of 3½ years, records of 1,428 serving men and women in the district, and have facilities for keeping up to date with information. Any new organisation or fund would have a tremendous task in building up records and, if it is the desire of those who feel that a welcome home gift should be given to every soldier, sailor, airman, ATS, WREN or WAAF from this district, then the only organisation capable of tackling this task is the War Comforts Fund. Any organisation wishing to further the committee's aim to build up a balance is invited to appoint a representative on the War Comforts Fund Committee, which consists of representatives of the Council, churches, works, clubs, WVS, etc, in the district. They would then be able to express their views and have some responsibility in determining, when the time arrives, how best to distribute any balance in hand. The War Comforts Fund has a steady income from regular subscribers and if other organisations will back them up, a substantial balance can be achieved to provide everyone with a hearty welcome back to civvy street. It is, therefore, hoped that the residents of the district will respond generously to efforts and appeals in the future so that the balance in hand can be substantially added to from time to time. If any organisation wishing to assist the fund would communicate with the honorary secretary or honorary treasurer, every assistance will be given to your efforts.*

The *Guardian* replied: *I mentioned some time ago that several ladies had approached me to tell me of their intention to start a Welcome Home Fund for the men and women serving in the Forces. They have, since then, put their scheme before the Council, and have been told that it is the intention to disburse any surplus funds lying to the credit of the War Comforts Fund among the men and women when they return home. That is a course I suggested several months ago; but I am still convinced that, in addition to the Comforts Fund - to whose good work I raise my battered tile – there is the room and the need for a fund such as these ladies have in mind. We have about 1,500 local men and women in the Forces, so that it will readily be seen that any balance left in the Comforts Fund – which is constantly depleting its finances by gifts – will not be exceptionally large. Even assuming that, at the end of the war, the balance in hand is £1,500 – and, because of periodic gifts, that is not likely – our returning warriors will receive the handsome sum of one pound each, or barely enough for one night's armistice celebration. As I observed on a previous occasion, if the Council is not prepared to tackle this new fund, the object of which should be to raise sufficient money to ensure that our returning servicemen do not have to endure the same bitter want that many experienced after the last war (not merely to give them a glorified tea party) then I strongly advise the ladies to go ahead with their plan. For my part, I shall be happy to do all I can to help.*

The *Guardian* wrote a description of the welcome home for Jack Jones, which took place on Saturday, 1st April. The article is beautifully written and gives a keen sense of the regard that Jack was held in the district: *Three weeks after he had returned from America, Jack Jones attended a welcome home gathering organised by the local branch of the British Iron and Steel Federation, at the Steelworks canteen. A concert was held and speeches of welcome were made for this Yorkshire-bred Lancashire man. Mr P.E. Holloway of the Lancashire Steel Corporation Ltd, presided over the gathering. Jack had worked at the Steelworks as a steel smelter for many years. In introducing Jack Jones, Mr Holloway said that the company was proud that out of all the thousands of trade unionists in the country one of their workmen had been chosen to represent this country in America, and said further that having met Jack on the same side, and the opposite side of the table, and round the fire, he knew that the Americans would be left in no shadow of doubt as to the part we over here are playing in this war. Mr Davidson, representing the British Iron and Steel Federation (local branches), and Councillor E. Owen, representing Local Government, supported and expressed their delight and pleasure in being asked to give Jack a real royal welcome home to this very ordinary township in Lancashire, which, by reason of the success which had followed him had not only put Lancashire on the map, but had made Irlam and Cadishead known to thousands who had never previously heard of the place. They also expressed the sympathy of the audience with Jack, who had received bad news that very day; a near relative had died on service in the south, Captain Audrey Hamilton, NAAFI. The high point of the evening was when Jack, suffering under a heavy sense of loss, put aside all personal grief in order that his co-workers in peace and war should not be robbed of the opportunity of giving him a real Lancashire welcome home. Jack gave a brief description of his visit to America. Then came another proof that Jack is like the rest of us, a man who has his point of view, a man who will fight for what he considers right, and yet a man who is human and whose emotions are soon aroused. He reached America just before Christmas and, on seeing the brilliance of New York lights and the abundance of good things in the shops, the huge Christmas tree in Times Square, he realised that Christmas in America was still something like the Christmases he used to know. Then he remembered how Irlam looked the night he left, with its blackout and rationing, the hundred and one inconveniences, the dangers of war-torn Britain, the children who were being robbed of so many of the things which Christmas should mean, he stood there and cried. That was not a confession of weakness but of the real humanity of this man who has made us feel so proud that he is one of us. And then he followed on with a bewildering picture of what he had done – 202 meetings addressed in 12 weeks, over 20,000 miles of travel, Pittsburgh to Birmingham, Alabama, and a score of other places, singing in negro choirs, teaching in a negro school, preaching in a negro church; a steel plant so huge that it beggars the imagination, factories where they turn out aeroplanes faster than we need to turn out midget cars, the high standard of living of the ordinary American, and finally the fact that despite all this high-powered efficiency and standard of living, he was glad to get back to this island with its blackouts and its shortages of all the main commodities. It was fascinating to hear the names of world-wide figures tripping off his tongue as if he was talking about his own workmates – Mr La Guardia, the mayor of New York, a dynamic personality, Henry Wallace, Eleanor Roosevelt, Lord Halifax, etc. till one began to wonder whether this really was the Jack Jones that we used to meet with the ordinary everyday greetings. But Jack Jones had not changed, and Kipling's question need not have been asked so far as he was concerned. You remember it – 'If you can talk with crowds and keep your virtue, or walk with kings nor lose the common touch.' Jack has always shown he can do that and we came away from the gathering feeling that we had not only welcomed home a successful British diplomatist but we had welcomed home, first and foremost, a man.*

The Battle of Kohima (north east India) commenced on 4th April when the Japanese attempted to capture the Kohima Ridge, the high ground which commanded the road used to supply the besieged British and Indian garrison of Imphal. The small British force at Kohima held the Japanese off until they were relieved in mid-April by the 2nd British Division and the 5th and 7th Indian Divisions, who had broken through the Japanese roadblock on the Dimapur-Kohima road. In early May the Allies counter-attacked and by 13th May the Japanese had been forced from the positions they had captured in April. Much of the Battle of Kohima was fought in appalling conditions brought on by the torrential rains of the Monsoon. The British and Indian troops pursued the fleeing Japanese, re-opening the supply route and ending the siege of Imphal on 22nd June. Local man, Private Tom Yates, 5 Platoon, B Company, 2nd Battalion, Manchester Regiment, took part in the battle. The 2nd Manchester Regiment was the machine-gun battalion of the 2nd Division and B Company was attached to the 5th Infantry Brigade within the 2nd Division. Tom, a machine-gunner, gave the following account of his time in India and the call to Burma to relieve Kohima: *From there they sent us to the Bengal jungle, after we'd been there a while for training for Burma, it's near Goa, Goa was actually only a few miles away. We had no transport then, you all just lived in the jungle. It was alive with bloody baboons and everything. Had some experiences but nothing like that. I sat with the T2s we were being the scouts this day, we sat down under this tree in front of the others. I looks up and saw this bloody snake, curled round this bough, we was off. And it was the same with the baboons, when we saw the baboons at first, it was just, the tree was like that, Billy Booth it was, he said 'they're bloody gorillas them.' We gets back, they said 'there's no gorillas in India, they're baboons.' Anyway we got a call then, we had to go into Burma, so of the whole of the 2nd Division, we move up like, and we drove all the way from Bengal and I had a bloody truck with no windscreen, and every day I used to be caked with sand and sweat, it must have been about 2,000 miles or more. We couldn't cross the Brahmaputra, the ferry didn't take vehicles over, we were carrying on to Calcutta, then we got on flat-tops on the railway and they took us north again, that's like to southern Himalayas. They put us off and then we finished up crossing this railway bridge with the vehicles over the sleepers, and I remember going along this road, Himalayas again, thousands of different people, lovely metal road, just gulleys like that every so far, and then we drove down to Dimapur, where all the supplies come through. That's where the Japs was heading for, Dimapur railhead. Able to supply anything. So I was put on this gun with my mate, Fred, and we were together all the time, you know you'd eat and sleep together, on the gun together, he was No 1, I was No 2, I fed the gun.*

During the battle Tom's gun team was located on the hills opposite the Japanese positions at Kohima and directly above them was the British artillery. When the British guns fired, the noise was tremendous. At the end of the bombardment the Japanese would emerge from their dug-outs to shake out their blankets to remove the dust and earth thrown up by the explosions. This was the machine-gunners' signal to open fire. Tom had no idea whether he hit anyone. He described the situation at Kohima: *We fought through Kohima and it took, I think it took about six weeks to take that place, anyway they were fighting there before we got there, we went on the other side, out of the tracks. But that was a bad fight that was, lost a lot of men there, the division. That was terrible that was. I forget what mob was holding that when we got there, repelling bloody attacks all the time, if they hadn't have done they'd have took bloody India. A lot of them was killed. They were doing all sounds, the Japanese were speaking English, you know, 'come on Tommy, it's all out now.' Shouting for help like a wounded soldier, you daren't go out, you daren't reply, that's what they said, 'come on Tommy.'*

Tom recounted how the Japanese had dug under the concrete tennis courts near the Governor's bungalow, where desperate hand-to-hand fighting took place. The Battle of Kohima was the turning point of the war in the Far East, and after the battle, the previously invincible Japanese would face defeat after defeat until the end of the war. Around this time Tom met another local man: *I came down this track with two or three others and we come round and this sergeant major came round to me and he said 'where've you come from?' and I said 'we've come down the track round, it's too steep that way.' He said 'do you know it's not cleared of Japs yet?' I said 'it must be if we've come down.' So he said 'that's good cos it's gentle, we can take food up and water.' And I saw this bloke stood by a tree and it was Tom Swindells, I used to know him from school, when he used to be in the Salvation Army playing in the band, and I just had a few words with him and I never saw him again. He was stood against this tree as I came down this track, and I spoke to the sergeant major and then I saw Tom, I went and had a word with Tom, only a brief word.*

Private Tom Yates, Manchester Regiment (right)

From there we went to Imphal, that was an airport, like an air landing strip. Tamu and Palel where the Gurkhas made another name for themselves, it was misty, the Japs were attacking and the Gurkhas just went out and made the bloody fighting there, they're great little fighters. Then we went up through the Kabaw Valley, that's where I got bloody malaria there. And I was flown out a couple of times, well once, and then with a suspected, but you didn't go far, just the forward hospital and these Americans used to fly us out. They were all volunteers from rich parents all these, and they just had these monoplanes and they could land on a football field. The first time I got in he said 'sit the lap down will you, and keep your feet off them wires.' And from there you just hitched your way back again, you know with aircraft, Dakota, they dropped us supplies, cos they supplied by air all the time then. Never saw bread for a long while. But when we used to come out of action, like you'd be in action for so long and then you'd say, you took a position and you'd stay there, and then the next day, then another troop would go in front, so you'd have a rest while they followed you for driving. Driving the West Africans forward, a sergeant said 'would you like a cup of tea?' I said 'aye'. 'What about a piece of bread?' I said 'bloody 'ell, you don't have bread do you?' He said 'aye.' Cut that up, crust like that, jam on it, they wouldn't eat the biscuits, the West Africans. But they were good fighting, they were good, mostly artillery, they were. So I was in there all the time.

Schoolchildren between the ages of 11 and 14 helped to feed the district by working on the allotments of Irlam and Cadishead. Francis Gold, Irlam Council's head gardener (and also a major in the Home Guard) said they had achieved amazing results. Originally, the Council had considered the standard 300 square yards of allotment to be too large for schoolboys to work, however, the children got over this difficulty by making business partnerships. Many of the boys came equipped with their own tools and many of them spent pocket money on artificial manure and also worked until late at night.

In mid-1942, the Cadishead branch of the WVS had started to garnish camouflage nets, and set themselves a target of 1,000 nets. The task required a high degree of skill and patience, with each net being garnished to a particular pattern. They reached their target in April 1944.

An appeal in Cadishead raised £53 for St Dunstan's Hospice for Blind Servicemen. Enid Bakker, the head of Cadishead WVS, received a letter from Sir Ian Fraser, CBE, MP and chairman of St Dustans: *My warmest congratulations to you and all associated with you on the great success which has attended your appeal in Cadishead. I am delighted to receive £53-4-3 and to note the substantial increase on your previous collection ... I extend to you and all who supported the effort so generously our warmest thanks ... The splendid help which has been rendered to us in your endeavour to place men and women blinded in the country's service in the careers to which they are best fitted by temperament and knowledge is deeply appreciated by all at St Dunstan's.*

Private Gladys Mona Daniels of the Auxiliary Territorial Service married Albert Sutton of Stoke-on-Trent on 12th April at St Mary's Church, Cadishead. Gladys was the only daughter of Mr and Mrs Frank Daniels of 2 Dorset Rd, Cadishead. She had been in the ATS for two years, stationed at an anti-aircraft battery in southern England where she saw action against enemy raiders. Albert was a sapper in the Royal Engineers who had spent 3½ years with the Eighth Army in Greece, Crete, North Africa and Italy.

Councillor Owen (the retiring chairman of the Council) gave his year-end review of the local Council on Wednesday, 12th April. In it he paid tribute to the various organisations in the district for the manner in which they had carried out their work during the year. He thanked Council members for the support they had given him during his year of office. Although the district had been free of enemy action, it had been necessary to keep the Civil Defence organisation in a state of efficiency. The Fire Guard had been kept busy reorganising and training, and he was satisfied that, under the leadership of the Fire Guard Officer, Leslie Jones, and his voluntary assistants, that the district had an excellent organisation. He also congratulated the WVS under Mrs Loxley and Enid Bakker, and the Savings Committee for the splendid efforts they had made. He expressed the hope that Salute the Soldier week would be even more successful than Wings week. He went on to state: *There is one item, however, to which I wish to call special attention, and that is that my year of office has seen the establishment of the British Restaurant, which was opened on January 15th by our local Member of Parliament. I have had the honour and privilege of being the chairman of the sub-committee running the restaurant, and it is pleasing to me to be able to state after 12 weeks' operations that the restaurant has been successful in every direction. It has given satisfaction to our customers, it has been well patronised, and it has been a financial success. We have a very large number of men and women from this district who are serving their country in the Navy, the Army, Air Force and Mercantile Marine, and they are stationed in all parts of the world. Some, unfortunately, are prisoners of war, others are in hospital, and a few have paid the great sacrifice. We extend to the relatives of those who have given their lives our deepest sympathy. To those in hospital we wish a speedy and complete recovery and to all those away from home a safe and speedy return. Before closing I do want to express my appreciation for the splendid efforts being made by the workpeople in the various industries in this district. They have quietly pursued their daily jobs and I know are determined to stand behind our fighting men until victory is won.*

During the month 25 year old George Vincent Borrino of 31 Lords Street, Cadishead, was promoted in the field to the rank of sergeant major as a reward for his gallantry in action. George was a pre-war soldier who had joined the Army around 1936. He participated in the costly Dieppe raid in August 1942, and went to North Africa in March 1943. He was wounded two months later. On recovery he participated in the Sicily operation and later, as the allies advanced through Italy, he was among the first troops to land on the Anzio beachhead, Italy. His father, William, was a First World War veteran who had re-enlisted into the Army at the outbreak of war. Two brothers were also serving in the Armed Forces: Chief Petty Officer William Alex R. Borrino of the Submarine Service and Stanley Peter Borrino. Peter joined the Royal

Navy in October 1942 and was commissioned in May 1943. All three brothers were known by their middle names: Vincent, Alex and Peter.

Another local man serving with the Submarine Service was Stephen Hayward (or Hayward-Lumber). Stephen was originally a fireman and, after witnessing the London Blitz, he resolved to enlist, volunteering for the Submarine Service. His brother, Private Edwin Randall Hayward (or Hayward-Lumber), served with the Royal Army Ordnance Corps.

Private Edwin Hayward, Royal Army Ordnance Corps

Mary Barrow of 7 Silverdale Avenue, Higher Irlam received the news that her brother, Guardsman 2719971 Patrick Burke of the 1st Battalion, Irish Guards had been wounded and was a prisoner of war. He lived with his sister in Irlam before joining the Army in January 1940. He first went overseas in February 1942, to the Middle East. Patrick was wounded at Anzio in Italy in April and was held at some point in Stalag IXC at Mühlhausen, Hesse, Germany.

Two of Patrick's brothers were also in the Armed Forces: Guardsman Martin Burke, also with the Irish Guards, and James Burke, Royal Navy. Patrick was the second member of Mary's family to be taken prisoner; her husband, Fred Barrow of the Royal Army Service Corps had been taken prisoner at Tobruk during the North African campaign. After the Allied invasion of Italy Fred escaped captivity and had almost reached the British lines before being recaptured.

1944

Stephen Hayward, Royal Navy

Twenty-three year old Sergeant (flight engineer) 1106196 **Cyril Whittle** of 103 Squadron, No. 1 Group, Bomber Command, Royal Air Force Volunteer Reserve, was killed on air operations on 23rd April.

On 22nd April Cyril was on board Lancaster bomber Mark I, serial no. LL913, code letters PM, which took off from RAF Elsham Wolds, Lincolnshire, at 11.16pm. This was one of 596 aircraft (323 Lancasters, 254 Halifaxes, and 19 Mosquitoes) which set off on a bombing mission to Dusseldorf, Germany. During the raid 2,150 tons were dropped on the northern districts of Dusseldorf, causing widespread damage to 56 large industrial premises, seven of which were completely destroyed. Two thousand houses were destroyed or badly damaged, 883 people were killed, 593 injured and 403 missing. Sixteen Halifaxes and 13 Lancasters were lost on the raid (4.9 percent of the force deployed). Whilst returning from the raid, Lancaster LL913 flew into the side of a hill near Thorpe Hall, Rudston, Yorkshire, at 4.55am on 23rd April killing all on board: Pilot Officer 172418 T.E. Astbury, Sergeant 1546820 D. Hopkins (navigator), Sergeant Cyril Whittle, Sergeant 911476 D.A.W. Leftly (air bomber), Sergeant 15858814 A. Jervis (wireless operator/air gunner), Sergeant 622825 W.B. Graham (air gunner) and Flight Sergeant AUS/436032 A. Hogg (air gunner).

Born c.1920 Cyril was the son of John William and Elizabeth Whittle and he had two brothers: Jack and Dennis. Before the war Cyril lived with his parents at 7 The Crescent, Higher Irlam, and worked at Royles Engineering Ltd. He joined the Royal Air Force in August 1940 and was stationed in South Africa for two years before being posted back to England. He was well-known in the district as a sportsman. His favourite hobby was cycling and he had won many trophies and medals in cycling events. He was also a keen footballer and had represented the RAF team. He was described as *one of the most popular young men in the district and his cheery and sunny disposition endeared him to his host of friends.*

On 29th April a service was conducted by Reverend Lee at the family home, 7 The Crescent, Higher Irlam. Reverend Lee said: *This young man has unselfishly given his life in the service of his country.* Later the funeral party moved to Newchurch churchyard, Culcheth, for the interment, where bearers from the Royal Canadian Air Force carried the coffin. Reverend Lee officiated at the graveside. Cyril is buried in a family grave along with his father. The grave is marked by a private headstone rather than a CWGC stone, but it bears the RAF's emblem and motto *Per Ardua Ad Astra* and there is a flowerpot on the grave bearing the epitaph *Cyril - One of the Few.*

Lance Corporal 24257 Ray Ward, serving with the Royal Signals, East Africa Command, wrote the following letter to the local newspaper: *Sir, many thanks for your*

Town Topics in the Guardian. You will appreciate from the address that the news is usually stale by the time it reaches me, but it is none the less welcome for that. I get a great kick out of your articles, and especially liked your remarks about people with 'parish pump mentalities.' Regarding hospitality to Allied Forces, I wonder if such people ever trouble to think what would have happened to us out in East Africa if the people there had closed their doors to us because of gossip? I can assure you that it has only been the wonderful kindness of such people – and let me tell you they entertain us for up to 28 days at a stretch – that has kept us from getting dreadfully fed up during the past three years. I am eagerly awaiting another bundle of papers to see who's going to get 'stung' next time. The whole affair is slightly reminiscent of a cinema serial, 'Who Done It?' with an unlimited number of instalments.

Another letter was received from Corporal James N. Howes, who was stationed in India, this time on the subject of a maternity home for the district: *Sir, may I take this opportunity of giving the local Council a big hand indeed in respect of the 'do or die' policy regarding the proposed maternity home for Irlam and Cadishead, and in putting forward this subject to the County Council with a view to the matter being brought before the notice of the Ministry of Health. I want to thank you, sir, and the few who have stuck to their guns in advocating this proposition. I quite realise the difficulties ahead in such a scheme, but they can very easily be overcome without any doubts whatsoever. If we are going to have this, it must be the very best of equipment and building materials required for such a project, none of the old ideas that this will do and that will do. If the Council had been more enterprising in days gone by things would not have had to be discussed to the extent that they have to be, for example, if the parks had been made into a paying proposition by the installation of tennis courts, bowling greens, swimming pool, putting greens, etc (which didn't need much, if any outlay at all) the profits would have paid for such things as a maternity home and I would even suggest a very much-needed hospital. May I also ask this question? Why can't we have back the rights of the roads through the district for the use of our own buses, which would also help considerably towards expenses for future undertakings for the betterment of the district? Also, two or three modern cinema which would certainly pay back in rates alone – a not to be sniggered at dividend. I know I may be jumping ahead with these ideas in the middle of a war which should, by now, be over, but they are worth keeping in the little note book for future action immediately hostilities cease. Would I be asking too much for you to broach this subject for a reply in the near future? Knowing you as I do through your column, I think not, Sir.*

The first effort of Salute the Soldier week was launched by two members of the Navy, Able Seamen Pallister and Jones. In the George Hotel they had decided to show the Navy's appreciation of the Army by organising a collection, which raised 10s-10d. The next night they decided that this sum would not salute many soldiers and decided to repeat the collection, raising a further 19 shillings, which was handed over to the manager of the hotel, Mr J.T. Remers. The George Hotel had raised £100 during the Wings for Victory week in June 1943.

Trimmers at the Partington Coaling Basin held a concert at the British Legion Hall which raised over £66 for the British Red Cross. The concert was organised by

Wilfred Loach who, in addition to being the labour officer at the coaling basin, was a well-known tenor. A party of nine Manchester artists provided the entertainment.

During the month the War Comforts Fund received contributions from the Irlam and Cadishead Gardening Association (£2), Nags Head Hotel (£3 raised during a Shrove Tuesday party), Mrs Seymour, British Basket and Besto Company (£2 from the proceeds of an effort), Mrs Shaw and Mrs Swindley (£10 raised by a dance), Irlam and Cadishead Welsh Society (£9 from a concert) and Mrs Genders ten shillings.

A Billiards Week was organised to raise money for the Aid to China Fund. The series of matches featured Arthur Cribbs, a former winner of the British Legion's national championship, who defeated all-comers in matches played throughout the week in various clubs in the district: The British Legion, Irlam Conservative Club, Cadishead Conservative Club and Irlam Catholic Club.

Fusilier Ernest Victor Sandercock (pictured) was wounded in Italy. He had joined the Army in 1940 and became a physical training instructor in the Devonshire Regiment, before transferring to one of the Fusilier Regiments. He first went overseas in November 1943. He was a native of Devonport and his mother was living in Openshaw Lane, Cadishead. He married Winifred Green in September 1943. Winifred had been a member of the Auxiliary Territorial Service for two years.

The 42nd Battalion, Home Guard opened the Worsley Salute the Soldier week on Saturday 22nd April with a demonstration at Parr Fold Park, Walkden, of Home Guard weapons, including sub-artillery types. Personnel from B Company, under the direction of Captain J.L. Jones, gave a demonstration of sentry duties – how not to do it – as well as how to do it correctly. The incorrect methods were deliberately exaggerated and caused amusement among the crowd of spectators. The bayonet fighting was carried out under the direction of Captain G.R. Haines of G Company, and NCOs and men from the same company. The programme also included a demonstration on gas discipline, organised by Second Lieutenant T. Johnstone, the battalion chemical warfare officer. The public had the opportunity to see what would happen to people who did not use their gas masks properly. The finale was an assault by a battle squad upon an enemy strongpoint, and the spectators watched with appreciation the way the squad overcame the obstacles and successfully captured the post. Throughout the demonstrations the public were given a running commentary by Major H.W.W. Whittle.

Two local men, Privates George Wilkinson and Noel Dobson, had a chance reunion in Italy and exchanged copies of the *Guardian*. George was the youngest son of Mr and Mrs G. Wilkinson of 295 Liverpool Road, Cadishead.

Private George Wilkinson

Educated at Irlam Endowed School and the College of Technology, George Wilkinson was, at one time, honorary secretary of the Rescue Party Social Club. He married Doris Monks of Warrington in 1933 and they resided at 2 Byng Avenue, Cadishead. Before joining the Army he was employed by his father in the firm of Wilkinson & Tonge (joiners and builders). He was called up in May 1943 into one of the Yorkshire Regiments (East or West Yorkshires). He first went overseas in November of the same year, and at some point he transferred to a different regiment in the 8th Indian Division. Noel Dobson was born in 1922 (birth registered at Barton I. in March 1922) and was educated at Flixton Senior School. His parents resided in Liverpool Road, Irlam.

Another chance meeting between local people occurred when Arthur Robinson of the Royal Army Service Corps met Mr and Mrs Roberts in Italy. All three were members of the district's Salvation Army, in which Arthur was a bandsman. Before moving to Italy, Arthur had served in the North African campaign. Mr and Mrs Roberts were engaged in the Salvation Army's Red Shield mobile canteen work supporting troops in Italy.

Thursday, 27th April saw the funeral of a member of G Company of the Home Guard. Thirty-eight year old Charles Durand Elcote Bower of 44 Harewood Road, Irlam had been killed in a collision with a motor lorry in Irlam. Charles was a native of Stockton-on-Tees who had moved to Irlam in 1932 to work as a pattern maker at the Steelworks. He was held in high esteem by his workmates and friends.

On Saturday, 29th April the Irlam detached flight of 292 (Eccles) Squadron, ATC played a football match against HMS Gosling V, losing 2-0.

The Knitting Guilds of the Centenary and Temple Methodist Churches in Glazebrook organised a highly successful bring and buy sale at the Centenary Schoolroom, raising £66 for the Victory Fund. Mrs Blundell, opening the function, expressed the hope that very soon they would be welcoming home all those serving with the Forces. Side-shows were organised by Mr G.H. Lewis and Peter Allen. After the sale Mr Lewis held a cinema show in the large vestry of the schoolroom.

On the same day (29th April), the Steelworks Division of the St John Ambulance Brigade held its annual awards evening at the Irlam Steelworks Club Annexe. A hot pot dinner was followed by a concert given by the Neonites Concert Party. The chairman, Superintendent A.F. Whittaker, divisional superintendent of the St John Ambulance Brigade at Urmston, proposed the loyal toast. He apologised for the absence of the president, James Sinclair Kerr, O St J, who was unable to attend because of transport problems. He thanked the wives of members for allowing their husbands to attend lectures and drills and he urged members to support their officers and to at least attend the required minimum of 12 lectures and drills each year. Edwin Jones, clerk of the Council, spoke next. He proposed a toast to the Order of St John and the Ambulance Brigade and also regretted the absence of Mr Sinclair

Kerr who, he said, was responsible for the success of many of the efforts in the district. He traced the history of the Order of St John from the Middle Ages. He went on to say: *Whenever I see a St John Ambulance man, I see a man who has taken time and pains to equip himself and to make him self-sufficient in rendering first aid, to relieve suffering and to be of service to the medical profession. Personally, I have always been impressed by the smartness and efficiency of the Steel Works Division.* Referring to the division's activities in war-time, he said that in Irlam, though there had been no serious enemy action, the authorities had always been confident that, in the time of need, the St John Ambulance Brigade would give a good account of itself. The local divisions had already given good service in other districts during raids. Superintendent F. Partington replied to the toast and said that when they saw a man in the uniform of the St John Association, they saw one who was proud to be an ambulance man. The divisional surgeon, Dr Drysdale, presented awards to the following members and congratulated them on their well-deserved awards; Superintendent Partington, Ambulance Officer Roland Watson, Sergeant W. Stewart, Sergeant S. Rogers, Corporal F. Nuttall, Corporal A. Massey, Privates T. Ashton, W. Astbury, J. Best, J. Best, F. Berry, W. Connolly, N. Greenhalgh, F. Hollinhurst, J. Lockett, J. Rollinson, W. Richardson, N. Sheppard, C. Simpson, A. Sproston, R. Thubron, G. Bell, W. Shaw, L. Goodwin, W. Wharton, P. Perrin, V. O'Brien, J. Mason.

MAY

During the month local charities and funds benefited from several fundraising efforts by local people. A number of children from the district went May Queening and donated the money to the Red Cross and the Salute the Soldier funds. A dance organised by the Royal Navy raised over £16 for the Red Cross. Miss M. Jones of 50 Addison Road, Higher Irlam, sold homemade shopping bags in aid of the Red Cross, and handed over £5 (her second donation). Ann Scotson and Beryl Barnes of Roscoe Road, Irlam, raised £2 for the Red Cross by selling homemade paper flowers and wooden animals.

Wilfred Kitching (service no. R293082), Merchant Navy, was on board the steam merchant *Janeta* (5,312 tonnes, owned by Maclay & McIntyre of Glasgow) when she was torpedoed and sunk on 1st May. Nine crew members and four gunners were lost, but Wilfred was one of the 35 survivors.

The unescorted *Janeta* was carrying ballast on a journey from Algiers to the River Plate, calling at Gibraltar (15th April) and Rio de Janeiro. At 4.11am on the morning of 1st May she was torpedoed and sunk by German U-boat U181, 900 miles south west of the Ascension Islands.

The survivors of the attack found themselves adrift on the open seas. Fifteen men were picked up by the Swedish merchant *Freja* about 150 miles south of Bahia and landed at Rio de Janeiro. Ten survivors were picked up on 12th May by USS *Alger* and landed at Bahia. The master, third officer and eight crew members were rescued and were also taken to Bahia, arriving there on 14th May two weeks after the sinking. Wilfred's wife was notified that he was safe in a letter dated 22nd May from Maclay & McIntyre: *Dear Mrs Kitching, we have been advised by the Admiralty that your husband, Mr W. Kitching, carpenter, is safe and well, but that the vessel on which he was serving has been lost. It will doubtless be some time before the crew are home, but any word we receive will certainly be passed on to you as soon as possible. Meantime we have been specially asked by the Admiralty to instruct you that the name of the vessel must not be mentioned.*

Wilfred Harold Kitching was born on 2nd March 1911 in Kildale, Yorkshire. He resided with his wife, Violet, at 14 Laburnum Road, Cadishead. He joined his first ship, *Ocean Valley*, on 29th May 1942 as a carpenter, and sailed on her until 14th October 1943. He joined the *Janeta* on 24th February 1944. After the sinking of *Janeta*, he spent a few months back in England, before returning to the seas again, this time on board the *Empire Ballad*. After three voyages, he joined *Richmond* on 2nd October 1945. He was discharged from the Merchant Navy on termination of war service on 2nd October 1946. His ability and general conduct were described as very good throughout his time in the service. He was awarded the George VI War Medal 1939-45, and campaign medals: 1939-45, Pacific, Atlantic and Italy Stars (the latter signified service in the Mediterranean Sea). His certificate of discharge described him as 5 feet 7 inches tall, with blue eyes, fair hair and a fair complexion.

The men of the Merchant Navy were largely unsung heroes, braving the dangers of the seas as well as the constant threat of attack from U-boats, E-boats, mines, surface raiders and aircraft, to bring essential supplies to Britain. Without these supplies the country could not have continued to wage war with Germany and the other Axis Forces. During the course of the war over 35,000 merchant seamen lost their lives and 2,426 British registered ships were lost. Three local merchant seamen were among those lost at sea: Joseph Frederick Barensche (1941), Samuel Whittle Anderson (1941) and William Proctor (1942). Another, Joseph Eric Talbot, died as a result of illness in 1945. Many local men served in the Merchant Navy, men such as Jim Best, Ernie Castle, Joe Brennan, Robert Outlaw, Henry Fleming and John Britton.

James William 'Jim' Best served as an Engineer Officer in the Merchant Navy on board MV *Innesmoor* in 1944 and later on the hospital ship MV *Abba*. The *Innesmoor* was built in 1928 (4,392 tonnes) and served with the Merchant Navy from November 1939. Jim joined MV *Innesmoor* as a junior engineer, probably in September 1944, when she returned to Falmouth after almost a year away from home. *Innesmoor* sailed from Falmouth on 6th September in a convoy of 56 merchants and five escorts, and arrived in Seine Bay two days later. Next day, they sailed for Southend in a smaller convoy and with only one escort. In October she went in convoy across the North Atlantic and spent two months visiting various Canadian and American ports before returning to Liverpool on 17th January 1945. At some point Jim transferred to the hospital ship MV *Abba* as fourth engineer.

Jim was born 1924 in Jarrow-on-Tyne, the eldest son of Mr and Mrs J.W. Best of Oakdene, Belgrave Road, Cadishead. His parents had moved into the district in 1937 to seek employment at the Steelworks. Jim was educated at Urmston Grammar School and then worked at the engineers' office of the Steelworks, until he joined the Merchant Navy in 1944.

Fourth Engineer (Seaman's identity no. NVJJ/57/1) Ernest 'Ernie' Castle enlisted into the Merchant Navy on 20th August 1943 and joined the merchant ship *Manchester Trader* eight days later. His first voyage took him from Liverpool on 5th September 1943 to Gibraltar as part of convoy KMS.26G. They left Gibraltar on 18th September and sailed to Bone, Algeria as part of a convoy headed towards Port Said in Egypt. One of his letters to his wife, Bertha, dated 19th September 1943 has survived: *Dear Bertha, just a few lines to let you know that we have arrived at our destination and am writing you at the first opportunity. We have had a very uneventful voyage and the weather has been grand, it is very hot here and I am brown as can be. I am pleased to say I am feeling very well and hope you and Jean and Jimmy are the same. I will have a look round to see if I can find anything to bring you all back. I have not been ashore yet, but am looking forward to doing so. I hope you are not worrying about me as I am quite alright. I might say I miss you a lot. It seems ages since I saw you. I am glad I brought your photo with me. I have got it alongside Jean's and Jimmy's where I can see it. I will write you a long letter in a day or so. All my love, Ernie.*

On 25th October they left Bone and sailed for Hampton Roads in the USA, passing through St John and Halifax on the way. They returned to Liverpool with convoy HX268 and arrived there on 11th December. In 1944 the *Manchester Trader* made six voyages across the Atlantic to Canada and the USA. She carried a variety of cargo including general stores, flour, grain and metal. Notably in July 1944 she carried explosives and ammunition from the USA to Britain and in September of the same year she carried amphibious vehicles.

Ernie was born 12th August 1906 at Northenden, Manchester. In 1928 he married Bertha Williams and they moved to 15 Chestnut Avenue, Cadishead in the mid-1930s. Ernie worked as a fitter/turner at British Tar Products in Cadishead and after the war he joined a haulage company in Cadishead. He was 5 feet 11½ inches tall, with brown eyes, brown hair and a fresh complexion. Throughout his time in the Merchant Navy his conduct and ability were described as very good. After the war Ernie was discharged from the service as physically unfit for sea service on 20th October 1945, aged 39.

Joseph 'Joe' Brennan served as a stoker in the Merchant Navy on board a variety of ships and he took part in convoys to Gibraltar, New York, Baltimore, Buenos Aires, Cape Town, Durban and Bombay. During the visit to Buenos Aires he saw the wreck of the German battleship *Graf Spee* at the mouth of the River Plate. He was a crew member on one of the block ships intended for the D-Day landings. Block ships were filled with ballast and sailed to Normandy where they were sunk to provide an artificial harbour. The convoy was attacked by E-boats off the coast of Scotland but these were driven off by their naval escorts. Shortly afterwards Joe was taken ill and had to be admitted to hospital at Oban. Next he served on a rescue ship with a Royal Navy captain and Merchant Navy crew on a convoy to Gibraltar (rescue ships accompanied convoys to pick up survivors from sunken ships). While at sea they had to rendezvous with a Royal Navy submarine to pick up a seaman suffering from appendicitis. Joe was born in Salford in 1924, the son of Patrick and Emma Brennan (nee Whitehouse) and was educated at St Joseph's RC School in Salford. Patrick was born in Eire and was a veteran of the First World War, having served in the King's Liverpool Regiment. He was gassed in Salonika. Joe worked as an apprentice joiner for a short while and then took up another job in a timberyard. The Brennan family moved to Irlam after having been bombed out of their house in Salford during the Christmas Blitz of 1940. They resided with Frank Brennan at 63 Eldon Road, Irlam. Joe worked at the Steelworks until volunteering for the Merchant Navy. He attempted to enlist in the Merchant Navy but was told that his job at the Steelworks was a reserved occupation. Two of his brothers, Frank and Patrick, were with the Merchant Navy and it was this that inspired him to join the same service. To get around issue of reserved occupation he travelled to Glasgow and found a coaster that was willing to take him on board.

Robert Outlaw served with the Merchant Navy, on board MV *Llangibby Castle*. In 1943 and early 1944 the *Llangibby Castle* was working in the Mediterranean Sea with voyages between North Africa and Italy. *Llangibby Castle* returned to Britain in March 1944 and sailed around coastal waters until D-Day when it appears that she was involved in ferrying cargo to Normandy. For the remainder of the war the ship was ferrying cargo from Southampton to Le Havre in France, in support of the war in northern Europe. It is not known when Robert joined the *Llangibby Castle* but as he was only 19 when the war ended, it is likely that he joined the ship in 1944 when it returned to British waters. Robert was born in late 1925, the eldest son of John Robert and Elizabeth Outlaw (nee Briston) of 3 Moss Lane, Cadishead. His father was a veteran of the First World War and had been one of the very first men from the district to serve on the Western Front. Robert was single during his time in the Merchant Navy and married Joyce Lowndes in 1948.

Henry Fleming and John Britton both served in the Merchant Navy but little is known about their service. Henry Fleming was born in Irlam in 1917, the son of John Henry and Florence Ann Fleming (nee Hankey). His father was awarded the Military Medal for gallantry in the First World War.

John Raymond Britton was born in West Hartlepool, Cleveland on 6th October 1917. He moved to Irlam in 1939 and married Margaret Elsie Carine in 1940. After leaving the Merchant Navy in 1945 he went to work as an engineer at the Steelworks.

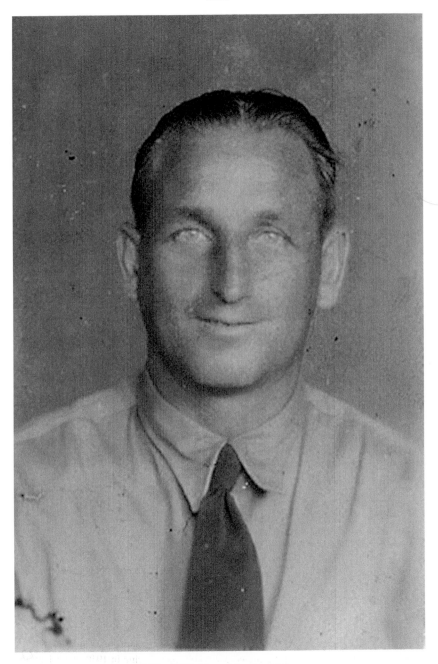

Wilfred Kitching, Merchant Navy

Engineer Officer Jim Best, Merchant Navy

Fourth Engineer Ernie Castle, Merchant Navy

Stoker Joe Brennan, Merchant Navy
Bombay, India

Robert Outlaw, Merchant Navy

At a meeting of the Savings Committee on Monday, 1st May Lieutenant Colonel Webb, who was acting as liaison officer between the Army and the Savings Committee, outlined his plans for the military events which would be held for the Salute the Soldier week, in June. An appeal was made for photographs of local servicemen and women for the Heroes Galleries which would be displayed at the four selling centres in the district. Residents were asked to send their photographs to Mary Bowker at the Council Offices. They were also asked to write the full name, rank and service, together with a few personal details such as length of service, theatres of war and the full home address (so that the photographs could be returned to their rightful owners). Each person who provided a photograph was provided with a card to display in their windows, bearing the figure of the Liberator and carrying the slogan *Salute the Soldier in this house.*

D Company, Home Guard, held a successful dance and cabaret at Irlam Conservative Club, which was attended by Lieutenant Colonel and Mrs F.D. Webb, Major and Mrs Whittle, Lieutenant Commander J.C. Hemmings, Royal Naval Volunteer Reserve, and Major Markham of the American Armed Forces.

On Wednesday, 3rd May the Irlam detached flight of 292 (Eccles) Squadron, ATC heard a talk by a Fleet Air Arm observer, on training in the Fleet Air Arm. The observer was an ex-cadet from 292 Squadron.

On 4th May the *Guardian* published notes of C Company, 4th Cadet Battalion, Lancashire Fusiliers, written by Cadet Captain Lowe. The cadets had taken part in the area boxing championships and the area football competition. In the boxing, C Company managed to get a cadet into the semi-final and another into the third round. The battalion football team, with two local boys, reached the semi-finals. One of the local boys scored ten goals, including four in one game. Boxing had been taken up in earnest by the cadets, under a good instructor. They had sufficient gym kit for the physical training of 30 boys, which was one of the main aims of the cadet movement. Cadet Corporal Ridgway and Cadet Prior attended Saighton Camp, Chester, for a week's intensive physical training. Lance Corporal Hartley, Lance Corporal Stewart and Cadet Trownson attended a six week course at Mulberry Street Army School of Physical Training. The instructor was Frank Swift, the famous international goalkeeper (Frank played for Manchester City and England before taking a career as a football correspondent. He was killed, along with eight of Manchester United's Busby Babes and 34 other passengers, in the Munich air disaster on 6th February 1958). The annual camp had been arranged for 12th to 19th August at Stanley Park, Blackpool and cadets were reminded to get their qualifying attendances in to avoid disappointment. Cadets were encouraged to adopt an infantry battalion and some of the cadets had written to the Cameronians. Two dances, attended by the commanding officer and adjutant, were held in aid of the cadets' Welfare Fund and over £4 was raised. The British Legion, British Basket and Besto Company, Cadishead Conservative Club, Major Hill, Dr Laing, Mr S. Dawes,

Mr W. Armitage and A.J. Wright and Sons were also thanked for their contributions to the Welfare Fund. The cadets held activities each day of the week, except Saturdays. The following is a typical programme: parade on Sunday at 10.15am, followed by 'attack,' boxing training at HQ on Monday (7.30pm), normal parade at HQ on Tuesday (7.30pm), band practice at Moss Lane on Wednesday (7.30pm), physical training class at Monton on Thursday (7.30pm) and physical training class at Irlam Central School on Friday (7.15pm).

The activities of the 42nd Battalion, Home Guard, in the Eccles Salute the Soldier campaign were brought to a successful conclusion on Saturday, 6th May when they held the last guard mounting ceremony at Eccles Town Hall. After Lieutenant Colonel Webb inspected the guard, the Mayor, who had arrived to witness the ceremony, thanked the Home Guard units for their contribution to the Salute the Soldier campaign. The *Guardian* commented: *All ranks in the 42nd Battalion were indeed proud to assist in the campaign, but such pleasing and unrehearsed incidents as the Mayor's speech are greatly appreciated by all.*

Sergeant (air gunner) 2210202 **Henry Dale** of 35 Squadron, a pathfinder unit serving with No. 8 Group, Bomber Command, Royal Air Force Volunteer Reserve, was killed on air operations on Tuesday, 9th May.

Henry was an air gunner aboard Lancaster bomber Mark III, serial no. ME620, code letters TL-C, which took off from RAF Graveley, Cambridgeshire, at 01.58am on 9th May to bomb railway yards at Haine-St-Pierre. The aircraft crashed at Estinnes-au-Val (Hainaut), 12 kilometres east south east of Mons, Belgium, with the loss of six of the seven crew aboard.

The crew members who were killed were: J.C. Kemp (wireless operator), Flight Sergeant R.C. Clark, Flight Sergeant A.G. Boam, Sergeant L.A. Lewis, Sergeant Henry Dale and Sergeant D.C. Rhodes. Sergeant W.G. Lawrie survived the crash and evaded capture.

Henry, who was 34 years of age, joined the RAF in June 1943. Prior to enlisting he was employed by the Eccles Co-operative Society. He was also a member of Irlam Police Force, which he had joined in December 1941 (presumably as a special constable). He was the only son of Mr E. Dale of Windsor Avenue, Higher Irlam, and he resided, with his wife, at 78 Ferry Road, Irlam. Henry is buried, along with the other crew members who lost their lives, in a collective grave at Chievres Communal Cemetery, Belgium. Henry's wife did not receive official notification of his death (he had previously been officially reported missing) until April 1945.

The local fire guards went through their biggest test on Wednesday, 10th May when the regional Fire Guard Plan test exercise was held in Irlam and Cadishead. The plan was designed to test Fire Guard communications, the movement of Fire Guard reinforcements, and the suitability of the operational equipment (for example tallies, diagrams, and so forth) used in connection with the plan. The *Guardian* made the following comments before the exercise: *The exercise, for which many of us have been training for months, is designed to test the all-round efficiency of the organisation. If we succeed, we can breathe easily once more. If we fail – but we shall not – then it will be just too bad. Personally, I see no reason why we should not come through with flying colours. Sector exercises have revealed the weaknesses of our organisation and these, I believe, have been remedied. They have also shown us that we can do our stuff with the best of them. Let's hope it will be so on Wednesday. Don't let's have any mistakes. You know what happened during our last invasion exercise, don't you? There was the incident, you will recall, when the chief warden was 'shot' by an enthusiastic Home Guard five minutes before the declaration of 'war' and several incidents when wardens and Home Guards were so fed up with being 'shot' (I know one man who was three 'casualties') that they packed up and went home to bed. Our exercise – the dance of the Civil Defence Cinderellas – must be so good that the other services will sit up and take notice. Water on!* Sixteen sectors (chosen by the region) took part in the exercise, but the names of these sectors were withheld from the fire guard officer until shortly before the exercise. Within these sectors, 32 incidents were staged for the Fire Guard and 16 for NFS assistance. The exercise covered the whole district and included large works and street parties. The NFS appliances from the three local stations and from Eccles were in use. The chief umpire was the regional training officer, Miss Barbara Crosland and 16 sector and assistant sector umpires were recruited from the Eccles authority, 16 from the Swinton and Pendlebury authority and 33 incident umpires from the local ARP service. The regional fire prevention officer, Mr A.D.R. Crowley, also attended the exercise. NFS stations were umpired by officers from the NFS. The sector and incident umpires were briefed at 7.30pm. The voluntary car pool provided transport for the officers and umpires. All the fire guards in the district reported for duty and the 33 sector points in the district were manned promptly. The first 'incident' occurred at 8.30pm. Reinforcing teams carried their equipment, stirrup pumps and empty buckets and all the fire guards wore their steel helmets and armbands. The success of the exercise depended largely on speed and efficiency and the area captains in the district: Harry Crawford, Harold Roberts, Mr J.B. Askew, Fred Davies and Mr J.C. Booth, along with 33 sector captains and 135 party and block leaders, were all given final instructions. Shift work, however, interfered with the strength of many of the street parties, and in some cases token teams had to be sent when reinforcements were called for. The exercise ended at 9.30pm and an hour later an inquest was held at Irlam Conservative Club. Sector umpires, the NFS and sector captains gave their verdicts and explanations. The sector umpires and NFS were unanimous in their praise of the efficiency of the sector points, although they levelled some criticism of the system of locating two or more sector points in the same building. However, the peculiar geographical features of the district made this system the only practical one. Miss Crosland summed up, saying she had nothing but praise for the exercise; there had been one or two minor slips which were of no real importance, and she felt sure they would not happen again. The shortage of personnel was a factor over which they had no control. Regarding the location of two or three sector points in one building, she said that this was not desirable but she understood it was unavoidable. She hoped, if it was possible, that steps would be taken to separate them as the present arrangement presented too high a risk. In summary she congratulated Leslie Jones, the fire guard officer, on getting the organisation into such a high state of efficiency. She thanked Edwin Jones, clerk of the Council, for the facilities offered by the local authority and for the great interest he personally had shown in the exercise. She also thanked Assistant Fire Force Commander Keeley, Column Officer Peet, and the personnel of the NFS for the efficient manner in which they had co-operated in a good job of work. Assistant Fire Force Commander Keeley gave a brief reply in which he said the good relations existing between the NFS and Irlam Fire Guard would continue and he assured the fire guard officer of their full support. He explained that the Fire Guard was carrying out important work in districts which had been attacked by the enemy. He urged those present not to be lulled into a false sense of security because of the district's recent immunity from enemy raids. Leslie Jones thanked fire guards throughout the district for their magnificent effort. They had co-operated to the highest extent, and he was more than delighted with the result. Turning to Miss Crosland, he remarked that he would back the local Fire Guard organisation against any in the country. He thanked the NFS for their help, and said he felt sure that the two bodies would always work well together. The final report stated that out of the 33 sectors, 16 took part in the exercise, and sectors were reported as fit for testing. The personnel involved were described as well turned out, showing keenness and interest in the exercise, they were well trained and efficient, their equipment was described as good and messages were well made. There was a shortage of personnel in some sectors due to shift work, as the timing of the exercise took place at a time when two shifts were changing. The report commented that there had been some difficulty getting accommodation for sector points and, as a temporary measure, this had been overcome by setting up three sector points in one room. This was unsatisfactory and every sector umpire raised this as a concern.

A letter from Signalman Jimmy Darnton, serving with the Royal Corps of Signals in the British North African Force (BNAF), to the editor of the *Guardian* was published in 13th May edition: *Sir, let me congratulate you on your untiring efforts to secure a British Restaurant for Irlam and Cadishead. I look forward to the Guardian and enjoy your criticisms and straight from the shoulder talks in column one. Let me congratulate Jack Jones on his successful goodwill tour of the USA. You can always depend on our Jack telling people some home truths. I enjoyed Corporal J.N. Howe's letter. He expressed the opinion of most of the boys in the services at home or overseas. I may say that I'm one of his personal friends, and I know what he is talking about. I used to like your comments on the Rescuing Perishers, of which service I was a member. We all used to take it in the spirit of fun. I don't suppose you know me, but just ask any of the Council tenants or anyone who works for the Council. I was an employee of the Council for 16½ years before joining up, and a member of the rescue service for four years. I have watched with interest your untiring efforts to make the district a better place to live in, and only hope that you will get support from the local civic fathers. I am looking forward to seeing a better and brighter Irlam and Cadishead when this war is over. We don't want to be let down with promises as our fathers were after the last war. I know we have someone on our side to speak for us while we are absent. It will be up to us young people to see that there is no more war when we get back to normal.*

Sergeant Jack Kelly was promoted twice within the space of a few weeks. He was promoted from sergeant to company quartermaster sergeant in April followed by a further promotion in May to Sergeant Major (Warrant Officer Class 1). At the time he was serving in North Africa, in charge of a Fire Brigade, the sections of which were so widely scattered that he had to travel 50 miles to visit them all. Jack, who was 29 at the time, was a former honorary secretary of the Irlam and Cadishead Nursing Association. In a letter to his mother, Mrs E.E. Kelly of 11 Hayes Road, Cadishead, he stated that at first the question of transport was difficult, but he had been issued with a motorcycle so that he could visit the sections. Apparently England is not the only country in which the weather cannot be trusted as he wrote: *Our weather is rather mixed just now. We have had it so warm and sunny that short sleeve order appeared on the notice board – then, with the announcement, came a change in the weather, with wind, rain and mud.* Jack was educated at Cadishead Council School and Urmston Grammar School and was an Associate of the Chartered Institute of Secretaries. Before joining the Forces, he worked in the CWS offices.

There was an astonishing editorial in the *Guardian: Another aspect – one even more alarming – is the increase in the number of liaisons between the wives of men serving in the Forces and transient servicemen who come to this district. This is no time to wrap anything up – no time for anything but straight from the shoulder talk, so let's call this the vilest and most shameful act of treachery that can be offered by any woman to a man who is risking all to protect our way of life. And let us be even more brutally frank and call these women what they are – harpies, traitors to their husbands, their children and themselves. Why do they do it? Simply for a good time, free cigarettes, free drinks and the chance, in some cases, to pinch the wallet from some drunken soldier or sailor. You may argue that this is not the sort of stuff that ought to fill this column. I don't agree. The duty of every newspaper – and particularly of every local newspaper – is to do all in its power to maintain the fair name of the district it serves. No matter how painful that duty is, this newspaper, at any rate, will attempt to fulfil that mission.* How this article was received when it was read by local soldiers can only be imagined.

Signalman Jimmy Darnton, Royal Corps of Signals

Sidney Baguley, a reader of the *Guardian*, wrote to complain about the above article: *Sir, after reading the remarks by Onlooker in the last two issues of the Guardian, I feel they cannot be allowed to pass unchallenged, because I believe that the picture presented by them is an exaggeration of the actual position in the district. In order to view the matter in proper perspective, I think the following points should be borne in mind. 'Rouging and raddling' are in themselves quite harmless, and are certainly not synonymous with immorality. I have occasion to pass a naval camp each week and can honestly state that I do not see an average of more than two girls a week who could be judged guilty of haunting at least that particular establishment. The implication borne by the word 'lucky' and particularly, its inverted commas, is an insinuation against the chastity of our girls which is as unsupported by facts as it is unwarranted, and will be resented by other persons besides those against whom it is directed. By far the worst blunder that Onlooker made in the Guardian was his indiscriminate attack on the wives of servicemen, alleging liaison between them and members of the Forces visiting this district. Onlooker must be fully aware that a very large proportion of the serving men from this district receive copies of your paper each week from relatives and friends, and that the thoughts, day-dreams and hopes of these men centre very considerably round their wives. In spite of this, his lack of diplomacy allows him to write the mischievous paragraph that is most calculated to shatter or overshadow their dreams, to start a gnawing doubt, and subsequently to cause a possible misinterpretation of letters, the effects of which might well prove disastrous. It is, admittedly, a generally known fact that there are a few servicemen's wives and a few young girls whose behaviour is very objectionable, that of a lesser number, indeed, is atrocious, but I remain convinced that the majority of them are suffering from an attack of 'uniformania' and the relationships are in most cases perfectly harmless.* Sidney lived in Glazebrook Lane, Glazebrook.

Staff and workers at the Steelworks raised over £38 for the Red Army Day, and other works and street sellers raised a further £62, bringing the total to £100.

A sign saying: *Plenty of fish and plenty of lemon* appeared in the window of a local greengrocery, a sure sign that the food situation in the district was improving. The *Guardian* commented: *If we had seen that notice in a greengrocer's window 12 months ago, we could perhaps have been excused for thinking the war was over, and having a private celebration in a quiet corner of the local. But at least one greengrocer displayed such a notice in his window last week and, believe it or not, there was no queue – no line of eager women tearing each other's hair and kicking each other's shins in their anxiety to get a helping before anyone else. One day, we shall waken up and see notices in shop windows telling us that there is plenty of meat, butter, eggs, bacon, tea, sugar, bananas, oranges, apples, pears, peaches, grapes and such like. But there's a long way to go and a lot of hard fighting and hard work in front of us before we reach those halcyon days.*

The members of Higher Irlam keep-fit and tap-dancing class held a concert on Wednesday, 17th May which raised funds towards a cot in Stalingrad Hospital.

St John's monthly parish magazine carried the following message from Reverend Lee, which shows that people in the district were expecting the invasion of Europe to start any day: *Ere this month passes we may all be on tenterhooks as to the result of the combined operations against the so called Fortress of Europe. We must pray earnestly for the success of our mighty venture. We are all involved in one way or another; we are all equipped in one way or another for defence or for any emergency. But we all have the offensive spirit as well, to overcome the worst tyranny the world has ever known. We should never be ashamed to pray for victory in such a cause. Victory means the defeat and overthrow of our enemies; that is what all our sons and brothers and husbands have been training for, and we need to send these warriors forth in God's name, with all the spiritual backing we can – praying that they may stamp out this great world evil and deliver from bondage the poor, half-starved and downtrodden souls who are under the Nazi yoke. There may be many surprises, even for us at home; so with our prayers we must be watchful, and every one of us rigorously perform our duties that we may all be worthy of our warrior sons and daughters who are in the battle line.*

Fusilier 3663241 Owen Eugene McCarthy, serving with the 2nd Battalion, Lancashire Fusiliers (11th Brigade, 78th Division, 13 Corps) in Italy, was awarded the Military Medal for bravery on 16th May. The award recommendation reads: *On 16 May 44 after an attack on the C. SINAGOGA feature on the GUSTAV LINE, the company was attacked by tanks when digging in. Heavy casualties were caused, but Fusilier McCarthy C Company stretcher bearer, without hesitation rushed forward under heavy fire and dragged the wounded to cover and applied first aid. He went out several times under intense fire, completely disregarding his own personal safety in order to tend to the wounded and to see to their evacuation. In the afternoon the company attacked again and on reaching its objective came under intense shell and mortar fire. One stretcher bearer was killed, so with the remaining stretcher bearer he organized the evacuation of the casualties, he himself taking part in the long carries to the RAP until the battlefield was cleared of casualties. His tireless energy and courage under the most difficult conditions of constant enemy fire, was instrumental in saving a good many lives.* Owen was, by all accounts, a very modest man. He broke the news casually to his mother in a letter with the words *P.S. I've got the MM.* Twenty-two year old Owen was single at the time and lived with his mother at 6 Baines Avenue, Irlam. He joined the Army in January 1942, and first went overseas in May 1943, serving in North Africa and later Sicily and Italy. Before joining the Army he was employed in the Steelworks cost office. He was educated at St Teresa's School, Irlam.

Able Seaman Ronald Bell wrote a letter from Port of Spain, Trinidad, to the editor of the *Guardian* newspaper: *Sir, I have been serving abroad now for 17 months. The last ten months I have spent in Trinidad. What I am really writing for is to say how much I enjoy reading the Cadishead and Irlam Guardian. I have been receiving it now regularly for the past seven or eight months now. I pass it on to some Warrington chaps after I have read it. It is wonderful what a little bit of home news can do to a fellow when he is away. It is sure swell to read that the old place is doing so well in the war effort and to see some of the old faces again. What I enjoy most of all is the article Town Topics. Anyway, I only wish I could send you all some of the lovely bananas, oranges, grapefruit, etc, that we get out here for practically nothing in exchange for the enjoyment I get from reading the local rag. Not forgetting the everlasting sunshine we get out here, you can have it all. I would give anything right now to be in the middle of a glorious snowstorm after being in this heat for so long.*

Ronald was the eldest son of Joe and Elsie Bell of 77 Victory Road, Cadishead (the family had previously lived at 94 Lords Street, Cadishead). His brother, Kenneth Sydney Bell, served with the Royal Artillery and would lose his life during the Normandy landings in June, whilst attached to the Army Commandos.

Two brothers, Clifford (left) and Fred Yates, met each other in Italy. Clifford wrote a letter to his father, Pharaoh Yates of 4 Hayes Road, Cadishead to describe how his brother had travelled over 200 miles to meet him: *I have a wonderful surprise for you. Our Fred came down on Friday and we spent all Saturday together. He looks fine and has put on a good stone since you last saw him.* The brothers spent an enjoyable time together, saw two film shows and for the first time in many months Fred slept under a roof.

Sapper Clifford Yates joined the Royal Engineers in 1941 and went overseas in 1942. His wife, Ellen Yates (nee Jaques), lived at 9 Fiddlers Lane, Higher Irlam. Ellen was the sister of Flight Sergeant Ronald Thornley Jaques, who was serving with the RAF and would lose his life on air operations in April 1945. Gunner Fred Yates joined the Royal Artillery in 1939 and initially served in India and was later posted to North Africa and joined the Eighth Army before the Battle of El Alamein. Fred was married to Nellie (nee Tootell) and they lived in Marlborough Road, Higher Irlam. Both Fred and Clifford were born in Cadishead and both worked as dockers for the Manchester Ship Canal Company.

The *Guardian* reported on the contribution of two local families who had served in both wars. The first, James McLean of 16 Oak Avenue, Cadishead, was a veteran of the South African War and the First World War. James was born in 1879, a native of Holytown, Lanarkshire, Scotland. He moved to Cadishead to work at the Steelworks shortly before the First World War. James had three sons and two son-in-laws who were serving in the Armed Forces. His eldest son, 33 year old Leading Aircraftman James Campbell McLean, was serving with the RAF. He was married and he resided at 8 Eldon Road, Irlam. Before joining the RAF in 1941 he was employed by Eccles Co-operative Society at Urmston. Another son, Leading Aircraftman John Pollock McLean joined the RAF in 1940, serving with the flying boat service. He had served for a time in the Azores but by May 1944 he was at a flying boat base in the Home Counties. Joseph's youngest son, 20 year old Sergeant Robert McLean, was with the Royal Marine Commandos. Prior to being called up in 1942 he had the distinction, at the age of 16, of being the youngest member of the district's Home Guard, which he had joined on 31st July 1940 (Private B95, 6 Platoon, D Company). He may have misled the Home Guard over his date of birth in order to enlist. His Home Guard record states his date of birth as 1921, whereas he was actually born in 1923. He joined the Royal Marines on 13th June 1942. Joseph's two son-in-laws: Robert Dickinson of Caroline Street, Irlam and Sydney Everett of Oak Avenue, Cadishead were also in the Forces. Robert was with the RAF and Sydney was an artificer in the Royal Navy.

George Lloyd of 4 Lines Road, Irlam, who had won the Military Medal whilst serving with the Royal Army Medical Corps on the Western Front during the First World War, was proud to have his four daughters all serving with the ATS, they were twins, Lance Corporal Daisy Lloyd and Private Mary Lloyd, 22 year old Private Gwen Lloyd and 19 year old Private Marjorie Lloyd who was a former member of the local WJAC where she had learnt Morse code. Gwen Lloyd gave this account in the Irlam, Cadishead and District Local History Society's publication entitled *Wartime Memories: I think a little bit of local history was made in the last war when my three sisters and I served in the ATS. My sisters, twins Daisy and Mary, volunteered in November 1941 and May 1942 respectively. I was called up in June in 1942 and Marjorie in March 1944. Daisy, Marjorie and I were all in the Royal Signal Corps as teleprinter operators, Daisy and I being stationed together at Luton Hoo. Mary went into the Royal Artillery with the 559(M) Heavy Anti-Aircraft Battery. Our father George Lloyd won the Military Medal in the 1914-1918 war during which he also lost a leg. That didn't stop him from 'digging for victory' on an allotment in Prince's Park where he was helped by my brother William (Bill). Bill was still at school when the war started. Later he worked on a farm on Irlam Moss where he stayed until the end of the war, farming of course being a reserved occupation. Our mother helped the food supply by keeping hens in the back garden. She also kept us up to date with all the news of relatives and friends by writing to each of us every week and by sending the Irlam and Cadishead Guardian.*

On Sunday, 21st May a concert was held at the Rialto in aid of the Comforts Fund. It was arranged by Wilfred Loach and the coal trimmers at the Partington Coaling Basin and was a follow up to a concert they had held earlier in the year, which raised £66 for the Red Cross. More than 700 people attended and over £90 was raised. During the interval, Councillor Albert J. Keal, chairman of the Comforts Fund Committee, thanked Mr Loach and his men for their fine effort.

Sergeant Fred Clarke gained his navigator wings during the month, while stationed at Malton, Ontario, Canada. Fred was born c.1912, the youngest son of Mr and Mrs Clarke of 5 Leader Williams Road, Irlam. Educated at St Teresa's School, he had won the George Thomas Scholarship and finished his education at Manchester College of Technology. He was married and lived with his wife in Flixton. Prior to joining the RAF in 1942 he had worked as a pattern maker at Royles Engineering Ltd. He was posted to Canada for training in November 1943.

Fusilier Dennis Westall of 15 Harewood Road, Irlam was interviewed by war correspondent, Cyril Bewley, near Cassino in Italy. The correspondent was collecting messages from men of the Eighth Army with the intention of sending them back to their families (Cyril was killed by a landmine shortly after the interview, on 18th May). In a greeting to his wife, Dennis said: *I am all right and hope to be home soon. This isn't a bad life but it will be grand to get back.* In civilian life, Dennis was a bus conductor. He had joined the Army in 1939 and served as a driver. In the interview he confessed that he had never known that driving could be so monotonous and much preferred his old conductor's platform.

Gunner Arthur Darnton, Royal Artillery, wrote to the editor of the *Guardian* on the subject of post-war planning: *Sir, your items by the men in the Forces deeply interest me. Some ideas proposed seem to me to be rather out of place. To build a local hospital may sound like a good idea; I admit we could do with one, but has your correspondent considered the capital expense and the running costs? It is a pity the local public don't take a greater interest in the local Nursing Association. By attending its meetings they may find a thing or two out, particularly regarding the upkeep of a hospital. In my opinion, such a project is looking too far ahead. Before we ever start talking about such matters, the first thing that must be done is to prepare an Irlam and Cadishead ready for the Forces when they return home. Most of us have jobs awaiting us, but there will be plenty who have not. Please don't have them queuing up at the labour exchange week after week. There are plenty of us who have married since the war started. We shall require houses of our own; our in-laws, etc, may be very nice people, but we don't want to impose on their generosity all the days of our lives. These plans must be made now. What I would like to see is a health-minded new generation in the district. We have evening educational classes, how about evening physical training classes? They could be started immediately. You never know, sir, you may be able to get that rugby team you would like to see in the district out of these lads. My final suggestion; how about a swimming bath in the district? I have heard of such places being converted into dance halls etc, during the winter months; the slipper baths could be kept open winter and summer. I am sure there are plenty of men who would make use of them when returning from work. Building space should be no excuse for abandoning such an idea.*

Arthur was unaware that physical training classes were held in the district, a public baths had been approved, together with a large new civic hall, which would include a large assembly hall and public library. All these plans were on hold until after the war.

Two local men, Private Tom Bryan and Naval Gunner William Powell, met each other while serving overseas. Thirty-four year old William was married and resided with his wife at 17 Allotment Road, Cadishead. His mother, Ada, lived at 10 York Road, Cadishead. William was educated at Irlam Endowed School and was later employed by the Steelworks until he joined the Royal Navy in 1941. His brother, Bertram, was serving with a Bomb Disposal Unit. Their elder brother, Joseph, was killed during the Battle of Passchendaele in 1917, while serving as a Lance Corporal in the Manchester Regiment. Tom Bryan was educated at Cadishead Senior School and was later employed by the Eccles Co-operative Society. His mother lived in Liverpool Road, Cadishead.

Private Tom Bryan and Gunner William Powell

A shoot by the Home Guard demonstrated that members of the 42nd Battalion could achieve scores with a Sten gun which, under Regular Army conditions, would qualify them as first class marksmen. A battle training school was opened during the last week of May which was managed by Captain G.N. Coop, the 42nd Battalion's training officer. The school provided instruction on the advanced phases of infantry warfare, including tactical training.

Two weddings involving local servicemen took place in the district on Saturday, 27th May; the first was between Cedric Arthur Borrino, Royal Navy, who married Annie Thomas at Cadishead Congregational Church. Annie was the youngest daughter of Mrs Thomas of 10 Rutland Road, Cadishead. The best man was Cedric's brother, Petty Officer Alex Borrino of the Submarine Service.

The second wedding was between Sapper Reginald Cottam, Royal Engineers, who married Julia Attenborough, the eldest daughter of Mr and Mrs W.A. Attenborough of 10 Hamilton Avenue, Cadishead. Reginald was the son of Mr and Mrs J. Cottam of

61 Lords Street, Cadishead. Two brothers, Lawrence and John, were serving in the Armed Forces.

Sapper Reginald Cottam and Julia Attenborough

Fire guards at posts 4, 5 and 6 raised the staggering sum of £120 for the United Aid to China Fund. House-to-house collections accounted for £51, in April a billiards week had raised £41 and a further £15 was raised by a dance. An effort organised by Mrs Banks made over £12.

New rations books were issued and, during the five weeks in May and June that the distribution centre was open, over 12,000 books were issued. Residents applying for the new books were required to provide personal information about themselves and their families on page 3 of the new ration book.

Around this time, two local men who had been prisoners of war since being captured during the Dunkirk evacuations in May 1940, Fusilier Harry Hutchinson and Private Hubert Jones, met each other in the German prisoner of war camp, Stalag VIIIB.

Members of 292 (Eccles) Squadron, ATC, including a number of cadets from Irlam detached flight, visited an RAF station in North Wales, where they received instruction on the firing range, on engines and on small arms.

JUNE

In the Far East, the closing stages of the Battle of Kohima were being played out. Local man Sergeant 3657233 Fred Bentham was serving with B Company of the 2nd Battalion of the South Lancashire Regiment (114th Indian Infantry Brigade). On 1st June the battalion came into the front line at Kohima, taking up a position known as Church Knoll, which was only 50 yards from the Japanese. The monsoon had started and the conditions for the troops were terrible. No man's land was thick with mud and there were the remains of many bodies strewn around. On the night of 1st June the 114th Brigade delivered a strong attack which forced the Japanese to withdraw and the next day the 2nd South Lancashires took over the enemy positions. Other battalions of the 114th Infantry Brigade pursued the retreating Japanese and on 5th June the 2nd South Lancashires went forward, covering over 20 miles in two days across difficult terrain. On 7th June the battalion occupied the village of Kezoma and then moved out across a high ridge. Patrols from C Company discovered that the Japanese were in a strong position near the village of Kidema. A and C Companies of the South Lancashires dug in 500 yards away from the Japanese positions, while the rest of the battalion took up positions behind them. For three days the South Lancashires probed and mortared the Japanese positions. On 12th June, after artillery and mortar preparations, the battalion attacked the Japanese positions. The battalion was split into two forces, with Force 1 comprising A and C Companies and Force 2 comprising B and D, plus the mortar platoon and medium machine-gun section of the 4th/5th Royal Ghurkha Rifles.

Force 1, who were to attack from the south, set off at 6.30pm on 11th June and Force 2, who were to infiltrate the village from the north, set off at 3.30am on 12th June. Force 1 had to cross difficult terrain and also ran into an enemy outpost which meant that they arrived at their assault positions after the planned start time. Previous orders were to withdraw if they were not in position at the appointed time, which they did. A and C unknowingly went ahead with the attack and were immediately met by heavy enemy fire which pinned them down. They managed to clear the first line of enemy bunkers but were held up at the second line and forced to withdraw. Two men were killed and 13 others were wounded during the attack.

Two days later a patrol found that the Japanese had withdrawn from the village and the battalion moved up to occupy the village, where they remained for a week. On 28th June they were moved back to a rest camp at Kohima. The regimental history of the South Lancashire Regiment had this to say about the battalion's first taste of action with the Japanese: *During its first experience of this front, the battalion had tasted to the full the rigours of campaigning in these wild and broken Naga Hills at the height of the monsoon season, and nobody who has not experienced it can appreciate the sheer misery and discomfort of struggling up and down the steep slopes in pouring rain and with clothes* perpetually wet. All supplies had to be brought forward on mule-back over slippery tracks, which were either ankle deep in mud or little more than torrents, and some of the men were beginning to show signs of malnutrition by the time the battalion was rested. Nevertheless, the enemy had been given no respite and the battalion had inflicted continuous casualties on him, while itself losing four other ranks killed and two officers and 19 other ranks wounded.

Sergeant Fred Bentham, South Lancashire Regiment

Fred was born in the district on 16th July 1917, the son of Arthur and Annie Bentham (nee Clarke). He resided in Lytherton Avenue, Cadishead, and worked as a labourer, and then as an oiler and greaser, at the Steelworks. In 1938, he married Josephine Beddows and they had a daughter, Beryl. Fred was called up on 15th February 1940. At the end of his service he received two testimonials from his commanding officers, both of whom clearly had great respect for Fred. The first described his military conduct as exemplary and stated: *This man has been an NCO for nearly five years and is capable of exceptional responsibility and of investing others under him. He is a hard and willing worker and is reliable, honest and trustworthy. He is moderate in his habits, clean and respectful.* The second testimonial from the Lieutenant Colonel of the 2nd South Lancashire Regiment was written on 15th November 1945: *Over a long period, much of it spent under the trying conditions of active service, this man has shown a constant devotion to duty. This has called for steadiness, reliability, honesty and a capacity for hard work coupled with initiative. He has at all times remained cheerful and willing in his duties.* Fred was demobilised in February 1946.

Sergeant Fred Bentham, South Lancashire Regiment

The massive preparations for the invasion of Europe could not be hidden from the Germans therefore the Allies staged a series of elaborate deceptions designed to keep the enemy unaware of the precise locations of the landings. As part of this, the 52nd (Lowland) Division, who, despite their Lowland name, were designated as Mountain troops, were in Scotland, preparing for a fake invasion of Norway. They were all kitted out with frost-proof boots, thermal clothes, woollen hats, rucksacks and red goggles for snow blindness. One of the men serving with the division was Lance Corporal 2601840 Harold Bate. In a later twist of irony, the 52nd Division would see action, in November 1944, on the Scheldt in Holland, which was below sea level.

Seaman Lawrie Cottam was serving with Landing Craft 180 which had been transferred from the Mediterranean to the highlands of Scotland as part of the preparations for the Normandy landings: *While we were in Invergordon, our officer told us to let it slip that we were going to invade through Norway. This was a ploy and it actually worked. Hitler did send divisions to Norway, expecting us to invade there. Fortunately for us, after our ship was repaired and tested, we suddenly on the 1st June 1944 were told to head post haste right down the coast to Brighton. We reversed into the canal, between Brighton and Hove gas works and were packed in side by side. On 3rd June the wagons started to roll up on the dockside bringing loads of assault troops. The soldiers simply walked across to the outside craft and filled each craft to the limit. It wasn't a bit like summer. The weather was dull and grey and cold. We set sail and sailed all night. Early the next morning we landed on the beach in Normandy. D-Day had started. There were five beaches.*

On Saturday, 3rd June the wedding took place at St John's Church, Irlam, between Signaller Roy Valentine, Royal Marines, and Radio Operator Silvia Mellor, who was serving with an anti-aircraft section of the Auxiliary Territorial Service. Born in 1922 (birth registered at Barton I. in March 1922), Roy was the eldest son of Mr and Mrs William Valentine of 24 Ash Avenue, Cadishead. He joined the Home Guard on 22nd July 1940, serving as Private 410 in 3 Platoon of D Company, until he joined the Royal Marines on 17th September 1941. Silvia was the only daughter of Mrs and the late Mr H. Mellor of 40 Ferryhill Road, Irlam. Before the war, both Roy and Silvia had worked for the Eccles Co-operative Society.

Control of the English Channel was essential for the Normandy landings to succeed. In particular, if U-boats were allowed to operate successfully in the Channel the invasion fleet would be decimated before it reached France. Anti-submarine warfare was therefore an important element of the Naval strategy for D-Day. Able Seaman Arthur Roberts was serving as a submarine detector (ASDICs) on board HMS *Hind*; a modified Black Swan-class sloop, which had been completed on 11th April 1944. She carried the latest design of surface warning radar and a standard fire control radar. She was also fitted with Hedgehogs (anti-submarine ahead throwing mortars). Arthur had previously served on HMS *Scylla* until she was damaged and returned to the UK for a refit in November 1943. When he left *Scylla* on 31st December 1943, he was sent for specialised ASDIC training to HMS *Nimrod*, an anti-submarine training base in Campbeltown on the Kintyre peninsula in Scotland. On 26th February 1944, he was sent to HMS *Osprey*, which was the Navy's main anti-submarine training base, located at Dunoon. When Arthur qualified as a submarine detector his trade certificate described him as: *A quiet and very reliable worker, good appearance and manner, above average intelligence.* He joined HMS *Hind* on 18th March in time for Acceptance Trials.

In May HMS *Hind* was nominated for service in support of the Normandy landings and transferred to G Force, where she was deployed as part of Escort Group 112. On 6th June she escorted convoy G3, comprising 24 landing craft carrying the US Build-up Division to the Western Task Force area. She remained on escort duties in the Channel during the month of June (after a refit, HMS *Hind* was posted to the Eastern Fleet in November and served out of Ceylon on escort and patrol duties in the Indian Ocean). Throughout his time in the Royal Navy, Arthur's character was described as very good.

HMS *Hind*

Another local man involved in anti-submarine operations to protect the Normandy Landings was Kenneth Barnaby, who served on board HMS *Starling*. Ken's regular duties on the ship involved dealing with stores, but during action stations he was either with the magazine crew or on the ammunition hoists where he would signal down the type of shells that were needed.

After a refit in December 1943, *Starling* returned to Atlantic convoy duties on 26th January and five days later she took part in the sinking of U592, south west of Ireland. On 8th February she was involved in the sinking of U762 and next day she had to fend off acoustic torpedo attacks from U238 and U734. Both these submarines were destroyed by the escort group after an extensive search. On 19th February she took part in the sinking of U264. At the end of the patrol (26th February), the group had sunk six U-boats and proven the effectiveness of creeping anti-submarine attacks, as perfected by the captain of HMS *Starling*, Frederick John Walker. On 7th March she provided support to convoys in the North West Approaches and on 15th March she worked with the aircraft carrier HMS *Vindex* and HM sloops *Magpie*, *Wild Goose* and *Wren* to sink U653, which had initially been spotted by a Swordfish aircraft from the aircraft carrier.

On 29th March *Starling* joined a Russian convoy and during the passage she sank U961. On 2nd and 3rd April the convoy came under a series of unsuccessful attacks by U-boats. After returning to the UK, *Starling* underwent some weather damage repairs in Liverpool (15th to 28th April) and then re-joined the group for anti-submarine support operations in the South West Approaches. On 6th May an operation by HMS *Starling*, *Wild Goose* and *Wren* forced U473 to surface, which was then sunk by gunfire. She returned to Liverpool and on 29th May she was deployed in support of convoys in the Western Approaches. In June and July she took part in anti-submarine operations in the English Channel, in support of the Normandy landings.

After the Normandy landings, *Starling* returned to Liverpool on 1st July and while there Captain Walker passed away on 9th July. From 28th July *Starling* was deployed in the South West Approaches, working with 3rd Support Group in combination with RAF aircraft, to prevent U-boats entering the English Channel and to intercept submarines in the Bay of Biscay before they could attack Atlantic convoys. Three days later she sank U333 and then on 6th August she sank U736. On 11th August she engaged U385 on the surface but lost contact with her when she submerged. U385 was later sighted and attacked by Sunderland aircraft of 461 Squadron, RAAF. *Starling* and other members of the group joined in the attack and the U-boat crew eventually abandoned ship.

During August the group sank four U-boats. In September *Starling* was deployed in the Western Approaches on convoy support operations and then on 30th September she was taken to Falmouth for a refit. In January 1945 she returned to convoy support operations in the Western Approaches and on 16th January she took part in the sinking of U482, after the escort carrier HMS *Thane* had been torpedoed in the Clyde. In February *Starling* was nominated for service in the British Pacific Fleet and was sent for a refit. The war with Japan ended before *Starling* could make the passage to the Far East and the ship returned to Devonport where the crew were paid off.

On the eve of D-Day, 5th June Horsa gliders took off from RAF Tarrant Rushton, towed by Lancaster and Stirling bombers across the English Channel to Normandy, France. These airborne troops are best remembered for their part in the action at Pegasus Bridge. Leading Aircraftman 1326402 John Llewellyn Williams was an armourer, stationed at RAF Tarrant Rushton, who worked on the Lancaster bombers that were used in this operation.

Leading Aircraftman John Llewellyn Williams

John enlisted into the RAF on 9th August 1940 and served as an armourer in Bomber, Fighter and Coastal Commands. He was, for a time, also attached to the USAAF at Norfolk. His basic training was undertaken at RAF Kirkham and Freckleton and he went on to serve all over the UK including Yorkshire, Lincolnshire, Dorset, and Stranraer in Scotland. Among the aircraft he worked on were Lancasters, Halifaxes, Mosquitoes, Spitfires, Hurricanes and Catalina flying boats. His son, Barry, remembered that, typical of his generation, John would tell humorous stories of service life, but was reticent about the darker side of war. Although he once mentioned the terrible losses of Bomber Command and that one of his jobs was to attend returning 'shot-up' aircraft to remove the gory remains of tail gunners from the rear turrets, and then wash out the turret with a hosepipe.

John was born in Rhuddlan, North Wales, on 8th May 1912, the son of John and Mary Williams. The family moved to The Crescent, Irlam, in the early 1930s to seek employment at the Steelworks. He married Gladys Skeels in 1936 and they set up home together at 5 Silverdale Avenue, Irlam. Before he was called up John was a member of the local Home Guard, serving as Private 353 in 1 Platoon of D Company.

D-Day Landings

After months of secretive planning and the massive build-up of men and materials the Allies were ready to invade the European mainland. The original landings were planned for 5th June and many of the assaulting troops had already been loaded onto the transport ships in readiness for the landings when a storm broke, which resulted in a 24 hour delay. Unfortunately the troops on the transports had to remain on board throughout this time and many suffered from seasickness. Finally orders were given and the invasion began with a massive airborne assault, with American paratroops landing near Carentan, France, on the west flank of the invasion area, and British paratroops on the eastern flank.

Despite the intensive preparations, the Normandy landings were a massive gamble and the fear and apprehension of all the men and women involved was tangible. Trevor Jenkins at Wanstead recalled: *I'd been on duty that morning when they went, oh it was chaos, bloody hell. The wires were red hot. All these all talking, the place was bulging, fear was all over the place, even round Wanstead and there, fields of tanks and God knows what, you know, all ready for the off.*

The following message from General Bernard Montgomery was read out to British troops on the eve of the D-Day landings. This document is from the personal collection of Sergeant Norman Jones of 39 (7th Lancashire Fusiliers) Anti-Aircraft Battalion, Royal Artillery.

21 ARMY GROUP

PERSONAL MESSAGE FROM THE C-in-C

To be read out to all Troops

1. The time has come to deal the enemy a terrific blow in Western Europe.

The blow will be struck by the combined sea, land, and air forces of the Allies—together constituting one great Allied team, under the supreme command of General Eisenhower.

2. On the eve of this great adventure I send my best wishes to every soldier in the Allied team.

To us is given the honour of striking a blow for freedom which will live in history; and in the better days that lie ahead men will speak with pride of our doings. We have a great and a righteous cause.

Let us pray that " The Lord Mighty in Battle " will go forth with our armies, and that His special providence will aid us in the struggle.

3. I want every soldier to know that I have complete confidence in the successful outcome of the operations that we are now about to begin.

With stout hearts, and with enthusiasm for the contest, let us go forward to victory.

4. And, as we enter the battle, let us recall the words of a famous soldier spoken many years ago :—

> " He either fears his fate too much,
> Or his deserts are small,
> Who dare not put it to the touch,
> To win or lose it all."

5. Good luck to each one of you. And good hunting on the mainland of Europe.

B. L. Montgomery
General
C.-in-C 21 Army Group.

1944.

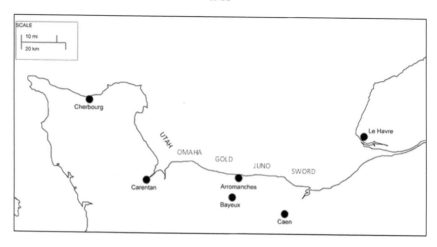

Normandy Beaches

During the night of 5th/6th June nearly 5,000 landing ships and assault craft carrying 130,000 troops, escorted by the Royal Navy, set sail for France. Tuesday, 6th June was a dull and wet day, with low cloud and choppy seas. After a night-time naval and RAF bombardment of the German coastal defences, the British, Canadian and Free French soldiers came ashore on three Normandy beaches: Gold, Juno and Sword, and the Americans on Utah and Omaha. The troops faced varying levels of opposition, depending on the strength of the local enemy forces and the effectiveness of the naval bombardment in each particular area. As the landing crafts came into sight the German troops opened up with artillery, machine-gun and rifle fire. The landing craft also had to negotiate mines and underwater obstructions and a number were lost. The men in the landing vessels would have been very aware of the artillery fire and the ping of machine-gun and rifle bullets hitting the sides of the craft.

Lawrie Cottam of Cadishead was on board Landing Craft 180 on that fateful day: *The British landed at Sword, Gold and Juno. The Americans landed on Utah and Omaha. It was rough on the three British beaches with an average of about 400 dead on each, but the Americans suffered severely; especially at Omaha, where three thousand young men were all dead, either on the beach or floating in the water. It was terrible. Even the German machine-gunners confessed, at a later date, that they were sick of killing young men – many of them only 19 and 20 years of age. We landed English troops on Sword beach, near Arromanches, and then took Canadian reinforcements to Juno beach.*

Irlam man, Able Seaman Jack Ainscough, was serving on board Landing Ship Tank No. 415 (or 'Large Stationary Target' as the crews commonly called them) during the D-Day landings. As suggested by their official name, these ships were used to land tanks after the first assault waves had cleared the beaches.

Landing Ship Tanks 320 and 415 on the Normandy Beaches on D-Day

Landing Ship Tanks on Sword Beach

When the landing crafts hit the beach the men charged down the ramps, sometimes into deep water, while shells and bullets struck the water around them and some troops were hit before they reached land. Once they reached the beach the men were faced with landmines and barbed wire, as well as the continuing shelling and machine-gun, mortar and rifle fire. By 8am the first assault waves had landed and the beaches were conquered quickly, establishing the bridgeheads necessary for the landing of the following waves of men and materials. On Omaha beach, however, the Americans were held up for several hours by heavy gunfire.

Once the beaches were secured, the next priority was to supply the troops with weapons, ammunition, fuel, food and clothing and reinforcements. The innovative Allied solution to overcome the lack of a deep water harbour in this region was to fabricate two artificial harbours in the UK, Operation Mulberry, and to transport them in sections across the Channel. One of these harbours was erected off the coast of Arromanches and the other at Saint-Laurent-sur-Mer. As the troops pushed inland from the Normandy beaches, more men and materials were arriving at the artificial harbours. Two local men helped to erect the Mulberries. The following letter written by Sapper James E. Arstall, Royal Engineers, was published in the *Guardian*: *Sir, I suppose local people have read about the pre-fabricated port at Arromanches. Maybe they would like to know that two local lads, Sapper K. Lennell of Irlam, and Sapper J.E. Arstall of Cadishead, helped to build sections of the port in England, floated and maintained sections of it during the dangerous passages across the English Channel on and after D-Day. The same company of Royal Engineers to which we belong set it in position with the help of the British and American Navies, and are still maintaining the port which the Navy has been given all the credit for. In my opinion the port has been the mainstay of the second front and is a credit to the Royal Engineers.*

James Arstall was born in 1911 (birth registered in Warrington). He married Hilda Renney in 1935 and they resided together at 94 Lords Street, Cadishead. On 14th July 1940 he joined the Home Guard as Private B100 J.E. Arstall, and served in 6 Platoon, D Company. He joined the Royal Engineers on 22nd November 1942.

Four local men would lose their lives on D-Day itself: James Sweeney, Benjamin Wilson, Kenneth Sydney Bell and Arthur Hilton.

Corporal James Sweeney and Private Ben Wilson, who were both serving with the 1st Battalion, South Lancashire Regiment, 8th Brigade, 3rd Infantry Division (I Corps), were killed during the Normandy landings on 6th June. Their battalion was among the first wave of troops to land at Queen White sector of Sword Beach at 7.30am between La Breche and Lion-sur-Mer. By 9am the battalion had captured its objective at Hermanville sur Mer.

Private 3655928 **Ben Wilson**, 1st South Lancashire Regiment, was wounded while wading ashore at Sword Beach and died shortly afterwards. His brother, George, serving with the same battalion, was with him at the time.

Ben was the youngest son of George and Elizabeth Wilson of 7 Francis Road, Irlam. He was educated at Irlam Central School and then went to work at the Steelworks. He married Lily Talbot on 28th November 1940 at St Mary's Church, Cadishead, and they set up home at 16 Partington Avenue, Irlam. Ben joined the Army on 12th November 1939, went overseas in February 1940 and was one of those evacuated from Dunkirk in May of the same year. He is buried at Hermanville War Cemetery, France. His gravestone has the epitaph: *Not a day do we forget you through the passing years, loving wife Lily and Carol.* He was 26 years old. Ben and George's sister, Ruth, served with the ATS, attached to a Royal Artillery unit.

Headstones of Kenneth Sydney Bell, Ben Wilson and James Sweeney at Hermanville War Cemetery

Corporal 3658740 **James Sweeney** was killed in action at some point during the landings on Sword Beach, or on the advance inland, on Tuesday, 6th June.

Born in the district in 1915, he was the eldest son of James and Caroline Selina Sweeney (nee Royle) of 12 Dixon Street, Irlam. He was educated at Irlam Endowed School. He married Thelma Gilmore in mid-1937, at Barton-upon-Irwell Registry Office, and their twin sons, Anthony and Terence, were born the following year. They resided together at 6 Rothiemay Road, Flixton, and James worked for W.H. Bailey, corn merchants of Urmston. He joined the Army in February 1941 and was stationed in the UK until the D-Day landings.

James is buried at Hermanville War Cemetery, France, and his gravestone carries the following inscription: *In loving memory of my beloved husband James. Killed in Action.* He was originally posted missing and it was September before his family learnt his fate. His name is missing from the Irlam and Cadishead War Memorial in Prince's Park but he is commemorated on the St Michael's Church Memorial in Flixton. He was 29 years old.

Corporal Ben Wilson, South Lancashire Regiment

Gunner 2082283 **Kenneth Sydney Bell** of the Royal Artillery was killed in action at some point during the fighting on 6th June. He was attached to No. 3 Commando, which was part of the 1st Special Service Brigade, 3rd Infantry Division (I Corps).

The brigade landed in the second wave at La Breche in the centre of Sword Beach, shortly after 9am. Their task was to link up with the 6th Airborne Division on the eastern flank of Sword Beach and to secure the high ground near Amfreville (Le Plein). The landing crafts came under artillery fire as they neared the beach and three of the craft were hit, sustaining casualties. Once ashore they made their way inland, but were held up at a narrow point of the route by No. 6 Commando. Later they advanced through Colleville and along the road to St Aubin d'Aquenay where they joined up with No. 6 Commando. They continued forward to a bridge over the River Orne, where they met Allied airborne troops who had taken the bridge early that morning. They then crossed the bridge, which was still under fire from German snipers. Airborne headquarters ordered the commandos to move to Le Bas de Ranville instead of continuing their planned advance to Cabourg. No. 3 Commando was detached and ordered to continue with their original objective to take Amfreville and Le Plein, while the rest of the commando took up their new positions. They were soon relieved and then completed their orders by holding the high ground around Le Plein.

Kenneth was educated at Cadishead Senior School and was formerly employed by the Irlam Brick Company, Rixton. He married Lillian Mary Barcroft in March 1941 and they lived together at Higher Ormond Street, Manchester. His parents, Joe and Elsie Bell, lived at 77 Victory Road, Cadishead and his brother, Able Seaman Ronald Bell, served in the Royal Navy. Kenneth joined the Territorials in February 1939, and first served with the Royal Artillery before volunteering for the Commandos. He is buried at Hermanville War Cemetery, Normandy, and his gravestone carries the following inscription: *Grant unto him O Lord Eternal Peace*. He was 23 years old.

Corporal PLY/X120196 **Arthur Hilton** was killed in action during the fighting on 6th June. He served with No. 48 (Royal Marine) Commandos, which was part of the 4th Special Service Brigade of the 79th Armoured Division (I Corps). No. 48 (Royal Marine) Commando was formed by the conversion of the 7th Royal Marine Battalion and the Mobile Naval Base Defence Organisations in March 1944. It was the last commando unit to be formed during the war.

Under the command of Lieutenant Colonel James Moulton, it carried out a shortened commando course at Achnacarry in the Scottish Highlands and then joined the Royal

Marine 4ᵗʰ Special Service Brigade alongside Royal Marine Commando Nos. 41, 46 and 47.

Corporal Arthur Hilton, 48 (Royal Marine) Commando

Assigned to the Normandy landings, 4ᵗʰ Special Service Brigade was given the task of capturing several coastal villages, including Luc-sur-Mer, St Aubin-sur-Mer and Langrune-sur-Mer. Their next task was to advance inland, capture the heavily fortified strongpoint near the radar station at Douvres, and hold the position for 48 hours. The lightly equipped and highly mobile commandos of 48 TM Commando were to follow the Canadian North Shore (New Brunswick) Regiment onto the beach. By the time the commando arrived the beach should have been cleared of German resistance. The commando were given the task of advancing two miles to the seaside town of Langrune-sur-Mer, clearing the coast as they went. Once they had secured the town, they were to attack the German strongpoint WN26 from the rear. A party was also to be sent eastwards to the hamlet of Petit Enfer to make contact with 41 (Royal Marine) Commando and linking Juno and Sword beaches.

On the evening of 5ᵗʰ June they left Southampton on board six Landing Craft Infantry (Small). Unlike the landing craft with a large ramp at the front which are often portrayed in movies, the commandos had to leave these landing craft via two stair-like landing ramps which were brought down at the front of the craft. By the time they arrived at Normandy many of the men were suffering the effects of seasickness.

Landing on sector 7 of Nan Red sector (Juno Beach) on 6ᵗʰ June No. 48 (Royal Marine) Commando was the first Commando unit to land near St Aubin-sur-Mer. Although the Canadians had landed at 8.05am, 35 minutes before the commandos arrived, it was soon apparent that the Canadians had been held up and there were still considerable pockets of Germans resistance in the beach area. Two of the six landing craft (those containing Y and Z Troop) were caught on undersea obstacles and the commandos were forced to swim for shore, many of them drowned, while others were shot as they assembled on the decks. Those that made it to shore, and the commandos from the other four craft, found the beach littered with dead and dying Canadians. Many of the commandos took shelter alongside a seawall, which protected them from most of the enemy fire. However, once in the shelter of the wall the commandos were pinned down and it was difficult to advance to their first objective. Eventually, they made their way off the beach and launched the assault on Langrune-sur-Mer, which was captured after severe hand-to-hand fighting and heavy losses. They then held the position awaiting the arrival of reinforcements and equipment from offshore. Once the rest of 4th Special Service Brigade had landed, 48 (Royal Marine) Commando made two unsuccessful attempts to take a hill near the village of Dozule. After being reinforced by 46 and 47 Commandos they bypassed the village of Dozule and occupied the high ground at point 120, cutting off a number of retreating Germans and destroying their vehicles.

Born c.1918, Arthur was the only son of Annie and the late William Hilton of 45 Marlborough Road, Higher Irlam. He was educated at Irlam Endowed School and Irlam Central School before being employed by the Steelworks. He joined the Forces in February 1940 and was posted overseas in February 1943, taking part in the African, Sicilian and Italian campaigns, probably with 7 Royal Marine Battalion. He was wounded at Salerno, Italy, in 1943.

Arthur was killed at some point during the fighting on 6th June and now lies buried at Bayeux War Cemetery, Normandy. He was 26 years old. There are two memorials commemorating 48 (Royal Marine) Commando at Langrune-sur-Mer and also one mounted on the side of an old German bunker at St Aubin-sur-Mer.

Corporal 2358748 Frank Dixon of the Royal Corps of Signals was attached to the American 4th Division. He landed at Utah Beach in the American sector; his role was most likely inter-allied communication and to facilitate coordination between ground units and air support. He was seriously wounded during an explosion as he went onto the beach after leaving the landing craft on D-Day.

Frank was born on 19th December 1919, the son of Mr and Mrs Joseph Dixon of 133 Liverpool Road, Irlam. His father was a veteran of the First World War who had been wounded and captured during the Manchester Regiment's famous stand at Manchester Hill in March 1918. On the outbreak of war, Frank was working as an apprentice at Brew Brothers, where he was involved in the construction of air raid shelters. He joined the Home Guard on 10th July 1940 as Private 137 Frank Dixon of 2 Platoon, D Company. While serving with the Home Guard he attempted to join the Army but was refused because his apprenticeship at Brew Brothers was classed as a reserved occupation. When his apprenticeship was complete he received his call-up papers in December 1940, shortly after his 21st birthday, and joined a Royal Signals unit at Derby on 2nd January 1941 for training. He was trained at Derby and Catterick. In June 1941 he travelled on the SS *Volendam* to Iceland, where he was stationed for about six months, living in a tented camp. He returned to Britain around Christmas 1941 and was then attached to Air Formation Signals and served at various airfields throughout Britain.

In May 1944 Frank was attached on Signals duties to the US Army (no doubt on joint communications work between US and British forces landing in the invasion) and stationed at an American camp in the New Forest, preparing for the invasion. Frank landed at Utah Beach on the Normandy coast, France, at H-Hour (6.30am) on D-Day with the 4th Division, First US Army.

As he ran off a landing craft with fellow soldiers they ran into a creeping barrage of enemy artillery and a shell exploded near to him. He was severely wounded in both legs, back and left arm and lay in an exposed position on the beach until being picked up by medics later that day. He spent the remainder of the day and night in a nearby wooded area until evacuated on the morning of 7th June onto a Landing Ship Tank and brought back to England. He was a patient at a hospital in Malvern and also at Sir Robert and Dame Magnus Hunt orthopaedic hospital where he spent the next two years. His wife, Jessie, visited him frequently.

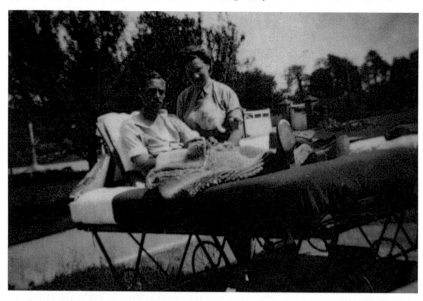

Corporal Frank Dixon, Royal Signals, in hospital, with his wife, Jessie

Corporal Frank Dixon, Royal Corps of Signals

Gunner Jessie Wilmot, Auxiliary Territorial Service

Jessie was the daughter of the late Mr and Mrs Wilmot. She served with the ATS as Gunner 235149 with 644 Medium (Anti-Aircraft) Battery, Royal Artillery. Jessie was born in Mayfield, New South Wales, Australia on 18th December 1922, and her family moved from Australia to Irlam when she was a young child. Jessie enlisted into the ATS in late 1941 and completed her training at Lancaster and Park Hall Camp, Oswestry. She then served as a radar operator at various anti-aircraft batteries across the UK. Jessie and Frank married at St Paul's Church, Irlam on 15th July 1943 and Frank's brother, Dennis, acted as best man. Jessie was given away by her brother-in-law, William Buckley, and her sister, Ellen Buckley, was matron of honour.

Frank was officially discharged from the Army on 6th December 1944, but remained in hospital until shortly before Christmas 1946. In a letter to one of the authors, dated 10th April 1991, Frank recounted some of his experiences: *The tin with the shrapnel holes in it. It was an elastoplast tin which I kept my cigarettes in the tin along with my field dressing pack and service issue pocket watch was all in my field dressing pocket. The shrapnel went through the lot and is still in my leg. Before we left England for the invasion on D-Day we had to take all badges and flashes off all uniform and were issued with one Combined Operations badge and told if we were captured to only give our rank, name and number, so I have no idea of any division. I haven't seen the Combined Operations badge since. With going over with the Americans, and leaving my old 30 Section Air Formation Signals unit behind, which was a south of England Company, I have not been to any reunions so lost touch with my old company. Since the American serviceman Bill Smyth wrote to my wife saying I had been killed on D-Day, we have written to each other every Christmas since, and along with his ex-ATS British wife he came to see me when they were over visiting her relatives about 25 years ago.*

Frank Dixon's shrapnel damaged Elastoplast tin

The leg wounds he received on D-Day affected him for the rest of his life. Frank died in April 1998, aged 78. Two of his brothers, Signalman W/2371018 William Dixon and Signalman Edward Dixon, served with the Royal Signals. Edward was born in 1922 and prior to being called up he joined the Home Guard (Private 550, 2 Platoon of D Company) on 22nd April 1941 and joined the Army on 28th June 1942. Another brother, Walter, served with the Royal Engineers on bomb disposal duty. A fourth brother, Dennis, who was born in 1924, joined D Company of the local Home Guard (service no. 505) on 24th January 1941, serving with 2 Platoon and later with HQ Platoon.

Signalmen William and Edward Dixon, Royal Corps of Signals
Syria 1944

Royal Marine PO/X 121855 Harry Bannister landed on Sword Beach with No. 41 (Royal Marine) Commando at 8.45am. The following is his account of D-Day, the bitter fighting that took place at Lion-sur-Mer and the days that followed: *We were taken to this tented place, in trucks, to this day I don't know where it was, but it must have been either Southampton or Portsmouth, or somewhere like that. Anyway they put us in... and we were guarded by these American troops, couldn't get out, security. I was in this tented camp for a fortnight and all we did, very little, was attend these, they had a sand plan [scaled plan of the beach]. Security, they'd told us it was Red Beach, and then it became Sword Beach, and just before we set off it was Lion-sur-Mer in France where we had to go. As you know it was deferred for 24 hours. Anyway they put us on these landing craft in harbour, somewhere in the south of England, still don't know where it was cos security was so critical. One troop to each landing craft, about hundred men in each troop; you'd about five troops to a Commando. And we was on this boat for 24 hours cos it was deferred like I said, and then we set off on the night of the 5th June, on the evening of 5th June, and we was going all night to Lion-sur-Mer, that's where we landed. A lot of them went down in the cabin, the sea was very choppy cos the weather had been bad. Anyway I stayed on deck and I went to sleep on a coil of rope on the deck. The next morning I opened my eyes and I could see all these similar boats to ours. It was like a motor torpedo boat, but no superstructure like, just a flat deck with a bit of a cabin on top. Anyway most of them were down below but I was on the top there. And it was a very grey morning and I could see all these other landing craft like ours. They weren't the flat bottom type, ours was a type that you had a ramp at each side and the Navy was supposed to put these ramps out at the front.*

Marine Commando Harry Bannister, No. 41 (Royal Marine) Commando

Anyway we were sent below for the approach to the beach and then they told us that we wouldn't be able to go down the ramps at the front because we'd received a direct hit and the craft was burning at the front. I didn't actually feel it, but the Navy couldn't put the ramps down because of the fire. So the order was: jump over the side. So I jumped over the side with all the stuff that was on my back, my big pack and my a little pack, ammunition and grenades, and everything, and I landed on my back in the water, very deep, and for them few, well it seemed like minutes but it was probably seconds like, I couldn't move, I couldn't get up. Anyway after a while I managed to roll over, of course I was like a bloody tortoise. I managed to roll over and I crawled to the beach, the edge of the water. None of my mates were in sight, I don't know where they were, all gone. Well the first sight that met my eyes was this bloke face down in the sand, still holding his rifle, but his legs had been blown away and he was at the water's edge, and I didn't know who he was, he was face down. Everybody else had gone, I was on my own. Anyway we'd had this talk with the sand thing and we had a rendezvous on the beach where I had to go. In front of us was the Cheshire Regiment, I think it was, and they were busy digging in on the beach, and the noise, and the smell, and the smoke was terrible on there. You couldn't see a lot because of the smoke, but I could see these men digging in on the beach. Of course we had to go, our orders were to go to the end of the beach to this house which was the rendezvous. It was over on the right, extreme right-hand side. We were supposed to advance and take Luc-sur-Mer further up the coast. Anyway like I say I was on my own, and I saw this tank coming up, and it was one of those flail tanks, knocking up mines and I got behind that and I went all the way to the rendezvous behind this tank. As I was getting towards the rendezvous a Bren Carrier came alongside me and a shell dropped right inside it, either a shell or a mortar bomb, and I was right next to it but I was saved, the explosion went up in the sealed sides and it stopped immediately, none of them was alive I don't suppose, but I was right next to it and I was alive. And as I got to the rendezvous the only people there were my commanding officer and the adjutant, all the rest of the blokes were missing. So any rate I was there, I'd only just joined the Commando of course a fortnight before, and I didn't know everybody. I was in P Troop, I knew my own troop sort of thing but I didn't know a lot of the people yet. The commanding officer ordered the adjutant and myself to go back on the beach and look for some of our guys, and I was frightened to death of going back on this beach because of all the bloody stuff flying about. The cordite smell was in the air and the smoke. Anyway I went with this adjutant and for a while we went along, I didn't see any of our men. Anyway the adjutant sent me back, don't know what happened to him, and I went back and by that time a few had filtered through. The next thing I remember we'd set off from this house, about eight of us, going across the road and one of us, one at a time we crossed this road, and as each of us crossed over a sniper had a go at each of us, and of course I took my turn, raced across this road and ducked behind and as soon as I got behind it took a chip off the wall, he'd had a shot at me, he took a chip off the wall, and he had a go at each of us this sniper. Anyway we survived that. Next thing I remember, we go into a farmyard and the Germans must have spotted us and we had to dive in this cellar, underneath the farmyard, and they splattered that farmyard with mortar bombs. Anyway after a bit we got out. That's the first time I felt scared, I'd been alright while I was along the beach, as soon as I got in that farmhouse I was shaking like a leaf. I thought, what the bloody hell's up with me. Anyway I was alright after a minute or two, and the next thing we were going along this road and I was my own again, I don't know why, and I'd just got beside this building and a shell hit the end of this building, all the masonry come down and I was covered in dust and muck, I survived that anyway. The next thing I remember, there's four of us and we was on this balcony of this house, looking down this street, and there was four of us taking turns on this Bren gun, looking for Germans coming up the street, and that's where I was for the rest of the day, D-Day. And I remember, it was a big house, we was in the bed taking it in turns having a sleep, making tea and God knows what, and we found some very old chocolate in the wardrobe what we ate. And after that everything seemed to go quiet after a while. We all assembled in this bungalow what there was left of us, there wasn't a great lot, I was told that after D-Day there was only 180-odd of us left of the five or six hundred men. How true that is I don't know. But each night the Germans bombed us and we lost some officers in one of these bombing raids, they bombed the headquarters. As soon as our aircraft went over, the German bombers came over and bombed us. And I remember, the only time I saw their aircraft in the daytime was three Messerschmitts come over one morning with all the guns firing at us and I got behind this tree quick, could see them coming, and then they were gone. They didn't get anybody but they might have done if we'd been in the open, they just scared us for a bit.

On 9th June the commandos were ordered to take over positions from the Black Watch around the radar station at Douvres - La Délivrande. The Germans had established a substantial pocket of resistance in the stations and the commando was ordered to contain them. The commando remained around the radar station until the Germans surrendered on 17th June. Harry continued the story: *Anyway things were very quiet for a while and then we were told this radar station had been by-passed by the advancing troops and they told us we were going to attack this radar station. And you couldn't see much above ground, it was all concrete bunkers underground. Anyway we had a go at it and we dropped a few grenades down this chimney and PIAT mortars at the entrances of these concrete blocks. Anyhow after a while they all come out, two hundred of them, Germans, that's the first time I'd seen a German, two hundred of these Germans come out. Anyway, things were pretty quiet after that, we was going all on patrols like at night time, you was always exhausted, tired out. The German commanding officer, he was a really arrogant bugger with a long leather coat on and you could tell, his manner. The others all had their hands up, but one had a bayonet wrapped in his blanket, holding a blanket over to hide a bayonet inside of it. Of course he got a telling off. Anyway our commanding officer and their commanding officer went off, inspecting round this radar station. After a while, our troop commander after D-Day, he was bomb happy, he was shell shocked, he was sent home. And after a week we got a replacement officer, Lieutenant Dietz, he commanded our troops, troop commander. I always thought that he's got a German name, you know, that's why I remembered it. I never remember the first bloke's name. Our commanding officer was a fella named Lieutenant Colonel Gray. There was a padre landed with our troop, I never saw him after the first day, never saw him at all* [Reverend Caradoc Hughes had been wounded on the first day].

Another local man who landed on Sword Beach (Queen Red Sector) was Sapper Albert Luke of 79 Armoured Engineer Squadron, 5 Armoured Engineer Regiment (known as 5 Assault Regiment, Royal Engineers). The regiment was part of the 79th Armoured Division but on D-Day was under the control of 3rd Mechanised Division. Albert was a crew member in a modified Churchill tank. He served in Europe with 79 Armoured Engineer Squadron from D-Day and took part in operations in northern France and Holland, including Walcheren in November 1944, and crossed the Rhine into Germany in March 1945. Albert was born in 1912, the son of William James and Emily Luke (nee Eccleshall) of 16 Lucy Street, Old Trafford. At some point prior to the war Albert moved to Irlam to take up employment at the Steelworks. In December 1943 he married Elizabeth Gillan, a nurse who worked at an Ipswich hospital and who had cared for Albert during a spell of illness. They set up home at 99 Eldon Road, Irlam and their son, James, was born in the following year.

Private Henry John Hayman, Royal Army Service Corps (Second British Army), was another local serviceman who landed on the Normandy beaches on D-Day. Henry was born on 24th July 1922, and resided with his parents at 9 The Bungalow, Dudley Road, Cadishead. He was called up in 1942. After the D-Day landings he served throughout north western Europe and, after the end of the war, he was posted to Palestine. He was demobbed in July 1946.

Private Douglas Ashton of the Royal Tank Regiment also served in the 79th Armoured Division (formed in 1942). Douglas had last been in France with the BEF in 1940 and was one of those evacuated from Dunkirk in May 1940. Douglas was the son of Mr and Mrs Ashton of 14 Rutland Road, Cadishead.

Private Douglas Ashton, Royal Tank Regiment (far right)

Private Henry John Hayman, Royal Army Service Corps

Private Henry John Hayman, Royal Army Service Corps

Sapper Albert Luke, with Elizabeth and son, James

1944

Sapper Albert Luke, Royal Engineers
Hanover, Germany 1945

Stoker 1st Class KX133391 Frank Taylor served with the Royal Navy on board the monitor, HMS *Roberts*. Frank's role on board the monitor was to keep watch and to carry out general engine room work. HMS *Roberts* was part of the offshore bombardment fleet on D-Day and was allocated for duty in Bombarding Force D attached to Force S. The monitor was stationed off Sword Beach to provide gunfire support by bombarding the Houlgate Battery, with Gorneville sur Mer as a secondary target. During the bombardment one of HMS *Roberts* guns was damaged and on 7th June she returned to Portsmouth for repair. On 16th June the Captain of HMS *Roberts* took time out during the refit to write to Frank's wife, Elsie: *Dear Mrs Taylor, very many thanks for your letter of good wishes for the ship. It was very nice of you to write. We have, as I expect you know, been having a very busy time lately and although our efforts have been somewhat eclipsed by being among so many larger ships. I think we have been very successful and that our work has been appreciated by our troops ashore. Everything seems to have gone surprisingly well and, from our point of view, it has been a much more peaceful affair than either Sicily or Salerno. I believe we have been mentioned once or twice by the BBC and the papers. I very much hope that before the summer is over, you will have your husband home on leave again, but I have no idea when. The ten days we had on arrival home went much too quickly and I scarcely feel I have had any. Thanking you again very much for your letter. Yours sincerely, R.E.C. Dunbar.*

After the refit HMS *Roberts* resumed support deployment in the Eastern Task Force area. On 26th June the monitor provided naval gunfire support for attacks in the Caen area and she continued to provide gunfire support for land operations until August when she was returned to home waters. On 31st October she sailed for Walcheren, Holland, as part of a Bombarding Squadron, to support Operation Infatuate. On 1st and 2nd November she provided gunfire support to land forces. In December she returned once again to home waters. Although she was nominated for duty in the British Pacific Fleet and prepared for foreign service in 1945, she was still in home waters on VJ Day. Throughout his time in the Royal Navy, Frank's conduct was described as very good and his efficiency ranged between satisfactory and superior.

Leading Sick Berth Attendant D/MX555965 James Alban Davies of Higher Irlam took part in the D-Day landings at Sword Beach as a ship's medic attached to Tank Landing Ship LST 420. As with many of the men involved, this was his first time in action. His son provided the following account: *As the huge Allied Fleet crossed the Channel he remembered that it almost had the atmosphere of a regatta, that is until the big guns from the battleships and cruisers opened up and began to saturate the distant shoreline with their massive explosive firepower; the roar of the big shells and multiple rocket batteries passing overhead, and the disappearance of the French coastline in a cloud of black smoke and flames; that was when the reality of it all began to sink in for Jim. After landing at Sword Beach, his duties involved setting up a field hospital on the beach to treat the badly wounded combatants of both sides before they could be ferried back to England. One of Jim's first big shocks of the day was seeing four Canadian soldiers drive over a landmine in a jeep and finding virtually nothing left of them to treat.*

Stoker Frank Taylor and his wife Elsie

Sometime later during the same day, Jim recalled intense sniper fire hitting the steelwork of the ship close by, which was quickly identified as coming from a church tower a short distance inland. One of the ship's 40mm Bofors was lined up and a couple of shells were let loose into the tower, after which Jim was called upon to give first aid treatment to the badly injured sniper. He was amazed to find a young French woman who, it seemed, was in love with a German soldier based in that area.

During the follow-up from D-Day, Jim crossed the Channel a further 19 times aboard LST 420, ferrying supplies and personnel to the expanding Normandy beachhead. After the Allied breakout from Normandy and the drive towards Germany, he took part in the Scheldt campaign, which was intended to clear enemy troops and open up the port of Antwerp to Allied shipping. After the 19th crossing, Jim and other medical staff were given 48 hours' leave before being posted back to Devonport for further training in preparation to be sent out to the Pacific.

Coder C/JX572640 Arthur Cordwell was serving on board HMS *Waveney*, the HQ Command ship of Assault Force J2, which was stationed off Juno Beach on 6th June, controlling the assault landing of the 8th Canadian Infantry Brigade on Nan White and Nan Red beaches. *Waveney* was a river class frigate which provided communication facilities for the assault troops.

Arthur was called up on 15th April 1943 and was first posted to HMS *Royal Arthur* (a shore-based training establishment) where he was trained as a coder. He then spent two months at HMS *Cabbala*, a naval communication training school at Lowton St Marys, Leigh. His next posting was to a shipyard in Birkenhead, where *Waveney* was being converted to a command ship. He joined the frigate on 7th February 1944 and spent the months leading up to D-Day training with assault force J2 for the invasion of Normandy. On 5th June they sailed from Spithead as part of convoy J10, bound for Juno Beach, Normandy. He remained with the frigate throughout the initial landings and the subsequent build-up phase. On 15th July he fell gravely ill with tuberculosis and had to be evacuated from the ship on a bosun's chair and was taken to Battle Hospital, Hastings. As a result of his illness he was medically discharged from the Navy on 7th September 1944.

Arthur was born in Pendlebury on 18th November 1924, the son of James and Alice Cordwell of 3 Burns Avenue, Swinton. Prior to the war he worked as a pork butcher. In June 1957 he married Bernice Fegan, the daughter of Tommy and Mary Fegan beginning his long association with the district. Her uncle, Nicholas Fegan, was a local veteran who had served in both World Wars, with the Royal Navy in the First World War and then the Royal Air Force in the Second World War. After the marriage they resided with Bernice's parents, at 92 The Crescent, Higher Irlam. They eventually moved into their own home in the newly built Exeter Drive, Irlam.

Coder Arthur Cordwell (circled)

Able Seaman Clarence 'Clarry' Handsley of the Royal Navy received shrapnel wounds while serving as an Oerlikon gunner on a defensively equipped merchant ship (DEMS) that was carrying troops and ammunition across the Channel. Clarry was called up in 1943 and took part in a number of Atlantic convoys. On one occasion he was on a ship that hit a British mine while leaving Liverpool harbour. Fortunately there were no casualties but the ship had to return to dry dock for repairs.

Clarry was born in Monton on 24th August 1925 and his family moved to the district c.1928. He was educated at Irlam Endowed School and Irlam Central School and then went to work at a coalyard in Eccles. After a time he took up a new job at Lancro and he was working there when his call-up papers arrived.

After the war, in November 1945, Clarry had the good fortune to be posted to Bermuda where he remained until September 1946. His journey out was quite an adventure. He sailed on the *Queen Elizabeth* to Canada and then took a train to New York. From there he was flown to Bermuda on board a Sunderland flying boat.

Clarry's father and elder brother, John William Handsley and Kenneth Handsley, were both pre-war members of the Territorial Army and were called up together shortly before the outbreak of war. After the war, Kenneth served in the British Army of Occupation, where he met and married a German woman.

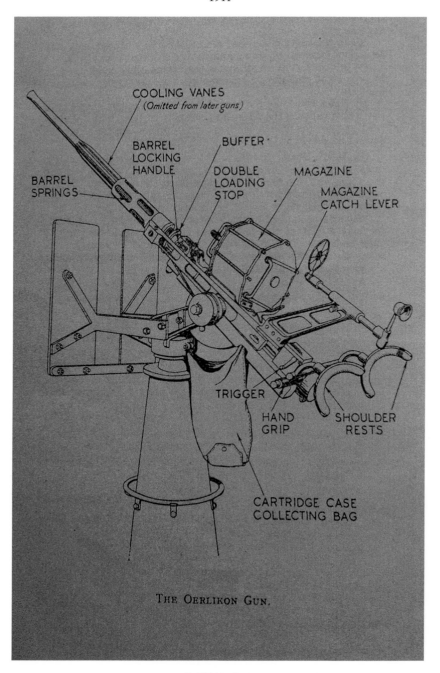

COOLING VANES
(Omitted from later guns)

BARREL
LOCKING
HANDLE

BARREL
SPRINGS

BUFFER

DOUBLE
LOADING
STOP

MAGAZINE

MAGAZINE
CATCH LEVER

TRIGGER

HAND
GRIP

SHOULDER
RESTS

CARTRIDGE CASE
COLLECTING BAG

THE OERLIKON GUN.

Oerlikon Gun

Able Seaman Clarry Handsley, Royal Navy

Private Kenneth Handsley (left)

Lieutenant 159735S Henry Rowland John was an officer in charge of petrol supplies on the beaches of Normandy. Rowland, as he was more commonly known, had volunteered for service in the Army in January 1940 and had been evacuated from France in June of the same year. After a time with No.1 Air Intelligence Section at Cambridge and later Oakhampton, he was sent to area HQ as a clerk to the education officer (September 1940). In December of the same year he was posted to Kilmarnock to join a newly formed company of the Royal Army Service Corps. He was promoted to corporal in April 1941, sergeant in December and staff sergeant in 1942. In January 1943 he was sent to Pre-OCTU (Officer Cadet Training Unit) in Wrotham, Kent, for two months, then to RASC OCTU at Southend-on-Sea for three months. He was commissioned 2nd Lieutenant on 12th June (service no. 281519) and then Lieutenant on 12th December 1943. In Spring 1944 he was posted to 246 Petrol Depot, which was forming at Barry in South Wales, preparing for the invasion. Final preparations were made at Wrotham before the Normandy landings. He was promoted captain in July 1944 and he was in the vicinity of Caen while the fighting raged around the city.

Sergeant 1090391 Walter Arstall of the Royal Engineers was involved in the D-Day landings. Walter's first posting was to Exeter in 1940 and from there he was sent to Iceland. His next post could not have been a greater contrast as he found himself involved in the North African campaign. He returned to England for a spell and then moved up to Scotland to prepare for the D-Day landings. He would later serve in Belgium, Germany and Poland as the Allies advanced through northern Europe. At the end of the war, Walter's service record described him as an excellent leader of men and his military conduct was recorded as exemplary.

Captain Henry Rowland John, Royal Army Service Corps

Sergeant Walter Arstall, Royal Engineers

Driver Norman Dakers, Royal Army Service Corps

Walter was born on 14th March 1915 in Manchester Road, Hollins Green, one of four sons of Walter Arstall and Minnie Arstall (nee Taylor). He attended Hollinfare Church of England School which catered for junior and senior pupils. After leaving school he worked at Partington Coaling Basin as a coal trimmer and, apart from a short spell at the Steelworks, he remained there all his working life. In 1942 he married Mary Young and they had two children, Joyce (born 1944) and John (1956).

The news of the long-awaited invasion of France was received with quiet restraint in Irlam and Cadishead. As the story of the landings unfolded on the radio there was an atmosphere of suppressed excitement, tempered by the sobering knowledge that this was the greatest test faced by the Armed Forces. Throughout the district churches were opened for prayer and special evening services were held.

On 7th June Driver T/14323168 Norman Dakers of 714 Company, Royal Army Service Corps, landed on Juno Beach: *From Dewsbury I went down to Brooklands in Surrey, waterproofed all the lorries for landing there, and then we went to Wanstead Flats. We were under canvas, we weren't allowed out, you couldn't get near the fence at all, because blokes were wanting to pass letters out and you couldn't do it, one or two tried it and they got into trouble. From Wanstead Flats we moved to the docks at London and boarded ship.*

I went over to Normandy on a boat called the Fort Henley and I boarded her in Queen Victoria Dock, that's where we got on and she'd come over from Canada with a load of coal and it had been emptied and we had to go in and sweep the bloody thing out and we were like chimney sweeps when we come back. We left for Normandy from Royal Dock, not from down south coast, we left from London and joined the convoy out in the Channel. I volunteered for it, they wanted five blokes for what they called deck picket and I thought I'd rather be up here than down there because there was no way out down there. The officers were in a section that was partitioned off and they had a ladder there and that was the only way out. Now had anything happened they could have got out but we couldn't have got out so I thought if anything's going to happen I'll be up there, so I said to this kid 'come on, let's get up on top. I'll volunteer for this, I feel a bit bloody safer up there than down there.' So we went up there and stayed there till we started to go. It was very fine, it wasn't rough weather at all, not at all. The rough weather started after we'd been ashore for a couple, two or three days, we had a storm and it made a mess of everything there. Hundreds of ships, you couldn't hardly put a finger between them. And somehow or other a submarine sneaked in and torpedoed one of them, they were going mad chucking bloody depth charges all over the place, our side. I couldn't get ashore on D-Day, they wouldn't let us ashore, we were standing offshore, we were about 200 yards offshore, they wouldn't let us in because somebody had said that they'd found mines that hadn't been taken away, we couldn't risk it. And then we went off the ship, down the rope ladder onto the barge and the boat was going up and down, bloody barge was going up and down, you'd got to be very careful when you step off, or you'd jump in the water, but we got off alright and got ashore. A lot were drowned, well they get trapped in there, between the ship and the landing barge, get crushed in between them there wouldn't be much of you left. They shipped them trucks off the ship with the ship's derricks onto the pontoons and took them in that way. Anyway eventually I got in, the truck had all been waterproofed, especially filled with waterproof, especially for dropping in deep water and we was lucky because when I came off the barge at the end to get onto the sand the water finished up here, water up to my chest, but anyhow I got out of it alright. It must have been about 4 o'clock in the afternoon something like that when I finally got ashore with my vehicle. And then I got onto the beach there, I had a bonnet rubber round the front, we'd had to put it on to stop water bubbling up into the cab, I had to stop and take this off, and the beach master, it was a bloke called Captain Bailey, screaming at me 'get off the so and so sand, get out of the road, you're holding things up!' So I had to get out of the road, I was frightened of my engine overheating with it blanked off, and it could have done because it was all sealed off and waterproofed, and I didn't want the engine to overheat and get stuck in the middle of the sand so while I could go I went. And it was a funny thing an all I was only ashore... I dropped the first load off, engineering stuff I had on, I dropped the first load and they told me to come back on the beach, and I came back to the beach and he said 'ere,' the ducks were coming in, you know these ducks, the American things that went in water and land, they were bringing stuff in, they dumped this in, he said 'there, that's the Yankee stuff, you'll have to take it over there.' I said 'over where?' he said 'over there, the Yanks are over there.' Well I said 'who the bloody 'ell do I see?' He said 'you'll find out, get on your way.'

We came out of that camp, that place, Wanstead Flats, and we had to go right past the house where Jack Gray lived but he couldn't do anything about it, and he wanted to get a letter to them but he couldn't get anything out there, and you know we were only over there two days and he got killed. He got killed with a mine and it was..., the engineers had been and put white tapes down and you drove between the tapes, if you wandered over you did it at your own risk and he must have wandered and he was shouting, Jack Gray was stood at the back and Johnny Schofield was driving this truck backwards and he shouted to him and he must have caught one and it exploded, hit him right in the middle, made a mess of him, so he never got to see home again. Actually my whole view of the beach and everything, my opinion was it was organised chaos put it that way, because nobody seemed to know where anything was going, every time you questioned the beach master 'get a move on, you're holding things up.' And as I say I was stuck with this bloomin' load of American gun barrels and I didn't know where to take them, I didn't even know where the bloody Yanks were, I knew they were over there somewhere, 'take it over there.' I thought it's a tall order and I kept asking blokes 'do you know where the Yanks are?' 'Down the road.' The Canadians landed with us, because I had a Canadian cousin that landed, he got his legs shot from under him before they cleared the beach he did, and last I heard of him they'd sent him back to Canada. Anyway I set off down the road toward where they were and coming the other way I got halfway there and a truck, a tanker come, a Yankee tanker coming the other way and he waved me down to stop me, and he was a coloured fella sat in the cab, he said 'where're you going kid?' I said 'I'm looking for this unit.' 'Oh', he said, 'they're up there on the right-hand side in a field, but be careful it's a bit unhealthy up there.' I found the unit and handed the stuff over to this Yank there, he said 'how're you going over there?' I said 'same as it is here more or less.' He said 'are you getting plenty to eat?' I said 'we've plenty of biscuits and corned beef.' 'Hang on a minute I'll fix you something up.' He gave me a sack and it was full of bloody tins and there was bacon rolled up inside it, all sorts of bloody food in tins that they'd been specially issued with and he gave me *a sackful of that, I took it back to the lads and we scoffed the lot. The first place we hit I think it was a place called Bayeux, that was the first sort of place we got to. It was a bit naughty at first because a lot of the German soldiers that had been stationed there, they'd been there a long while, and they'd married into the local girls and they didn't take too kindly to us wading in there and making a mess of everything there, they started taking bloody potshots at us as well, and I didn't want to be there any more than anybody else. Then you know the FFI, they landed with us as well, the Free French of the Interior, they carried the Cross of Lorraine, and of course they went searching for collaborators, and we heard this racket going on and there was two of these FFI blokes and they had a bloke sat down against a tree, on the floor with his back against the tree and a girl there and they'd cut all her hair off, and I said 'what's going on?' 'Nothing to do with you.' You know, sod off, get out of it sort of thing. So what had happened, they'd said that these were collaborators these two, and they'd cut the girl's hair off and then they'd shot the bloke, he was just sat down dead, they'd shot him. I thought heartless buggers you know, to do a thing like that, it's alright saying fight on and fight on when you're safely in England but when you're stuck there and somebody sticks a gun in your head and says if you don't do what you're told I'll kill your family it's a different ball game altogether isn't it. And then we heard the loss of, we lost a sergeant, a sniper shot him, a motorcyclist, he got shot, but they said it wasn't a German they said it was a French girl that had done it, it was a rumour but we never found out really. Sammy Hogg his name was, Sergeant Hogg. Well after that we were behind them, passing stuff up all the time. It was quite an experience.*

Norman was born in Irlam on 17th May 1924, the son of Andrew and Dorothy E. Dakers of 15 Mond Road, Higher Irlam. His father, Andrew, was a native of Scotland who had served as a sergeant in the Black Watch during the First World War, having been seriously wounded twice and gassed. Andrew came to Irlam from Brechin in Scotland in 1919 to work at the Steelworks. In 1920 he married Dorothy Hill and they had two children, Margaret (born 1922) and Norman. Norman was educated at Irlam Endowed School and was later employed as a joiner at Wilkinson & Tonge. At the age of 16, Norman was compelled to join the Local Defence Volunteers (later the Home Guard) and was stationed at the HQ on Fairhills Road, Irlam. He was called up into the Army on 30th November 1942.

Gunner 1109637 Thomas Vaudrey of 209 Medium Battery, 53rd (London) Medium Regiment, Royal Artillery, landed on Sword Beach on 7th June. A few days earlier on 1st June reconnaissance parties from the regiment had embarked on two Landing Craft Tanks and the gun groups followed on 4th June. At around 7.30am on 5th June they weighed anchor and set off across the English Channel and, by 10am on D-Day, they were lying within sight of the Normandy shoreline, opposite Sword Beach. The failure of the Rhino ferries delayed the regiment's landing until 7th June. Once ashore their guns were deployed between Hermanville and Colleville. At 10.10pm the batteries fired blind in support of the 1st Battalion, Royal Norfolks, who were heavily engaged in Lebisy Wood. During the first weeks in Normandy, the batteries were situated in an area near the River Orne and fired in support of 3rd Division, 6th

Airborne Division and then later, in support of 51st Highland Division. They suffered their first casualties when two guns were put out of action by night-time bombing and C Troop's operating post was hit by a shell; one man was killed and two were wounded. A few days later a bomb hit D Troop and one man was killed.

Gunner Thomas Vaudrey, Royal Artillery
(second from right)

Tom was born in Irlam on 14th December 1908, the son of Herbert and Alice Vaudrey of 27 Baines Avenue, Irlam. Prior to the war he was employed as a soap labourer at the CWS Soap Works. He married Amy Dora Thorpe in 1936 and they had three children: Alice (born 1937), Leslie (1947) and Susan (1955). Amy's brother, Joseph Richard Thorpe, served with the Army in North Africa. Tom and Amy resided at 22 Princes Avenue, Higher Irlam. His younger brother, Herbert, served in a unit in the 8th Indian Division. Tom was called up on 12th December 1940 and enlisted at Newtown. The regiment was stationed in the UK as part of the 48th Division, situated in Bude, Barnstaple and Westward Ho during 1941. Later in the year they moved to Bedfordshire then Buckinghamshire. In September 1941 they were re-equipped with 4.5 inch Howitzers and in the same month they moved, with the 48th Division, to Lincolnshire, then to Sleaford in March 1942. In the autumn of 1942 they moved to Woodhall Spa, where the Howitzers were replaced with the new 5.5 inch medium gun. In April 1943, they became part of 4th Army Group Artillery and moved to Blairgowrie, Perthshire. In the summer of 1943 they were earmarked for the invasion of France and were allocated to I Corps, under the command of 3rd Division. The regiment prepared for the Normandy landings by waterproofing their vehicles, testing their performance over sand and practicing the unloading and marshalling of vehicles ashore and into action. They also practiced quick survey techniques for identifying and ranging on targets. By September every driver had practiced driving their vehicle in 4 feet of water for a minimum of 50 yards. All the drivers and some non-commissioned officers were sent in batches to Inverary, where they practiced beach landings from a Landing Craft Tank. In April 1944 they moved southwards and carried out dress rehearsals for the invasion.

On Thursday, 8th June, 22 year old Stoker 1st Class D/KX136480 **Clifton Hillyard**, Royal Navy, serving on board His Majesty's Landing Craft Tank 390, was lost at sea when the ship was sunk off the Normandy coast.

On the morning of D-Day, LCT 390 of the 4th LCT Flotilla, 'K' LCT Squadron, had been assigned to the 'swimming tanks' of the Canadian 1st Hussars, 7th Infantry Brigade, 3rd Canadian Division, who landed at Courseulles sur Mer on the western flanks of Juno Beach. After landing the Canadians, LCT 390 returned to England to take part in the 'shuttle service' between England and France. Her next voyage to France would end in disaster. Shortly after 4am on 8th June LCT 390 was hit in the stern by a torpedo fired from an E-boat. LCT 1025 was alongside and managed to save some of the men from LCT 390. Another ship in the vicinity, Landing Craft Infantry (LCI) 105, was also hit by a torpedo and further lives were lost. Clifton was one of the men killed. He has no known grave but the sea and is commemorated on the Plymouth Naval Memorial, Devon.

Born in 1921 (birth registered at Saddleworth in March 1922), he was the son of Walter and Ada Hillyard (nee Daniels) of 2 Addison Road, Higher Irlam. He was single and resided with his parents. Before the war he worked at the Steelworks and on 8th April 1941 he joined the Home Guard (service no. 534) and served in 2 Platoon of D Company. He joined the Royal Navy on 24th August 1941. During his military service he took part in nine convoys to Russia and was on board HMS *Onslow* when it was attacked in the Barents Sea by the German heavy cruiser *Hipper* on 31st December 1942. At the time *Onslow* was escorting convoy JW51B to Murmansk. She was badly damaged and suffered many casualties, however, all the merchant ships were successfully defended. Captain Sherbrook, who was badly wounded, won the Victoria Cross for his part in the defence of the convoy. Clifton later transferred to landing craft, serving in the Italian campaign before taking part in the Normandy landings.

Clifton's youngest brother and two sisters all served with the Forces. Herbert (birth registered at Saddleworth in June 1925) served in the Royal Navy; Corporal Irene

Hillyard (born Saddleworth, June 1920) was a member of the WAAF, which she had joined in 1940; and Driver Annie Hillyard (born Saddleworth, December 1923) was in the ATS.

Private Frederick 'Eric' Holt, Royal Army Service Corps, celebrated his 21st birthday, on Thursday, 8th June while on active service in Italy. His parents, Mr and Mrs Holt of 8 Palatine Close, Irlam, sent their son a 'key to the door.' Eric joined the Army in July 1942 and first went overseas in January 1943 to join the North African campaign. He was in Africa when King George VI visited troops there and he had also met the Prime Minister's son. On one occasion, he had acted as guide to General Montgomery who wished to find a certain officer. Characteristically, 'Monty' left Eric and his friends 1,000 cigarettes and six large bottles of meat extract. Eric participated in the allied landings in Sicily and Italy and his division took part in much of the fighting during the Italian campaign, including the Battle of Monte Cassino, the fighting at the Gothic Line and the Battle of Argenta Gap.

Eric provided the following description of his time in Italy: *After North Africa Monty decided to rest 78th Division and march to Sousse* [Tunisia] *but the advance after the initial invasion had problems moving through the German resistance and Monty changed his mind and decided he would need 78th Division to spearhead this change in strategy and so 78th Division went across to Sicily. The boats taking the division across to Sicily were called LCI's (Landing Craft Infantry), all welded craft, they were so thin metal that the remark was made that they were so thin even the fish could be heard talking with one another. On 25th July* [1943] *Mussolini was dismissed and his council was disbanded, on the same day 78th Division arrived in Sicily and began operations to clear the Germans out of Sicily. While we were there we slept in tents on the slopes of Mount Etna, the volcano, and many men went down with malaria and were shipped to Malta for treatment. On the 3rd September 1943 the leading troops of 13 Corps landed in Italy, the Italian coastal troops and their supporting artillery were quickly silenced by the RAF attack and the invasion was complete. In the middle of Italy, near Lake Trasmeno* [Umbria region] *a notice came up on the HQ notice board that a truck would be going into Rome to have an audience with the Pope. I put my name on the list and lo and behold I went in the Sistine Chapel and saw the Pope. Monti Cassino was the most talked about operation in the Italian campaign which will never be forgotten. 78th Division (including me) looked over the battlefield at Cassino from the mountain opposite and watched a 1,000 bomber raid on the town by American planes. We had to take (well the Poles did) the town because the Germans had control of the highway running in the valley in front of Monti Cassino and no transport could use the road without being shelled. It was a costly operation taking many lives. On the 6th June 1944 Allied forces landed on the beaches of Normandy and began the long march to Berlin and the heart of Hitler's Third Reich. At this point the spotlight switched away from the campaign in Italy to events nearer home, the war in Italy became a backwater. At this point Monty decided 78th Division had served its purposes in Italy and should go to Egypt for training and some relaxation and so we all jumped on a train of cattle trucks and went south to Taranto and sailed across the Med. We, Division HQ, had our camp compound across from the Pyramids and the Sphinx.*

We had many trips to Cairo but had to go in pairs because the Arabs showed reluctance to our being there and the prices in the shops and cafés increased. However after some time at Cairo, the Germans realised what had happened in Italy and began to take advantage of the situation and began to win battles so Monty called 78th Division back to Italy and we sailed back across the Med and took our positions back and pushed to finish all action in Italy. [The 78th Division was sent to refit at Egypt between July – September 1944 and on its return took part in the fighting at the Gothic Line]. *As the Italian campaign closed 78th Division moved into Austria because it was thought Tito was about to move into Austria, this did not happen and 78th Division moved in along with the Americans who had moved through Italy along the west coast of Italy, they took Rome.*

Able Seaman Harry Lowndes was seriously wounded when HMS *Halstead* was torpedoed off the coast of Normandy at 2am on 11th June. Harry was the youngest son of Mrs and the late Mr F. Lowndes of 12 Baines Avenue, Irlam. He was educated at Irlam Central School and employed by Taylors (butchers) of Liverpool Road, Cadishead. He joined the Navy in April 1943. His brother Thomas Lowndes served in the Royal Air Force.

Another local man wounded in Normandy was 19 year old Private 14414250 William Arthur 'Bill' Taylor of the 7th Battalion, Seaforth Highlanders, 46th (Highland) Infantry Brigade, 15th (Scottish) Infantry Division.

Bill was born at 7 Vicarage Road, Irlam, on 18th April 1925, the eldest son of Mr and Mrs A. Taylor, later of 185 Liverpool Road, Irlam. His father was a First World War veteran who had been wounded on the Western Front. Bill was educated at Irlam Central School and later gained an apprenticeship at the Stretford & District Electricity Board, whilst continuing his studies at Stretford Technical College. On 10th December 1942 he tried to volunteer but was turned away because he was in a reserved occupation. The next day, he went to another recruiting office, told a different story, and was promptly enlisted into the General Service Corps. He joined this unit, which delivered basic training to recruits, on 21st January and following training was posted to the Highland Regiment on 3rd March 1943. He undertook some of his training at the 11th Infantry Training Centre, Fort George, Inverness, Scotland.

Bill was transferred to the Cameron Highlanders on 28th May 1943 and subsequently served with A Company, 1st Lovat Scouts until being transferred to his father's old regiment, the Seaforth Highlanders, on 13th September 1943 and served with the 7th Battalion. He landed at Normandy on 13th/14th June with the 15th Scottish Division and participated in heavy fighting. He was wounded, probably during Operation Epsom, and was evacuated to the UK on 28th June.

Private Bill Taylor, Seaforth Highlanders

Private Bill Taylor, Seaforth Highlanders

IRLAM URBAN DISTRICT COUNCIL.

EDWIN JONES, A.C.I.S.
CLERK.

REFERENCE.

YOUR

OUR

TEL'S.: 24 & 25 IRLAM.

Council Offices,
Irlam,
Lancashire.

29th June, 1944.

Dear Mrs. Taylor,

On behalf of the Irlam & Cadishead War
Comforts Fund Committee I desire to tender to you
their sincere sympathy in the sad news conveyed to
you that your dear son, Arthur, has been seriously
wounded.

I sincerely hope that you will soon have
more comforting news, and that his youthful vigour
will reassert itself and help him to overcome his
disability.

May you be given strength and courage to
carry you through these very anxious days.

I am,
Yours sincerely,

Gh. E. Bowker.

Hon. Secretary.
Irlam & Cadishead War Comforts Fund.

Mrs. Taylor,
185 Liverpool Road,
IRLAM.

Letter received by Mrs Taylor from the Irlam & Cadishead War Comforts Fund

Corporal John 'Jack' Hilton was serving with the 9th Battalion, Royal Tank Regiment, which arrived in Normandy between 19th and 21st June. The advance party of the battalion had left Aldershot on 11th June and the following day, the rest of the battalion moved off by train to the marshalling area near Gosport. Jack worked as a clerk in the battalion headquarters, which formed part of the advance party: *I was a clerk as I wore spectacles and had poor eyesight. We were posted to Aldershot in preparation for the invasion. On 6th June, a beautiful morning, we had been advised that the RAF in great force would be bombing the Normandy coast. We were ready for moving and our HQ and office would be a soft top three tonner. A tarpaulin cover was slung inside which held all our equipment, typewriters and personal gear to make sure it would be dry when we landed. Our personal weapon was a bazooka.* The battalion moved from the beaches and concentrated in the area of St Gabriel. Jack was one of the first to land and move inland: *We landed and took out our gear. We, as part of HQ, had to follow a certain coloured tape which landed us in an assembly field. There were other coloured tapes for other parts of the unit. We were soon reminded it was war and we were in it. In this field a German had been buried, his rifle stuck in the ground and his helmet on top, but they had left one of his arms sticking out vertically and his fingers were peeling back like banana skins. This was my first experience of death, there were many more. Our colonel and many of the Churchills* [tanks] *were unable to land for about a week because of the wild gale blowing.*

Jack lived at 45 Marlborough Road, Higher Irlam and worked at the Steelworks as a shunter from 1933. In November 1939 he took a job as a clerk in the scrap department at the Steelworks. He joined the Home Guard on 5th July 1940, serving as Private 416 in 1 Platoon of D Company, until he was called up on 8th February 1943.

Lance Corporal (later Sergeant) 1062503 Gerald Bannister of the 49th Reconnaissance Corps, 49th West Riding Division, landed on Juno Beach, along with the Canadians, on D-Day plus six (12th June). Gerald described his experiences: *We were reconnaissance, our job was to go out in front and scout. We were scouts really. I mean really you were supposed to be, you'd become mechanised cavalry, so you were doing what in the old days the cavalrymen would do. Going out..., scouting out in front of the rest of the units. We had started getting these Bren gun carriers. I was at the front with the driver, and there were two men behind, and I was literally in command of that carrier. We were part of a kind of unit with different roles, each with a different role but all in carriers or armoured cars. The armoured cars were the spearhead really, and we were coming up behind the armoured cars. We went to somewhere, getting ready to go on the invasion. Anyway we went down to London and we were in a holding camp and my role then was as a 3 inch mortar, that was our weapon, we had it on a Bren gun carrier, but it was fitted out to carry this 3 inch mortar. It was 3 inch diameter of course with a point, and sights and bombs to go in it. And one of the things about being in a carrier in the back, was that the exhaust was at the side and if you got your boots on it you'd burn your boots and your foot as well. Then of course we boarded a ship, one of these Empire ships, in London docks, and nobody was supposed to know where we were going but when we passed Dagenham they were all there waving to us. We went with the Canadian Army for some reason or other, probably to reinforce them or what, land on*

Juno Beach. But I've never seen as many ships in all my life, the whole horizon was full of ships, and one of the warships was firing, near us, firing beyond the beaches, and some of those shells was nearly as big as this. Anyway we got onto a landing craft, and I remember the ship was going up and down and the landing craft was going up and down and you'd got all your gear on and a rifle in your hand and you'd got to get onto the bridge and then into this landing craft, and the carriers are on the landing craft, so you want to get on the landing craft, go up the beach, get the carriers, and so that's what we did. But it was quite an adventure jumping off that ship onto that landing craft [laughter], with a full kit, you know, everything on me that you could have really. We were pretty well clued up as to what was going to happen, yes. Montgomery was pretty keen on that kind of thing and everybody knowing what they were going to do. Well I was alright but there was a whole..., as you can imagine on these Empire boats, they'd been made in America and you were all stuck there really, there was nowhere you could get away, get out of anything, but I was alright, I didn't have any sea sickness or anything like that, but we did have sea sickness pills, we were issued with that kind of thing. Well you were apprehensive to say the least, scared to death probably [laughter], but you know it was part of the adventure really. We landed at the beach and we went forward into what they called the bocage country. Well when you've a Tiger tank first shooting at you and you hear that whistle, well I suppose if you hear the whistle it's gone past you, you don't hear the one that hits you. It's quite frightening really, oh aye, frightening. On the odd occasion you got closest to them [German tanks], you know. On my crew I had a shepherd from Wharfedale, now I was a sergeant with a big pair of binoculars but he could see things that I never saw. My troop commander, we had to, him and I, went forward this particular time to reconnoitre a place for the mortar troop, this is a troop of mortars, more than just me, more than my carrier, there was a troop who were looked to go forward beyond our own lines and fire at a target of course, and then take mortars and come back, but when we were coming back, the troop officer and I, we walked through a gate and it was booby trapped and it went bang of course. I said 'you've been hit,' because there was blood coming out of his tunic at the back. I'd been hit as well, I'd got shrapnel in various places but mostly in this leg. We kind of made it back to where we'd laagered as we called it (we used cavalry terms). And it was one of our own booby traps, it wasn't a German booby trap, it had been set by our own people but we didn't know. And he was so badly injured that he was sent back to his father's hospital, his father was a surgeon in Scotland, and he was taken back to Scotland. Eventually he came back in about a year, but I'd gone by then. And I stayed with an old Commando doctor, you know he had been a Commando doctor, he was out of doctoring by then, and I was just in this first aid place which was actually a kind of church, and we had a spotter thing in the spire. A first aid bloke had been trying to get this shrapnel out with a scalpel and this doctor said to me, 'leave it, it'll go septic, and as soon as it gets septic squeeze it and it'll come out.' I was only in the first aid dressing unit. I was only wounded slightly, I wasn't kind of you know, if you'd been wounded really badly we'd have gone back. And of course I had to gather all my gear up when I got back to the unit because they'd all sorted it out amongst themselves. Anyway I stayed with him perhaps two or three weeks really, while we were still moving on, and at about this time we got round a place called Troarn.

Corporal Gerald Bannister, Reconnaissance Corps

Driver Sidney Burrows, Royal Army Service Corps

Henry Burrows, Royal Corps of Signals

Gerald Edward Bannister was born in 1922 (birth registered at Northwich in December 1922), the son of Alfred and Edith Bannister of Lostock Gralam near Northwich. The family came to Cadishead in 1933 to live with an aunt and uncle at Kings Road, Irlam, before moving to Rosebank, New Moss Road, Cadishead. On 4th June 1941, Gerald joined the Home Guard, serving in 3 Platoon. He joined the Army on 15th January 1942.

Another local man serving in Normandy was Driver 4042147 Sidney Burrows, Royal Army Service Corps (RASC). Born in 1922, Sidney was the son of Samuel and Ellen Elizabeth Burrows (nee Malin). He resided at 17 Marlborough Road, Higher Irlam. On 6th June 1940, Sidney joined the Home Guard (service no. 261) and served with 1 Platoon, D Company. He was called up on 15th January 1942 into the King's Shropshire Light Infantry. Some months later he signed on as a regular soldier for seven years' service and five years on the Reserve. In 1942 he transferred to the RASC and became a driver and mechanic. In early 1944 he was working in Huddersfield at a motor works, assembling American trucks. In late June he was posted overseas, disembarking at Normandy, where he served with 707 Station Maintenance in France, Belgium and then Holland. During his time overseas he was a recovery truck driver whose task was to retrieve unserviceable vehicles for repair. In 1945 he was posted to Egypt and served at Tel-el-Kebir and then later in Palestine attached to the West African Frontier Force, stationed near Giza and at Haifa.

Sidney returned to England on medical grounds and after treatment at Netley Hospital, he was posted to 398 (Airborne) Divisional Composite Company RASC, 6th Airborne Division. He was demobbed in January 1946 but was subsequently recalled to complete his period of engagement with the Regular Army and was based at the Depot Battalion RASC, Thetford, Norfolk. He was discharged on completion of his term of engagement in 1949 and remained for a period in Norfolk working as a civilian for the Army, and then at the USAAF Base at RAF Lakenheath. He then worked in a saw mill until returning to Irlam where he worked at a number of places including the Steelworks, the CWS Soap Works and the CWS Margarine Works at different times. His father, Samuel Burrows, was a veteran of the First World War. Sidney had a sister, Katherine and three brothers: Joseph, Henry (Harry) and Roy. Harry saw active service with the Royal Corps of Signals in Italy and Katherine served with the Auxiliary Territorial Service.

Two friends from Cadishead met in Normandy shortly after D-Day, Signalman Stanley Bell (pictured left) and Trooper Thomas Reginald Hodges. Both Stanley and Thomas arrived in Normandy on D-Day. Stanley wrote to tell his father of the meeting, stating they were both well. In February 1942, the two friends had joined up together in the Border Regiment. Stanley later transferred to the Royal Corps of Signals and Thomas went to the Royal Armoured Corps.

Lance Corporal Thomas Hodges, Royal Armoured Corps

Thomas was the youngest son of Mr and Mrs Robert Hodges of 8 Hamilton Avenue, Cadishead. He married Amy May Rogers on Saturday, 1st April 1944 and, prior to enlisting, he worked at the Steelworks.

Twenty-one year old Stanley was the youngest son of Mr and Mrs Lance Bell of 12 Laburnum Road, Cadishead. He was educated at Cadishead Senior School and was later employed by Lancashire Tar Distillers Ltd. His elder brother, George, was an engine room artificer in the Royal Navy. George was born c.1922. He attended Cadishead Senior School and worked at the Steelworks before joining the Home Guard on 6th June 1940 as Private 237 George Bell, 3 Platoon, D Company. He joined the Navy in November 1942. Another brother, Sydney, served with the Armed Forces although details of his service are unknown. He was born in 1924 and joined the Home Guard on 18th December 1940 as Private 496 Sydney Bell, 3 Platoon, D Company, before joining the Armed Forces in February 1942. Their father, Lance Bell, had served in the Royal Navy during the First World War.

While the Normandy landings were in full swing, the home front was suffering the wrath of Hitler's latest weapon of terror as the V1 (or doodlebug) attacks intensified during June. By the middle of the month 60 V1s a day were striking the capital.

Whilst working on the exchange shortly after D-Day, Signalman Trevor Jenkins overheard an officer reporting that a German aircraft had crash landed at Stratford but there was no pilot. This must have been one of the first V1s to hit London (the first V1 attack was on 13th June 1944). *Aye, that's when they started with the flying bombs, you know, the V1 and V2. I remember I was on duty, cos we used to listen to obviously because you could listen quietly, and we used to listen, and this duty officer, and one was on from Scotland Yard and they brought this plane down they said and I think it was Stratford, they brought it down, then he come on again and he started effing and blinding, and he said 'there's no pilot in it.' I can remember that, remember that vividly, wondered what was going on. They'd just started and they hadn't seen them then. And then when they got this one, no pilot in, Stratford I think it was, I'm sure it was Stratford in London.* Trevor also saw the aftermath of a V1 attack which destroyed a block of flats near Wanstead, the nearby trees were littered with clothing and handbags. He commented: *They just carried on, these London people, marvellous people, very resilient, I don't know how they did it.*

Wilf Drum, Home Guard, spent some time in London during the V1 attacks: *I also remember on a visit to London during the war when Hitler was sending 'flying bombs.' The driving force was timed to cut out when it travelled as far as London and then the bomb dived to earth. People watched and listened to its engine showing pleasure when it passed over their district but hoping it would cut out over waste ground.*

Craftsman George Evans, Royal Electrical and Mechanical Engineers

Another witness to the destructive power of the German V weapons was Craftsman 14823464 George Evans of the Royal Electrical and Mechanical Engineers (REME): *Whilst I was at Canterbury, when I first went in the Army, of course it's not far from Dover and the V1s are coming over all the time there. I mean we just didn't take any notice but you'd see the big barrage over Dover and then often the RAF planes followed them and soon after as soon as they got past Canterbury, where there was loose wild ground, they would attack them then. I saw one tip it, the thing landed just at the end of the field, so they were coming through all the time there. They were all aimed at London of course. Afterwards I was at Woolwich for a short time with the Royal Artillery barracks there and the officers' quarter was destroyed with a V1. I was on demolition duty for a short while. I went to London later and I think by then the Allies had driven the V1s further away but at night on the stations people were still lying out there, you could hardly walk on the platform, you know they'd got so used to it and of course after the Blitz had stopped they thought everything was okay and then the V1s started. With the V1s when I went to Woolwich what they said was if you hear it coming towards you and it gets very loud above and then it cuts out you're alright cos it's going into a dive, but if it's on the way up and you suddenly hear it cut out, get undercover. There was steel staircases there, it was the old artillery, I suppose that was the main place, Woolwich, for the Royal Artillery, and I know the beds are all steel what you lay on, and we used to dive under the staircase because they were massive, really heavy steel, so that was the only V1 I got under. While I was on a special course at Croydon, we were all working one day and suddenly there was this noise like an express train and a huge explosion nearby, not right on us, and the instructor said 'that's a new V2 weapon.' And that was all you heard just whoosh and that was it, BANG. I just heard this V2 and you can imagine there's nothing you can do about it is there, just a whoosh, just like an express train, then BANG. I understood afterwards it had exploded in Thornton Heath. We were sort of halfway between Croydon, there was an old barracks there, Mitcham Road it was called, so we were a bit nearer to it so we heard it well and truly. But that was the only one I heard when I was there but obviously they were landing in London at that time.* After his spell in London, he was posted to the REME workshops near Bicester, where they repaired and maintained damaged tanks: *It was a huge workshop and it was just full of tanks. I was on a purely electrical section, we did all the electrical work. I think that was the main repair depot for the… France. Damaged ones came back, ones that were really damaged because there used to be squads going on cleaning them out. Because you can imagine if a shell comes through it just ricochets round and there's no chance for the guys then that's inside it, so there was a gang went in and cleaned everything out and then the parts were stripped down and we went and maintained them all or repaired them, whatever you know. So that was mainly what I did.*

George was born in Chorlton-on-Medlock, Manchester, and his family moved to Twenty Row, Liverpool Road, Irlam, after their house had been damaged in the Manchester Blitz (December 1940). His father worked at the Steelworks and, at 15 years old, George started an electrical apprenticeship: *When you went to the Steelworks you were expected to do a little stint in the offices first. Strangely enough, in the office I was working in, the work's cost office, Peter Borrino worked there and this chap who got the double Military Medal, Owen McCarthy. So they both worked the next desk to me.* George turned 18 in the middle of 1944 and was called up: *I went for a medical, I think it was a Naval one. I had and they said 'what do you want?' I said I wanted to keep in electrical if I could and they said 'oh well you'll have to have what we give you otherwise you're in the Army.' So I was in the Army.* But of course when you go in they give you all sorts of tests, they soon root out who are the people for tradesmen's jobs as opposed to future soldiers who are going to do the fighting.

Just after 11am on 18th June a V1 struck the roof of the Guards Chapel in Bird Cage Walk, London, causing the concrete roof to collapse. Leading Aircraftwoman Kitty Green, who was working in the casualty branch of the Air Ministry on Oxford Street, witnessed the V1 attack: *I was coming back from church one day and I was just a little way past the guards chapel when it was bombed and a doodlebug came down and I believe quite a few of the guardsmen were killed. I was in the street, I was coming home from church, I'd got past this and I kept going, I was practically running.* The church was packed with guardsmen from the nearby Wellington Barracks, together with their families and friends. It was the worst V1 disaster, 121 guardsmen and civilians were killed and 141 seriously injured. During her time in the Air Ministry, Kitty saw and heard many V1 attacks: *Oh yes, many times. It was frightening when you were waiting for it to cut out, it was very frightening. It went in spasms, sometimes there were quite a few and then you'd get a few days when nothing. It was frightening. I was with one girl, I think she was working her ticket, we heard the doodle bomb, and it was quite near, it stopped and she just threw me on the floor and herself, I was filthy, my uniform was dirty. She got finished after that, she got her ticket, she wanted out. She'd had enough.*

Three children from Higher Irlam: Marjorie Bate, Joyce Haydon and Pam Middleton, organised a jumble sale which raised 16 shillings for the Prisoners of War Fund.

The wedding took place at St Paul's Methodist Church, Irlam, on Saturday, 17th June between Ellis Thomas Baxter, RAF, and Doris May Ankers, daughter of Mr and Mrs T.H. Ankers of Shropshire. Ellis was the eldest son of Mr and Mrs E.T. Baxter of 87 Eldon Road, Irlam. He was stationed at an RAF base at Beningbrough, York.

The district's Salute the Soldier campaign started on Saturday, 17th June. The next day, a Combined Services parade was held, organised by Major Gold and consisting of members of the Army, Home Guard, ATS, Rangers of the United States Army, Army cadets, ATC, WJAC, ARP wardens, pre-service youth organisations and all branches of Civil Defence Services including the NFS, rescue squads, first aid parties, St John Ambulance Nursing Division and cadets, WVS, fire guards, together with scouts, guides, and street group secretaries. The Cadishead contingent assembled at Lords Street, while the Irlam group congregated at the Nags Head Hotel. Both parades set off at 2.20pm for the Council Offices. The Cadishead parade marched along Liverpool Road, left the main road at Cooper Road, and went along Tramway Road to join the Irlam contingent. Headed by the Salford Home Guard band they marched past the Council Offices, where the salute was taken by Lieutenant Colonel E.H. Tattersall, DSO, along with Councillor Melville and Edwin Jones. At the saluting base the band of the Lancashire Fusiliers played marching tunes. British military units marched past to the tune of *The British Grenadiers*, and the music switched to a stirring Sousa march as the Americans paraded past. After the salute, they marched to the Central School playing fields, where they formed a large square, and watched as the Home Guard demonstrated Army tactics such as bayonet fighting, the right and wrong way to mount a guard, unarmed combat, gas drill and an assault over walls and barbed wire. The weapons used by the Home Guard were also put on display, including mortars, bombs and a rocket gun. Throughout the week a ceremonial guard was mounted (presumably at the Council Offices), which was inspected each evening by an officer, who then placed the latest total on the indicator. The target set for the week was £100,000.

The Combined Services Parade passes the Council Offices

Several fundraising events were held during the week. An Army exhibition was opened by Councillor Melville at 3pm on Saturday, 17th June in the hall of Irlam Conservative Club, which remained open throughout the week. The exhibition included a Heroes' Corner displaying the photographs of local men serving in the Forces were on view. The photographs were catalogued by Mary Bowker, secretary of the Irlam and Cadishead War Comforts Fund. Posters carrying the slogan *Salute the Soldier in this House* were distributed to households which had a family member serving in the Forces. There were also a series of sporting and social events such as the bowling handicap at the Steelworks Club on Saturday, followed on the Sunday by a concert at the Palace cinema by the REME concert party. On Monday, a boxing match was held on the Central School playing fields and a challenge bowling match

They'll reach their objective—

SO MUST WE!

Whether it's a shell spattered bridgehead . . . . a bullet-swept beach, or a rain-sodden swamp, rely on the British Tommy to get there. We, at home, don't need such courage, such fortitude to reach our objective. Just determination—to reach and pass the savings figure fixed for our SALUTE THE SOLDIER WEEK. Show our fighting men we're crack marksmen too—on our savings target.

SALUTE THE SOLDIER WEEK

INVEST ALL YOU CAN IN—
3% Savings Bonds 1960-70 • 2½% National War Bonds
1952-4 • 3% Defence Bonds • Savings Certificates
Savings Stamps • The Post Office Savings Bank • A Trustee Savings Bank

JUNE 17th - 24th

IRLAM & CADISHEAD

OBJECTIVE £100,000
Cost of moving a Division to Berlin

took place at Unsworth's ground in Cadishead. On Tuesday, there was a baseball match between two American teams at the Steelworks cricket club. On Wednesday afternoon, Irlam Central School held its sports day and, in the evening, a cricket match took place between personnel of HMS *Gosling V* and Lancashire Steel on the club ground. On the next day, the Steelworks club hosted a challenge bowling match. Friday saw a flood of sporting events. At 6pm, Irlam and Cadishead Schoolboys played Manchester Schoolboys at cricket and, at the same time on the Steelworks club ground, a representative local team played a team of Northern Command professionals at football. Cadishead Conservative Club held a bowling challenge match on their green. The final day of the campaign was devoted to cricket on the Steelworks ground, and there was a mixed foursome and the final of the open bowling handicap on the club's greens.

A total of £23,862 was raised on the first day of the Salute the Soldier campaign, but this was followed by a noticeable tailing off over the next three days. On Wednesday, the total stood at £44,121 and on Thursday there was a considerable increase to £65,318 but this still left the district £35,000 short of the target with only two days remaining. The district made a final push on the last day and, when all the receipts were counted, the total stood at £117,421.

Over 60 percent of the money received came from small investors, who invested as follows: Certificates £23,315; deposits at Post Offices and Trustees Savings Bank £20,508; Defence Bonds £23,900; stamps £1,549. Major investors included: £10,000 from an anonymous investor; Halifax Building Society £5,000; Royles Ltd £3,500, Eccles and District Co-operative Society £3,500; British Basket and Besto Company £2,500; South Lancashire Transport £1,000; Britannic Assurance Company £3,250; British Iron, Steel and Kindred Trades Association £1,000; Prudential Assurance Company £700; Irlam and Cadishead War Comforts Fund £500; Lancashire Steel Corporation Employees Recreation Club £300; Irlam Catholic Club £300; Irlam Band

£300; Cadishead Conservative Club £200; Nursing Association £200; CWS Soap Works Recreation Club £200.

One disappointing result was that free gifts only accounted for £170, the lowest ever recorded in the district. Most of this sum was raised by local pubs; Mr G. Remers and patrons of the George Hotel raised £50, the Boat House Inn, Irlam, raised over £14 by holding a concert organised by Mrs M. Baxter and Alice Sutor. Patrons of the Railway Inn, Irlam, the White Lion Hotel, Higher Irlam and Nags Head Hotel, Higher Irlam, raised over £67. The mixed foursomes played on the Steelworks Club's bowling green attracted many entries and raised over £35. Other free gifts included £1-8s collected by Bernard Leslie, Gerald Finch, and Sheila and Jean McKay of Higher Irlam, and £1 from Fay Johnson, Beryl Yates and Mary Holt of Irlam. A group of local children from the Ferryhill estate: Michael Connolly, Kathleen and Maria Ellison, Joan Wilde, Maureen Clutterbuck and Fred and Leslie Hall, raised 12 shillings by holding a concert.

The Salute the Soldier campaign came to an end on Saturday, 24th June with a pre-service youth parade. Captain Lowe of the Army Cadets had invited all youth groups in the area to take part, regardless of whether they were uniformed organisations, or not. The parade assembled at Lords Street at 3pm and then marched along Liverpool Road, to the Council Offices, where the salute was taken by Lieutenant Colonel Webb of the Home Guard. After the salute, they marched along Liverpool Road to St John's Church, where they left the main road, travelled down Vicarage Road, turned into Chapel Road, and then proceeded back to the main road, opposite Ferryhill Road. They returned to the Council Offices and were dismissed on the field behind the offices. After the march a large crowd of several hundred people gathered at the Council Offices to find out whether the campaign had been a success. A great round of applause broke out when the indicator changed to £117,421.

Councillor Melville later received a letter of congratulations from the president and chairman of the National Savings Movement, Lord Kindersley and Sir Harold Mackintosh: *Dear Councillor Melville, we write to offer our congratulations upon the successful result achieved by Irlam in its Salute the Soldier week. We should be glad if you would kindly convey to your fellow citizens our warmest thanks for the support they have once more rendered to the war savings campaign. We are very much indebted to the Local Authorities for the prominent part they have taken in stimulating interest in this effort and for the assistance they have so generously given to our local savings committee. We send both to you and your colleagues our best thanks and appreciation.*

On 18th June, destroyer HMS *Fame* attacked and sank German U-boat U767 using hedgehogs and depth charges. During the attack the destroyer was shelled from shore batteries in northern France. Able Seaman Ronald Green, youngest son of Mrs and Mrs J. Green of 10 Woodbine Avenue, Cadishead, was among the crew. He had joined the Navy in February 1941, and prior to this was employed by the Steelworks.

A chance meeting took place in Normandy between two brothers, Harry and Gerald Bannister. Royal Marine Commando No. 41, Harry's unit, had landed at Lion-sur-Mer on Sword Beach on D-Day, then moved along the coast to Luc-sur-Mer. Harry explained: *After the radar station, the next thing I remember we took over the position where my brother was in this 49th Division and we were a small Commando, we were a small unit taking over their positions, and we had to be very quiet. As soon as I saw the polar bear division sign on their shoulders I said 'can you tell me if Sergeant Bannister's about?' And this bloke said 'I'll go and see.' And as we were marching through a few minutes later he comes up walking beside me, that's the first time I'd seen him for a while, he'd been wounded, but it was only a slight wound.* Gerald also recounted the meeting: *Soon after that I met our Harry and he'll have told you about meeting in Normandy and they'd actually took over the positions that we were holding so that we could go on this beginning of the kind of advance, and it wasn't till later on that I heard that he'd been wounded and that he'd gone back to England.* Harry carried on the story: *Anyway we took over their positions, and all I remember about that was of being exhausted all the time. We were underground like, digging in these dugouts what they'd made. By the time you'd done your sentry duty, the first thing you had to stand to in a morning for an hour, stand to at night for an hour, which of course dawn was very early because it was summertime. Stand to at night, and you probably had to do sentry duty as well, and then patrols as well at night, listening patrols. Went out one night on patrol and we was digging for mines with your bayonet in front of you, you had to prod the ground before you stepped on it, and I went to sleep in no man's land and the bloke behind me had to shake my foot to wake me up. We was so bloody exhausted. Anyway one of these patrols what we went on, it was the dead of night and there was about, I think there was half of the troop, I don't think there was a full troop, be about 50 of us, and this shot rang out and a bloke, this is in the dark, one of our blokes was shot right between the eyes, and Lieutenant Dietz sent me back on my own, in the dark, over no man's land, back to our lines for a stretcher. I took it back again, 'good man Bannister, good man.' Anyway we had to take his body back, to see, they thought it was perhaps an English bullet what had killed him, anyway they took him back to the post mortem, it was a German bullet. How's that though in the bloody dark, right between the eyes and the only one shot, I don't know how that happened at all to this day.* After the meeting, the 49th Division, including Gerald Bannister, continued the advance. Gerald explained: *We did have some wireless sets because you needed communication really, it was very important really, and what wireless sets we carried they had lights, and my particular troop sergeant went forward with his wireless on and of course the Germans must have been able to see him, he was a very brave man, Sergeant Tatlow his name, he came from Derbyshire. And about this time my carrier driver went bomb happy, he was sent back. Quite a few of my friends were wounded. I was made a corporal, just about what time I'm not sure, but I was promoted to corporal. Of course when people start getting killed they had to have somebody to take their places. And we moved up from there, we went on the advance through France. I remember going through Rouen at night time, over a bridge that had been blown and the sappers had put a temporary bridge over, and I remember seeing this lone MP stood in the middle of the road guiding us. It was supposed to be dangerous, you were supposed to be able to last, your expectation of life was a week, but I mean that's ridiculous really, cos I'm still here [laughter], and I'm nearly 90.*

Able Seaman D/JX399961 Herbert Eric Allsey (known as Eric) was a Royal Navy gunner who served on defensively equipped merchant ships. Immediately after the Normandy landings he was serving on SS *Lakewood* (570 tonnes, built 1919) which made several voyages from Barry, South Wales to Seine Bay, France, to deliver supplies and ammunition to the Allied troops in Normandy. He took part in convoy EBC.13 (15 merchant ships and two escorts) from Barry to Seine Bay on 16th to 18th June and then the unescorted return convoy on 29th June to 1st July (convoy FBC.13), along with four other merchant ships. By the end of August he had sailed from Barry to Seine Bay four more times (convoys EBC.31 to Seine Bay on 4th to 6th July, no record of return convoy; EBC.41 to Seine Bay on 14th to 16th July; unescorted return FBC.32 on 20th to 22nd July; EBC.59 to Seine Bay 1st to 3rd August; return FBC.45 on 5th to 7th August and EBC.81 to Seine Bay on 23rd to 25th August). His shore leave passes show that he was serving on SS *Lakewood* out of Glasgow in October 1944.

At some point, probably 1945, Eric transferred to the *Dominion Monarch* and served in the Pacific theatre of war, calling at South Africa on the way out and including visits to Sydney, Australia and Wellington, New Zealand. He also served on board SS *Orion*, which was involved in convoys in the Mediterranean (dates unknown).

Able Seaman Eric Allsey (right) and colleagues

Eric, the son of William and Helen Mary Allsey (nee Foster), was born in the village of Costessey in Norfolk on 24th October 1909. At some point in the 1920s the family moved to Milton Avenue, Irlam and later moved to 27 Cutnook Lane, Higher Irlam. Eric worked as a bricklayer at the Steelworks and in 1935 he married Nellie Adams (daughter of First World War veteran and Military Medallist, Walter Adams). They lived at 67 Belgrave Road, Cadishead.

Able Seaman Eric Allsey, Royal Navy

Able Seaman Eric Allsey, Royal Navy (left)

Eric was called up on 15th February 1943 and did his basic training at HMS *Glendower* (a former Butlin's camp at Pwllheli) between 15th February and 23rd April. He was 5 feet 7¾ inches tall with light brown hair, grey blue eyes and a fresh complexion. He completed his gunnery training at HMS *Wellesley* between 24th April and 21st May, passing his gunnery qualifications on 21st May and was promoted from ordinary seaman to able seaman on the same day. He transferred to active service on 22nd May 1943 (under the administration of HMS *President III*, the shore base which managed DEMS accounts).

Meanwhile in Italy, fighting continued as the Allies headed north. Fusilier 4460264 **Ernest Thompson** of the 1st Battalion, Royal Fusiliers (City of London Regiment) died, presumably killed in action, on Wednesday, 21st June. The 1st Royal Fusiliers were part of the 17th Indian Brigade, 8th Indian Division.

The 8th Indian Division was involved in the Battle of Cassino and their heavily opposed night crossing of the Rapido in May 1944, supported by Canadian tanks, was critical to the Allies' success in the final Battle of Monte Cassino. Following this, they advanced over 200 miles in June across mountainous country, fighting many actions against German rearguards and defended strongpoints. In late June they had reached Assisi where the division, which had been fighting since November, was rested.

Born in late 1916 (birth registered at Bucklow, Cheshire) Ernest was the son of Colin and Mary Thompson (nee Yates). He joined the Army in 1940 and prior to this he was living in Cadishead and had been employed as a milkman for the Eccles and District Co-operative Society. In late 1941 he married Ivy Cook and they had one child. He lies buried at Assisi War Cemetery, Italy. At the time of his death, his parents were living at 40 Cecil Road, Eccles.

On Monday, 26th June Captain 169780 **Leslie Herbert Hilton** of the Royal Army Dental Corps, serving with 199 Field Ambulance, died in the United Kingdom.

Born 1912 (birth registered at Stockport in June 1912), Leslie was the son of Herbert and Lillian Hilton (nee Charlesworth). He married Queenie Elizabeth Harvie at Wallasey in 1939 and they resided in Cadishead. He lies buried at Hollins Green Cemetery and his grave is marked by a private headstone. He was 32 years old.

Readers of *A District at War* (the authors' first book which described the district's involvement in the First World War) may recall the naming of a tank 'Irlam' during the First World War. When the 9th Royal Tank Regiment was re-constituted in November 1940 the names of the First World War tanks were re-used and a Churchill tank, serving in C Squadron, was named after the district. On 26th June, during

Operation Epsom, *Irlam* went into action for the first time. It was hit and put out of action before it could fire a shot, its track was smashed and the turret seized. Fortunately the crew were uninjured but the tank's short war was over.

From L-R: Leslie Shaw, H.G. McVey, Thomas Norton, Joseph Fairclough

Two local men, Corporal Leslie Shaw of the Royal Inniskilling Fusiliers and Sapper H.G. McVey of the Royal Engineers, met each other in hospital in Italy while they were both recovering from wounds. Twenty-nine year old Leslie was the youngest son of Mr J. Shaw and the late Mrs Shaw of Higher Irlam. He had joined the Army in 1940 and first went overseas in March 1943, serving in North Africa, Sicily and Italy. He had been taken prisoner while fighting in Tunisia but was released a few days later when British troops entered Tunis. He attended Irlam Central School and, before joining the Army, was employed by the CWS Soap Works. He was married and had one baby daughter who, at this time, he had not seen. Sapper McVey was a resident of Flixton, who had previously lived in Irlam. He was 25 years old and had joined the Army at the outbreak of the war. He had been overseas for 2½ years.

Captain Joseph N. Fairclough of the Royal Army Service Corps was injured in a motorcycle accident in Halifax, Yorkshire. He was returning to his post when he collided with a motor car, receiving extensive injuries. Joseph had joined the Army in December 1939 as a private. He received his commission in April 1943, and was promoted to Captain in August of the same year. Born c.1913, Joseph was the only son of Mrs B.E. Fairclough of 10 Massey Avenue, Lymm. He moved to the district in 1936 and lived with his wife and two children at 17 Ferryhill Road, Irlam. He was employed as manager-salesman by Fords of Warrington.

Private Thomas Leslie Norton of the North Staffordshire Regiment received serious chest wounds whilst on active service in Italy, only six weeks after arriving in the country. He had celebrated his 28th birthday six days before being wounded. Thomas lived with his wife at 1 Alexandra Grove, Irlam and worked as a checker at the Steelworks until he was called up in 1942.

Private Jack Senior, Staffordshire Regiment

Another local soldier serving in the Staffordshire Regiment was John 'Jack' Senior. It is not known which particular battalion of the regiment or which theatres of war he served in. He had previously served with a battalion of the Cheshire Regiment and finished the war in a Welsh regiment. Jack resided at 205 Liverpool Road, Irlam. His brother, Irvin Senior, was a despatch driver with the Sherwood Foresters, based at Sherringham, Norfolk. Irvin resided at 36 Lyndhurst Avenue, Higher Irlam.

Two brothers from Glazebrook, Trooper Joseph and Private Harold Knowles, met each other in Italy. They had both made attempts for several months to meet up and finally achieved this, and spent six days' leave together at a rest camp.

The brothers were born in Cadishead, Joseph in 1911 and Harold in 1920, and were both educated at Cadishead Council School. Joseph went on to Urmston Grammar School. He was transferred to headquarters just three weeks after joining the Forces, in September 1940. He served with the Royal Tank Regiment in Africa, Egypt, Persia, Iraq and Italy and his unit took part in the Battle of Cassino. At the time of the meeting he was serving with the British Liaison Unit at headquarters in Italy. Harold joined the Army in 1942 and first went abroad in December 1943. He served in North Africa, Sicily and Italy. Their mother lived at Bel-Airs on Glazebrook Lane, Glazebrook.

The *Guardian* interviewed a number of local people to ask their opinions on what they would like the post-war world to look like. Here are some of the views they expressed: A 17 year old girl, who worked as a clerk, said that the first job after the war was to make sure that the men and women who had been fighting for their country got fair treatment: *Their sacrifices must not be in vain and the mistakes made after the last war must not be repeated.* She said that when the 1914-1918 war came to an end there were no jobs for thousands of ex-servicemen and hundreds could be seen queuing outside the labour exchanges in search of employment. *There is no necessity,* she said *to mention the poverty and miseries brought about by unemployment, so that after the war our slogan must be 'Work for all!'* A university student said that she was one of the lucky few whose parents had been able to provide her with a good education, but she said that in the future every boy and girl must have the same opportunities of acquiring knowledge and after the war there must be a standard of education available to all, whether rich or poor: *There must be schools, which will enable the dustman's son to study alongside the Cabinet Minister's son with an equal chance of success.* A young female factory worker who had been brought up in poverty in Manchester was of the opinion that the housing plan would play an important part in the post-war world: *It is revolting to see some of the dirty little hovels in which people have to make their homes. The houses in these overcrowded areas* (referring to the area of Manchester where she had been brought up) *should be razed to the ground as they are a disgrace to humanity, and out of the rubble and ashes must arise new cities of beauty and culture. Well planned estates must be erected in the fields of our countryside, away from the smoke and grime of the industrial factories.* An 18 year old female shop assistant felt that there should be more opportunity to travel abroad at a price that could be afforded in the post-war era: *Travel broadens a person's outlook on life, improves his education and enables him to see how his fellow beings live and work.* She thought that if we understood our fellow-men better, the world would be a happier place.

The following verses were written by an anonymous pilot officer from Cadishead. They contain his hopes and ideals, those he held in common with hundreds and thousands of young men who were prepared to fight and, if need be, to die for them:

PRAYER OF THE COMMON MAN

To live in peace beside my fellow-man
Nor seek to conquer, subjugate, subdue
But to encompass in this little span
The task my Maker set for me to do,
To strive, not for mere fortunes gained nor nations praise,
But to advance that knowledge dearly bought
By ancestors, whose single aim to raise
A nation fitted both in deed and thought
In amity its neighbours' interest to comprehend,
And, comprehending, so to act
That malice, envy, greed and strife
May vanish evermore from mortal ken
And every man pursue his chosen course in life.
To hear again the sullen thunder of the breakers roar
Upon this island's rock-bound coast remote,
Or pause mid downland's rolling sweep
To catch the plover's plaintive, piping note
To see the moon's bright orb illume the distant vale
Nor dread the drone of death plane's deep exhaust
Discern the flame of sunset 'gainst the darkling sky
Its glow betokening no holocaust,
To sleep, serene and undisturbed, at close of daily task
These things, these little things, O Lord, are all I ask.

Donations for the Irlam and Cadishead War Comforts Fund continued with contributions from the Small Pig Keepers' Club (Mr H. Day) £1, Irlam and Cadishead Darts League raised almost £7 (the proceeds of matches at the Coach and Horses, George Hotel and Railway, Cadishead) and Miss J. Rollinson donated the proceeds of a dance, which amounted to £9. Mrs Cope and Mrs Dale arranged an effort at the Ship Hotel which raised £23 and Mr Remers of the George Hotel, Cadishead contributed £50 from a Salute week effort. The War Comforts Fund wasn't the only fund to benefit from the district's efforts as women at the CWS Soap Works collected the sum of almost £2 for the Prisoners of War Fund, and a boxing match in

Cadishead raised £1 for the Red Cross. Mary Lewis and Audrey Dennett of Marlborough Road, and Edna Bickerton of Mond Road, Higher Irlam, donated almost £3.

A letter written by George Anderson, a prisoner of the Japanese, was received by his stepfather and mother, Samuel and Martha Ann Whittle of 18 Fir Street, Cadishead. The letter, the third one he had written, was dated shortly after Christmas and had taken six months to arrive in England. In the letter he stated that he was receiving better treatment than usual. It was apparent that he was unaware that his half-brother, Samuel Anderson Whittle, Merchant Navy, had lost his life in 1941, as he asked in the letter to be remembered to him. At the time, George was being held in Keiyo POW Camp, Chosen, Korea.

Another man in Japanese hands was Corporal Ron Sampson, Royal Marines. During his three years in captivity Ron faced appalling physical treatment and ritual humiliation at the hands of his Japanese captors. Ron, a proud man, who, at the time of the Czechoslovakian Crisis in 1938, had joined the Royal Marines to fight for his country, had to suppress the urge to fight back, as any form of resistance would have been met with immediate death. He maintained his dignity through passive defiance, refusing to bow properly to the prison guards and swearing at them when he bowed, which often resulted in savage beatings. The following firsthand account of his time as a prisoner of war gives some idea of the treatment he received while at Soengei Geroeng camp, situated near the old harbour in East Palembang, about 1.5 miles north east of the centre of town on the north bank of the River Musi: *The food was terrible. It was shocking, it really was shocking. And we used to have ubi kayu, which is like a sweet potato but it's all spikes all round and they used it for poster paints normally, for posters, and that was our main food, ubi kayu, that's what we used to eat mainly, it was, we used to call it glop, but it's something and in the prison camp when you're hungry you'd eat practically anything. I've eaten all kinds of animals: cats, little puppies, iguanas, you mention it, monkeys, snakes, anything edible we'd eat to exist. You wouldn't dream of it normally but it was, when you're hungry it was better than nothing, even the Japanese were hungry on the island so you can imagine what state we were in, you'd eat anything. We had to go to work, and it's all kinds of tasks, unloading ships and you'd be in the hold of the ship and flour or cement, normally cement, and the burst bags, that cement would be pouring down on the men below and at the end of the day when they come to have a wash the skin used to go white with the cement, they couldn't get rid of the cement, oh dear, when you think of it now. Yes, and we never had any shoes, they never gave us any shoes, but we used to cut out imprints in pieces of wood and put a lap over, tap those out, I could do it now, I could make you a pair of those, and it would save the feet. But the soles of the feet used to go hard, and you can walk over stones, you couldn't possible do it normally but the soles of the feet got hard. But then they took us to this searchlight battery and we had to dig a grey clay from the bed of the Musi, dig it up this grey clay, then you'd pass it to the men and they'd pass it up, and they used to pack that round the searchlight battery, pack it, and when the sun dried it it went hard, but we had three days doing that and the body from here, the tide used to come up to about here, the river used to swell and we used to come out pickled, you know your skin goes wrinkled. I thought I'll be crippled after this. Anyway the hard sole became soft because we were three days in the water and when it dried, when we come out eventually, when this dried the sole of the foot it came off, it peeled away and it left bare flesh underneath. I didn't know what to do, the whole sole came away, just like a sole of a shoe and when I got back to the camp eventually my feet oh they were killing me, and I was afraid of dirt and dysentery because men had dysentery and they were passing motion all over the place, you couldn't help but tread in it, it was a nightmare. They made a toilet, put planks across and a hole and just squat down, that was a toilet but many people couldn't get as far as the toilet and this excreta was all over the place and if you tried to make the toilet at night time, you had to walk through this. I used to have a kerosene tin and I used to put water in that at night time when I was asleep so that if I went to the toilet I can come back and I could wash my feet, I used to go to that trouble, other men didn't do that, I don't know how they survived at all, I used to wash my feet.*

Oh terrible. Terrible, really terrible. I got repeated beatings for nothing at all, no reason, they'd just come in and start battering you and you couldn't understand it. To ease the boredom an artist had drawn a dartboard on a wall, we made our own darts through curtain rods, cut them up and knocked nails through them and it became quite successful, we made our own darts and cut them at the top and put paper in, they were quite good. But the Japs came in and an artist, he was an artist and he'd drawn an aircraft alongside the dartboard, you know he'd no intention, it wasn't a Japanese aircraft or an English it was just an aeroplane and this Jap came in and said we were throwing darts at a Japanese aeroplane. All those playing darts got a beating for that, a really terrible beating, we were throwing darts at a Japanese plane, and it wasn't a Japanese plane at all it was just an aeroplane. Oh dear. But they were very hard and we had Koreans, now one or two of the Koreans we could get through to, they didn't like the Japanese but they were part of them and they were the guards, and we had one Korean and he used to tell us, he used to come and tell me the Japanese are going to make a search so if you've got anything to stow away get rid of it now. I think they knew that I used to keep a record every day and bury it, I wanted to write a book when I came home, that was my intention and if I didn't make it I thought I'd leave the records and they knew what had gone on because there were a lot of atrocities, and Chinese, they didn't like the Chinese, and they'd bayonet the Chinese, line them up and bayonet them, there's no compassion.

And we had this camp commander, he came and it must have been two or three months before the end of the war really, and he was all dressed up and he had a smart rig-out but he had an evil face and you'd only got to look at him and you'd think oh dear me we're in trouble now. He was a really wicked Japanese, and I think he must have come from a front, he'd been fighting in the front and I think they'd sent him to the prison camp for a rest. Anyway I was drawn out with nine of us, nine of us, and he picked us out for no reason. He wanted the names of people who brought in oil, and they used to wait for an air raid, and if there was an air raid the Japanese couldn't search you and most people had little cans of oil or bottles of oil stowed away and they knew the Japanese wouldn't search you if there was an air raid on, they'd just rush you in, and it was a good opportunity what you'd stole to take it into camp.

Corporal Ron Sampson, Royal Marines

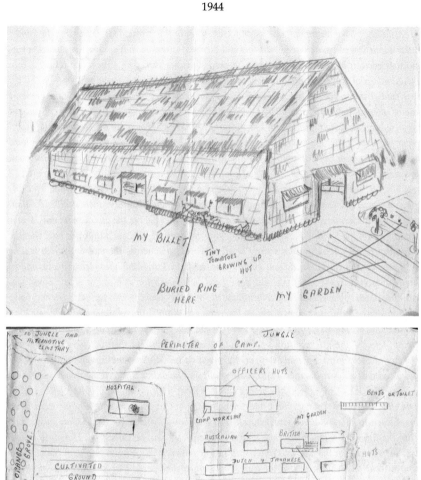

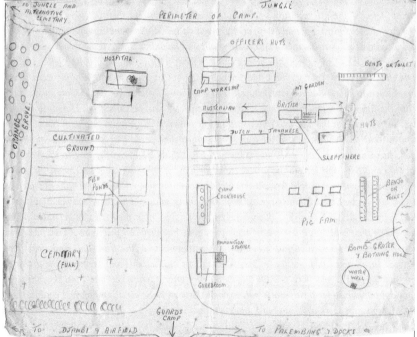

Sketches of Soengei Geroeng POW Camp by Ron Sampson

Anyway this guard commander he was all dressed up in this tropical kit, it was starched and I must admit it was smart but he had this evil face and it was such a contrast because the rig-out was good, it looked nice and it was starched so it was stiff. And anyway he takes me into the guard room and he wanted me to give the name of at least two people who brought oil in, so I said 'I don't know, I've no idea.' And I can remember now, 'saya tidak tahu, I don't know.' I knew he'd understand that because it's Malay or Indonesian, but he kept on and because 'saya tidak tahu,' that's all I kept saying. And he goes away to the corner of the guard room, it was quite long, and I thought oh he's leaving me alone, because the guard commanders never partook with punishment, none of them, they never did any punishment themselves, but this fella wanted to you could tell. So he took me into the guard room and I wouldn't tell him the names of the men who brought oil in, he went berserk, and he had this piece of wood, it was about that long, and an inch thick and about 2½ inches wide like that, and he put his hands round it and he walked from the other part of the guard room and he was tapping in on his hand, I thought he was trying to, as it were, show authority, but when he comes up to me without any warning at all he slashed me across the face with this, and he split my eye and the blood, do you know I can feel it trickling, the head bleeds freely, and in the tropics even more so, if you cut your head you lose a lot of blood, and the blood was running down my eye, and I had a beard, a little one, I'd grown it, and I used to try and singe it off to shape it. But instead of stopping he kept on with this lump of wood and he was hitting me like this on my face, and if you get beaten for a while you lose feeling, and in the end I couldn't feel, I think it's nature's way, you stand so much and then you don't feel it, and although he was hitting me and with all the blood on my face and that it was splattering and my blood was all over his nicely starched rig-out and he didn't notice it, he was so engrossed in battering me. And he had two young soldiers fresh from Japan, only young fellas and he said, the interpreter told us 'he's told them they've got to learn to kill. It's important they must learn to kill, and don't forget it, put it in your mind, you've got to kill, that's your job.' And the interpreter told them this, now this interpreter said he came from Honolulu but he was in Japan when the war was imminent, he knew there was going to be a war. Some funny things went on. Anyway when the camp commander discovered that his shirt was in such a mess he went stark raving mad, and you could tell, I think he'd been fighting in the front for so long and they sent him to the prison camp for a bit of a rest but he didn't want that, he'd rather be killing, I could tell. And all this blood all over his rig-out, that's the only satisfaction I got, and he sent me in the charge of these two young soldiers and they took me down, they had bamboo slits and they put them between my fingers, now they tried to get them down here, well they could only put one or two down here, but they can put more if they put them on that first joint, so they put a bamboo slit between those, the first joint and then they pressed them, and I had one Jap on this side and one on that side and they kept the pressure on, now at first it was very painful but then again after a while you don't feel it, with pain you can only go so far then I think nature comes in, you can't feel it any more, I couldn't feel it although they were pressing hard and even now my fingers at the end are dead, these are dead, no feeling in these, that first joint on both sides, and my hands ache, they hurt regularly. Now I don't know what caused that, whether it was the malnutrition or whether they'd done something to my hands when I was unconscious, because they knocked me unconscious a couple of times these young soldiers by thumping me and kicking me, and they thought they'd killed me, they thought they'd made a good job eventually, and they left me in this clearing and I was unconscious, I think they'd hit me on the head with something and knocked me out. But my friends came and they thought they'd bury me, and take me back to the camp, and they'd organise a burial. There was no coffin, no clothing, nothing, when they were buried they were buried naked, there was nothing there just a body, and if you didn't make it long enough it was awful. I remember we had a Dutchman, he must have been about 7 foot I think and we dug this grave 6 foot, it was probably less than that, we were trying to cut down, but when they brought this body up for burial we put him in and pushed his feet down to the bottom and we put his shoulders down but his head wouldn't go in, his shoulders went in and his head came up as we pushed him down, his head came up on his chest, and I thought oh my. So this chap I was with, he said 'we'll have to try and get him out.' So we put the spades in under his body and we couldn't get him out, he was jammed tight, fancy having to muck around with a dead body like that, but you'd no alternative and you couldn't leave him there, the Japs would be looking for us, he had to be buried. So anyway this chap he goes away and he says 'hang on, leave it to me.' And there was a lot of bracken been cut down and he brought that then and he put it over this body and he goes away and takes a few steps back and he starts running up and jumping on this body trying to push it down, but his head wouldn't go down of course so we tried cutting around to let his head go down, can you imagine it, you know, you wouldn't dream of such a thing but there was no alternative, and I thought this chap was going to chop his head off to tell you the truth, he knew we couldn't leave his head above the ground, there was wild boars they'd come and eat it, wild boars in the jungle, big ones with the tusks, and they would attack humans too.

Oh yes, it was quite common [to bang prisoners' heads together], *for punishment and to save injuring their hands I think, they'd get them and bump them together and they used to hit on the ears, they perforated my ears doing that, just bashing them together, oooohh, it's like concussion, and this ear used to bleed, my right ear, I've had several operations on this ear when I came home, they've operated several times because they were perforated and they've got now if I take this out I'm deaf and yet I can hear, it's like a language I've learnt, it's really odd because I don't know where it's come from. Well they had the women's ward and we had to pass the women's ward to go to the wash basin and in the wash basin they had a dripping tap and it was separated by a bit of a border built up, and the women used to go the other side to wash and you weren't supposed to speak to them, and they'd have a guard there watching if you tried to wash and it was only a trickling of water, it was terrible. Anyway I went towards the men's wash place and the women were there on the other side, and this guard came and he wanted me to bow and I felt humiliated at that time, bowing to the flamin' Japanese, you know that was terrible, so they were showing me how to bow, down like this and holding it, you had to do it properly, bow from the waist. Well when I was bowing instead of bowing from the waist I was just giving them a nod and the guard went mad 'No! No! No! No! No!' He was going and shouting, and these women could see what was happening so they said 'oh for goodness sake give him a bow.' I said 'I can't, I can't.' I couldn't humiliate myself and I was still bowing, I couldn't understand what he meant by bowing right down but this guard came out and he went mad. And those women, it was supposed to be a so-called hospital really, these women they used to sing at night, it was quite good, it made a change, and one she said her name was Annie Laurie, that was her name she said, but they used to sing all songs, and we used to try but we didn't sound at all nice, I don't think we were very talented generally, at least the Marines weren't, I was with the Marines, they were only taught how to kill, they never give them any musical lessons.*

Well they used to take us to the docks, working on the docks, and this guard commander there he used to come and sit by me every day and I used to say 'Ohayou, you stupid old so and so,' and choice words, and the men used to roar, they used to think it was funny so I used to try and think of more words to call him, you know. But he eventually learnt what I was saying, he must have asked somebody what it meant because this day I called him some nasty words and he come running at me, started battering me, and you weren't allowed to resist, if you resisted they used to hand you over to the Impi and if you'd shown resistance by holding them they'd hand you over to the Kempeitai and this was like the Gestapo, but anybody that went to the Kempeitai they were never seen again, so you knew if you go that far you're not going to come back. Impi, that was like the local police, they'd give you a battering, but that was it, but if they handed you over to the Kempeitai because you'd resisted that's it, that's the finish, they'd just execute them. They were very cruel the Japanese. Oh dear.

I was in Soengei Geroeng camp, Palembang, and at the entrance to the camp they had five skulls on poles and these skulls had got bleached with the sun, they were white and they were at grotesque angles, some this way some that way, and we had to pass them every morning and the Japanese used to say 'your friends,' they used to like saying that, 'your friends.' But they were Air Force, they must have been Air Force because they had particles of Air Force uniform at the bottom of the poles, so we presumed it must have been airmen, perhaps planes that had been shot down, they did shoot down one or two, and they put the crew on parade in Palembang, in the town to let the local people see that they were winning the war sort of thing, you know.

The beds were bamboo slats laid out and bound together with, oh what do you call it? Anyway you used to soak it in water and it used to dry hard, but we bound these slats together and that was our beds to lie on. But they used to get covered in bugs and body lice, and I used to wake up in the morning and I'd be covered in blood, and it's my blood that the bugs had been sucking and in my sleep I'd been crushing them and bursting these bugs and there was blood all over me, and you got that way you accepted it, you knew what was going to happen each day, there was no way round it, you had to accept it. It would send you mad, normally it would send you mad, I think it sent some mad. I saw people lose their mind, I could be talking to somebody like you and then suddenly they'd stop and they'd start speaking a lot of jumble, rubbish, and I used to look at them but then I realised their minds had gone and only a few minutes before I could talk to them, it was as quickly as that, it was an education to me.

A sick man who couldn't go to work they used to have the dead bodies and they used to pile them up in one section of the huts and they'd all be lined up, all the dead bodies, and a sick man who couldn't go to work they had sticks and they had to keep banging them to chase off the rats because the rats would start eating them, even the rats were hungry. And we had one *chap he'd even ate a rat, I only remember one chap eating a rat, oh dear you just didn't fancy that, that was the last straw, and he got some disease and he never got over it but they reckoned it was through eating a rat. Fancy eating a rat, you've got to be hungry. I've eaten all kinds of animals, animals you wouldn't dream of eating.*

Gunner Len Wright from Hollins Green was another prisoner of the Japanese. After a time at Changi Jail he was sent to No. 1 Camp, Siam (modern day Thailand), where he was put to work on the Bangkok-Moulmein railway (notoriously known as the 'Death Railway' and made famous by the film 'Bridge over the River Kwai'). Len worked on the railway until September 1944, and found the conditions very hard. One compensating factor for the cruelty of the Japanese was the kindness that the Siamese people gave to the British prisoners. The following is Len's account: *Then they said 'you're going to Thailand' and we landed in Thailand and we had nothing to sleep in only a field and then we started building huts and I had to go and I were wounded because I'd gone up with 'em and we had to fetch poles down on a tripod, so these two fellas said 'come with us and pretend to pull Len', and I was just going like that you know, and we did all that job and built us own hut and then we went in and then we started on the railway. And I was 2½ years on that railway. You know the big bridge over the River Kwai, we loaded it, we was at Nong Pladuk and we fetched the bridge off onto a..., because going to the bridge was a narrower gauge railway and all the sidings, we went in the morning and got in for about one o'clock. And then they said right you're going off at six with this bridge. Hell, we thought we'd finished. We started the bridge, two engines, one at front and one at back and it took us till eight o'clock to get them all there, they was only crawling, didn't want it to fall off the road. And we got to the River Kwai bridge and we had to unload it and it poured down all the time we was unloading it in there. When we unloaded it we went back to Nong Pladuk then we finished there.*

There was five Australians in the camp, Nong Pladuk Camp where we was most of the time, and they went one time, they were going to try and get a little boat and sail down to Australia if they could, they caught them. And do you know what their punishment was? They laid them on their back, held their mouth open and poured water down with kettles and they did that about six times I believe. They looked terrible when they came back to the camp. Have you ever heard of anybody escaping because I didn't, no. We never had anything proper to eat, it was all rice. I went to work after a while on the railway proper and you got tea with no sugar or milk and in a morning you always got rice with a spoonful of sugar. Cooked rice. Then the Japanese opened a Chinese shop, you could get stuff from there if you had the money, inside the camp. There was a Jap seeing that you didn't do anything. You could buy bacca and you could buy things to eat, you could pick as many bananas as you wanted, it were full of bananas that camp. I can't say they were rotten to me. If they tried to be clever, do you get me, they got hit, good and proper. But our gang we worked and we finished at 2 o'clock and they'd say 'Yazmi' so we all sat down and then I'd go and fetch some water from over the railroad behind the station, used a pump, come back, brew it and we had tea to put in it and we didn't do anything then till 5 o'clock and come back in, cos we finished at 2. Some were awkward, but they were nasty the Japanese, they were nasty, very nasty.

Bridge over the River Kwai (modern day view)

Gunner 14337244 Raymond Cookson, 439 Battery, 55th Field Regiment (West Somerset Yeomanry), Royal Artillery, arrived at Arromanches in Normandy on 27th June. His regiment was attached to the 3rd Battalion, Irish Guards, which was part of the Guards Armoured Division. The regiment was loaded onto a liberty boat where they remained for one week before making the crossing to France and landing at Arromanches. The battery fired 25 pounders and Raymond's role as signaller was to take up an advanced position and direct artillery fire onto German positions using a wireless from inside a Sherman tank. The following is his account of his call-up and his arrival in France: *I was called up on 19th November 1942 and I went to Middleton Towers Holiday Camp near Morecambe for my six weeks basic training. Then New Year's Day 1943 I was posted to the 55th Field Regiment, 439 Battery, at Codford near Salisbury. I went in as, well I went in the Artillery as a gunner, came out as a gunner. You see, you could only get promotion if somebody got killed in your sort of doings, and there were very, very few signallers in the higher ranks, like sergeants and bombardiers, cos you see in the Artillery you're a bombardier you're not a corporal, they didn't get killed, so I couldn't get promoted. But when I got called up I was glad because all my mates were going and I was at the Steelworks from being 16-18 and when I went to the manager and said 'I've got my call-up papers to go in the Army,' he said 'lad, I can get you off because you're on war work.' I said 'oh no, I'm not going to be called a bloody coward.' I can remember my Uncle George, and so I was delighted to go in really. And the fact that all my mates were going, and women were coming taking the jobs at the Steelworks. I did my basic training, the six weeks, like I say at Middleton Towers and then I went to the 55th Field Regiment. You see when you're on your basic training you get all different tests and it's strange but when I was working at Clarke's when I was 15 to 16 there was a lad I knew who was going in the Merchant Navy as a wireless operator and he used to get me sending him Morse code while he was training and so I got quite good at Morse code, and then when I went to my training at Middleton Towers you get all these exams to do, well of course I could do the Morse code so I got automatic posted as a potential signaller, wireless operator, and that's what I was training as, a wireless operator, when I joined the 55th Field Regiment. And I passed out to be a wireless operator and then we went from Codford to West Tofts Camp, that's between Norfolk and Suffolk, West Tofts. From West Tofts we went to Hovingham, Yorkshire near Malton. And then from there we went all the way down to Pevensey, Pevensey Bay where we were in the practice landings, it's not Hastings it was at Pevensey, a place called Battle near Pevensey, and that's where we got ready to go to Normandy. The vehicles had to be waterproofed, when you had what you called a wet landing, your exhaust and your inlet for your engine you've got extended pipes for the air to go in or come out, so that's where we had our training to get to Normandy. Now then I can't actually tell you the date but it was somewhere around about 14 days after D-Day we landed on the Normandy beaches and that was at Arromanches. We went across, we were a week on the bloody boat, it was what they called a Liberty boat. You see you can't have artillery on a landing barge, all the guns and limbers and that and you name it were on a big boat and then they hauled us all off the big boat onto a huge raft made of oil drums and steel plates with a ramp on it, so we got pulled with a tug and then the tug let us go and we drifted to where we grounded, course we were still in the water. They let the ramp down and you drive off up the beach, that's how we landed. I got on the raft down a rope ladder, down the side of the boat, which wasn't very nice looking down and seeing the water. The first impression that you get, the weather was nice, it was June, middle of June, the first impression you get is the smell of death believe it or not, but not necessarily men, all the cows and horses in the fields in Normandy, Normandy's a farming area, you never saw any live animals, they were all dead and full of maggots and bloody flies and the smell lingers with you for ages and ages and ages. And I mean from then on really it's a case of you're doing your job, you're frightened to bloody death cos there's always shells landing, the mates I lost, got killed, I was just one that was lucky. I was in a tank from Normandy, all the way when we landed in Normandy. You see I was like a signaller in the captain's vehicle, a 15cwt vehicle, and then the captain had to go to the front to direct the fire, well of course it's no good going to the bloody front in a little lorry otherwise you'd get shot up in no time, so we got a tank from the Irish Guards and the driver and co-driver were guardsmen but the two signallers were me and another bloke called Bill Tannett, and Captain Ludgrove.*

Born in Irlam on 11th June 1924, Raymond was the only son of Samuel and Elsie Lillian Cookson (nee Brewer) of 8 Woodbine Terrace, Irlam. He was educated at Irlam Endowed and Irlam Central School and then, at the age of 14, he left school and took up employment at Clarks Atlas Works at Patricroft. At 16 he joined the Steelworks. Raymond was called up on 19th November 1942 and when he informed his manager at the Steelworks he was told that he was in a reserved occupation, however, Raymond wanted to serve because of his uncle George - he remembered stories about his uncle who was killed in action during the First World War. At 17 years old, George, a well-built young man, had been given a white feather which compelled him to lie about his age and join up. Raymond's cousin, Reginald Brewer, was killed at Anzio in February 1944.

Gunner Raymond Cookson, Royal Artillery

Private 3657072 **William Porter** of the 2nd Battalion, Border Regiment, 100th Indian Infantry Brigade, 20th Indian Division, died of wounds on 28th June.

William was born 1917 at Warrington, the son of William and Mary Porter (nee Bennett). He was educated at Beaumont Council School, Warrington. Before the war he lived at 35 Victory Road, Cadishead, and had worked for the Council. He was a Sunday School teacher at Cadishead Wesleyan Church and was very popular with the schoolchildren. Before joining the Army he was a member of Irlam Fire Brigade. He joined the Army in January 1940. However, at the height of the Blitz, he was released from the Army to serve with the AFS for 18 months. William first served in the South Lancashire Regiment and then transferred to the Border Regiment. He went overseas in December 1943, seeing service in India and Burma. He was stationed at Imphal, India when the Japanese attacked, and he took part in the Battle of Imphal. When the siege ended on 22nd June his division counter-attacked towards Ukhrul, north east of Imphal. William was wounded at some point, probably during this counter-attack. He was healthy enough to write a letter to his mother informing her that he had been wounded and was on his way home and the family made preparations to visit him as soon as he was back in the country. Sadly he died of wounds on board the hospital ship and was buried at sea. He is commemorated on the Rangoon Memorial, Burma. He was 27 years old. After the war, in September 1949, William's sister, Doris, married Len Wright, former prisoner of war.

Thirteen year old Margaret Savage of 23 Addison Road, Higher Irlam made a gift of an Ocean Library to the Merchant Navy. To achieve this, she sold all her toys and saved and collected, until she had seven guineas. On Friday, 31st June she visited the Jutland Rest Home on Trafford Road, Salford, and handed over her donation to the Port Chaplain, Reverend F.M. Hodges-Roper. The chaplain arranged for the library to be installed in a merchant vessel using the port of Manchester. Margaret's name was inscribed on the cabinet.

Corporal James N. Howes, South East Asia Command, wrote to encourage other servicemen and servicewomen to write to the *Guardian: Sir, may I take this opportunity of speaking to the local boys and girls in the Forces, through the medium of the Guardian. Now, boys and girls, where are those letters that our great friend Onlooker asked for in previous issues of the Guardian? Come on, don't let him down, also myself and the few who do let the ancient Council know just what we want and what we are going to have when we finish this little argument. I know that most of you are thinking the way I am, but what gets me is that you are thinking these things and doing nothing about it. Come on, now, the more we are together, the happier we will be when we get back to the old home town. Most of you think that you are fighting for far better things in the future than you have had in the past. You feel that way as much as I do, so let's give it big licks and snow Onlooker under with bags of what we want; then, as he says, he will hold the fort until our return. Then we will have bags of fun kicking some semblance of life into the old town. Don't let this letter be in vain. Let's be having them in bulk – don't store them.*

Private William Porter, South Lancashire Regiment
(later served with the Border Regiment)

The *Guardian* published a letter by R. Taylor, titled 'Somewhere in France': *Sir, you don't know me, and probably you'll not be any nearer by the time you've finished reading this little note, but I would really like to say how much I enjoyed reading your articles in the Guardian – your news is just the stuff you need for the troops, and as I sit here in a truck in the front line in France, I would like to thank you for a couple of minutes' laughter a few of us had when I read your bit about 'Pheep' – the train journey in your article (June 10th). Keep at ye olde Council for some good homes for us when we come back! Cheerio for now – best of luck.* R. Taylor's home address was 4 Bradburn Road, Irlam.

JULY

During the month, Don Dickson won his 'wings' and was commissioned at Manitoba, Canada. Don had joined the RAF in May 1943 and in November of the same year he was posted to Canada for training. He also received training in Oklahoma, USA. Before going overseas he had, in August 1943, taken part in an RAF clay pigeon shooting competition and was the first of 4,000 contestants to get 14 'kills' out of 14 shots, from seven different angles. He was awarded a silver cup for this achievement. Don, the eldest son of Mr and Mrs K.A. Dickson of 16 Prospect Road, Cadishead, was educated at St Mary's School and Cadishead Senior School. Before joining the RAF he was employed in the offices of the CWS Soap Works.

Mr and Mrs F.W. Richardson of 81 Victory Road, Cadishead, received a letter from their son, 26 year old Guardsman Stephen W. Richardson of the Scots Guards. This was the first letter they had received in eleven months. Stephen had been captured at Tobruk in 1942. He was held as a prisoner of war in Italy and whilst there made two escape attempts. On the third attempt he escaped from the camp (most likely at the time the Italians capitulated) and was given sanctuary by an Italian farmer. In his letter Stephen stated he was in Naples and awaiting transport back to England: *During the time I was free, I had a very exciting and sometimes not too pleasant time. I had two goes at getting through but was unsuccessful and since then I have been living on an Italian farm, believe me, I've been treated excellently by the people who sheltered and fed me, and looked on me as one of their own sons. They were all broken hearted and crying when I left and begged and implored me to stay with them, but, of course, that was impossible.*

On Wednesday, 5th July a chance, fleeting meeting of two Irlam friends took place in Italy between Albert Drum, Royal Signals and Eric Holt, Royal Army Service Corps. Albert wrote of the meeting in a letter to his mother, dated 6th July: *Now here's a bit of news. Yesterday I was out on a job and the truck I was in broke down. We knew one of our trucks would be along later in the day so we just lay down in the sun and took things easy. I got in the cab after a while because the sun was pretty hot but I soon found that the truck cab was hotter still and got down. As I got out and started to stroll over to the grass where my mate was I noticed two big control trucks coming along and just as they were passing a voice howled 'hallo there, Albert' Well! I jumped about a foot in the air and spun round and spotted a fair head, (the face of which was split by a big grin) and an arm waving wildly. I recognised him straight away. It was the lad I've been looking for all over Sicily and Italy – Eric Holt. I just had time to shout and wave back and he was gone. Unfortunately the truck was in convoy and could not stop so that was that. Hard lines you know, four years since I saw him and then a split second meeting and away again. You can tell his father that in the little time I had to notice, he looked exceptionally fit and well, and has changed very little in the face since I last saw him except he looks much stronger and very much more tanned. From the direction they were going I think he may be able to visit a place I described to you recently in a very little while. I'm afraid the combined shouts of he and I had a very startling effect not only on my mate who was dozing gently on the grass and jumped like a startled rabbit, but also on Eric's pals some of whom sitting on the roof of their huge vehicle nearly fell off with the shock. Still a passing like that can hardly be carried out in silence.*

Eric Holt recalled the sighting in a letter to the authors in 2013: *In Italy 78th Division moved through on the Eastern side of Italy. Part of the way 78th Division was moving to a new destination and while I was plane spotting in a brief flash I saw a person I used to work with at the Irlam Steelworks, yes there was Albert Drum on the side of the road, unfortunately we were in convoy and could not stop but that was an experience I shall never forget.* Albert and Eric worked in together in the offices at Irlam Steelworks before joining the Army.

Private Eric Holt (front left), Royal Army Service Corps
(in the left background is the armoured HQ vehicle that Eric was in when he spotted Albert Drum)

Service medals were awarded to several members of the district's St John Ambulance Brigade, to commemorate 15 years continuous and efficient service: Superintendent Herbert Weston, Ambulance Driver Tom Hazlehurst, Sergeants E. Mason and T. Walton, Corporal R.W. Meakin, Private H.R. Selon and Sergeant W. Stewart (who had transferred to the Lancashire Steel Corporation Division). These members were among the original 16 men who founded the district's division in May 1929. At the outbreak of the war the division had placed itself at the service of the local ARP

Committee and had provided excellent service at the local first aid posts. Over 20 of its members had joined the Armed Forces during the course of the war, including Private Harold Rosbottom, who was a prisoner of war in Germany. Three other members of the original 16 were still serving with the brigade in other areas: Sergeant F. Collier DCM, MM (Stockport Division), Cadet Superintendent W.R. Tonge (Altrincham Division) and Sergeant D. Charnock (Warrington LMS Division). In addition, the president, James Sinclair Kerr and vice president, Edwin Jones, had given good service during the 15 years of the division's existence.

A letter published in the *Guardian* from Leading Aircraftman Stan Stringer, serving with the RAF of India Command, gave his views on post-war planning: *Sir, I have been receiving the Guardian out here for almost three years now, and in your April edition, the latest to arrive here, you invited us to write our views on post-war planning, and say we are shy or too busy to write. I don't think it is 'shyness,' far from it. It's the proverbial 'one-won't-get-blood-out-of-a-stone' feeling that may have prevented a lot of letters. Look how long the B.R. [British Restaurant] took to get established! Incidentally, I followed Onlookers campaign with much interest and amusement. He is the most interesting part of the paper, I think. Well I haven't given this post-war planning much thought, there is still a war on in this part of the world, though most people at home don't seem to realise it, and as can be imagined, we are kept busy. Still, here is what I should suggest as improvements to our district. First and foremost, housing. There is quite a lot of overcrowding, cramped living accommodation, houses that should literally be blown up, and houses that should never have been built at all. In your 'Readers Forum' of the edition I have here, a J. Cassidy of Flixton, says that the Irlam and Cadishead Council has built four 'modern' estates in the past 20 years. What a poor conception he must have of the modern house! They are, of course, built solidly, but they are as modern as the 'bashas' we exist in here. So, when the Council decides to carry out its post-war housing plan, assuming it is intending to do some, I hope it will give every consideration to health, convenience, comfort and labour-saving in their new houses, and keep in mind what was good enough 30 years ago isn't good enough now. Next, the roads of the district, none of which can be compared to the bullock tracks we use for roads here, unless, of course, there has been drastic changes while I've been over here, but there was one road I remember quite well, and that was Laburnum Road, off Fir Street. I often saw a car or lorry bogged during the winter months, and the people who had to walk up the same road had to do a spot of navigating. That's just one example, Bankfield Avenue is another, and there are many more. Something has got to be done about it. In the way of entertainment and recreational facilities, the district offers very little. Those two super cinemas, Rialto and Palace, are hardly the last word in luxury and comfort are they? Also, how about Sunday shows? Cadishead on a wet Sunday night is similar in some respects to this place in the present monsoon, except one can choose between a pub and a church. This may annoy some people, but it is correct. As the Rev. Bakker says, the youth of today is not so religious as he was a generation or so ago, so what? One doesn't have to attend church regularly to live like a Christian. Still, I'm wandering off on another subject now, so 'nuff said. To get back again to recreation, I would like to see a swimming pool, public tennis courts, better sports grounds, and lastly but most important, a public library, with a large selection of technical reading. I say important, for when the higher education scheme comes into being, a library would be both helpful and instructive. That just about concludes all I have to say for the present. I hope to see letters from a few more of the locals in the services in your paper. I have not seen any from any of the girls who are serving, as yet, which is strange, for women can usually find something to say without invitation (this should bring something).*

One week later, *Lancashire Lass* accepted the challenge in Stan's letter: *Sir, referring to Stan Stringer's letter of last week. Good shooting, Stan! You certainly hit the nail on the head. Believe me, young fellow, Cadishead hasn't altered one bit for the better. You will need your top boots on if you visit Belgrave Road and Bankfield Avenue when you return. The Sunday evenings are just as quiet; only pubs and churches open, and some of the people here are still minding other people's business instead of their own. Of course, they find pleasure in it. So, why worry? Now to post-war planning. May I suggest the Council Chamber be changed into a library? It would certainly serve a better purpose than at present. A good name for that place would be 'Sleepy Valley.' Holidays at home? No, not here! Too much expense and trouble. But if the 'civic daddies' had a chance to go to a conference and stay at a posh hotel that would be different. With due respect to Mr Muir and the scouts' hut, why not a cottage hospital or maternity hospital? Which do we need most? 'Londoner' was right when he said 'wake up Irlam.' I say wake up Cadishead. By the way, it would be very interesting to know how many ARP chaps have volunteered to go to London and exchange with those chaps for a rest. It's quite common to see them either sat in the newsagent's shop or standing at their depot door passing remarks about people on their way to work. They have not much to grouse about, and a little exercise would do some of them no harm. Some of them nearly shed tears to get in the ARP, now they don't want to leave here. They have as much right to do their share as the NFS. Never let it be said you failed to do your share. I expect when they sound the last all-clear the councillors will be greeting the lads with a couple of bob and a toffee apple, and the lads will be singing 'We don't know where we're going till we're there.' So with patience we'll wait and see.*

The reference to the ARP in Lancashire Lass' letter stirred up a hornet's nest and two letters were published in the *Guardian* both from people who called themselves *Lancashire Lad*, and both serving with the ARP: *Sir, in answer to Lancashire Lass, maybe she doesn't know that most of the Civil Defence is run by part-timers. If they could get someone to take their place at work, they would be only too glad to help in any way. They did not run when Manchester got it in 1940-41, and would not run away again. Don't forget that some of the NFS are also part-timers. How do they go on? What is Lancashire Lass doing in this? Yours, etc. Lancashire Lad (part-time ARP).*

Sir, referring to Lancashire Lass, it would be interesting to know how she obtained information that was confidential to the ARP only. It seems she has a very poor memory. When volunteers were wanted in 1939 did they fail then? No, nor since. They have always been ready when wanted, but, of course, there was no exception for the ARP chaps. They didn't fail the public because of that. They carried on until their papers for the Forces came. If it is, as Lancashire Lass states, quite common to see ARP chaps sitting and passing remarks about people on their way to work why has she not the courage to name the ARP chaps and not class them all the same. From one who did not change his job to keep from the Forces, or any other organisation – Yours, etc. Lancashire Lad, guard room A Sec. 1.

Corporal 644189 Stanley Stringer served overseas with the RAF. He enlisted in 1939/40 at the age of 19 and originally served as ground crew. He was in Malaya in January 1942 and by February he had moved to Singapore and was there when it fell to the Japanese.

Corporal Stan Stringer (centre)

Corporal Stan Stringer during flight training

Corporal Stan Stringer, Royal Air Force

Stanley was badly wounded at some point around this time but managed to escape the clutches of the Japanese Army. After recovering he volunteered for flight crew and received his training at Kohat RAF Station in India (now Pakistan). In December 1943 he was in Calcutta and in August of the following year he was at Bengal. By March 1945 he was stationed in Ceylon.

Reverend Lee expressed emphatic views about the post-war planning in the parish magazine: *I am all in favour of raising money for work for our boys when they return. This is a far better provision than gratuities and parties. After a rest from all their labour and perils they will want to settle down normally with some sense of security; the kind of secure independence which they deserve, and it is to be hoped that there will be work and adequate wages for all. One requisite that will be homes for all and I trust that our imaginative and creative genius will contrive something better than the temporary prefabricated houses at present in mind. There can be nothing more unsettling than to feel that you are temporarily housed and everything about you and your surroundings just a makeshift. It will have an unstable influence on the parents and children. We could build beautiful homes for all which would last not ten years but 500 years. You may see in many parts of our country vestiges of Roman villas 1,900 years old, with the floor tiles and footings just as good and ornate as ever. There are beautiful circular Roman baths in French Morocco with the mosaic patterns in tiles which are a pleasure to look at. Glazed tiles and brick will last for centuries. Why should we fall behind these architects and artistic builders and hustle up as though our land were like some Wild West cow town – a lot of frowsy low-ceilinged concrete habitations? When a man leaves his factory with its ferro-concrete mass to take the weight of the machinery, shafting and the like, he wants to come home to see warmth and colour and beauty – the charm of a real English home with its garden and scope for hobbies and interests of a personal nature. Every man should own his own home and have a say in the design. To my mind, building charges are far too high. Even in poor Italy many of the houses are beautifully and artistically built with polished bedroom floors and even as you lie in bed you look up at a ceiling charmingly decorated because it is the part of the room which you see more than anything else. We are satisfied with whitewash. I may be treading on someone's toes in saying all this, but we will all agree that the time is ripe for the building of homes which may represent the mind, culture and art, as well as the genius and practical skill of our nation. Time, it might be argued is the factor – but many of our young men have trained arduously for over four years and have waited patiently to have a smack at the enemy, and I feel sure they would work with zest and eagerness a little longer to possess the kind of home which they deserve. Many of our young men may be home sooner than we think, and we must strive to see that after their perils and wounds they have the same advantages or more so, than those who, however hard they may have worked, have had the privilege of working for their country at home. We are asked to strengthen their hands in war. Do not let us forget them in peace.*

On 8th July the Allies launched Operation Charnwood, which was a renewed attempt to capture Caen, using three divisions; 3rd (British), 59th (British) and 3rd (Canadian). On 7th July, as a prelude to the operation, wave after wave of RAF Lancaster bombers bombed the city of Caen. This was the first time that bombers had been used en masse in support of ground troops. At 11pm, massed artillery launched a powerful bombardment which continued until the ground attack started at 4.30am on 8th July. The 3rd Division struck south south west from Biéville towards the north eastern part of Caen. The initial phase of the battle went well and by dawn, the British 3rd and 59th Divisions had advanced one and a quarter miles into German territory and captured Lebisy. At 7.30am, after a further RAF bombing raid, the second phase of Charnwood commenced. Fresh brigades continued the advance south and were met by stiffening resistance from interlocking German strongpoints. On the eastern flank, the 3rd Division secured Hill 64, a key objective. By the end of the day, the Allied forces were 950 yards north of the city. Gunner Thomas Vaudrey of 209 Medium Battery, 53rd (London) Medium Regiment, Royal Artillery, was one of the local men involved in Operation Charnwood. His regiment fired over 300 rounds in support of 3rd Division during the operation.

On Saturday, 8th July, 21 year old Private 14206410 **John Kenneth 'Ken' Longbottom** was killed. Ken served with the 2nd Battalion, East Yorkshire Regiment, 8th Infantry Brigade, 3rd Division,

On D-Day (6th June), the 3rd East Yorkshires had landed on Sword Beach at about 7.30am. On the beach they met considerable opposition; cross-fire from artillery and mortars caused casualties, and snipers were very active. However, once off the beach they advanced inland. The battalion took part in Operation Perch (9th-14th June) and Operation Charnwood (8th-9th July). It was at some point during the 3rd Division's advance on the first day of Operation Charnwood that Ken lost his life. He is buried at La Delivrande War Cemetery, Normandy, France. The epitaph on his grave states: *In Loving Memory of John. He died for those he loved and those he loved, remember.*

La Delivrande War Cemetery

Private John Kenneth Longbottom, East Yorkshire Regiment

Private John Kenneth Longbottom, (right) with Eric Dale

Lance Corporal Albert Clare of the 1st South Lancashire Regiment (in the same brigade as Ken) helped to bury his body and later went, with his father, to visit the Longbottom family to explain that Ken had been buried underneath an oak tree. He was later re-interred at La Delivrande War Cemetery.

Ken was the son of Harold and Lily Longbottom, and had two sisters, Nancy and Hilda. He was educated at Cadishead Council School and Cadishead Senior School. He resided at 11 Green Lane, Cadishead and worked at Brew Brothers, Cadishead. Ken was called up in February 1942 and first went overseas with the invasion force on D-Day. His cousin, Eric Dale, was surprised that Ken was accepted into the infantry because he wore glasses and had poor eyesight.

On Sunday, 9th July, 29 year old Private 3455758 **Herbert Arstall** of the 2nd Battalion, Essex Regiment, 56th Infantry Brigade, 50th (Northumbrian) Infantry Division, was killed in action.

The 50th Division landed on Gold Beach at 7.25am on D-Day, and headed inland towards Bayeux. Following this the division took part in Operation Perch (9th – 14th June) during the battles in Normandy. Although not directly involved in Operation Charnwood they took part in one of the 'side-shows' designed to relieve pressure from the main British/Canadian thrust around Caen. On 7th July the battalion was at La Butte where they prepared for an attack that had been arranged at short notice. The war diary records that: *the battalion prepared cheerfully for battle and all appeared very calm and normal at eventide.* At 6pm the company commanders received their final orders and reveille was set at 4am for the next day. On 8th July the 56th Infantry Brigade was tasked with getting across the main road to the west of Hottot les Bagues. They achieved their objective during the afternoon against heavy opposition, but were counter-attacked and by evening the two leading battalions had been forced to withdraw to the north of the road again. At 6am the following morning the Germans attacked again on the 2nd Essex's front with three infantry companies and between 20 and 30 tanks. The Germans were thrown back with heavy losses, and eight tanks were 'knocked out'. It is likely that Herbert was killed during this engagement.

Born 15th March 1915, Herbert was the youngest son of James and Susannah Arstall (nee Taylor) of 134 Lords Street, Cadishead. He was educated at Cadishead Council School and was employed by the CWS Soap Works before joining the Army in June 1940. In late 1941 he married Doris C. Bennett of 86 Woodsend Road, Flixton. Herbert is buried at Hottot Les Bagues War Cemetery, Normandy, and his gravestone bears the inscription: *Still linked with love and memories no parting can divide – wife Doris.* As well as being commemorated on the Cadishead plaque of the Prince's Park War

Memorial in Irlam, he is also remembered on the War Memorial in St Michael's Church. Flixton. Herbert's brother was serving in France at the same time.

Bombardier Sydney Brooks of the Royal Artillery was serving with the 50th (Northumbrian) Division, and played a part in the bombardment of the German positions around Caen. Called up in 1939 he was originally posted to the 7th Battalion, Loyal Regiment (North Lancashire), attaining the rank of corporal. At some point before D-Day he transferred to the Royal Artillery (probably one of the following: 74th, 90th or 124th Field Regiment, Royal Artillery or 102nd Anti-Tank Regiment, Royal Artillery, who all served with the 50th Division during this period). He had landed on Gold Beach around noon on D-Day. Sydney was born in Irlam in 1911, and his parents lived on Liverpool Road, Irlam. He was educated at Irlam Council School and then worked at the CWS Soap Works. On 17th December 1938 he married Violet Lowndes. He was a talented musician in civilian life and played the saxophone in an Army Band.

Private James Muskett of the Argyll and Sutherland Highlanders, was wounded during the fighting around Caen. James was the son of Walter and Hilda Muskett of Irlam. He spent some time in hospital in London and after recovering from his wounds he returned to the Argylls, and was posted to the Orkney and Shetland Defence Organisation, which protected the naval base at Scapa Flow in Scotland.

Gunner Raymond Cookson was also involved in the relief of Caen: *Our first real engagement, we were on the relief of Caen, we were advancing inland to Caen and I think we were actually assisting the Canadians there. We were attached to the 3rd Battalion, Irish Guards, our battery, 439 Battery was supporting the Irish Guards but we went across before the Guards. The battery captain asked me and another bloke would we be his radio operators in a Sherman Tank see cos he was to go to the observation post at the front so we said yes. So we did, we were in a Sherman Tank for a few months, going to the OP, that's like directing the artillery fire. We broke out of course from Caen and we actually went through France into Belgium. I can remember one position we were in, and bearing in mind I don't know how true it was it was only something that was actually said at the time, but during the relief of Caen when the Canadians went in, I believe they lost about 98 tanks relieving Caen, and them tanks were the Shermans, and that was the tank that I was in, course you can imagine my bloody feelings can't you when 98 of them got bloody shot up. After the Battle of Caen you see, until we got to Brussels I don't remember any towns but believe it or not, and we didn't know at the time, but there's a word that they use when they're advancing called swanning, and when you're swanning the only part of the territory that you actually are relieving or conquering is the ruddy road and at times when we'd been swanning we only owned the road and bits and pieces at the side, Germans were either side of us. And I can recall one place we were eating German bread, we were that far in front the supplies couldn't get through to us, we were eating German bloody bread, and I can remember two of our blokes went into a farm, oh and the farmer was bloody blazin', they shot a pig, [laughter] shot a pig through the head so of course we had pork then, all that sort of thing was going on. Oh laugh, memories.*

Sydney Brooks, Loyal Regiment (North Lancashire)
(later served with the Royal Artillery)

1944

Private James Muskett, Argyll & Sutherland Highlanders

Lance Corporal Gerald Bannister witnessed the aerial bombing of Caen: *By the way, no doubt you've heard about the bombing of Caen, well when those bombers came over we knew nobody was going to shoot at us while they were there cos it was tremendous, tremendous.*

German V1 attacks had caused mass evacuations of children from London and other towns and cities in the south east of England. In early July appeals were made in Irlam, Cadishead and Rixton-with-Glazebrook for housing to accommodate the evacuees. Volunteers from Irlam and Cadishead were asked to write to the billeting officer, Norris Dale, at the Council Offices. The response to the appeal was magnificent and soon there were more offers of rooms for the children than were needed. In some cases, however, mothers had been evacuated along with their children, and people were less enthusiastic about sharing their house with another adult. Appeals were made at the cinema to ask householders to voluntarily accept mothers with one or two children into their homes. If sufficient voluntary billets had not been found, the Council had it within their authority to order compulsory billeting. Fortunately this measure was not needed.

On Sunday, 9th July there were emotional scenes at the receiving centres at Hollins Green Day School and the Centenary Methodist schoolroom, when 120 bewildered and bedraggled children, evacuees from the London area, arrived in Rixton-with-Glazebrook. On Saturday afternoon, 15th July the evacuees attended a party held in the Hollins Green Day School, which was organised by Miss Farrington. The headmistress, Mrs Vickers, and her staff helped to entertain the children and, after tea, they were treated to a cinema show provided by Mr F.R. Witty. At Glazebrook, Warrant Officer Eric Fanshaw and his team made toys for the children, and ladies living on or near the Carlton estate arranged a weekly 'make and mend' meeting. Mrs Fanshaw set up a lending library for the evacuees at her home.

On Friday, 14th July 52 young evacuees and an adult arrived in Cadishead from areas of London which had been affected by the German V1 flying bomb attacks. They were received at Cadishead Congregational Church and although most appeared happy there were some cases of homesickness. Local children soon gathered outside the church and friendships were struck up with the evacuees. After the reception the evacuees went to a rest centre where they were provided with a hot meal and a bed for the night. On the next day, the billeting began and by 11am all the evacuees were safely in their new homes. The district had mobilised all its efforts to accommodate the evacuees. The stationmaster and staff at Irlam Station handled all the train arrangements and employees of Lancashire United Transport helped with transport arrangements, as did volunteer car pool drivers, and drivers of the Council and NFS vehicles. The British Restaurant opened its doors to the visitors and the WVS made its two rest centres available. Norris Dale, the billeting officer, assisted by officers and members of the Council staff, did splendid work in dealing with such a large group of evacuees. Mrs Remers of the George Hotel, Cadishead, set up a fund for providing books to the evacuees and by late July she had collected £5. At this time the total number of evacuees billeted in the district was 124; comprising 27 adults and 97 children.

Later, Edwin Jones received a letter from the clerk of the London County Council: *Dear Mr Jones, thank you for your telegram informing me that 52 children from this district had arrived, and that they were very comfortable and happy. I am sorry that conditions have arisen which made it necessary for the evacuation of children from this area, but it is a satisfaction to know that they are being received in other districts, where they will obtain rest and quietude, and I am sure that the people of your urban district will do everything possible to make them happy.*

The headmaster of the London school which the children attended also wrote to Edwin: *I was delighted to have an account from Mrs Goldsmith, the escort, of the magnificent welcome you gave our children on Friday. It was true Lancashire, and I've lived in Lancashire and know how warm their friendship is. Their friends here are content, knowing that the children will be happy in the homes of your people, and I would like to express our gratitude to all who are giving such true hospitality.*

Councillor Melville (chairman of the Council) and James Adams (chairman of the Irlam ARP Committee) wrote an open letter which was published in the *Guardian* to thank local residents: *Last weekend this district received 52 evacuees from the southern counties, and they were all fixed up in billets in various parts of the district by 11am, following their arrival. The residents who opened their homes to them and extended such a wonderful welcome to our little visitors are deserving of our grateful thanks for their generous hospitality. We feel certain that any future calls of a similar nature that may be made on this district will be met with the same spirit of goodwill and we feel we can rely on the residents of Irlam and Cadishead to do everything possible to make our visitors happy and comfortable during their stay in our township.*

A second letter was received from the Clerk of London County Council: *The thanks of the Council are accorded to the local authorities concerned in the reception areas, for the great kindness with which many thousands of people, sent there at short notice by the Council, under the Government Evacuation Scheme, were received, and that they may be asked to communicate to those concerned, the Council's appreciation of the work done by their staff and volunteers, and by the householders on whom the evacuees are billeted. I am directed to bring this resolution to the notice of the respective local authorities referred to, with the request that the Council's warmest thanks may be indicated by them in any appropriate manner, and also to their staffs and volunteers and to the householders concerned.*

Mrs V.E. Miller, organising secretary of the Aid to China Fund, wrote to Edwin Jones to thank all those responsible for fundraising efforts: *Lady Cripps has asked me to thank you very much indeed for your extremely generous contribution of £250-10-3, given by the people of Irlam to the United Aid to China Fund. Will you please also convey our most grateful thanks to the Fire Guard organisation, who helped so splendidly to obtain this magnificent sum. You may be interested to know that your contributions to date total the grand amount of £494-6-6, which must surely be a record for so small a population. Your continued interest is a great inspiration, the task we have undertaken is so huge, and it is the staunch support of such districts as yours that make it possible for us to carry on.*

Nineteen year old Miss H. Dixon of 68 Marlborough Road, Higher Irlam, was one of the probationers chosen by the Ministry of Health Emergency Medical Services to transfer from a Manchester Hospital to a north western Second Front casualty reception hospital. She had passed parts one and two of the preliminary State Examination of the General Nursing Council of England and Wales in April 1944.

On Thursday evening, 13th July, a social evening was held at Irlam Conservative Club to thank members of D Company, Home Guard, for mounting the guard during the Salute the Soldier week. Major Gold, officer commanding D Company, personally thanked the men for their smart turn-out.

Two local men were killed in Normandy on Monday, 17th July: Lance Corporal 4202357 **Thomas Gratrix** of the 7th Battalion, Royal Welch Fusiliers, 158th Brigade, and Private 3389328 **Ronald Driscoll Southern** of the 1st Battalion, East Lancashire Regiment, 71st Brigade. Both the 71st and 158th Brigades were part of 53rd (Welsh) Division, XII Corps.

Thomas Gratrix was called up at the end of June 1940. He first went overseas to Normandy on 25th June 1944. At 10am on 15th July the battalion commanders attended a briefing by Brigade Command on their next objective, the Farm de Mondeville, which was situated about 1,200 yards across a tributary of the River Orne on the south side of the road from Evrecy to Eterville. At 2am the next day the 7th Royal Welch Fusiliers (RWF) left for the assembly area east of Mondrainville, arriving there half an hour later. They spent the morning resting and then at 2pm, the commanding officer and intelligence officer attended a final briefing.

A reconnaissance was made in the afternoon and final orders were given out at 8pm. At 9.30pm they moved up to the battalion start line, approximately 3,000 yards from the objective, and were in position by 11pm. By this time it was pitch black and a heavy mist developed which would be a serious drawback to the whole operation. At 11.30pm the 7th RWF crossed the start line, with A Company on the right, B Company in the centre and a company from the 6th RWF on the left. C Company and D Company were in reserve. Two companies from the 4th RWF protected the flanks of the attacking companies. The line of the Evrecy road was reached by all companies and by 0.45am the command post had caught up with them. The attacking companies advanced but in the mist they lost touch with each other and could not provide their locations to the command post. As a result it was not possible to bring up battalion support weapons or to coordinate the consolidation. They had to hope that the mist would clear at dawn, but this was not the case and at 7am Brigade Command ordered the battalion to withdraw. However, as they withdrew the mist finally cleared and they were exposed to heavy mortar and machine-gun fire. The commanding officer called for smoke and, except for a few stragglers, most of the men took cover in the cornfields and the dead ground beyond. Thomas was killed at some point during this operation.

Thomas was the son of the late Mary Gratrix of Irlam and resided at 108 The Crescent, Higher Irlam. His mother had died at the beginning of 1944 and Thomas had appointed Mr H. Ryles, 112 The Crescent, Higher Irlam, as his next of kin. It was Mr Ryles who received notification of Thomas' death. Thomas had worked in the grocery department of the Eccles and District Co-operative Society, before joining the Army. He is buried at Banneville-la-Campagne War Cemetery, Normandy.

Private 3389328 Ronald Driscoll Southern was killed in action whilst the 1st East Lancashire Regiment was engaged in fighting near Granville-sur-Odon. The 1st East Lancashires had landed at Juno Beach on 25th June.

Ronald was the adopted son of John and Sarah Arstall of 24 Lytherton Avenue, Cadishead. He married Lance Corporal Gladys May Ashley, Auxiliary Territorial Service, on Saturday, 30th October 1943 at St John's Church. Gladys was the youngest daughter of Mr and Mrs George Ashley of Prospect Grange Farm, Irlam. Ronald is buried at St Manvieu War Cemetery, Cheux, Normandy. He was 24 years old.

At some point during the month Lieutenant Herbert Johnson was wounded in the arm by a mortar shell while his platoon was attacking an enemy position in Normandy. He was the second of four sons of Mr and Mrs Bert Johnson, undertaker, who were serving with the Armed Forces. Herbert joined the Army in 1940, was commissioned in 1943, and went overseas with the invasion force on D-Day. By mid-July he was recovering in a hospital in England and he had nothing but the highest praise for the Army medical and hospital services which he considered had *reached an unbelievably high standard of efficiency on the beachhead.*

The following men are also known to have been wounded in Normandy around this time: Driver George Peacock, Lance Corporal Albert Clare and Sapper Kenneth Taylor.

Private Ronald Southern, East Lancashire Regiment

Lance Corporal 3656880 Albert E. Clare served with the 1st Battalion, South Lancashire Regiment, 8th Brigade, 3rd Infantry Division. Born 6th October 1917, he was the only son of Mr and Mrs Albert Clare of 65 Victory Road, Cadishead. His father was a veteran of the First World War. Albert was educated at Irlam Central School and, after leaving school, was employed by the Eccles & District Co-operative Society at Irlam as a street vendor, selling fruit and vegetables from a horse and cart. In February 1938 Albert married Annie Crozier and they shared a house with her sister, Kathleen and her husband, Thomas Norton at 1 Alexandra Grove, Irlam. Their son, Albert, was born a year later. Albert later worked at the Co-operative Society in Urmston as a fishmonger, then the Steelworks and finally Metropolitan Vickers in Trafford Park. He was a talented musician, playing trombone for several bands including the Irlam and the Cadishead Public Brass Bands. He could also play alto saxophone and violin. Albert joined the Army in 1940, enlisting in the South Lancashire Regiment. He was a member of the battalion band and, as a member of the band, his role in battle was stretcher-bearer. He went overseas with the invasion forces on D-Day, taking part in the fighting around Caen and was in the front line until being wounded. At some point he transferred to No. 3 Company, Royal Army Medical Corps (probably after recovering from his wounds). Albert was awarded the 1939-45 Star, the France & Germany Star, the Defence Medal and the George VI War Medal 1939-45.

Forty-one year old George E. Peacock served as a driver with the Royal Electrical and Mechanical Engineers. He joined the Army in December 1941, and went overseas with the invasion force in June 1944. He was the third son of Mrs Peacock and the late Mr G. Peacock of Chester Road, Hulme, Manchester. He lived with his wife at 27 Addison Road, Higher Irlam, and worked in the cleansing department of Manchester City Corporation.

Sapper Kenneth Cyril Taylor, Royal Engineers, was seriously wounded in Normandy, while working as a driver-wireless operator of a Royal Engineers' truck, which came under enemy mortar fire. The truck received a direct hit and Kenneth received injuries which resulted in the amputation of a leg. He was the second son of Mr and Mrs C.G. Taylor of 1 Sandy Lane, Irlam. He married Myra Whiting at St John's Church, Irlam on 19th May 1941 and they set up home in Brereton Grove, Cadishead. Myra was the only daughter of Mr and Mrs J. Whiting of Cadishead. He was formerly employed as a joiner at the Steelworks.

By mid-July Albert Clare and George Peacock were recovering in hospitals in England and Kenneth was in a hospital somewhere in Wales.

Lance Corporal Albert Clare, South Lancashire Regiment
(note the Anderson shelter in background)

Lance Corporal Albert Clare, South Lancashire Regiment, with his son, Albert

Fusilier 3461589 **Joseph Thomas Ackerley** of the 2nd/5th Battalion, Lancashire Fusiliers, 197th Brigade, 59th (Staffordshire) Division, was killed in action on Tuesday, 18th July, aged 33.

The 59th Division had arrived in Normandy in late June or early July. Their first action was during Operation Charnwood (8th to 9th July). They liberated Combes-en-Plaine and then they were deployed in the north western outskirts of Caen, fighting against the 12th SS Panzer Division. Between 16th and 18th July they took part in Operation Pomegranate, during the Second Battle of the Odon. This was a series of attacks southwards towards Noyers-Bocage (east of Caen) which were intended to divert German attention away from the Second Army's preparations for Operation Goodwood on 18th July. It was the first time the division had fought in the Bocage (French rural land crisscrossed by sunken roads and ancient hedgerows). The 49th (West Riding) and 53rd (Welsh) Divisions also took part in the operation. In three days of heavy fighting, the division suffered 1,250 casualties, including 167 men of the 2nd/5th Lancashire Fusiliers. Joseph was killed during this operation.

Joseph was born on 7th September 1909, the son of Thomas Hampson Ackerley and Elizabeth Ackerley (nee Hankinson) of 12 Caroline Street, Irlam (his entry on the CWGC Roll of Honour has the wrong names for his parents). His parents both predeceased him; his mother died in 1916 and his father in 1925. His siblings were Lucy (1904), Nellie (1906), May (1908) and Margaret born 1911 but sadly died in 1912. Joseph was educated at Irlam Council School and was later employed by Mr E. Mosedale, coal merchant. He married Betsy Hodson at St Mary's Church, Cadishead, on 31st July 1937, and they set up home at 91 New Moss Road, Cadishead. He joined the Local Defence Volunteers (which later became the Home Guard) on 5th June 1940, shortly after the Dunkirk evacuations. His Home Guard number was 210 and he served in 3 Platoon of D Company, 42nd County of Lancaster Battalion, Home Guard. He transferred to the Army on 14th March 1942 and first went overseas with the invasion force.

He is buried at Fontenay-le-Pesnel War Cemetery, Tessel, Normandy. Betsy was pregnant at the time and suffered a further tragedy in December when their baby was stillborn.

The wedding of Marine Edwin Williams and Esther M. Hayes took place at St John's Church on Saturday, 22nd July. Born in 1922, Edwin was the only son of Mr and Mrs J. Williams of 47 Eldon Road East, Irlam. He had joined the Home Guard on 5th June 1940, as Private 67 in 2 Platoon of D Company and served until he joined the Royal Marines. He subsequently served on board a landing craft and had just returned from Normandy where he had taken part in the D-Day landings. Esther was the eldest daughter of Mr and Mrs J.P. Hayes of 29 Prospect Road, Cadishead.

On Sunday, 23rd July the 42nd Battalion, Home Guard, staged the annual first aid competition for the Jessel Challenge Cup (named after the battalion medical officer, Major G. Jessel) near Worsley station. Teams consisting of one NCO and four stretcher-bearers from each company took part in the competition which lasted for the best part of a day. The competition consisted of a display of theoretical and practical first aid under war-time conditions using the RAMC methods they had been taught. Each team test was part of a tactical exercise with the stretcher-bearers following a battle squad of Home Guards. A small assault on a party of 'enemy snipers' was staged for each team, who had to go through the various stages of approach to casualties, including treatment in the field and safe removal to a casualty post, while overcoming the obstacles and difficulties which had been planned as part of the exercise. H Company won the competition, closely followed by teams from E, F, A and D companies. The competition served a dual purpose, by winning the Jessel Cup, the winners had also won the first round of the Webb Trophy competition and the marks awarded to each company would count towards the finals for the trophy.

Leading Aircraftman 1014423 **Henry Jones**, Royal Air Force Volunteer Reserve was killed in an accident in Egypt on Sunday 23rd July, aged 32.

Harry, as he was known, was the youngest son of Henry and Eva Jones of 4 Devon Road, Cadishead. The family originated from Thornaby-on-Tees, Yorkshire, and had moved to Cadishead in 1932. He worked at the Steelworks until joining the RAF in May 1942. He went overseas to Palestine in August of the same year. Harry is buried at Tel-el-Kebir War Memorial Cemetery, Egypt.

A local soldier using the pseudonym *One of the many waiting to return*, wrote to the *Guardian*: *Sir, being an Irlam resident I was pleased to read in the Guardian (so gladly received weekly from home) that two local gentlemen had promised a weekly subscription of one shilling each in the good cause of the scout movement (nice work!). May I add that the scout movement is of very good value to the youth of today and certainly deserves every consideration in its upkeep. May I ask you to put this extra few shillings towards the scout movement? I feel sure that if some folks start the worthy subscriptions, there are many good and generous people in Irlam and Cadishead to keep it going.*

Sergeant Herbert Harry Dugdale, Royal Artillery, wrote to his wife, Mabel, to tell her about his good fortune in receiving an invitation to visit the Viceroy of India and, whilst at the palace, he attended a concert and had dinner with Lord and Lady Wavell. In his letter he wrote: *I had a wonderful time at the Viceroy's House. Just imagine rolling up to the palace in a smashing limousine! We came to the entrance of the Viceregal gardens and proceeded along the road which was all floodlit, which made it possible to see for miles along the road with its beautiful gardens. At every mile there were policemen directing us to the palace and, oh, boy! What a palace! When we arrived we were shown the way along tremendous passages and staircases made of marble and supported by huge marble pillars and in every hall there were lights coming from beautiful cut-glass chandeliers. The walls were adorned with priceless tapestries and portraits of the Kings and Queens of England and previous Viceroys of India. The reception room took my breath away, and there were the Viceroy and Viscountess Wavell on thrones of Gold. I don't really remember shaking hands with their Excellencies, but I do know this – it sent a thrill down my spine. They looked a wonderful couple amidst all this elegance and luxury. After the presentation was over we were shown into the concert room where we were entertained by Noel Coward for over an hour. And after that, amid a fanfare of trumpets, we were shown to the dining room where dinner was served. I can't describe the dinner, but if you think of everything, that's it.* In the letter, Herbert explained that General Auchinleck and his staff were also present at the dinner. Herbert and his wife lived with Mabel's parents, Mr and Mrs Miller, at 75 Marlborough Road, Higher Irlam. He joined the Army in 1940 and had been in India for over two years, where he had taken part in jungle actions on the frontier. He was formerly employed by the CWS Soap Works.

Another local man serving in India was Gunner 1822643 Frank Bickerton, who was serving with 21 Battery, 8th (Belfast) Heavy Anti-Aircraft Regiment, Royal Artillery. He enlisted on 17th January 1941 and, after training, he was posted to Belfast, Northern Ireland. On 28th May 1942 he was posted to India where he remained until after the end of the war. On 10th September 1945 he left India and returned to England, where he was demobbed on 8th March 1946. He was married to Lilian May

Bickerton and they had three children and lived at 26 Francis Road, Irlam. He worked at the Manchester Corporation Works at Boysnope, Barton.

Corporal 3453165 Thomas Melling of the Royal Electrical and Mechanical Engineers (REME) served in India (and later Singapore). Tom was called up in January 1940 and joined the Lancashire Fusiliers at Bury. After basic training he was to have joined his battalion in France but the Dunkirk evacuations occurred before he could be posted. At some point around 1942/1943 he transferred to the REME and attended Wandsworth College to train for radar operation. After training he was stationed at Hull for a while and then he was posted to Liss, Hampshire, to join another unit. When he arrived at Liss he found that the unit required a fitter whereas Tom was trained as a clerk. He was told to take two weeks' privilege leave and then to return to his original unit. When he returned from this leave he found his unit had sailed for Burma. Tom was sent to India. When he arrived in India he was ordered to collect equipment from Bombay Docks – this involved a three day journey by goods train. When he arrived at Bombay he was told that the shipment had not left England and he would have to wait for it. He spent two months in Bombay, and during this time he was fed on a diet of spam and chapatis, supplemented by fish that he caught angling from the dockside, using spam as bait. Tom was born in Ince, near Wigan, on 8th November 1919. He was educated at Hindley & Abram Grammar School and then started his working life in the wages office at Irlam Steelworks. After the war he returned to the Steelworks, where he progressed to the position of transport manager, and later moved to live in Cadishead.

Corporal James N. Howes of South East Asia Command wrote the following letter to the *Guardian*: *Sir, reading with interest the election of Councillor F.J. Melville as chairman of the Council, also the election of standing committees, I wish to make this week's contribution more of a question than a letter to the public. The question is, has Councillor Hesford, as chairman of Housing and Town planning, any ideas or propositions towards easing the burden of the old-age pensioners in any post-war planning of his? My reasons for asking this question is that I don't think – in fact, I'm sure, that the aged pensioners have not had a square deal or any help whatever in previous years, either from the Government, or from their own district council. He must admit that they have been sadly neglected by the Government in previous years. We all know that is so, without being told (unfortunately at the moment, I'm not in a position to criticise the people I'm working for!) so I think that the needs of the pensioners is of primary importance in the rehabilitation of the district after the war. Wouldn't it be possible to build a small estate of cottages at rents within the meagre means afforded by the Government? I think it could be done. If Councillor Hesford reads this article I hope he treats it as a man-to-man talk, as I should hate him to think I was criticising his ability or his work. I only wish to point out just what the boys and girls in the Forces are thinking and, as we all realise that someday we, too, will grow old. The hub of this great wheel is only too conscious of the great help of these people when they are young and healthy but, alas, the importance grows dim in later years with lack of gratitude shown. I sincerely hope Councillor Hesford will keep this in mind while holding the position he does at the moment.*

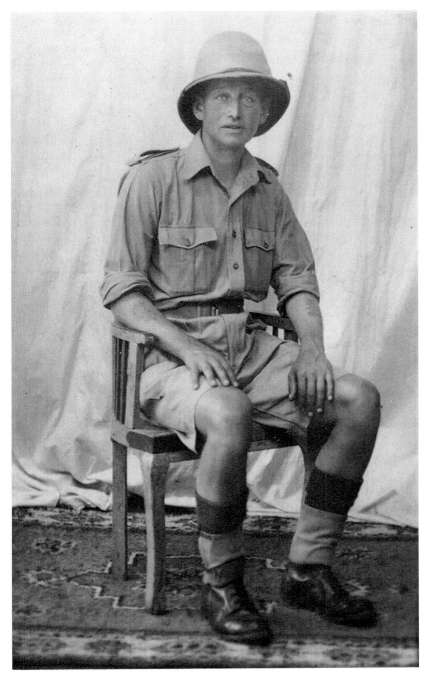

Gunner Frank Bickerton, Royal Artillery

Corporal Thomas Melling, Royal Electrical and Mechanical Engineers

Lance Corporal Hubert Williams, prisoner of war, sent a postcard and a few German Marks to Mary Bowker, honorary secretary of the War Comforts Fund, to thank the local Red Cross for the valuable work of the Red Cross Prisoners of War Fund. He wrote that: *Unless one was a prisoner, one could never fully appreciate the great work the Red Cross is doing.* Hubert was the son of Mr and Mrs W. Williams of the Nags Head Hotel, Higher Irlam.

Two friends, William Norman Wright (left) and Reginald Roberts, met each other unexpectedly in Normandy. They were old school friends who had joined the Army together in 1940. Unfortunately they could not stay together; William was posted to the Irish Guards, and Reginald to the Welsh Guards. During their service they had both spent time in the district on leave but never at the same time. William resided at 1 Brereton Grove, Cadishead, and Reginald at 25 Henley Avenue, Irlam.

Private Stanley Morris of Irlam was mentioned in dispatches for gallantry and devotion to duty. No further information is known about the nature of the deed which earned him this distinction. Stanley had previously been awarded the Military Medal for gallantry during the Dunkirk evacuations in May 1940.

The Red Cross received a donation of 25 shillings which was the proceeds from a backyard concert arranged by local children: Vera Allen, Doreen and Brenda Tinsley, Pauline and Sheila Vinton, Joan Corlet, Margaret Ravenscroft, Valery Booth, Renee Shaw and Phyllis Hindley (most of whom lived in Atherton Lane, Cadishead). Doreen and Brenda Tinsley also handed over a further 15 shillings which they had collected over three months.

AUGUST

Lance Corporal 2617483 **Sydney Ernest Hall** of the 4th Battalion, Grenadier Guards, died on Sunday, 6th August. He was 24 years old.

The 4th Grenadiers was an armoured battalion which was part of the 6th Guards Tank Brigade. Sydney served as the driver of a Churchill tank. On 4th August the 4th Grenadier Guards, along with the 8th Royal Scots Fusiliers, attacked and captured the village of Montcharivel. They then spent two days resting and overhauling their vehicles, including 6th August, the day Sydney died. It is possible that he died of wounds received in the earlier August battle. He is buried at St Charles-de-Percy War Cemetery, Normandy.

Doris and Sydney Ernest Hall

Lance Corporal Sydney Ernest Hall, Grenadier Guards

Born in 1919, Sydney was the eldest son of Mr and Mrs Ernest Hall of Lower Stanley Bank Farm on Cadishead Moss. His father had served with the South Lancashire Regiment during the First World War. Sydney was educated at Cadishead Senior School and then worked for T. Blundells, farmers, of Cadishead Moss, until enlisting into the Army in December 1939. On 14th February 1942, he married Doris Hutchinson of Warrington, and they had a son, John, who was only four months old at the time of Sydney's death.

Twenty-seven year old Private 4204985 **John Patrick Beirne**, 2nd Battalion, Argyll and Sutherland Highlanders, was killed in action on Sunday, 6th August during the fighting in Normandy.

The 2nd Battalion was part of the 227 Brigade, 15th (Scottish) Division. Although his battalion landed in Normandy on 21st June 1944 it is believed that John joined them later as part of a reinforcement draft as he was still in England in early July. He had served in the Army for 4 years.

Born in Wrexham in 1917, John was the son of John Price Beirne and Margaret Beirne, produce merchants from Wrexham. He was well-known in the Rixton Moss area, having from his boyhood days accompanied his father's vehicles on their regular visits for farm produce. John married Ellen Austin of Lymm View, Manchester Road, Rixton, on 12th July 1944. He is buried at Bayeux War Cemetery, Normandy. He is not commemorated on any local War Memorial.

Private Clifford Hughes, the only son of Mr and Mrs Hughes of Lines Road, Irlam, was taken prisoner in the Falaise Gap on 7th August. He had joined the Army in June 1940, and went to Normandy in June 1944.

Lance Corporal 2720865 **Robert Whittaker** of the 3rd Battalion, Irish Guards, Guards Armoured Division, died of wounds on Wednesday, 9th August.

On 8th August the battalion was positioned south of Montchamp. There was mortar and small arms fire throughout the day and the Irish Guards suffered three killed and seven wounded. Robert was one of those wounded. He survived long enough for his brother, Norman, to visit him, but succumbed to his wounds on the following day. Robert, like Sydney Hall, is buried at St Charles-de-Percy War Cemetery, Normandy. He was 25 years old. Robert was the son of Robert and Alice Whittaker (nee Etheridge) of Higher Irlam. Before the war he resided at 37 Princes Avenue, Higher Irlam, and worked at Royles Engineering Ltd. Three of his brothers served: Alfred with the Lancashire Fusiliers in Burma, Jim (possibly Thomas J.) with the Royal Army Service Corps and Norman with the Royal Artillery.

Lance Corporal Robert Whittaker, Irish Guards

Gunner Norman Whittaker, Royal Artillery

Fusilier Alfred Whittaker, Lancashire Fusiliers

Private Jim Whittaker, Royal Army Service Corps

Engine Room Mechanic P/MX502273 **Kenneth Irvin Morgan**, Royal Navy, was lost at sea when the repair ship HMS *Albatross* was struck by a torpedo whilst off Courseulles, on the Normandy coast, on Friday, 11th August. The ship did not sink but over 50 officers and ratings were killed, including 34 year old Kenneth, of Irlam. He has no known grave but the sea and is commemorated on the Portsmouth Naval Memorial, Hampshire.

Corporal 3454498 **Albert Ward** of the 9th Battalion, Durham Light Infantry (DLI), 151st Infantry Brigade, 50th (Northumbrian) Division, was killed on Saturday, 12th August. On this day, the 9th DLI attacked a German strongpoint (point 262) near La Plesses, in Normandy. As they advanced they came under heavy mortar and artillery fire. They took the objective and beat off a counter-attack later that day. Albert resided at 7 Haig Avenue, Cadishead. He had a brother, Cyril, and a sister, Annie. He is buried at St Manvieu War Cemetery, Cheux, Normandy. He was 27 years old.

Sidney Higson was wounded at Falaise (probably sometime between 6th and 17th August). At the time he was serving with the Sherwood Rangers Yeomanry, which was equipped with Sherman tanks. He had landed with his unit at Normandy on D-Day. He lived at Woodbarn Farm on Irlam Moss.

Pilot Officer Eric Williams was shot down on the night of 12th/13th August while on air operations over Russelsheim, Germany, and was captured. His wife, Millicent, spent an anxious few weeks not knowing the fate of her husband, before being informed in late September that he was a prisoner of war. The manner in which she received the news was fortuitous; a woman in Heaton Norris, whose husband was also missing, was listening to German radio broadcasts in the hope of hearing some news. During the programme, it was announced that Pilot Officer Eric Williams of Higher Irlam was a prisoner. The report provided Eric's service, a description and his wife's maiden name. She immediately contacted the Police Station at Irlam, who in turn broke the good news to Millicent.

Eric was the eldest son of Mr and Mrs J. Williams of 74 Caroline Street, Irlam, and the husband of Millicent Williams (nee Owen) of 11 Fiddlers Lane, Higher Irlam (her parents' address). At the time they had a three month old baby. Before joining the RAF he was employed by Hill-Smiths, chemists, Irlam. He joined the RAF in October 1941 and had taken part in over 30 operational flights. He received a commission shortly after being taken prisoner and was promoted from pilot officer to flying officer in a German prisoner of war camp.

Portsmouth Naval Memorial (Kenneth Morgan)

During the month, Private Thomas L. Wrench (pictured) was captured in Normandy. Thomas was the son of Mr and Mrs P. Wrench of 6 Ash Avenue, Cadishead. Before being called up in 1942 he worked at the Nuttall Street butchery branch of the Co-operative Society. He had married Olive Edwards on 1st July 1944, at St Mary's and set up home at 23 Nelson Drive, Cadishead. Only days later, he was posted overseas, to Normandy.

Royal Marine PO/X 121855 Harry Bannister, 41 (Royal Marine) Commando, was wounded on 20th August. Two commando units, 41 and 48, were to support 6th Airborne who had advanced from the Troarn Bulge, secured the road and railways crossings, but had been held up at Dozulé. On 19th August the commandos assembled at Goustranville, three miles east of Troarn. In the early hours of 20th August they marched to Point 134, a commanding feature south of the Dozulé. Here 41 Commando took up positions between 46 and 48 Commandos. By 4pm they had moved up to Panniers. At 5.45pm a patrol from P Company, 41 Commando, moved northwards up the Dozulé road towards St Léger-Dubosq. It is likely that Harry was wounded during this patrol. The following is his account: *It was about 20th August by that time, and we'd gone all this day like advancing and then we slept out in this field. The following morning I was sick as a dog, thick white jelly on the ground, I thought, oh I feel rough; anyway I thought I'll not go sick otherwise they'll think I'm scared, anyway I didn't go sick. I carried on, I went on that day, we heard these either mortar bombs going off or rockets, anyway we took cover and we went in the prone position. And then I just felt this terrible pain in my feet, well it wasn't a pain, I just felt as though I had no feet on, and I was scared to look at my feet, anyway when I did I could see my boots were hanging off, and my gaiters blown off. Lieutenant Dietz said 'anybody hurt?' and I said 'yes, I am.' And I was the only one who was hurt. So anyway they stripped my trousers off and took my pack off and everything and threw it in the hedge, and then next thing two blokes carted me off to the sick. I'd got these shrapnel wounds in my feet and my legs, and my side, and my shoulder. If I'd had my head where my feet were I'd have been dead, but luckily… Anyway I was taken to this sick bay and one of the blokes who was carrying me on the stretcher, he'd been wounded, his trousers had been slit at the back and I could see blood running down his leg. Anyway they treated me in…, I said 'where are we?' and they said 'Troarn'. That's where the dressing station was anyway. Anyway they took me then to a tented hospital, there's two stretchers on top of a jeep, like metal work and then two stretchers carried on this. I was in this tented hospital for about a week, Germans on one side, British on the other, and they kept taking the Germans for attention, and they never come, apart from giving me meals, they never took me in. Anyway after about a week they said 'you're going back home.' And they took us in the ambulances, and I was in a bit of pain by then and somebody opened the back door of the ambulance, 'does anybody need attention?' I said 'yes, I do.' He said 'well if you go now you'll miss the boat.' So I said 'oh, carry on then.'*

Anyway we went on the boat and it was one of these tank landing ships that they'd converted to taking back stretchers, all on stretchers, rows of stretchers on the floor of this ship. They said 'does anyone need attention?' I put my hand up and said 'yes, I do.' I was in quite a bit of pain then. Anyway he took me in this little operating room, it wasn't big, and this lieutenant surgeon played heck about me being in that condition, everything had gone septic. Anyway he put white powder in all the wounds. I took that to be penicillin cos it had just been invented then. And he gave me a full glass of whisky and water and I knocked that back, and I can't remember anything else then. But he gave me priority off the boat, I was the first off that boat. My wounds had been neglected, I wasn't badly wounded but they were neglected and I was in such a bad way. Went to Haslar Naval Hospital at Gosport and they operated on me in there and they put splints on me and whatnot, I was in there for a fortnight. And they took me to a hospital in Basingstoke. Oh while I was in there they sent a telegram to my father and my stepmother to go, because I was dangerously ill, and they came and stayed one day, they were frightened of the bloody doodlebugs going across, anyway I told them to go home. And about a week later, no, a fortnight later, I was sent to this hospital in Basingstoke and they played heck again because my dressings, the gauze what they put on, my flesh was growing through it. Anyway it was only a sort of a distribution centre that, and luckily from there I went to Manchester Royal Infirmary. I was very lucky because the next lot were going up to Scotland. Anyway it was lucky I went to Manchester Royal Infirmary and I was in there for about four or five months, and then they sent me to Didsbury. I had a good time in there, in Manchester Royal, because they were sort of walking wounded, we had plasters on and sticks. A gang of us used to go out, and we used to call for a couple of blind lads at the Eye Hospital, and there was about six of us used to go out in Manchester, in Nelson Street there, in that road. And we used to go in these pubs and we used to start singing and all the pints would come over you know. We had quite a good time, free football matches, and United were playing one week and City another week, but it was on City's ground cos United's ground had been bombed. And free travel on the buses so I could get home on the bus, and I often used to go home, I used to take a lad from London home, we were lifelong pals really. He's dead now poor lad, he died not long ago. But we had a good time in Manchester. Then I was sent to Didsbury College for convalescence, it was a place for Catholic priests really I think to train, but they'd changed it, it was a convalescent home for soldiers when I went there. I was there a month and then they sent me back to Wrexham Barracks and there they gave me a soft job looking after the billiard tables, ironing the billiard tables, putting tips on cues and whatnot. So a few weeks after that they starting getting a bit strict and they said everybody had to wear boots. Cos my feet were injured I didn't want to wear boots, so I went sick and then they sent me to Seaforth Hospital for some X-rays, and I had X-rays on my feet, the next day or two I was discharged. Well they sent me to Upton, Portsmouth, covering the Portsmouth Division. They sent me to Portsmouth and I was on their parade ground and I had my brown shoes on and everyone else was in blues, you know [laughter]. I was in my green beret and my brown shoes, all the rest were in blues. Anyway this adjutant come up on his horse and had a few words with me, he could see I was in the sick parade part, anyway he sent me into Portsmouth with a chit to get some black shoes [laughter]. A couple of days later I was in front of a medical board and discharged. So that was the end of my career in the Marines. I was only in it from 6th June, active service till 20th August, I think it was when I got wounded, and all the rest of the time I *was either training or in hospital [laughter]. But while I was in hospital my, 41 Commando was in the invasion of Walcheren Island, and the other, quite a few Commandos with them, and they really got another battering there as well, but I wasn't with them then. That's what I was told. So I was lucky really that I'd been wounded otherwise I might have been killed there.*

Private George Haslam of Glazebrook was wounded in the right leg during operations in Normandy. He was brought back to the UK where he was treated in a hospital in Penarth. George was only 18 at the time.

Born in October 1925, he was educated at Cadishead Council School and then became a linesman on the railway, stationed at Glazebrook. He attended the Temple Methodist Church and Sunday School. He joined the Army as a volunteer in October 1943, after serving with the Rixton Home Guard. He spent time training in Northern Ireland and Norfolk, before going overseas to Normandy on D-Day. He had two brothers in the Army, William in the Royal Engineers and James in the Durham Light Infantry.

Supply Assistant D/MX580335 Denis Townsend of the Royal Navy found himself in the unusual position of serving on board three Italian cruisers, which were captained and crewed by Italians, and also included a British officer and eleven other ratings. The former ally of Germany had surrendered in September 1943 and then declared war on Germany in October of the same year. As a result the ships of the Italian Navy had been put at the disposal of the Allies. Denis joined the *Scipio Africana* at Fort St Angelo in Malta on 19th August and, over the next 18 months, he served throughout the Mediterranean on the *Scipio Africana, Attilio Regolo* and *Pompio Magno*.

Italian Cruiser *Attilio Regolo*

Denis Townsend (right), Royal Navy

Kenneth Townsend, Fleet Air Arm

Denis was born on 10th June 1925, the youngest son of Charles and Gertrude Townsend. The Townsend family moved to Irlam c.1924 from Chesterfield. In 1941 he started working for Brew Brothers in Cadishead before being called up on 8th July 1943. He received his basic training at HMS *Royal Arthur*, which was a shore-based training establishment at a former Butlins camp, Skegness, which Denis described as *no holiday*. He transferred to HMS *President V* at Highgate on 23rd July for further training and then on 4th October he was posted to HMS *Drake* at Devonport for two weeks. Between the 16th October 1943 and 7th August 1944 he was stationed at HMS *Turtle*, a shore-based establishment at Poole, where he was involved in victualing (supplying) the troops in preparation for D-Day. On 8th August he returned to HMS *Drake* for ten days, including a short period of leave, before being posted to the Mediterranean to join the Italian cruiser *Scipio Africana*. On 17th March 1945, while serving on one of the Italian cruisers, he was promoted to leading supply assistant. He was demobbed from the Navy on 28th December 1946. After the war he became a Methodist local preacher in 1949 and a year later he married Mary Blundell of Cadishead. He was a producer-actor for St Paul's Dramatic Society and was involved in local churches joint services and social work.

Kenneth John Townsend was called up around the same time as Denis (July 1943) and served in the Fleet Air Arm, working his way through the ranks to become Petty Officer FX09373. He was a member of 816 Squadron, based mainly in Scotland, where he was responsible for servicing radios for aircraft carriers and ground staff. He was demobbed in October 1946.

Kenneth was born in Irlam on 14th March 1924. He worked in the laboratory of the CWS Soap Works and later became manager. In early 1951 he married Audrey Gilbert. In 1953 Kenneth was badly injured when lightning struck the cricket pavilion of the CWS Soap Works during a cricket match to celebrate the coronation of Queen Elizabeth II. Three members of the team were killed. His brother, Denis, was in the pavilion but was unhurt. One of the men killed by the lightning strike was an ex-serviceman, Herbert Vaudrey.

Other local man who served in the Royal Navy included Maurice Briggs and Leading Seaman Walter Whitfield. Walter resided in Fir Street and then later Essex Gardens. Unfortunately no further details of his service are known.

Maurice Briggs was born in 1923, the son of George and Mary Briggs of 2 Marlborough Road, Higher Irlam. Two brothers served in the Army: Harry and Ernest Briggs. Maurice had originally joined the Home Guard as Private 723, 1 Platoon, D Company, on 22nd April 1942 and was called up in September 1943.

At a Council meeting on Tuesday, 22nd August Councillor Adams proposed that the Press and public be allowed to attend meetings of the Post-War Planning Committee, to allow them to hear the Council's discussions. It was entered as a motion for the next meeting.

Leading Seaman Walter Whitfield, Royal Navy

Maurice Briggs, Royal Navy

On Thursday, 24th August the NCOs of D Company, Home Guard, held their monthly mess night. During the evening a presentation was made to ex-Company Sergeant Major George Ogden in appreciation of his service from the LDV days. He was a veteran of the First World War [possibly Private 15863 George Ogden, 8th King's Own (Royal Lancaster Regiment)] and his experience had proved invaluable when he joined the LDV in June 1940. He had been platoon sergeant to the old 4 Platoon and was quickly promoted to company sergeant major. Captain Carberry, in the absence of Major Gold, paid tribute to George, describing him as an outstanding example to all ranks of the Home Guard. In his reply, George recalled many incidents of the early training days – which he described as more to do with enthusiasm rather than efficiency. He remarked on the help and encouragement he had received from old soldiers and new, including Regimental Sergeant Major Butterfield: *Our instructors would hold their own with any within the battalion, both for enthusiasm and ability.* He stated that he deeply regretted leaving the Home Guard, but felt compelled to accept medical advice. Regimental Sergeant Major Butterfield apologised for the absence of Colonel Webb who was unable to attend, however, he welcomed the chance to express his own personal regret at losing such a competent company sergeant major who, by the high standard he had set, would be hard to replace. At the end of the speeches, Lieutenant Thomas Grundy, on behalf of officers of D Company, expressed the appreciation of all present.

The Rixton-with-Glazebrook Forces Canteen at the Centenary Methodist Church celebrated its first anniversary. Its first three months in service had started slowly with poor take up from members of the Armed Forces and it had almost closed. Instead, the opening days were extended from three days to six and money was spent to increase the amenities on offer. By the end of the first 12 months it had been used by more than 8,000 servicemen and servicewomen and no fewer than 12,000 meals had been served.

On Saturday, 26th August the Irlam detached flight of 292 (Eccles) Squadron, ATC played a return cricket match against their colleagues from the squadron at Eccles, and once again the Irlam team came out winners. The Irlam players included Cadets Cooke, Porthouse, Ferns, Bailey, Elliot, Davies, Warburton, Bagnall and Bostock. Cadet Porthouse top scored with 56 not out and Cadet Bailey was the pick of the bowling with four wickets.

On Sunday, 27th August Private 1607306 **Fred Corder** of the 2nd Battalion, Essex Regiment, 56th Infantry Brigade, 50th (Northumbrian) Infantry Division, was killed in action in Normandy.

Three days before his death, 2nd Essex Regiment had been involved in an attack on Cormeilles. After two days' rest, they advanced eastwards to Pont-Audemer, a small town on the river Risle. All the bridges across the river had been destroyed by the retreating German Army and the town had to be taken in order to establish a bridgehead which would allow 1st Corps to push through to the River Seine. The 2nd Essex and 2nd South Wales Borderers were ordered to cross the river and to eliminate enemy positions on the north bank. At about 11.30pm the leading platoon crept down the bank of the river to cover the arrival of a boat party, when several Spandau machine-guns opened fire from the opposite bank. The platoon was in an exposed position, without cover and suffered a number of casualties. A Company of 2nd Essex Regiment returned fire with PIATs (Projector, Infantry, Anti-Tank) and eventually won the fire fight. Two other companies were engaged in similar battles across the river. One company from the South Wales Borderers made it across the river but were cut off from the rest. A few sections of A Company made it across the river and took cover in some part-demolished buildings. Here they were surrounded by enemy troops and held out until the early afternoon on 27th August when the Germans finally withdrew. By late afternoon Pont-Audemer had been cleared and the two battalions had crossed the river. The 2nd Essex suffered a number of casualties at Pont-Audemer and the commanding officer later complained that they had to make a river crossing at night without proper preparation or unit training.

Born in the district in 1913 (birth registered at Barton I. in June 1913) Fred was the son of Benjamin and Elizabeth Ann Corder of Irlam. From the insignia on his uniform Fred must have served with the Royal Artillery before joining the Essex Regiment. He is buried at St Desir War Cemetery, Normandy. He was 31 years old. His brother, Fusilier Benjamin Corder, served with the Lancashire Fusiliers and a younger brother, Private Ronald Corder, also served in the Army (regiment unknown).

Mr and Mrs Robinson of 95 Fir Street, Cadishead received a fieldcard from their son, Private John Robinson, who was a prisoner of war in Japanese hands. In the card he said he was well and in a prisoner of war camp in Thailand. Although he was captured when Singapore surrendered in February 1942, it was a year before his parents were informed that he was a prisoner of war. This fieldcard was only the second piece of news that John had been able to send to them.

Fusilier William Ernest Micklewright was wounded in north west Europe, sustaining injuries to his face. This was the second time that he had been wounded, the first was during the Dunkirk evacuations when he was serving with the BEF. William was the 30 year old son of Mr and Mrs Micklewright of 541 Liverpool Road, Irlam.

Private Fred Corder, Royal Artillery and later Essex Regiment

Private Ronald Corder

SEPTEMBER

The *Guardian* (2nd September) carried the following editorial from Onlooker entitled 'Aftermath': *Swiftly, inexorably, the war in Europe is drawing to a close, and the visions of a sweeter, cleaner world, about which our sons, brothers and husbands have died becomes clearer with each passing hour. Are we really ready for the dawn of peace? Or will it, as it did last time, catch us unprepared and leave us to wallow in a sea of chaos and confusion? Some time ago, I addressed a meeting and, in the course of that address, I said, quite flatly, that after the war we did not want a country cluttered up with war memorials to those who had given their lives while the survivors, unemployed and half-starved, walked the streets in despair. That statement caused a gasp of surprise, and I am sure many people present were offended. It angered them and I believe they thought I had insulted their dead when I called war memorials senseless lumps of stone. Well, that's my opinion. I am quite convinced that the men who died in the last war and those who have died in this would much rather have died secure in the knowledge that their wives, children and dependants would be adequately cared for, than in the knowledge that the reward for their sacrifice would be the inscription of their names on a slab of granite. Yes, we want a memorial after the war – but not a cold, unfeeling pile of stone. Our memorial must be a national memorial – a living memorial expressing itself in better living conditions, security, work and the happiness and welfare of the nation. If we get that, our boys will not have died in vain... I ask you quite seriously – and this particularly applies to my servicemen readers – whether you would prefer ornate and elaborate war memorials or pensions on which you could live in reasonable comfort if you were disabled.*

Onlooker missed the point; the men who died would undoubtedly have wanted security and happiness for their families, but the families left behind would want both; a better world but they would not want the sacrifices of their loved ones to be forgotten. It should never have been a question of one or the other.

At the request of the King, Sunday, 3rd September was set aside as a national day of prayer. St Mary's Church, Cadishead, observed the day of prayer with a special evening service which was attended by the chairman and members of the Council, and by contingents from the ARP service, WVS, NFS and St John Ambulance Brigade. In reference to the day of prayer, Reverend Bakker wrote in the parish magazine: *In the past 12 months events have moved with great rapidity and the end of the struggle is now within measurable distance. We can rejoice that the overthrow of an appalling form of tyranny is now becoming apparent. But the approach of the end directs our attention urgently to the problems which lie ahead, the task of reconstructing a world that lies in ruins. Whether this problem will be successfully solved depends very largely on our approach to it; we can approach it from the angle of revenge pure and simple, in which case we shall make an even worse mess of it – a mess which someone else will have to clean up years hence; we may approach it from the point of view which regards the Allies as entitled to all they can get – in which case they will probably fall out among themselves; or we may approach it from the point of view which realises that a stable and contented world is the only guarantee of peace. How to build a stable and contented world will tax the wisdom and resources of our statesmen to the utmost, and for that spirit of wisdom and counsel we need most earnestedly to pray. But it cannot be left to the statesmen; in fact it won't be, for in the long run the shape of things depend on the desires of the ordinary man; if his desires are high we shall see a better world; if they are indifferent or selfish we shall get a selfish world.*

Onlooker commented: *And now for Reverend Bakker's letter. He asks how we are going to tackle our post-war problems and how we are going to treat Germany. Well, I've heard a lot of suggestions about what we should do with Germany and the Germans once the war is over. In the heat of battle or under the stress of bombing many of us have expressed violent opinions about Germans and have also said what we would like to do to them. But, on sober reflection, we have perhaps modified those opinions. How would you treat Germany after the war, and how would you deal with the Germans? I want you to write to me – servicemen and ex-servicemen especially – giving me your views on what should be done with them.*

The Minister of Home Security's announcement that blackout restrictions could be eased reflected the improving fortunes of England, however, it did not mean the immediate abolition of the 'starlighting' system in the district or a return to more normal street lighting. The announcement only applied to districts whose lighting systems were controlled by a single master switch. The lighting system in Irlam and Cadishead was controlled by three separate switches at different substations and, in the opinion of the Stretford Electricity Board, which only maintained a skeleton staff in the district, a considerable time would elapse between the sounding of an alarm and the total blackout of the district. Henry Nurse advised that once permission was given to lift the blackout restrictions, the normal lighting could be restored in three or four days. As a partial measure towards normality, gas lamps along Liverpool Road were once again returned to operation on 16th September.

The marriage took place at Cadishead Congregational Church on 7th September between Guardsman Stephen W. Richardson, Scots Guards, of Cadishead, and Edna Yates. Stephen had been in the Army since 1939 and had been taken prisoner at Tobruk in 1942, later escaping as the Allied Armies advanced through Italy. He had only recently returned from Italy. Edna was the second daughter of Mr and Mrs P. Yates of 12 Nelson Drive, Cadishead.

Whilst in a rest camp in the Middle East, Fusilier William Henry Sharp met his younger brother, Leading Aircraftman Thomas Sharp. Thomas was educated at Irlam Central School and, before joining the RAF, he was employed by the Maypole Dairy Company. Twenty-three year old Thomas originally served in 3 Platoon, D Company of the local Home Guard for a short spell before joining the RAF at the end of 1940. He went to the Middle East in May 1942. William and Thomas were the sons of Mr and Mrs R. Sharp of 65 Baines Avenue, Irlam. Another brother, Robert Sharp (born 1903), also served in the Home Guard as Private 919, in 4 Platoon of D Company. He joined the Home Guard on 28th August 1940 and resigned on 22nd December 1942.

Mrs T. Taylor of 31 Fiddlers Lane, Higher Irlam, was informed that her husband, Trooper Thomas Taylor (pictured), was missing in France. It later transpired that Thomas had been captured and was a prisoner of war in Germany. Tom was the youngest son of Mr and Mrs S. Taylor of 75 Bridgewater Street, Farnworth. He joined the Army in February 1940 and first went overseas on D-Day. Before joining the Army he was employed by the Lancashire United Power and Transport Company as a conductor.

John R. Marsland, Royal Air Force Volunteer Reserve, sent word to his parents that he had received his air gunner's wings in Scotland. John, who was 19 at the time, was the only son of Mr and Mrs W.J. Marsland of 31 Liverpool Road, Cadishead. He was educated at Cadishead Senior School and, prior to joining the RAF in March 1944, he was employed as an apprentice fitter at the Partington Gas Works (almost certainly a reserved occupation).

Two local men met each other in France, Sapper Horace Massey and Sapper W.H. Hampson. Twenty-seven year old Horace was the only son of Mr and Mrs W.A. Massey of 31 Fiddlers Lane, Higher Irlam. He was educated at Irlam Endowed School and worked at the Steelworks. He was married with one child. He joined the Army in January 1940 and went overseas on D-Day. Sapper Hampson resided at 24 Tramway Road, Irlam. He also joined the Army in 1940 and first went overseas on D-Day. Prior to joining the Army he was employed by the Manchester Ship Canal Company.

Jack Fluck, an Irlam reporter for the *Guardian* who had been called up into the Army, wrote the following article describing his service with the Manchester Regiment in Italy: *Nine months in Italy – yes, with wheels never still; sometimes high up in the mountains of Cantabria; then hurtling down to the plain of Foggia with its oppressive heat, and next perhaps the mighty Maiella, with its marvellous snow-capped peaks and remarkable mountain roads. No wonder the Italian is a crack racing motorist. To negotiate some of these routes you would want to be at least a Malcolm Campbell. In fact there are precious few spots of this country which is already in our hands that I have not seen. I have bathed in the dirty yellow waters of the Sangro, and inspected the graves of our lads who fell in forcing the crossing of this wicked river. I've stood and studied Monastery Hill and Cassino and marvelled that the Allies could have overcome such a bastion. Rome, in many ways, is a wonderful city, but Naples and Vesuvius interested me far more. Censorship regulations prevent me mentioning many things of more current interest. It has been hard slogging practically the whole of the time, but I did manage to get a week's leave at Amalfi, near Salerno, on the Italian Riviera. In peacetime it is the playground of this pleasure-loving nation and tourists from all over the world. It was for me seven days of swimming, surf-riding and boating on the picture-book blue of the Mediterranean. A highlight was a trip to*

Capri with some Canadian doctor friends of mine, but the happenings there are better told in the atmosphere of a bar parlour than in a letter!! Please don't think that the Mediterranean is always as pictured – deep blue and brilliant sunshine; it can be as vicious as the North Atlantic in January, and I had one experience of its wiles which I shall always vividly carry in my mind. By the way, close to Amalfi is Revello, where the old King of Italy and Umberto resides. The old King moves about almost unnoticed. Incidentally, we turned out to see our own King a few weeks back, and what a reception he got from the many thousands of troops. We go for long periods with a minimum of sleep, but plenty of really good food, with any amount of fruit, melons, monster peaches, plums and grapes being in profusion at the moment. I never cease to marvel at the administration which looks after the well-being of the Army out here. Welfare is always to the front. ENSA plays its part in first class style, with live shows and films of very recent issue; swimming baths are very quickly overhauled and opened for the lads to disport themselves in, then, mobile libraries are quickly going the rounds and they don't carry a lot of junk. This week, for instance, I managed to get 'The Battle Within,' a recent Philip Gibbs. Personally, I think time and shipping space are wasted in sending newspapers to troops, as our own sheets are first class and get right forward very promptly, if sometimes not on the day of issue. Newspapers from home still take as long as seven weeks to get here, so you will realise their value is practically nil. However, what is popular is the man's home-town weekly, and you find the soldier stuck in all sorts of queer corners getting the 'gen' on home-town affairs. We have 'Parade,' our own pictorial magazine, while 'World's Press Review' is a really excellent publication which reprints material which has been published already, but would not otherwise be available to us. Its admirable selection of articles enables service readers to follow the trend of public opinion as shown in the Press of Great Britain and other countries. A variety of topics is covered and every attempt made to give a balanced view. Another feature of this campaign is the work of the APO. Rarely does a letter go astray, and at the moment troops in the line are reading messages from home on a Thursday which have only been written by their folk on the previous Sunday. Nothing keeps the morale of the troops up better than a prompt receipt of mail from home. I have known mail on many occasions to have reached a destination before the men actually got to the spot. Generally, everything out here is fine; the troops are all in great heart and on their toes to finish once and for all the Nazis and all their creed stands for.

Despite the unity that the war demanded there was still the ever-present risk of crime. The following letter appeared in the *Guardian*, under the heading 'Soldier's Wife's Loss', which appealed for stolen property to be returned. As there was no subsequent follow-up in later editions of the newspaper it can be assumed that the appeal fell on deaf ears: *Sir, may I, through the medium of your paper, appeal to the conscience of one who has been the means of causing much suffering to the wife of a serving soldier? On August 31st I attended the clinic at Longfield Lodge and while I was there a pouchette containing £6 and a wallet with photographs of myself and my four children was taken from my child's pram. It is hard enough for the wives of soldiers to make ends meet in these days; and the photographs and the pouchette have a value beyond mere cash. Yours, etc. Mrs L. Hodson, 319 Liverpool Road, Cadishead.*

Tom Swindells, serving with South East Asia Command (SEAC), wrote the following letter which was published in the *Guardian*: *Sir, I feel I must write to let you know how much I enjoy reading your articles in the Guardian. I receive them often and look forward to reading your juicy bits in Town Topics. I read with interest your readers' views on post-war Cadishead and Irlam. Although leaving the home-town at the age of 14, with only a few visits since then, I still take a great interest in the progress of it, and hope one day to see a really large and prosperous town. I wish you would convey to the people of Irlam and Cadishead how much we lads out here appreciate these excellent efforts in the way of war comforts. And, believe me, we are most grateful to them all. I have often heard the remark passed by other lads that they wish they came from a place so thoughtful. You are doing a fine job and I wish you and the Guardian all the best for future years.*

Mr A. McPhee of 11 Birch Avenue, Cadishead wrote the following letter to the *Guardian* on the subject of war pensions: *Sir, while on the subject of inadequate pensions for ex-servicemen, I would like also to draw attention to the dependants of fallen servicemen who receive no pension and for whom no provision whatever is made after reaching the age of 21, even though those dependants are incapable of work owing to infirmity and sickness. Their fathers gave their lives for their country, and died believing that the country would care and provide for those children, but in no circumstances whatever is provision made for these dependants after the age of 21. I think this also a great injustice. I hope those who have the luck to come through and also those who have their welfare at heart and appreciate those who fought and died will look into these cases and see if some provision cannot be made for those who cannot help themselves, then these men will not have fought and died in vain.*

Battle of Britain Sunday, 17th September was celebrated by services at 10.30am in St John's Church and Cadishead Wesleyan Church, with members of the Civil Defence Services attending. In previous years the day had been celebrated by parades of Home Guard and Civil Defence Services, however, this year the parade was scaled down with only the scouts and cubs marching. They assembled at the Scout Hut at 9.50am and moved off at 10am to Cadishead Wesleyan Church.

During the month Aircraftwoman (ACW2) 2114619 Gladys Moody was posted to RAF Dallachy in Scotland. The following is her account of her time from joining the WAAF: *I wanted to go into the services and I chose to go into the WAAF. My brothers were all in the Army, and my sister was in the Land Army. I said I'm not going in the ATS, I'm going in the WAAF, be different. It was a month before my 18th birthday. I was desperate to do something because the rest of the family were all doing something. I think that was the reasoning behind it. The day I went into the WAAF was the day that Rome fell to the Allies. The next day was D-Day. I went to Wilmslow for six weeks to do my training and they asked where we'd like to be posted. Because we all came from Middlesbrough we all said we'd like to go to Thornaby, RAF Station Thornaby and I was the only one who actually went there. It was just normal service life. I made a lot of good friends along the way and while I was at Thornaby I was able to go home at times, about 15 miles home. We'd scrape enough money together between half a dozen of us, get the bus fare and go home on the bus or the train and scrounge some money off my parents to go back so we could all exist until the next pay day. But I wouldn't say there was anything outstanding, we just got on with our work.*

Gladys and Douglas Moody

Gladys, Frank and Betty Moody

I was there for two months and in September I was posted to Dallachy in Scotland, RAF Station Dallachy. I was in Coastal Command, in operations block. We didn't get out an awful lot. We'd see the planes coming back after they'd been out on flights round the coast. They engaged sometimes with enemy aircraft and you wondered when you saw some of them how they got back from that trip (RAF Dallachy had a strike wing of Bristol Beaufighters which operated against heavily defended coastal shipping, mainly off the west coast of Norway. They also flew radar-equipped Wellingtons for submarine detection). *We didn't think anything of it, it was just part and parcel of life. I didn't have any adventurous times sort of thing, we were just getting on with our duties as WAAF. While I was up at Dallachy it was fairly regular sight, seeing damaged aircraft, then the war was tailing off and they weren't getting as much stuff coming in. obviously the invasion had started so they weren't getting the U-boats coming in towards the end of the war. It was hazardous for the crews because they never knew what was going to be around there, with German planes flying about and dodging around all the barrage balloons that were up round the areas, things like that, often tangled with them. There was nothing adventurous for me, like the men going out to fight or the girls on the balloon sites. My best friend at home, her sister was on the balloons. The adventures she had made my hair stand on end. That was what started me off wanting to go in the WAAF, but nothing like that happened to me. We saw German aircraft occasionally, but only in the distance because they didn't come over our station, we didn't see any coming over our 'dromes. The only aircraft that we saw was when we were living at home, we had the air raids and one of the aircraft crashed on the hills. That's the only real sighting I had of enemy aircraft. And then from Dallachy, I was a clerk in signals and we became surplus to requirements as the war was finishing, they were closing our 'drome down and they posted me to the Records Office in Gloucester, RAF Innsworth. It was clerical work, actually we worked for the officers in charge of the signals, just doing ordinary clerical work but all dealing with the work associated with the signals. So I was in the operations block so we couldn't talk a lot about what went on. But when I went down to Gloucester I was re-trained to a clerk general duties, which was more or less the same as I'd been doing in Scotland. We did ordinary clerical work. I finished as sergeant in charge of the office. That was basically my WAAF service. I came out in September 1947.*

Gladys was born on 13th July 1926, at South Bank, Middlesbrough, the daughter of John William and Hilda Beatrice Moody. Four of her brothers served in the Army and one, Trooper Eric James Moody, was killed while serving with the Royal Armoured Corps in 1941. Frank, a regular soldier who had served in India for seven years before the war, was wounded at Salerno, Italy, whilst fighting as part of the East Yorkshire Regiment. Douglas served with the Queen's Royal Regiment in France (Dunkirk and then Normandy invasion). Windsor Moody served with the Royal Engineers in Normandy. Gladys' father, John William Moody, was a veteran of the South African War and the First World War, and re-enlisted in the Second World War. He was honourably discharged at the retirement age of 60. After the war Gladys married Cyril Dawes and moved to Cadishead.

Operation Market Garden (also known as the Battle of Arnhem) took place between 17th and 26th September in the region of the Dutch town of Arnhem. Allied paratroops were dropped in Holland on a mission to capture bridges and towns at strategic points along the Allied line of advance. At the northern end of the battlefront, the British 1st Airborne Division, supported by men of the Glider Pilot Regiment and the Polish 1st Independent Parachute Brigade, landed at Arnhem to secure the bridges across the Nederrijn. Very little opposition was anticipated and the expectation was that the British XXX Corps would relieve the men within two or three days. Unfortunately they landed some distance from their objectives and met unexpected resistance, especially from units of the 9th and 10th SS Panzer Divisions. The main group of paratroops were held up on the outskirts of the town and only a small number made it to the road bridge at Arnhem. The advance of the XXX Corps was delayed and the small force at the bridge held out heroically for four days before being overwhelmed. Meanwhile, the rest of the Airborne Division was caught in a small pocket to the north of the river and could not be relieved or re-supplied by either the Polish or the XXX Corps, nor could they be re-supplied from the air. Eventually, after nine days in action, the surviving members of the division were withdrawn. As a fighting force, the 1st Airborne Division was shattered, losing 75 percent of its strength. It would not see combat again. The failure to capture any bridges over the river stalled the Allied advance. The Battle of Arnhem was a costly failure, with brave men fighting heroically to achieve almost impossible objectives.

Several local men are known to have participated in Operation Market Garden: Sapper Edward Mahon, Hugh Mahon, Sergeant Charles Taylor, Private J. Dixon, Gunner Joseph Hindley, Gunner Raymond Cookson and Fusilier Albert Edward George Hayman.

The wife and parents of Sergeant Charles Taylor, a glider pilot who took part in the airborne assault on Arnhem, received two letters which caused great distress to the family. During the battle his wife received a letter from the secretary of his regiment's fund which asked if she needed any financial assistance and making additional offers of help. Shortly afterwards, his parents received a letter in Charles' own handwriting, which contained the following words: *If you receive this you will know that I have done my bit, and not coming back.* The letter also contained farewell messages to his wife, brother, sister and sister-in-law. It was a tradition for soldiers going into combat to write farewell letters to their families in case anything happened to them. These letters were held by the Army and posted out if the worst happened. As there was no official notification, and to ease the suffering of the family, Reverend Bakker contacted the military authorities. As a result of his enquiries a telegram was received which stated that he was alive and well and that the letters had been posted in error! Charles later recalled the operations at Arnhem where he landed on Sunday, 17th September: *The flight across was the easiest part of it, and afterwards things got very warm.* It was reported that like most men who have looked death in the face he was loath to talk of his experiences but he did say: *the only thing I'm glad about is to be home.* Charles returned home on leave in October.

Sapper Edward Mahon, Royal Engineers (Airborne Forces), was in a reserved occupation when war broke out but volunteered to serve in the Army. Before the war he had successfully obtained his glider pilot's certificate at a Surrey flying club; however, he did not achieve his ambition to become an Army glider pilot, instead he opted for parachute training and service with the Airborne Engineers. His brother, Hugh (birth registered at Barton I. in March 1918), also fought at Arnhem. Edward was educated at St Teresa's, Irlam and De La Salle College, Weaste. Edward and Hugh were the sons of James and Mary Ellen Mahon of 11 Bradburn Road, Irlam.

Private J. Dixon (pictured) of the 7th Battalion, Kings Own Scottish Borderers (part of 1st Airlanding Brigade, 1st Airborne Division), was reported as missing following the Battle of Arnhem. Private Dixon was a member of the glider borne troops that landed at Arnhem. He was later confirmed to be a prisoner of the Germans. Private Dixon was 22 years old, the son of Mr and Mrs J. Dixon of 15 Baines Avenue, Irlam. He was educated at Irlam Council School and, before enlisting, he was employed in the rod mill of the Steelworks. He joined the Army in 1941.

Gunner 14337244 Raymond Cookson was a signaller/ wireless operator with 439 Battery, 55th Field Regiment (West Somerset Yeomanry), Royal Artillery, Guards Armoured Division, 21st Armoured Group, XXX Corps, 2nd Army. During the Battle of Arnhem his battery was stationed on 'The Island' to provide artillery support to the Allied troops at Arnhem. The Island was a polder between Nijmegen and Arnhem, bounded by the Lower Rhine on the north and the Waal River on the south. It was below sea level and the flood waters were held back by dikes. The hills on the north side of the Lower Rhine provided the Germans with excellent positions for artillery spotting and the nearby Rhine industries provided plentiful supplies of ammunition for their 88mm guns. The battles on the Island took the form of artillery duels between rival gun batteries.

The following is Raymond's account of his time on the Island: *We were, as far as we know, we were the only regiment that fired artillery from the middle of Brussels, we were in the action in the middle of Brussels with the artillery. And then of course we went through Nijmegen, Grave, Eindhoven up to a few miles from where the paratroops landed, Arnhem. Yes we went in action in Brussels and then we pulled out of Brussels but the Americans actually relieved Grave. We went to Nijmegen and Eindhoven and across, I think it's where two rivers are, with the sea and the rivers it makes it like an island and they called it The*

Island, and we were supporting the paratroopers at Arnhem. We didn't go anywhere near Arnhem but the artillery were supporting them, and that's where… I think it was American Boston bombers, they were getting shot down like bloody flies over Arnhem the American bombers were. It was only a small slow bomber, it wasn't very quick, they shot the bugger down quite easy. And we were there for a few days at Arnhem and I can never remember the film star's name, but a prominent English film star was a captain in the regiment that relieved us at Arnhem, that's when we pulled back to Teenin. We were just outside a town like Irlam and Cadishead, at a village called Best and we'd only been there a few days and about three o'clock in the morning, like when you're in static positions you don't use the radios you've a line of telephones. About three o'clock in the bloody morning the phone rang, it was the adjutant to the Regiment to tell us we were going to move to the Ardennes near Namur to help the Yanks out. Then we came back to Teenin and had a month with them. We were billeted in houses then with people.

Raymond's regiment first went into action at Putot-en-Bessin and was involved in the battles for Carpiquet Aerodrome, Caen and the Miny Bocage. It advanced from the Falaise Gap with the Guards Armoured Division, was involved in the capture of Brussels and in the assaults on the Albert and Escaut Canals. Following on from Arnhem they were moved up to support the Americans during the German Ardennes Offensive and then advanced into Germany where they were when the war came to an end.

Fusilier Albert Edward George Hayman was also at Arnhem. He was a member of 2nd/8th Battalion, Lancashire Fusiliers, which was a Territorial Army unit. The battalion was on home service until after D-Day when it was used to provide draft reinforcements to other battalions to make up losses from the Normandy battles. He served in northern France, Belgium, Holland during 1944 and it is likely that he went into Germany in 1945. During one encounter with the enemy he owed his life to a pocketbook which stopped a bullet for him.

At some time during the month Flight Sergeant Kenneth Browne (bomb aimer) was wounded while on air operations over Arnhem. In September alone he had flown nine missions in support of Operation Market Garden, dropping supplies to British troops at Arnhem. As his Short Sterling (call sign LJ622) was turning to return to base it came under heavy and sustained German flak and machine gun fire and the plane was hit several times. Kenneth was seriously wounded in the head and arm. The plane was so badly damaged that it barely made it back across the North Sea to the nearest emergency landing ground, RAF Manston in Kent. Kenneth was treated for his injuries and made a full recovery but he was no longer able to fly and his RAF career ended at the age of 22, with nearly 380 flying hours logged.

Gunner Raymond Cookson, Royal Artillery

Fusilier Albert Hayman, 2nd/8th Lancashire Fusiliers

Flight Sergeant Kenneth Browne, RAFVR

Born c.1923, Kenneth was the only son of Mr and Mrs J. Browne of 17 Albert Street, Cadishead (formerly of Eccles). He attended St Mary's Primary School and Cadishead Senior School and, before joining up, he was employed by Irlam Council in the surveyors department. At the age of 18 he volunteered for the RAF Volunteer Reserve in September 1941 and was called up for training in March 1943. He went to Canada on board the *Queen Mary* and trained at No. 7 Bombing and Gunnery School, RCAF Station Paulson, Manitoba where he qualified as an air bomber and navigator. After further training at the Air Observer School, Ontario and the Advanced Flying Unit at Millom, Cumberland, Kenneth joined his first operational unit at the end of 1943 when he was posted to No.10 Officer Training Unit at Abingdon, Oxfordshire. In April 1944 he converted to heavy bombers at 1665 Conversion Unit at Tilstock, Shropshire and a couple of months later he joined A Flight 298 Squadron (38 Group) and flew many SOE (Special Operations Executive) missions over occupied France and Holland, sometimes towing Horsa gliders full of troops.

Around this time, Lance Corporal Harold Bate, a wireless operator with 155th Infantry Brigade of the 52nd (Lowland) Division, was stationed at Chalfonts St Peter, in the south of England. Shortly before the start of Operation Market Garden, a mock transport aircraft was placed in a field close to the base. Next, the motor transport sergeant was ordered to teach all the wireless operators to drive and to practice driving up a ramp into the rear of the transport aircraft. The idea was to reduce the weight of the wireless units by doing away with the driver. Although they were eventually stood down it was apparent that they were training for airborne operations at Arnhem. Later in the month, 52nd Division was posted to France to take part in operations in Holland.

Reverend Lee later wrote the following tribute to the men of Arnhem in the parish magazine: *The very sound of these words seem legendary and perhaps there is no other event in our history that will rank higher than their exploits in the ten days on short rations – the latter days without food and water, and fighting on grimly to the last. Their hardships scarcely bear thinking about and their heroism and endurance stir our deepest emotions. These brave men who have left so many of their comrades behind to consecrate the soil of Holland will never forget their desperate fight. It is to men like these, enduring hunger and thirst to defend us and bring us victory that we owe our security and the blessings we enjoy. I suppose none of us had any patience with the grumblers at home as we recall these sacrifices.*

On Saturday, 16th September Cadishead WVS held a party for 100 evacuees, made up of unaccompanied children and mothers with children. They had tea at the British Restaurant and then went to the Congregational School Rest Centre for entertainment consisting of games, magic tricks and an hour's film show. Edwin Jones and Norris Dale (billeting officer) attended the party. One young lad commented as he was leaving: *It was a smashing show.* In spite of Government warnings that the danger of enemy attacks had not passed, a number of evacuees billeted in the district had drifted back to their homes in London. Of the estimated

457 evacuees in the district, 72 had returned to their homes, most of them being mothers with children.

Trooper 3458870 **Charles Mort**, serving with the 51st (Leeds Rifles) Royal Tank Regiment, Royal Armoured Corps in Italy, was killed on Tuesday, 19th September 1944, aged 30. The regiment was part of the 128th Brigade of 46th Infantry Division.

This regiment was equipped with Churchill tanks and had seen action in the Tunisian and Italian campaigns. It appears that his unit was in action at Coriano Ridge. The ridge was an important position and its capture was vital for the Allies to advance on Rimini and then the River Po. The ridge was captured on 12th September but the following week saw heavy fighting between Allied and German forces. Born in Salford in 1914, Charles was the son of Alfred and Ann Mort and lived in Irlam.

He is buried at Coriano Ridge War Cemetery. The cemetery is located a couple of miles west of Riccione, which is a seaside resort on the Adriatic coast of Italy.

Coriano Ridge War Cemetery, Italy
(Inset: CWGC headstone of Charles Mort)

Signalman Trevor Jenkins of the Royal Corps of Signals was posted to Italy in 1944: *Once D-Day started you see we was cut out then. We got posted to different sections and that's when I got my posting to 61st Artillery Regiment. Go and find them, they were in northern Italy, I thought we're alright here. When I first went abroad, I was on my own again, when I say on my own I'm on a troopship but I'm on my own, I didn't know anybody and being a signalman I'm fully on duty. They put me on duty on a bloody boat, put me on the bridge just to help the... forget what they call it now, real old salt he was, don't know what they call them on board ship, 'ah just keep your eyes open' he said. We'd been out three days, I was on top then I could see this glimmer, I thought what the bloody hell's that, so I shouted this bloke, the senior hand, 'There's a light over here, what, what...' 'You bloody pillock' he said 'that's Liverpool lighthouse!' [laughter]. We'd been out three days. Well they were dodging bloody U-boats see, you go out in convoy and it went up north of England, and then doubled back and came back down again and after two days we were passing Liverpool again [laughter]. He said 'you bloody idiot, Liverpool lighthouse.' And then we got to Naples and I got off the boat, there was no docks when I got there, we had to climb over boats to get off at Naples. They slapped us into this big holding camp, 'we weren't expecting this boat in' they said. It was Christmas Day, corned beef butty that's all we had and it was bad, and we all finished up, you can imagine about 500 troops under canvas all with dysentery, oh what a bloody mess it was in. It was terrible. I said 'where's this field regiment?' 'Well you'll have to look for them.' I said 'well where do I look?' Italy, you're talking hundreds and hundreds of bloody miles. Well they're up near Florence and I'm in Naples, on my own. There was a bloke told me in the end, sergeant major he was, he said 'look, you're getting your food here aren't you?' 'Yes.' He said 'there's an ammunition depot over there, go there, eventually someone'll have to come back for some ammunition.' So that's where I finished up looking for one of these field regiments coming in for ammo. I could have cried honestly, could have cried. All on my own, nobody to talk to.*

I got to this, eventually, on an ammunition wagon, I was going up the hills near Florence, we had to stop, got out the back like had a drink, asked them what we were waiting for. He said we can only go up every so often, this pass it comes round the mountain, the mountain pass, so many come down, when they got down so many to go up. Well every time they opened the pass up the bloody Germans shelled it, I'm in the back of a bloody ammunition wagon on my own. You can imagine, I was only bloody 20, I could have cried, again. We got there alright obviously. I got up there and joined this regiment then the sergeant come, this sergeant, the Signals, he said 'find your new job' his name was Alf, he was a goalkeeper and he ended up as manager of Wigan Athletic, we'd only a few of us, you know, and that was where he come from, Sergeant Alf, can't think of his second name. Here again I wasn't with them all that long because I was moved about all the time and then I was with the Yanks for about six months, Yankee Fifth Army, I had to put a Yankee badge on, Yankee Fifth Army badge I had on. My job was to keep in contact with each regiment. Every regiment has their own Signals but for the main signals they've got to have Royal Signals, all the headquarters you know. That's what I was doing all the time, passing messages and going up the observation post when the colonel wanted to go up the observation post. First time I went up there I was putting bloody sandbags on the floor, thought what the hell am I doing this for, didn't sink in first time, there was sandbags in the bottom of the jeep if you went over any bloody landmines like [laughter]. That's what I was always filling sandbags for. There you go, busy times.

I think it was in Padua, we heard about rations coming so you'd jump in the queue and I was a heavy smoker then and I jumped in this queue for this NAAFI, some fags coming in. You're toddling forward one at a time and all of a sudden this bloke's pushing me in the back, two or three times then I started losing my rag, I thought what the bloody hell... a bloke called

Sherratt [possibly Jack Sherratt] *from Albert Street, Cadishead, he was doing it on purpose, he kept pushing me because he'd seen my face, in the end I turned round 'bloody hell, who are you pushing.' Sherratt his name, he lived in Albert Street.*

When asked about his time in the Army, Trevor replied: *Good days, but I don't reckon nothing to war, terrible. Not only that the people that were getting killed, what upset me most was these women and kids bloody starving, wandering round, nowhere to go, oh bloody horrible. Terrible. Poor buggers all starving, and I've actually seen an English soldier throw butties in mud knowing the kids are going to fight for it, I saw him do it, terrible, there's good and bad everywhere isn't there, yeah I saw him bloody do it. I've always said you seem to forget about it, you don't want to talk about the rough times, you always think about the good times that you had you know the camaraderie that went on, that sort of thing is far greater than looking at the bad stuff you know cos there was some bloody bad stuff during the war, terrible. Terrible. It was chaos and all them bloody women and kids running about, nobody'd got any food at all, it was bloody sickening.*

Gunner Charles Melton was wounded during the month while serving with the Royal Artillery in Italy. Charles had joined the Army in 1939 and had served throughout the North African campaign, receiving the Africa Star. He was educated at Cadishead Senior School and had worked at the Kinder Branch of the Wallpaper Manufacturers Association. He was married and his wife, Edith Melton, resided at 66 Fir Street, Cadishead.

(L-R) Gunner Arthur Massey, Sapper Fred Massey and Gunner Charles Melton

Two brothers, Gunner Arthur Massey and Sapper Fred Massey, met each other while on active service in Italy and spent the weekend together. They were the sons of Mr and the late Mrs J. Massey of 9 Atherton Lane, Cadishead. Thirty-six year old Fred joined the Royal Engineers in December 1942 and went overseas in July 1943. He served in North Africa, Egypt, Palestine and Italy. He was married, and lived with his wife at Elwyn, Kenmore Grove, Cadishead. Before joining the Army he was employed by the CWS Soap Works. Arthur was 28 years old at the time. He had worked for the Manchester Ship Canal Company before joining the Army in 1940. He went overseas the following year; serving throughout the North African campaign, before moving on to Italy.

On Thursday, 21st September Irlam WVS held a bring and buy sale in the Irlam bandroom which raised £10 for the Welcome Home Fund. In addition, Mrs Seddon of 4 Prospect Road, Cadishead made and auctioned a satin cushion, which realised £8 for the Fund, and six year old Joan Partington and 13 year old Glennis Evans raised a further £3. A backyard concert staged by girls of Rutland, Lancaster and Devon Roads in Cadishead raised ten shillings for the Red Cross. The concert, organised by Barbara Walton, Anne Ellison, Alma Philips, Maureen Higham, Nancy Broughton and Lillian Broughton, consisted of tap-dancing and acrobatics. The scouts raised £5 for the Red Cross POW fund.

On Saturday, 23rd September the members of Headquarters Platoon of D Company of the 42nd Battalion, Home Guard, were entertained to dinner at the British Restaurant, Irlam by Lieutenant E. Woods, Officer Commanding Headquarters Platoon and amongst the guests were Major Gold (Officer Commanding D Company), Captain P. Carberry (second in command), Reverend Lee (Padre for D and G Companies) and Henry Nurse (controller of the British Restaurant) and the ladies of the Headquarters staff. Major Gold thanked Lieutenant Woods on behalf of the guests and paid tribute to his untiring efforts since the formation of the Home Guard and to his enthusiasm, which had set an example to his platoon and also to the company. He also complimented the ladies of Company Headquarters, who had been with the company since the early days. He welcomed Reverend Lee and reminded the group that the Padre had assisted as an instructor and had been a philosopher and friend to the company. Finally, he thanked Henry Nurse and the British Restaurant for the catering. In reply, Henry complimented the Home Guard on the tremendous amount of work they had carried out in the district, although they had not always received the credit they deserved. Reverend Lee added that his own involvement with the Home Guard had been a great pleasure to him; he had enjoyed the weekly meetings with members of the company and he hoped that the great spirit of comradeship among the men would not lapse as a result of the relaxation in Home Guard duties. Sergeant F. French and Miss A. White (on behalf of the ladies of the staff) added their thanks to Lieutenant Woods.

Gunner Thomas William Humphreys, Royal Artillery, was wounded during fighting in France. He had joined the Army in 1939 and landed in France on D-Day. Educated at Cadishead Senior School, he had worked at Cadishead Post Office before joining up. His mother, Mrs A. Humphries, lived at 17 Moss Lane, Cadishead. By mid-October Thomas was recuperating at a hospital in Derbyshire.

OCTOBER

Sergeant 2045586 Norman Jones served in northern Europe with A Troop, 356 Searchlight Battery of 39 (7th Lancashire Fusiliers) Anti-Aircraft Battalion, Royal Artillery. He had been posted overseas after D-Day. Searchlight batteries were essential for the defence of Great Britain in containing the threat of German bombing raids and, in the preparations for D-Day, they were an important element of the Allied strategy for air supremacy over northern Europe. Without searchlights, anti-aircraft batteries would have been blind during the hours of darkness. Pairs of searchlights were spaced at known distances apart and as well as illuminating an enemy aircraft for the anti-aircraft batteries, they were used to calculate the height of the aircraft using triangulation. This allowed the anti-aircraft batteries to set the fuses of the anti-aircraft flak shells. The searchlights also hindered the eyesight of German bomb aimers, making it difficult for them to make out targets. The following summary is taken from 356 battery's war diaries for the period between the 2nd October and 18th November and gives some idea of the duties of the battery during their time in northern Europe.

On 2nd October 356 Battery was ordered to the Nijmegen area (Holland) to undertake an unusual role. Instead of their main anti-aircraft use, they were deployed on river and bridge defence. Their task was to illuminate anything floating down the river, for example mini-submarines, to prevent the bridge being destroyed. One searchlight was deployed continuously on the water and the second of the pair would be used to follow anything that was sighted. Other pairs of searchlights were deployed on the railway bridge and the main road bridge to Waal to prevent sabotage. Each searchlight was manned by five men and illuminated between the hours of 6.30pm and 6.15am. During the battery's time in Nijmegen the bridges and surrounding areas were subject to intermittent shell fire and mortar bombs. During the night of 9th October there were several searchlight sightings of aircraft but most of these were assumed to be friendly. The positions around the bridges were shelled heavily and one of the searchlights was put temporarily out of action. The shelling eased off on the next day. The constant running of the searchlights and their generators began to have an effect on the battery's equipment and, with no spare parts available, they experienced several outages. On 11th October two bombs fell near one of the searchlight positions but overall the shelling of Nijmegen was much reduced. Two men were wounded by a bomb which was dropped from a high fast flying enemy aircraft. Several enemy aircraft flew over the positions during daylight but none were reported during the night.

On 15th October A Troop's two searchlights were replaced by four Lyon lights which were more suitable for constant use. On 17th October three low flying aircraft attacked the searchlight positions and the searchlights were temporarily put out of action and one man was wounded. At first the raid was thought to be the prelude to a seaborne attack but nothing further developed. The shelling of the Nijmegen bridges increased in magnitude with approximately 80 shells being fired on 17th October, 200 on the following day and over 350 on 19th October. Next day, the role of the searchlights was changed from river and bridge defence back to anti-aircraft duties. Three Messerschmitt ME 109 fighter aircraft were seen during daylight but the anti-aircraft batteries held their fire as Allied aircraft engaged them. Enemy air activity increased over the area and a few bombs were dropped without causing any damage. On 22nd October a Focke-Wolfe 190 was hit by light anti-aircraft fire and claimed as down and a further two enemy aircraft were spotted.

Members of A Troop, 356 Battery (Sergeant Norman Jones standing centre)

Lance Sergeant Norman Jones was one of ten men from the battery promoted to Sergeant on 23rd October. The next day an enemy aircraft was spotted during the night. All previous sightings had been during daylight hours. On 29th October there was considerably more air activity as ME 262s flew over in pairs and three bombs were dropped close to the railway bridge. A Messerschmitt ME109 was shot down during daylight on 2nd November. On 4th November there was more aerial activity and several Me 262s and 109s were sighted. A bomb was dropped but did not cause any damage. The next day, despite heavy rain, high winds and low cloud, two Heinkel HE111s were spotted at 8.03pm and 9.05pm respectively. Each time they were illuminated by the searchlights for 25 seconds but there was no anti-aircraft fire at the first aircraft and only a few wild shots at the second. At 6am on 8th November a shell landed in the back of a vehicle and killed one of the gunners. Two days later a number of aircraft were engaged by the searchlights and a Heinkel HE 111 was illuminated for 45 seconds but there was no anti-aircraft fire. On 11th November the bridge areas were shelled throughout the day and night and there was some air activity between 8pm and 9pm. Enemy shelling of Nijmegen continued for the next three days and was particularly heavy on 14th, with mortar fire ('Moaning Minnies') during the night. On 15th November the battalion HQ and most of the battery moved to Belgium and A Troop followed on 18th November.

Norman Jones was born in Cadishead on 10th September 1919. He was a printer by trade. He was a pre-war Territorial soldier, having enlisted into the 7th Battalion, Lancashire Fusiliers at Flixton on 27th October 1937. He was described as 5 feet 6 inches tall, with blue eyes, dark brown hair and a sallow complexion. In September 1939, the battalion was converted to anti-aircraft duties, becoming 39 Anti-Aircraft Battalion, Royal Artillery, based in Salford. The battalion comprised four batteries: 354, 355, 356, 357. In August 1940, the battalion became 39 (Lancashire Fusiliers) Searchlight Regiment, Royal Artillery (TA), and a further change took place in May 1943 when they became 356 (7th Lancashire Fusiliers) Independent Searchlight Battery, Royal Artillery. Up until D-Day, Norman served in various locations in Great Britain, including Kirkwall in the Orkney Islands and also near Liverpool. In 1942 he married Eva Owen Marshall, daughter of First World War veteran, Frank Marshall of 1 York Road, Cadishead. Norman and Eva lived at 15 Allenby Road, Cadishead, and later at 22 Bankfield Avenue, Cadishead. In May 1944 he was in Ipswich, when he received the news that his daughter had been born.

On Wednesday, 4th October members of 292 (Eccles) Squadron, ATC, including five cadets from the Irlam detached flight, visited a North West aerodrome. They were shown around the aerodrome and later they were treated to flights. The detached flight was established in 1942, and in that time the flight had sent 19 cadets and two civilian instructors to the Forces. Six cadets and one instructor served with the RAF, three with the Fleet Air Arm, three in the Royal Navy, four cadets and an instructor in the Army and one in the mines. One cadet served with the United States Army Air Corps and another cadet served with a Canadian Paratroop battalion.

One of the former ATC cadets who joined the RAF was Leading Aircraftman 3012777 Jack Lilley. Jack was born on 21st December 1924 in Ashton. Prior to enlisting, he had worked as an electrician at the Steelworks. Originally Jack applied to join the Navy but, at the time, they were only recruiting stokers. Therefore, because Jack wanted to use the skills he had learnt as an electrician at the Steelworks, he joined the Air Force. He was stationed at Manby in Lincolnshire where he was involved in servicing aircraft. On one occasion he had to run and dive for cover when a German Messerschmitt ME109 fighter flew over the airfield and fired on the planes on the ground. He also spent time in London helping to clear bomb damaged buildings. On one occasion he was sat on the back of a flatbed truck with another man when a V1 exploded in front of the vehicle and killed the driver and his mate. Jack and the other man spent a few days in hospital with temporary deafness due to perforated ear drums. After the war, Jack returned to work at the Steelworks, attaining the post of chief electrical engineer.

Norman and Eva Jones

Leading Aircraftman Jack Lilley, RAF

On Thursday, 5th October members of Irlam and Cadishead British Legion visited a north western Royal Canadian Air Force station (presumably Dam Head Hall at Glazebrook) to take part in a snooker match (which they won). The Canadian airmen made the visitors feel at home, and while the snooker was in progress others played cribbage and table tennis. Clearly this event, and many others, helped to strengthen the bonds between the district and the Canadians.

On Sunday, 8th October the 42nd Battalion, Home Guard, held a shooting competition to enable those members who had passed the snipers' course to qualify for their 'Skill-at-Arms' badge. As a result, Private A. Overton of G Company and Lance Corporal Frank Hubert Herricks of D Company, achieved the marksmen standard by scoring 95 or more out of a possible 140. In addition, several members of the local Home Guard companies achieved the service shot standard, scoring more than 75 out of 140: Corporals Pickering, Banks, Southern and Halliday, Lance Corporal Page, Privates Darby, Clealand, Pilling, Wilson, Perkins and Worthington.

Flight Sergeant 1235933 Harold Townend (navigator) had a lucky escape when, on the night of Tuesday, 10th/11th October, his Wellington bomber got into difficulties. They had taken off at 10.25pm from RAF Benbecula in the Outer Hebrides in order to protect a large convoy which was inbound from Halifax in Nova Scotia. After 2½ hours in the air, and in atrocious weather conditions, the starboard engine iced up and the aircraft dropped 2,000 feet. When the skipper re-started the engine it kept faltering, and they had no alternative but to return to base, dropping their depth charges safely into the sea and then jettisoning some of their fuel. When they arrived back at the base, it was completely shrouded by cloud so they asked for SANDRA to be ignited – this was three searchlights converging on the centre of the airfield. The crew couldn't see the lights and were advised to either bale out or make their way to the mainland. Neither option was possible; they had insufficient fuel to make the mainland and baling out in a force 14 gale would have been suicidal. Harold bowed his head and said a prayer asking for the safe deliverance of the crew. At that very moment, a clear area of sky appeared and SANDRA shone through. The skipper circled around the beams and when they got down to 300 feet they found the cloud base was clear. They landed safely and almost immediately the engines cut out – his prayer had been answered. On Harold's next leave he visited his grandmother in Buxton, Derbyshire. During the visit, his aunt asked him whether he had been in trouble on 11th October. On this day, at 1.10am, his grandmother had called her two daughters who were living with her into her room to kneel and pray because she said: *The lad is in trouble, we must pray for him.*

Harold was born at the New Inn, at Walton near Wakefield in Yorkshire, on 12th May 1923. He provided the following summary of his enlistment and his service: *I was in the Air Training Corps. I worked in the engineering branch at New Sharlston Colliery Company in Yorkshire and the son of the enginewright, who was the head engineer there, he came in in his uniform and he was in Guy Gibson's squadron and he said to me 'aren't you* going to join us Harold?' and of course working in the mines was a reserved occupation, the only way you could get into the service, and they couldn't stop you, was either going in submarines, which I didn't fancy, or going into air crew, because you had to volunteer for both of those, so I volunteered for air crew. I went to Huddersfield and got taken on there and they sent me to Cardington to be kitted out and when I got there they said 'you're only 17¼, you'll have to go in the ATC in Wakefield and then we'll call you up when you're 18 in May.' May '41, and that's what they did and then I was sent for air crew training. I was stationed at RAF Madley in Hereford when I did my first flight. We were the first squad to use that airbase, it was newly built in '41. So I was flying in Dominies, twin-engined Dominies there, a Proctor as well. And then I went on to Yatesbury. I did my morse training at Yatesbury, I got 22 words a minute, when I'd got that they sent me down to 280 Squadron at RAF Detling in Kent to await my final… oh I had to go to Penbrey on a gunnery course, everybody had to be taught how to use guns. And then I was sent to Limavady in Ireland, then Detling in Kent, on 280 Squadron. I flew from Detling over to RAF Rhos on the Llyn Peninsular because they'd taken all the navigators off the night fighters because they'd lost that many on Bomber Command that they had to replenish them so we did a short course of four months to become radio observers, with having got my 22 words a minute we were doing radio observers and at the end of it they gave you a flight badge 'RO' which they eventually took off us and gave us an 'S'. They gave me the option when I finished the course, of either carrying on and doing the full navigation course or going as a second navigator on Coastal Command, well I wanted to get into action so that's what I did, I went as a second navigator on Coastal Command. Then I was sent to Limavady in Ireland and joined a crew there and from there we were sent on Wellingtons, we were sent to Turnberry in Scotland, you know where the golf is, and crewed up. We did practice runs with torpedoes, it was a torpedo Wellington, we carried two torpedoes and did dummy runs on Ailsa Craig and things like that. I lost my best pal there, well when I was at Turnberry I lost him, he was a chappie, before the war he was a wonderful pianist and he broadcast as a young teenager during the war, Reg Comley. It was whilst we were training at Turnberry they took off on a night exercise with dummy torpedoes and they never gained height and they struck the electric power cables and the whole lot were killed and because he was my pal the CO asked me to escort the coffin down to Erdington in Birmingham which is where he lived. His father was a manager of a brewery there, and I said I would never do it again because you can imagine, power cables, all incinerated, the mother wanted to see her son, they couldn't open the coffin, and I said I would never do it again [23 year old Sergeant Philip Reginald Comley died on 28th March 1943]. Then I was sent to Talbenny in Wales and then sent to India to join 99 Squadron at Ceylon on torpedo Wellingtons. We flew via North Africa, Morocco, landing at Fez then going across the battlefield at North Africa to Cairo, stopping en route at various places and then from Cairo through Habbaniya, Iraq and various places, various stops to Karachi in India. And then we went to join our squadron in Ceylon and we got as far as Allahabad in India and we were told to hold fire, the squadron were being posted back to the Middle East, to Italy, for the invasion you know, and the CO of the squadron took off and he crashed his aircraft about five miles away, came back, pinched our aircraft and left us stranded in India. So then we were sent from Allahabad back to Karachi and we joined 21 Ferry Control there which was delivering aircraft to various parts of India and then suddenly they decided they wanted us back in the

UK for the second front. We were sent home by ship, the Stirling Castle, the first ship through the Suez Canal after it was cleared, to St Augustus in Sicily to pick up 2,000 Americans after they had a successful landing there, and we said well where are the lads of the 51st Division, so we waited for a day and half while they brought 200 of the 51st Division onto the ship. We proceeded to Algiers and then the Americans said they wanted to take all their troops on this ship back to the States and so they shipped us off that and took us on the Princess Beatrix which was one of Lord Louis Mountbatten's tank landing craft. We went from Algiers to Gibraltar, I had one or two humorous episodes there and waited and then they decided we would then go on this Princess Beatrix back to Falmouth in Cornwall which we did. It was one of these no keel things, when we crossed the Bay of Biscay it did everything except loop the loop, and whilst we were doing that we'd loaded up with fruit because fruit was scarce in England and halfway across the Bay of Biscay the fruit was smelly and we'd taken on some U-boat prisoners and they were down in the cells on the ship and they overpowered the marine guard and the U-boat commander, he was a typical German chappie, you know beard, he looked the part of a U-boat captain, and they came up on board, they thought they were being gassed, that's the reason they gave for overpowering the guard and coming up. Anyway we had a lieutenant commander in charge of the ship and he drew his revolver out and said 'I'll count to ten and if you don't go back I'll shoot you' and he explained, he could speak some German, he explained to them what it was, anyway they did go back down and eventually we got to Falmouth. Then we were sent home on leave and then I got a telegram to say that I had to go to Silloth in Cumberland and I got an entirely different crew then apart from one chap that I was with in India. Then we were sent onto to Leigh Light Wellingtons at Silloth.

As Harold had volunteered to serve as air crew in the Royal Air Force Volunteer Reserve, he was, like all members of the Volunteer Reserve, not subject to the normal rules of conscription and could opt out at any time. In addition, as he had come from a reserved occupation he often received letters from his employer asking him to return to the mines: *Every two or three months I had a letter asking me to return to the mines. The CO wanted to see me, 'I've got another of those requests' he said 'are you fed up with the Air Force, do you want to go back to the mines?' I said 'I don't. I don't know why they keep sending, I've told them I don't want to go back.' But they kept asking me to go back.*

Harold's connection with the district began after the war, when, in 1947, he married Betty Dawson of 25 Chapel Road, Irlam. Betty served as a telephonist in the WAAF. She was born on 17th December 1923 and was educated at the nearby Irlam Endowed School and then Irlam Senior School. After leaving school, she was employed by the CWS, working in a clothes shop opposite the Ship Hotel. After war broke out she decided to enlist and in 1940 she joined the Women's Auxiliary Air Force. She was first posted to the Balloon Centre at Bowlee, near Middleton and then was posted to the Bomber Command station at RAF Witton near Cambridge. On 24th August 1943, her friend, Flight Sergeant Vernon Lewis DFM (whose father, Hubert, won the Victoria Cross in 1916), was killed on air operations over Germany. As a result Betty left the Air Force for a time. She later re-joined and, in 1946, was posted to RAF St Eval where she met and married Harold on 24th May 1947 (see later entry).

Flight Sergeant Harold Townend, RAFVR

Betty Dawson (later Townend), Women's Auxiliary Air Force

Aircraftman Charles Roberts, RAF and Beryl Dean

Air Mechanic Charles Roberts of the RAF was stationed at RAF Cambridge where he was involved in servicing and repairing aircraft. Born in 1917, Charles was the son of Charles and Louie Roberts (nee Clark) of Cadishead. His father, Sergeant Charles Roberts of the 11th Manchesters, was killed in action on 18th May 1918 during a trench raid in the First World War. While stationed at Cambridge, Charles met and married Beryl Dean in 1944. After the war they settled in Cambridge.

There was a growing optimism about the chances of the war ending in victory for the Allies and this was reflected in rumours that the Home Guard was about to be stood down on an imminent and specific date. The *Guardian* issued a statement denying the rumours and advised that the Home Guard members would be given at least one month's notice of the date of the stand-down.

The wedding of Able Seaman Roy Marshall, Royal Navy, and Ellen Matthews, took place at the Church of St John and St James, Bootle, on Wednesday, 11th October. Roy was the third son of Councillor William Marshall and Mrs Marshall of 290 Liverpool Road, Irlam. Prior to enlisting, Roy had been a member of 1 Platoon, D Company, Home Guard (Private 497), from 31st October 1941 to 2nd March 1942. Ellen was the elder daughter of Mr and Mrs Matthews of 7 Ballantyne Grove, Orrell, Bootle. Roy's two brothers both served in the Royal Navy, Able Seaman Tom Marshall and Able Seaman Herbert James Marshall. Herbert married Annie Hayes in February 1942.

Irlam WVS held a mock Lord Mayor's Banquet at St Paul's schoolroom to raise money for the Welcome Home Fund. Edwin and Mrs Jones acted as Lord Mayor and Lady Mayoress and received the 100 citizens who attended the banquet. Mr H. Fairhurst acted as toastmaster and proposed toasts to the King, Lord Mayor and Lady Mayoress, our friends in HM Forces and the WVS. Dance music was provided by Mrs L. Roberts and Madame N. Tynan and, after the banquet, Mr Broadhurst. The Welcome Home Fund benefited by £23.

Sergeant (air gunner) 545369 **James Henry Prince Jibson** of 178 Squadron, Royal Air Force Volunteer Reserve, Mediterranean Allied Air Force Command, was killed on air operations on Saturday, 14th October.

At 5.39pm on Friday, 13th October Liberator Mark VI, serial no. EW280, took off from Terria airfield, Libya, to bomb the Szekesfehervar marshalling yards in Hungary. The aircraft was shot down by a German fighter with the loss of the entire crew: Warrant Officer (pilot) Keith W. Bardsley, RAAF, Sergeants Robert H. Hughes (flight engineer), Louis W. Fiest (navigator), Joseph Gerrard (air gunner), John J. Robinson, Joseph R. Chambers (air gunner), James Jibson (air gunner) and Norman B. Molyneaux (air gunner). They were all buried at Budapest War Cemetery, Hungary.

Another appeal was made by the War Comforts Fund, in the *Guardian* (14th October) for the overseas addresses of local servicemen. The purpose was to ensure that they all received gifts. In previous appeals, the addresses had been collected on scraps of paper, which had proved difficult to administer. This time special forms were made available at the Council Offices, and the Rialto and Palace cinemas. Additions to the fund included £43 from a Sunday Concert given by Bolton Civil Defence Concert Party, £6 from Guard Room A Social and Comforts Committee, £4 from Mrs Williams of the Nags Head Hotel, £12 from the CWS Soap Works 'Salute the Soldier' effort, £1 from the LSC Blast Furnace Bowling Handicap, ten shillings from Jean Crawford, £50 from the Steelworks (£25 for the Comforts gifts and £25 for the Welcome Home gifts), £1 from Cadishead Congregational Benevolent Fund, £2 from Lancashire Tar Distillers and £7 from Irlam and Cadishead Trades Council.

On Sunday, 15th October 42nd Battalion, Home Guard, held its inter-company shooting competition at Crowden rifle range in brilliant weather. F Company won the competition with a total of 635 points out of a possible 800 points. Irlam and Cadishead's D Company were runners-up with a total of 592 points.

The St John Ambulance Brigade suffered a severe loss on Sunday, 15th October when 45 year old Ambulance Officer Thomas Hazlehurst died at his home, 30 Lancaster Road, Cadishead. Tom was a founder member of the Irlam and Cadishead Division of the St John Ambulance Brigade when it was established in May 1929. He was appointed divisional storekeeper in November 1929, receiving high praise from the inspecting officer who visited the division. He was promoted to corporal, then sergeant, before attaining the rank of ambulance officer and divisional secretary in March 1935. At the outbreak of the war he devoted himself to the training and organisation of first aid parties and was in charge of the Longfield Lodge section of the local Civil Defence first aid parties. His obituary stated: *The thoroughness of his training was apparent in the efficient state of the parties under his control, and his devotion to his duty won him the esteem of all who knew him.* He was awarded the Service Medal of the Order of St John in July 1943. Thomas was a native of Partington, who had moved to Cadishead around 1924. He took a keen interest in Cadishead Wesleyan Church. The funeral took place at Hollins Green Cemetery on Thursday, 19th October after a service by Reverend Ayres at Cadishead Wesleyan Church.

On Monday evening, 16th October at Irlam Central School, Lieutenant Colonel Webb of the Home Guard presented the district with a plaque to commemorate the successful savings effort during Salute the Soldier Week. Despite Irlam having the highest total of small savings in the Manchester area, the turnout was disappointing as only 150 people attended. Lieutenant Colonel Webb congratulated the Savings

Committee, who had organised the campaign. He stressed that savings would continue to be important after the war as the country was reconstructed and he urged the audience to maintain the district's high standard in saving. He concluded by commenting on the relaxation of war-time measures, which he described as anticipating the end of the war, as he felt it was too early for some of the measures. Councillor Melville thanked Lieutenant Colonel Webb and reiterated that the public understood how important savings were and that, at this stage, there would be no relaxation in the district. Councillor Owen agreed that the Government had been premature in allowing a slackening of some war-time restrictions and he also agreed that savings would continue to play an important part in the re-construction of post-war Britain. Mr Wilde, deputy regional commissioner, thanked the district, on behalf of the National Savings Association, for its efforts in the Salute the Soldier week. Lieutenant Colonel Webb presented merit certificates to street group secretaries.

The officers and NCOs of D Company held a cabaret dance at Irlam Conservative Club, with guests including Lieutenant Colonel Webb, Major and Mrs H.W. Whittle, Lieutenant and Mrs J. Lyle, and Regimental Sergeant Major J. Butterfield and his wife. Major Gold presented Miss A. White of Company Headquarters, with a cheque as a token of appreciation of all ranks of D Company for her invaluable services to the company almost since its formation. Lieutenant Colonel Webb traced the history of the Home Guard and thanked the men for the excellent work they had done. He also thanked the ladies for lending their husbands, without complaint, to the Home Guard, but warned that their most testing time was still to come – what to do with quarrelsome and disgruntled husbands when they had no Home Guard work to do!

James Rogerson of 11 Haig Avenue, Cadishead, serving with HM Forces in Italy, wrote to give his views on post-war planning: *Sir, I have just received, in Italy, the Guardian dated July 15th, in which Corporal J. Howes makes an appeal for bags of letters from us boys in the Forces which Onlooker asked for in previous issues of the Guardian. Well you've asked for it, now you're gonna get it, and here is my contribution. While quite in favour of all the post-war reforms suggested in Reader's Forum from time to time, e.g. hospitals, maternity homes, baths, and reference libraries, etc. I can't see how these things are to be achieved under any system of Government similar to that which existed before the war. As long as private ownership continues in Britain, how can we look forward to improved conditions after the war? For all that private enterprise offers are the conditions which prevailed before the war – mass unemployment, slums, waste of materials, poor planning, and all the other disasters common to the people of Britain previous to the war. The one answer to this is common ownership of all the means of production, factories, workshops, etc., and the land. Only then, when all is in the hands of the people, when it is really our country can all our plans, hopes and desires be put into practice and become realities. I add, in conclusion, all power to the Common Wealth Party of Sir Richard Acland which is doing so much with regard to the things I mention above, also that the majority of the boys here overseas I talk with are becoming 'common ownership minded.'*

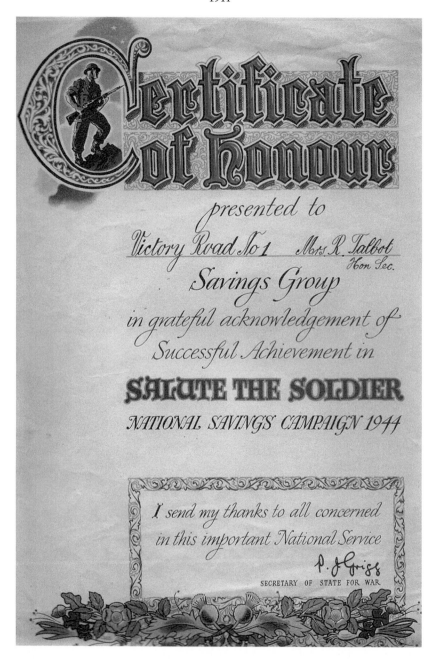

Certificate of honour

presented to

Victory Road No 1   *Mrs R. Talbot*
Hon Sec.

Savings Group

in grateful acknowledgement of
Successful Achievement in

SALUTE THE SOLDIER

NATIONAL SAVINGS CAMPAIGN 1944

I send my thanks to all concerned
in this important National Service

P. J. Grigg

SECRETARY OF STATE FOR WAR

On Saturday, 21st October an Anglo-Canadian wedding took place at St John's Church, Irlam, between Wireless Operator George E. Urquhart, Royal Canadian Air Force, the youngest son of Mr and the late Mrs K.J. Urquhart of Williamstown, Ontario, Canada and Margaret E. Scott, the eldest daughter of Mr and Mrs W. Scott of 581 Liverpool Road, Irlam.

On Tuesday, 24th October Irlam Council continued to improve lighting in the district by bringing the gas lamps on the Victory site back into operation. The estate was reported to have shone with almost peacetime brilliance.

A number of German and Italian prisoners of war were put to work on local farms. Each day, they were brought from the POW camp under armed guard. Some of them worked on Barton Grange Farm, which was owned by the Shacklady family, and was situated at the top of Fiddlers Lane. In 2011 Peter Shacklady recalled: *Mother used to make them meat and potato pie and apple pie and they used to measure the pieces exactly to all get a fair share (in true German style). They worked threshing and if there was any particularly dirty or horrible jobs the Nazi POWs did them, they got the worst jobs. The German POWs were proud of the fact that they had served under Rommel. Italian POWs stayed on the farms overnight. These were the ones the locals hobnobbed with. A threshing machine used to go round the farms, this was owned by a fairground person and operated by reserves. After the war a German bought it, stayed in this country and married a land girl.*

Wartime Memories, a publication produced by the Irlam, Cadishead and District Local History Society, carried the following story from Stan Berry (Cadishead Moss): *When a prisoner of war camp was set up at Haydock racecourse some of the prisoners were asked to volunteer for farm work. My dad applied for help and two prisoners were sent from the camp to help on the farm. Bernard Kipper and Werner Hesse. My father had been a POW in the first war and had a lot of sympathy with the plight of these men. He instructed my mother to feed them as he said men could not work off an empty stomach. Both lads settled in and became good and reliable workers. They both continued to write to my parents after the war, right up to my father's death in 1954. At various other times especially harvest times other nationalities of men became available for farm work. We employed Italian POWs dressed in British Army battledress dyed a purple colour with diamond shaped patches. We had French sailors with blue uniforms with a red pompom on top of the cap. British soldiers and airmen were also used to harvest the potato crop.*

An article appeared in the *Guardian*: *One youngster who volunteered for the work* [Potato picking] *was given two meat pies by his mother for dinner. He asked the farmer's wife if she would warm them for him and was told that she could only do it on that one occasion as she was BUSY LOOKING AFTER THE ITALIANS. Shades of Libya and Tripoli!*

Marie Burgess (nee Brady) recounted an exciting incident which happened at St Teresa's School when word spread through the playground that a 'German' soldier was trapped in the trench shelter at Clarendon Road playing field. The curious children rushed to the trench and found a mud bespattered man at the bottom of the trench. Marie's father, Francis Brady, was the headmaster of St Teresa's School and a member of the Home Guard. He was called to the incident and found an Italian prisoner of war in the trench. The Italian had been drinking and had taken a shortcut through the playing field, presumably to return to the farm on Astley Road where he was working. He had stumbled into the trench and, in a drunken state, could not get out. The authorities were called and the chastened prisoner was taken away.

With the Allies advancing across Europe, thoughts were turning to the end of the war. Irlam Council gave the district's surveyor, Henry Nurse, authority to purchase £56 worth of bunting, flags and flood lamps in preparation for the celebrations. It would still be some time before these items would be used!

Bombardier Edgar Crozier, Royal Artillery, was awarded a Certificate of Merit signed by the Commander-in-Chief, Mediterranean Forces, for outstanding service. Edgar was a pre-war soldier who had joined the Army in July 1939. He served in India, Persia, Iraq and Egypt, and by October 1944 he was in the Lebanon.

Edgar was born in 1918 at Barrow-in-Furness, the youngest son of John Sansome and the late Alice Maud Crozier (nee Riseley). At some point before the war the family had moved to 255 Liverpool Road, Cadishead.

(L-R) Bombardier Edgar Crozier and Privates George and Ernest Gardner

Private George Gardner travelled 400 miles to see his brother, Private Ernest Gardner, in hospital in Italy. George joined the Army in 1940 and went to West Africa the same year. His brother, Ernest, served with the Royal Marine Commandos. Before the outbreak of war, he was in the Territorial Army and was mobilised in 1939, serving in France and Belgium before being evacuated from Dunkirk in May 1940. He was serving in Italy in the summer of 1944 when he was wounded. They were the sons of Mr and Mrs G.W. Gardner of 12 Liverpool Road, Irlam, and both worked for the family business, G.W. Gardner and Sons, carriers.

Two Cadishead soldiers, Sergeant Thomas E. Vann and Private Harold Wilde, met each other in Karachi, India (now Pakistan). In civilian life they were next door neighbours, living at numbers 39 and 41 Allenby Road, Cadishead respectively. Thomas had been in Karachi when a convoy came in but at first he did not recognise his former neighbour. Harold saw him first and they had a happy reunion, followed by a night out. Harold had joined the Army in 1942 and served as an Army transport driver. He had been in India for 12 months. He was formerly employed by Metropolitan Vickers in Trafford Park.

Mrs Roberts, a former officer of the local branch of the Salvation Army was with her husband, Adjutant Roberts, in Italy where they were engaged in Red Shield canteen work behind the front line. She wrote a letter which was published in the *War Cry* and the *Guardian*: *I am sending this note by one of the boys to assure you that we are all right for I know you will be anxious for all of us in the forward areas. We arrived before the main body of the division, so we were greeted with hearty cheers and waves as the convoy drew in. tomorrow, after only three days here, we go to an old country inn – the only place standing in a hamlet much shelled and bombed, to set up a semi-static canteen. Adjutant will run the mobile to the units too far away for me to serve. I shall make the cakes until the divisional bakery comes within easy proximity or until we come to a sizeable village. I can't tell you how much the instruments are appreciated by the boys whom we are very happy to contact. This is a peaceful break between very intense gunfire. The sun is setting in marvellously tinted splendour. I find it hard to think of fighting and bloodshed so near – but there go the guns again, just to remind me.*

The annual meeting of the Rixton-with-Glazebrook Red Cross Fund was held in Hollinfare Schools on Saturday, 28th October and Reverend Firth presided. Mr Witty (co-treasurer with Mr A. Pitchfork) read the financial statement which had a balance of £47, £31 of which had been set aside for the men and women who were serving in HM Forces but were not entitled to benefit from the local Red Cross fund. Miss Farrington presented the committee's report which stated that gifts were sent to 110 men and women, each with a postal order for 15 shillings. In addition, a further 28 men and women had been sent a similar amount, thanks to the effort of Mr Vickers and the school staff; £20 was sent to St Dunstan's Hospice for Blind Servicemen and £20 to the Aid for Russia Fund. She thanked the organisers of the 'bring and buy' sale which had raised £62 and also thanked Lady Stopford's gift of wool which had enabled knitters to send 36 woollen garments (mostly pullovers) to the Merchant Navy and local boys had received 24 woollies. In addition, collectors had raised over £900 in the year which was donated to the Duke of Gloucester's Red Cross Fund.

On 31st October the WVS held a 'bring and buy' sale at St Paul's School, which was opened by Mrs A.J. Neal, and realised £21.

NOVEMBER

As the Allies advanced northwards through Europe it became necessary to open Antwerp up as a port to allow supplies to reach the Allied troops in Holland. The Allies had taken the city of Antwerp with its port facilities intact but the Germans still controlled the Scheldt estuary leading to the port. The Battle of the Scheldt began on 2nd October and raged until 8th November when the area was finally cleared of Germans. The final phase of the operation, the capture of Walcheren island, was dubbed Operation Infatuate. Walcheren island had been strongly fortified by the Germans as part of their Atlantic Wall defences. The Canadian 2nd Infantry Division had attacked the causeway on the island's eastern side on 31st October but they were held up here by the Germans. On 1st November amphibious landings took place with No. 4 Commando, followed by 155th Infantry Brigade, 52nd (Lowland) Division, being ferried from Breskens in small landing craft to Uncle Beach in the south east of the city of Vlissingen.

Lance Corporal Harold Bate was with 155th Infantry Brigade. At Breskens he witnessed the devastation caused by the previous battles which had flattened all the buildings. On 1st November his brigade was marched to the quayside at Breskens and ordered to board the amphibious landing craft, which he described as: *large tanks which could carry 150 men*. They were ordered to board the craft but there was little order on the quay and all the troops became mixed up. As they boarded the landing craft they were each handed a life jacket but when it came to Harold's turn they had ran out. Harold could not swim. As the crafts 'chugged' across the two mile wide estuary towards Vlissingen German shells were landing in the water alongside them. When they arrived at Uncle Beach the men were ordered to jump into the water and onto the beach. Fortunately, the Commandos had forced the Germans northwards which allowed the landings to continue unopposed. However, there were chaotic scenes on the beach as men searched for their individual units. Harold decided the best course of action was to stay on the beach, however, an officer rushed up and ordered him, along with two other soldiers nearby, to follow him into the city. As they walked along the road a soldier came running towards them and warned them off the road as there were snipers about. They waited five minutes in a nearby house and then the officer, with a change of mind, ordered them back to the beach. As more troops began to arrive on the beach order was restored and the various units were gathered together.

Harold was a wireless operator and his role was to sit in a 'Weasel' (a vehicle with armour plating covered by a canvas roof with plastic windows) and maintain communications between the infantry and the Brigade headquarters. On 2nd November Harold was sitting in the back of the Weasel, when he felt something pass through his hair at the back of his head. He turned around and noticed a small hole in the plastic window and a corresponding tear in the canvas roof above him. A German sniper, hidden in a windmill behind the vehicle, had taken a shot, probably at a different target, which must have ricocheted off the road and narrowly missed Harold. He remained with the 155th Brigade during the fighting across Holland and into Germany, crossing the Rhine in March 1945 and advancing into Germany. At the end of the war they were sent to Bremen where a divisional Victory Parade was held. He served mainly in a unit consisting of a driver and two wireless operators in a jeep but later in the war he spent some time as 'Brig Recce' (brigade reconnaissance), travelling between the various infantry battalions with Brigadier McLaren and his intelligence officer. He finished the war with the rank of corporal.

Another local man in the 52nd (Lowland) Division was Private James 'Jimmy' Yates, who served with the 4th/5th Royal Scots Fusiliers, 156th Infantry Brigade. Jimmy was the son of Mr and Mrs James Yates of Nelson Drive, Cadishead.

Sapper Arthur Appleton, Royal Engineers, served throughout the campaign in northern Europe and was involved in erecting bailey bridges. Arthur, who was born in 1920, moved with his family from Wigan to Hampton Road, Cadishead at some point before the war and worked as a bricklayer at the Steelworks. After the war Arthur married Kitty Green of MacDonald Road, Irlam. Kitty served as a leading aircraftwoman in the Women's Auxiliary Air Force. They later resided in Hargate Drive, Higher Irlam.

Captain Norman Wilson wrote the following letter to the *Guardian* to describe India, where he had been stationed for over three years: *I have read with great interest the many letters you receive from members of the Forces and would, indeed, be lax, if I did not convey my, and I'm sure, all our thanks for your interest and help. It is now some 3½ years since I left home, and I never fail to look forward to my Guardian with its portrayal of events at home. May I congratulate you on a first class production. Specially would I thank you for the help you have given our Scout Troop – of which I was - and still am a proud member. May they and the Cubs enjoy a new year of good, happy scouting! I recall that you have had many letters from India – unfortunately, I have not met any of their writers, except one, Ernie Bassett – whom I met on the boat coming out. To describe India, even in a longer letter, would be manifestly beyond my powers. It is a vast, strange, wonderful country. I never tire of discovering its marvels, and they are many! Its vastness, apparent from the map, can only be realised by travelling from the brown, barren hills of the North West Frontier to the forests of the south, from the western ghats to the jungle-covered hills of the east. I remember, with no uncertainly, the longest train journey I ever made at home, from Thurso to Euston – interminable it seemed. The difference here is that one settles down, after the inevitable rush for berths to three or perhaps even four days travel. Even a 17 day convoy by road does not occasion surprise. To the naturist it is truly a paradise, with its multitudinous multi-coloured butterflies and birds, its insects carefully camouflaged by nature, from the quaint praying mantis to the small destructive white ant and his ugly queen. Its animals – Kipling knew them only too well – and its reptiles, some ugly and venomous, but with no 'precious jewel in his head,' as Shakespeare said of the toad. But then I forget – perhaps the toad is an animal?*

Private James Yates, Royal Scots Fusiliers

Sapper Arthur Appleton, Royal Engineers

Animals and reptiles remind me of Kipling's Jungle Book. Remember Ricky-Ticky-Tavi, the mongoose? They are everything he describes. I've had three, their names as above – my favourite Ricky. I could write many tales of her, of her playfulness, her amusing habits, her sometimes unbridled ferocity. Truly delightful pets, and sometimes very useful. Digression seems to be my main theme. So back again to India! Perhaps the prettiest place I have ever visited is Darjeeling. I was fortunate enough to spend a short leave there. Perched high in Bengal it commands a marvellous view of the snow-capped Kanchinjinga peaks some 28,000 odd feet above sea level, and its neighbouring Himalayan peaks. I tried to see Everest at sunrise, but was rewarded with a magnificent view of a cloud. 'Better luck next time,' my guide – a sturdy Nepalese boy – smilingly informed me. In passing I would say the railway from the plains to the hills – miniature it seems – is one of the most outstanding engineering feats I have ever seen. In so short a letter I could never describe India. I doubt if anyone ever will. It has its 'things of beauty' and its 'objects of ugliness.' I will not dwell on the latter. There are too many in this world already. Books on India, inevitably, not without some truth, describe those peculiar to this vast country. But before closing, I must mention the Indian Army. I have been in it some three years now, and am justly proud of it. The men who comprise it are all great fighters and good soldiers, all volunteers, from the independent Pathan, the proud Punjabi of the north, to the smiling Madrassi of the south, from the Mahratta of the west to the hill tribes of the east, never forgetting 'Johnny Gurkha' of the kingdom of Nepal. All stout fellows. Records and epics speak for themselves. And so, space forbidding more, I must say adieu, with all best wishes to the people of Irlam and Cadishead. May Christmas be a happy one and the New Year brighter.

Soon after the outbreak of the war patrons of the Red Lion Hotel in Hollins Green had established a War Comforts Fund in order to send cash gifts to its members who were serving with the Armed Forces. Between its formation and November 1944 it had raised over £1,000. The patrons also set up a small Welcome Home Fund.

Ex-scout, Driver 'Rowley' Thompson wrote from Belgium to the 1st Cadishead Scoutmaster, Duncan Muir: *I am meeting with scouts every day over here. They are patrolling the bridges and roads, directing traffic and clearing up the houses, ready for occupation.*

Signalman Harry Smith, Royal Navy, wrote to the *Guardian* giving his views on post-war planning: *Sir, I have been inspired by the appeals of Onlooker to write this letter expressing my views on the post-war planning which is to be undertaken by our local Council, and to whom I address this letter through the medium of the Guardian. Very little information regarding any such plans has reached me, and so I am in a position only to make suggestions which I feel sure many other servicemen of our town will agree with. I am convinced that in this manner the post-war planners will gain valuable assistance, and I have every confidence that they will succeed. After this war and on returning home, we want to see some material reward for our sacrifices, and to be able to say, truthfully, that 'this was worth fighting for.' In my opinion the housing problem will be the greatest and one which must have priority consideration. For those who have married since the war, and those who contemplate post-war marriage, what will enable them to appreciate the blessings of peace more than a home of their own? I sincerely hope that the importance of this is realised to the fullest extent. The issue depends entirely upon united effort. My personal interest is centred around the pre-fabricated housing scheme, which is unique in its principles. A swift and satisfactory plan, and in my opinion wholly practicable in our own locality. The ultra-modern and superbly hygienic devices which these homes will provide is surely the young housewife's dream. If the Council has any intention of utilising this scheme, then I appeal to the councillors concerned to commence the solution of this vital problem now whilst they have the advantage of time.*

H.R. Bate, South Atlantic Command, sent in his views: *Sir, in reply to your impassioned appeal for letters from local members of the Forces, may I take this opportunity to express my views. First I would like to see more public places of entertainment, a library, at least one decent theatre, and last but not least a good public playing field. More 'young blood' in the Urban Council, 'lads' and 'lassies' who have fought in this war, and who know what the younger generation want. The Cadishead and Irlam I left was a district of ancient ways, and if I remember correctly a place of muddy roads and cart tracks in some parts; surely we are seeing enough mud on the battlefields? The suggestion of J.N. Howes (in July 29th, 1944 edition), is an excellent idea. Why not a Memorial Hospital? It would be a magnificent gesture to all our brave friends who have fallen in this fight for freedom. They died that we might live, and I for one, would like to live in a modern Cadishead and Irlam, a growing township which they would have been proud of had they survived. One other thing I should like to see, and this is more encouragement of sports.*

On Sunday, 5th November air cadets of the Irlam detached flight of 292 (Eccles) Squadron, ATC went with other cadets of the squadron to an operational airfield in the North West. Most of the cadets enjoyed 1½ hours flying experience.

On the same day, the local branch of the British Legion held its annual meeting. At the meeting Tom Walton (veteran of the First World War, who served with the 11th Battalion of the Manchester Regiment) proposed a resolution, which was seconded by Mr Williams, to send a resolution to the Area Conference urging that a man who was passed as medically fit for service should be regarded as fit for a pension. There were grave injustices in the granting of pensions; when a man was called up he was given a medical examination and, if he was fit, he was passed for service without considering his previous medical record. However, if, after a period of service, he was discharged and applied for a pension, his entire medical history from the time of his birth was taken into account as evidence that his disability was not attributable to war service. The slogan 'Fit to Serve – Fit for Pension' was coined and the resolution was unanimously approved. At the meeting, Benjamin Neville, chairman of the branch, outlined the support provided to ex-servicemen and women and their dependents. The Benevolent Fund had awarded immediate grants to 23 cases from the local fund, amounting to £29. In addition, special grants amounting to £15, including £5 towards a funeral account, had been received in four cases. In addition, six members had been sent to Byng House Convalescent Home, Southport.

Servicemen and ex-servicemen had sought advice on pension matters but he regretted that in one case which went before the Appeals Tribunal, the case was lost.

Signalman Harry Smith, Royal Navy, wrote a second letter to the *Guardian*: *Sir, copies of the Guardian, I am pleased to say, reach me regularly from home and I find myself developing a greater interest in home affairs, in particular, the activities in our own locality. Firstly, I wish to congratulate the billeting officers on their success with regards to the evacuee problem. In spite of their many inconveniences and trials experienced, I have no doubt that they proved the genial hospitality of the north countryman. On those members of our community who without sound reasons denied the 'guests' a friendly welcome, I do not intend to waste words. We all know how the horrors of this war have been brought to their very homes and I feel sure that it is the moment of bitter suffering which hides their gratitude. Post-war planning! I am more than eager to agree with Councillor Adams' proposals to allow the Press and public to attend the meetings of the Post-war Planning Committee. I do hope that the folks at home will take advantage of this opportunity. It is useless to express one's views within family circles alone. A more apparent interest is required. In addition to my previous statements on the importance of the housing problem, I trust that an adequate amount of attention will be paid to higher education, the success of which depends, to a great extent, upon equal opportunities. In my opinion, an educational reform is forthcoming. To conclude, a word of appeal to my fellow servicemen. Our expressions of opinion are needed now more than ever, as I have realised, and a few minutes spent on putting pen to paper is worthwhile. How about it then?*

Able Seaman D/JX237857 **William 'Bill' Taylor** of HM Landing Ship Tank 420, Royal Navy, was lost at sea on Tuesday, 7th November, aged 26.

LST 420 left Dover on 7th November carrying a party of airmen, together with trucks and supplies for RAF personnel stationed in Belgium. It was unable to enter the port of Ostend because of a severe storm and the captain decided to return to England. The ship was about a mile off the Middelkerkbank and still within sight of Ostend when it hit a mine, caught fire, broke in two, and sank. Fourteen officers and 224 other ranks, including Bill, were lost and only 31 of the crew and passengers survived. It was the greatest loss of lives on a British landing craft during the war.

Bill, the sixth son of the late James and Mary Taylor of Irlam, was educated at St Teresa's School, Irlam. He resided at 2 Liverpool Road, Higher Irlam, and worked at the Steelworks. He was a member of the works football team and had won 13 cups and four medals for football. In October 1940 he joined the Navy and served in the Mediterranean for two years and in 1941 he took part in the evacuation of Crete. He also served in the Indian Ocean. Since D-Day he had been engaged in operations in the English Channel. His guardian, Mrs A. Doolan, received the news on Saturday, 18th November that Bill was missing, presumed killed. He has no known grave and is commemorated on the Plymouth Naval Memorial, Devon. Bill Taylor's younger brother, Stoker 1st Class Frank Taylor, also served with the Royal Navy.

Able Seaman Bill Taylor, Royal Navy

Frank and Bill Taylor, Royal Navy

James 'Jim' Alban Davies of Higher Irlam, should have been on LST 420 that day but, after taking part in the previous 19 crossings of the English Channel from D-Day onwards, he was given a 48 leave pass. It goes without saying that Jim considered his leave pass to have been the luckiest he had ever been given. One of his colleagues who was on board at the time had a very lucky escape. When he tried to exit the sick berth compartment via a watertight door, he found the door jammed shut due to the force of the explosion. He then turned to find, of all things, a crowbar, which he used to lever the door open and make a safe exit. Jim and his friend could never understand why a crowbar should be in a ship's antiseptically clean sick berth compartment. In a long list of essential medical equipment, a crowbar would have been the last thing you would ever expect to find.

Two brothers, Gunner Harry Wright and Fusilier William Wright of Hollins Green, met each other in Florence, Italy. Both had been in Italy for some time. On Wednesday, 8th November Bill went on a week's leave to Florence and, knowing Harry was stationed somewhere in the neighbourhood, he made enquiries which led to their reunion four days later. They spent four days together, swapping experiences and enjoying the sights of Florence. This was their first meeting in three years. Harry said that he had never enjoyed meeting anyone so much, and both considered the experience was a foretaste of the family reunion they would have when the war was over. They had two other brothers serving in the Forces: John and, Len, the youngest, who was a prisoner of the Japanese.

James Alban Davies, Royal Navy

Members of the WJAC (Irlam Unit) and cadets of the Irlam detached flight of 292 (Eccles) Squadron, ATC held a dance at Cadishead Conservative Club, on Saturday, 11th November to raise funds for both the WJAC and ATC.

On Monday, 13th November Leading Stoker Gwilym Brown, Royal Navy, married Sergeant Mary A. Nugent (Auxiliary Territorial Service) of Liverpool, at St Mary's Church, Cadishead. Gwilym was the second son of Mr and Mrs W. Brown of 16 Graham Crescent, Cadishead.

Topical film displays were held in Irlam for members of the 42nd Battalion, Home Guard, which gave a good indication of the different types of warfare that the servicemen abroad were engaged in. During the show Lieutenant Colonel Webb, commanding officer, mentioned the stand-down. He thanked all those who had supported him so loyally during the previous 4½ years, and particularly the wives and sweethearts who, by their restraint and forbearance, had allowed their menfolk to carry on the work and training which had earned the battalion so high a reputation among Home Guard battalions. He also expressed the hope that the many friendships which had been created as a result of the Home Guard would be maintained in the future, and would be as binding in the peace as they had been during the war. He referred to the Old Comrades Associations which were being formed and he hoped that there would be many gatherings in the future. He also referred to the Stand-down Parade, which was planned for 3rd December within the battalion area, and he expressed the hope that every available man would turn out for the final parade of the battalion.

On Thursday, 16th November a ceremony took place at the British Legion when Jack Carter presented Mr J.A. Massie (president of the local branch) with a petrol driven wheelchair for use by its members. Jack and a small sub-committee had organised a number of events to raise funds for the purchase of the chair. Mr Massie paid tribute to the work done by Jack and the sub-committee and said it was evident that their hearts were in the right place. In the past the Legion had had a chair on loan from the United Services Fund, but now, thanks to Jack and his friends, the branch would have one of its own.

The local branch of the British Legion had received less than its usual allocation of poppies for Armistice Day in 1944, however, the total receipts, when counted, were found to be only slightly less than the previous year. Peter Barrow, DCM, secretary of the Irlam and Cadishead Branch of the British Legion, thanked all those involved in selling the poppies and described it as a good return for the number of poppies available. *Only 21 boxes were out*, he said, *but the sum realised was £90-16-4. Wreaths amounted to £9-1s, making a total of £99-17-4. This is a good return for the amount of poppies obtained, as we were unable to make any refills to sellers, nor to send our usual amounts to different organisations who have come forward to help in this worthy cause.* Peter said that though the results had fallen below last year they were hoping, in view of a pending change in the distribution of poppies, to obtain a greater supply next year, and make their effort a record.

A Toy Sale was held at the British Restaurant, on Saturday, 18th November which raised a total of £85 for the Irlam and Cadishead War Comforts Fund. One of the toys, a Perspex model which had been made by a Polish airman, raised £20, and a doll dressed by Mrs Cordwell of Dixon Street, realised £11.

Lance Corporal 3659994 **Frederick Roberts Allen** of the 2nd Battalion, Green Howards (Yorkshire Regiment) died in Burma on Tuesday, 21st November, aged 29.

During the summer of 1944, the 2nd Green Howards spent time with the 116th Indian Infantry Brigade, 39th Indian Infantry Division. The 116th Brigade provided specialised jungle conversion training, and infantry battalions would spend four to six months' training with the brigade before relieving a battalion at the front. On 19th September the 2nd Green Howards moved to the Arakan area of Burma and joined the 4th Indian Infantry Brigade, 26th Indian Infantry Division, to take part in the Third Arakan Offensive.

Frederick was the son of William and Margaret Allen and the husband of Clare Allen (nee Dobbin) of Cadishead, who he had married in 1940 at Leigh. Frederick is buried at Taukkyan War Cemetery, Burma. His name is missing from the Irlam and Cadishead War Memorial in Prince's Park.

Leading Sick Berth Attendant James Alban Davies married Margaret J. Dakers on Saturday, 25th November on a leave pass. He had travelled up from Devonport in the guards van of an overnight goods train, and walked all the way from Manchester to Irlam with his kitbag over his shoulder on the morning of his wedding. He wore his 'Number One' uniform for the wedding service at St Teresa's Church on Liverpool Road, and Margaret wore a wedding dress made from parachute silk. Shortly after the marriage, Jim was posted to Harland & Wolfe in Belfast to join the escort aircraft carrier HMS *Arbiter* (CVE-51), which at the time was being re-fitted and re-armed for service in the Far East.

Margaret was the daughter of Andrew and Dorothy E. Dakers of 15 Mond Road, Higher Irlam, and the sister of Norman Dakers who, at the time, was serving in northern Europe with the Royal Army Service Corps. Norman was a friend of Jim's and provided the following information: *My sister was in the Forces as well, she was in the NAAFI. She had to either go in the ATS or the NAAFI, but they wouldn't have her in the ATS because she'd had an operation when she was a kid, they wouldn't accept her so she went in the NAAFI and she was in the NAAFI all of the time during the war. We were mates Jim and I. We were mates right up to him going in the Navy. He was on the D-Day landings an all, it's a wonder I didn't bump into him somewhere because they were carting blood packs. His real name was…, they never called him Jim, his family always called him Alban. I was away in the Army when our kid got married and Jim, he got demobbed before me I think. We used to box together when we were lads, his older brother was a good boxer, he used to train us in the back garden.*

Jim was born in Abram, near Wigan, on 4th October 1921. His family moved to Irlam in 1935 during the great depression years, following the closure of several coal mines in the Wigan area where both his father and older brother had worked as underground coal cutters. The loss of work caused many families to uproot and relocate to areas where there was work, and at the time Irlam was such an area. At 15 years old, Jim went to work on the 32 inch rolling mill at the Steelworks. By 1939 the family was living at 1 Mond Road, Higher Irlam. Jim did his bit on the home front, first as a member of the St John Ambulance Brigade, and then in the Home Guard, on first aid and fire-watch duties at Irlam Hall, before volunteering for 'Hostilities Only' service with the Royal Navy. After receiving basic training Jim went on to be trained in battlefield first aid at the Royal Naval Hospital, Devonport, Plymouth.

Flying Officer Frank Mosedale (pictured) of Fighter Command was shot down during air operations over Italy. It would take two months before his mother, Hilda G. Mosedale of Brook House, Rixton, received official confirmation that her youngest son was a prisoner of war. His elder brother, Thomas, was shot down over Germany, and had been a prisoner for nearly two years.

On Sunday, 26th November 292 (Eccles) Squadron, ATC, including members of the Irlam detached flight, visited a North West aerodrome, where they were shown around the hangars and workshops. In the morning, two ex-cadets, Sergeant Cyril Bagshaw and Aircraftman (2nd Class) Edward Thwaites of the RAF, visited the squadron and gave a demonstration of life-saving.

Cyril recounted his early experiences with the RAF: *I joined the RAF in 1943 to serve as aircrew. In September 1943, at the age of 18, my parents waved me 'goodbye' from Irlam Station on my short journey to RAF Padgate, having volunteered for aircrew operations. I can remember very little of the RAF Padgate itself just outside Warrington, as it was purely an aircrew receiving centre where we were interviewed for suitability for aircrew position, i.e. be it PNB (pilot, navigator, or bomb aimer) or wireless operator/air gunner, or purely an air gunner. After arriving at Bank Quay Station in Warrington, I found myself with my little suitcase gathering up with a crowd of young men, also with their sole belongings, and being hustled into awaiting transport, then in no time at all, marching through the Camp gates. So it was at this camp, where my brief visit lasting only a couple of days, that I got my first taste of communal hut life for the next four years. After nine months training at RAF Yatesbury in Wiltshire, I completed my training there to become a sergeant wireless operator/air gunner and the photo is one of the day we were presented with our promotion. That was in June 1944, and we were held there waiting to replace lost crews. The war in Japan needed air sea rescue volunteers and for capable wireless operator mechanics for Catalina flying boat service in the Pacific, so after hanging around waiting for a posting in the UK I put my hand up for the conversion course. After completing that course at RAF Cranwell the war in the pacific ended and mercifully came to my rescue. After several postings in the UK and Middle East, I was finally posted back to RAF Burtonwood, which had then been returned from USA control. I spent my last couple of months of RAF service in the accounts section there before being de-mobilised back into Civvy Street.*

Sergeant Cyril Bagshaw, RAF
(middle row, standing 4th from left)

On 29th November the Irlam and Cadishead War Comforts Fund sent a five shilling postal order to all local men who were serving overseas. The letter on the next page was received by Private Joe Tighe, 2nd Somerset Light Infantry, who was stationed in Greece at the time.

DECEMBER
On Friday, 1st December Mrs Golda-Barr, a Polish refugee, gave a talk about her experiences at a meeting of the Irlam branch of the Commonwealth. She had been evacuated from London to Irlam in August 1944, and had been billeted with Mr and Mrs J. Robinson of Beech Avenue, Higher Irlam. Her husband, who was English, was serving with the Royal Army Service Corps. She thanked the people of Irlam and Cadishead for their kindness and hospitality, both to herself and baby, and other evacuees who had sheltered in the district. By the end of the month she had returned to live in London.

The Chairman and Committee

of the

IRLAM & CADISHEAD WAR COMFORTS FUND

send Greetings and Good Wishes for

Christmas and the New Year, and hope you

will accept the enclosed gift of 5s/-

with their compliments.

    Kindly acknowledge receipt on the

enclosed postcard.

                          Chairman.

Council Offices,
   I R L A M,
      Near Manchester.

29 NOV 1944

The 2nd December edition of the *Guardian* carried the following letter from R.T. Jackson, serving with the Royal Artillery: *Sir, no matter where I am stationed I am always sure of keeping in touch with local affairs through the Guardian. I am very interested to find that just as long ago, things at home are still the same, they have not changed and honestly I am more than disturbed when I see how other places are going so speedily ahead with their post-war planning. Years ago the people of the district wanted a public swimming bath, a library, proper sports and recreation fields. All they got was promises, now all those things could have been paid for now if they had been taken up at the time. Would anyone expect the district to get bigger and better if there are no means of attracting outsiders to come and live there? I am quite sure they could not, and 99 percent of the population would not live here if it were not for the local industries, which are their bread and butter. What is needed is younger brains with more modern ideas on the Council. I was very interested in Rev. W. Motson's subject, of men and women returning from the Forces, and I write to you as a soldier in the ranks, and who knows the soldiers' hardships, his temptations, his sufferings. I also write as one who knows what a fine fellow the British soldier is, for believe me there are no braver men beneath God's all beholding sun than our lads have proved themselves to be. They are fighting for something great, and high and holy, they are contending against tyranny, lies, savagery. Never did a nation have a greater, grander cause than we. And when they have won this glorious victory for you, do you expect them to return to the same drab, uninteresting town? I say this deliberately, it is nothing short of crime, to call men from the four corners of the earth to fight for a great cause like ours, and then to allow them to come home to nothing but promises. The least every man and woman of the district can determine God helping them that they will leave nothing undone until they see that the post-war plans of the district are something to be proud of, and really get carried out.*

On Sunday, 3rd December a great Home Guard 'stand-down' parade was held in London, and Private Robert Mort was chosen to represent Irlam and Cadishead. Robert was a veteran of the First World War, a member of the British Legion and an original member of the Local Defence Volunteers (LDV). His son, Stanley Mort, was serving with the Highland Light Infantry in France. Stanley was born in 1924, the son of Robert and Daisy Mort of 29 The Crescent, Higher Irlam. He joined the Home Guard on 15th January 1942 as Private 658, serving in Transport Section, D Company. Stanley was called up into the Army on 31st March 1943.

By this stage of the war, the strength of the Civil Defence Services had largely been dissipated, with a drastic reduction in both personnel and material. The number of personnel at first aid posts had been reduced, full-time members of the Civil Defence Services and fire guards had been discharged and surplus vehicles and materials at defence posts and centres had been sold off. The emergency mortuary on Springfield Lane, Irlam had been released, fortunately without having to be used, and the wardens' guard rooms, warden posts and first aid posts were closed.

The wedding took place at St John's Church between Driver Derek Birch, Royal Engineers (REME), and Joan Stanbank, only daughter of Mr and Mrs Stanbank of 19

Silverdale Avenue, Higher Irlam. Derek's brother, Frank K. Birch, Royal Navy, was the best man. Derek and Frank were the sons of Mr and Mrs Birch of 6 Elsinore Avenue, Irlam.

On Tuesday night, 5th December Flight-Sergeant Charles William Hood of the Royal Canadian Air Force, who was visiting the district, was knocked down by a passing American Army truck whilst crossing the road at the junction of Atherton Lane, Cadishead. He was taken to Eccles and Patricroft Hospital suffering a suspected fractured skull.

On Thursday, 7th December a local scout, Eric Bolton, left the district to join the Royal Engineers. He had been a scout patrol leader and drummer in the Scout Band. He was the fifteenth scout from the district to join up. He later served in northern Europe and a *Guardian* report mentioned that he was home on leave from Holland in October 1945.

Sapper 1941239 **William Palin** of No. 4 Bomb Disposal Company, Royal Engineers, was killed whilst engaged on mine clearance duties on a beach along the south east coast on Monday, 11th December, aged 32.

William joined the Army in 1940 and his unit was responsible for the disposal of many unexploded and time-bombs which fell during the Blitz, a job which required the strongest of nerves.

Born in Sale in 1912 (birth registered at Bucklow), he was the son of James and Elizabeth Ann Palin (nee Davies) of 27 Fir Street, Cadishead. He was educated at St Martin's School, Ashton-upon-Mersey. In late 1936 he married Lena May Hamilton at St John's Church, Irlam, and they resided at 27 Fir Street, Cadishead (an address they shared with William's parents). Before the war he was employed as a bricklayers' labourer at the Steelworks.

Members of a Royal Artillery rocket battery acted as bearers at his funeral. Reverend Lee officiated at the service at St John's Church and at the graveside and the mourners included William's widow, his parents, his three sisters, Mrs Burgess, Mrs Walker and Miss M. Palin, and his brother, Private J. Palin. He is buried at Irlam (St John the Baptist) Churchyard Extension and his headstone bears the epitaph: *He gave his life that we may live. Sadly missed by his loving wife May.* He is also commemorated on the St Martin's War Memorial, Ashton-upon-Mersey.

The Welcome Home Fund and the War Comforts Fund were amalgamated into a single fund, which required the approval of the County Council who had to amend the certificate of registration accordingly. £500 was already invested and the committee's aim was to maintain a substantial balance for a fitting welcome home to those who were serving from the district in the Forces. At November's meeting of the fund, the members discouraged the formation of individual street welcome home groups and emphasised that it was illegal to collect money unless the fund was properly registered under the War Charities Act, 1940. The committee considered that the central fund together with the combined efforts of the district would provide a more suitable welcome home gift to the servicemen and women. Members of the Engineers' Works Committee of the Steelworks donated £19 to the fund. In a letter to Mary Bowker, secretary of the fund, Mr A. Callaghan, secretary of the Engineers' Works explained that the money had been raised by collections at the works: *We send our best wishes to the lads and girls who have left our township for the Forces.*

On Saturday, 16th December Arthur Day passed away at the house of his son, at 11 New Moss Road, Cadishead, aged 74. Arthur was a native of Ilford, Essex, who had moved to Cadishead to escape the V1 flying bomb attacks.

During the week of 16th to 23rd December three local soldiers, serving in the South East Asia Command, appeared in a newsreel which was shown in a Manchester cinema. They had been given the opportunity to send messages to their families. From Bombay, Corporal Jack Drummond, RAF, assured his parents that he was fit and well. His parents were Mr and Mrs J. Drummond, the steward and stewardess of Irlam Catholic Club. In the words of his mother, the film showed he was in the best of health and spirits. Also in India, Sergeant Thomas E. Vann of 39 Allenby Road, Cadishead, gave a message to his parents and friends. The third person to speak was called Roberts of Cadishead (unfortunately his Christian name is not known).

WS/Sergeant 4345345 John Wrench, East Yorkshire Regiment attached to 2 (NY) King's African Rifles (the Battalion was part of 21 (East African) Brigade, 11 (East African) Division, 33 Indian Corps) was awarded the Military Medal for gallantry in the Assam. His award recommendation read: *During the period under review 16 Aug – 15 Nov 44, though on the strength of the Battalion as a Mechanist NCO, Sergeant Wrench volunteered for and has led the Battalion HQ Platoon from the time the Battalion first went into action. Throughout the whole period his devotion to duty, his coolness under fire, and his desire to get to grips with the enemy, have been fine examples of the highest military qualities. Sergeant Wrench has led his platoon in an assault in an entrenched enemy position at ZIBAW, BURMA, in November 44. With great bravery and dash he went forward at the head of his men and was completely successful in carrying out the difficult task given to him. Shortly after this action, this NCO took out his platoon as protection to two officers making a reconnaissance of another enemy position. An enemy light machine-gun opened fire at very short range, and Sergeant WRENCH was hit in two places. Despite his wounds, the NCO continued to lead his platoon in carrying out its mission successfully and he refused to withdraw till the reconnaissance was completed. Sergeant WRENCH has shown that he is a leader who inspires his men to undertake cheerfully the most hazardous tasks and his displays of bravery and determination without thought of his own safety are of the very highest order.*

Leading Aircraftman Colin Campbell, RAF met his elder brother, Sergeant Major Leo Campbell, Royal Artillery, in Holland. Thirty-six year old Colin was married and lived with his wife at 38 Francis Road, Irlam. He had joined the RAF in 1941 and went to France in October 1944, and then moved to Holland. Thirty-eight year old Leo resided at Lorne Grove, Urmston. He joined the Army in early 1940, and went overseas shortly after D-Day. Both men had worked at the CWS Soap Works. Another brother, Sergeant Major Frank Campbell, was serving in the Army in India. A fourth brother, Miles, had served, but had been discharged from the Army (c.1943) after a motorcycle accident in Dorset while carrying despatches. They were the sons of Mr and Mrs M.C. Campbell of 29 Dixon Street, Irlam.

(L-R) Leading Aircraftman Colin Campbell and Sergeant Major Leo Campbell

The Germans launched the Ardennes Offensive (also known as the Battle of the Bulge) on 20th December. Gunner 1109637 Thomas Vaudrey of 209 Medium Battery, 53rd (London) Medium Regiment, Royal Artillery, was one of the local men involved in opposing the offensive. His regiment first heard rumours of the offensive late on 20th December and were ordered to prepare to move next day. At 8.15am on 21st December they moved to positions north of Genappe (about 40 miles south of Antwerp). 209 Battery then moved to Gochenée to provide artillery support to 23rd Hussars (29th Armoured Brigade). By 7.30pm the guns were in position but remained silent. On Christmas Day they moved to Givet and by 9.25am they were in action, firing east of the River Meuse, as the 23rd Hussars advanced towards Beauraing. Mopping up operations continued throughout Boxing Day, with the guns firing on the instruction of air observation posts at pockets of enemy troops. On 2nd January the battery received orders to support the Fife and Forfar Yeomanry who were advancing eastwards towards Bure and Grupont. The next day 209 Battery supported the 7th Parachute Battalion into Wavreille.

Gunner Thomas Vaudrey, Royal Artillery

Between 4th and 7th January they rested and then on 9th January they supported the Royal Ulster Rifles. They continued to support the advance until 12th January when the battle moved out of range of the guns. 209 Battery moved into billets in Ave-et-Auffe and remained there until 18th January when they were ordered to move through Tilburg towards Loon op Zand, in Holland. Here they experienced poor living conditions but the period was not very busy, with an average of only eight rounds a day being fired.

Prior to the Ardennes Offensive 53rd (London) Medium Regiment, Royal Artillery had been involved in the Normandy landings and had taken part in Operation Charnwood in support of the 3rd Division (8th to 9th July 1944) and Goodwood in support of 51st Highland Division (18th to 20th July). Both operations were attempts to relieve the city of Caen, which was finally cleared of German opposition on 20th July. On 17th August the regiment came under the command of 7th Armoured Division, which was tasked with clearing the high ground east of Lisieux. This was a new form of warfare for the artillery as they had to support fast-moving armoured units. They remained with the division until 29th August when they paused near Routout while the armoured units raced across north east France and into Belgium. Next they supported the 49th Division's attack on Le Havre. On 29th September they moved, in poor weather conditions, to Scherpenberg in Belgium to support the 2nd Canadian Division. Two days later they came under the command of 1st Polish Armoured Division and supported the capture of the village of Merksplas. The battery was with the Poles at Rouwleegd but then on 18th October they left to take part in a joint operation with 49th and 4th Canadian Division around Wustwesel, near Antwerp.

53rd (London) Medium Regiment, Royal Artillery, rejoined the Polish Armoured Division on 28th October for a short time and on 11th November they rejoined the 3rd Division at Oploo, near Overloon in Holland, to clear the left bank of the River Maas. At 9.55pm on 1st December they fired a counter bombard for the attack on Wanssum. In a country as flat as Holland any high point was invaluable as an observation post and windmills and church towers were often used by both sides for this purpose. This made any elevated man-made structure a target for the artillery. On 2nd December 209 Battery moved to positions at Hoogerbroek, south east of Venray, to engage the windmill at Larenbeck, which was being used by the Germans as an observation post. After reconnaissance on 3rd December 50 rounds were allocated to the task and by 12.40 on 4th December the windmill had been demolished. The next day they were ordered to destroy a church tower north west of Wellerooi, on the east bank of the River Maas. This was demolished on 6th December. On 7th December they moved to La Hulpe, south east of the Belgium capital, Brussels, where they took time out to clean their guns and vehicles.

At the end of December the 'Town Topics' columnist wrote 'a warning note' due to recent damage that had been caused across the district, he wrote: *The outbreak of window smashing seems to have subsided, but it has been followed by damage of another kind.*

Recently, RCAF personnel uprooted a signpost at the corner of Glazebrook Lane and carried it several hundred yards away. What good purpose this piece of senseless nonsense served it is hard to say. The time has come for some plain speaking to our Canadian cousins, but first of all let me make it quite clear that this is not a general attack on all and sundry. I have many good friends among the Canadians – men whom I am proud to call friends – and I know they don't agree with that small minority of their countrymen whose one means of expressing themselves when they have had one over the eight is by going around smashing things. To this minority – who appear to be eternally walking around with chips on their shoulder – trailing their coats as the Irish would say – it must be made quite clear that we will stand for so much hooliganism – and no more. Rightly or wrongly this particular element seek to assert their imagined superiority over the decadent Britisher (whom, I might remind them, has been considered decadent by everybody from the Romans onward) by seeking quarrels, damaging public property and generally making an infernal nuisance of themselves. In the process they have earned for themselves the reputation of being 'crackers' – or, in other words, fit candidates for the nut-house. We, in this district, have consistent contacts with overseas visitors in peace and war. We have entertained Canadians, Americans, Poles, Danes, Norwegians, Belgians, Free French, West Indians, Chinese and people from every quarter of the globe. All in all, we have found them friendly and law-abiding. Whatever opinions they may have had of us they have politely kept it to themselves – and we have respected that. They have also fallen in with our ideas of the sacredness of public property and observed them. Nor have they walked around looking for trouble. During their brief periods with us they have been content to do, as we do, to conform to the law and to behave as they would behave in their own home towns. But, decadent or not, we will not tolerate a minority of men, no matter what their nationality, whose idea of a good time is to make themselves as objectionable as possible. In doing so they bring contempt on themselves and discredit to their own great country. If the fact that they are earning the dislike of many people does not deter them in future, perhaps a minute's reflection on the harm they are doing to their country's reputation will induce them to remember they are soldiers, and presumably, men, and, as such, should be ambassadors for their nation. When American troops first came to Britain they behaved like gentlemen. That standard has been maintained and, as a result, Americans are welcomed in thousands of British homes. So are thousands of Canadians. But it seems a pity that a senseless and irresponsible minority should be allowed to besmirch the fair name of Canada.

A letter appeared in the 23rd December edition of the *Guardian*, written by Mrs E. Atkinson and Mrs F. Houghton, under the title *Marlborough Road Remembers*: *Sir, we would like to thank friends and neighbours of Marlborough Road, Higher Irlam, for their co-operation in helping us to send to the 55 men and women of Marlborough Road serving in HM Forces, a Christmas gift of 10s each.*

Members of the foundry department of the Steelworks had formed their own Comforts Fund back in November 1940 for employees of the department serving in the Forces. By Christmas 1944 the fund had sent £1,030 to the 15 members serving overseas. Each member of the department received regular gifts of 7s-6d, an amount that was doubled at Christmas time.

HMS *Renown*

HMS *Renown* served with the Eastern Fleet throughout 1944. She arrived at Colombo, Ceylon (modern day Sri Lanka) on 27th January and then sailed for the naval base at Trincomalee. Leading Stoker Walter McArthur was aboard HMS *Renown*: *I served most of my time down in Ceylon there, Trincomalee. Well the reason for that being that when they surrendered Singapore, they'd no main supply base, so they made one in Ceylon, not Colombo but the other side, Trincomalee side. They had a massive harbour, a very, very deep harbour, so they could make a base there, and they moored it into there. We operated from there. We could go from there right up to Burma as far as the top end and right down to Australia. Well that was our main run, up and down there, stopping the Japs getting the oil from Burma. Go out for ten day runs, go out so far, Indian Ocean, they had some idea where there was something happening and go and bombard them, go back. They called them club runs, ten day runs, five days out, bombard them, five days back again.*

Between 21st March and 1st April *Renown* took part in Operation Diplomat, which was an exercise to get various units operating together as a fleet and also to rendezvous with USS *Saratoga* and her escort, in the Bay of Bengal. During the operation the fleet practiced re-fuelling at sea, which was a relatively new and difficult procedure.

Normally the carrier was with us and maybe two destroyers, or three destroyers, there was other ships with us an all. We'd oil at sea and water at sea. My mother's name was Phoebe, I've got a picture in there, it's when we're getting oil off, one of the ships was called Phoebe funnily enough, and when we were getting oil off her I'd written on the back 'oilly from Phoebe' she wasn't well pleased with it like. What used to happen was we'd come alongside, we'd couple up oil, couple up with our crane, then steam alongside one another for about four hours, quite perilous you know if you weren't aware, a time or two we'd spring apart and that'd snap, and get a new one in. Then the smaller ships would come along, the destroyers would come along and get some oil off her. We could burn an awful lot of oil, I forget now, 100 ton a day, something like that. And fresh water an all because your boilers are used with water, so fresh water was a big thing with it you see, and you'd get a water tanker come as well and top up with water. They had a small boiler for that but it wasn't big enough, it was only used in harbour, it was only a small one but at sea in four or five days you could use your oil up, you know, if you're doing economical steaming, about 17 knots, 18 knots, you could last for 12, 14 days, but if you started doing high speed, you get up to 26, 27 knots, four days and it's gone. You had a chief petty officer in charge of you but you were doing it with him anyway. Me and this chief used to work great together, he had two or three under him and I'd have one under me, and I'd be switching tanks or pumping tanks whatever, water, to keep him, if he was taking oil on the port side I'd take water on the starboard side to try and keep it dead, because the skipper wanted it level so he could fire his guns.

HMS *Renown* oiling HMS *Phoebe*

On 16th April the combined British and American fleet, left Trincomalee to carry out Operation Cockpit, an air strike on port and oil facilities at Sabang Island (off the northern part of Sumatra). At 5.30am on 19th April the aircraft carriers, HMS *Illustrious* and USS *Saratoga*, launched their aircraft. The air strike damaged two merchant ships, oil tanks were set alight, the barracks and communications station at Lho Nga airfield were damaged and 24 enemy aircraft were destroyed on the ground. At 7am, the aircraft began to return to the carriers. Later that day the Japanese launched an air attack on the fleet but this was beaten off by a concentrated barrage from the fleet. During 30 minutes of action, HMS *Renown* fired 700 rounds of

4.5 inch anti-aircraft shells. Six Japanese aircraft were shot down. On 21st March the fleet arrived back at Trincomalee.

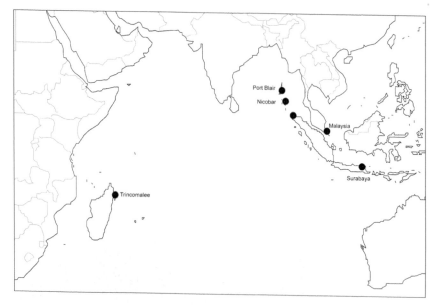

HMS *Renown*'s Theatre of Operations

Walter explained: *Our job mainly after that was escort duty with the carriers, loaded with twenty 4.5s, 60 or 70 Oerlikons, three sets of Chicago Pianos, them bang-bang-bang things; Oerlikons that used to fire bullets as big as your finger, twin Oerlikons, there was 40 or 50 of them aboard loaded with anti-aircraft fire so when you got two or three ships protecting the destroyers and the other ships, protecting the aircraft carriers mainly, they could knock anything out of the sky, the Prince of Wales and Repulse was a big warning to them.*

On 6th May the fleet departed to carry out another air strike, Operation Transom, this time to attack the port of Surabaya on the island of Java. At 6am on 17th May the fleet was stationed 180 miles south of the target, and the carriers launched their aircraft, which arrived over the target at 8am. Ten ships were attacked in the harbour, oil tanks were destroyed as were the dock facilities and 14 aircraft on the ground. After the attack the fleet sailed to Exmouth Gulf in Western Australia, where they bade farewell to USS *Saratoga*. After refuelling, the fleet departed for Trincomalee.

Now when you went to sea you had a sea job then, you was either in the boiler rooms, they didn't need you in harbour you see so immediately you went to sea you'd got boiler rooms, engine rooms, all the jobs, anti-flooding systems, was always on watch somewhere. You doubled up on all the conning tower where the skipper and all the crew was at the top, was organised, right down at the bottom there was a duplicate of every one so that if the top was wiped out they could continue with the orders from down below. And every so far was big doors with dogs on, was all shut so if you'd got a bomb with a hole through it would only flood so far, it didn't matter about you being in there but then it wouldn't go that way or that way, it'd be confined to that small area.

Leading Stoker Walter McArthur (standing right) and crew mates

When asked whether the crew accepted that they may be locked into a flooding area, Walter replied: *Oh yeah, yeah, oh aye and you didn't know, the boiler room has a loudspeaker you could hear it, but in engine rooms and gear rooms on the outside and all the other outside auxiliary machinery you didn't have owt, so you didn't know whether you were firing or they were firing at you, you'd hear a bloody big bang and the ships go over when..., when the 15 inch go off the ship goes over, the backlash kind of thing, but you didn't know whether they'd hit you with one and it was going over that way. You'd be like wondering what the hell's happening till the phone would ring or you'd ring up the boiler room 'Chief, what's happening?' 'Oh you're alright, nothing's happening.' They called us a lucky ship, we was very fortunate. Mind you we always used to operate mostly with good armament and also with carriers, like I say next door but one, Stan Wilson, he was on the Illustrious, we was with her a lot.*

On 19th June the fleet sailed for the Andaman Islands to carry out an air strike against the harbour and airfield at Port Blair (Operation Pedal). At 4.45am on 21st June *Illustrious* launched its aircraft, which were over the target at 5.30am and back on board the carrier by 7am. The next day, they sailed back into Trincomalee.

The skipper, he was bomb happy. We were 100 mile off Singapore when he pipes over the loudspeaker 'we're now 100 mile off Singapore. We hope the Japanese will come out and fight.' And everybody's saying 'we hope the buggers stop in.'

HMS *Renown*

At 4pm on 22nd July Task Force 62 (comprising four battleships, two aircraft carriers, seven cruisers and nine destroyers) sailed from Trincomalee to undertake Operation Crimson. This was an air strike and bombardment of the harbour and oil installations at Sabang. In addition, two submarines were deployed off the coast of Sabang for air sea rescue. By 3am on the morning of 25th July the fleet was in position and divided into two distinct groups: bombardment and air. *Renown* was part of the bombardment group which contained four battleships, six cruisers and seven destroyers. The air group was made up of the two aircraft carriers, one cruiser and two destroyers. The strike force of 51 aircraft and eight spotters started to take-off from the two carriers at 5.35am. The spotters were tasked with reporting fall of shot to the four cruisers, each of which fired shells that burst with a different colour to help the spotters. The bombardment group opened fire at 6.30am and continued for 20 minutes, in which time the four ships fired almost 300 rounds of 15 inch shells. At 7am the destroyers went into the bay to attack targets of opportunity, at 7.30am the strike aircraft returned to the carriers. On the return voyage the fleet was attacked twice by Japanese aircraft, five of which were shot down. They arrived back at Trincomalee on 27th July.

On 15th October *Renown* took part in Operation Millet, which was a series of air strikes and bombardment of the Nicobar Islands. At 5pm, Task Force 63, divided into three groups: two bombardment groups and an air group, sailed from Trincomalee. Two days later they were in position to launch their attack and at 6.30am on 17th October the first strike aircraft took off from the carriers to attack the airfields on Nicobar Island. Later in the day the two bombardment groups attacked Malacca on Car Nicobar Island and Nancowry harbour on Nancowry Island. Two days later, after refuelling, the fleet resumed air and bombardment on the islands. During the day, nine Japanese aircraft attacked the fleet, seven of which were shot down for the loss of three allied aircraft. Unfortunately, Operation Millet caused little damage to the Japanese due to a lack of worthwhile targets. This was the last time that *Renown* fired her main armament in anger. The fleet arrived back at Trincomalee on 22nd October.

On 8th December *Renown* left Trincomalee for Durban for a refit, remaining there until 26th February 1945. On this day she set sail for Trincomalee, arriving on 7th March. After a short time, she was ordered to return to the UK to replace HMS *Rodney* in the Home Fleet. *Renown* left Trincomalee on 30th March, sailed through the Suez Canal and arrived at Scapa Flow on 14th April. On 16th April she was moored off Rosyth: *We got in, came back to Scotland. What happened was, we'd just been to Durban for a refit, only for a short one, about a fortnight, three weeks, and they ordered us home straightaway because they thought old Jerry was gonna escape on one of his pocket battleships, so they ordered us home fast. We left Durban, the Old Lady in White singing there, you know the big microphone, famous for it, every ship that left she was there, an opera singer singing away, beautiful it was, quite a scene really. We steamed out, we didn't hardly stop, we were coming flat out but halfway through the Med word came that Hitler was dead, or it was over, so we kept on coming home then and we got to Scotland and they gave us immediately 14 days leave.*

King George VI visiting HMS *Renown*
1945

Postscript: On 10th May 1945, shortly after VE Day, the German Naval Delegation boarded *Renown* to make arrangements for Allied warships to enter German ports. Two days later *Renown* sailed for Portsmouth where she remained for a month. On 23rd July she sailed to Plymouth where she was repainted and smartened up for a visit by His Majesty King George VI and American President Harry Truman on 2nd August. This fine ship was placed on the disposal list in 1948 and sold for scrap.

On Christmas Eve, the Germans launched 35 V1s towards Manchester. The crew of the anti-aircraft unit situated at the back of Peel Green Cemetery were called to action when a V1 was reported in the area. By the time they got the gun ready for action the V1 had passed and it went on to explode in Worsley, killing five year old Brian Walter Ainsbury of 20 Woodstock Drive, Worsley. Local man, Arthur Wilkins, was a member of the gun crew which was commanded by Sergeant George Stephenson (in peacetime, a linesman in professional football). There were several such anti-aircraft units in the region, mainly along the Manchester ship Canal, which the Germans used as a navigation aid for the raids on Manchester, Salford and Trafford Park. There were four units on the canal between the Boat House Inn and Peel Green, two of which were dummies. It is believed that these guns had one confirmed 'kill', a German aircraft which had been damaged over Liverpool, shot at from Irlam and which then crashed on a hill outside Stockport.

Arthur of 29 Princes Avenue, Higher Irlam, was a pre-war Territorial (7th Battalion, Lancashire Fusiliers), who was called up at the beginning of the war. He spent about nine months in the Regular Army but, once the threat of invasion had receded, he was recalled back to the Steelworks for war work under the Essential Works Order. He joined the Home Guard and one day saw a notice at the Steelworks calling for volunteers for gun crews. As his training and experience in the Territorial Army was as a gunner he immediately volunteered.

On Boxing Day, the Captain class frigates HMS *Capel* (K470) and HMS *Affleck* (K462) were patrolling, along with HM Ships *Cranstoun*, *Burges* and *Lochkillin*, in the English Channel, in the vicinity of H8 buoy ten miles north of the Cherbourg breakwater. *Capel* and *Affleck* had been built in America under the Lend-Lease Agreement and operated out of Belfast with the 1st Escort Group. A submarine's snorkel had been spotted the day before so all ships were on high alert. At 12.24pm, a torpedo fired from German U-boat U486 struck *Capel* forward of the bridge and a second torpedo struck her hedgehog magazine. The explosion destroyed the bridge and it seems probable that it broke the ship in two.

An eye witness, Roy Worley, was on board HMS *Affleck* and saw the torpedoes strike *Capel*: *Suddenly before my eyes, the Capel was torpedoed and everything forward of the bridge disappeared in a cloud of smoke, and what was left of the ship aft of the bridge started sinking.* Soon *Capel* was bow down and stern up in the water. After the second explosion, Able Seaman Stan Wilkinson hurried aft to render safe the depth charges before abandoning ship. As he completed the task he saw a third torpedo race towards *Capel* and then pass under her raised stern to hit *Affleck's* stern. *Affleck* had turned to pick up survivors from *Capel*. While *Affleck's* crew worked to keep her afloat, the frigate started to drift onto the partly submerged *Capel* and unsuccessful events were made to avoid a collision. *Affleck* struck *Capel* a glancing blow on her port side, just forward of the projecting stern and then the two ships drifted apart. Another witness to the sinking of HMS *Capel* was Able Seaman Charles Campbell: *Action stations sounded and we all rushed to our positions. We closed watertight doors and on arrival on deck we saw Capel on her starboard side with no bows. Her magazine must have blown because she was now only two thirds of a ship. The stern half was wallowing and there were many men in the water. We saw survivors jumping overboard or launching life rafts. In these few minutes it struck me as being such a lovely day, so why this?* Seventy-six of *Capel's* crew lost their lives, along with eight from *Affleck*. Survivors of both ships were taken to Cherbourg where they were fed and cared for by the US Army.

HMS *Capel*

Able Seaman JX296940 Stanley Wilkinson was one of the survivors from HMS *Capel*. He was wounded during the sinking and at first his family was informed that he was missing at sea. Fortunately a second telegram was sent on 1st January from the Royal Navy at Portsmouth to his sister, Mrs Elizabeth Lomax, which read: *I am sorry to have to inform you that your brother, Stanley Wilkinson, A.B. P/JX 296940, has been injured while on war service and admitted to hospital at Cherbourg, France. His condition has not been reported as serious or dangerous, and no further communications will be sent to you unless any such report is received. I hope you will soon hear reassuring news from him direct.*

On 1st January 1945 Stanley was moved from Cherbourg to England, arriving in Portland at 6pm. The next day he was received at Royal Naval Base Portsmouth at 6.15pm.

Stanley was born in Warrington on 5th March 1923 and his war-time address was 76 Fox Street, Bank Quay, Warrington. His pre-war occupation was rubber washer cutter. He enlisted on 18th September 1941 and volunteered to serve until the end of the war. His description was 5 feet 4½ inches tall, with brown hair, brown eyes and a sallow complexion. He did his basic training at HMS *Collingwood* between 18th September 1941 and 2nd January 1942 before joining HMS *Canopus*, a shore-based establishment in Alexandria, on 5th January and remained there until 10th June. On 11th June he joined his first ship, HMS *Roberts*, a Roberts class monitor. On 17th August Stanley was promoted from ordinary seaman to able seaman. HMS *Roberts* took part in Operation Torch (the invasion of North Africa between 21st October and 7th November 1942), where she was damaged by two 500lb bombs. Stanley left HMS *Roberts* on 12th February 1943 and, after a stint in the UK, he went to the USA where he was allocated to *Saker* BDE, which was a shore base in Washington for servicemen waiting for ships under construction. On 4th September he joined the newly built HMS *Capel*, which, on 9th April 1944, was attached to the 1st Escort Group working out of Belfast. *Capel* was employed on patrols in the seas between the Irish Sea and the Scottish Isles and then anchored in Moelfre Bay in Anglesey awaiting a role in the Normandy landings. On 5th May she sailed to the western end of the English Channel to undertake anti-submarine screen patrolling to protect the landings. On 18th June she returned to Belfast. After Cherbourg fell to the Allies, *Capel* escorted convoys across the Channel to and from Cherbourg with rest periods spent in Plymouth. In late 1944 the group was involved in patrolling the convoy route to Antwerp.

After recovering from the injuries Stanley suffered in the sinking of *Capel* he joined Landing Ship Tank 3505 on 20th June 1945 and remained with her until New Year's Eve 1945. He was demobilised on 21st March 1946. He re-enlisted into the Navy on 3rd September 1947 for a period of 12 years (seven in the Navy and five in Reserve) as Able Seaman S/MX766330, and was employed in connection with the naval stores and victualing, messing and clothing work in the Royal Navy. On 9th April 1949 Stanley married Bessie Marshall, the daughter of First World War veteran, Frank Marshall, and at first they resided with Bessie's parents at 1 York Road, Cadishead, before moving to 2 Warwick Road, Cadishead. He was invalided from the Navy on the grounds of ill-health on 21st August 1951. His character throughout both stints in the Navy was described as very good.

Able Seaman Stanley Wilkinson, Royal Navy

One of the longest standing members of the local Home Guard was William Hughes of 11 Moss Lane, Cadishead. Born in 1911, Robert joined the Home Guard when it was established on 6th June 1940, serving as Private 272 in 3 Platoon and later 4 Platoon of D Company. He was still in the Home Guard when it was stood down on 3rd December 1944.

In the years when our Country

was in mortal danger

WILLIAM HUGHES

who served 8 JUNE 1940-31 DECEMBER 1944

gave generously of his time and

powers to make himself ready

for her defence by force of arms

and with his life if need be.

George R.I.

THE HOME GUARD

CHAPTER EIGHT
1945

Do not think they are forgotten – indeed theirs has been the greatest sacrifice of all

1945 would be a memorable year, with victory over Germany in May followed by the defeat of Japan in August. The successes of 1944, with the collapse of the Italians, achievements in the Far East and the D-Day landings in Normandy, had been followed by swift but hard fought victories in France, Belgium and Holland. The year would start with the Germans being pushed back over their own frontier. At the same time, the Russian Army was advancing through east Germany, overwhelming defiant German resistance.

By the middle of the year the Japanese Army was all but defeated but stubborn resistance would have made the final battles extremely costly in terms of casualties. The Americans brought the war to a swift conclusion by using the newly developed atom bomb on the cities of Hiroshima and Nagasaki.

Locally, many people were becoming concerned with what the district would be like after the war, with housing for the returning servicemen and women at the top of the agenda.

JANUARY
Air supremacy was a vital ingredient of the Allies successes since the Normandy landings. The anti-aircraft units of the Royal Artillery and RAF Regiment played an important role in controlling the airspace over Europe. On 1st January the Luftwaffe launched Operation Bodenplatte, a series of attacks on Allied airfields that attempted to wrest back control of the skies from the Allies in an effort to support the Ardennes Offensive (Battle of the Bulge). Although the attack caught the Allies by surprise and destroyed many aircraft on the ground, it did not achieve its objective. There were very few casualties among the Allied airmen and the destroyed aircraft were replaced within a week. The Germans, on the other hand, suffered a major setback, losing aircrew which could not be replaced.

The following account was written by Gunner W. Price of 48 Lords Street, Cadishead, about his experiences while serving with an anti-aircraft unit in north west Europe: *Sir, reading in the Guardian that you would welcome letters from local men in the Forces I thought I would like to send you an account of the exploits of my regiment; on New Year's Day, the day Jerry dared to send his planes over in force and suffered heavily for it. On the particular day my regiment had four troops in action, and two in rest, my troop being one of those in rest. It was a lovely morning with a clear sky following a heavy overnight frost. About ten o'clock the sky was suddenly filled with that particular sound associated with fighter planes and suddenly followed by the sound of Ack-Ack bursting. The next minute the sky seemed to be full of Jerry planes flying just over the tree tops, they were FW 190 and ME 109. My colleagues busily engaged in cleaning the guns were suddenly galvanised into action, and ran the guns into vantage points, and within minutes of opening fire an FW was observed to have smoke pouring from it, and it was watched till it crashed. Meanwhile the four troops who were officially in action were having the time of their lives. This was what they had longed for since the early days in France. D (for dog) troop had a grand time. One of their detachments shot three planes down and had a share in a fourth. Altogether the regiment shot down seven planes, had five probable kills and a share in two others all in less than an hour. The total score of planes constituted the largest official score to the credit of any single LAA regiment in this action, and the regiment can now claim 59 German aircraft in NW Europe, 42 certainly destroyed and 17 probably destroyed. One of the troops went ashore on D-Day. In closing I might add that I eagerly await the arrival of the Guardian each week. There are also a number of Warrington men in my regiment.*

One of the anti-aircraft units involved in repelling the attack was 2873 Squadron. Leading Aircraftman 1540731 William Sidney Perrin, RAF Regiment, was serving with this squadron. On 1st January the squadron fired 565 rounds from entrenched positions in Helmond, southern Holland, shooting down four German planes and damaging others.

William was born in 1923, the son of Peter and Mary Ellen Perrin (nee Yates) of 68 Bank Street, Glazebrook. William later moved to Cadishead. He enlisted on 6th August 1941, aged 18 years and six months. He married Annie Alldred in February 1942 and their son Alan, was born in April of the following year, while William was stationed at RAF Shawbury. William was posted to 2873 Squadron on formation in June 1943. This was an anti-aircraft unit equipped with vehicle mounted Browning machine-guns. The squadron moved to Eastbourne where its first task was to combat the Luftwaffe's 'tip and run' raids. The squadron converted to the light anti-aircraft role within 2nd Tactical Air Force in April 1944 and went overseas to Beny-sur-Mer, France on 19th August 1944. The unit served in France, Belgium and Holland. William kept a record of his movements through Europe: 28th August to Boisney, 7th September to Fresnoy Foley, and on 20th September to Fort Rouge at St Omer. Between 20th and 27th September they were stationed at Ghent (Belgium). On 8th October they moved to Eindhoven (Holland) and then on 29th November to Helmond. 3rd January 1945 to Gilze, 5th April to Grave, 7th April to Nordhorn (Germany) and on 1st May to Lingen. After VE Day, they moved on 18th May to Varrelbusch, 26th May to Langenhagen, 30th May to Hustedt. In June 1945 they were stationed on the Dortmund Ems Canal, 20th November to Wesendorf and finally to Dedelstorf on 1st December 1945, where the squadron was disbanded. William returned to England and was demobbed on 3rd December 1945.

Leading Aircraftman William Sidney Perrin, RAF Regiment

William's brother, Osborne Peter Perrin, also served with the RAF. Prior to being called up he was a member of D Company of the local Home Guard, which he had joined on 20th October 1941. Osborne was born on 27th December 1920.

The presence of so many American and Canadian servicemen resulted in a number of weddings with local women, most of whom would emigrate after the war. One such wedding took place on Saturday, 6th January at St Mary's Church, Cadishead, between Leading Aircraftman David James Thomas, eldest son of Mr and Mrs D.J. Thomas of Welland, Ontario, Canada and Ida Molyneaux, youngest daughter of Mr and Mrs W. Molyneaux (possibly William Molyneaux a veteran of the First World War) of 36 Kitchener Avenue, Cadishead. A wedding took place later in the month, at Cadishead Wesleyan Church of Sergeant Richard B. Phillips (USAAF), from Lansery, Michigan, USA and Dora Leighton, the younger daughter of Mr and Mrs G.W. Leighton of 158 Liverpool Road, Cadishead. Other weddings of this nature throughout the year included the marriage at Cadishead Wesleyan Church of Corporal Robert R. Lesy (RCAF) of Lafleche, Saskatchewan, Canada, and Winifred Street, the second daughter of Mr and Mrs H. Street of 22 Fir Street, Cadishead (possibly Harry Street, a veteran of the First World War). Leading Aircraftman Gorman of Ontario, Canada, married Jean Dixon, eldest daughter of Mr and Mrs Frank Dixon of 14 Lords Street, Cadishead, at St Teresa's Church, Irlam. The bride's brother, Flight Sergeant Frank Dixon, acted as groomsman.

On 8th January a patrol of the 2nd Manchesters, including Private Tom Yates, was ambushed by the Japanese in Burma. In 2012, Tom described the ambush to the authors and explained how he came to lose his friend, Lance Corporal 3533341 Frederick Fitzsimmons. Even after all these years the raw emotion was evident and Tom welled up as he spoke: *I think January '45, the end of the bloody war. We were there another 12 months after. He was a bloody good mate. This was why I lost touch with other people. He got, we got ambushed. We got ambushed that's, where the hell was that…, once, twice. Once outside Swaybo and that's where he got done, we were taking this place and we walked in and it was all low shrub like that, about this high you know, we was with the infantry out there, not behind like they used to be. When you stopped you always had to form a box, you'd have infantry and you'd have troops here, we helped on the corners, and you'd be attached to say the company of the Camerons today and perhaps be with them for a week or two, then the next time you'd be with a company of Worcesters, and Dorsets, you see machine-gunners just going out with the infantry. What upset me with Fred, he got captured and tortured and killed, and we couldn't find him for two days, and I never wrote to his parents, cos I thought I'll just let them think he got killed ordinary. You were blazin' bloody mad with 'em when you found out. I mean they didn't take prisoners when we was advancing down there you know. They didn't take prisoners, the Japs. But to do that to people. I'm glad I got that out again. The atrocities you see, it's bloody wrong.*

Members of 'Q' Company of the 42nd Battalion, Home Guard held a smoking concert at Irlam Conservative Club on Saturday, 6th January with entertainment from Fred

Tipping's concert party, with Tommy Gormley as compere. During the evening Benjamin Neville JP, a member of the Old Folks' Treat Committee, appealed to the guardsmen on behalf of the fund and was met with a great response, raising over £6. G Company had already given generously to the fund and this further effort was highly appreciated by the committee.

The district had a well-represented and active British Legion which was organised by stalwart veterans of the First World War; men such as Benjamin Neville (a former member of the RAMC) and Peter Barrow, DCM (ex-member of the 11th Battalion of the Manchester Regiment). In preparation for the long awaited return of servicemen and servicewomen the *Guardian* published the following information about the Legion: *I am writing this note especially for my service readers in this country and overseas. In a recent issue of the Guardian I outlined something of the work the British Legion is doing for servicemen, ex-servicemen and their dependants. That work is deserving of the highest praise and, if a soldier's best friend on active service is his rifle, it can be truthfully said that his best friend when he returns to Civvy Street is the Legion. The British Legion has a nine point programme, most of which has already been put before the Minister of Labour and National Service. That nine point programme deals with the speedy and adequate creation of homes, the training of disabled men, priority training and employment for men who have lost their skills during service, opportunities for agricultural and ancillary industries, completion of interrupted education at universities and technical colleges, entry and re-entry into small businesses and, of course, a higher and more comprehensive standard of pensions. These are some of the points covered by the programme – and they are all of vital importance to the man now in the services. One thing, however, is essential if this programme is to be put into operation. The Legion must be strong enough to make itself heard. It will be useless if, say, 200 of our district's 1,500 servicemen join, while the other 1,300 remain outside and expect the minority to shoulder the responsibility of fighting for the ex-serviceman's rights. Make no mistake about it, the ex-soldier and ex-sailor and ex-airman will have to fight for their rights. They won't get them by sitting back and expecting a more or less benevolent Government to see a fair deal. The Government in office is always more concerned with saving money rather than spending it. If they can get away with it on pensions and allowances, or on anything else, you can bet your boots they'll do it. In the heat and excitement of war many promises are made. In the calmer days of peace those promises are apt to be forgotten. They were last time – and, so far, we have no proof that this time will be different. The end of the last war caught the ex-servicemen unorganised and unprepared – and they got the rawest deal in history. This time there is the Legion – but, to get justice for the ex-serviceman, it must be a strong Legion – so strong that not even the most reactionary Government will be able to ignore it.*

Private Douglas Williams received a shrapnel wound in his back during the Battle of the Bulge (16th December-25th January), when a German tank fired on the water tanker he was driving, blowing the water tank off the back of the vehicle. Doug was the son of John and Mary Williams of The Crescent, Higher Irlam. The family was originally from Rhuddlan, North Wales. His brother, John Llewellyn Williams, served in the RAF and he also had two sisters, Gwen and Olwyn Williams.

A Certificate of Merit was awarded by Field Marshal Montgomery to Corporal Sidney J.J. Yates (Royal Electrical and Mechanical Engineers).

Born in 1911 at Walsall, Sidney was the youngest son of the late Mrs W.A. Yates of 56 Dixon Street, Irlam. He was educated at Urmston Grammar School and prior to joining the Army he was employed by Barlows, potato merchants of Irlam. He married Doris K. Neesom at Manchester in June 1939 and moved out of the district to reside in Middleton. He joined the Army early in 1943, and first went overseas shortly after D-Day, serving in France and Holland.

During the month two Irlam brothers, Trooper Frank Barrow and Guardsman Herbert Barrow, unexpectedly met each other while on active service in Holland.

Frank, Herbert and Fred Barrow

Herbert, fourth son of the late Mr and Mrs F. Barrow of Cadishead, was married and resided in Leigh. Prior to joining the Army in May 1940 he worked at the CWS Soap Works. He went overseas to France during the Normandy landings in June 1944. Frank was the second son. He resided with his wife at 8 Victoria Road, Irlam, and worked at the Steelworks. He joined the Army on 1st September 1939, and went to France almost immediately. He returned to England at Christmas. In January 1940 he was posted to the Middle East and he was wounded at Tunis. He returned to the UK at Christmas 1943 for six months and then went to Normandy in June 1944. He later served in Holland. Earlier in the war he met another brother overseas, Driver Fred Barrow. Fred joined the Army in 1941, and went to the Middle East in June of the same year. He was taken prisoner by the Italians at Tobruk. He escaped to Messina, and was at liberty for three months before being recaptured by the Germans.

Guardsman John Hesford of the Grenadier Guards was commended for his work on a patrol into No Man's Land, when his unit defeated a larger group of German soldiers. His company were holding a section of the Second Army line on German soil and, in order to gather intelligence about the enemy units opposing it, a patrol was sent out to try and take a prisoner. As darkness fell, the patrol, consisting of seven men including John, was led out into No Man's Land by a sergeant. They dug themselves in and waited until, suddenly out of the darkness, came the flash and rattle of automatic weapons. Grenades began to fall around the patrol and ten Germans came charging forward, shouting to the patrol to surrender. The Grenadiers returned fire, and a fierce battle raged for about ten minutes. Then two Germans ran for their own lines, followed by bombs from the patrol's two-inch mortar. Another German tried to get away but John shouted: *Come in with your hands up*, and the soldier surrendered. The patrol, having completed its mission, returned to the British lines, with John and the sergeant carrying the wounded German soldier between them. Though actually an anti-tank detachment, the patrol had performed a successful infantry job. John resided at 64 The Crescent, Higher Irlam.

Throughout the war, local men serving overseas were sent copies of the *Cadishead and Irlam Guardian* which kept them up-to-date with events in the district. The Readers Letters column of the newspaper often carried letters from servicemen, who took a keen interest in local news. The following letter was sent by local serviceman Sergeant Roland Powell, RAF: *As a regular reader of the Guardian when, and if it reaches me, and one of the servicemen who is interested in what his country and his home town will have to offer on his return, I am writing these few lines. I see in the Guardian of October 28th, just received here, that the local Council is making a financial crisis and spending £50 on flags, floodlighting, etc. for V Day. Now surely this money could be put to a far greater use such as a start to a local hardship fund for the benefit of the wives and families of local men killed or disabled in this war. At least that would be appreciated, and from the serviceman's point of view how many servicemen or civilians will worry if all the lights in Irlam fail that night? And I'm sure we have all seen enough flag waving in the last five years or more! Isn't it time we all gave a little more thought to the necessities now and post-war, instead of thinking of one day, and having to face stark reality in the next? In closing I should like to say how much I appreciate and admire Onlookers articles. Here's wishing you all the best in 1945, and may you succeed where others fail.*

Roland served in India with SEAAF (South East Asian Air Force). Roland was the son of Mr and Mrs W. Powell of 4 Walker Road, Irlam. Prior to being called up he worked at Metropolitan Vickers in Trafford Park. On 10th January 1942, Roland married Dorothy Lowe, a Sunday school teacher at Boundary Road Church, Higher Irlam and they resided at 20 Buckingham Road, Cadishead.

Private Edward Mace returned home on 28 days' leave from Burma, after being overseas for over four years. He joined the Army in March 1940, and in August of the same year he went to Egypt. He went through the siege of Tobruk and the fighting in the Western Desert, before going to Syria, and then Ceylon (present day Sri Lanka), India and Burma. He served with General Wingate in the Chindits, and was later with General Lentaigne's 'ghost force', which Tokyo radio falsely claimed had been completely wiped out. The 'wiped out' force returned and forced the Japanese out of their dug-in positions between the Indawgi Lake and Mogaung.

Edward experienced many hardships during his time in the Far East, such as going without water for two or three days and making three days' rations last five days: *Many times, we have slept through monsoons in the open, wet through to the skin. Many men were full of malaria and other illnesses, and with regard to food, I have seen days when we had to kill the mules to provide meat.* On 14th March 1944 he met his nephew, William Mace, in Burma. Four days later William was killed in action (see earlier entry). During the same month he also met Alf Whittaker (Lancashire Fusiliers) of Princes Avenue, Higher Irlam. On Edward's return to England, the only welcome he received was when he landed at a port in the North West and a policeman patted him on the back and said: *Glad you're home Tommy.*

Private Edward 'Ted' Mace and his wife, Esther

Edward was born c.1917. Prior to joining the Army, he worked as a pitch crusher in the Steelworks coke ovens. He married Esther Kirk in June 1938, they had two daughters and resided at 12 Vicarage Road, Irlam. His visit unwittingly sparked controversy in the district, with the following letter being published in the *Guardian*: *This concerns every organisation in our district – religious, political and civil. It is in respect of men in the Forces coming home on leave after long service abroad. I know one who has been away 4½ years on the Burma front. His 28 days' leave is up this weekend, and not a soul, with the exception of the Press and two others, has been to visit him. Where are the Council, the British Legion, the ministers of religion, the Comforts Fund administrators, etc? Where are they all? Noel Coward, after his visit to Burma, said they were the Forgotten Army. This was contradicted, but he was right. No one has cared a snap of the finger for this lad. He's forgotten now – and if he came out of the Army tomorrow, he would be entirely forgotten. Mass patriotism is OK as long as it is carried out 100 percent. Concluding his letter, my correspondent states that members of the Council and officials live in the vicinity of this man's home and have never even called to wish him luck. Of course, there is another aspect. Each week, we have a number of local lads home on leave from active service. Mostly, they are Navy men. In recent weeks, we have had several men home on leave from Holland and Germany. Naturally, except in rare instances, it is not generally known to the authorities that these men are at home and it would be a pretty stiff job to keep track of their arrivals and departures. But I agree that, in this particular case, something could have been done in the form of welcome – even if it were only a letter – if only for the reason that the soldier referred to is, to the best of my knowledge, the only local man to return from the Burma front (Edward Mace). Perhaps the neglect on this occasion will be remedied in the future.*

One week later the newspaper published an apology: *The recent note in Town Topics regarding the arrival home from Burma of a local man, and the letters which appeared in last week's Guardian have induced my original correspondent to tender an apology. He writes 'The Vicar has certainly got one home on me and there's no doubt I was labouring under a misapprehension for which I am to blame, and it is the right thing to apologise. I very sincerely apologise if my letter hurt those whom the cap did not fit, for I was truly labouring under a misapprehension. I am glad to know that our friend was visited for I feel sure his visitors experienced a personal joy at so doing.' That I take it is the amende honourable.*

Also serving in the Far East were three local officers: Thomas Wright, Julius Leonard Kreibich and George Warrior.

Thomas Wright was born c.1906, the son of Thomas and Emily Jane Wright of 49 Moss Side Road, Cadishead. He was educated at St Mary's School, Cadishead and Urmston Grammar School. After leaving school he worked at the CWS Soap Works. Shortly before the outbreak of war, he had moved out of the district to Blackpool. Thomas served as a captain in the Royal Artillery.

Born in late 1923, Julius Leonard 'Len' Kreibich was the eldest son of Julius Wilfred and Gladys May Kreibich of 11 Victory Road, Cadishead. His father had served in France during the First World War and was in charge of a Home Guard platoon in Cadishead during the Second World War. His grandparents were natives of Germany. Len joined the Home Guard on 14th October 1940, serving as Private 47 in 3 Platoon of D Company (his father's platoon). He resigned from the Home Guard on 8th October 1941 and enlisted into the Welsh Regiment. He later served with the King's Royal Rifles and then the Royal Electrical and Mechanical Engineers (REME). At some point in 1945 he was stationed at Mussorie, India.

Major George Warrior served with the Royal Army Ordnance Corps. George was born on 12th July 1918, the son of George and Meggie Warrior (nee Green) of 653 Liverpool Road, Cadishead, and later the family moved to 2 Drake Avenue, Cadishead. He worked at the Steelworks as a mechanical engineer, a reserved occupation, and so, on 6th June 1940, he responded to the call for volunteers for the local Home Guard, enlisting as Private 192, HQ staff of D Company. He was called up in April 1942 and spent the next four months at the Officer Cadet Training Unit of the Royal Army Ordnance Corps and was commissioned as second lieutenant. He married Alice Johnson on 8th August 1942 and lived at 8 Albert Street, Cadishead, and later 4 Russell Drive, Irlam. At some point after August 1942 he was posted to India and was promoted to captain. On 28th July 1945, he joined 515 Command, Indian Electrical and Mechanical Engineers (IEME), Workshop, Small Arms, in Bangalore, India. By this time he had received a further promotion to the rank of major. On 13th June 1946 he was posted to Medan in Sumatra, where he joined the 26th Indian Divisional Indian Electrical and Mechanical Engineers.

Gunner Edward Golden was home on leave during January. He was the first man from Irlam to be granted leave from Belgium and was also a member of the first heavy battery of British guns to fire on German soil for more than a century. Edward was born in 1920 at Northwich, the son of Robert and Rose Golden (nee Bannister) of 16 Mond Road, Irlam. He attended Irlam Central School and, prior to joining the Army, was employed by Bloch's of Patricroft. He joined the Army in January 1941, and went overseas shortly after D-Day, where he served in France, Holland, Belgium and Germany. When asked what life was like over there he said, with typical British understatement: *Oh, it's alright! Sometimes you see some excitement.* In his opinion the average German soldier was the same as the British 'Tommy' but he had seen old men among the German prisoners which indicated their shortage of manpower.

Mrs H. Calderbank of 14 Woods Road, Irlam, received a letter from her husband which informed her that he was serving with his unit in Holland. Until she received the letter it had been thought that he had been taken prisoner of war in November 1944. The confusion arose when a neighbour thought she heard his name read out as a prisoner of war over the German radio. It later emerged that the name read out was Calderbrook not Calderbank, and the address was Woods Street, Irlam O'th Height. Private H. Calderbank, who was 35 years of age, joined the Army in 1940, and went overseas on D-Day. He was the eldest son of Mr and Mrs J. Calderbank of 44 Cumberland Road, Urmston, and he was educated at Urmston Grammar School. Before joining the Army, he was employed as a bricklayer at the Steelworks.

Captain Thomas Wright, Royal Artillery

Lieutenant Julius Leonard Kreibich, Royal Electrical and Mechanical Engineers

Major George Warrior, Indian Electrical and Mechanical Engineers

At 3am on 16th January a German E-boat fired two torpedoes into HM Landing Ship Tank no. 415. On board the ship was Irlam man, Able Seaman Jack Ainscough.

Landing Ship Tank No. 415 aground in the River Thames at Grays, Essex

The BBC website 'WW2 People's War' contains the following firsthand account from Private John MacKenzie of the Gordon Highlanders, who was on board LST no. 415 that night: *Around 200 troops embarked at Tilbury on HMLST415 (Landing Ship Tank) on 15th January 1945. The ship was already loaded with heavy transportation and other supplies for the BLA (British Liberation Army), and we moved off Southend to join several other supply ships waiting to cross the Channel. LST 415 sailed that evening, at the tail-end of the convoy. Conditions on board were crowded and uncomfortable, and the lighting subdued. With two companions, I sought a space to sleep on a small area of gangway outside the ammunition store. In the early hours of 16th January we were rudely awakened by crew entering the ammo depot. Almost immediately all hell broke loose. The ship's warning siren sounded 'Action Stations', we felt two dull thuds which brought the ship to a shuddering halt, and naval guns opened up from various directions. In the general confusion, there was no need to tell us to assemble immediately at our boat stations on deck where we watched flares and tracers light the night sky over a cold, but fairly calm, North Sea. LST415 had been hit by two torpedoes (at the crews' quarters in the stern) from a Nazi E-boat which had been lurking in the shadow of a large buoy to avoid radar detection. By use of her watertight compartments the ship stayed afloat, with its stern now partially submerged. The E-boat had lost no time in escaping into the night and, soon, LST159 manoeuvred skilfully alongside. The assembled troops were then ordered to leap from the rail of our stricken ship to the deck of the rescuing vessel – not the happiest prospect on a dark night, but fear of the cold North Sea below lent us wings! All aboard, LST159 sped us back to Tilbury, soldiers without weapons or equipment, many without boots. LST415, which had seen action at Sicily, Salerno, Anzio and Normandy, was towed to land and beached on the south coast of England. I later learned that six Royal Navy crew died that night, with many more injured. I believe there were a few Army casualties during the transfer, but numbers I cannot confirm.*

Reverend Lee wrote in the parish magazine, about the disturbance of the traditional life of Europe and its far reaching effects: *War brings many evils but this war is different; it has struck much deeper into human consciousness and will than the usual bloodshed, hatred and bitterness which are the handmaids of war. The root evil is often money – there has been too much for our young people at home and the squandering on drink, pleasure and lust is appalling, but these are just the outward symptoms of the chaotic unbalance of mind and lamentably poor foundations upon which many young lives are built. They show the weakness of home life and control, and these in turn show the carelessness and selfishness of parents. What the outcome of all this will be I do not know, but for me it is the greatest fear for the future. The liberty and animal freedom for youth is another great evil we owe to German thought and methods – the Hitler Youth, with its vulgarity and its dirt is an abomination. All that is worst in the human appetite has been encouraged in them, and there are many in this land who are no better than those Nazi leaders who have destroyed the fair flower of youth in the Reich to their own profit and lust. Youth at the helm is all right if the course is set by wiser heads than theirs, and all this chatter about youth having their way is an ignorant fallacy. There was a fool king once (and he was the son of the wise Solomon) who took the advice of youth and said 'my little finger shall be thicker than my father's loin.' This king didn't last long. Those who shout about this age of youth should note that our three great leaders of today are all eligible for old-age pension and the spryest of them all is a young man of 70, who has been the salvation of our land in these dreadful days. Our efforts must be to direct youth aright, to set forth industry, dignity, self-respect and Christian character as the great needs of this age, rather than allowing them to run wild like untamed horses and to provide them with everything they covet in the way of leisure, pleasure and a nincompoop spoonfed existence. If we do not get back to real industry and labour and bring to an end this minimum of production, for whatever reason this may be preached or practiced, we shall have neither money nor trade. Germany's mighty effort is amazing in the industrial sphere; they have always worked and do work like ants – only they have had fool leaders. Their efforts have been so prodigious that at this present moment they are withstanding the whole world. If they had been lovers of peace they would have captured world trade long ago – and who will deny that those who labour hard do deserve the fruits of the earth? I may be wrong, but I believe that all the noise and shouting about shorter hours, more pay, more leisure, security, and all the rest is doing immense harm to our land, and that we are now living largely on a harvest gathered by our forefathers. The sour grapes of a very industrious and prosperous past are too bitter for us. When we relearn that giving and not gain, sacrifice and not self, industry and not ease are the stepping stones to greatness we shall begin again to rise to greater heights than ever.*

John H. Reed, an ex-member of the Hollins Green Home Guard, died at his home 21 Victory Road, Cadishead, on Sunday, 21st January. John was an ex-soldier who had served on both the French and Italian fronts during the First World War. He was a native of Sunderland, who came to Cadishead c.1930, to take up employment as a pipe fitter at the Steelworks. He served in the Home Guard for two years, and had many friends both in Hollins Green and in Cadishead. His funeral took place at

Hollins Green Cemetery on Friday, 26th January after a service at St Mary's Church, Cadishead, conducted by Reverend Bakker.

Councillor Enticott, chairman of the Public Health Committee commented on the reports of the medical officer and the sanitary inspector, at the monthly Council meeting on Monday, 22nd January. The annual reports on the health and sanitary circumstances of the district were, in peacetime, important documents concerning the welfare of the population. In war-time, for security reasons, the department's statistics were not published: *I do feel, however, that it will not be a contravention of any regulation if I say that during the war years the health of this district has remained surprisingly good. Longer working hours, lowered food standards, the blackout, and all the sundry trials and annoyances have not, to any notable extent, affected the health of the people of this district. In fact, during one year the death rate was the lowest that has been recorded for more than 34 years. I personally am interested and pleased to learn, too, that during the period 1940-43 no maternal deaths occurred in this district and the deaths of infants under one year of age in relation to the number of births have given some of the lowest figures in the history of the district. No outstanding outbreak of infectious disease has been reported, but it is pleasing to say that the annual figures for the notification of diphtheria have dropped correspondingly with the increasing success of the Council's scheme for the immunisation of children against this disease. The immunisations started in 1941 and at the end of 1943 2,155 had been completely immunised and between 300 and 500 children were undergoing this treatment. This represents the better part of all children of pre-school and school age. As regards the sanitary circumstances of the district, the Council's housing demolition plan has, of course, been held over during the war and only six houses have been demolished during the period. House repair work has been difficult throughout the war owing to the shortage of labour and materials and owners of property are asked to do only essential work. We are fortunate in knowing that the inspection of the district's food supply has been continued on the high levels we have been led to expect by our officials, and though we know of the prevailing milk shortage, the quality is kept under careful watch, particularly the milk supplied to schools. The new service of rat disinfestations performed under the general direction of the Ministry of Food is an excellent scheme, and as I have taken a personal interest in this work I know that it is based on sound lines of organisation. It is one of the new services arising out of the war for which we should be pleased. The public cleansing and salvage staffs have performed excellent work. Domestic refuse is not moved weekly as in pre-war times, but the best service that was possible with the available labour and conditions has, I know, been given. This section of the Health Department's staff has had the additional burden of salvage collection and, whilst no spectacular results have been reported, a steady output of valuable salvage has been maintained for the war effort. I should like to record my thanks to those who have and are carrying on this good work. I should also like to refer to the Council's ambulance service. This has been maintained at its pre-war efficient standard in spite of many difficulties. I have heard of no serious complaint concerning its operation. Lastly I would like to comment upon the way in which the officials of the Health Department – the medical officer and sanitary inspector and their staffs – have carried out their work and the additional duties imposed upon them by war-time conditions.*

During the month the donations to the Irlam and Cadishead War Comforts Fund included: Irlam Hall Social Club £8-12-3; Cadishead Conservative Club £10; Cadishead Conservative Club (Wait and See Committee) 10s; Poplar Grove Firewatchers 5s; Immediate Action Squad Social Club £5; Irlam and Cadishead Darts League (George Hotel) 16s-8d; Mr J. Robinson, Beech Avenue, Higher Irlam 10s; Engineers Works Committee (LSC) £19-6s; LSC Employees Recreation Club £9-8s; CWS Soap Works Comforts Fund (proceeds of a dance) £8-10s; St Mary's Mothers' Union £3; H. Dawson, Liverpool Road, Cadishead £2; Mrs Read, Astley Road, Irlam £2-10s; Joseph William Hayman, Dudley Road, Cadishead 10s; Mrs Adair, 25 Moss Side Road, Cadishead £1; Mr A. Richardson, Lion Hotel, Cadishead (effort) £10; Irlam Primrose League £5; St Paul's Dramatic Society £2; and Miss G. Byrom, Boat Lane, Irlam (proceeds of effort) £3-18s. Other fundraising efforts included a dance arranged by the WVS at the Conservative Club, Irlam, on Friday, 19th January for the Welcome Home Fund. Refreshments were provided by the committee, Mr F. Ashley was MC and Fred Broadhurst's band provided the music. £24 was raised and a further £44 was raised from the sale of a rug made by Mr Henderson. Mr James of Fir Street, Cadishead, raised £7 for the local Red Cross through an 'over the counter' collection and a house party.

As well as collections for local concerns such as the Red Cross, the local War Comforts Fund and the Welcome Home Fund, there was a national drive for war savings to support the country's economy. On Monday, 22nd January local members of the National Savings Movement were shown films at Irlam Central School which demonstrated what was done with money invested in National Savings. The films were introduced by Stacey Lintott, a well-known sports writer of the time: *The excitement of war keeps the savings movement alive but after the war it is up to you, the group secretaries and the committees, to keep the public interested. I ask you not to give up your posts after the war. Even if you have to give up, try and keep other people interested in the movement.* In support of the movement, Councillor Owen stated: *the war is not over yet. Many people in this district think that now we are getting nearer to Berlin the war is all but over. I wish I could think the same. We may have many setbacks yet, and let us hope they are not in the form of those things that fly straight into the middle of our village. Savings are as vital today as they were two or three years back. Many people think that the high prices after the war will not affect them as they are getting high wages. People were getting high wages after the last war but they dropped quickly. You know that if you haven't got money, the shopkeeper won't serve you. I remember after the last war people selling rings and fur coats at ridiculous prices so as to be able to buy the necessary things of life, therefore you can see the advantage of investing your money in war savings now, and be prepared for later. Money is most valuable when you need it. By investing your money, you are not only helping yourself, but the nation as a whole. You are helping to bring the lads and lassies in the Forces home.* The films were Walt Disney's *Donald's Decision*, *Sons of Britain*, *Victory Wedding*, *Wheels of Freedom* and *Savings Cavalcade*. *Sons of Britain* told the story of the war up to the campaign in Libya, with a recorded talk by General Montgomery. *Wheels of*

Freedom showed different war vehicles and guns being made, and *Savings Cavalcade* demonstrated the sums that the small saver had invested since 1916.

On Saturday 27th January Leading Aircraftwoman Veronica C. Givens (WAAF), daughter of the late Mrs Sarah Givens of 28 Ferryhill Road, Irlam married Corporal Robert Bales (RAF), third son of Mrs and the late Mr R. Bales of 16 Mansfield Lane, Norwich, at St John's Church. Veronica was given away by her brother Mr G. Givens and Leading Aircraftwoman W. Burgess (WAAF) and Miss J. Tipling (bride's niece) acted as bridesmaids. Both bride and groom had been in the RAF since 1941.

Another brother, James Richard Givens, was serving with the Royal Navy in the Far East (Ceylon). James was born in 1922. He joined the Home Guard on 19th July 1940 as Private 466 Givens and served in 1 Platoon, D Company. He joined the Royal Navy on 30th June 1943.

The 27th January was also an important day for Signalman Trevor Jenkins, his 21st birthday. Trevor was stationed, with another signalman, in a farmhouse in northern Italy, serving with the 61st Heavy Regiment, Royal Artillery. The role of the signalman was to patrol along and behind enemy lines to act as an observer for the artillery. On this day, Trevor was due to go out on patrol with a major and the other signalman offered to take his place because it was his birthday. He declined the offer and set off with two days' rations, in a jeep with a floor that was lined with sandbags to offer some protection against landmines. At some time during the patrol, the officer parked the jeep and, with Trevor carrying a heavy wireless set on his back, marched up a nearby hill. When they got to the top of the hill, the officer took out his field glasses to scout the area in front. To Trevor's chagrin, the officer decided that the hill next door would provide a better view, so they marched down the hill and up the next one. From here the officer spotted a party of Germans near a river and ordered Trevor to call in the coordinates over the wireless to the artillery to: *entertain a bathing party*. Shortly afterwards a shell screamed over the hill towards the Germans. The officer and Trevor immediately packed up and made their way quickly to the jeep, knowing that the Germans would soon be searching for them. In all, the patrol lasted a day and a half but when they returned to the farmhouse they found that it had been hit by a bomb. The signalman who had offered to take Trevor's place was dead.

Another local man who was on active service in Italy was Trooper George Leslie 'Les' Gibbon, who was a tank crew member. Born in 1922, Les was the son of George

William and Jessie Gibbon of Moss View Farm, Barton Moss. He joined 1 Platoon, D Company of the local Home Guard on 26th June 1940 (service no. 11). He joined the Army in December 1941. He later served in Austria.

Ever since Germany had declared war on Russia in June 1941 there had been a great outpouring of sympathy from the British public for the Russian people (somehow overlooking the fact that the Russians had originally been an ally of the Germans and had participated in the attack on Poland which had brought Great Britain into the war in September 1939). Once the Russians became allies, both the Americans and British supplied them with massive amounts of military, medical and other aid. Irlam and Cadishead followed the general mood of the nation by setting up a committee for Soviet Medical Aid. The first meeting was held on Thursday, 25th January and the main agenda item was the election of officials. Mr S. Wolstenholme was elected chairman, Mr Gold, vice-chairman, Mr Horne, secretary, Miss E. Barlow, assistant secretary and Mr G. Thomas, treasurer. Fundraising was discussed, and it was agreed to hold a flag day and to stage an Anglo-Soviet friendship exhibition. An immediate appeal was made for voluntary collectors and flag sellers and a further appeal for medical aid and supplies was posted to works, organisations and local residents.

Around this time, Private Dorothy Mae Moore, who had joined the American Women's Army Corps (WAC) in 1944, was performing as a member of the cast of a musical revue in Paris which had been specially arranged for members of the United States Armed Forces. Most of the cast were former professional show people. Twenty-one year old Dorothy was born in Samville, Ohio, and came to England c.1934, residing at 40 Dean Road, Cadishead. She was well-known in the district, and was the sister-in-law of Mr W. McNulty, producer to the Irlam and Cadishead Children's theatre.

Pilot Officer 184192 John Hill of 619 Squadron, was awarded the Distinguished Flying Cross (DFC), the first award of its kind in the area. The circumstances surrounding the award are unrecorded but the family believe that he took over an aircraft after the pilot had been wounded and landed it safely, saving all the crew. John was a former pupil of Cadishead Senior School and Urmston Grammar School. He was an all-round sportsman who had represented Lancashire in both school cricket and football. He joined the RAF four years earlier as an aircraftman class 2 and was commissioned eight months before his award. He was an air gunner who had taken part in many operational flights. John was the second son of Mr and Mrs J. Hill of 25 Kitchener Avenue, Cadishead. On Saturday, 17th July 1943 he married Constance Sheila Dale of 6 Dean Road, Cadishead at St Mary's Church, Cadishead. John's older brother, Gunner Charles Hill, served with L Battery, S/L Unit, Motor Transport Section of the Royal Artillery, based at Oswestry. He was born in Fir Street, Cadishead, and later resided at 25 Kitchener Avenue, Cadishead.

Trooper Les Gibbon (second from right)
Pictured with his crew and their Sherman Firefly tank

Pilot Officer John Hill, DFC

Gunner Charles Hill, Royal Artillery

FEBRUARY

Lance Corporal 3651387 **Henry Harris** of the 2nd Battalion, Border Regiment, 100th Indian Infantry Brigade, 20th Indian Division, was killed in action in Burma on Friday, 2nd February, aged 34.

Henry 'Harry' was the second son of Lizzie and the late Herbert Harris of Baines Avenue, Irlam. His wife, Elsie, resided at 12 Kenmore Grove, Cadishead, with their son, Gordon. Harry was a pre-war regular soldier who had served in the Army for nearly 14 years, including seven years in India before the war. Having completed the terms of his service prior to the outbreak of war, he was placed on the Reserve, and worked at the Steelworks for 18 months. On the outbreak of war, he was recalled from Reserve and was sent to France. In February 1940 he broke his leg and, as a result, he was returned home. After recovering, he was posted to the Isle of Man guarding prisoners of war. On 13th November 1943, he left for India, and later served in Burma. On 2nd February 2nd Border Regiment was engaged in fighting in the village of Satpangon on the northern side of the Irrawaddy River. Companies B and D of the battalion assaulted the Japanese position in the village, but had to withdraw to their starting position after suffering heavy losses, one of whom was Henry. The village was finally cleared next day.

Henry is buried at Taukkyan War Cemetery, Burma. The epitaph on his headstone states: *His presence was our greatest pleasure, his memory our greatest treasure.*

During the month, 42 year old Thomas Hatcher Bilsborrow applied to be reinstated at his old job. Thomas of Mond Road, Higher Irlam, was a pre-war Territorial soldier who had worked as a steel dresser at the Steelworks. In November 1944, he was discharged from the Army on medical grounds, after five years' military service. He was suspected to be suffering from silicosis (a lung disease caused by inhalation of silica dust), which he could only have contracted while employed by the Steelworks. If he was reinstated as a steel dresser he would be eligible to be examined by the Silicosis Board, but without reinstatement he would be debarred from claiming compensation, chiefly because of the time that had elapsed while he was in HM Forces. The Steelworks contested the case on the basis that there was no proof that he was suffering from the disease and it would be inhumane to employ him in his old job which would put him at risk of silicosis. The chairman of the tribunal was sympathetic to his plight, but ruled that no reinstatement could be made. It was a shabby way to treat a soldier with five years' service behind him.

Lance Corporal 1887407 Cyril Frederick Hankinson, Royal Engineers (Heavy Mechanical Equipment (3a) Sec RE), 21st Army Group, received a certificate of commendation from Field Marshal Montgomery: *It has been brought to my notice that you have performed outstanding good service, and shown great devotion to duty, during the campaign in North West Europe. I award you this certificate as a token of my appreciation, and I have given instructions that this should be noted in your Record of Service.* At the outbreak of war, Fred had walked to the recruitment office in Warrington to enlist.

After more than four years' service abroad, 29-year old Signalman George Cordwell returned home on leave from Italy. He had joined the Army in May 1940 and went overseas in July of the same year, serving with the Eighth Army in India, Iraq, Persia, Egypt and later in Italy. In India, he found that the English and Indian women in the cities showed great kindness to the soldiers, managing the canteens and organising dances for all the service personnel. In North Africa, he met Jimmy Darnton of Cadishead in the American Red Cross Club at Tunis. At one point he was taken prisoner in Italy, but, after two weeks in captivity, he and many others were fortunate to be rescued by an infantry patrol and tanks working behind enemy lines. While escaping, he was wounded when a shell hit the truck in which he was travelling. During his leave he expressed his gratitude to the War Comforts Fund, Miss Ashton, welfare officer at the CWS Soap Works, and the people of Dixon Street from whom he received regular parcels and money orders. Before joining the Army he had worked at the CWS Soap Works, on the landing stage. He was the only son of Mr and Mrs John Jubal Cordwell (First World War veteran) of 71 Dixon Street, Irlam.

Irlam and Cadishead Children's Theatre production of the pantomime *Babes in the Wood* raised £60 for the Duke of Gloucester's Red Cross and St John Fund during a three day showing at St Paul's School, Irlam. A letter to Jean Alldred (honorary secretary) of the Children's Theatre, from Mr A.S. Campbell, assistant secretary of the fund, conveyed the thanks of the Appeals Committee.

Lance Corporal Cyril Fred Hankinson, Royal Engineers

The air raid wardens of guard room C, Cadishead, at a general meeting chaired by Reverend Bakker, decided to dispose of the Social Fund (£26) and the Penny-a-Week Fund (£34). The Penny-a-Week Fund had been set up to help wardens who met with accidents whilst on duty, however, the need for the fund had diminished as the threat of bombing raids reduced. The Social Fund was divided between the Irlam and Cadishead War Comforts Fund, the Duke of Gloucester's Red Cross and St John Fund, and Irlam and Cadishead Nursing Association. The Penny-a-Week Fund was divided equally between St Dunstan's Hospice for Blind Servicemen, Salford Royal Hospital and the Limbless ex-Service Men's Association.

On Monday, 5th February Able Seaman D/JX176309 **Jack Ainscough** was killed in an explosion on board Landing Ship Tank 415. It occurred while the ship was being repaired as a result of the damage caused by an E-boat attack in January (described earlier).

Jack was born in Ince near Wigan, on 8th September 1919, the eldest son of Sarah and James Ainscough. He had two brothers, James and Fred. Jack was educated at Rosebridge Council School at Ince. The family came to Irlam c.1933 when their father, James, took a job at the Steelworks and set up home at 143 Eldon Road West, Irlam. James later became keeper of No.3 blast furnaces and Jack worked in the chart house at the Steelworks until he enlisted on 1st January 1940.

The wedding of Jack and Lily Ainscough
Also on the photograph are Fred Ainscough (far left), with his parents also on the left. His other brother, James, is to the right of Jack.

In 1942 Jack met Lily Beevers at Newton-le-Willows while visiting an aunt and uncle and they married in September 1943 at St Peter's Church, Newton-le-Willows. Their son, John, was born in December 1944 and Jack had the pleasure of meeting his son once before his death.

During his service, Jack had been involved in the Dunkirk evacuations and then spent three years in Ceylon and Africa. In 1944 he was serving on board Landing Ship Tank 415 and was with the ship during the D-Day landings. Two days before his death, on 3rd February, Jack wrote to his Aunt Edna and Uncle John. The letter was sent from Mess 32, LST Repair Base, c/o FMO, Tilbury, Essex: *I'm sorry for the delay in writing, I was hoping for a reply to my last letter. Anyhow earlier this week I had a letter from uncle Fred saying you were ill in bed, so that explains everything, and I do hope you are well on the way to improvement by now. He also gave me the news about Eve expecting an increase, I was quite surprised. It's nice to know she's keeping well these days and hope she keeps that way. I was also home for last weekend and enjoyed it very much. Elsie came on Saturday night and stopped until Monday morning. I'm sure you would have enjoyed it at the Boat House on Saturday night. There was quite a crowd there and of course lots of singing. The big son is doing fine these days. Unfortunately he's been showing his red-headed temper a little as well. The reason for it I think is not being able to go in the back garden in the pram for his daily sleep due to the foggy atmosphere. He had to be nursed most of the time and Lily's had her hands full. When I got home I washed a few nappies and a couple of night dresses while she attended to him. On the Sunday he managed to get a few hours fresh air and did him a world of good. You'd be surprised if you saw him now, he's a lot bigger. My mother says he has a belly on him like my dad. He looks fine and he's beginning to take notice a lot more now. Everyone was OK when I left and according to my latest letter sent Thursday. There isn't a great deal of news to pass on from here. The weather's changed quite a lot from last week, in fact been almost like summer this afternoon. I've been busy just lately making a toy engine and took it home last week. At the moment I'm in the middle of painting a racing car, it looks alright. We still have a few rockets dropping round here but haven't seen any flying bombs. If things keep moving as they have, they won't be dropping them much longer. I'll have to ring off now Edna, I have several more letters to write. So for a while I'll say cheerio, hoping it finds you much better and John OK as well. Here's wishing you Both the Best of Everything, yours Jack. P.S. hope to hear from you soon.*

After his death, the Royal Navy wanted to inter Jack in the London area but his wife, Lily, insisted that he be brought back to Irlam. At the time, the Royal Navy would only return a body to the nearest railway station (Irlam in this case) and the family would then have to arrange for the body to be collected from the station. Bert Johnson, the local undertaker, heard about this and kindly made all the arrangements and also covered the cost of the funeral. Jack is buried in Irlam (St John the Baptist) Churchyard Extension. The epitaph on his gravestone reads: *No sun ever sets, no dawn awakes, no smile can take our secret aches.* Medal entitlement: George VI War Medal 1939-45, 1939-45 Star, Africa Star and France & Germany Star.

Able Seaman Jack Ainscough, Royal Navy

Able Seaman Jack Ainscough, Royal Navy

CWGC headstone of Jack Ainscough (Irlam Cemetery extension)

The Allied advance through Belgium and Holland continued into Germany. On the night of 5th/6th February the 53rd (London) Medium Regiment, Royal Artillery moved into Germany to take part in a major artillery operation, which employed every artillery piece in each of the four Army Group Royal Artillery (AGRA) numbers 2, 4, 5 and 9. Irlam man, Gunner Tom Vaudrey served in 209 Battery of 53rd Regiment. At 5am on 8th February 53rd Regiment, along with 183 other gun sections, opened fire on German positions. The guns continued to fire for the next three days, with the final round being fired on 10th February when the battle moved out of range. Each gun had fired 229 rounds. The next day the regiment moved south to St Agatha, to support the 51st Highland Division which was having a difficult time in the Reichswald Forest. They remained in action, firing vigorously, until 18th February. They had two days' rest and then entered Germany to take up positions near Bedburg-Hau, south east of Cleve. During this time they fired in support of 3rd Canadian Division, which was advancing on the Hochswald Line.

Mrs Hilda G. Mosedale of Brook House, Rixton, received official confirmation that her youngest son, Flying Officer Frank Mosedale of Fighter Command, was a prisoner of war, being held in Stalag Luft I, near Barth in Germany. News that he was a prisoner was also given in a German radio broadcast. He had been reported missing on air operations in Italy at the end of November 1944. In a postcard received by his mother on Tuesday, 7th February he informed her that he was in good health. Frank was 22 years of age and had joined the RAF in 1941, and gained his wings in Rhodesia. He became a ferry service pilot, then a test pilot and finally a member of the crack 92 East India Squadron, reported to be one of the finest fighter squadrons in the Central Mediterranean Force. He was educated at the Boteler Grammar School, Warrington, and afterwards joined the family business of Thomas Mosedale and Sons, brickmakers of Rixton.

Lance Corporal 3536857 **Horace Bowen** of the 10th Battalion, Highland Light Infantry (City of Glasgow Regiment), 227th Infantry Brigade, 15th (Scottish) Division, died of wounds on Friday, 9th February.

Born in late 1910 in Irlam, Horace was the eldest son of Reginald and Mary Ann Bowen (nee Newton). In 1911 the family were living at 190 Liverpool Road, Irlam and his father was employed as a fireman at the paper mill. By 1914 the family had moved to 18 Caroline Street, Irlam. His father, Reginald, was a veteran of the First World War and was the first known Irlam soldier to be wounded in 1914.

Prior to enlisting Horace was employed by the CWS Soap Works and was well-known in the district through his activities with Irlam Public Prize Band, which he had joined at the age of 15. He enlisted into the Army in

February 1942 and in June of the same year he married Gladys Bent and set up home at 13 Falcon Avenue, Urmston. He went to France in June 1944 and, during the same month, he was wounded in both legs by German soldiers who opened fire while apparently in the act of surrendering. After spending ten weeks recovering in a hospital in England he was posted back to his unit in France on 4th September.

On 8th February 30 Corps launched an attack on a five divisional front as part of Operation Veritable. The 15th (Scottish) Division were in the centre of the attack and had to advance through a narrow zone of attack, bordered between the thick woods of the Reichswald Forest and the flooded low country south of the Rhine. Their objective was to break the Siegfried Line north of the Reichswald forest and then to take Cleve. Allied artillery opened its barrage on the German defences at 5am, at the same time as the 227th Brigade passed through the gun area. Dawn opened on a grey and miserable day, with low cloud and it rained almost continuously for several days. At 10.30am, the infantry launched its attack, with 227th Brigade on the left and 4th Brigade on the right. 227th Brigade's objective was to secure the general line Frasselt to Kranenburg. The enemy's defensive fire was heavier on 227th Brigade's side than on the neighbouring 4th Brigade. The 227th Brigade started the attack on a one battalion front, led by the Argylls, with the 10th Highland Light Infantry following up on their left. The rifle companies of the Highland Light Infantry followed the Argylls through a gap in a minefield which had been laid by the Americans in September 1944 (fortunately the mines had been laid on top of the ground and were visible to the advancing troops). By 11.40am they had reached the Dutch-German border. Here, the Highland Light Infantry passed through the left of the Argylls, pivoted left and then swung up into the line to the northward to advance on Kranenburg with their left on the Wyler-Kranenburg-Cleve axis. Very soon the Highland Light Infantry found themselves in an anti-personnel minefield. Unfortunately their flail tanks, which could have cleared the mines, had been bogged down earlier and they had to advance through the minefield, losing several men. Horace was wounded when the Bren carrier he was driving ran over a mine and it is possible that his injuries occurred at this stage of the assault. By 6pm the 15th (Scottish) Division had achieved all its first phase objectives. Horace is buried at Jonkerbos War Cemetery, Nijmegen, Holland. His brother, Harold, was also in the Forces and was serving in Belgium at the time of Horace's death.

Following successful shows at Irlam and Wigan, the Irlam and Cadishead Theatre Group gave performances of the pantomime *Babes in the Wood* at the Centenary Methodist schoolroom, Glazebrook on Friday and Saturday, 9th and 10th February in aid of the Rixton-with-Glazebrook Victory Fund. Both nights were sold out. The shows were promoted by the local Forces Canteen Committee and Mr R. Allen jnr (president), Mr E. Sinton (secretary), and Mr J. Baguley (treasurer) supported the chairman of the committee at the performances. Mr A.C. Harrison opened proceedings on the Friday night by describing the cause as one of the finest in the world. He understood that between 110 and 120 men and women from the area were serving in various capacities in HM Forces and he hoped that they would soon be returning victorious. He stated that some would return fit and well, while others, less fortunate, would return suffering from the effects of wounds and he hoped that they would soon be restored to health and strength. There were those who had made the supreme sacrifice and to their loved ones who were left behind he offered his heartfelt sympathy: *Do not think they are forgotten – indeed theirs has been the greatest sacrifice of all.* The balance of the Victory Fund at this time stood at £932, but he described this as inadequate. Initially the Victory Fund, by an unfortunate oversight, did not include those who had joined the Merchant Navy, thereby failing to recognise the heroic work they carried out. The oversight was soon corrected; it was not only the amount of money they would receive but the satisfaction of having their names added to the list of those who had served their country. Mr A. Lewis of Culcheth presided over Saturday's performance. He said that the good that the Forces Canteen at Glazebrook was doing extended far beyond the village. They had received many letters of appreciation from people who had passed through the camp at Glazebrook but were now stationed elsewhere.

Mrs Loxley, the centre organiser of Irlam WVS, recapped the year's work to members at the annual meeting at the bandroom on Tuesday, 13th February and expressed pleasure at the success they had achieved. For example, the production of camouflage nets had increased every quarter until it was officially decided in April 1944 that no more were necessary. Six WVS members had attended at the Citizens Advice Bureau, three at the Babies Clinic and two at the NAAFI Services Club, Manchester. The large stock of clothing held for distribution in an emergency had been well-maintained and cared for by the clothing officers. In August 120 evacuees, mothers and children, had arrived from the south coast, and were catered for at St Paul's Rest Centre until billets were found for them. War Savings were well-maintained, and members had worked hard and helped in many ways during Salute the Soldier Week. A savings group based at the Babies Clinic had done well and, during the year, the takings of the WVS group at the bandroom had amounted to £4,724. The voluntary car pool had proved of great assistance to the district, and in the knitting of comforts, 64lbs of wool was knitted into vests, 48lbs into shawls for occupied Europe and 84lbs into cap scarves for the Forces. In addition, a regular monthly parcel of oiled wool had been transformed into stockings and mittens. After the statement of accounts was given by the treasurer, it was decided to send fifteen guineas to the British Red Cross, and a similar sum to the fund for the war blinded. The efforts for the Welcome Home Fund had been very successful and £360 had been handed to the Irlam and Cadishead War Comforts Fund.

In addition to the larger fundraising efforts, there were many contributions from individuals, for example, Renee Shaw of 14 Fir Street, Cadishead, raised 17 shillings for the British Red Cross by making golliwogs and selling them to neighbours, as did Phyllis Hindley of 14 Oak Avenue, Cadishead, who raised 16 shillings.

Private Raymond Johnson of 10 Dorset Road, Cadishead, was involved in fierce fighting in Holland. His infantry company, supported by tanks and flamethrowers, fought for St Joost, a Dutch village near the German border, and after violent close-range fighting, captured 43 prisoners from a crack German paratroop battalion. A firsthand account written by a 'military observer' appeared in the *Guardian*. It described how: *Raymond and his colleagues were sat round a stove which was giving out more smoke than heat, in a windowless and shelled house near the Roer River. Many of them wore fur collars made from the skins of rabbits killed by the soldiers, which were stitched onto their battledress for extra warmth. Ferocity and contempt for the enemy was very evident, and one soldier leaning forward to pat a dog's head, late Wehrmacht property said: Fritz, you're the only decent German among 'em. The strength of the enemy in the village was unknown before the attack, but it had been estimated to be about 40 infantrymen. The attack started with an artillery barrage followed by tanks opening fire on the outlying houses. Flamethrowers spat jets of burning tar at the nearest buildings, the buildings began to flame – and the infantry went in. About 20 yards beyond the third house, there were more German troops occupying two houses on either side of the road running through the village. After tanks had provided an initial softening by shellfire, the leading platoon rushed them. A party of eight Germans drove women with babies in their arms ahead of them to make sure of a safe surrender. After capturing one of the houses two British soldiers sat on a bed for a rest, which caused two Germans, who had been hiding there, to complain. The Germans were promptly taken prisoner. About 50 yards further up the road there was a solitary house with a long communication trench leading towards it. In the trench lay 40 or 50 civilians waving white flags. As the men crawled up the trench, being sniped and machine-gunned, they were patted on the back by the laughing civilians, even while the troops were in the unavoidable act of stepping on shoulders and legs. Fifteen yards of open ground lay between the end of the trench and the house from which a Spandau was firing. The men charged across the gap, sniped and spandaued, without suffering a single casualty, although one of the soldiers had the wool of his khaki glove snipped. They captured the machine-gun and another eight prisoners. As a result of interrogation on the spot, the company commander realised his men were pitted against a battalion of German paratroopers. Six self-propelled guns had been shelling the British tanks throughout and now the enemy began to mortar the house, but they underestimated the range and the majority of the bombs fell in houses occupied by their own troops. The supply of grenades had practically run out and it was decided to move back to the next house. All door exits were covered by Spandau fire and the men were forced to leap out of windows. Shortly after they had left the house, two 88mm shells shattered it. During the night, the enemy reinforced the garrison by another company of paratroops, and it was not until late afternoon the next day that the village was taken (by another battalion) after the following message from the German commander to his superior officer had been intercepted: We are having heavy casualties and cannot hold out.* Raymond was the only son of Mr and Mrs F. Johnson. At the time he was 19 years old and had joined the Army in November 1943. He went to France on 6th July 1944 (one month to the day after D-

Day). Later he served in Belgium before arriving in Holland. Before joining the Army he was employed by the Manchester Ship Canal Company.

The annual report of the Irlam and Cadishead War Comforts Fund described how more than 1,600 men and women of Irlam and Cadishead were serving or had served in HM Forces during the war. The number serving on 31st December was reported as 1,334 men and 142 women. In addition 51 men and 22 women had been discharged, 36 men were prisoners of war, and three had been repatriated, whilst 13 men were missing and 53 men and one woman had been killed. The honorary secretary, Mary Bowker, stated that there had been an increase in the number of men and women serving in the Forces, and 1,334 gifts of five shillings had been dispatched during 1944. In addition, three special gifts of ten shillings, and one of five shillings had been sent to wounded local men in hospital. Thirty-one parcels of cigarettes and tobacco were sent to local men in German prisoner of war camps and nine gifts of ten shilling each were forwarded to the nearest relatives of men who were prisoners of war in Japanese hands. Mary commented: *Communications from prisoners in the Far East are still far from satisfactory, but I understand that a few relatives had letters and cards at Christmas time. One relative received as many as nine letters and cards, and the most recent communication was dated September 1944.* As in the previous year, a grant was made to each family with children of the men who were prisoners of war, on the basis of five shillings for the wife and five shillings for each child.

John and Norman Smith

Two Irlam brothers, Sergeant John R. Smith who was stationed at Alexandria, and Electrical Mechanic Norman Smith, met when Norman's ship docked at Alexandria, Egypt. This was their first meeting in over four years. John was born c.1918 and Norman c.1925. They were the sons of Mr and Mrs J.G. Smith of 49 Marlborough Road, Higher Irlam. John joined the Army in January 1940 and went overseas in

December of the same year. He had served in Malta and Palestine before being posted to Egypt. Prior to joining the Army, he was employed by Lancashire United Transport as a bus conductor. Norman joined the Royal Navy in April 1943, and left England in July 1944. He was employed by Fords Ltd, Trafford Park. They were both ex-pupils of St Teresa's School, Irlam.

Twenty-one year old Guardsman Harold Smith (pictured), was wounded in western Europe. He was born on 31st January 1924, the fourth son of Mrs Clara Smith of 26 Harewood Road, Irlam. He joined the local Home Guard on 6th August 1941, serving as Private 595 in 1 Platoon of D Company. On 31st August 1943 he joined the Army and first went overseas a few days after D-Day. He served in France, Holland, Belgium and Germany, and was among the first troops to enter Brussels. Two of his brothers served in the Forces, one in the Royal Marines, and the other in the General Service Corps. Prior to joining the Army Harold was employed by the Steelworks in the boiler shop.

Guardsman William Norman Wright was wounded in action in Achon, Germany. William (born c.1914), was the youngest son of Mr and Mrs W.H. Wright of 1 Brereton Grove, Cadishead. He joined the Army in 1940 and went overseas on D-Day, serving in France, Holland and Belgium. Before joining the Forces, he worked at Kinder and Company.

Dai Jones returned home on leave from the Merchant Navy for the first time in 4½ years. Born c.1913, the second son of Mr and Mrs Owen Jones of 542 Manchester Road, Hollins Green, he resided with his wife and three children at 13 The Weint, Hollins Green. Dai joined the Army c.1939 and served with the Loyal Regiment (North Lancashire) in Iraq, North Africa and Italy. For reasons not known in July 1944 he had been discharged from the Army and had joined the Merchant Navy.

The first local man to be taken prisoner during the war, 32 year old Fusilier Harry Hutchinson, returned home to his wife and family at 125 Eldon Road West, Irlam after more than 4½ years in German prison camps. In that time he had been in three different camps, had lost an eye and had survived experiences which convinced him that the Nazis, in particular the younger element in Germany, were rotten. He had witnessed a comrade shot by a German guard for whistling while returning from work. Immediately after his capture, he was taken to Stalag XXIB at Posen in Poland and later moved to the notorious Stalag VIIIB at Lamsdorf. From there he was transferred to Stalag 344. Harry said that the older Germans realised that the war was lost but it was being kept going by the younger Nazis, who knew that an Allied victory would mean the end of the Nazi Party. *The food situation too, was acute, and had it not been for the Red Cross parcels many of the prisoners, including myself, would have gone under. The shortage did not only affect the prisoners; local children would beg food from prisoners. If they were caught the guards would frog-march them down the street, and shave their heads, to make an example of them. Many were hit with rifle butts, too.* One of the most heartening sights for him was to see Allied bombers roaring over the camp at almost the same time every day: *They usually dropped pamphlets to warn the civilian population of impending raids, but when the actual bombing started the authorities told the prisoners that they had to remain above ground.* Harry was the eldest son of Mr and Mrs M. Hutchinson of 42 Spenser Avenue, Scunthorpe. Harry had worked at the Steelworks until he joined the Army in September 1939. He was posted to France in March 1940 and taken prisoner, at Bethune, on 27th May 1940.

A decision was taken to form a Cadishead and Irlam Branch of the 42nd Lancashire Battalion Home Guard Old Comrades. The Old Comrades Association of many regiments had done valuable work in the past, not only by their annual reunions at which the 'old sweats' met and fought their battles over again, but by various benevolences to sick and needy members. The Home Guard Old Comrades Association was intended to work on similar lines, and all local ex-members of Britain's citizen army were invited to a meeting.

The *Guardian* contained the following comment: *Incidentally I see that the British Legion, at the Annual Conference turned down the resolution that Home Guard should be allowed to become members. Well that, of course, is the Legion's domestic affair, and in the past they have proved themselves quite capable of running their huge organisation. But reading a report of the conference I did most strongly object to one reason put forward for refusing Home Guards to become members. That reason was that 'the British Legion did not want in its ranks men who had to be conscripted to the Home Guard between 1942 and 1944.' In my opinion the argument was illogical. How many men who were conscripted during the last war are members of the Legion today? How many men who have been conscripted during this war will be allowed to become members when the war is over? And, finally, if conscription more or less on the continental model, becomes the law here after war, will the British Legion refuse to accept the conscripts as members when they have finished their service. The whole point is that this has been a total war, and there are civilians and Home Guards who have seen more action, and more death and destruction than some servicemen. That is only to be expected in a war of this kind. No, the British Legion was entitled to do just as it wished in the admission or non-admission of Home Guards, but to refuse them on the score that conscripts were not welcome was a gratuitous insult to the men who, if the call had come, would have had to have borne the brunt of the attack on this country. Incidentally most Home Guards are as proud of their units as we were – and are – of our own mobs. Harking back to those days should remind us that we were not so much concerned with whether a man was a conscript as long as he was a good pal and a staunch friend.*

The issue of whether members of the Home Guard would be allowed to join the British Legion continued to be an issue in the district. The following article appeared in the Town Topics column of the *Guardian*: *I would like to clear the air regarding the Home Guard and the British Legion. Misunderstanding seems to have arisen owing to various reports in the Press giving the impression that this matter has been dealt with and the question of membership turned down. This is not so, but is a matter for the Annual Conference and will probably be decided this year. According to the Legion Journal, Brigadier-General E.R. Fitzpatrick, chairman of the British Legion, at a meeting last November stated: 'Under the terms of the Royal Charter of the British Legion, ex-members of the Home Guard are not eligible for membership of the Legion. The Charter can only be amended by a two-thirds majority of a national conference. At the same time, a large number of Home Guards are already eligible by reason of previous service, and a further considerable number who have gone from the Home Guard into the Navy, the Army and the Air Force will become eligible on the completion of their service.' The above should make the position quite clear, and I might add the question of whether men were conscripted into the Home Guard or the services does not enter into the matter in any way.*

On 15th February Private William Arthur Taylor (known to all as Bill) of the 7th Battalion of the Seaforth Highlanders was wounded in action at Tilburg, Holland. This was the second time that he had been wounded. The first time was in France in June 1944. He was evacuated to the UK on 28th June and after recovering he was posted back to his battalion in France on 2nd August 1944. Bill took part in heavy fighting at Best, Holland, before being wounded for the second time. He was admitted into a hospital in Belgium. He later went on to Germany where he remained until returning to the UK on 26th May. On 1st November 1945 he was transferred to the Cameron Highlanders and served in Gibraltar from 12th December 1945 until 25th February 1946. Bill was demobilised on 23rd March 1946 and posted to Class W (T) of the Army Reserve, resuming his career as an electrician. On 4th June 1953 he enlisted into a Territorial Army battalion of the Parachute Regiment (Regimental number 22802484). Bill served with the TA until 15th August 1962 when he was discharged, at his own request, having attained the rank of sergeant.

The Cadishead and Irlam branch of the British Legion proposed a resolution to the Legion's Annual Conference at Preston, on Saturday, 17th February. The resolution, which had first been raised by First World War veteran, Tom Walton, was a protest against the actions of medical tribunals. Benjamin Neville, chairman of the local branch, and Peter Barrow, DCM, were the branch delegates at the conference. Both men were veterans of the First World War. The resolution, moved by Peter Barrow, read: *That this branch protests in the strongest possible terms against the actions of the medical tribunals in the treatment of applicants appearing under the heading of psycho-neurosis, and we protest against the consideration of an applicant's medical history being taken from when he was a child and submit that his medical history begins when he is accepted A1 on enlistment, Fit for service, fit for pension is the considered view of this branch.*

Private Bill Taylor, Seaforth Highlanders

The resolution was seconded by delegates from another branch from the floor of the conference hall and received the support of many others. The area chairman, Lieutenant General Sir James Wilton O'Dowda, said the resolution was one of the most important of the day and that a special committee would be set up to go into the question. Their views would be put before the Ministry of Pensions at an early date. Sir James agreed that many men had been discharged with psycho-neurosis and it was a matter which the British Legion would take up very seriously.

Miss Joan Rollinson, teacher of the Newcroft School of Dancing, and Jimmy Gill organised a staging of the pantomime *Cinderella* on Thursday, Friday and Saturday, 15th to 17th February at St Paul's schoolroom, Irlam. The proceeds went to the Welcome Home Fund. They had already raised over £200 from previous fundraisers. Robert Milner, who was back in Irlam on leave from the RAF, helped with the scene-shifting.

Private 14246188 **Frank Shaw** of the 2nd Battalion, Seaforth Highlanders, 152nd (Highland) Brigade, 51st (Highland) Division was killed in action in Germany on Sunday, 18th February.

On 18th February the 2nd Seaforth Highlanders were ordered to attack south from Hervuist and to take and cross an anti-tank ditch which was in their path. This was a preliminary operation which was intended to secure the way for a night attack on the town of Goch.

Private Frank Shaw, Seaforth Highlanders

Modern day view of Frank Shaw's headstone, Reichswald War Cemetery

Frank was the only son of George and the late Martha Shaw of 41 Baines Avenue, Irlam. His father, George, was a veteran of the First World War and had been wounded twice. Frank joined the Army in August 1942 and was posted to France in August 1944 where he joined the 2nd Seaforths which had been fighting in Normandy since June. Frank was educated at Irlam Central School and prior to joining the Army, he was employed in the general office of the Steelworks. He is buried at Reichswald War Cemetery, Cleves, Germany. The inscription on his headstone states: *He gave his life that we might live.* He was 21 years old.

Private 14762696 **John Victor Thomas** was killed in action on the same day as Frank Shaw, Sunday, 18th February, aged 18.

John served as a light machine gunner with the 6th Battalion, King's Own Scottish Borderers, 44th Infantry Brigade, 15th (Scottish) Division in Belgium and Germany. On this day 15th (Scottish) Division was tasked with clearing the area north of the River Niers to east of Goch, in preparation for an attack by the 51st Highland Division on the town of Goch, Germany, scheduled to take place the following day.

John was the youngest son of the late William and Mrs E. Thomas of 22 Victory Road, Cadishead. Educated at Cadishead Senior School, he went on to work for the Eccles Co-operative Society until May 1944 when he was called up into the Army and posted to the King's (Liverpool Regiment). He went overseas in November 1944 and at some point was transferred to the King's Own Scottish Borderers. Only three weeks prior to his death, John had been home on compassionate leave to attend the funeral of his father. He is buried at Rheinberg War Cemetery, Germany.

Private John Victor Thomas, King's (Liverpool Regiment) and later King's Own
Scottish Borderers

On 24th February Flight Sergeant (navigator) 1235933 Harold Townend was on board Vickers Warwick PN748K, when it made radar contact with an enemy U-boat. Depth charges were dropped and shortly afterwards large amounts of debris and oil appeared on the surface. It was later confirmed that U927 had been sunk. Harold served with 179 Squadron, Coastal Command, which, at the time, was operating out of RAF St Eval in Cornwall. The squadron was tasked with protecting supply and troop ships from submarine attack.

On 24th February the local Committee for Soviet Medical Aid had arranged a Red Army Flag Day, to raise funds. Collections took place in most of the works. In spite of numerous offers of help, there was a great shortage of flag sellers, and the committee made an appeal for volunteers. Wolstencrofts store on Liverpool Road, Lower Irlam, distributed the flags and collection boxes. The committee felt that most people, realising the tremendous needs of the Red Army in its advance to Berlin, and the suffering involved, would not hesitate to give promptly. Along with the Flag Day, but held later, the committee had arranged an Anglo-Soviet Exhibition which consisted of posters, drawings and photographs of life in the USSR. It showed graphic pictures of the relief of Stalingrad, which was described as probably the world's most heroic city. The exhibition took place on Saturday, 3rd March at the Congregational Schoolroom, Cadishead, and was held again on the following Saturday, at a schoolroom in Higher Irlam.

Leading Aircraftman Wesley Lawrence Green, Royal Canadian Air Force, of Arthur, Ontario, Canada, married Gwendoline Evans, the daughter of Chief Petty Officer Harry Evans, Royal Navy and Mrs H.H. Evans of 44 Princes Avenue, Higher Irlam. Harry, who participated in the Dunkirk evacuations in 1940, was a First World War veteran who had lied about his age to join up aged 14. He later ran the penny ferry across the Manchester Ship Canal and earned himself the nickname 'The Admiral'.

Housing was a real concern for the soon to be returning servicemen and women and the Council was considering whether to erect temporary housing in the form of prefabricated houses. Although the district had established a post-war housing plan to build 100 new houses, there was little chance of these being built for at least two years. With over 1,000 names on the housing waiting list prefabricated houses offered a partial and short-term solution. Many servicemen and women who had married during the war years, had made temporary homes with their parents but the thought of returning to live with their parents after the war would not appeal to most and they would rightly feel that they deserved a home in recognition of their service. The prefabricated house may not have been the ideal solution but at the time it appeared to be the only one. They would at least provide temporary shelter for young married couples with one or two children.

Flight Sergeant Harold Townend, RAFVR

The *Guardian* led the campaign to urge the Council for a solution: *It is their job, too, to make up their minds – in the very near future – to provide some sort of temporary homes for the men who have fought for them. If they fail to do this; if the boys return home and have no homes to go to, the Council will have failed in its duty as the elected representatives of the people.*

A questionnaire had been sent by the Council to local servicemen asking them if they were in favour of prefabricated houses as temporary homes to help alleviate the housing shortage. Although the results were not published, the overwhelming majority had voted in favour, but this did not sway the Council and the majority of its members remained against prefabricated houses. The *Guardian* decided to keep up the pressure on the Council by sending out its own questionnaire on the subject; almost all the questionnaires received were in favour of 'prefabs'. It was significant that the vote by three women's organisations (attached to local churches) cast 140 votes in favour of the 'prefabs' and only nine against. Servicemen, too, were in favour. The Council was faced with a quandary; they recognised the urgent need to provide adequate housing accommodation for the men and women who would soon be returning home but, with little money available, the majority of the Council members were against this type of home, preferring instead to invest in permanent brick-built houses. This led to a great deal of prevarication and it would take several months before a decision would be made. Quotes from the monthly meeting of the Council gives some idea of the debates that were being held within the Council Offices: *We have the housing space. If the Council are only going to have good intentions they won't get so far. We have sent out deputations to various housing sites and done all sorts of things except making an attempt to save this ground. Some time ago, Mr Nurse (the surveyor) submitted plans of a bungalow that was, in my opinion, an ideal house. It was of steel and asbestos exterior, but it did not suit our wishes. These dwellings could certainly be let at a rent not exceeding 15 shillings a week, and well in reach of everyone's pocket. That was an excellent proposition and we should not delay the matter any longer. Very soon, we hope, hostilities will have ceased in Germany. We will be able to rejoice, wave flags and make it nice for ourselves. But it won't help the boys; they can't live in fields. We should do all we can to obtain some accommodation additional to what we have already got and we should apply for a large number.* Councillor Adams.

The boys should have something to come back to. I do think it is our duty to find houses for them. Waving flags will not be enough. Councillor Enticott.

In a land fit for heroes we want houses fit for heroes to live in. We have had no concrete facts from the Government, but we have had some steel and concrete houses. I have yet to hear the ladies' organisations in this district who have seen these 'prefabs,' speak well of them. The blame does not rest with the Council, but with the Government. They will not make a move in this problem. We have heard about different types of 'prefabs,' and now we have the chief of the AA Gunners as housing adviser. During the war there have been one and a half million marriages and the Government say that one in ten will get a house; the other nine will be unlucky. Manchester is already trying to force the Government's hand as far as temporary and permanent houses are concerned. We in Irlam want houses for the soldiers, and not steel and concrete pill boxes. Councillor R. James.

While I have no objection to these men who have done so much for us having houses, I agree with Councillor James that the fault is with the Government and not with us. If we put soldiers in these temporary 'prefabs' they may be satisfied for a year or so, but after that they would want permanent houses. These lads are worth everything we can do for them. Councillor Hesford.

The Town Topics column of the *Guardian* commented on the above meeting of the Council and its position with regard to the housing shortage: *On Tuesday, by a majority, Irlam Council threw out an amendment by Councillor Adams that they should apply for 50 prefabricated houses. Let there be no misunderstanding. Those who argued against the amendment made a good case for themselves – a case equally as strong as the argument in favour of the amendment. But they missed one salient point – or failed to ask themselves one question. That question was; what is going to be done to provide houses for returning servicemen? It is all very well to say that we must wait until we have seen 'prefabs' erected; it is all very well to demand permanent houses. We know they are needed, but what is going to happen in the interim period – the time between the homecoming of the men and the erection of the first permanent homes? Are we to have – as many towns had after the last war – squalid caravan colonies which were a disgrace to our alleged civilisation? And a hideous monument to our lack of foresight?*

One of the prefabs on Fairhills Road, Irlam

Prefabricated houses may not be ideal; there is no claim made for them in that direction. But they will fill the gap until such time as permanent homes can be erected. Within the next few months, it is likely that many of our servicemen will come home. To what? To sharing a home with 'in-laws' or strangers, to overcrowding, to lack of privacy and to all the troubles and evils these things can breed. I agree that our fighting men do deserve good, permanent homes – but I am convinced that, rather than share a home with others, they will willingly for a period make do with a prefabricated home for, after all, it will be a home and not a lodging. I believe that the Council – individually and collectively – is doing what it considers is for the best and that it is honestly concerned with the question of providing good homes. They have proved that on their own housing estates. But there still remains the fact that these permanent homes cannot be erected yet – perhaps not for several years. In the meantime the surplus population must have somewhere to live. It cannot live in fields and it must not be allowed again to erect huddles of shacks and caravans. The solution to the problem is, whether we like it or not, prefabricated homes that will fill the breach. In the meantime, there has been some mention of a questionnaire which was sent to members of the Forces asking their opinion. I am informed that the bulk of the replies were in favour of the 'prefabs.' If this is the case, why has the amendment been turned down? However, we can perhaps arrive at some idea as to whether 'prefabs' are wanted or not. To do this, I ask all servicemen and, for that matter, residents, to let me know their opinion. At the end of Town Topics is a small form. Fill it in and post it to 'Onlooker', Guardian office, Liverpool Road, Irlam. That should give us some indication whether readers are in favour of prefabricated houses.

Over the next few months up to the end of the war, several letters were published in the *Guardian* on the subject, from servicemen overseas:

Sir, having written one letter to Reader's Forum, and as yet had no threatening letters by return, I venture on a little more correspondence regarding post-war planning. Re the housing problem – I myself being one of the hundreds in Irlam and Cadishead who hope to have a roof over my head after this war! I see that in a copy of the Guardian which has just arrived out here the question of a loan to cover the initial cost of building was raised, i.e. that a sum of say £50,000 means that over the period required for repayment, the initial amount plus interest becomes more like £100,000 owing to the very high rate of interest? Now as the Government is prepared to grant loans to local Councils for the purpose of housing and education schemes, etc. at 3 percent, where does the very high interest rate enter this problem? Isn't it time some of our local 'fathers' got down to a few hard facts regarding the housing problem instead of thinking up imaginary ones to fill in the time? After all this war won't last forever, and I think the least we can ask for is a home of our own to come back to! Looking forward to the next parcel of Guardians. Sergeant Roland Powell, RAF, India.

Sir, on Saturday, February 24th, I, with a friend in the building trade, went to see one of the temporary pre-fabricated houses which have been erected in the Kasr el Nil Barracks, Cairo. We went mainly to see exactly what it was like and to 'pull it to pieces.' After queuing up for an hour on what to us was a very cold day, and looking at what appeared to be a glorified Army hut, we went inside to receive a surprise. I take my hat off to the man who thought it out; it was good and the only fault we could find was that the living room was a bit too small for a temporary home (say three years). It was ideal for two people, but not with children as well. The kitchenette was the best, and built in a permanent house with a similar design would be 'just the job'. My friend was puzzled about condensation from the bathroom and kitchen. Our guide couldn't explain that. Perhaps some person with knowledge of the matter could enlighten us. How long are we to live in these temporary houses? And what will happen to them when they are no longer required? They would make ideal holiday chalets. Any enlightenment on these matters would be appreciated. J.R. Howard, Mediterranean Expeditionary Force.

I take this opportunity to express my thanks for the way you are endeavouring to find out whether or not the need and wish of the people is for or against prefabricated bungalows. I think that you are doing an excellent service to the district in this way. I am enclosing a letter to the councillors of Irlam and Cadishead expressing my views on the matter, and would be pleased if you would bring it to their notice either through your paper or direct. I have only just received the Guardian for April 7th, so trust that my hurried views meet with your approval.

To: - The Councillors of Irlam and Cadishead, Gentlemen – This question of prefabs or not seems to be causing you a bit of a problem, personally I feel the solution is in the answer to the following questions:

Does our present housing situation cater for the needs of our present population?

How many men and women returning from the Forces will require accommodation?

Have we enough, or can we erect sufficient permanent dwellings now?

I do believe that you are giving this problem your honest and sincere consideration, and that you do want to provide better houses than those termed by Councillor James, Steel and concrete pillboxes. But can you? Try to visualise the present communal homes of our men and women in the Forces; hideous, ugly looking Nissen huts or worse, occupied by 20 to 30 people all getting in each other's way, with not one minute of privacy. Then imagine how they are going to welcome their own little prefab castle. They don't want to return to civilian life as lodgers, or be under an obligation to people and still pay barrack room damages; neither do people want them as such. The outward appearance of these temporary houses may not be all that is desired, but inside is going to be a home for someone; that's something you can't build you know; you can only put up the walls. What is to prevent someone using a little initiative and improving the outside appearance a little? As you are aware 'prefabs' can be erected quickly and in the main by unskilled labour. They will be more hygienic than lots of houses at present occupied by local residents, so why not get on with the job as a temporary measure then start making your plans for permanent houses and go all out to get them. After all, what is the use of your excellent idea of a questionnaire if you are going to over-rule the result? So, come on, let's get going. The boys will soon be home and by the way I hope you consider my application and put my name on the list. 2nd Lieutenant J. Shaw, Pioneer Corps.

Sir, being an ardent admirer of your column, I think it only right that I should state my views on prefabricated houses more fully than you have asked. Here, then, are one or two ideas. Prior to joining the Navy I was employed as a bricklayer by T.E and J.A. Brew of Albert Street, serving a total in this one trade of 5½ years. I think by now I should have a good knowledge at the rate 'good' houses can be put up, or don't you agree. Here, then, is why I'm against prefabricated houses. I believe that the speed the Council acts, it would take just as long to put this type of house up on a respectable site and get them ready for accommodation. Also I believe the rate at which men will be released from the Forces will allow for the building of decent houses to last a hundred years, not five or ten. I saw the state of roads, etc. (independent of Liverpool Road) in built up sites in Cadishead and Irlam 12 months ago, so I have a good idea what a 'prefab' site will look like after some of our typical weather. Can you tell me this – why hasn't it been suggested yet, that when houses are built for lads returning home, the house after a reasonable deposit and paying weekly or monthly till the price of the house becomes his. I'm sure this would be welcomed by everyone in Cadishead and Irlam if only openly suggested. I must close now, hoping my small but crude letter will have been of some assistance to you for a better Irlam and Cadishead. Norman Mason, Royal Navy.

Sir, I have been taking a keen interest in the development of the post-war housing problem. Speaking for myself and, no doubt, a good many others, I am looking forward to coming home and getting married, but in my home there is not sufficient room for another person besides myself, and that goes the same for the other chaps I have met out here who come from Irlam and Cadishead. For us chaps out here in Ceylon and SEAC, and other places abroad, all we can do is hope that the people at home are not just looking at the immediate housing problem, but are trying to do something for us chaps who are away. I think the majority of people are looking at the prefabs in the light that they will have to buy them outright and, of course, they can't afford the amount of money, £500 or £600, whatever, they may cost, so they do not wish to press for the prefabs, just in case they may have to buy them outright. It is definitely up to the Council to buy these and rent them. We don't want to come back to paper streamers and brass bands – we want a home, and peace and quietness. Yours etc. James Richard Givens, 28 Ferryhill Road, Irlam.

Sir, re: the articles by C. Mallett on prefabricated houses (Guardian 21st April), I think his statement sums up practically everyone's views on the subject. I as an individual do not think that prefabs are satisfactory, because, in the first place, this is 1945, and I consider it a disgrace that one should have no choice but to live in what are nothing more or less than glorified Army huts! That is, of course, referring to the wooden bungalow types. But, one has to face facts, and as we have already been at war for practically six years, there is obviously a serious shortage of men and material in the building trade. This obviously leaves prefabs as the only way out of the very critical situation that has arisen through the aimless and drifting policy that has been pursued in the past. If, then, as it appears, we have to accept prefabs as a temporary measure, we must also ensure that these temporary dwellings do not become permanent. In effect, with the release of men and materials after the war there is no reason why permanent dwellings should not be erected irrespective of whether the prefab have been in use five days or five years. Sergeant Roland Powell, South East Asia Air Force, India.

Sir, yes, we should have the prefabricated bungalows. They would be much better than some of the houses we have to live in and bring children up at present. Let's have less talk and more action. Thanking you for your interest in us. Gunner Vaudrey of 16 George Street, Higher Irlam (home on leave from the British Liberation Army). Gunner Thomas Vaudrey, Royal Artillery.

Gunner Thomas Vaudrey, Royal Artillery

Sir, I have read in two recent issues of the Guardian the Council's attitude towards prefabricated houses. Surely, if it is a fact that only 100 houses can be built two years after the war, then there should be no doubt about the building of the 'prefabs'. I must say that a 'prefab' is not my idea of a home, but if we can't have the real thing, surely we can have a temporary home. Let us hope that after two or three years in a 'prefab' we haven't to start a war to get a real home. One war is enough for any man. But I suppose a house war could be arranged at a push. I think my local friends in the Army will agree that we've been pushed around enough in the Army without being pushed around when we eventually come home. A friend of mine who reads your article on the Council's views towards 'prefabs' remarked 'They are a dithery crowd at your place, aren't they?' Why is it that our civic fathers are so much against these 'prefabs'? Is it the cost? Surely if the country can keep the war going for all these years we can have built these 'prefabs' to last two or three years, or is that too much to ask? Perhaps it is thought that having had so much experience of living in a hole in the ground, we can do the same when we come home. Let's hope our civic fathers get mobile on the job. Why wait till the war is over? Why not a home to come home to? Perhaps, sir, you could give them a few digs in the Guardian; I must say you've done very well in the past. 'Local Lad Browned Off' of the British Liberation Army.

Now something about prefabricated houses, having seen them by the hundred, I would think twice before I put pigs in them. T. Ashton, RAF.

Sir, enclosed is my Guardian questionnaire. As you can see my answer is yes. Irlam and Cadishead should have some of these prefabricated bungalows until such time as labour and materials permit the building of houses. I should like to make one point, and that is that those who are allotted these prefabricated buildings should have the first chance of a brick house. Now a little in praise of Councillor McLean's idea of being available one night a week to help and advise those who need it. I hope many take advantage of this offer and, as we say in the Army, Councillor McLean you're proving that 'You're just the job' for the job. Here's a bouquet for Onlooker, keep on punching in your column of Town Topics. We'll get somewhere one of these days, and carry on giving us lads serving overseas the 'griff'. J. Hamilton, serving overseas in Greece with HM Forces.

Sir, I would like to thank you for the interest you are taking in the district housing problem. I for one am all in favour of the prefabricated houses, as I see no other way out of the difficulty. The district, when I left it, was badly in need of houses; what is it like now I cannot imagine with so many of the servicemen getting married and needing homes. I would like to know why the Council is turning prefabricated houses down. If they are good enough for other towns, they are good enough for us and I think they will tide us over till the Council starts building. S. Taylor, Central Mediterranean Force.

Although the prefabs provided some additional housing, there was still insufficient provision for the many servicemen and women who would return from the war. Cliff Cole was amongst those affected when he was demobbed and returned to the district: *It was a bloody worry, because I'll tell you what I'd nowhere to live, no, ... now it so happened that when I come home I'd nowhere to live, finding a place, in Irlam, I got my name down in the council offices that used to be opposite the Catholic Club and I used to go all the time down, 'any news?' So there was nowhere, couldn't get a home or anything, there was nowhere to live, and what happened that, our Dave married Peggy Broad, Graham Crescent, and to cut it short he got married, she was married before, she was married to an Air Force crew lad who got killed, Donkin, and they had this boy Gerald Donkin and of course they got married and she had a house in Warrington, which was a police house, so it was her house so she said while you've got no house you go and live in Warrington and live there for a while, this was before they got married. So I went there when I come out of the Forces and I got a job in Warrington, wire drawing, the thing was I kept going back to Irlam asking 'have we got a house?' 'Oh yes you're alright, you've got so many points cos you were away all that time, first time you've got a prefab down Fairhills Road.' I said 'just the thing.' She said 'where do you live now?' I said 'I'm living in Warrington.' 'Oh, you've had it.' If only I'd kept my gob shut, but I didn't get it.*

It would be May before the Housing and Town Planning Committee of the Council finally recommended that an application should be made to the Ministry of Health for an allocation of 50 temporary bungalows. The total area of land in the Council's ownership available for building was 36.83 acres, which would allow for the building of approximately 457 houses. The 1946 building programme for the district was an allocation of 100 houses. These were to be erected on the Moorfield Estate, Irlam, and the land between Lords Street and Fir Street, Cadishead, in equal numbers. In addition, 40 temporary bungalows – 20 in Irlam and 20 in Cadishead were to be built. The second year's programme was for 200 houses and these again would be equally divided between the Cadishead recreation site and Fiddlers Lane, Irlam.

MARCH

On Saturday, 3rd March at St Mary's Church, Cadishead, Miss Frances Jean Patterson married the highly decorated Lieutenant John Bridge, BSc, AKC, and only holder of the George Cross, George Medal and bar.

Frances was the youngest daughter of Mr and Mrs Frances Patterson of 146 Liverpool Road, Cadishead. She was the adjutant of No. 1147 (Irlam) Unit of the Women's Junior Air Corps (WJAC), and also a member of the Cadishead Junior Unionists. Reverend Bakker officiated at the ceremony. The bridesmaid, Miss Alice Bridge, was the sister of the groom, and Lieutenant Commander C.G. Staines, OBE, Royal Naval Volunteer Reserve, acted as best man. After the ceremony, a reception was held at Hole Mill Farm, and later John and Frances departed for their honeymoon in the Lake District. At the time they resided at Maghull, Liverpool.

Born in 1915, John was the youngest son of Mr and Mrs Joseph Edward Bridge of Hole Mill Farm, Culcheth. He was educated at Leigh Grammar School and King's College, London, where he gained an honours degree in science and mathematics. He worked as a physics master until he was called up. He had a most distinguished military career, joining the Navy in June 1940, and serving with a bomb disposal unit at Plymouth, Scapa Flow and South Africa. He also took part in the invasions of Sicily, Italy and France. He volunteered for bomb disposal work because, as he explained later, it involved saving lives rather than taking them. In September 1940, while stationed in Cornwall, John safely disarmed an extremely dangerous bomb fitted with a delayed-action fuse, for which he was awarded the George Medal. In March 1941 he received the King's Commendation for Brave Conduct after dealing with 15 bombs, one of which had fallen near the dockyard at Devonport, Plymouth. John examined the bomb and found that one of the fuses was ticking. He could not deal with the ticking fuse until he had dealt with the first fuse, as the slightest movement would have set off the fuse. He applied liquid discharge to the first fuse, which took him one hour, all the while, with the ticking fuse next to him and no idea of when the bomb would explode. When he had finished with the first fuse, he applied a magnetic clockstopper but this only slowed the ticking. After several attempts he decided to remove the fuse, despite knowing that they were often fitted with anti-withdrawal devices. Once the fuse had been removed the bomb was taken away and dropped into the sea. The fuse fired shortly after it was taken out. In October 1941, he disposed of a bomb which had fallen into the sluice valve chamber between two graving docks at Falmouth and failed to explode. He climbed 35 feet down a shaft using the cross girders to get to the water level. The bomb was at the bottom of the chamber in 6 feet of water. He disarmed the bomb and saved the docks from damage. As a result he was awarded a Bar to his George Medal, the first naval officer to be honoured in this way. He was awarded the George Cross for defusing enemy depth charges at Messina harbour, Sicily in May 1943. A previous bomb disposal party had been killed while attempting to defuse similar devices. He made 28 dives to render the depth charges safe and recovered the mechanisms which were of a previously unknown type. He also rendered safe a further 207 depth charges situated above and below the water. As a result of his bravery Messina harbour was cleared of depth charges and declared open one day before the assault on Italy. The citation read: *For the most conspicuous and prolonged bravery and contempt of death in clearing Messina Harbour of depth charges. The recommending officer stated that he had never before had the fortune to be associated with such cool and sustained bravery as Lieutenant Bridge displayed during the ten days of the operation.* He also served in Normandy and was involved in the D-Day landings as naval bomb safety officer. He later served in Belgium and Holland. By the end of the war, John had reached the rank of lieutenant commander.

The members of Cadishead Conservative Club elected Mr A.C. Harrison as their club president for the third year running. Thanking the members for the confidence they had shown in him, Mr Harrison, in his acceptance speech, made reference to the two world wars: *This year will, I have not the slightest doubt, see a general election.* Mr Harrison continued: *We have had a political truce in Parliament for the past five years and certainly, in so far as the vast majority of the House of Commons is concerned, that truce has been faithfully observed. I am sure we will continue to honour that pledge and I believe all other parties will do so until the day of final victory. Victory is now certain, and when it comes members of the Liberal and Labour parties can leave the Coalition Government – to use the words of Mr Herbert Morrison – with good grace. The essence of Conservative politics is national. Our objectives, broadly, are the maintenance of the Empire and the elevation of the condition of the people. We earnestly seek a lasting peace. Whether that search is successful will depend upon all the peoples of the United Nations. In World War One, we fought to make the world safe for democracy. We failed. Hitler rose and the Second World War came on because we were not sufficiently concerned with the plight of the common man the world over. We did not realise that economic democracy must be combined with political democracy or political democracy would die. Hitler exploited our failure to establish an economical democracy by starting World War Two. If we are to prevent a second Hitler and World War Three, we must be more daring than we were 25 years ago. We must fight, not merely to make the world safe for democracy, but to give democracy first place in the world. The slogan 'Democracy First' needs the supremacy of freedom in both the economic and political world. Freedom means respect for the dignity of the individual. No man should be free to take another man's freedom away from him. If we plan aright there can be freedom from hunger – freedom from the fear of a poverty-stricken old age. Our new declarations must go on to cover freedoms we have not yet got, but we must have. The time has come for a new declaration of freedom which I would define as freedom from worry about a job, sickness and poverty-pinched old age; freedom which will enable the scales of justice to be held with equal poise between employers and employees; freedom from strife between races and creeds; freedom and support to inventors of new ideas to expand the production of needed goods without the fear of repressive cartels; excessive taxation or excessive Government regulations. Above all, we are fighting for peace – but peace will not last long if it doesn't bring to the common man everywhere, these freedoms. On February 25th, 1942, at the 50th annual general meeting, I concluded with certain words, and I am sure they are worth repeating again – Though the future is unknown, we believe that freedom will stand and that justice will survive all the wrongs of dictatorship. That is what we stand for – that is what we believe; that is what our boys have gone out to preserve – this freedom, this liberty for all the world to share.*

There had long been calls for a maternity home to be set up in the district and the local *Guardian* took up the case. The following article appeared in the edition published on 17th March: *From hospitals, the topic leads naturally to the maternity home. So far, in spite of agitation, nothing appears to have been done in the matter. Yet, recently, I heard of an instance where a soldier's wife with one child is living in lodgings and sharing the only available bed with the daughter of the house. The wife is expecting her second child and, in view of the circumstances, she has been asked to find alternative accommodation. To ask anyone to do that in a place so crowded as this district is, of course, ridiculous. But what can the householder do? This is only one instance; there must be others, and all these difficulties could be solved if we had a maternity home in the district. Imagine the feelings of the soldier-husband, who is abroad and whose wife is expecting a baby, when he knows that his wife has nowhere to go. Can that man possibly give his best service? Sooner or later something will have to be done about the provision of a maternity home – and if it is done sooner, the better for all concerned. But we shan't get anywhere if we sit twiddling our thumbs waiting for official Bumbledom to get a move on.* Despite pressure from various quarters the maternity home never materialised.

Private Edward Winder and Private Thomas A. Blundell, met each other in France. They had only been overseas for three weeks. Born c.1927, Edward was the only son of Mr E. Winder of 47 Lancaster Road, Cadishead. Before joining the Army he was employed by Kilvert and Sons of Trafford Park. He joined the Army in August 1944, and went overseas in February 1945. Thomas (born c.1927) was the youngest son of Mr and Mrs T. Blundell of 6 Graham Crescent, Cadishead. He joined the Army in August 1944 and went overseas on 13th February, serving with the 15th Scottish Division. He was previously employed by Mr W. Motley, coal merchants, of Cadishead. Both Edward and Thomas attended Cadishead Senior School.

A German radio broadcast in March confirmed that Rifleman Ernest Wrigley (pictured), reported missing in December 1944, was a prisoner of war. His mother, Mrs M.J. Wrigley of 62 Nelson Drive, Cadishead, received letters from Whalley Range and Chiswick, sent by people who had heard the broadcast. Ernest was born c.1921 and he attended St Mary's School and later, Irlam Central School. He was employed by Wilkinson & Tonge of Cadishead before joining the Army in May 1940. His first overseas posting was to Italy in early 1944, where he was captured.

The AGM of the Irlam and Cadishead St John Ambulance and Nursing Divisions was held on Tuesday, 6th March. Superintendent Herbert Weston remarked that the strength of the divisions had been well-maintained during the period of the war. As this was the first AGM since returning to a peacetime footing, he thought it appropriate to pay a tribute to the loyal manner in which the members had placed their services at the disposal of the authorities on the outbreak of war, and for the way they had carried on until the breaking up of the Civil Defence parties. They were still prepared to carry on any duties they may be called upon to perform in any emergency that may arise. He said the ambulance division was 50 strong, out of which 18 members were on service with HM Forces – four in the Navy, eight in the Army and six in the RAF. One member, Private Harold Rosbottom, was a prisoner of war in Germany. The division had suffered a great loss in the form of Ambulance Officer Hazlehurst, who had died in 1944, and the meeting paid silent tribute to his memory by standing. Sergeant S. Higginson was appointed acting ambulance officer, and Corporal (Acting Sergeant) W.W. Meakin, pending their passing examinations for promotion. The divisional treasurer (Transport Officer J. Daniels) then produced the balance sheet, which showed a balance in hand of over £70. A discussion took place on the future of the divisions, and the need for expansion.

The brigade had given good service prior to the war, and there would still be a great need for their work when peacetime conditions were again restored. There was also a need for more members, and the opinion was expressed that many of those who had relinquished Home Guard and Civil Defence duties might want to continue giving public service, and they would all be welcomed into the brigade's ranks. It was felt, particularly with the acquisition of the ambulance, that the brigade should possess a headquarters of their own, and a committee was duly selected to arrange suitable methods for raising a building fund. This would give improved facilities for training and duties. The Nursing Division also wanted to increase its numbers. The ladies would be of great assistance if the cottage hospital, so much talked about, materialised. As it was, these ladies had given invaluable part-time assistance in other districts besides Irlam and Cadishead. The Cadet Divisions, despite war-time conditions, had continued in their good work of training the boys and girls in the humanitarian work of St John, but they also were in need of recruits if they were to continue in their function as 'feeders' to the adult divisions. Boys and girls between the ages of 12 and 16 were asked to apply to Cadet Superintendent H.J. Lehrle, or Cadet Superintendent Mrs Jackson respectively.

On Wednesday evening, 7th March Flying Officer Ernest Mason, an ex-boy scout, visited his old scout troop in the district to attend the investiture of five scouts. He was home on sick leave from Belgium. During the ceremony, the Troop Flag was carried by Corporal V. Hayes, a Canadian serviceman who was stationed in the area. Afterwards, Ernest told the assembled scouts of a monument erected in Brussels to the memory of seventeen Belgium scouts who were shot for defying the Germans in keeping loyal to their Scout promise.

Ilford, one of the most badly blitzed places in the south, had been adopted by Lancashire County under the Good Neighbour Scheme, which helped districts that had suffered as a result of enemy action. The Good Neighbour Scheme was launched to help towns like Ilford to replace lost homes, clothing and furniture. The local WVS appealed for bedding, china and glassware, cleaning equipment, cutlery, floor coverings, furniture, garden tools and plants, house decorating material, household linen, kitchenware, ornaments and soft furnishings. The WVS arranged collections, and organised transport for the bulkier and heavier articles. They also set up receiving centres, which were open from 5th to 19th March at the WVS Centres, 107

Liverpool Road, Cadishead, and 604 Liverpool Road, Irlam. The WVS organisers were Mrs Loxley of 360 Liverpool Road, Irlam, and Enid Bakker of 278 Liverpool Road, Cadishead.

Charles Taylor, a local butcher and a member of the Irlam Food Control Committee, complained that nearby districts were getting preferential treatment in the matter of supplies: *The principal reason for our failure to get these supplies is because the Food Committee lacks punch and will not fight. Right through the war this district has never had a fair crack of the whip in the matter of food supplies. When it comes to allocations of various commodities we are off the map. But we are not off the map when it comes to calling our boys and girls up for service in the Forces.* Throughout the war there had been shortages of certain types of goods. An application had been made for a cooked meat and pork shop in Cadishead, which the Food Control Committee approved. The deputy meat agent from Manchester endorsed the committee's decision, but a higher authority turned down the application on the grounds that the district did not need such a shop. He continued: *In Cadishead and Irlam we have approximately a population of 15,000 people and no pork butchers or cooked meat shop, yet in Eccles, with a population of about 40,000, there are three or four of them. Urmston, with an almost similar population, is also well provided for. The official explanation is that we do not require a cooked meat shop because all the butchers get an equal percentage on their meat ...* (words missing due to damaged newspaper) *for the purposes of manufacture. That argument is idiotic, because every butcher in the area – whether they are cooked meat shops or not - gets a similar percentage. This discrimination against a small district has been going on ever since war broke out, and I am convinced that though the Food Control Committee have good intentions, they do not have enough punch and drive behind them. For example at Christmas, one was lucky to see a turkey in Cadishead or Irlam, yet people could leave here on the bus, go to Manchester, and get a double helping of turkey in the café of a well-known departmental store. How many women in this district haven't had to scrape up something for tea – not on one day a week, but on several? Yet in Eccles, Manchester and other towns' shops – and particularly big stores – are loaded with goods. I know two tripe shops, one in Manchester and one in Eccles – each of which gets more tripe in one week than comes into the whole of Irlam and Cadishead in a month. Yet we sit back and do nothing about it. One of the worst features of the whole thing is that most of the women in this district are working. They have not the time to go to Manchester and Eccles to do their shopping. The whole system is unfair to those women who are helping the war effort. Fish is another commodity which seems to be in eternal short supply here. Yet it can be got at Shudehill Market. Only this week I got a big piece at one shop, a piece of hake, a fish which has never been seen in Cadishead since the war broke out, and I was told I could have as much as I wanted. Confectioners and sweet shops are also being played with by the Ministry. There are shops in the district with thousands of sweet coupons – and the shopkeepers cannot get the sweets for them. Applications for these coupons to be translated into sweets have been turned down by someone in Liverpool. The whole thing is farcical, for people can go to Manchester and buy any amount of sweets. There the shops are loaded with them, and if you have the coupons you can get as many as you want.* Charles urged the Food Control Committee to make the strongest possible protest about the food restriction in the district: *The trouble in the past has been that we have not scrapped it out with the Ministry of Food officials as we should have done, and the result has been that they believe anything is good enough for this town. It is up to the Food Control Committee to show them that it isn't,* he concluded.

In the next two weeks' the *Guardian* published further letters on the same subject, the first from someone named 'J.H.' and the second by E. Potts:

Sir, it was with a great amount of interest that I read the statement made by Mr Charles Taylor at a recent meeting of the Irlam Food Control Committee. Every word spoken was an absolute 'straight from the shoulder' fact. When it happens that our womenfolk have to look farther afield than the village in which they live, just for packing up for lunch alone, it is evident that there is something radically wrong as regards the allocation of food in this area. Irlam and Cadishead for its size is a busy industrial area, and the workers in it want its fair share of food, just as the nation expects its share of war production from us, apart from the recruitment of man and woman power for the Forces, and I can honestly say that for the size of it, Irlam and Cadishead bears a great contribution. I have known of instances when I have myself gone to work and thrown myself to the tender mercy of the canteen for a meal because my wife has been unable to get anything in the village, and what have I received there? Jam and bread and, perhaps, a small sweet cake. After this delicious meal, I am expected to work like a Trojan and keep the production pointer at its peak, and it just can't be done. How many times have you got your daily papers and read that the health of the nation today is as good, if not better than ever it was. Well, in my opinion, there is only one answer, 'Poppycock!' Just come with me and watch workmen unwrapping their parcels of lunch at meal-break and listen to the remarks. Not gentlemanly, but we do realise the woman's talk of making the best of a bad job and, believe me, it's a damn bad job. We raise our hats to the housewives of Irlam and Cadishead.

Sir, in reply to your heading in last week's Guardian: 'Food Control Committee Lacks Punch. Do Irlam and Cadishead get a fair share of certain foodstuffs?' Some years ago while visiting St Paul's Cathedral, London, I read the following words written as a tribute to Wren, the great architect and builder 'If you seek his monument, look around you.' Today, as I look around at the British women, children and men, I think we could pay a similar tribute to the Ministry of Food for its care, thoughtfulness and foresight in designing a scheme of food rationing and supply which has kept all of us so fit, and healthy during six years of war, unequalled in the history for ferocity and severity. As a district, we have done well. To my knowledge, we have had no reports of malnutrition, through lack of food which could be laid at the Ministry of Food. True, I admit there are anomalies in the distribution of certain classes of food. Fresh salmon, turkeys, rabbits. Where these luxuries go to in war-time is beyond me. Might as well ask me where flies go in the winter. I can assure the public of Irlam and Cadishead that their Food Control Committee does not lack punch. With reference to the cooked meat trade; two shops were licensed in the early months of the war for this type of trade, but unfortunately did not take advantage of those licenses, hence we have a situation today of 'what we have never had, we never miss.' This seems to be the Ministry of Food attitude on this matter. We have our canteens at the local works, the British Restaurant, and school feeding centres. The local shops are full of cooked meats on points. With reference to sweets; due to the zoning system, with a view to economising in transport, we are unfortunately in a zone where our favourite pre-war brands of sweets are not manufactured. The Food Control Committee is alive to the situation. We have a very capable staff at Irlam, who have been complimented by Ministry of Food officials for their administrative ability.

A Cadishead soldier's letter from the Japanese prisoner of war camp Keiyo Camp at Chosen, Korea, revealed something of the uncertainty and anxiety felt by men who had been in captivity for some time. The letter from Lance Corporal George Anderson was posted on 21st September 1944 and finally reached his home on 8th March: *Here I am writing to you again, and still a prisoner of war. I am beginning to give up all hope of ever getting home now. I have received letters from you, the latest being 18/2/44. Glad to hear you are all doing well. For myself I am not doing too badly under the circumstances. Things could be a lot worse, but not much. The Red Cross seem to have forgotten us; we have not had any parcels since January 1944, and that was American. My only consolation is that someday I shall be a free man again, and able to make up for these years of misery that I am spending here.* At the close of his letter, George stated that all he wanted when he returned home was a steady job. *If that isn't available I shall probably sign on to complete 21 years' service.* He was the stepson of Samuel and Martha Ann Whittle of 13 Fir Street, Cadishead. Before joining the Army, and during his Army service in the Far East, he was a well-known cyclist, and the winner of many cups and medals. He had joined the Army c.1931 and was captured during the fall of Singapore. His stepbrother, Samuel Anderson Whittle lost his life in 1941 whilst serving with the Merchant Navy (see earlier entry).

The Irlam Industrial Sub-committee of the National Savings Movement had been a great success in a short time. Much of the success was due to the committee members and, in particular, to the energy, drive and organising ability of Mr H. Wilde, the assistant commissioner, whose enthusiasm was described as so infectious that it had spread not only among members of the local Savings Committee, but among workers and managements. The management of the various works in the district had supported the industrial savings scheme, unlike the management in firms in several nearby towns who, if not exactly opposed to the idea, were described as, at best, only lukewarm about it. This cooperation between management and men was described as one of the most pleasing features of the industrial life of the district.

Private Joyce Thompson, Auxiliary Territorial Service, married Corporal Davie Nichols, Royal Artillery, of Kirkbrae, Galashields, Scotland, at St Mary's Church on Saturday, 10th March. Joyce was the second daughter of Mr and Mrs A. Thompson of 246 Liverpool Road, Cadishead.

Nineteen year old Guardsman Roy Hilton, serving with the Irish Guards, was seriously wounded in the fighting in Germany on Saturday, 10th March. The armoured vehicle driven by Roy had been hit in the front by a phosphorous shell and flames had entered the cabin through the gaps provided for the driver and gunners to see through. His main injuries were severe burning of the legs, arms and face, and his condition was described in the official letter as dangerous. He was visited in hospital in the south of England by his parents, Ben and Emma Hilton of 256 Liverpool Road, Cadishead. Ben had nothing but the highest praise for the courtesy, kindness and consideration shown by the hospital authorities and the Red Cross to the relatives of wounded men: *The treatment I received from them was such that it made a deep impression on me, and though no parent likes the thought that his son was seriously injured, my visit to the hospital, and stay at the Red Cross hostel, will always be remembered by my wife and myself with the deepest gratitude. No parent or relative – even those who are not too well off – need have any hesitation. The Red Cross does all it possibly can – even to paying fares and providing transport to and from hospital – to make the visit as pleasant as possible. Not only that, but at the hostel they refused to take anything and asked me – if I wished to pay anything, to put it in the Red Cross box. I have never in my life contributed more willingly than I did then.* Before joining the Army, Roy worked at his father's coal business in Moss Lane, Cadishead. He went overseas shortly after D-Day.

Two of Roy's brothers served in the Forces, Guardsman Fred Hilton (born 1916) served with the Irish Guards and Driver Wilf Hilton (born 1918) with the Royal Army Service Corps. Their sister, Ellen Hilton and Wilf's wife, Eva, were employed on war work at the Royal Ordnance Factory at Risley. A side effect of working with munitions was that it turned their skin yellow and it took several months for their colour to return to normal. After the war Roy worked on security at the Steelworks and was a very popular figure in the area. The authors spoke to several people who knew Roy and they all spoke of his great sense of humour and good nature.

Private Tommy Denton of Irlam, who was serving in Italy, wrote a letter to the *Guardian*. In it he wrote that he was in the same company as Jack Callaghan of Cadishead and Bill Holding, the Warrington fullback. Tommy, who had played many matches with Lancashire Steel Cricket Club, stressed that when the war was over, he was coming home again to restart his old window cleaning business and his Saturday afternoon cricket. He didn't appear to have any desire to roam once he got his feet under his own table, for he stated: *If anyone after this war starts talking of taking a Continental tour, I shall feel like crowning him – or her, for that matter. These foreign countries aren't a patch on old England and however these dirty thieving Ities ever thought that they would lick us passes my comprehension. In sanitation they are about 100 years behind the times. Can you imagine people keeping sheep, goats, fowl and even cattle in their homes?* Private Denton had been overseas for nearly three years having served in North Africa and Sicily, before moving north through Italy.

Tommy's letter caused some controversy and in mid-May a letter was published in the *Guardian* from Corporal James E. 'Eddie' Hampson, who was serving in Italy with the Royal Corps of Signals. He took exception to the phrase: *dirty, thieving Ities*, which appeared in Tommy's letter: *Sir, ever since I have been overseas, now more than three years, I have regularly received my copy of the Guardian, and enjoy reading anything concerning Cadishead and Irlam, especially your topical local column. In fact, in me you have had a secret admirer, but since reading your column in the issue of March 17th, your stock has gone down somewhat in my estimation. I refer to the extracts you quoted from Mr Denton's letter regarding 'Dirty Thieving Ities.' Believe me, my dear 'Onlooker,' they are not quite so bad as all that, and I did not think you were the type to quote such a statement without inquiring more deeply into the state of affairs in this country. Please don't think I am a champion of the Italians or that I have anything but loathing for the late lamented fascist regime, but I would like to give you a picture of the Italians as I have found them. No doubt there are dirty Italians, also thieving Italians – I've met them, but are there not dirty and thieving people in other countries, I think so. I will agree that their domestic amenities in the small towns and villages do not come up to our standards at home, but as one proceeds north a distinct improvement is noted. The Italians are easily led – hence Mussolini, but they are a likeable and pleasure loving people. When I say pleasure loving, I mean the finer things of life. Would this world not be a happier and better place if all people learned how to live, instead of just struggling to go one better than their neighbours. Again, don't interpret my reference to love of pleasure as laziness. Some of the craftsmen in the country have turned out some marvellous work. Surely there must be some good in a country that has produced Caruso and Gigli, to mention just two famous Italians. As a lover of good music I will go as far as to say that my greatest musical treats have been enjoyed in Italy, and in this respect I think you will find that many servicemen who have been in this country will agree with me. Friendliness and hospitality, I have received more in Italy than anywhere else since I have been in the Army – including one's own country! Again, don't forget that since the Armistice in 1943, Italy has provided divisions to fight with the Eighth Army, and in addition, the work of the Partisans against the Germans has not been negligible. Many an Italian family has risked its very existence by sheltering and feeding escaped Allied prisoners of war in German-occupied parts of the country. This I know because I have myself spoken to these ex-prisoners. If you could speak to these fellows about the Italians, you wouldn't get bad reports, and they should know! Well, that is all I have to say, but I think it is enough to convey a different impression to that made by Mr Denton's bald statement. The Italians have had a very bad time in this war – no doubt due to their tamely accepting the fascist regime, but they have already been much maligned, so please show a little tolerance, for without tolerance towards others we shall never have permanent peace.*

Born 1914 in Cadishead, Eddie was the eldest son of Charles H. and Sarah Hampson (nee Hoyles) of 11 Allotment Road, Cadishead. Charles and Sarah had married at Runcorn in 1913 and must have moved into the district shortly before the birth of their first child. Two other brothers served in the Army: Gunner Charles Raymond 'Ray' Hampson (born 1918) of the Royal Artillery and Corporal Eric Hampson of the Royal Army Medical Corps. All three brothers were born in Cadishead.

Guardsman Roy Hilton (right) and his brother, Fred

Roy (recovering from wounds) and Wilf Hilton

On Tuesday, 13th March 23 year old Private 3663060 **James Henry Hancock** was killed in action in Burma. He served with the 2nd Battalion of the Green Howards (Yorkshire Regiment), 4th Indian Infantry Brigade, 26th Indian Infantry Division.

On 12th March the 4th Brigade embarked at Kyaukphyu on Ramree Island and was transported by the Navy to the Arakan mainland. Their objective was to advance south towards the main Japanese base at Tangup (Taungup). Little was known about the Japanese strength in the area but it was believed that the enemy had two or three 7mm guns covering the landing position. At dawn on 13th March they transferred onto landing craft and, supported by the gunfire of four destroyers, they made their way up the Kaleindaung River to the Ma-i Chaung, where they landed unopposed on the north bank, at Pyin-Wan. At 9.30am the 2nd Green Howards were on shore and pushed through the village to inland positions covering the beachhead. Despite the unopposed landings the 2nd Green Howards lost four men that day, including James.

James was the youngest son of Frank and Florence Hancock of 9 Lancaster Road, Cadishead, and he was an ex-pupil of St Teresa's School. Before joining the Army he was employed by Sir Lindsay Parkinson at Risley. He joined the Army in January 1942, and served in the Orkneys before going overseas to Burma in March 1944. James has no known grave and is commemorated on the Rangoon Memorial, Burma.

Flight Sergeant Ernest Loftus, RAF, and Leading Aircraftwoman Elsie Bentley were married at the English Baptist Church, Rhyl. Elsie was the only daughter of Mrs and the late Mr A. Bentley of 16 Grosvenor Avenue, Rhyl. Ernest was the elder son of Mr and Mrs J.H. Loftus of 356 Liverpool Road, Irlam. He had joined the RAF in 1935 and served in the Middle East for over four years with the Eighth Army and Western Desert Forces. Elsie had joined the WAAF in 1941.

The Irlam District Branch of the National Farmers Union, on behalf of the hospitals, realised the sum of £120 through various events throughout the previous 12 months. A dance held in the Irlam Conservative Club on Friday, 9th March had realised £44. The Fred Broadhurst Orchestra provided dance music, and the MCs were Mr J. Moulder and Mr W. Hurt. The remainder of the £120 was made up from subscriptions.

As the war in Europe drew to a close, preparations were being made for the return of local servicemen and women, and funds were needed to cover the cost of celebrations. One of the fundraising ideas suggested was a £100 bowling handicap ran by the Steelworks Recreation Club. On Saturday, 10th March members of the club, at an extraordinary general meeting, approved the scheme. The idea had first been put before members at the annual meeting in January but there had been an objection on the grounds that the word 'invitation' suggested that the number of local players allowed to enter the competition would be limited. It was against this background that the extraordinary meeting took place and the following is a summary of the interesting debate which took place: Jack Jones was in the chair. In support of the proposition, Mr R. Watson said the idea of an invitation handicap was first raised by the social committee with a view to raising funds for the Welcome Home Fund for members of the Forces. In 12 months, by various efforts, £270 had already been raised for this purpose. In 1944 the club had 400 members serving in the Forces and each of them had received ten shillings. To raise further money for the fund, the social committee had approached the bowling section and, after discussion, it was decided to go in for a bowling handicap on a big scale. Their principal reason for an invitation handicap was to attract spectators, and they, therefore, intended to invite the best bowlers in Lancashire and Cheshire areas and, if they could get them, he felt sure they would get many spectators. With local players only they would not be able to attract the same number of spectators. With regard to the number of entries, Mr Watson said they were swayed in favour of 64 players, which would allow 16 local players to participate (though he was doubtful they would get so many of the calibre they required). Concluding, he said the committee had gone very deeply into the matter, and they were convinced it would be something the district had never seen before. Mr W. Small, opposing, said he had interviewed a number of members on the question of the handicap, and it was surprising how many objected to it. The rules of the invitation handicap would exclude their own players who had contributed to the upkeep of the club for years. His second objection was the time the green would be occupied. At the general meeting he had mentioned that it was highly likely that this year the two greens would be more in demand than for the past five years, due to the standing down of the Home Guard and Civil Defence Services in which they had many members. In 1944, the club had great difficulty in obtaining sufficient refreshment for members with the result that it was closed more often than any other club in the district. He was anxious to know what the position would be this year if they ran a handicap such as the one proposed and non-members took the refreshment intended for members. The secretary of the local bowling league had told him that it was the League's intention to run a handicap, the proceeds of which would go to the Comforts Fund. The right and proper thing for the club to have done at the annual general meeting was to start a special fund and ask for a grant of £500 which the club could well afford. Supporting the resolution, Mr G. Standish (almost certainly George Standish of Cadishead who had served with the Manchester Regiment during the First World War) said they had gone into the question in a constitutional manner. In running this handicap they were hopeful of getting well-known bowlers and they would be creating a bigger interest in bowling. Irlam and Cadishead was a recognised centre of bowling, and it was only by efforts of this sort that they could maintain an interest in the sport. As sportsmen they ought not to object to sacrificing some time on the No. 1 green for the benefit of their members in the Forces. He maintained that if Irlam and Cadishead had sixteen players in the handicap they were getting a very fair quota. Mr J. Hambleton, opposing, said they were using the Welcome Home Fund as a lever to force the voting. When the handicap was first mooted there was no mention of a Welcome Home Fund, but merely of a £100 handicap. Mr W. Halliwell, chairman of the Cadishead, Irlam and Partington Bowling League, who also opposed, said most of their members would be with them again this summer and more people would be using the greens than had ever used them before. If they were going to invite outsiders to use the green for two-thirds of the season they were depriving the members of its use. On a show of hands the resolution was carried and Mr W. Small, who had opposed, came in for warm applause when he said he was satisfied that it was a majority vote and asked all present to support the club in the handicap.

The progress made in works savings since the formation of the Irlam Industrial Sub-committee of the National Savings Movement was outlined by the secretary, Mr S.U. Robinson, at a meeting at the British Restaurant, on Wednesday, 14th March. The meeting was attended by representatives of the firms involved in the scheme, and was presided over by Councillor Owen, CC (chairman of the Irlam Industrial Sub-committee). The figures quoted by Mr Robinson showed an all-round increase and the average per week was: Brew Bros £9, British Tar £6, CWS Margarine Works £42, CWS Soap Works £78, Lancashire Corporation £266, Royles Engineering Limited £19, Wilkinsons Transport £8. Mr E. Tynan, a member of the North West Regional Advisory Committee, spoke about the link between savings and the National Savings Movement. He said it was not easy to convince people that saving was the right thing to do, but at exceptional times such as these they had to ask people to save, and it was their duty to convince people of this necessity. National finance was not on all fours with individual finance. Money was only worth its true value when the goods were there, and at present the goods people really wanted were not available. If they bought unnecessarily they merely forced up the prices of unwanted goods. It was in the interests of all of them to save. Mr J.C. Robertson, CC, constituency representative on the Regional Industrial Committee, stressed the importance of saving to prevent inflation. The nation's wealth was in the hands of the people and it must come from production. Any surplus of money left over after material wants had been supplied should be saved. What he would like to see was a system under which a man's savings could be deducted from his pay on lines similar to PAYE. That, in his opinion, was the ideal way of industrial saving. Mr J. Osborn, deputy commissioner for the North West region, said that there would be a difficult period after the war and the need for saving would still be there. This would be necessary to maintain a sound financial basis. Some of the difficulties encountered in forming works savings groups were mentioned by Mr H. Wilde, assistant commissioner, who said it was essential that there should be co-operation between managements and men and men and managements. He had found it far easier to get the co-operation of the men than of the managements, but was glad to say that had not been the case in Irlam and Cadishead. Once that co-operation was obtained they should set up a committee, no matter how small, and let them iron out the difficulties. There were no cut and dried schemes for works savings. At the close of the speeches, a discussion was opened by Jack Jones, who said that they wanted schemes which would give a man the confidence that his future was secure.

Sergeant (air gunner) 1481728 **Herbert Darbyshire** of 49 Squadron of the Royal Air Force Volunteer Reserve, was killed during air operations on Friday, 16th March.

Born in 1922 (birth registered at Bucklow in September 1922), Herbert was the youngest son of Mr and the late Mrs A.E. Darbyshire of 6 Roscoe Road, Irlam. He was educated at Irlam Central School and was employed by the Cheshire Lines Committee at Irlam railway station.

Herbert enlisted into the RAF in June 1941 and was posted overseas to Egypt in February 1942. He spent 2½ years in the Mediterranean theatre of war and was awarded the Africa Star. He also served in Sicily and Italy. In June 1944 he returned to England to train as an air gunner. During his three years of active service he took part in many flights over enemy territory.

On 16th March 17 aircraft of 49 Squadron took off to join the 5 Group attack on Wurzburg in Germany. One of the aircraft detailed to take part in the attack was Lancaster ME454, piloted by Flying Officer Douglas Whent. Herbert was the rear air gunner on this flight. This was the crew's fourth flight together. In total, 225 Lancaster bombers and 11 Mosquitos took part in the raid. This was the first time that the city had been targeted and post-war reports suggested that 90 percent of the built-up area was destroyed. Six Lancasters failed to return from the raid, including two from 49 Squadron.

Sergeant Herbert Darbyshire, RAFVR

One of the Lancasters brought down that night was ME454. The following is a summary of the RAF report into the incident:

ME454 took off from Fulbeck in Lincolnshire at 8.03pm. Having dropped its payload at Wurzburg, ME454 turned for home. At 10.40pm, the aircraft encountered heavy flak over Strasbourg/Kehl, and at a height of 8,500 feet, a heavy jolt was felt from the port wing and the aircraft started to turn over and dive to port. After falling 2,000 feet the pilot regained control. A jagged edge was seen near the outer tip of the port wing, which had been caused by heavy flak. Now flying at 7,000 feet, the pilot took weaving action to avoid more flak but two minutes later the aircraft was hit again, this time through the bomb bay door immediately beneath the navigator's table, seriously injuring the navigator and wounding the bomb aimer in the left arm and shoulder. There was also a large hole in the wireless operator's seat but fortunately he was not sitting there at the time. Almost immediately, fuel seeped into the fuselage of the aircraft and the port inboard engine started to overspeed causing a further loss of height. As a result, the pilot ordered the crew to bail out. After some crew members had bailed out, a fire started in the rear fuselage. The flight engineer opened his parachute inside the aircraft and refused to jump. The pilot arranged to jump holding the flight engineer so they could both descend together. Tragically, the flight engineer could not hold on and was swept away by the slipstream of the aircraft without his parachute. The rear gunner position was notoriously difficult to escape from and, although there is no information about Herbert's death, it seems likely that he was unable to leave his post, and went down with the aircraft. The aircraft crashed ten miles from Dieuze in France, which was behind Allied lines. It is possible that the final hits on ME454 were caused by a night fighter, as Hauptmann Helmut Gaul claimed a Lancaster near Strasbourg at 10.30pm. Four members of the crew managed to bail out and survived but Sergeants Frank Haylock (flight engineer) and George Leeke (air gunner) were killed, along with Herbert. At first he was reported missing and the family would have to wait until December 1945 for official notification of his death. He was 23 years of age. He has no known grave and is commemorated on the Runnymede Memorial. His elder brother, Leading Stoker Walter Darbyshire, was reported missing in 1942 and, like Herbert, the family would have to wait until December 1945 before being officially notified of his death (see earlier entry).

With the stepping down of the Home Guard in December 1944, the men's thoughts turned to how they could keep the comradeship alive that they had developed during the many hours of patrols, sentry duty and training together in the previous 4½ years. The first steps for the formation of Home Guard Old Comrades Associations within the area of the 42nd County of Lancaster Battalion, Home Guard had been completed. In January and February well attended meetings had been held in Eccles, Swinton, Walkden and Irlam and a branch of the association had been formed in each of these districts. Local committees had been elected and a programme of social and other events had been drawn up. In mid-March representatives from the four branches, who constituted the Executive Committee of the 42nd Battalion Association, met under the chairmanship of Lieutenant Colonel Webb, the commanding officer of the battalion. Each of the branch secretaries gave a short progress report and an outline of their future programmes which included dances, light entertainment and smoking concerts in the different areas. Rifle clubs were established within the various branches and Colonel Webb announced that there was a good chance that the War Office would help by providing miniature rifles and range facilities. Membership of the association was open to all members of the 42nd Battalion and an appeal was made for members.

Though most household goods were in short supply the district responded generously to the WVS appeal for household articles for the bombed out people of Ilford. Crockery, soft goods, cutlery and cooking utensils had been given and ten chairs and two beds had also been promised. Though the appeal in its early stages met with small success, the drive and energy of the WVS under their centre leaders, Mrs Loxley and Enid Bakker, proved more than equal to the task and their efforts were amply rewarded. In the week before 31st March piles of furniture, cases of crockery, beds and bedding and household utensils, enough to fill a large furniture van, were assembled at the ARP depot in Liverpool Road awaiting dispatch. The piles included tables, chairs, at least one three-piece suite, a wringing machine, a sewing machine, beds, bedding, hundreds of cups, saucers, knives, forks and spoons, cooking utensils – in fact, everything that was necessary to establish several families in new homes. Mrs Loxley said that though the work had been exacting, they were more than satisfied with the results: *I think it has been a marvellous effort.*

A similar scheme was organised by the members of Hollinfare Women's Institute. During a meeting at the Social Club, Hollins Green, with Mrs Marsh presiding. Miss Farrington (hon. secretary) reported that a splendid collection of goods had been received for Ilford, including a marble top wash stand, easy chairs, three bedsteads and bedding, new sheets, cutlery, crockery, enamel and hardware, good clothing, and footwear, and also monetary donations. Mrs S. Openshaw Taylor, the delegate at the Preston LFWI meeting gave an interesting report. Mrs Bury and Mrs Dyke did good business at the trading table and Mrs Hugh Blundell and Mrs Heath acted as tea hostesses. The social half-hour was spent dancing, with Mrs Bate playing the piano. Two new members were elected: Mrs Barrow and Mrs Shakeshaft.

The 15th ordinary general meeting of Lancashire Steel Corporation Ltd was held on Monday, 19th March at the register office, Bewsey Road, Warrington. Mr John E. James presided (chairman and managing director) and spoke of the changeover from war to peacetime working: *As you no doubt realise, the production of your undertakings has, in one form or another, continued to be confined almost entirely to the national war effort. I think, however, it is reasonable to hope that during the present year we shall be allowed to return, to some extent, to the manufacture of our normal peacetime products. You will, I am sure, appreciate that a changeover to peacetime requirements from those demanded by total war will be a task of considerable magnitude, involving both technical matters and problems of personnel. During that changeover period we must also, without interfering unduly with our manufacturing production, carry out the necessary arrears of repairs and maintenance of plant and buildings in order to restore these to the high standard of efficiency we observed in pre-war years. The reinstatement of employees now serving with the Forces, whom we shall welcome back to civilian life, is a further matter to which much patient thought and foresight will be given. The cessation of development for nearly six years in the iron and steel industry in this country, unavoidable as it has been, has given considerable advantage to other countries which have been able to pursue their development unhindered, or even to add modern units to their manufacturing resources. This loss of comparative efficiency must be rapidly overtaken, and as we are credited as a nation with resourcefulness and adaptability – a view which the war has proved to be well-founded – I have every confidence that the steel industry will be able to deal satisfactorily with such a situation. I am not one of those who think that this country should be content with the capacity for making iron and steel products which it possessed at the beginning of the war. The industry technically was, I believe, in much better shape in 1939 than it had been for many years, but I should not like to think that we had then reached the limits of our productivity either in degree or in kind. None the less, not only the expansion of our output but the maintenance of the old level of production will, in my opinion, depend largely upon the raw material factor, especially if the industry is to be able successfully to export its finished products. In closing, may I extend our deepest sympathy to the relatives of those from our works and staff who have fallen or have been wounded in the gigantic struggle with Germany and Japan. We who are left can repay our debt only by bending all our energies to the creation of a better world. I should also like to pay warm tributes to the staff and works employees of the corporation and its subsidiary companies for their services during the year. I am sure you will join with me in according to them the thanks of this meeting.*

Home on leave from north west Europe, Private Robert Henry Smith, youngest son of Mrs and the late Mr A.R. Smith of 11 Francis Road, Irlam, was married at Riccarton Parish Church, Kilmarnock, on Thursday, 22nd March to Miss Elizabeth Wylie Fisher, eldest daughter of Mr and Mrs G. Fisher of Bruce Street, Riccarton. Robert had joined the Army in 1940 and went to France shortly after D-Day. He was formerly employed as a hairdresser in Irlam and later in Manchester. He was treasurer of the Fairhills Road Methodist Sunday School.

Gunner John Dodd, Royal Artillery, son of Mr and Mrs J. Dodd of 38 Hayes Road, Cadishead, married Constance Morgan, daughter of the late Mr Morgan and Mrs A. Westbrook of 113 Liverpool Road, Cadishead. It was a joint ceremony with his brother, Harry Dodd, who married Olive Sudall Morgan, daughter of Pastor Thomas W. Morgan, and the late Mrs Morgan of Greenwood House, Moss Side Road, Cadishead. Pastor Morgan officiated at the Congregational Church, Cadishead. The bridegrooms acted as best man for each other. A joint reception was held at Cadishead Wesley School.

Robert and Elizabeth Smith (left) and John and Constance Dodd

On the morning of 24th March Corporal Harold Bate of 155th Brigade, 52nd (Lowland) Division, was visiting the nearest village on the west bank of the Rhine, when he heard a tremendous noise from above. He looked up to see the magnificent sight of over 500 aircraft towing about 1,300 gliders across the Rhine. As he described it: *My ears started aching with the noise of planes. The sky seemed black with planes and gliders as they flew overhead crossing the Rhine.* He was witnessing Operation Plunder, the last mass parachute and glider assault of the war, as the 6th Airborne Division and 17th US Airborne Division dropped east of the river Rhine near Wesel. Within 5½ hours they had taken all their objectives.

Fusilier Harry Killon, Royal Scots Fusiliers (probably 6th Battalion, 15th Scottish Division) was one of the local men who were involved in the crossing of the Rhine. Harry was born in Wigan in 1924 and his family moved to the district before the outbreak of the war and resided at 14 Hamilton Avenue, Cadishead. He enlisted into the Home Guard on 4th March 1941 and is believed to have served with 8 Platoon, H Company until he was called up (probably in 1943, aged 19) and joined the Royal Marines. At some point before the Normandy landings he transferred to the Royal Scots Fusiliers and served in northern Europe, including the crossing of the Rhine. After the war he married Catherine Mona Fowler, sister of John and Frank Fowler. His brother-in-law, John Fowler, was killed in action in 1942 (see earlier entry).

Gunner Tom Vaudrey of 209 Medium Battery, 53rd Medium Regiment, Royal Artillery (4 AGRA), was involved in the crossing of the Rhine. On 19th March they had moved up to new gun positions near Udem, close to the River Rhine. Four days later, on 23rd March they opened fire as part of a planned counter battery operation. The next day, they bombarded Rees and various other targets in support of the airborne troops. Next, they fired constantly throughout the night and day in support of the Airborne and 43rd Division's assault on Isselburg and then 30 Corps link up with the Ninth US Army, across the River Lippe to Dorsten. They ceased fire on 30th March. The next day they moved to Till where they fired 50 rounds per gun during the night at the woods beyond Emmerich. After a day's rest on 1st April they were again in action, this time supporting the Guards Armoured Division and Canadians. They then spent two weeks in Till, resting and carrying out various jobs, including clearing the battlefields.

As the Allied troops advanced through Germany, they witnessed the devastation wrought by Bomber Command on the cities of Germany. Driver T/14323168 Norman Dakers, Royal Army Service Corps, witnessed the devastation of Germany: *Do you know I got done, I got done a week's pay. We were waiting to cross the Rhine, it was a place called Emmerich and the place was a shambles, and we were waiting to get across the bloody river there. I was just leaning on the cab door, you know there was seven trucks in line, and there was a little kid wandering around in the ruins and he must have only been about six this kid, and alright he was a German but you can't blame what happened on the bloody kids there, and I shouted to him 'eh' and he looked up and I threw him a couple of bars of chocolate and I made a mistake, a bloody Red Cap saw me, and they charged me with consorting with the enemy and I lost a week's pay for that. Poor little bugger didn't know what had happened, the place was in ruins and he was just walking round looking for his mother and father and he couldn't find them. It's terrible really, the kids weren't to blame for what happened.*

They stopped us one day, this bloke stepped out into the road and stopped us and said 'you can't go any further, stop.' 'What's on?' 'Never mind what's on, just stop, stay there and don't budge, keep your engine running.' There was two or three of us there and all of a sudden, there's a church on the right-hand side, and then all of a sudden there was such a bloody BANG! and the top of the church disappeared. I thought what the hell's that, and they said there was a German observer up there and he wouldn't come down so they blew the top off the bloody church with him in it.

I got as far as, over the German border near Bocholt that way, and they turned us round, it seemed that this bloody, was it Patton, this American general, he was sifting all the bloody stuff out to his side of the war and ours were getting nothing. So they sent us back to bring all the stuff that had been left because they couldn't use Antwerp at that time. And we come back, and it was while we came back to pick this stuff up, it had been raining and they must have waved, shouted for me to back the lorry in, to put this bloody stuff on they were putting on and I didn't hear him, and I was climbing off the truck and one of the blokes mustn't have realised what I was doing and he jumped in the cab and he was only a little short fella, well it was a Leyland, a big heavy clutch you know, and he mustn't have shoved the clutch in far enough and the truck jumped forward and chucked me off and broke my back. So they sent me back to England and I was in hospital in Yorkshire for quite a while and then I came out, in a convalescent depot and I went to Thetford and from Thetford I went back out to the Middle East. But as they say it's all part of life's rich tapestry.

Fusilier Harry Killon, Royal Scots Fusiliers

The Irlam Committee for Soviet Medical Aid announced that the sum collected to-date was £98. This amount had been raised by the Flag Day donations, an exhibition and an effort. With other monies still to come in and further efforts being held, it was hoped they would raise at least £150. The committee thanked all who had assisted in the efforts. A suggestion had been made that the work of the committee might be broadened and that further activities to strengthen the bonds of Anglo-Soviet friendship be entered upon. It was felt that much could be done in Irlam in the way of cultural activities such as music, another exhibition, study classes, and inviting speakers who have had the opportunity of seeing the Russians at war.

On Saturday, 31st March Stoker Charles Egerton, Royal Navy, eldest son of Mr and Mrs H. Egerton of 5 Eldon Road, Irlam, married Eileen Hoare, only daughter of Mr and Mrs H. Hoare of 8 Clarence Street, Taunton, Somerset. The marriage took place at St James' Church, Taunton. Charles' sister, Mabel Egerton, acted as bridesmaid. Mabel was serving with the Army Territorial Service at the time. Before joining the Navy, Charles was employed by the Steelworks. He enlisted in 1942 and was stationed at Devonport, near Plymouth.

Stoker Charles and Eileen Egerton

Mabel Egerton was born in Stockton-on-Tees in 1926 and in the early 1930s the family moved to Irlam. She volunteered for the Auxiliary Territorial Service in 1944 at the age of 17½. She was trained at Dalkeith in Scotland and was then stationed on the south coast at Brighton, Hastings and Folkestone. She worked as a physical training instructor at Brighton and while there witnessed V1 attacks on the city. Later she supervised German prisoners of war in the officers' mess at Folkestone.

Corporal Mabel Egerton, ATS

Another local woman who served in the Auxiliary Territorial Service was Private Joan Field. Joan was born in 1923, the daughter of Arthur and Lily Field of 33 Fiddlers Lane, Higher Irlam. Her father had served as a chief petty officer in the Royal Navy for 20 years, including during the First World War. Joan was educated at Irlam Endowed School and then worked at J&N Phillips in Manchester. She volunteered for service in 1942 and enlisted at the recruitment centre in Manchester after seeing a recruitment poster. She was sent to Lancaster for training and then went to Cardiff University to be trained in accountancy. Between 1943 and 1946 she was stationed at the Ordnance Corps depot (tank repairs) at Chilwell, Nottingham.

Whilst doing what he described as a 'job' at a Burmese harbour, Marine Thomas E. Williamson, son of Mr and Mrs A. Williamson of 19 Boundary Road, Higher Irlam, noticed a destroyer coming alongside. He recognised the ship and, when it was tied up, he asked if anyone of the name of Douglas Cooke was on board. In his own words: *Then who should pop up but Doug. So I went on board and had a talk with him. He got permission for us to go on board at night to have a slap up feed and to see a film show. Well, it just had to be as it always is. I had to go out on a job and, of course, that put paid to the invite. Anyway, I am hoping to see him again.* Marine Williamson, who was formerly employed as a window cleaner by Tommy Denton, mentioned in his letter that his former employer had written to him. Before joining the Navy, Ordinary Seaman Douglas Cooke was also employed by a local window cleaner.

Marine Thomas Williamson and Seaman Douglas Cooke

Donations to the Irlam and Cadishead War Comforts Fund included: Miss Jean Crawford of 81 The Crescent, Higher Irlam donated ten shillings (collection of one shilling per week from friends); Mrs Hughes of 59 Lyndhurst Avenue, Higher Irlam £3-16s (proceeds of effort); Mrs Lewis of 280 Liverpool Road, Cadishead £2-10s; Royles Engineering £1 (monthly contribution); Directors and employees of the British Basket and Besto Company £3-1s; air raid wardens, guard room C (per Mr F. Clarke),

£10; proceeds of children's pantomime *Babes in the Wood* at Cadishead Senior School £20-16-11; proceeds of County Charity Handicap 1944 (per Mr B. Rushton), £2-12s; Irlam WVS (proceeds of effort for Welcome Home Fund), £360-4-6; Miss I. Gostridge (donation from scholars of St Mary's Sunday School) 2s-6d; proceeds of children's pantomime *Cinderella* given in St Paul's schoolroom, 15th to 17th February (per Miss J. Rollinson) £64-13s; Mrs Tyer, 26 The Crescent, Higher Irlam 5s.

APRIL

Guardsman William Norman Wright, Irish Guards, was wounded in action on 2nd April and taken prisoner by the Germans. This was the second time that William had been wounded in action, the first being at Achon in Germany in February 1945. His parents received a letter from his commanding officer: *I regret to inform you that your son, Guardsman William Norman Wright is reported missing believed wounded on April 2nd, 1945, in western Europe.* Shortly afterwards, they received a letter from William who was in a British hospital in western Europe: *Just a few lines to let you know that I am all right. Again I got slightly wounded and the Germans took me prisoner. I was only in their hospital four days and was treated all right, but the food was no good. Anyway I am safe and you have nothing to worry about.* The German hospital had been overrun by advancing Allied troops.

Sapper 14812244 Douglas Stewart Menzies, a driver in the Royal Engineers, was stationed at Knokke-sur-Mer on the Belgium/Holland border, where his unit was re-supplying British troops across the Germany border: *We were loaded into cattle trucks and went up to near the Belgium border. We transferred to lorries then went to Ostend. We were stationed at the North Sea Hotel in Knokke-sur-Mer. At night we were taken to the depot where many trucks were waiting for us to go to the front. It was pitch black and all I could see in front were the small convoy lights on the back of the truck in front. We went to Xanten in Germany, which was in a forest, there were plenty of trees about. We did this about 14 or 15 times. The noise of the convoy was tremendous, you couldn't hear yourself speak.*

While at Knokke-sur-Mer, Douglas witnessed the Belgians taking revenge on people who had collaborated with the Germans: *While we were in Knokke the White Brigade were coming round taking steps against collaborators. They came with bugles and a white flag and photographs of women who had their hair shaved. They lit fires and smashed hotels but we couldn't get involved. I couldn't say you could trust them. 'Nothing to do with you' they said. There were only a few Canadians and about ten or 15 of us.*

Douglas was born on 9th July 1926, the son of David and Elizabeth Menzies of 9 Byng Avenue, Cadishead. The family lived at Berwick-on-Tweed and then Perth in Scotland, before moving to Cadishead in the late 1920s or early 1930s. His brother, Charles Menzies, had lost his life on war service in February 1943, when HM submarine *Vandal* was lost with all hands. Douglas was called up on 3rd August 1944, shortly after his 18th Birthday. At the time he was employed by the Steelworks. His service record describes him as 5 feet 8½ inches tall, with blue eyes, brown hair and a fresh complexion. At first he was sent to the King's Own Scottish Borderers training camp at Berwick-on-Tweed where he received his basic training and also was trained on machine-guns. Douglas must have impressed an officer with his shooting skill because he was soon asked whether he would like to apply as a sniper. At the time his fitness had been rated as B2, so he was sent on a special course at No.1 Physical Development Centre, at Hereford. After a gruelling six weeks' physical training and good food, he was passed A1 on 28th September. He returned to Berwick-on-Tweed for a time and was then transferred to the Royal Engineers and posted to Gibraltar Barracks at Aldershot. While at Aldershot he met many Canadian troops who were stationed there over Christmas and New Year 1944. Doug recalled: *They were itching to get over there* [northern Europe] *to avenge the mates they lost at Dieppe in 1942.* His training continued at Aldershot; on 10th January he passed the HQ driving test, and the next day, the HQ maintenance test. He also passed the DM gas chamber, and the fire range course in the month. Next he was sent to barracks in Halifax, then on to Knightsbridge, Dover and finally, to Calais. He was demobbed in 1948. In typically understated fashion his military conduct was described as 'very good.' Douglas re-enlisted into the Regular Army in 1950 and served in Egypt as driver 22535524.

Sapper Douglas Menzies (centre) of the Royal Engineers, with colleagues

Meanwhile, in far off Burma, the 'Forgotten Army' was still involved in hard fighting, advancing south through the Arakan and pressing the Japanese back towards Rangoon. Private 3659903 John Vaudrey of the 2nd Green Howards [or, to give it its full name, the 2nd Battalion, Alexandra, Princess of Wales's Own (Yorkshire Regiment)] was one of the troops involved in the campaign. He had joined the battalion on 8th July 1944 which, at this time, was serving with the 116th Indian Infantry Brigade, 39th Indian Infantry Division. The brigade provided specialised jungle conversion training and infantry battalions would spend four to six month training with the brigade, before relieving a battalion at the front. On 19th September 1944, the 2nd Green Howards moved to the Arakan area of Burma and joined the 4th Indian Infantry Brigade, 26th Indian Infantry Division. During the Third Arakan Offensive and subsequent operations, the 26th Division took part mainly in amphibious operations, including the unopposed capture of Akyab Island, and the Battle of Ramree Island (21st January to 9th February). On 3rd April the 2nd Green Howards captured Hill 370, three miles north of Taungup, however, two days later, the Japanese launched a determined counter attack which drove the Allied troops off the hill. Two further attacks were launched on this day to re-take the hill and the second succeeded in driving off the Japanese. On 15th April troops from the 4th Indian Brigade entered Taungup, a town situated on the southern bank of a stream of the same name, surrounded by paddy fields and dominated by a large jungle clad hill to the east of the town. Unfortunately they could not gain a foothold.

Two days later the brigade was relieved and transported to Ramree Island, however, the 2nd Green Howards remained in the battle zone, having been transferred to the 4th (West Africa) Infantry Brigade, 82 (West Africa) Infantry Division. The 2nd and 4th West Africa Brigades were ordered to take and hold Taungup and, during the night of 26th/27th April the 4th (West Africa) Brigade crossed the Taungup stream against slight opposition, while the 2nd Brigade attacked the large hill to the east. By the end of the next day, the 4th (West Africa) Brigade had occupied Taungup, having cleared the area of Japanese. They then linked up with the 2nd Brigade which was established on the large hill.

The next day patrols from the division extended out some seven miles east of Taungup. Next, the 4th Brigade pushed on south along the coast, occupying Sandoway on 10th May and Gwa three days later. By now, all organised Japanese resistance in the Arakan had stopped, although some small groups continued to emerge from the jungle over the next two or three months. On 12th July the 2nd Green Howards returned to India and was at Meerut from 27th July to the end of the war.

John's testimonial, completed by the commanding officer of the 2nd Green Howards, on 10th December 1945 at Barrackpore, India, recorded that his military conduct was 'Good', and that he was of: *quiet disposition. He is a conscientious worker, reliable and trustworthy.* He returned to the UK and arrived at No. 8 Military Dispersal Unit, Hereford on 24th December. The next day he was released for leave until 18th February 1946. He transferred to Class Z, Army Reserve on 13th March 1946.

John Vaudrey was born on 6th March 1913. He married Maria Wilson in September 1936 and they lived at 10 Mersey Avenue, Irlam. His mother lived at 59 Boundary Road, Higher Irlam. He worked at the Steelworks. He was called up on 24th June 1940 and joined the South Lancashire Regiment. Four months later, on 8th November he transferred to the Royal Artillery for a spell but re-joined the South Lancashires on 10th June 1941, and served with the regiment until 8th July 1944 when he was transferred to the 2nd Green Howards.

Another local man serving in Burma was Lance Corporal 14722432 Harold Albert James, who was with the 1st East Yorkshire Regiment in India and Burma during the period February to September 1945. Harold was called up on 2nd March 1944 and was posted to the training camp at Berwick-on-Tweed. He transferred to No. 6 Infantry Training Centre on 13th April. He joined the 5th Battalion, West Yorkshire Regiment on 22nd August and then the 11th Battalion on 2nd September. He embarked for India on 11th December and arrived there on 11th January 1945 and went to the Kalyan Transit Camp next day. On 5th February he transferred to the 1st Battalion, East Yorkshire Regiment. The 1st East Yorkshire was a regular battalion which had been in India since before the war. He was admitted to 63 India Field Ambulance on 15th February and spent five days there and then entered a concessional area.

Harold returned to the 1st East Yorkshire Regiment on 21st May which had served with the 99th Indian Infantry Brigade since March 1945. During Harold's time with the East Yorkshires they fought in the battles of Rangoon Road and the Sittang during the advance southwards through Burma. In August the 99th Brigade was attached to the 19th Indian Infantry Division and fought along the Kalaw road. On 28th September Harold was posted to HQ 505 district of SEAC (South East Asia Command).

At the end of his service Harold was with GHQ 2nd Echelon India Command and his commanding officer provided the following testimonial dated 20th March 1947: *Exemplary Military Conduct. Has been employed as a clerk in which capacity he has done well. A keen, conscientious and capable worker. Strictly honest and sober and correct in his attitude towards his superiors at all times. Smart and well turned out.* He arrived back in England on 16th April 1947 and was demobbed on 11th July.

Harold Albert James was born in Irlam, the son of Robert Edward and Mary Agnes James (nee Lumsden) of 583 Liverpool Road, Irlam. The family moved to a house on the Victory estate in Cadishead and Harold was educated at Cadishead Junior and Senior Schools. He was employed as a storekeeper at Royles Engineering in Irlam. Harold was a very good footballer and represented the Royles Engineering team. On 1st February 1935 he received a letter from Herbert Chapman, the manager of Arsenal Football Club which offered him a trial with Arsenal. Harold had two brothers, Ernest and Robert, who may have served in the Armed Forces. On 26th October 1940 he married Irene Daniels and they lived together at 34 Baines Avenue, Irlam.

Private John Vaudrey, 2nd Green Howards

Lance Corporal Harold James, East Yorkshire Regiment

Lance Corporal Harold James, East Yorkshire Regiment

Lance Corporal 14863386 James Taylor of the 1st Battalion, Cameronians (Scottish Rifles) was another local man serving in the Far East. The 1st Battalion had first entered Burma in February 1942 to counteract the Japanese invasion, however, they were forced to take part in the long retreat to the Indian frontier. They remained in India for a time regaining their strength and training for long-range operations with the 3rd Indian Division (the Chindit expeditions). In March 1944, the battalion, as part of 11th Brigade (or Profound column as it was known within the second Chindit expedition), was flown by gliders into Burma. They operated behind enemy lines for four months, disrupting lines of communication. They were supplied from the air and also had to rely on their own jungle craft to survive. The Japanese caught up with the column at Namkin and forced them to withdraw. The battalion remained in the Far East until the end of the war, helping to push the Japanese from Burma. James was born on 27th October 1925, the son of Leonard and Helen Taylor (nee Makinson) of Irlam.

Lance Bombardier 1077016 Robert Jackman served in India and Burma with 322 Post Battery, Royal Artillery. Born on 7th December 1912, he resided at 14 Rutland Road, Cadishead, and later at 5 Dixon Street, Irlam. He was called up on 15th August 1940 and posted to 25th Training Regiment Royal Artillery. His first operational posting was to 479th Field Battery, 114th Field Regiment, Royal Artillery before going out to India. His brothers also did their bit; John served in the Army and Henry briefly served in the Royal Engineers and then the Home Guard. Private 13086706 John Jackman, Pioneer Corps, was called up on 1st May 1941. His final unit, in 1946, was the Army Fire Fighting Centre. He was discharged on 28th April 1946. He resided at 5 Dixon Street, Irlam, and was employed as a soap process man at CWS Soap Works.

Another local man in the Pioneer Corps was Private 14358422 Frederick Walter Boydell of 350 Company. Frederick was born in Leigh on 17th January 1913, the son of Fred and Gladys W. Boydell (nee Bootle). He married Olive Blay in 1937 and they resided at 223 Liverpool Road, Cadishead. Before joining the Army he was employed by Brew Brothers of Cadishead. He was called up in November 1942 and his service record describes him as 5 feet 6½ inches tall, with brown eyes and brown hair. He was demobbed on 12th April 1946.

In Germany, Sergeant Peter Walsh of the Royal Army Service Corps, was badly wounded when his truck ran over a landmine near Munster. He had been collecting wounded and displaced British troops from the area and was returning to camp when the mine exploded. He received serious wounds including facial scars and, as a result of his injuries, he was invalided from the Army. Peter had previously been mentioned in dispatches for bravery. He was a dispatch rider, normally riding motorcycles, but was driving a truck when the incident happened. Prior to joining the Army he worked in the rolling mills of the Steelworks. Peter was the brother of Edward Walsh who lost his life in Tunisia in 1943.

Lance Corporal James Taylor, Cameronians (right)

Lance Bombardier Robert Jackman, Royal Artillery

Private John Jackman, Pioneer Corps

Private Frederick Boydell, Pioneer Corps

Two friends, Driver Michael Lynch and Driver Ronnie Allcock, met each other in Italy. This was the first time they had seen each other in three years. Michael lived at 23 Birch Avenue, Cadishead, and Ronnie at 12 Oak Avenue, Cadishead. In a letter to his mother, Michael said that Ronnie had found out where he was stationed and obtained a three day leave pass. In that three days the two friends, in Michael's words: *made up for lost time*. Michael (born c.1921), joined the Army in 1940 and went overseas two years later, serving in Africa and Italy. Before the war Michael was employed by Singleton's butchers. Ronnie, who had also joined the Army in 1940, was at Dunkirk and Narvik (Norway) and then served throughout the North African campaign.

Private John Lynch was wounded while taking part in the assault across the Rhine, and was making a slow recovery in hospital. John joined the Army in 1940 and went to France just after D-Day. He served in France, Holland, Belgium and Germany. Prior to joining the Army he was at Longfield Lodge first aid post on ambulance work, and before the war he was employed by Royles Engineering. Born c.1906, he was the eldest son of Mr and Mrs J.A. Lynch of 78 Lords Street, Cadishead. John resided at 13 Chestnut Avenue, Cadishead.

On the evening of 9th April D Company, 2nd Battalion, Lancashire Fusiliers (11th Infantry Brigade, 78 Division, 5 Corps) took part in an attack on the floodbank of the River Senio near Imola, Italy. During this attack, Lance Corporal 3663241 Owen Eugene McCarthy, a stretcher-bearer, showed *exceptional bravery and a complete disregard for his own life*. On four occasions, Owen went forward to positions below the floodbank to evacuate casualties. Undeterred by heavy enemy concentrations of shell, mortar and machine-gun fire, he succeeded in evacuating casualties to D Company HQ, involving a carry of 600 yards. Throughout the attack he was called upon by both C and D Company to give first aid and to evacuate casualties. As a consequence of his bravery his commanding officer Major J.A.H. Saunders recommended that Owen be awarded a Bar to the Military Medal that he had earned in 1944: *His great courage and daring in the heat of battle, being all the time under heavy enemy fire was a great example and an inspiration to the men in his company and by his gallant conduct was instrumental in saving life.*

Born in 1922, Owen attended St Teresa's School, Irlam, before taking up employment in the cost office of the Steelworks. He resided at 6 Baines Avenue, Irlam. Owen had joined the Home Guard on 14th February 1941 (Private 521, 3 Platoon, D Company) before transferring to the Army in January 1942. He went to North Africa in May of the following year and later served in Sicily, the Italian mainland and Austria.

Twenty-five year old Fourth Engineer Officer **Joseph Eric Talbot** died in hospital on 10th April. He had served with the Merchant Navy for a number of years on board the SS *Manchester Port* (Manchester).

Joseph Eric Talbot, Merchant Navy

Joseph was the son of George Edwin and Rose Talbot of 8 Victory Road, Cadishead and the husband of Isabella Talbot (nee Buckingham), who was a native of Stretford. They had married at Salford in September 1943.

Joseph was cremated at Manchester Crematorium, Barlow Moor Road, West Didsbury and is commemorated on panel 21 of the Memorial Screen Wall in the war graves plot at Manchester Southern Cemetery.

Private Winifred Dutton of the Auxiliary Territorial Service (Royal Corps of Signals) married Charles Hannon, only son of Mr and the late Mrs Hannon of 23 Victoria Road, Irlam. Winifred was the fourth daughter of Mr and Mrs S.E. Dutton of 61 Dixon Street, Irlam. The marriage took place at St Teresa's Church. Before enlisting, Winifred was employed by the CWS Soap Works.

Around this time, two friends, both former members of the Lancashire Steel football and cricket elevens, Petty Officer George Edward (Eddie) Barnes and Stoker Frank Connor, met in a Middle East port. During their meeting they talked about home affairs and sport, and before they parted, they had arranged a football match, destroyers versus minesweepers, with Eddie in charge of raising the destroyers' team, and Frank, the minesweepers.

Leading Stoker Frank Connor and Petty Officer Eddie Barnes

Before joining the Navy, Eddie Barnes was one of the Steelworks Club's outstanding athletes. He gained honours on many running tracks, including winning the Earl Cup for the 100 yards at the Lancashire Steel sports day. During his time in the Navy he won the silver cup for cross-country running and, when serving on board the *Queen Mary* during her period as a troop carrier, he was chosen to represent the ship's company. He completed the quarter mile in a time which was only two seconds slower than Lord Burleigh.

Eddie took part in the invasion of Sicily, the Battle of Anzio and operations in the south of France. He was born in Irlam, the son of Alfred and Lilian S. Barnes (nee Dixon) and resided with his parents in a shop at 544 Liverpool Road, Irlam. Eddie was an ex-boy scout. His father had served with the Lancashire Fusiliers in the First World War and had been gassed during the war, which caused him illness throughout his life until he passed away in 1940.

Leading Stoker D/KX136468 Frank Connor volunteered in 1940 and was called up in the following year. He was first posted to Malvern, Worcester, for kitting out and training, and after a fortnight he was posted to HMS *Drake*, Devonport. From here he went to Renfrew, Glasgow, where he joined the new minesweeper, HMS *Fly* (pennant J306). The ship underwent trials at Tobermory Bay and then joined the fleet at Aberdeen (the ship was commissioned on 10th October 1942). The ship's first assignments involved convoy duties to Iceland and sweeping duties in and around Iceland. After 12 months in the Arctic the ship returned to the UK and was then sent to Gibraltar and the Mediterranean. Frank took part in the naval operations during the Allied landings at Sicily, Salerno and Anzio. In the last year of his service he left HMS *Fly* at Malta and returned to UK on the troopship *Empress of Scotland*. He was demobilised in June 1946.

Born in 1921, Frank was the son of James and Annie Connor (nee Dickinson) of 30 Baines Avenue, Irlam. He ranked as one of Steel Cricket Club's best all-rounders, and his good humour made him popular with his team mates in the cricket and football elevens. Frank had two brothers who served in the war, James and Martin. James Edward Connor, the eldest brother (born 1913), served with the 2nd South Lancashire Regiment in Madagascar and Burma, and Leading Aircraftman Martin Connor (born 1920) served with the RAF in the Middle East, North Africa and Italy.

The following article appeared in the *Guardian* complaining about the meagre rations that serving men received while on leave: *What is the value of a soldier's meat ration when he is home on leave? The civilian ration is, of course, 1s 2d a week, but a friend tells me that when an acquaintance of his came on leave the butcher allowed him only one shillings worth of meat during the entire nine days. This, I suppose, is what is meant when we piously protest that our servicemen will get an adequate reward for the services they have rendered to the country. Well, three ha'prth of meat per diem might be the butcher's idea of a fighting man's meat requirements, but it certainly isn't mine. Nor is it, I believe, the Food Ministers.*

Although the blackout had ended some time ago when the threat of air raids diminished, the district was still subject to a 'dim-out'. In April there were rumours that the dim-out would shortly be removed. The district's 'dim' lighting compared very favourably with other towns, though there were some cities, such as Blackpool and Salford, where the lighting was significantly brighter.

On Thursday, 12th April the wedding took place at St John's Church, Irlam between Corporal Arnold Wrigley, only son of Mr and Mrs J. Wrigley of 20 Victory Road,

Cadishead, and Margaret McKinnell, elder daughter of Mr and Mrs O.G. McKinnell of 536 Liverpool Road, Irlam. Two days' later, on Saturday, 14th April Petty Officer Joseph Malin married Nora Pollard, only daughter of Mr and Mrs J. Pollard of Vine Cottage, Dunham Massey at St Mark's Church, Dunham Massey. Joseph was the only son of Mr and Mrs J. Malin of Rose Avenue, Irlam. Nora's brother, Sergeant John Pollard, RAF, was best man. Nora was employed as a shorthand typist by the Record Electrical Co. Ltd, Broadheath.

Arnold and Margaret Wrigley (left) and Joseph and Nora Malin

While en route to an overseas posting, Corporal William Grills of the RAF, met his brother-in-law, Captain Ernest K. Robinson. William lived with his sister and brother-in-law at 640 Liverpool Road, Irlam. This was their first meeting for over two years. William was the bandmaster of the local Salvation Army corps band and Ernest was a member of the band and a Salvation Army officer.

Corporal William Grills and Captain Ernest Robinson

Ernest had travelled overseas in 1943 to serve with a Red Shield canteen. He was in the victorious campaign from El Alamein, and it was during this period that he met one or two local men who were served with refreshments from his mobile canteen. He was awarded the Africa Star.

William was posted to Cairo, Egypt, early in 1945. Here he visited the Red Shield club, the rendezvous of many servicemen, and he met up with his brother-in-law. After this first meeting they were able to meet up again on a number of occasions. During their time together they joined the Cairo Red Shield Band, which was composed of Salvationists serving with the Forces in Egypt.

The following account appeared in the *Guardian* from 'A Military Observer' and is worth reproducing in full:

In theory, as the Royal Electrical and Mechanical Engineers' representative at Brigade HQ, I am liaison officer between the battalions and 70 infantry brigade workshops, REME. I arrange for all jobs beyond capacity of the Light Aid Detachments with the battalions to be repaired through brigade workshops,' said Captain Kenneth H. Davies, REME, of Irlam, with mock pomposity. 'In practice, however,' he added with a smile, 'I go anywhere in the brigade area and deal with any mechanical problem.' Captain Davies was far from his office when I met him. Notebook in hand, and with a preoccupied look on his face, he was here and there in the workshops, cajoling and chiding alternatively, pressing for his work to be hastened – and getting his share of pressure too. An ROAC officer spotted him and came over to where we stood chatting. 'Bill, that back axle, any griff?' he asked. In equally terse engineer – cum- soldier language, 'Bill' gave him the 'griff'. A REME lieutenant joined them, and an involved discussion on a workshop problem ensued; Captain Davies reached down, plucked the problem by the roots, and presented the solution. The group split up. 'Get him to tell you about his trip into No-Man's Land,' was the REME lieutenant's parting shot. Captain Davies was reluctant to talk about this exploit which was the talk of the workshops. It appears that in the face of overwhelming opposition during the heavy fighting in north Belgium, a battalion was forced temporarily to withdraw, leaving five carriers and three anti-tank guns, bogged in very bad ground, between the German lines and our own. The nature of the ground, rather than the weather, caused the difficulty, and nothing the battalion possessed in the way of equipment would move them. When a message reporting the fact reached Captain Davies, he decided to do a recce himself to find out exactly what condition the vehicles were in, and to form an idea of how to set about getting them back. Captain Davies went out at ten o'clock in the night under cover of darkness. Owing to the proximity of the enemy, he could not take his jeep past a certain point, and had to do most of the recce on foot. The drivers, who were the only people who knew exactly where all the vehicles had been left, were not available, and as the vehicles were all in different places, it was early the next morning before Captain Davies found them. Weighing up the advantages and disadvantages of both day and night recovery, he decided in favour of the former considering that its benefits outweighed the admitted danger of possible enemy observation. Despite a weariness resulting from his all-night adventure, he took up a breakdown wagon and crew comprising CFN G. Dovey of London, CFN W.G. Bradbury of Sale, Cheshire, CFN J. Dix of Selly Oak, Birmingham, Corporal H.D. Hughes of Madley, Hereford and CFN P.L. Hibberd of Upper Tysoe, Warwick, and a section of REs. The party removed two anti-tank guns and two carriers the first day, and the engineers placed booby traps round the remainder to stop the Boche from 'playing about' with them overnight. The following day, the party returned and removed them. Despite the very flat country, and good observation posts, making it easy for the enemy to observe their activities, so skilfully did they work, they were not observed until just as they were leaving on the second day, when the enemy began to mortar the area. But their luck held. They were 50 yards on their return journey when the first mortar bomb fell, and the craftsmen chuckled, as they gathered speed, to see a 'stonk' falling on the area where the vehicles had been.

Kenneth Davies resided at 68 Baines Avenue, Irlam, and at the time of the above account he was 27 years of age. His parents lived in Argentina. When he had returned to Irlam on leave in February his aunt had noticed that he was wearing the ribbon of the Military Cross, but he refused to say why it had been awarded. Kenneth joined the Army in December 1942 and was commissioned in May 1943. Prior to joining the Army he was employed as an engineer by Mather and Platt of Manchester. A keen rugby player, he was a wing forward for Walton Park.

The *Guardian* took up the rights of mothers to receive a war pension if they lost an unmarried son: *One of the most glaring anomalies of this war is that of pensions. A woman whose husband is killed on service is entitled to a pension – not an adequate one by any means, for no one will ever accuse the British Government of undue generosity towards the dependants of those who give their lives to make democracy safe for bureaucrats. Still, niggardly though the sum is, it is a pension. But a mother may lose one, two, three or even four unmarried sons, and she still does not get a pension of any sort without submitting to a humiliating means test. The gross injustice of this has attracted the notice of several Members of Parliament, but, against the ramparts of bureaucracy – against the Government determination not to part with a penny if it can be avoided – their best efforts have failed. A reduction in the pensions of Civil Servants would provide something towards meeting the cost of pensions for mothers. Or perhaps our Civil Serpents, as I once heard them called, wouldn't like it that way.*

Rationing was a major talking point throughout the war and, in stark contrast, was compared to what was seen by many as the good treatment handed out to German prisoners of war. An article in the *Guardian* stated that one of the best existences was to be a German prisoner in England. *Not only does he do a minimum of work, but he gets a maximum of rationed foods – about twice the amount a British civilian gets, according to the grocers, who have decided to call the Ministry of Food's attention to this state of affairs. Of course, the official excuse (officialdom is as full of excuses as a dog is of fleas) that, by the Geneva Convention, a prisoner of war is entitled to the same rations as a soldier of the country by whom he was captured. Of course, Germany was also a signatory to the Geneva*

Convention, but recent photographs received proved conclusively that British prisoners are certainly not getting the same rations as the German soldier. Repeatedly one hears from repatriated British prisoners that they would have starved if it had not been for the Red Cross parcels. In addition, British prisoners have been compelled to work in mines, or clearing up air raid debris, and on scores of other tasks forbidden by the Hague Convention. Yet British farmers have had a hard task to persuade the head lads of British Bumbledom to allow them German prisoners for farm work. It is becoming increasingly obvious that the Government – or at least its permanent and semi-permanent officials – are completely out of touch with public opinion. This latest revelation that German prisoners live, comparatively speaking, on the fat of the land, whilst our own people scrape along on a bare minimum, and our own lads who are prisoners are literally starving should prove to all who previously had any doubts that Whitehall rule is a poor substitute for Westminster democracy. In fact it certainly looks as if the Whitehall Wallahs are determined that everybody – Jerries, wops and Japs – will come out of this war better than the poor, blooming British. Well last week I wrote about decorating lamp posts with Civil Servants. Maybe when rope gets a bit cheaper and out of the clutches of whatever controls rope – we'll be able to do something about it.

Flight Sergeant 1522705 **Ronald Thornley Jaques** was killed on air operations on Wednesday, 18th April, aged 21. At the time he was serving with 640 Squadron, No. 4 Group, Bomber Command of the Royal Air Force, which was based at Leconfield, Yorkshire. Ronald was the flight engineer on board Halifax bomber Mark VI, serial no. RG564/P.

On Wednesday, 18th April Halifax RG564/P took part in its first operational 'sortie,' a raid on a fortified German naval base at Heligoland in the North Sea. The 12 inch guns of the base commanded the approaches to the Weser and Elbe estuaries. 969 aircraft took part in the raid, consisting of 617 Lancaster bombers, 332 Halifax bombers and 20 De-Havilland Mosquitoes. The raid, carried out in the absence of any serious flak and no sign of German fighters, was a success and not a single building was left standing. Three Halifaxes, including RG564/P, were lost on the raid.

Sergeant Gerry Mallin, navigator of RG601/Y, witnessed the end of RG564/P: *On the squadron's penultimate raid (on Heligoland) Pilot Officer Pugh and his crew were 'downed' in broad daylight when one of their engines was knocked out by a bomb falling from an aircraft high above. The flight to the target was uneventful, visibility being perfect. On the run up, the sky seemed to be full of Halifaxes. The anti-aircraft fire was desultory, probably because the raid was well in progress before we arrived. I noticed several small ships below heading away from the port facilities. We bombed visually at 1325 hours. Most aircraft were at our level, as instructed. I didn't see the bomb strike Pugh's aircraft, but the pilot or bomb-aimer drew my attention to it, out of control and with several 'chutes spilling from it. Though they were equipped with Mae Wests, we feared the survivors wouldn't have lasted long in the cold waters of the Heligoland Bight in April.*

Ronald was born in the district on 16th May 1923, the eldest son of Joseph and Gertrude Millicent Jaques (nee Turner), who resided at 6 Silver Street, Higher Irlam.

Before enlisting Ronald worked at the Steelworks. He joined the Home Guard (service no. 273) on 25th September 1940, serving in 2 Platoon of D Company, and at some point during the war he also joined the Irlam detached flight of 292 (Eccles) Squadron, ATC. On 13th January 1942, he enlisted into the Royal Air Force Volunteer Reserve aged 19, at the rank of Aircraftman 2nd Class. He qualified as a wireless operator, and rose to the rank of Sergeant in 1943. A year later he became a Flight Sergeant (flight engineer). In 1945 he joined 640 Squadron, which had been formed in the January of the previous year (it was disbanded in July 1945, shortly after the end of the war in Europe).

The other members of the crew were: Flying Officer H.K. Pugh and Warrant Officer H.K. Franklin (both of the Royal Australian Air Force), Flight Sergeant W. Probert and Sergeants G.A. Knowles, A.R. Lishman and J. Whittenbury. Ronald has no known grave and is therefore commemorated on the Runnymede Memorial, Surrey.

Runnymede Memorial
(Inset: Ronald's inscription on the memorial)

A Cadishead glider pilot, Sergeant Charles Taylor, youngest son of Mr and Mrs Charles Taylor of 100 Liverpool Road, Irlam, was seriously injured when riding his motorcycle back to his unit on Wednesday, 18th April. Charles had been home on leave and left Cadishead on his own motorcycle in order to be back with his unit on the following morning. He was only five minutes ride from his destination when his motorcycle struck a roundabout and he was thrown to the ground, sustaining serious head injuries. After several days he regained consciousness and his condition had improved slightly. Earlier in the war, news was received that Charles had been killed at Arnhem, but fortunately this proved to be false. Due to an error, his 'farewell' letter was posted to his wife and the secretary of the regimental fund made an inquiry asking if his wife was in need of financial assistance. This led to the belief that he had been killed but subsequent enquiries made by Reverend Bakker proved that he was alive and well and shortly afterwards he returned home on leave.

The hope that the district would soon be in a position to build a new nurses' home was expressed by Mr H. Booth, chairman of the Irlam, Cadishead and District Nursing Association, in the committee report which was presented at the annual meeting of the association, in Fairhills Road Methodist Church on Wednesday, 18th April. Mr Booth stated that by the combined efforts of the public, Cadishead Conservative Club, management and patrons of the Railway Hotel, and the employees of the British Basket and Besto Company, they had now invested £702-10s in Defence Bonds and the Post Office Savings Bank. When they were in a position to build the nurses home they hoped the Council would give them the necessary land as near the centre of the district as possible. *It would make a very suitable and useful war memorial and, whilst we hope not; it may be that returning members of HM Forces would require the services of the nurse or nurses, as much as anybody from the effects of their war service.*

The membership of the Irlam and Cadishead branch of the Home Guard Old Comrades Association had grown to 91 members since its inauguration in January and in its brief existence had made very definite progress. At a general meeting of the branch at Irlam Conservative Club, on Thursday, 19th April the president, Lieutenant Colonel Webb was present. Robert Pears, chairman, reported on the progress made. A meeting had been held with the Committee of the Irlam Conservative Club, with the result that the club had granted to all members of the branch full refreshment and recreation facilities, with the exception of the use of the bowling green, which was run independently. Robert stressed that the Old Comrades Association was non-political and the use of the Conservative Club's facilities did not imply any political bias. He urged members to take advantage of the club facilities, and pointed out that the use of the club was only a temporary measure until the association could acquire a headquarters of its own. Robert stated that an executive committee of three had been elected to represent the Irlam and Cadishead branch at an Executive Committee meeting in Eccles. At that meeting, which was attended by representatives of the other three branches, it was decided to form a sub-committee of one member from each branch to frame a set of rules which would be uniform throughout the branches. Robert gave the membership from the various companies in the district as D Coy 15 and G Coy 12. He expressed thanks to Alan Royle of Royles Engineering, who had sent a donation of five guineas as a token of his appreciation of the services rendered by the Home Guard in the past. After the general meeting two further donations to the branch funds were received. One of £5-6s from Mr H. Hulme of the British Basket and Besto Company, Irlam, and one of £2-2s from Mr C.A. Murray jnr, of British Tar Products, Cadishead. The president, Lieutenant Colonel Webb, before presenting certificates to Lieutenant Ernest Woods, Quartermaster Sergeant R. Tupling, Sergeant Arthur Phillips, Private J. Cundall and

Private George Twigg, said: *The time has gone when you had to sit down and listen to me whether you liked it or not. No one is more grateful than I, because it is a sure sign that we are winning the war.* He congratulated the branch on the progress it had made; he had visited the other branches, and Irlam was not lagging behind. Lieutenant Colonel Webb mentioned that the miniature rifle range at the nearby naval camp had been put at the disposal of the Old Comrades Association. At the moment he realised that a lot of work was falling on a few shoulders in the formation of the branch, but he urged all present to ask their friends to join. Following the general meeting, the Old Comrades Association made pleas for branch members who wanted to join the Rifle Club to contact John Hamer Hughes, captain of the club, or the branch secretary. Referring to the recent photographs of atrocities which had appeared in the Press, Lieutenant Colonel Webb said that, if it had not been for the Home Guard, that sort of thing might have been happening in this country. Officials of the local branch of the Old Comrades Association were: Lieutenant Colonel Webb, president; Robert Pears, chairman; Mr William Douglas Smith, hon. secretary; Francis Gordon Gold, hon. treasurer; and a committee comprising: Daniel Moore, Emanuel Harris, Mr G. Coulthard, Ernest Woods, Harry Thorne and Harry Goodier. A Rifle Club was formed: John Hamer Hughes, captain and assistant captains; Mr W. Houghton and Mr L. Burns. In addition, a Sports Committee was established which consisted of: Joseph Wrigley, John Atkinson, Mr F. Copeland and Frank Readman.

The second of two loads of household goods collected by the WVS in Cadishead and Irlam under the Good Neighbour Scheme, had reached Ilford, Essex and they showed their appreciation in the following letter: *The second load of furniture, etc. which you so kindly sent us arrived quite safely last Saturday morning. I cannot tell you how grateful we are for this marvellous gift. All the articles are excellent, there are no breakages, they are just what we needed. We have already disposed of quite a number, these have been gratefully appreciated by all who have received them. The sideboard, tables and chairs, have been hailed with delight. So few have been able to salvage such as these from the wreckage of their homes. Will you be good enough to thank all who have given so generously or taken any part in sending these gifts for our people. Thank you most heartily for your great help.*

The figures issued by the Irlam and Cadishead War Comforts and Welcome Home Fund showed that 1,674 men and women were serving or had served in the Forces. The number actually serving was 1,474 and of these 715 men and 82 women were from Irlam and 619 men and 58 women from Cadishead. In addition 29 men and 11 women from Irlam and 27 men and 17 women from Cadishead had been discharged. Prisoners of war totalled 35, 19 from Irlam and 16 from Cadishead, and three Irlam men and one Cadishead man had been repatriated. Four men from Irlam and ten from Cadishead were officially reported missing, whilst 30 Irlam men and one woman and 32 Cadishead men had been killed or had died on service. Donations to the fund included £1 from the sale of toys by Fay Johnson, B. Masters, A. Bolton, B.

Fletcher, G. Johnson, C. Eckersley and B. Millington, and £2-14-2 from the directors and employees of the British Besto and Basket Company.

Thomas Sharp, serving overseas with the RAF, sent the following letter to the *Guardian* regarding sports in the district: *Sir, I have read with interest your article on the sportsmanship of the Irlam and Cadishead residents. It seems to me that there is certainly something wrong with them when they are unable to supply a ground for one of the best hockey teams ever produced in the district; and then again you say that there are lots of locals who say that a Rugby club will never again 'go' in the district. All that I can say to that is that I wish the other local lads and myself from out here could get home to help you with the job of making one go. I should imagine that your article in the Guardian every week goes a long way to waking the locals up, and from all reports they need it, its time they got together and made the district a place to be proud of.*

The marriage took place at Cadishead Congregational Church, between Leading Aircraftman George Wheelton and Ethel Savery, only daughter of Mr and Mrs A. Savery of 72 Caroline Street, Irlam. Mr E. Dawson (late of Parachute Regiment) was best man and the groomsman was Private E. Price, RAMC (the bride's cousin). George, who was on leave from the British Liberation Army, was formerly employed by the Steelworks, as was his bride, Ethel. He was the younger son of Mr and Mrs F. Wheelton of 74 New Barton Street, Irlam O'th' Heights, Salford.

Fusilier 14775385 **Frederick Talbot** died of wounds on Sunday, 22nd April, aged 18. Fred had joined the Army in June 1944 and served with the 6th Battalion, Royal Welch Fusiliers, in France, Belgium and Holland. The 6th Battalion was part of the 160th Infantry Brigade, 53rd (Welsh) Infantry Division.

The division landed in Normandy on 28th June (D-Day+22) and was placed under command of XII Corps, which was defending the Odon Valley position. The division took part in heavy fighting in this area in the days leading up to Operation Goodwood. In August it pushed out of the Odon region and crossed the River Orne, helping to close the Falaise Pocket. They advanced into Holland and on 28th October, after five days of heavy fighting, they liberated the city of s-Hertogenbosch. In December the division took part in the Battle of the Bulge, and helped to isolate the northern tip of the German salient. It also took part in Operation Veritable which was a pincer movement conducted by 21st Army Group to clear and occupy the land between the Rhine and Maas rivers. The operation took place between 8th February and 11th March.

Frederick was the second son of Frederick and Hilda Talbot of 30 Lancaster Road, Cadishead (later of Sinderland, Cheshire). Educated at Cadishead Senior School, he then worked at Mosedales Brickworks in Rixton, before gaining employment at the Steelworks. He is buried in Becklingen War Cemetery, Soltau, Germany.

The 'dim-out' in Irlam and Cadishead was finally removed on 22nd April much to the relief of the local population. There had been much controversy when the blackout first changed to dim-out in September 1944 as to whether the new lighting added or hindered the motorist. The war-time measure that cyclists should have red rear-lights resulted in many summonses which persisted even though the seriousness of their act was impressed upon offenders.

A letter from Adjutant Roberts and his wife, Mrs Roberts, who were stationed with the Salvation Army in Italy on canteen work with the Forces, contained a donation towards the band's new instrument scheme and they also sent best wishes to their many friends in the district.

As the campaign against the Axis Forces in Italy was coming to an end, the Allies reached the River Po on 22nd April. One of the most important considerations was to find a way of crossing the river, as the Germans had destroyed most of the bridges. The Royal Engineers were given the task of erecting pontoon bridges and one of the local men who helped to span the River Po was Sergeant Roy Taylor. At one point, they inadvertently found themselves behind enemy lines: *We were looking for a river crossing, when we saw an Italian bloke with blocks of timber. We wondered whether he had been sent to work for us. We followed him for a while and then stopped him. We asked him whether he was working for the British and he answered 'No.' When then asked him where the Germans were and he replied 'All around,' we got out of there sharpish. Another time, we built a bailey bridge and a sergeant went across in a jeep. He came back with 90 prisoners. They were starving and were looking to give themselves up. We didn't have much ourselves but we collected corned beef and biscuits to feed them. We found them to be quite pleasant. There's not much difference between Germans and the British.*

The following images are from Roy Taylor's collection:

ONE MORE RIVER!

But it isn't only "one more river" - this time it is THE river!

It is the mighty Po!

Do you remember the hell of the rivers Sangro, Rapido, Liri, Volturno and Garigliano? Do you remember the lives that were sacrificed in crossing these rivers?

Put these rivers all together and the result will be smaller than the

Po!

Also when you crossed these rivers, the Germans, were in retreat and had no time to prepare defenses.

But covering the Po you will find a blanket of death... Artillery, Nebelwerfers, Mortars and Spandaus.

The whole Po area is a network of canals and is impassable for tanks.

Push
In!
Various
Exiting
Revelations
Prepared -
Oh Boy!

And here are a few facts about the Po:

At its shallowest part (between Adda and Mincio) it is 7 ft. deep.
At the deepest part (near Faenza) it is 20 ft. deep.
The width varies from 208 to 1,040 yds.
The banks are mostly sheer and between 18 and 30 ft. high.
The speed of the Po exceeds 20 m.p.h.

"PO" means death and suffering -
P.O.W. means security and comfort!

Think it over, only

Fools rush in..!

★ 1303-1-45

German propaganda left for the Allied troops to read

Pontoon bridge over the River Po

A destroyed bridge on an unknown Italian river
Note the devastated houses in the foreground

Sergeant Roy Taylor (second from left) with colleagues
Longarone, Italy

Sergeant Roy Taylor (second from left) with colleagues

Sergeant Roy Taylor, Royal Engineers

Sapper Jack Marshall, Royal Engineers

Sapper Noel Nelson, Royal Engineers

Lieutenant Gerard Riordan arrived home on Friday, 27th April after being released by the American Ninth Army from a German prisoner of war camp. He was taken prisoner on the Greek island of Leros in November 1943 and spent time in several prisoner of war camps and was at Oflag 79 at Brunswick when it was liberated by the American Forces. He was 22 years of age, and joined the Army in 1942, subsequently serving in the Middle East and the Dodecanese. He was full of praise for the Red Cross, whose parcels helped the prisoners to maintain their health. One of the greatest hardships for him was when, for some unknown reason, the Red Cross parcels stopped arriving at the camp. Gerard was the youngest son of Mr and Mrs M. Riordan of 29 Francis Road, Irlam. He attended St Teresa's (RC) School and later De La Salle Grammar School, Weaste. Prior to joining the Army he was employed in the general office of the CWS Soap Works.

Sapper 1901343 Harry Toal, Royal Engineers, was also engaged on constructing Bailey bridges to aid the Allied advance. He had been called up in 1939 and had served throughout the Middle East campaign. After the Allied invasion of Italy in 1943, Harry accompanied his unit to Italy, disembarking at Taranto. During this period he saw the horrific battlefields of Monte Cassino. From Italy his unit was posted, briefly, to Greece before returning to Italy. Later in 1945 he served in Austria as part of the occupation force. He then disembarked from Naples, Italy, for England and was demobilised on 2nd June 1946.

Another two local men who served with the Royal Engineers were Sapper John Robert 'Jack' Marshall and Noel Nelson. It is not known which theatres of war they served in. Jack was born in 1920, the son of Mr and Mrs W. Marshall and resided at 25 Poplar Grove, Cadishead. He had joined the local Home Guard on 5th June 1940, and served as Private 64 in 3 Platoon of D Company. Jack joined the Army on 21st May 1941. Noel Nelson, nicknamed 'Nippy,' was born on 11th January 1919, the son of Mr and Mrs R. Nelson. He resided at 2 The Crescent, Higher Irlam and worked as a boiler maker at the Steelworks. He joined the local Home Guard on 28th March 1941 as Private B535 of 1 Platoon, D Company. He resigned from the Home Guard on 14th February 1942. He served on active duty but was then returned to the Steelworks because his trade was a reserved occupation.

Signalman Trevor Jenkins, serving with the American Fifth Army, was one of the first across the Bailey bridges over the River Po. On the other side of the river, he found the roads littered with bodies and it was impossible to avoid running over them. As they came off the bridge his driver made an error and the vehicle came off the road and rolled over down a bank. Trevor was knocked senseless but remembers turning off the wireless set before losing consciousness. After recovering, they joined in the pursuit of the Germans, who had no petrol and had to resort to using cattle and horses to pull their transports. Trevor recalled that the Germans were trapped on the roads with nowhere to go. Allied aircraft strafed and bombed the columns and the artillery shelled them as they retreated northwards. The places he visited included Monfalcone, Padua and, shortly after the war, Trieste. He commented that: *The Americans wanted to bomb everything, including Venice.* During his time in Italy, a Canadian aircraft crashed in a nearby copse, killing all the crew. Trevor volunteered to bury the crew and remembers the badly burnt corpses and was struck by the red hair of one of the men which had somehow not been destroyed by the fire. After the war, he wondered whether the graves had been found by the Imperial (now Commonwealth) War Graves Commission.

Italy's entry into the war had shattered a long, friendly relationship between Italy and England which had lasted for many years. Overnight the smiling, friendly, easy-going Italian became a hated enemy. Many local men had mixed experiences at the hands of the Italians, as shown by the letter from Tom Denton in March 1945 and the response by Corporal James E. Hampson in the same month. At times the Italians were seen as being as brutal as the Germans and sometimes, even worse. It is therefore surprising to find that some people found true friends among the Italians; one such case was Thomas Lowe. His mother, Mrs S.E. Lowe of 16 Kitchener Avenue, Cadishead, received news about him in a letter from an Italian mother, Mrs Dora Fabi Gentili of Torentino, at whose house he had stayed. The letter dated 24th April is presented below (without corrections): *Dear Mrs, I think your son Tommy, has let you know our hospitality during his free hours in our home. We was very glad to have him with us, because he is a very well good boy. He left this town on the April 10th, 1945, since then we didn't receive any news from him because he can't write to any civilians and even we cannot write to any Allied soldiers. We was very sorry for his departure and hoping that this war ends soon, and he will come back to his dear home safe and healthy. I hope to receive a letter from you very soon, and I shall be glad to hear all the news you can give to me from Tommy. When he was spending his free hours in my home, always mention you and his father and the brothers. My children cannot forget him because he was playing with them always. I understand your anxiety and trepidations. I am a mother myself, but don't worry the war will ends properly into this month and you will see your son very soon. Me and my husband sending to you and family our best wishes and believe in us.*

MAY

Mr E. Winder of 47 Lancaster Road, Cadishead, received word on Wednesday, 2nd May that his only son, Private Edward Winder, had been wounded in Germany and was in hospital in Belgium. Edward, who joined the Army in August 1944, went overseas in February 1945 and in that time had seen service in France, Holland, Belgium and Germany. He was 19 years of age at the time and, before joining the Army, was employed by Kilvert & Sons Ltd, Trafford Park.

Air Mechanic Mary Smart, WRNS

On the same day, (2nd May), the wedding took place at St Catherine's Church, Barton Bridge, of 22 year old Walter McArthur, second son of David and Phoebe McArthur of 20 Marlborough Road, Higher Irlam, and Mary Smart, daughter of Mr and Mrs G. Smart of 120 Kingsway Road, Davyhulme. Walter's older brother, Leslie, was the best man. After the ceremony, a reception was held at the bride's home, and later the couple left for Staffordshire. Walter served as a Leading Stoker on board HMS *Renown* from 1942 to 1946. Walter explained: *On the way back they said the war with Germany was over but we still had the war with Japan, was still going on, so we thought we'd probably reach home or reach Malta and then they'd turn us round and send us back but they didn't, we kept on coming and we went right up to Scotland, Rosyth, put in there. They immediately gave us 14 days' leave, both watches, one watch come, I went the second watch so's I could get married, give Mary time to get some gear together, you know give her a fortnight [laughter]. So I got married then from there, and then went back to the ship, we went down to Plymouth, just tied up there and it never moved again, well it only moved to get scrapped.*

The McArthur family had a distinguished military pedigree. David, their father, was a First World War veteran and holder of the Military Medal. David also had a short stint with the local Home Guard, serving as Private 379, in 1 Platoon of D Company. He joined the Home Guard on 14th July 1940 and resigned on 14th January 1941. Both Leslie and Walter served in the Second World War; Leslie with the Lancashire Fusiliers and then as a Corporal in the Durham Light Infantry and Walter as Leading Stoker on board HMS *Renown*. Mary served as a Wren (air mechanic) with the Women's Royal Naval Service.

Gunner John Cassidy, who had been held as a prisoner of war, returned home on 2nd May after being liberated by the British Second Army. John, who was 27 years of age, joined the Army in July 1939, and went to France in January 1940. He returned via Dunkirk, and went to North Africa in December 1940, where he was taken prisoner at El Agheila, Libya, on 24th January 1942. He was taken to Italy and, 17 months later, was moved to Stalag 411 in Germany. During his captivity, he spent time in six different prisoner of war camps. He said every prisoner had looked forward to the distribution of Red Cross parcels. Prior to joining the Army, he was employed by the Cheshire County Council and resided at 99 New Moss Road, Cadishead.

Twelve children from Poplar Grove, Cadishead, who went 'May Queening,' raised over a £1 for the Red Cross Penny-a-Week Fund. The children were: Kathleen White, Ann Hugill, Kathleen Plater, Betty Bell, Arleen White, Norma Russell, Shirley Nock, Dudley Nock, Arthur Nelson, Billy Hargreaves, Brenda Miller and Carol Knight. A further £1 was raised for the Penny-a-Week Fund by eight children who lived in Allotment Road and Rivington Grove, Cadishead. The children were: Betty Hilton, Audrey Doton, Aileen Battles, Anne Shakeshaft, Evelyn Bailey, Joyce Hodgkiss, Ann Rust and George Wharton. The Red Cross also benefited by £1 as a result of another May Queen organised by H. Andrews of Chestnut Avenue, Cadishead. The girls taking part were; D. Jordan, P. Whittaker, P. Toft, J. Lynch, J. Waldron, J. Wright and C. Elliot. The boys were: R. Roberts, C. Brown, E. Eddon and J. Cassels.

The district had been planning for VE Day for some months, however, when the day finally came the celebrations were low-key; the war against Japan was still being fought and many local men were out in the Far East. Even in Europe, it would be many months before local men and women serving in the Forces would be allowed to return home. Although Germany had been defeated, there was still another enemy, Japan, to be dealt with. Many local people had sons, brothers, husbands in Burma and elsewhere and they, naturally, did not feel inclined to enter into any rejoicings – not of the riotous sort anyway – for, though half the war was over, the other half in which their near ones, and dear ones, were engaged was still far from finished. The *Guardian* carried the following article: *Few, I am sure, will indulge in any hysterical flag waving demonstrations when VE Day is announced. Naturally, there will be that element which will take advantage of the declaration – as they would take advantage of the slightest pretext – for an orgy of riotousness, but, for the most part, I believe the general feeling will be one of thankfulness for perils safely passed.*

As a result it was decided that the official VE Day programme for Irlam and Cadishead would be more in the nature of a thanksgiving. The following appeared in the *Guardian: There are no present indications that the district will go wild with joy or that there will be an outbreak of hysterical flag waving. The imminence of the cessation of hostilities in Europe has been received with sober satisfaction and a feeling of relief. If VE Day comes on a week-day the Council will appeal to local traders to do all in their power to ensure that the public gets an adequate supply of foodstuffs – particularly bread and milk. The British Restaurant will be open all day. Whatever celebrations there are will be on a minor scale – possibly a band or bands in the district – and cinemas will be asked to provide some sort of entertainment for schoolchildren. On the Sunday following VE Day it has been suggested that open air services should be held at Prince's Park and Cadishead Recreation Ground. Local churches have already made their plans for VE Day. Town Topics suggested that one way in which the Government could help the district to celebrate VE Day was to allow everybody a double week's ration of foodstuffs. For five years and more we have been told what a gallant and valiant people we are and a spate of propaganda has drummed it into our ears that we have been – and are still – fighting for the freedom of the common man. Having got half-way to our objective, the Minister of Food might stretch a point and let us have a week's extra rations to help us to carry on with the other half of the task. Or, perhaps, there is only enough in stock to ensure that our Jerry prisoners get theirs.*

On Monday, 7th May the war in Europe finally came to an end with the German unconditional surrender to General Dwight D. Eisenhower at Rheims, France, and to the Soviets in Berlin. The next day, 8th May was declared the long anticipated Victory in Europe (VE) Day.

It is not known for certain who fired the last shell of the war in Europe, however, one unit which has a claim is the 53rd (London) Medium Regiment, Royal Artillery, which included Gunner Tom Vaudrey. On 15th April the regiment had deployed near Duiven, east of the River Ijssel and north of Nijmegen to support 49th Division's attack on Arnhem, which was over by 17th April. They moved to Meppen in Germany and remained here until 28th April when they moved to support the 3rd Canadian Division's attack on Leer. On 2nd May the battle moved out of range. On 3rd May the regiment moved to Detern under the command of the 1st Polish Armoured Division. The next day they moved to Halsbeck. At 8.30pm, on 6th May the news came through of the German surrender and that hostilities would cease at 8am next day. The Poles, not trusting the Germans to stick to the truce, asked for counter battery fire to continue until the last minute. The last shell was fired by 53rd Regiment at 7.59am and 35 seconds, with a recorded flight time of 24 seconds.

Tom was demobilised from the Army on 22nd February 1946. His discharge papers stated that his military conduct was exemplary and his commanding officer provided the following testimonial: *Trustworthy, reliable and sober. A keen hardworking man who has given first class service.*

A local man, Lance Corporal Jack Sherratt of 11 Ash Avenue, Cadishead, was given the job of delivering the victory messages for Field Marshal Montgomery. Being attached to the HQ of the 21st Army Group, his unit was asked to provide a driver to deliver the victory messages to various Army units and, after loading up the car, his first job was to take Monty's secretary to an airfield to enable him to fly to England for VE Day. After a 150 mile dash over the war-torn roads of Holland, Jack succeeded in carrying out his orders of delivering before midnight with a few minutes to spare. When he returned to HQ in Germany he was thanked by the Field Marshal's Chief of Staff. As a reward he was asked if he would like an autographed victory message from Monty for which he had to wait whilst the chief of staff entered the commander's room. Jack kept the message as a war souvenir. Before entering the Forces in September 1939 he was a member of the local Salvation Army Band, and had played in many prominent Salvation Army bands throughout the country. Jack's brother, Joseph Arthur Sherratt, was lost at sea when HMS *Glorious* was sunk in 1940.

Able Seaman Roy Brotherton heard the news in America: *The end of the war, the European war, we was over in... I told you where we had the collision, and finished up at Quebec, we were at a place called Lauzon which is on the other side of the river, it's only a little place but that's where the shipyard was because we had to go to a place where they had a dry dock to mend this and the nearest dry dock we could get who could take us at that time was this one there, so we came up the St Lawrence and went there. But we used to go just down to a place to get the ferry across and go to Quebec when we went ashore at night, so officially we were at Quebec but actually we were staying on the other side of the river. We were over there and then it came through that the war in Europe had finished, well Quebec is very, very much a French state, very strong, they're not very keen on the English it's well-known, in fact they don't bloody like us at all, and it was a dry state, there was no pubs or anything in the state of Quebec, so what they used to do is when we went over there, and we* used to go to a place and we used to get a liquor permit which allowed you to buy a bottle of gin or a bottle of whisky, but we never used to, we used to just get the liquor permit then we used to sell it for $2 and then go and have a feed with the money, so that was it. So of course when we were over there the only time you could perhaps get one can of ale on the ship cos they didn't encourage drinking, we didn't used to drink, and you didn't drink when you was ashore and course you couldn't go out and get drunk or anything. And the only place you could go to get a drink was if you went, apparently there was a Canadian naval barracks where we could have gone and got a couple of cans of beer but nobody bothered trying to find out about some obscure barracks for a couple of cans of beer, so that was it. And you'd have thought that the war had just started, there was no festivities, no nothing, there was a great huddle about the place but all it was that weekend there was something to do with the Catholic church where they go round and bless the houses, provided you pay. Oh they had shrines on the bloody corners, all for this festival, blessing, never mind about the bloody war finishing and people not gonna get killed and all that lot going on there.

The victory message below, signed by General Dwight Eisenhower, is an example of the victory messages distributed to servicemen and women.

SUPREME HEADQUARTERS
ALLIED EXPEDITIONARY FORCE

TO ALL MEMBERS OF THE ALLIED EXPEDITIONARY FORCE:

The task which we set ourselves is finished, and the time has come for me to relinquish Combined Command.

In the name of the United States and the British Commonwealth, from whom my authority is derived, I should like to convey to you the gratitude and admiration of our two nations for the manner in which you have responded to every demand that has been made upon you. At times, conditions have been hard and the tasks to be performed arduous. No praise is too high for the manner in which you have surmounted every obstacle.

I should like, also, to add my own personal word of thanks to each one of you for the part you have played, and the contribution you have made to our joint victory.

Now that you are about to pass to other spheres of activity, I say Good-bye to you and wish you Good Luck and God-Speed.

Dwight Eisenhower

Leading Aircraftman 1487651 John Ryan, serving in No. 4 Flight, 2844 Squadron of the RAF Regiment, received the news while stationed at Quakenbruck in north west Germany. He would later take part in the Victory Parade in Berlin. John took the following photographs during his time in Germany:

VE Day at Quakenbruck, Germany

2844 Squadron on the road to Berlin

2844 Squadron in convoy

Bomb damage in Berlin

The road from Berlin to Luneberg

More bomb damage on the road to Luneberg

Victory Parade in Berlin

The RAF Regiment march past

Leading Aircraftman John Ryan, RAF Regiment

Born on 22nd June 1922, John was the son of Michael and Johanna Ryan of 34 Addison Road, Higher Irlam. His brother Thomas Ryan served with the Maritime Royal Artillery. John was educated at St Teresa's School, Irlam and then worked at a local butchers before taking a job at the Steelworks. He joined the Home Guard on 8th April 1941 (Private 533) and served in 2 Platoon, D Company. John's job at the Steelworks was classed as a reserved occupation, however this did not stop him volunteering for the RAF at the age of 19. He joined the RAF Regiment on 9th August 1941 and trained as a mechanical transport driver and also as a gunner at Filey in Yorkshire and then joined 2844 Squadron.

2844 Squadron was originally formed as 844 Squadron at Barrow on 19th December 1941, having been unnumbered from the previous April. On 1st February 1942 all RAF Regiment Squadrons had 2000 added to their numbers. The squadron moved to the RAF Depot at Belton Park in 1942, becoming a field squadron in October of the same year. The squadron converted to the light anti-aircraft role in May 1943 and became a rifle squadron in October 1944. The squadron moved to the continent in May 1945, being deployed to Luneburg, where it remained until being disbanded in March 1946. John was demobbed on 22nd January 1946 and returned to work at the Steelworks. His character throughout his military service was described as very good and his proficiency as superior.

Trevor Jenkins, Royal Corps of Signals, remembered how they celebrated VE Day

Yeah I was in Italy, I remember what I was doing yeah, supping ale. They gave us four bottles, I don't think they had a glass, NAAFI bottles they were, for celebration, four little bottles of beer. We were obviously elated you know. We were never bloody sober once they'd let us loose, because once it had finished I must admit the Forces sort of went out then, gone. No discipline, nothing. You could do what you want, go where you want, nobody seemed to bother, no one signing in and out of camp, things like that. You wandered about, did what you wanted, no, especially on our job because we weren't attached to a regiment, we were only attached to them but we weren't part of them, you just did what you wanted. I had a great 18 months I had. Aye if you got called up in the Canadian Forces you had to volunteer to come overseas, if you didn't then they used to stay in Canada. I was always keen on dancing and we went to a place where the Red Cross used to have a dance on a Saturday night and I went there this time and they had this American idea where they had girls as dance hosts, you know you could go, and every week there was trouble because they could tell. If they'd volunteered to come over they had a flash or something on their arm so these girls knew whether they were, and if you didn't have one of these flashes they used to call them zombies, and they were supposed to dance with anybody that asked but they wouldn't dance with the bloody zombies, they all had headaches or somebody had just trod on their bloody foot, and of course the zombies used to get mad, used to be like pitched battles but that was how it was going on and you would have thought that the war had just started, it was the most miserable bloody day you could ever imagine and we'd been looking forward to this all them years, so that was it.

On 8th May Flight Sergeant Harold Townend was a crew member on board a Vickers Warwick which escorted a French cruiser into Brest harbour: *We went with the SS Duquesne, the French cruiser, we escorted her into Brest, all the nurses came out on the hospital roof waving to us, we circled round and let the Duquesne go in and take over.* After this they continued on anti-submarine patrol and it was ironic that after all the many many hours they had spent searching for U-boats – the German Naval Command had given an order for all U-boats to surface and surrender: *They were popping up like corks to be escorted to Londonderry in Northern Ireland.* Later on the crew of the aircraft were able to go aboard one of the U-boats.

Meanwhile back in the district people had hung out flags and bunting on Monday evening (7th May) and by the morning of VE Day shops, houses, offices and works had been decorated. Anything containing red, white and blue (the colours of the United Nations) served as a decoration. Many works were closed, although some, because of the nature of their work, had to remain open until after the Prime Minister's speech. Many men turned up at work to find them closed or insufficient men had turned up.

A heavy downpour on the morning of VE Day prevented any outdoor celebrations but in the afternoon the rain stopped and the pace of the celebrations quickened. Shortly before the Prime Minister's speech, the stage had been set. There would be rejoicing on the day and on those that followed, however, they were largely restrained and with little incident. The *Guardian* made the following comment: *It was as if the people, after 5½ years of war in Europe, were too thankful to come through the peril and hardship, through a seemingly endless hideous nightmare into the full light of day, to indulge in the riotous orgies that marked Armistice Day 1918. For 5½ years people had lived on their nerves; they had lived, too, through bitter disappointments and defeats that would have crushed a smaller and less vital people; they had become inured to expecting the worst while hoping and fighting for the best and the imminence of the end of hostilities in Europe found them rather inclined to think there might be just one more of those last minute disappointments which marked the course of the war. For those reasons and because people realised that this was only the end of the first half of the war, the celebrations were restrained.*

Special thanksgiving services were held at churches throughout the district on VE Day and the following day. At St Mary's Church, Cadishead, there was a thanksgiving service on the evening of VE day and an official thanksgiving on the following Sunday. At St John's Church, Irlam, there were services all day, a children's thanksgiving service at 5.30pm, a further service at 7.30pm and a Communion at 8.30pm. A service was held at 7.30pm at Cadishead Wesleyan Church and there were similar services at Rixton and Glazebrook. Prior to the evening Salvation Army service on VE Day the band and comrades of the corps made a special 'Victory' march around part of the district. The representatives of the district's religious orders shared their wisdom with their congregations.

Reverend Lee compared the passing of Adolf Hitler with that of Judas Iscariot: *The real reason for celebrating should not so much be for the retribution that had overtaken our enemies. That would be a low conception of victory, a beating down of our enemies because we were physically stronger and in greater numbers. That was a conception of the Middle Ages. The true thought of victory came from the thought that good had triumphed over evil. While a great number were celebrating because they had no personal loss, victory was also a time of sorrow for those who had sons, husbands and sweethearts killed. One man with four sons in the Forces had summed up victory in his own case as a time for thanksgiving because they were all safe and alive.*

Reverend Ayres addressed a large congregation at Cadishead Wesleyan Church: *We are gathered here to give thanks to God who had given us the victory and brought an end in Europe to the horrors and brutalities that war always brought. The people had been called to pray many times during the war when the country had been in dire straits and it was only right and proper, when we had triumphed, to give thanks for the overthrow of a diabolical tyranny which had caused so much suffering and pain. But as Christians they must recognise that the sacrifices of the past would need to be continued in the days ahead if they were to avoid this constant negation of all their principles. The Christian had his duty to his own land but he must know that his overriding loyalty was to God and his fellows wherever they may be.*

At St Paul's Methodist Church in Irlam, Reverend W. Motson felt that language was too inadequate for such an occasion. He urged the congregation to sing their hymns of praise and offer their prayers of intercession and then go back with the determination to rid the world of the vile and unspeakable horror which men called war. He went on to explain a terribly sad experience: *I was jostling in the crowds of Manchester today and sharing in the revelry of victory celebrations. In the midst of that excited thong a Methodist Minister told me that a few hours previously he had visited a house where a family had received word on VE Day that a son had been killed in battle. That was sufficient evidence to remind me of the awful price which has been and is still being paid for our freedom.*

Speaking at Boundary Road Church in Higher Irlam on Wednesday, Reverend Motson said: *It is natural that people's feelings should be mingled at this hour. We all feel a great sense of relief, liberation and great joy and out of these feelings rises that act of thanksgiving. But we rejoice with a special sense of restraint; the victory was only partial and fellows were still facing the perils of war. Before complete victory is won great sacrifices will have to be made. When the war really ended we will be presented with a challenge and an opportunity, a challenge which will demand more courage and sacrifice than the days of the war and the opportunity to build that kind of world which will be a worthy tribute to those who had made it possible to live in freedom and peace. We are grateful to God for everything that is ours tonight, we should rejoice with sober minds remembering the grim tragedy through which we have passed and realising the desperate need of peoples whose homes and countries have been destroyed. We must dedicate ourselves to the high task of living our religion out in such a way that the people might catch a vision of Jesus Christ as the only hope and salvation of the world.*

At St Mary's Church in Cadishead, Reverend Bakker spoke: *At last the night waned and the dawn has begun to lighten up the horizon. Yet we should remember that it was only the dawn. Even at that moment, war raged over a quarter of the globe; English, American and Chinese troops were passing through the fire. Many of the men who have won us victory in Europe will have to screw up their courage to face the ordeal again. Yet when all is said it remains a moment of immense deliverance. It is not that for the first time in five years, Europe no longer bears the sound of guns and that our ships can sail the seas without fear of attack. It is rather the knowledge that children are playing on the swings of Belsen and that all over Europe the slave workers of Germany are trudging homewards, weary but free. At present we have solved nothing. But at least we have stopped the onrush of evil. We have won the right to hope. And hope for what? That the voice of Christian men and women may again be heard in Europe, that men may listen to their only hope, the brotherhood of hope which springs from the fatherhood of God. In the past, no doubt, the voice of the churches has often been faltering, yet on the whole it has remained an authentic voice. And it is a hope for a shattered world.*

The Council Offices served as the focal point for the celebrations on VE Day and VE Day plus one. The offices had been decorated with a huge 'V' for Victory, with an illuminated crown in the middle and flanked by the flags of the United Nations which stood out against the floodlit background of the building. On both nights crowds assembled in front of the offices and 'made merry', singing to tunes relayed through loudspeakers from the Council chamber. People celebrated with mixed emotions, the older people, perhaps with memories of the last Armistice in their minds, celebrated quietly, while the teenagers danced and sang in the streets. Everyone in uniform who passed through the streets was greeted with loud cheers. The British Restaurant was floodlit and music was played through loudspeakers. The impromptu street parties for children sprung up in streets up and down the district. Jean Tilston of 76 Marlborough Road, Higher Irlam later recalled that momentous day: *Parties were in full swing all over the place, the air was full of excitement, one felt is this really happening? People were hugging one another yet they were complete strangers, but no one cared. If I remember rightly, some of the street lights were lit for the very first time. It was wonderful not having someone shout 'put that light out!' It was crazy, as one walked through the streets there were parties everywhere. One couldn't help but laugh at the antics of someone who was so drunk staggering from one party to another. My friend and I heard someone talking about a party at Irlam Council Offices which was on Liverpool Road, then practically facing the Savoy cinema. As we approached the Ship Hotel there were that many people it was unbelievable. I have never seen that many people. There were flags everywhere. On the balcony of the Council Offices stood the officials and I think it was someone with the chain of office (like a mayor would wear). The American soldiers were doing the jive with the local women and girls, sailors from the Gosling camp were there too. I remember a band playing. One had to fight your way through to listen to a speaker on the balcony and that was a waste of time, the noise was horrendous. What time the party finished I don't know. I lost my friend and on the way home parties were still going on. That was a night that was!*

VE Day celebrations were held throughout the district. In Lancaster Road and Warwick Road, Cadishead, electric lights were strung across the streets, and tea parties were held. Similar children's street tea parties were organised in Caroline Street, Irlam, Lords Street, Cadishead and Devon and York Road, Cadishead.

VE Celebrations on Lords Street, Cadishead

Devon Road and York Road, Cadishead

A Canadian airman, who was billeted with his wife in Cadishead, attended the Devon Road and York Road festivities. The photograph was provided by Jean Merrick (later Evans), who is seated near the centre, wearing spectacles. Four children to the right of the airman is Winifred Shepherd, the cousin of Royal Marine Leslie Arstall, who in later life has done so much to keep his memory alive.

VE celebrations through the streets of the district

VE parade through the streets of the district

Private Fred Barrow of 7 Silverdale Avenue, Higher Irlam, arrived home in time to take part in the Silverdale Avenue VE celebrations, and to sit down to tea with the children, who gave him a hearty reception. Fred had joined the Army in 1941 and went overseas in June of the same year. He served in Libya and was at Tobruk before being captured in June 1942. He was liberated by the Americans near Munich on 30th April. Like all the returning prisoners of war he highly praised the Red Cross and the Irlam and Cadishead War Comforts Fund.

Another returning prisoner of war was William 'Bill' Nicklin, a mid-gunner on a Lancaster bomber that had been shot down over Germany. Bill was born outside the area but at some point he moved into the district and, in 1937, he married local woman Louisa Barbor. They lived together in New Moss Road, Cadishead. Bill was a joiner by trade and worked for Gerrards of Swinton. Before joining the Royal Air Force Volunteer Reserve, he was engaged in building radar structures in Scotland.

Jean Tilston was one of the local children who participated in the VE parties. The following is an account which she provided to the authors about the party which took place between numbers 60 and 76 Marlborough Road, Higher Irlam: *Like all Irlam and Cadishead residents, in fact, all over the country parties were in full swing when news came the war was over. I was in awe as the neighbours dragged tables, chairs and the piano, just about everything, from their houses out into the street. What amazed me was where on earth did all the food come from, as they lay their white bedding sheets across the tables? I remember making paper cone hats then put knicker elastic on them with the rest of the kiddies. A Mr Lewis played his accordion, someone played the piano, my dad played a tin whistle, and someone put two tables together tying the table legs so they didn't move. There was always someone singing even dressing up acting the fool. I and two friends did a tap dance, Oh boy! What a party that was, our mums and dads were hugging each other with lots of tears, it's something I will always remember as for the works hooters and ships on the canal. How long we played in the street I don't know, I know the dawn was breaking as we fell into bed that morn. I awoke as the men were cleaning up all the mess. When my sons ask me was I frightened during the war my answer was no, but as for my parents they must have been petrified seeing us off to school not knowing if they would see us again.*

VE Day in the parish of Rixton-with-Glazebrook was not marked by an outburst of public rejoicing, such as had taken place in the more populous parts of the country, most of the residents celebrated the momentous occasion according to their own private taste or fancy. Nearly every house had a display of flags, bunting and patriotic decorations. At Hollins Green there were two open air parties for the children, who afterwards had a sing-song to the accompaniment of a gramophone. Near the Glazebrook station cottages a bonfire and fireworks brought together members of the Royal Navy and the Royal Canadian Air Force, and an impromptu dance ensued. There was genuine thankfulness and relief that the years of strain and tension were at last over. A moustached effigy of Hitler was strung up on a telegraph pole and it remained there for a week. It was finally taken down and removed to

Hollins Green Police Station, where it remained on show, hanging by its neck. On Monday night, 7th May the St Helen's Church bell was tolled by the vicar, Reverend Firth, and a few people entered the church for a short service. Holy Communion at 7.45am, and the Evensong service at 7.30pm on VE Day were well attended. At the Centenary Methodist Church, Glazebrook, there was a large congregation at a morning service conducted by Reverend Motson. Lessons were read by Messrs H. Dodd and E. Yarwood. Reverend Ayres conducted an impressive and well attended evening service at the Methodist Church, Rixton. Both at Glazebrook and Rixton a special form of thanksgiving service prepared by the Methodist Church was used. At St Michael's Church, Rixton, Reverend Ball conducted the service of Benediction in the evening.

On the night of VE Day, adult celebrations continued in Irlam and Cadishead. All the local hotels were filled to capacity with well-behaved and orderly crowds. British, American and Canadian servicemen mingled with the crowds, sailors wore soldiers' hats and soldiers wore non-regulation hats such as paper cups or hats borrowed from female relatives or friends. The celebrations were joyous and full of the spirit of comradeship, hilarity and good-natured fun and horseplay and the air was full of laughter, shouting and singing. Total strangers shook hands with each other and laughed, chatted and joked. Every so often a firecracker or rocket was let off in the street. The only disappointment was that the buses stopped running in the early evening which prevented local people from joining in the more hectic celebrations in Manchester city centre.

On Wednesday, 9th May (VE Day plus one), The Vista, Cadishead, decorated with flags, was the scene of a street party which was attended by about 200 children and parents. The guests enjoyed a bumper tea provided by residents of The Vista and Kitchener and Haig Avenues. Games were played after tea and later 'Hitler' met a well-deserved fate on top of the Victory bonfire. Each child received a present of sixpence and everyone at the tea had a slice of victory cake. Mrs Lloyd of The Vista, the main organiser of the function, also conducted an auction sale which realised £5-5s, for the Red Cross.

Rain prevented the holding of the planned open air VE Day Thanksgiving Service on Sunday, 13th May so the hall at Irlam Central School was taken over for the occasion and, as a result, was packed to capacity. As well as members and officials of the Council, there were representatives of the Home Guard and all the Civil Defence Services. Pastor Thomas William Morgan (First World War veteran) of the Pentecostal Mission conducted the service attended by representatives of the Church of England and Salvation Army. The Benediction was pronounced by Reverend Bakker and the address was given by Leslie Jones of Cadishead Congregational Church. Leslie warned the congregation that his first words might come as a shock to many of them: *Did he want their thanks? The answer was Yes. He was like a parent whose child made a little article – something which he already possessed. Did that parent need it? He did not – but he wanted it. They were there to render praise and thanksgiving, but if they were there simply because they thought it was the thing to be there, they were wrong. In view of the fact that they were there to give thanks for victory, it would not be a true thanksgiving unless they counted the cost of victory. If their thanksgiving was only going to remain a sentiment in words, it was useless. There must be a resolution about it all, and he asked all present to check over our tools so that we can make something useful out of victory. It was the wish of God that they should have life and have it abundantly.* During the service the National Anthem, and the hymns *Praise, my Soul, the King of Heaven, Rejoice, O Land* and the *Old Hundredth* were sung.

Charles Green, the headmaster of Irlam Council School since 1941, left to take up a new position in Loughborough. He came to Irlam from St Lawrence's School in Denton. During his stay in the district he played his part in the war effort. He was secretary of the Irlam and Cadishead War Savings Committee and was largely responsible for the success of the various special savings weeks and for the general increase in the district's savings. He took a keen interest in the Air Training Corps and, along with Mr T. Goddard, was instrumental in the formation of the Irlam detached flight of 292 (Eccles) Squadron and was given the rank of pilot officer. Charles was a veteran of the First World War, having served as a pilot in the RAF. He was replaced at Irlam Council School by Mr C. Hargreaves of Aintree Council School, which was destroyed during the Blitz on Liverpool.

Sergeant Fred Edwards returned on leave to his home at 29 Hayes Road, Cadishead. He was grateful to his former workmates at the Steelworks, and the ladies of Cadishead Conservative Club for the gifts they had sent to him and asked the *Guardian* to thank them on his behalf. Leave, he said, was too short to thank them all personally. Joining the Army in January 1940, he went with the BEF to France and was one of the last soldiers of the BEF to leave France in June 1940, via St Nazaire. After a short spell in Scotland, he was sent overseas again, this time to Africa, Oran and then Gibraltar. He returned to England for a short time and then went to Normandy on D-Day. Since then, he had taken part in fighting across France, Belgium, Holland and Germany. Before joining the Army, he was employed as a bricklayer by the Steelworks.

While Canadian and American troops were largely welcome visitors to the district, there was also an element of the Canadian servicemen who were described by the *Guardian* as *Hooligans in Uniform*. The following article appeared in the Town Topics column: *On several occasions in these notes I have called attention to the wanton damage and childish behaviour of many Canadians who use this district for recreational purposes. In the past, we have had gates taken from their hinges and thrown in the middle of the road, signs and signposts removed, street lamps smashed and house and shop windows broken. A variation of this idiotic behaviour is to go into a public house, order a pint of beer and steal the glass. Even more recently, a group of Canadian airmen sat in the front row of the balcony in a local cinema. They drank beer from bottles, talked loudly, made themselves generally objectionable and 'improved' matters by throwing the caps off the beer bottles among the people in the pit. Let us admit that many Canadians are real gentlemen – men whom we are proud to call friends. But there is another element which takes a delight in walking around with a chip on its shoulder, looking for trouble – and, generally finding it. It may be pleaded that they are young and full of animal spirits but there is no reason why he should behave like one. When the Americans first came to this country each man was issued with a book instructing him in our customs and code of social conduct, warning him of the pitfalls and telling him what was expected of him. It seems a pity that a similar book was not issued to the Canadian Forces. Of course, it may be that we in this district have been less fortunate than others. But, in almost every town I have visited there have been complaints about the behaviour of Canadians. In one town which, at various times, billeted Poles, Australians, Free French, Belgians, Americans and Canadians, it was the men from the land of the Maple leaf who earned an unenviable reputation – who took a delight in wanton damage and destruction. It has been pointed out to me that the men responsible are not the best of Canadian manhood. I can readily believe that, for, as I have said, I have scores of good friends among Canadians – and quite a few relatives in the Canadian Armed Forces in different parts of the world. I know, too, that the better element does not condone the conduct of the unruly minority – but that minority makes such an infernal nuisance of itself that the average Britisher is apt to get a very distorted view of Canadians generally. It will be remembered that, at one time, there was trouble with naval personnel. But, with true naval discipline, the camp authorities jumped in at once. Naval patrols covered the district – and the trouble ended.*

The following article appeared in Town Topics of the *Guardian: I talked this week to a soldier who was in the force which overran the Belsen horror camp. For those of you who thought it all propaganda – and there were some people who refused to believe the evidence of the camera – I will quote his words: 'The pictures published were nothing compared to the actual thing. When one of our officers entered one of the compounds to make his report he vomited – and left the compound. It is something I will never forget.' Incidentally this boy – who has fought through France, Belgium, Holland and Germany, has something to say about the food situation in those countries. In France, there were some shortages, in Belgium the situation was worse; in Holland it was desperate – but in Germany, glutted with the loot of the occupied territories, they had full and plenty.* Sergeant Norman Jones of 39 Anti-Aircraft Battalion, was another local man who was on the scene when Belsen was liberated. The terrible sights would stay with him for the rest of his years.

Sapper Douglas Menzies of the Royal Engineers was another local man who was stationed near Belsen. He had been posted to the Independent Field Company of the Royal Engineers, in the Ruhr, and was billeted in a small house outside Dortmund: *We went to Dortmund, Dusseldorf and other small towns. How they ever lived, after being bombed, I don't know. Next we went to a barracks near Belsen. The main executioners, Pierrepoint and his son, came out. Two that I know of, a man and a woman, were strung up there by Pierrepoint, after the war. They were in charge of Belsen, which I never saw, but it was only up the road. Disease was rife there, typhus. The doctor told me he couldn't go there.*

Although the war in Europe was now over, there had been men wounded during the final battles leading up to VE Day and news was still filtering through. Mr and Mrs W. Micklewright of 541 Liverpool Road, Irlam, received word that their second son, Fusilier Norman Micklewright (pictured), had been wounded in Europe and was in hospital in Belgium. Norman joined the Army in April 1942, aged 19, and went overseas just after D-Day with the Royal Artillery. He later returned to England for six weeks' infantry training and then went back to France, where he served with a Fusilier regiment. His brother, William, was serving as a fusilier in the Army and had been wounded twice; the first time in May 1940 during the retreat to Dunkirk and the second time in August 1944 during the battles in Normandy.

The overrunning by British, American and Russian Forces of the many prisoner of war camps in Germany meant that by early to mid-May released prisoners returned to the district and were reunited with their families. These prisoners of war, particularly those who had spent five years in captivity after being captured during the retreat to Dunkirk, had suffered terrible depravations during their time in the camps. Food in the camps was generally in short supply and of very poor quality, toilet facilities in some camps were totally inadequate. The poor diet, unhygienic conditions and hard work led to disease and lice and other vermin were rampant. Many of the returning men credited their survival to the Red Cross parcels which they received in the camps. Some of the men suffered as a result of cruelty from their captors, while others suffered neglect.

Pilot Officer Thomas Mosedale, the eldest son of Mrs Hilda G. Mosedale of Brook House, Rixton, was liberated from a German prisoner of war camp. He praised the Red Cross, saying that if it had not been for their parcels every prisoner in Germany would have starved. Of the treatment meted out by the Germans, he said *Sometimes it was good, and sometimes it was bad*. Joining the RAF in May 1940, he had been shot down and captured en route to Cologne, on 22nd June 1943. When liberated he and his colleagues had been constantly marching for three months, as the Germans tried to keep away from the advancing British, American and Russian Forces. Prior to joining the Forces he worked for the family's business, Mosedales Brick Works at Rixton. Shortly after Thomas' return, his younger brother, Flying Officer Frank Mosedale of Fighter Command returned home. He had served first as a ferry service pilot, then a test pilot and, finally, a member of the crack 92 East India Squadron. He had been reported missing on air operations in Italy in November 1944. It later transpired that he had been a prisoner of war at Stalag Luft I.

Another local airman returning home from a German prisoner of war camp was Pilot Officer Arthur William 'Billy' Dean, son of Mr and Mrs Arthur Dean of 21 Fir Street, Cadishead. He was reported missing on operations in January 1944, and was later notified as a prisoner. He had joined the RAF in 1941, and completed his training in Canada, where he gained his wings. Billy gave the following account of his escape from the camp: *I speak good German because obviously it was part of my exposure. We went on there* [Stalag Luft III] *until the Russians advanced from their divisions at Stalingrad, Von Paulus had surrendered. The Russian divisions were breaking through that part of Poland and Silesia, and the Germans decided to move us and we had that long march of maybe 200 miles to a place called Luckenwalde near Berlin. It was very tragic the whole thing, two of my friends died, one of gangrene, the other one died of a heart attack. I had some strange escapades during the march; we came across several German platoons which were in ambush, ready for the Russians, one of them, the chappie next to me was pulling a sledge, one of the guards from the camp and this German officer started shouting at me something in German and although I had a knowledge of German but I couldn't understand what he said, he was too fast, but my friend, one of my friends, said 'Bill, get hold of that sledge, he's telling you you mustn't be allowing a German to pull a sledge while you are there!' and at the same time he held this Luger against my forehead, I tell you it's a nasty feeling to have a gun, and I can see his finger tightening on the trigger. I'll tell you something, you remember it all your life, like a fraction of a second off a dead body lying there with a hole front to back through its head. Snowy White saved my life by shouting at the German 'he doesn't understand!' and the German put his Luger down and went back into hiding. At Luckenwalde there were Polish officers who had violins, and gave a wonderful violin concert. While the concert was on I decided to escape and I made myself a window catch and I filed it to make it sharp so that when it was double it was like a pair of scissors. It took me a long time filing it with a piece of rock and stuff. I cut through the barbed wire while they were all in the concert and I escaped and I was on the loose for the rest of the war. I was on the loose for about two months. Walking as the crow flies to avoid treading on mines, the roads were all mined and to keep out of the way of the Panzers, tanks. I came across a great big house, like Chatsworth, I don't know who it belonged to, not far from the Elbe River. It was empty so I put my foot through a French window and got in. Ooh you should have seen that, full of antiques, hundreds of thousands of pounds worth of rare pictures, a gun room full of beautiful shotguns but there was one thing I was interested in, that was something to eat. You can imagine, something to eat, I'd gone five or six days with not a thing to eat and I went through the cupboards and all there was was three big tins of sauerkraut, no thank you, not sour cabbage, not the way I was. And one cupboard, most of them being empty, one cupboard had one tin at the back of it, so I got my bayonet and pulled it out and you know what it was, a tin of Heinz baked beans with pork, a large tin, oh and that saved my life. Heinz would laugh if they knew they saved the life of the soldier, because I was on my last legs. And from there I tried to get into a bunker, I knew that this bunker wasn't ammunition. Ammunition bunkers were built in a certain way, it was what they called a storage bunker. I blew the door open with a Panzerfaust. I found big tins in it, long tins, 15 inches in length. You know what it was, and don't forget the Germans were starving? Tins of goose, I opened it, pulled it out, goose, made myself ill of course eating it. That's one of the stories. There's one I've not told you about because it's very gruesome. Well I was walking along and two German soldiers, Wehrmacht, passed me, I said 'Guten Tag' and when they passed me they stopped, they shouted 'halt!' and one started lifting his gun up so I had a Panzerfaust, a grenade, so it was either him or me, do you follow me? He knew I was something wrong, I threw the grenade and killed both of them. Oh, the sights were terrible. There'd been several platoons of Germans with armoured vehicles that had been attacked by Russian troops, they were dead, lying all over the place. I looked at this dead man and he had wonderful leather boots on and I looked at mine and I thought he won't miss them now so I put my foot in his crutch and pulled the boot and it pulled the boot off and he went 'Uuurgh' and opened his eyes but he was dead, it was the gas in his stomach and with pressing on his crutch the gas was pushed out through his lungs, but I remember that all the days, all the days, when I go to bed at night I can see that man's face. Well I left this place where I was talking about to get some food for us, there was chickens running about and geese, course they were just wild, you know, not being looked after, but they were all over the place, chickens and ducks, so I went bang, that was our dinner sort of thing. Anyway, I was at the side of the road looking for something to eat and I could hear this all of a sudden, 'RrrrrRrrrrr RrrrrRrrrrr' and round the corner came an armoured American vehicle, I could see his gun at the back went round, I said 'Kriegsgefangene! Prisoner of war! Prisoner of war!' This man said 'God damn it man, what the hell are you doing here? God damn, get on' so I got on the truck and he took me to a big camp where they had must have been a hundred tents ready for the last stages of the invasion and there they sent me to Brussels. At Brussels they gave me a clean uniform, powdered me with DDT and I had three baths, and I had three lots of lice, I had chest lice, hair lice and genital lice, so you can imagine I wasn't very clean.*

You see, there was nothing glorious about the war, now I want you to put in the book, as an individual you don't need to name me, but there are people and particularly one man who considers that medals were not medals but were certificates of murder, I'm not proud at all about what I did. I don't go on parade; I don't want my medals of service. I consider that the war was a very tragic episode in my life; no way should we be at war now (a reference to the war in Afghanistan). *If we had any brains, whether or not it was a matter of talking with terrorists, whether or not it was a matter of compromise, whatever it is, all those things are far better than the death of one person.* Billy had been sheltered by a German woman for several weeks before being picked up by American troops. After the war he remained in the RAF and in the 1950s attained the rank of squadron leader with the City of Chester Squadron.

Fusilier Norman Winstanley returned to his home, 99 Fir Street, Cadishead, after five years in German prisoner of war camps. He was taken prisoner at Bethune on 27th May 1940 during the retreat to Dunkirk. As a result of his many years in German hands his view was that the Germans were: *a nation of barbarians who deserved no mercy for the way in which they had treated not only the people of the occupied countries, but their own political prisoners and prisoners of war.* During his years in captivity, he was employed in various working parties, and was also put to work in the mines. The German rations supplied to prisoners were totally inadequate and, had it not been for the Red Cross and the generosity of many local people who sent gifts, he would have found it impossible to keep going. When the Russian breakthrough came, he was being held in a camp in Silesia (now part of Poland). The prisoners were quickly gathered together by their guards and marched away. In all, they covered an estimated 700 miles on foot before they were interned in another camp in western Germany. Then came the breakthrough by General Patton's American Forces: *We had a small radio set and we could keep track of the American advance. As they drew nearer the Germans told us we would have to move again. We refused, and nothing they did could shift us. Then, one day, tanks appeared, and at first we thought they were Jerry's. When we found out they were American, we didn't know whether to laugh or cry. The Americans could not do enough for us. They gave us their rations and cigarettes and then went through the village taking food from shops and sharing it out amongst us. When the Germans protested the Yanks said 'You've had it your way long enough. These boys haven't eaten real food for a long time, and they're going to start right now.' They would not let us do a thing, and then they attended to our guards. It did me good to see them being kicked around by the Yanks after all the kicking around they had done.* Norman had no patience with those people who doubted the truth of the atrocity stories. He had seen men, women and children literally starved to death. On one occasion he saw 30 railway vans packed with Jewish people. They had travelled for four days without food, and all were in a pitiable condition. Russian prisoners, he said, got the worst treatment. If one fell on a march the guards simply flung him on the side of the road and shot him.

Also home was Lance Corporal Hubert Williams, eldest son of Mr and Mrs W. Williams of the Nags Head Hotel, Higher Irlam. He went overseas in December 1939, and served in Palestine, Egypt and Crete. Hubert was captured during the fighting on Crete and remained on the island for seven months before being sent to Stalag VIIIB at Teschen, located in the east of Czechoslovakia. When the Russians broke through, a body of prisoners, including Hubert, were marched 700 miles by their guards in order to elude the Russians. This march, later known as the Lamsdorf Death March, took the prisoners through Czechoslovakia, towards Nuremburg and then to Moosburg (Stalag VIIA) in Bavaria. They were liberated by the American Third Army on 3rd May. In 1944 he had written to Mary Bowker, secretary of the Comforts Fund, to thank her for the gifts sent to him and promised to make a substantial donation to the fund but the difficulties of money exchange made it impossible. One of his first calls after arriving home was to the Council Offices where he made good on his promise, and donated £16 as a mark of his appreciation for the work of the fund. At least two other men, George Glover and Frank Brown, were held at Stalag VIIIB and took part in the Lamsdorf Death March.

Lance Bombardier George Glover was taken prisoner in the Middle East in June 1942. After his capture, he spent time in three Italian prisoner of war camps and, on the capitulation of Italy, he was transferred to Stalag VIIIB. George returned home during the month.

The Italians are worse than the Germans, was the opinion of Private Frank Brown of 9 Atherton Lane, Cadishead. Frank had joined the Army in April 1940, and served in Egypt, Cyprus, Iraq, Syria and the Libyan campaign, before being taken prisoner in the Western Desert. He was taken to a prison camp in Italy and when Italy surrendered was moved to Stalag VIIIB. Frank was another of the many who praised the Americans who liberated them: *The Yanks gave the prisoners everything they wanted.* Like Hubert Williams, he was among those who were forced by the Germans to take part in the Lamsdorf Death March in an effort to escape the Russians. Their column was on the march for three weeks, and he had been forced by frostbite to drop out. Later, they were again marched away, this time for a month, but the Allied net closed around them and the prisoners were freed. He stated that if it had not been for the Red Cross parcels he and many others would not have survived.

Lance Corporal Alfred Wright (POW No. 126593) of the 1st Battalion, Irish Guards, was released from Oflag VIIB by General Patton's men. Whilst a prisoner he had to carry out work both in the camp and in working parties outside, including working in a brewery and tending the gardens of a convent. When he returned to the district he commented: *The treatment was pretty fair but if it had not been for the Red Cross parcels we would have had it.* During his time in a prisoner of war camp Alfred was witness to an unusual event. The camps were a mix of nationalities including British, Russians and Polish servicemen and various international football matches were staged in the camps, however, these often resulted in brawls. The German camp commandant came up with a novel solution. Every football team had to include at least three British players, one of whom had to be the captain of the team. He reasoned that the British sense of fair play would keep the players under control. Once Alfred was liberated from the camp he and others spent two or three weeks rounding up German troops. After the war he returned to live in Laburnum Road, Cadishead and took an active part in many local activities. He became a churchwarden at St Mary's Church, Cadishead, and was also a school manager and governor at St Mary's Primary School for many years.

Another returned prisoner who described his treatment in a prisoner of war camp as *not too bad* and the Red Cross parcels as *very good indeed,* was Private Clifford Hughes, the only son of Mr and Mrs Hughes of Lines Road, Irlam. He was taken prisoner in the Falaise Gap, Normandy, on 7th August 1944, and was sent first to a prison camp at Luneberg and later to Moosburg. He was released by American troops. Clifford had joined the Army in June 1940.

Lance Corporal Alfred Wright, Irish Guards

Lance Corporal Alfred Wright with his wife Mary

Sergeant Geoffrey Gillibrand, youngest son of Mr and Mrs J. Gillibrand of 11 The Crescent, Higher Irlam, escaped from captivity while being marched away from the advancing Allies. He was taken prisoner at Crete on 1st June 1941. He was later transferred to Stalag 383 in Bavaria (near the Swiss-German border) and spent 2½ years there before making his escape.

Rifleman Ernest Wrigley of 62 Nelson Drive, Cadishead, who returned home from a prisoner of war camp on Wednesday, 16th May, was full of praise for the Red Cross. He was so impressed with the good work they performed for the prisoners he decided to donate his first week's pay, when he returned home. He joined the Army in 1940 and went to Italy in March 1944, where he was captured. He was well-treated while a prisoner and described the food as good, which was a sharp contrast with conditions at other POW camps. He was released by General Patton's forces and was full of praise for the way that the Americans, who liberated the camp, dealt with the released men.

Another of the returning soldiers was Private Hubert Jones, who resided at 27 Fiddlers Lane, Higher Irlam. Jean Tilston, a local schoolchild at the time, remembered the celebrations that greeted his return: *Irlam at one time was a small village where everyone knew each other, when front doors were left open and children were safe on the streets. When we were all settling down after the war and street parties were becoming a part of the last few months, news would filter through with neighbours talking of Mrs so and so's husband is coming home from the war. Mrs Jones who had the hardware shop in Fiddlers Lane, passed comment to someone that her husband was due home any time after being a prisoner of war and that she couldn't wait to see him. Around this time we had a fairground in Fiddlers Lane somewhere around the car park. If I remember rightly this was the first fairground I had seen, the air was full of excitement for us as children and teenagers. Then someone passed word round we all had to meet at the corner of Marlborough Road and Boundary Road. Everyone was given a candle with a piece of cardboard near the bottom to catch the drips I guess, through this a knitting needle with the elders lighting these. There must have been about 30 to 40 people and we all walked slowly towards the hardware shop, some carried torches, there was a quietness, people were joining in until we arrived at the shop. Then someone shouted 'We want Mr Jones' then all hell broke loose with everyone joining in, some were crying, it was quite emotional, then all at once the upstairs sash window was lifted up with Mr Jones practically hanging out waving his hand. I can't remember how long we stood there it seemed ages then Mrs Jones stood beside him. I remember someone climbing up the drain pipe giving him a Union Jack flag; there were lots of tears too that night as I walked home with my sister and parents.* As a result of the above welcome, Hubert wrote to the *Guardian* to thank all the well-wishers: *Sir, may I solicit*

the good offices of your paper to extend to all the good people of Irlam and Cadishead my sincere and heartfelt appreciation of the almost overwhelming expressions of gratitude for my safe return. Also my gratitude and thanks to the Irlam and Cadishead War Comforts Fund Committee, whose parcels, received in captivity, were always a source of comfort, and greatly appreciated by all the lads out there. Thank you very much neighbours and everybody.

Captured in August 1944, Private Thomas Wrench of 23 Nelson Drive, Cadishead, was held at Stalag IIIA (a camp known for its inhumane treatment of prisoners). He was liberated by General Patton's forces and arrived home on Monday, 14th May.

Leading Aircraftman Harold Rosbottom was released from Stalag Luft I (located at Barth, Germany) when the Russians broke through on the Eastern Front. At first, like many of the Allied prisoners liberated by the Russians, he feared that they would not be released back to Britain, however on Monday, 14th May he returned to Cadishead. He described his treatment in the prison camp as *fairly good*. Like many other men who spent a considerable time in German prisoner of war camps he considered that the Red Cross parcels had kept them alive. He had been taken prisoner on the island of Kos in October 1943.

Lance Corporal John McDonagh of 20 Beech Avenue, Higher Irlam, was liberated on 24th April by American troops, after 18 months in captivity. He was taken prisoner on the Greek island of Leros on 16th November 1943 and received what he described as fair treatment while in German prison of war camps. He, too, was an admirer of the work of the Red Cross: *I don't know how we would have gone on without their parcels.*

The fire-watchers of Kings Road, Irlam held a winding up meeting at the Labour Hall, on Tuesday, 15th May and decided to distribute their funds, amounting to £192 to the Red Cross and the District Nursing Association. The meeting also decided that the firefighting and protective equipment purchased by the groups should be sold, with the proceeds divided between the two organisations. In addition, the group's first aid box was donated to the local St John Ambulance Brigade. The Kings Road fire-watchers had been established before fire-watching became compulsory and was one of the largest and most efficient groups in the district. The committee included Mr J. Brown, as chairman, Mr A. Wilkinson, secretary and Mr A. Waterman, treasurer.

Reverend Lee wrote the following in the Irlam parish magazine: *We all believe that the mills of God grind slowly, but they grind exceedingly small. The process of grinding works in diverse ways beyond our comprehension - nevertheless the issues are always certain. Nemesis follows in the steps of evil, retribution follows close upon the heels of aggression and brutality; fears and remorse follow folly. You can never estimate the full extent or nature of the judgement of retribution when it comes; people usually make their estimate from the outward appearance of things, from what they see – the dead body of an SS man or the bullet-riddled body of a Mussolini exposed to public gaze and lying in a gutter – or the possible suspending body of Hitler hanging from a lamp post. When people see these things they think that this demise is the complete end. The punishment, however, is much deeper than that; there is the terror of mind; the accusations of the conscience, the fear of the beyond; the spectre of past crimes with their hundred denouncing voices, the bullet that brings death or the cord that snaps the spinal column may to some be welcome, and those who see such swift retribution may be quite oblivious to the deep mental torment and fright of the criminal. Only martyrs in holy causes die in peace because that peace is peace with God. Who could have thought that the Idol of Italy whose gospel was the 'Song of the Machine-gun' and 'A Million Bayonets' – this man, the gesticulating despot, shouting from Roman balconies – would lie in death, his body spurned and spit upon in his own native Italy? The mills have indeed ground very small. Do we ever ask what was wrong with the character and the life of such men – they began in innocence as children – power brought pride and pride, destruction. Both Hitler and Mussolini were gifted men – they were modernists and realists – both their countries benefited by their industry and ideals – in great thoroughfares and highways – fine public buildings, public health, land reclamation as in the Pontine marshes – the care and physical training of youth, the example of which we ourselves followed and are following in this land. These men were great on housing, social amelioration and all that a modern world preaches with all the aids of science and discovery. All our boys who return from Germany tell of fine houses and flats with central heating, refrigerators, and the like. Where then was the snag, where was the wrong turning in their lives and leadership? Hitler, if all reports are true, was a clean living man unlike Benito. He neither drank nor smoked, and unquestionably worked like a slave in the cause for which he was fanatically responsible. Both men were nationalists and socialists, with fervour, even frenzy, behind their political outlook. The answer is that you cannot enthral man – or be ourselves enthralled, body, mind and spirit, to the exclusion of all God's claims upon life – in dues and duties without courting and ending in disaster. The error of these men was that everything should be subservient to the State. Man, maid, material, the whole energy and power of the community devoted to maximum powers for conquest. The question of Right – or God's claim on a nation was usurped by the belief that might was right for the master race. The sovereignty of God was eliminated and sovereignty of man established and dominant. This dominance is seen in the horrors of Buchenwald and elsewhere – where man in the image of God and created by God is tortured, burned and the fragments scattered. Cain slays Abel again, and the blood cries for vengeance from the earth. So the mills grind, and grind exceedingly small. We leave the souls of these men in the hands of God – they have not lived in vain for their evil ways and the retribution are for the generations to see and for all to learn the lessons afresh – that sin and evil, even of a much lesser kind has its reward. It is the warning to the world that as human justice is meted out – behind all is the judgement and the wrath of God.*

On 21st May Marian Blackburn of the Auxiliary Territorial Service, married Warrant Officer Richard Corser at Cambridge. Richard served in Bomber Command as a member of the Royal Air Force Volunteer Reserve. Marian was the only daughter of John and Ada Annie Blackburn of Irlam. Her only brother, Sergeant John 'Eric' Blackburn, who had also served with the Royal Air Force Volunteer Reserve, Bomber Command, had been killed on air operations in 1942. Richard and Eric had met each other during their service in the RAF and became firm friends.

Wedding of Marian Blackburn and Richard Corser
(L-R: George and Muriel Corser, GI James Kelly, Richard Corser, Marian Blackburn, John and Ada
Blackburn and Heather Corser)

A certificate of merit for outstanding good services and devotion to duty during the campaign in north west Europe was presented by Field Marshal Montgomery to Fusilier William Cubbin. William, who resided with his sister, Mrs Madge Booth, at 23 Victory Road, Cadishead, was 27 years of age at the time. He was born in 1918 at Wigan and prior to joining the Army he was employed by Andersons of Trafford Park. He joined the Army in November 1939, and first went overseas three days after D-Day, and served in France, Holland, Belgium and Germany. He had been wounded earlier in the year while serving in Belgium.

Sapper Frank Johnson, Royal Engineers, returned home to his parents' home at Alma Villas, Glazebrook, on Thursday evening, 24th May. To mark the occasion the house was decked out with flags. Frank had been a prisoner of war in German hands for four years. He was captured in Greece in 1941, only a month after landing there, and his journey to Wolfsberg, Austria (Stalag XVIIIA) took him through Corinth, Salonika, the Balkans and Hungary. He was at Wolfsberg until April 1945, being employed on work such as road-making and lumber work. When the Russian Army approached to within 45 kilometres of Wolfsberg, the

Germans marched the prisoners to Markt Pongau where on 12th May they were liberated by the Americans. They were moved by truck to Salzburg, then by plane and truck to Rheims, where they were taken over by the RAF. Frank had no complaints to make as to his treatment at the hands of the Germans. Occasional games of football helped to break the monotony of camp life, which at times was very dull. The food provided was the worst feature, being both meagre and of poor quality. It was only the parcels received through the British Red Cross that enabled the prisoners to keep going. They received one parcel each week until November last year when the supply became less regular. He was described as perhaps a stone or so below his normal weight, but he looked fitter than might have been expected in view of his experiences.

The local Council were criticised for their lack of preparedness for the VE Day celebrations, particularly the lack of entertainment for the children. To be fair, the Council were aware that most people in the district preferred a low-key celebration. Looking back on the VE Day celebrations, the chairman, Councillor Joseph McLean (pictured), said that the Emergency Committee had tried to organise a free cinema show for the children, but after talking to the managers of local cinemas and representatives of the Education Committee it had proved too difficult. Councillors Owen and Hesford still felt that some form of entertainment should be arranged. They had also tried to find a band to play on VE Day but were unsuccessful. At least the decorations and floodlighting arranged by Henry Nurse around the Council Offices were a success.

Officers of D Company of the 42nd County of Lancaster Battalion, Home Guard held a dance cabaret at Irlam Conservative Club on Friday, 25th May for the NCOs and men of the company, and their wives. Although the Home Guard has been 'stood down,' the officers' mess had remained open, and mess funds were used from time to time for social gatherings. Among the officers who attended were Lieutenants Daniel Moore, Ernest Woods, John Hamer Hughes, Albert Hughes, Robert Pears, Charles Horace Gardner, Harold Wilson and James Ferguson, and Second Lieutenants William Douglas Smith, Ernest Tupling and L. Burns. The artists were Fredorio and his band, Lieutenant Charles Horace Gardner (guitar and ukulele), Miss Mary Wright (songs at the piano) and Frank Readman (entertainer). Lieutenant Colonel Webb and Major Gold were unable to attend.

The Town Topics column in the *Guardian* published the following article about the Home Guard: *Some of you people are remarkably slow at coming forward. Recently I asked if you had any Home Guard or Civil Defence anecdotes – true ones, I mean – that would help us all to recall something of the spirit of comradeship, the good natured fun, and even the difficulties of those days when Jerry was our nightly visitor. So far, I have had one: In the early days of the Home Guard, a musketry instructor was taking a class. They had rifles but no ammunition, blank or otherwise, and the instructor was anxious to show them how to load. So the motions of loading had to be gone through. The class was in the prone position and the order was given to load. Bolts were drawn back, imaginary clips were pulled out of imaginary ammunition pouches, the rifles loaded and bolts closed. All went well – all, that is, except for one man who appeared to be having trouble. 'What's wrong with you?' the instructor asked. Quick as a flash the answer came back, 'I've got a jam.' But the instructor, an ex-soldier, was just as quick. 'Well, if you've got your imaginary cartridge jammed in the blankety breech, you can stay behind and have some more instruction when the others have gone.' After that, there were no more jams.*

One week later the following reply from A.D. Smith, honorary secretary of the local branch of the Home Guard Old Comrades Association, appeared in the newspaper: *Sir, the notes on the local Home Guard which appeared in the Cadishead and Irlam column VE week, were noted and discussed with interest by the committee of the local Home Guard Branch of the Old Comrades Association. While the historical facts published were mainly correct, names, etc were not. The two mobile platoons of H Company were commanded by Lieutenants Harris and Minshull. The second in command G Company was Captain G. Haines. Mr Story was given a title (which to be quite fair to him) he has never claimed for himself. All ranks of the 42nd Battalion, would, we feel, be unanimous in support of the compliment paid to Lieutenant Colonel F.D. Webb, whose service to the battalion could be described as incomparable. On the lighter side, your playful reference to the 'shooting up' of our friendly chief warden ten minutes before zero of a practice exercise may have been true, but we feel the shock did not upset that gallant gentleman, who, no doubt, had been 'shot at' before, both in service and in private life, without losing his equilibrium or in any way being perturbed. Now the local Home Guard have never assessed themselves as military masterpieces. Nevertheless, they were conscious of their strength as well as their failings. We had quite a number of tough, well-trained battle platoons in whose ranks were resolute men who meant business. We had leaders, too, who organised other things beside war savings parades. They did not wait for the invasion of the continent to learn the modern values of sniping or of flooding tactics from the enemy. With unerring instinct all the necessary data for flooding a certain area was worked out long before D-Day. In our defence exercises the use of snipers was stressed long before the Normandy battles drew attention to those delaying tactics thought by some people to be out of date. We do not wish to commend ourselves to anyone in particular, and we feel any praise on the Home Front should be subdued, and particularly so as far as individuals are concerned. There are so many. For instance, the same boys who dug the first trench in 1940 filled in the last one in 1944; the not so young fellows who gave up their annual holidays to take a gruelling course of instruction at more than one War Office school; the boys who slogged for months, and when called to the Regular Forces, spent several hours at HQ the night before they went away to ensure they left the job tidy for their successor. Many such tales of devotion to training and attention to detail could be told. Occasionally, tired and with frayed tempers, we waxed sarcastic and cussed, but we stuck it because we were needed. To relieve the monotony there was a humourist about. Even the chappie who was happiest when he was miserable commanded our affection. But sincerely, we who have sacrificed so little in comparison, reserve our praise rather for the brave and proved in battle. To the skyfighter; to those who held the sea lanes and secured our food; to the boys of Falaise, or Arnhem; the lads in the steaming jungles of Burma; to the mothers and sweethearts whose lot it was to feel a tug at the heart when the BBC announcers gave out 'forty of our bombers are missing' – and a land battle announcement – 'our casualties were not light' – or 'Five of our ships are missing.' The Home Guard have generally a sense of feeling and of proportion; a wish to fade out decently with a mutual respect and understanding of the part played by other services, both at home and overseas. We rejoice with those with newly found freedom; our hearts go out to those less fortunate; our prayers are with those facing future hazards.*

On Saturday, 26th May the wedding took place at St John's Church, Irlam, between Anne Prendergast and Edward Patrick Flanagan of 12 Brief Street, Manchester. Anne had served in the Women's Auxiliary Air Force since the outbreak of the war. She was the daughter of Mr T. Prendergast of 63 Baines Avenue, Irlam. Her husband, Edward, had joined the Royal Navy in 1935, and had served in the Mediterranean, India and Ceylon. He served in Greece and Crete, and took part in the Malta and Russian convoys.

During the month two local women married Canadian airmen. St Teresa's Church saw the wedding of Leading Aircraftman William J. Kaine of Ontario and Kathleen T. O'Shaughnessy of 78 Caroline Street, Irlam. Yvonne Stewart, third daughter of Mr and Mrs W. Stewart, 80 Marlborough Road, Higher Irlam, married Morris Lynn Peterson of the Royal Canadian Air Force, at St Michael's RC Church, Rixton.

Prisoner of war Albert Houghton came home from Germany at the end of May after being liberated at the beginning of the month. He was very thankful for the gifts from the Irlam and Cadishead War Comforts Fund, and Welcome Home Fund. The Red Cross parcels, he said, were marvellous, and if it had not been for them he probably would not have survived. He joined the Army in January 1941 and went overseas in March 1943, where he served with the First Army in North Africa. He was taken prisoner by the Italians in May 1943, but was later moved to Germany. Born on 27th July 1922, he was the second son of Mr and Mrs S. Houghton of 74 Baines Avenue, Irlam. He was employed by the Steelworks before joining the Army. Albert's friend, Ernest 'Ernie' Perryman, also from Irlam, enlisted into the Royal Engineers but at some point he transferred to the Royal Army Medical Corps. He married Vera Hall in 1943 and their son, Alan, was born in 1944, followed by a daughter, Joan, in 1952. He served with the Royal Army Medical Corps in Malaya.

Another liberated prisoner of war, Flying Officer Eric Williams, returned home to his wife and son at 11 Fiddlers Lane, Higher Irlam on Monday, 28th May. He had been released from a German prisoner of war camp by the Russians on 22nd April. During his captivity in Germany he was held in Stalag Luft VII at Bankau, near Kreuzburg in Silesia (now Poland). He was one of the many forced by the German Guards to march over 300 miles in order to elude the Red Army. The march started on 19th January when 1,500 men were forced to march in blizzard conditions, before later being loaded onto cattle trucks. The route took them via Lamsdorf (Stalag 344) and Görlitz in Poland (Stalag VIIIA), eventually arriving at Stalag IIIA at Luckenwalde, 20 miles south of Berlin. The food they received on the march, he said, was laughable; one day he had only received one potato. On the whole he considered that the food had been awful, but the treatment had not been so bad. In common with all the returned local prisoners of war he was full of praise for the Red Cross parcels. Eric was the eldest son of Mr and Mrs J. Williams of 74 Caroline Street, Irlam.

On Monday, 28th May a small party of evacuees, consisting of four mothers and eight unaccompanied children, returned to London. They were one of the last remaining groups of evacuees who had arrived in the district in July and August 1944, during the V1 and V2 attacks on southern England. Irlam and Cadishead had been home to more than 400 evacuees (including over 100 mothers, more than 200 accompanied children, 90 unaccompanied children and 23 other adults). Norris Dale, who had acted as billeting officer for the evacuees, accompanied the children to Mayfield Station, Manchester, together with Mrs N. Hampson of the WVS, who travelled to London with the party. On arrival at Mayfield Station, Mrs Hampson took charge of the party. Norris said: *Everything went like clockwork. The train left Manchester dead on time, and arrived in London only five minutes late. The only accident was that we forgot a baby's dummy, but that was soon put right.* On arrival at London, they were welcomed back by Mrs Winant, the wife of the American Ambassador to England.

The distribution of the new ration books to local people began on Monday, 28th May and continued until the end of 23rd June. The Fire Guard Office, 625 Liverpool Road, Irlam (next door to the Food Office) was used as the distribution centre and was open from 9am to 6pm, Monday to Friday and 9am to 12 noon on Saturday. Each person was required to produce their identity card with the correct address shown on the reference leaf, and to give the complete particulars relating to children aged five and six, especially the name of the milk retailer. Residents were asked to attend in the week allotted to the initial letters of their surnames in order to avoid queues. Within four weeks the Food Office had distributed 12,000 ration books.

VE Day celebrations continued long after the actual day. A group of about 30 children celebrated at the Number 1 War-Time Nursery, on Wednesday afternoon, 30th May by playing games and having a sing-song. After the games, the children sat down for a party, every child wearing a red, white and blue hat, made by the nurses and probationers. There was a special VE cake, and many red, white and blue iced buns, amongst other things. A similar party had been held at the Fiddlers Lane Nursery a fortnight before, where nearly 40 children were present. The parties were organised by the matrons and staffs of the respected nurseries.

Of course, there was little celebration in Germany, homes had been destroyed, and food, water, sanitation and shelter, all basic human needs, were all in very short supply. The defeated Axis countries were destitute, their governments had been overthrown, infrastructures, transportation and utilities such as water, electricity and gas were all affected, people were starving and crime was rife. Refugees were roaming across Europe in search of food. The Allied Armies had to take control and bring order and, most importantly, provide food to the defeated nations. Trevor Jenkins was a witness to the effect that the war had on civilians: *I finished up, we went into Austria and what was it called, Eudenberg, and we had little bivouacs with us to sleep under and we had to give them all in to these…, there must have been five hundred women and bloody kids in this field, didn't belong to anybody, they'd been wandering and wandering and wandering between Italy, Austria, Germany you know what I mean, and they were just wandering about, bloody kids starving and oh it was terrible. I used to play hell with my kids when they were young if they left any food, I used to go bloody mad, seeing it all over there, seeing kids starving and fighting for food, I used to say 'people in occupied countries today they'd be glad of some of that bloody food.' I used to hate them wasting food.* Trevor also witnessed the return of Russian prisoners of war, who had been forced to work for the Germans, to the Russian Army. The prisoners believed that they would be shot for aiding the Germans but there was nothing that could be done to help them.

Gunner 14337244 Raymond Cookson of 439 Battery, 55th Field Regiment, Royal Artillery, was with the Guards Armoured Division. He took the photographs on the following page while he was stationed in Hamburg shortly after the end of the war. They clearly depict the destruction of one of Germany's major cities and give some idea of the scale of relief work that the Allies had to undertake.

Leading Aircraftman 612874 **Harold Southern** died on 30th May while serving with 2750 Squadron, Royal Air Force Regiment,. Harold was killed when he stood on a landmine, during clean-up operations in Germany.

Members of the RAF Regiment were trained as infantry and were primarily responsible for defending airfields. In June 1943, 2750 Squadron converted to a light anti-aircraft role. In April 1944 it joined 2nd Tactical Air Force and became a rifle squadron in September of the same year. The squadron moved overseas in December 1944 and initially served at Mons, Belgium, and later moved into Germany, serving in Bonn, Achmer, Bochum and Osnabruck in 1945.

Harold was born in Irlam in June 1918, the son of Herbert Wright Southern and Elizabeth Southern (nee Standish) of Dixon Street, Irlam. He has no known grave and is commemorated on the Runnymede Memorial, Surrey. His brothers, Thomas Edwin (Eddie) and Ellis, also served with the RAF. He had a sister, Doris.

1945

Leading Aircraftman Harold Southern, RAF Regiment

Private Albert Houghton (left) and Ernie Perryman

Albert Houghton in a German POW camp

Albert Houghton (front right) with two guards (left) during his time in captivity

1945

Ernie Perryman, Royal Army Medical Corps
Malaya

Page 1165

Now that the war was over the district started to dismantle some of the fire service measures that had been set up, such as the emergency water supply points that had been installed earlier in the war. The first to go was the static water tank in Victory Road, Cadishead, which was removed. The Council approached the NFS to arrange the removal of other water tanks in the district. The only surviving indication of these war-time fire precautions is the yellow painted EWS (emergency water supply) sign on a wall on Liverpool Road opposite the junction with Fairhills Road

Relic of the Second World War
Emergency Water Supply sign still to be seen in 2014

Sergeant Gerald Bannister, 49th Reconnaissance Regiment, was with the 49th West Riding Division which had fought its way from Normandy, through Belgium and Holland, and eventually found itself in Germany. The following is his account of those last few days of the war: *We went, you remember the Arnhem thing, now the River Waal and the River Rhine form an island and you've got to go over Nijmegen bridge to get onto this island, and the other bridge was the 'bridge too far', you know the Arnhem bridge. We lived at various places. We lived in farms, we lived in some cottages, and we were billeted with a family, they didn't have a man, there was two girls, Anna and Dorna and the mother, and we were billeted in this house. So we'd be there for a week and then we'd go round and get ready, get over the bridge before the Germans could shoot it, in the carriers, down and across and onto the island and we'd be on the island. We had white suits then because it was snow, it was wintertime, very very cold and the rifle bolts and that had to have special oil on because of the cold. So then eventually what they called artificial moonlight, we had searchlights, and they went forward and took Arnhem. This was the Second Battle of Arnhem [April 1945], and we were in Arnhem then and more or less isolated from the war then really. Every house in Arnhem had holes through it, every house, and I went there after the war and you couldn't tell that there'd ever been a war, marvellous it was. For some reason or other I was selected to*

*take a party of blokes from Arnhem to Brussels for a few days and then to Paris for a few days,
and then back to Arnhem. And from there I went to Germany, to Frankfurt, and we spent
some time there patrolling and looking for arms in German houses, and of course they'd
capitulated then. And I was in a farmhouse in Holland and we used to get a ration of rum
during the wintertime and I'd saved mine in a bottle. I was in a barn in Holland and they said
'the war's finished,' and I got this bottle and had a good drink. And then we went from there
to a place in Holland, because I remember our convoy was overtaken by some reporters in a
jeep, and you know they must be brave, anyway they went forward and suddenly they were
coming back again, still some German soldiers, they scooted back again pretty quickly because
of these Germans. But we had to put barbed wire round the carriers to stop the Dutch
children and that from getting to us because they were all clamouring for food, they were
really hungry people, they were starving people. At that time I was a sergeant and I went to
Frankfurt, and I went to headquarters to volunteer, they'd asked for volunteers to go to Japan,
and I volunteered and when I got there, Ianto was there, and he'd volunteered as well, he was
a sergeant by this time. And actually there was a sergeant called Jack Redray, he'd been a
policeman in Manchester, he was a sergeant in the Guards he was, there was a sergeant from
the 3rd Carabiniers, and there was another sergeant, I forget his name, there was five of us.*

Sergeant 2208941 Ron Tonge was sent to South Africa for flight training. The
following is his description of his enlistment into the RAF Volunteer Reserve on 6th
February 1943 and his subsequent training in 1945: *Towards the end of 1942, because of
their heavy losses, the RAF mounted a publicity campaign for workers in reserved occupation
to volunteer for air crew duties. I volunteered and after three days at RAF Padgate for medical
and educational assessment I was enlisted into the Royal Air Force Volunteer Reserve. I
enlisted on the 6th February 1943 but the success of the recruiting campaign was such that I
was put on deferred service until 13th May 1944. To show that we were in the RAFVR we
were issued with a numbered RAFVR badge which was made out of silver. We were advised
to join the Air Training Corps which I did at Urmston Grammar School. We learnt drill and
Morse code and airmanship for which we used a Westland Wallace aircraft which had flown
over Everest in 1930. On 13th May 1944 I reported for duty at Scarborough College and
became AC2 2208941. Apart from basic trainings we had three days of aptitude tests in the
Floral Pavilion. These decided what we were to be in the air crews of the Royal Air Force. It
was amazing that even from day one we were issued with two white sheets in our bedding
pack and this caused some consternation amongst ground staff as they only had the rough
blankets. This is where I was on D-Day. Based on the Aptitude tests I was graded pilot or
navigator and consequently had to go for a flying assessment regarding my pilot aptitude. I
was posted to Brough, No. 3 Air School, where I did 12 hours dual flying and ten minutes
solo on Tiger Moths. I was graded pilot and from there we went on our first home leave.
Returning from leave at the end of July I was posted to the ITW* [Initial Training Wing] *at
Newquay, Cornwall. We were billeted in the Trebarwith Hotel. All of August was very hot as
I remember it and we were officially taken into the sea to cool down three times every day. In
early September the ITW unit was moved to the RAF aerodrome at Stormy Down in South
Wales. It was while I was here that I met Audrey* [they married on 6th September 1947].
Prior to our arrival the aerodrome had been an air gunnery school.

Sergeant Ronald Tonge, RAFVR

Sergeant Ronald Tonge, RAFVR in a Harvard training aircraft

Early in November we passed out and after more leave I was posted to Heaton Park, Manchester, which was a holding centre for air crew waiting to go overseas to continue their training. The camp was absolutely full and so, as I could travel, I was billeted at home. We were eventually issued with our flying kit before getting on a train to Liverpool to be posted overseas. We embarked on the 28,000 ton Royal Mail ship Andes which was then of course painted grey. For the first three days we were escorted by two destroyers and then we cruised on at 22 knots and arrived and anchored off Freetown [Sierra Leone] after seven days. We picked up fresh water and fuel and after a further seven days arrived at Cape Town. We fully expected to train in Southern Rhodesia but 30 or so of us had been selected to train in South Africa. We went by train on the 1,000 mile, 24 hour journey to Johannesburg, the first time I had slept in a bunk on a train. We then took a local train for the 60 odd mile journey to No. 6 Air School at Potchefstroom. We spent a few days getting acclimatised. The airfield was 5,500 feet above sea level and the colour bar, etc. was explained to us, and after a few days sightseeing in Johannesburg and Pretoria we went on 14 days' leave to Zeerust close to Mafeking and the South Rhodesian border. Don Smith and I stayed with the Martin family who looked after us very well. We happened to be there on VE Day which was really quite a subdued affair in this quiet backwater. Back in camp early one morning it snowed. Some of the South Africans had never seen snow before but it had all melted and gone away by nine o'clock. The course was made up of about 15 South African Cadets and 15 British Royal Air Force Cadets and I had my first flight in a Tiger Moth in South Africa on the 28th June 1945. I soloed again at 7.30am on the 16th July. We all sported scarves, mine was orange and black. We covered all aspects of flying and at the end of the course I had flown 49 hours 20 minutes dual daytime, and 32 hours five minutes solo daytime, two hours 45 minutes dual night flying and 15 minutes solo night flying. We celebrated VJ Day at Potchefstroom and had a riotous time. In fact I bribed one of the servants to bring me breakfast in bed on VJ plus one. He brought it on a huge silver tray which was the centrepiece of the sideboard in the mess room. Soon afterwards we moved to No. 22 Air School at Verreniging to fly the advanced trainer, the North American Harvard. I had my first flight in a Harvard on September 6th 1945 and although the war was over things were fairly chaotic and training continued as normal. In fact we only had two days off for VJ Day. Officially low flying was at 100 feet but in practice we had to fly at 50 feet to get below the radar. Unfortunately Bunny Hare and his instructor hit a telegraph pole and both were killed. Another accident occurred when one of my colleagues was coming in to land during night flying. They were too slow and the aircraft flipped over. Fortunately it was so strong that both the pupil and instructor crawled to safety uninjured. In early December we moved to No. 24 Air School at Nigel [Dunnottar]. My last flight was on February the 14th. It was a night solo, cross country, starting at 2000 hours and lasting one hour 45 minutes. It was a triangular course and I had thunder, lightning, thunderstorms and much of it was flown in cloud. I was glad to see the welcoming red flashing beacon of Nigel. Two days later we had our Wing's Parade. We were course 49, 50 was the last and everyone had at least one fatality. We moved to Cape Town where we enjoyed the sights, Table Mountain, etc. We had a lovely mess and a good life while waiting for a boat to take us home. The Spotted Café was near the camp and was a favourite stopping place. We did volunteer to help wives and families to board the Caernarvon Castle but there wasn't room for us. We eventually went to Durban and embarked on the motor ship Dominion

Monarch. We stopped at Mombasa to load ground nuts and so had a chance for more sightseeing. The final leg took us through the Suez Canal and the Mediterranean to arrive at Southampton. We docked at Southampton on Saturday the 21st June, Audrey's 21st birthday. We went by train to Market Harborough and after a couple of days we went on disembarkation leave. After returning to Market Harborough we were posted to Pembray in South Wales where we were interviewed and told if we wanted to continue flying we had to sign on for three years. Only Sergeant Oliver did out of the whole flight. I thus joined the 100s of redundant air crew and after interviews took the easy option of becoming a clerk under training for movement control. I was posted to the Liver Building and because of the acute shortage of accommodation I was posted to Salford Docks so I could live at home. I was within a mile of where I used to work. I was released early under a special scheme on 22nd October 1946 and I returned to work at Trafford Park Exchange after some demobilisation leave.

On the completion of his service Ron had flown a total of 241 hours 40 minutes. Two of his friends from Hollins Green also served in the RAF, Kenneth Edmonds and Flight Lieutenant James Henry Eaves (known as 'Henry'). Kenneth was killed on air operations in 1942 (see earlier entry).

James Henry Eaves was born in 1922, the son of James and Elsie Eaves (nee Pitchfork) of Elmhurst, Hollins Green. He was educated at Hollinfare School and Urmston Grammar School and then worked for a short time in the administration department of the Royal Ordnance Factory in Risley. He volunteered for air crew in the Royal Air Force Volunteer Reserve in 1942. He was posted to South Africa in 1943 where he spent six months training as a bomb aimer, and he celebrated his 21st birthday there.

James went on to serve as a bomb aimer in Bomber Command and he also took part in operational duties with a special squadron of American Super Fortresses, which flew ahead of the bombers to render enemy radar ineffective. After several operational flights he was selected as a trainer and was posted to a training unit in Wales. After the war he went out to Australia where he was put in charge of a supply depot, spending nine months there before returning to a Norfolk station for demobilisation. In total he served in the RAF for seven years.

After the war he became a highly respected and well-thought of teacher at Irlam Central School, before taking the post of deputy head at Woolston School. He was also a keen sportsman, one of the best tennis players in the district and a follower of Manchester United FC. He married Jean Gordon of Graham Crescent, Cadishead, at Cadishead Wesleyan Church on 24th May 1947. They lived at Carr Road in Irlam for a time and moved back to Rixton in 1961. Tragically James lost his life in a car accident on 11th January 1962.

Flight Lieutenant James Henry Eaves, Bomber Command, RAFVR

Private T/14649965 Harold Lowe served with the Royal Army Service Corps in Trieste and Venice, Italy, after VE Day. Born on 11th June 1923, he was the son of William and Lillian Lowe of Allenby Road, Cadishead. Before the war he was employed as a milkman. Harold joined D Company of the Home Guard on 12th August 1940 and served as Private 186 in 5 Platoon. He was called up on 1st July 1943 and enlisted into the General Service Corps at Warrington. On 4th November 1943, he transferred to 247 Company, Royal Army Service Corps. He had an unusual trade, waterman, and while in Venice he was engaged for a time as a steamboat ferry escort. He later recalled with sadness the destruction and poverty that he had witnessed in Italy. He was demobbed on 8th September 1947 and married Edith Cooper in 1948. They lived at 165 Fir Street, Cadishead. His military conduct was described as exemplary.

Private Harold Lowe, Royal Army Service Corps, at Trieste

JUNE

Peter Barrow DCM, the honorary secretary of the local branch of the British Legion, wrote the following letter in the *Guardian* to advertise the support that the Legion could provide to help servicemen and women to return to civilian life: *Sir, now that hostilities in Europe have ceased and service personnel expect to be demobilised, there will be some problems arising for the services. The British Legion, since the last war, has built up an organisation which is at the disposal of all ex-servicemen and women or dependents of ex-services personnel. This branch (Irlam and Cadishead) invites all such to bring their difficulties to us and these will be forwarded to the appropriate quarter for action (if any) to be taken. Mr B.B. Neville has consented to be in the office at the club each Tuesday evening, commencing 5th June, from 6.30pm to 8.30pm, to meet anyone interested.*

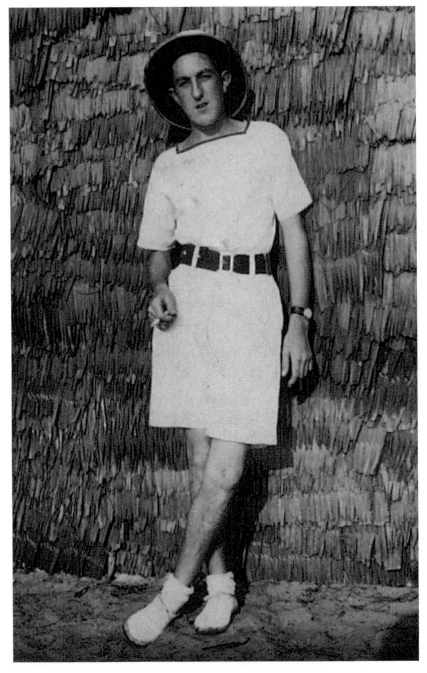

Private Harold Lowe, Royal Army Service Corps

Collections for the War Comforts Fund continued and contributions were received from the following: Miss Jean Crawford of 81 The Crescent, Higher Irlam (proceeds of a penny-a-week collection from friends) 10s; Royles Engineering (monthly contribution) £1; No. 3 Platoon, Home Guard £5-10s; Irlam Branch Primrose League £3; British Legion Club £7-7s; the directors and employees at the British Basket and Besto Company £3-10s; scholars of St Mary's Church, Sunday School 2s-6d; Mr W. Hollinhurst, Railway Hotel, Cadishead (proceeds of effort) £10; proceeds of collection boxes from the Ship Hotel, Irlam (per Mrs Cope) £2-7s.

Mrs Clorley, Mrs Fairhurst and Mrs Bailey organised a party in Victory Road, Cadishead, on Friday, 1st June for more than 60 children from the road who had missed the earlier VE Day street tea parties. Long trestle tables were placed in the semi-circular green and trees were decorated with flags and bunting. Music was relayed through three loudspeakers perched on the top of an adjacent air-raid shelter and tea, consisting of sandwiches, cakes, jellies, and a variety of treats were provided by residents in the street. At night there was a bonfire and fireworks display.

Victory Road VE Party

Bank Street in Glazebrook staged its own VE Party (date unknown) to celebrate the end of hostilities in Europe. In many of these street parties it was the children who were the focal point of the celebrations.

VE Party in Bank Street, Glazebrook

1. Michael Scanes 2. Master Scholes 3. Brian Perrin 5. Tommy Action 9. Ray Shaw 10. Maurice Hatton 11. Lillian Acton 12. Joan Hatton 15. Ruth Moss 16. Mary Moss 17. Alwyn Shaw 18. Mrs Cleworth 20. Ethel Cleworth 21. Mrs Betty Jones 22. Kathy Action 23. Scholes 24. Mrs Scholes 25. Gladys Acton 26. Mary Acton 27. Mrs Hatton 29. Mrs Acton 30 Mrs Perrin 31 Mr Perrin 32 Mrs Bancroft

On Saturday, 2nd June all public and communal shelters within the district were formally closed, however, it would be some time before they could be demolished due to the shortage of labour. At the same time, householders were offered the chance to buy their Anderson or Morrison shelters for £1 or £1-10s, respectively. Alternatively, they were instructed to dismantle their shelters (unless it was connected to a drain) and the Council would arrange collection of the materials. Householders were responsible for storing and taking reasonable steps to preserve the material on their own premises.

On Sunday, 3rd June Reverend A. Bott preached at the morning and evening services at St Paul's Methodist Church, Irlam. He had just returned to England after seven years in India. Before that he was a minister in the Manchester Mission. During his time in India, he had been chaplain to the Forces, and had broadcast on the radio many times.

Robert Kirkham of 4 Albert Street, Cadishead, a member of the Salvation Army Band, wrote the following letter to the *Guardian*: *Sir, in reply to the first article of Town Topics published in last Saturday's Guardian I feel that this cannot pass without comment, and so I would like to make this reply and so clear up a so called bit of amusement on the part of Onlooker. We as Salvation Army bandsmen have, during the past years, struggled hard against the misfortunes of war, and so far have been able to keep the interests of the band together while the boys are away on active service. Having lost the cream of the band to the fighting services we have been left with about a dozen players, 75 percent of these are the young ladies and boys who have been taught during this period. Owing to the local prize band being disbanded for the war period, we 'the never say die' of the Salvation Army were asked if we could provide a band for the Whitsuntide procession. This we did, and although both bands combined would have drawn some 'untuneful' remarks from a keen band critic, we tried to make the most out of a bad job. The weather, of course, intervened, the walk was therefore cancelled, and we were again left with the task of providing the band. In the circumstances a number of the bandsmen volunteered to come back from Liverpool to give a helping hand the following week, among them being our friend on the cornet who played and steered the old velocipede at the same time. Having the misfortune to be crippled in both legs, this man has certainly a great spirit within him and his enthusiasm has enabled him to overcome a great handicap. Having said all, we certainly take the Christian spirit to forgive and forget the little bit of sarcasm about the tandem, but sincerely hope that the spirit of overcoming the most severe handicap will still continue in our ranks.*

The 'Fit for Service, Fit for Pension' resolution which the Irlam and Cadishead Branch of the British Legion moved and had carried at the North West Area Conference was approved at the Annual Conference of the Legion in London. The resolution read: *That this conference protests in the strongest terms against the action of the medical tribunals in the treatment of Applicants appearing under the name of psycho-neurosis, and protests against the consideration of an applicant's medical history being taken from when he was a child and submits that his medical history begins when he is accepted A1 on enlistment. Fit for Service – fit for pension is the considered view of the conference.* Peter Barrow, DCM, secretary of the Cadishead and Irlam branch and one of the branch's two delegates, said: *As movers of this resolution they protested against the treatment by medical tribunals of applicants suffering from psycho-neurosis and contended that when a person had been accepted by a court of medical referees on attestation for the Forces and accepted A1, the Government should take full responsibility for that person. They considered that when a man made an appeal for a pension after being discharged as unfit, he should not have to submit a medical history covering his whole life as was the case when persons were discharged with psycho-neurosis. If they were fit for service they were fit for a pension. The majority of these persons were not fully cured when they were discharged from hospital and they either finished up in PAC mental ward or under the care of their own doctor which rendered them unfit to go back to their civil employment.* Peter Barrow instanced a case taken up by the Cadishead branch where an applicant was discharged in 1942. After being brought out of a public assistance ward he applied for a pension. The British Legion took up the case but failed. *This man's sole means of existence was ten shillings a week. I ask you, gentlemen,* Mr Barrow said, in conclusion, *if this is sufficient to live on? We wish this conference to press the Government to see that these cases are fully recovered before they leave hospital and not to leave them without a means of livelihood. Fit for Service, fit for pension is our considered view.* The resolution, which was supported by Penwortham Branch, was carried. The resolution received national coverage in 1946, when Baron Denning took up the resolution and attempted to reform the pension arrangements. He ruled that it was up to the Pension Tribunals to prove that an injury was not due to war service, reversing the previous state of affairs when a claimant had to prove their injuries were due to war service. He also allowed for judges to grant time extensions for claimants to gather more evidence when the extension had been rejected by the Tribunal. These two cases made a large difference to applicants and Baron Denning received praise from the British Legion and the general public. The Government refused to backdate the rulings to those servicemen who had previously been rejected. This provoked public outcry under the slogan 'Fit for Service, Fit for Pension', which were the words put forward by the Irlam and Cadishead branch of the Legion.

On Friday, 8th June a farewell concert and smoker was held at Irlam Catholic Club for members of the Royal Canadian Air Force, who were leaving for home, having been at Dam Head Hall for a considerable time. On the same night a dance was held at Irlam Conservative Club in aid of the Welcome Home Fund. Members of the Forces and civilians attended and dancing continued from 7.30pm to 2am. Music was provided by J. Tyrrell's Band, and the event, which was organised by Mr Tyrrell and Mr T. Gillett, was expected to raise £10 for the fund.

Irlam and Cadishead said farewell to the district's Civil Defence Service at a disbandment parade, on Sunday, 10th June when wardens, policemen, rescue parties, St John Ambulance Brigade, Nursing Divisions, WVS, and boy scouts who had acted as messengers throughout the war, marched along Liverpool Road for the last time.

The parade assembled at Fairhills Road, and to music by Irlam Public Prize Band, passed the saluting base at the Council Office, where the salute was taken by Councillor McLean, chairman of the Council, and Councillor J. Adams, chairman of the ARP Committee.

Civil Defence Services Disbandment Parade

Civil Defence Disbandment Parade

At Irlam Central School, the services formed three sides of a square to hear farewell messages from national, county and local heads of Civil Defence. Councillor McLean, who opened the proceedings at the Central School, said that on this day of dismissal it was well that they should remember the brave men and women of the Civil Defence Services who had lost their lives. The assembly preserved a minute's silence in their memory. Councillor Adams, thanking the services for the work they had done during the war, said he had a long and close association with all branches of Civil Defence: *This afternoon's parade brought some thoughts. In the first place it means that this land, which had for so long been subject to attacks by the enemy was free from danger. Now we can go back to our ordinary way of living. The occasion also brought a certain amount of regret, because in days to come they might let slip the friendships that had been made during the danger years. When danger was threatening they made friends – true friends – and in the days to come I hope we will be able to maintain those friendships.*

The saluting base at the Civil Defence Disbandment Parade

Councillor Adams expressed thanks on behalf of the local authority for the work the Civil Defence Services had done. Whatever call had been made on them had been answered unfailingly and uncomplainingly, and in spite of many difficulties they had done their duty.

After reading an Order of the Day from Herbert Morrison, announcing the disbandment of Civil Defence, Edwin Jones, clerk of the Council and the district's ARP Controller, read a message from the chairman of the Lancashire County Council, which stated: *As chairman of the County Council and chairman of the Emergency Committee, I wish, on behalf of the County Council, to associate them with the sentiments conveyed in the Order of the Minister, and to express our sincere appreciation and gratitude to all members and past members of the County Services. We will recollect the unceasing devotion to duty displayed in the different parts of the county in those difficult days when we were subjected to enemy attack, and the sacrifice in time and effort so ungrudgingly given by all of you training and undertaking your respective responsibilities as members of a service which has made such a vital contribution to bringing the war in Europe to a successful conclusion. The County Emergency Committee have encouraged stand-down parades or other appropriate ceremonies to be held throughout the county so that they may have the opportunity of wishing you farewell, and saying that they know that you will face the problems which lie ahead in the same spirit of cooperation and goodwill as has existed in the war years. The county is proud indeed of its Civil Defence Service, and to each of you the County Council send very grateful thanks and wish you well in the years to come.*

Before dismissing the parade, Edwin expressed the Council's grateful thanks and appreciation for the help and cooperation they had all given. The Civil Defence Services in Irlam and Cadishead had compared favourably with any part of the county, and had earned high praise at inspections. The Council were proud of the service and each member could look back with pride on the part they had played. The Council and the ARP Committee appreciated the help and support they had been given in very trying years. He emphasised that though this was a disbandment parade, and Civil Defence, as such, ceased to exist, there would still be members whose services would continue for some time, among them the WVS. Concluding, he said: *Goodbye and thanks for a very good job.* The parade ended with the singing of the National Anthem, and Auld Lang Syne, and later those on parade were entertained to tea at the British Restaurant and Irlam Central School. The Scout Band played at the parade and was to receive congratulations from many prominent citizens on their performance.

The *Guardian*'s Town Topics column by Onlooker carried the following article on the disbandment parade: *On Sunday, the Civil Defence Service in Irlam and Cadishead was disbanded. 'Knock off, and make up' as the Fire Guards used to say, was the order of the day. Personally, I viewed the final parade with mixed emotions; I was glad because, at long last, we had completed the first and, for us, the most dangerous leg of a dangerous journey and I was sorry because the final parade signalled, if not the end, at least a partial severance of those friendships which we formed when the wail of the sirens was as regular as meal times and much more regular than sleep. I am not, as a rule, given to nostalgia; but I look back with something akin to longing to those nights – those winter nights particularly – when, after the sirens sounded and the menacing 'thrum-thrum' of enemy bombers overhead keyed up exquisite and dreadful excitement. There was something strangely thrilling and stimulating about it all, mingled with a barely concealed fear that, if and when 'it' came it would be for us, or even worse, for the ones we loved. Under these conditions, the friendships in the Civil Defence Services were made. They were made by long spells of duty together in the streets and the guard rooms and the battle-posts. Friendships which had their genesis under such conditions are friendships which will last even though those who made them may be separated. Yet, here we are today – those who were friends and are still friends – on different sides of the political fence, now that the danger which engendered those friendships has gone. It seems a pity. During the raids we didn't ask the man working next to us on an incident, whether he was Tory, Labour, Liberal or Communist. All we knew was that he was a man – doing a man's job at the risk of his neck, doing it willingly, cheerfully and without pay, and with the thought in his mind that he was playing his part in the common effort for the common weal. As I say, it seems a pity that party politics should intervene. But I am convinced they will never break up the friendships formed in the war years. If only we could get that spirit of comradeship and mutual aid and understanding into our everyday life, we should have a happier people and a happier country. After all, we are all Britons, living in Britain, and each and every one of us should be – even if he is not – concerned not only with his own welfare and interests but with the welfare of the whole community. All parties, of course, say they are concerned with it; but each advocates its own policy as the one panacea for the ills of the country and the world. There is only one panacea – only one universal remedy for those ills; the people, high and low, rich and poor, will have to recapture the spirit of the danger years – the spirit which, more than any one man or party, welded them together and made them determined to see the thing through no matter how hard and long the road nor how bitter the sacrifice it entailed. Yes, we have said farewell to Civil Defence – and it seems that, at the same time, we have also said farewell to the spirit of unity and comradeship. From now on, it is to be every man for himself and the devil take the hindmost.*

A friend tells me he was rather surprised to see wardens and others smoking during the march past on Sunday, and also on parade. So was I, and I must admit it didn't look good. There has, also, been some criticism because the members of the Civil Defence Services were later entertained to tea. Well, it's a poor lookout after nearly six years in many cases – or more than six years in many cases – for the wardens' service was formed long before the outbreak of war – if men and women who have done a good job of work are begrudged a cup of tea and a simple meal of non-rationed food.

On Tuesday 12th June six former servicemen took up the British Legion's offer of advice and help. Two were in respect of pensions since discharge; two in respect of appeals to the Pensions Appeals Board; one for advice and help from the Legion and for convalescent treatment, and one in respect of release from the brick building trade.

Food rationing was never far from the minds of local people and would continue to be a concern for several years after the war. Certain rationed foods had been cut and, for the first time in nearly six years there was a shortage of potatoes. Meat rations had been reduced. They had been reduced before, but the deficit had been made up with corned beef. This time, the value of the meat ration had been cut and so had the corned beef ration. At the time, the nation was being told that it was next to impossible to reduce the rations again and still be able to maintain the health of the nation. As one RAF Sergeant remarked: *I have fought for five years and been in at the liberation of several countries and every time have helped to liberate a country my family in*

England have had less to eat. The *Guardian* added: *And that, to my mind, is the daftest part of a daft war. At the present rate if we go about liberating any more countries, we shall find ourselves on Belsen and Buchenwald rations.*

Throughout the war there was a continual attempt in the district to ensure a fair distribution of food, however, occasionally cases of unfairness would surface. One such instance involved the selling of potatoes, where it was not unheard of for a shopkeeper to refuse to serve a customer with potatoes if they were (a) not a regular customer or (b) not registered with them for other rationed goods. There had also been instances where a shopkeeper had refused to sell potatoes unless the customer purchased a lettuce. Local people were encouraged to report any instance to the Food Office but in reality they would have been afraid of being refused service in the future and would probably also be glad to receive the goods.

On Wednesday evening, 13th June, Councillor Joseph McLean (chairman of the Council) and representatives from various organisations within the district met with Miss Dora Dawkins, area organiser of the King George's Fund for Sailors. The meeting, which was organised by Councillor McLean, was held at the Council Offices. He had received requests to issue an appeal on behalf of various marine benevolent societies, and in selecting the King George's Fund for Sailors, he had in mind that the Lord Mayor of London, the Board of Admiralty, and the Ministry of War Transport recognised it as a central fund for those societies. Miss Dawkins stated that all money received by the King George's Fund for Sailors was divided equally between the Royal Navy and Merchant Navy, and separate Royal Navy and Merchant Navy distribution committees considered and recommended the allocation to be made to the marine benevolent societies. She explained the objects supported by the fund, which included seamen's hostels, homes and clubs, rest homes and club facilities at foreign ports, schools and orphanages, rehabilitation centres, and grants to widows and dependants. The meeting unanimously decided to appoint a local committee consisting of representatives of local organisations to run the appeal: Councillor McLean was appointed president, and Councillor James Galloway Enticott JP, chairman of the committee; Mrs E.M. Woodcock was asked to act as honorary secretary, and Mr H.L. Jones, honorary treasurer. It was decided provisionally to arrange the local appeal for the period 22nd to 29th September 1945. A fundraising concert was arranged for October (this was subsequently postponed until the middle of November).

Dorothy Laverty, serving with the Auxiliary Territorial Service, married Craftsman Leslie Wood, Royal Electrical and Mechanical Engineers, at St Mary's Church, Cadishead on Wednesday, 13th June. Dorothy was the eldest daughter of Albert and Annie Laverty of 39 Princes Avenue, Higher Irlam. She was a former secretary of the Cadishead Junior Unionists. Her younger sister, Joan E. Laverty, was a member of the Women's Land Army. Leslie was the youngest son of Mr and Mrs Wood of Basingstoke.

Private James Gallichan, a 19 year old Cadishead soldier, was awarded a certificate for outstanding gallantry and devotion to duty by the commanding officer and officers of his battalion, the 1st Gordon Highlanders. James joined the Army in February 1944 and went overseas in August of the same year, serving in Holland and Germany. He was wounded twice, the first time about February and the second time two days before VE Day. In June he was recovering in hospital in Germany. Before joining the Army, James was employed as an operator at the Rialto cinema. He was the eldest son of Mrs and the late Mr Gallichan of 18 Birch Avenue, Cadishead.

On Saturday, 16th June the Silver Street Victory Club held a victory party at the Eccles Co-operative Hall, Silver Street, Higher Irlam. 50 adults and 50 children, all residents of Silver Street, were given tea and entertained by Misses Mary Behan, June Cassidy, Marie Moores, Maureen Moores, Dorothy Broom and Master Richard Moores, whose singing was greatly appreciated by all present. Music for dancing was provided by Mr Mitchard's (Flixton) Dance Orchestra. During the evening ice cream was served. The outstanding event of the evening was the cutting of a large victory cake by Mrs Farnworth, to celebrate the great European victory by the Allied Forces. The secretary, Mr J. Winskill thanked the committee, and Mrs Farnworth and Mrs Vaughan for their great help in providing tea. He urged all present to spare a few precious moments for those relatives, friends and neighbours still fighting in the Far East, and wished them a speedy and safe return to their loved ones. The Silver Street Victory Club had been formed in November 1944, when it appeared certain that the war in Europe would probably end in the spring of 1945. It was then decided that the residents of Silver Street would hold a grand Victory party on the first convenient date after the cessation of hostilities in Europe.

German attempts to mine the Manchester Ship Canal were mentioned by a public relations officer of the Ministry of Transport, when he accompanied Lord Leathers, Minister of War Transport, on Tuesday, 19th June, at the end of a two-day tour of ports in the North West. The officer stated, in Manchester, that the Manchester Ship Canal had, on many occasions in the war years, recorded a higher daily tonnage of goods dispatched than any other port in the country. *Total imports for one war year average 6,000,000 tons, as against 5,000,000 tons before the war,* he said. *In the past three years, Salford docks has exported over 250,000 tons of goods to Russia, including the mobile generating stations which helped the Russians during their spectacular advances. Very little of this has been lost as a result of enemy action.* During the war 34 million tons of cargo, mostly war material, was brought up the canal to Manchester. He stated that German bombers tried to knock out the canal by mining, but all attempts failed, and the canal never closed for a single day. There were a number of near misses along the canal, and a few ships were sunk in the docks, and though there were ships in Salford docks loaded with enough explosives to wipe out the whole of Salford, the raiders failed to cause any big disasters.

Silver Street VE Party

Mond Road VE Party

The *Guardian*'s Town Topics column carried the following article: *The announcement by a Ministry of War Transport official that the Germans attempted to lay mines in the Manchester Ship Canal is no revelation to those of us in the district who live within a stone's throw of that unlovely strip of water. Nor is it news to us that those attempts were unsuccessful – though that was not because Jerry had not got his heart on the job. He tried hard, but failed because of a well-organised and strategically-posted defence. At Irlam Locks, for example, was one Bofors gun that earned the nickname of 'Coughing Clara,' because of its staccato bark when low-flying Fritzes neared the locks. That gun, and its crew, never shot down a plane, but they made the vicinity so uncomfortable that Jerry never registered a hit. Subsequently the gun was removed and the crew went overseas. That was still in the period when there was danger of an aerial attack, but the enemy gave the place a wide berth. Whether this was because the crew left a perfectly realistic dummy Bofors gun in place of the original article, I can't say. However, it was defences such as this, coupled with rigorous sweeping of the canal that enabled the Port of Manchester to remain open. To be able to claim that the canal never closed for a single day is something of which the Canal Company can be proud. They should feel even greater pride in the fact that the narrow strip of water enabled millions of tons of essential cargo to reach this country for our war effort and to leave it to aid our Allies.*

Irlam parish magazine carried the following article written by Reverend Lee: *This war has taught us that evil does not pay – that it survives in its iniquity only for a time and then, like the birds which return to roost, never receive the reward of good or iniquity. We all come home in the end to the justice which is greater than life, however violent it may be. No greater crime has ever been inflicted on humanity than by Hitler and his colleagues. But where are they all now? Hitler with his intuitions, Goebbels and his sounding brass, Goering and his pompous buffoonery, Streicher and his Jew baiting, Himmler with his patch over his eye – the limited sight and much more distorted and cruel mental vision; Dr Ley and his lying and drunkenness, Hess and his perverted mental persuasion. What a list – what a story, what a reckoning! There are others, too, by the hundreds of thousands – not the least Ribbentrop and William Joyce – but the axe which has severed the root will, in time, top the lesser branches. What have we learnt from these wicked men – from their rock-bottom sin of Godliness? Have we learned to stamp from ourselves their varied wickedness and shame? There is just one last thought; we remember how we used to think of Mussolini as the jackal which devoured what the Nazi beast had left – the invasion of south east France and the pretensions and claims in Albania and Greece. Where the carcass is, the eagles are gathered together. God forbid that the carcass of Germany, Italy or any occupied territory, should become the snarling ground for any of the Allied nations. There are many unmistakable signs of unlawful acquisitiveness that could lead to divisions and war. We must hope and pray for wise statesmanship to carry us over many delicate situations.*

Around this time a Canadian Airman, Sergeant V. Hayes, RCAF, left the district for another camp in England. During his time in the area he had become involved with, and made many friends in the 1st Cadishead scout troop, helping out with instruction in swimming and games.

An un-named Canadian airman (but possibly Sergeant Hayes) who, for a considerable time, had been stationed at a nearby camp, and who had made many friends in the district, sent the following letter which he'd copied from a RCAF magazine. He said it expressed, better than any words of his own, his thoughts on the eve of his departure for Canada: *On the eve of returning to Canada I feel urged to pen these thoughts to you, as I feel they are representative of the thought of many Canadians who have had the privilege of serving overseas and will also soon be going home. The job we came over to help do is finished; we hope this time, for all time. Now we are going home, some of us after only few months with you, more of us after several years. Others of us are remaining with you, some have elected to stay and share with you the full life of England, many more are to sleep eternally in the soft, warm earth of your wind-swept fields and in the further reaches of this Old World continent. To most of us it is goodbye, for it is not likely that we will have the opportunity to return. To others, more fortunate, it is only 'au revoir,' and they will return at the first opportunity to renew acquaintances, to visit your reconstructed cities and towns, to enjoy your rich hospitality and to see your ancient land in all its splendour. It is with a pang of regret that we bid you farewell – farewell to the people who befriended us when we were lonely and who took us into their hearts to share the meagre comforts that were theirs during those long, dark years. Farewell, then, to these fair little isles and to Mother England, the England that we have come to know – and to love.*

The *Guardian* replied that: *the people of Irlam and Cadishead who have made friends in the RCAF are proud to have had the privilege of playing hosts to the fighting men of the Dominion. As they leave us, we say 'Come again – but under the happier conditions of a war-free world.'*

The last of the evacuees from the London district who came to Irlam and Cadishead in July and August 1944 returned to London on Saturday, 23rd June in a special train from Manchester. The contingent from this district consisted of five unaccompanied children; Norris Dale, the billeting officer, who was in charge of the party, handed over to an escort from London, at Manchester. The children had all enjoyed their stay in this district, and it was with very mixed feelings that they left. In the autumn of 1944 there were 446 evacuees accommodated in the district, and these had all returned home, with one or two exceptions, where they were remaining with relatives or friends for the present. There was no single occasion when compulsory billeting had to be resorted to, and the householders who took in evacuees did so voluntarily, and there were very few complaints either from evacuees or householders. Norris Dale and the Irlam and Cadishead sections of the WVS had carried out an onerous task with thoughtfulness and efficiency, and they were congratulated on the smoothness with which all the arrangements had worked in the district.

A meeting of the Executive Committee of the Irlam and Cadishead War Savings Committee was held in the Council Offices on Monday evening, 25th June with Councillor Albert James Keal presiding. The main business of the meeting was the arrangements for a Thanksgiving Week in connection with the autumn campaign. It was decided to go ahead with arrangements for the middle of October and to fix the target at £100,000. A Campaign Sub-committee was appointed consisting of representatives of the Publicity, Industrial and Social Sub-committees.

The plaques received for Warship Week and other special savings weeks were taken out of storage and displayed for two weeks in every school in the district, probably in response to a complaint that had appeared in the *Guardian* earlier in the year.

Two Anglo-American weddings took place in the district in June. The first, at St Mary's Church, Cadishead, was between Technician Terry Mattingly (USAAF), and Joan Massey, only daughter of Mr and Mrs Massey of 2 Jellicoe Avenue, Cadishead. At St Teresa's Church, Corporal B.J. Urbanek (USAAF) married Eileen Reilly, the elder daughter of Mrs C. Reilly of 34 Dixon Street, Irlam.

JULY

A tribute to all those who participated in the Red Cross Penny-a-Week Fund, was contained in a letter which Reverend Lee, chairman of the Irlam Branch, wrote: *Now that the weekly collections for the above have terminated, may I express the appreciation and thanks of all our workers to all those who have so generously and constantly given to this fund. We got our organisation in working order by the month of June 1942. Since then the total amount collected and by donations and efforts has reached the fine total of £1,320-12s for the parish of Irlam, which includes Barton and Chat Moss. There have been many contributions, and those realising the splendid aid for our prisoners far exceeded the penny per week, which was at first asked for. The children have played their part, and from juvenile efforts we have had many gifts, as well as the large sums from adult socials and dances. There has been a great deal of work for all concerned, not the least the collectors – one lady alone collected £105, and this by regular visitation from house to house in her district. All our collectors have responded well to the call, and they must be deeply sensible of the value of their work now that so many of the returned prisoners of war relate how they would not have survived without the parcels. Those who were prisoners before the parcels arrived speak of their despair and malnutrition – the parcels came as gifts from heaven. All our work could not have been carried on without an efficient secretary and treasurer. These tasks were carried out wholly voluntarily and without any charge whatever on the funds by Miss E. Melville and Mr John Gibbon. It is to their great credit that their tasks have been undertaken with ungrudging and untiring zeal. It is our experience that the people of Irlam have given – as they ever do – most generously to any good cause. I have the hope that many who have been giving to the Red Cross Fund might like to give a little towards the 'Soldiers', Sailors' and Airmen's Family Association. Quite a large amount of money has already been disbursed in Irlam and Cadishead for cases, most deserving, which are outside war service grants and particular benevolent funds belonging to naval, air or military societies. The needs of some families will continue for a long time. Up to the present we have been asked to give nothing to this fund, although some of us have been greatly exercised to deal with innumerable cases.*

Will you please think the matter over? With the thanks of all our workers for the generous response to our calls and invitations to aid the British Red Cross Fund.

Aircraftman 1st Class 1116011 **John Arthur Jacklin,** Royal Air Force Volunteer Reserve, died on Monday, 2nd July while being held as a prisoner of war by the Japanese in Indonesia.

He was better known by his middle name, Arthur. He joined the RAF in 1940, went overseas in November 1941 to South Africa, and was later moved to the Far East. He was captured when the Japanese invaded Singapore but it would be months before his father Mr A. Jacklin of 135 Fir Street, Cadishead, and his family, received the news that John was a prisoner in Japanese hands. After that nothing more was heard for over a year and the family waited anxiously for more news. In July 1943, his father received a card from his son, who was in a prisoner of war camp in Java: *Dear Dad, I am still alive and well, but I was ill last year with dysentery. Hope to be home this year.* Another postcard was received on 24th September 1945 which stated: *Dear Dad and Len, feeling fine and very optimistic. Hope you are all fit. Remember me to all relations and keep smiling. Love, Arthur.* Unfortunately, by the time this postcard arrived John was already dead. His father did not receive official notification from the Air Ministry until Tuesday 16th October. John is buried in Jakarta War Cemetery, Indonesia.

Gravestone of Aircraftman John Jacklin, RAF

On Wednesday, 4th July St John's Church was the venue for the wedding of serviceman Ronald Bell to Hilda Royle, elder daughter of Mr and Mrs E. Royle of 11 Caroline Street, Irlam. Ronald had recently returned from 2½ years' service overseas with the Royal Navy. He was the eldest son of Joe and Elsie Bell of 77 Victory Road, Cadishead.

On Thursday, 5th July the first German U-boat to sail along the Manchester Ship Canal, passed through Irlam locks. The U1023 spent a week on view at Pomona Dock. She was a 220ft, ocean-going submarine with a cruising range of 10,000 miles. She was fitted to carry 18 torpedoes. Her two 1,400 HP oil engines gave her a surface speed of 17 knots, and two 500 HP motors a submerged speed of 8 knots. A second U-boat went through the canal the following week (right). The bottom photograph shows one of the U-boats passing through Cadishead.

U-boats in the Manchester Ship Canal

Stoker 1st Class R/KX 603312 **Alfred Hunt Holley** died of wounds in the Pacific on 9th July. He served with the Royal Navy on board HMS *Barricade*.

Alfred was born in the district in 1908, the son of Alfred and Mrs M. Holley. He married Beatrice Taylor in 1931, and they had five children: Keith H. (born 1932), Raymond (born 1934, died 1934), Geoffrey (1937), Audrey (1940) and Michael (1944). They resided at 64 Fiddlers Lane, Higher Irlam, and Alfred worked as a shunter at the Steelworks. Prior to his call-up he was a member of the local Home Guard, which he joined on 1st July 1940, as Private 329 in 3 Platoon of D Company. He was 36 years old and had been with the Navy for two years. HMS *Barricade* was a boom defence vessel which was used to lay and maintain anti-submarine netting. Alfred is buried at Mombasa (Mbaraki) Cemetery, Kenya.

Mombasa (Mbaraki) Cemetery, Kenya
Two local sailors are buried in this cemetery

A meeting of members of the Ferryhill Fire-watchers' Association, held at the Boat House Inn in the second week of July decided to present the balance of its fund, amounting to more than £42, to the British Red Cross. The meeting also decided that the association's equipment, including stirrup pumps and first aid boxes should be sold, and the money also handed over to the Red Cross. At the close of the meeting, the Chairman, Mr O. Delaney, thanked the members for what they had done in the past, and spoke of the good fellowship that had been engendered by the association. A vote of thanks to Mr Delaney was unanimously approved. The Ferryhill Firewatcher's Association had been formed in the early days of 1941 and soon became one of the largest associations of its kind in the district. It was wound up on the introduction of the compulsory fire-watching system in 1941.

Questions about queues and what constitutes 'conditional selling' were asked at the monthly meeting of the Irlam Food Control Committee, on Wednesday, 18th July. A Mrs Hunt told the committee that an Irlam greengrocer had refused to let her have a piece of cucumber unless she bought a lettuce. The food executive officer, Edwin Jones replied he was not quite sure whether it was right or not. A case of conditional selling had been reported in a newspaper and the Manchester Food Committee was taking it up. He assured Mrs Hunt that he would raise the question with the divisional food officer and if it was found to be correct he would caution the retailer. A member of the committee pointed out that retailers were forced to submit to conditional buying and selling at the Manchester Market and most of the fault lay there. Also at the meeting, a Mr McGowan asked if there was any way of preventing unnecessary queues. For example, people no longer had to queue for potatoes because, by this time, they were now in plentiful supply, but queues were still forming. Councillor Melville stated that people queued for goods that were in short supply and the problem was worse at Higher Irlam where there was only one shop to cater for the needs of so many people. When Mr E. Potts asked what the queues were for, Mrs Stringer replied that they were for fish and fruit. *Some people*, she said, *like queuing, and because they like it and form queues others who don't want to queue have got to.* Mrs Hunt made a plea for the workers. *I feel sorry for the workers. If I can't get the stuff through people going from shop to shop and queuing, how do the workers go on?* she asked. The 'Queue question' ended when Mrs Stringer stated that, at this late stage, it seemed that queues would have to be put up with.

Sergeant William Beisly of 241 Liverpool Road, Irlam, was due to visit Berlin in his role of deputy conductor of the Royal Air Force Regimental Military Band. The band had been specially flown from England to Norway to take part in the Oslo celebrations for the homecoming of King Haakon after five years absence from his country. William was described as well-known and popular, not only in Warrington and Irlam circles, but nationally. He joined the RAF in 1940, and before going to the regimental band was deputy conductor with, first, the Training Command, and then the Coastal Command bands. His mother, Mrs M. Barrow, was a well-known Irlam music teacher. William's favourite instruments were the piano and clarinet, and he played solo clarinet in the regimental band.

Before the war he had held important musical appointments in London and the provinces, and for four years before the outbreak of war had been the musical director at the Tivoli Theatre, Grimsby. The RAF Regimental Band was a war-time combination formed around 1942, which consisted of 36 musicians and was equipped for both ceremonial duties and orchestral concerts. It was the first RAF military band to visit the continent after D-Day. During a seven week tour it had travelled 3,000 miles across France, Belgium and Holland, giving more than 40 concerts to Allied troops and civilian audiences, including broadcasts from liberated Brussels and Eindhoven. It had also been broadcast by the BBC and was booked up for the summer of 1945, the programme including concerts at several holiday resorts in England. During a concert in Oslo the band was mobbed by crowds who were delighted to hear British music again. During his time with the band William played for four Kings and two Queens; King George and Queen Elizabeth of England; King Haakon of Norway; King Peter of Yugoslavia; King Farouk of Egypt; and Queen Wilhelmina of the Netherlands. From the age of four he had developed his musical talent. For his piano work, he received the LLCM (Licentiate of the London College of Music) at the age of 13, and two years later entered the Royal College of Music, Manchester. In his younger days, William attended Bradbury High School and Barrington Grammar School.

Another local man stationed in Berlin was Corporal Joseph James Warburton, Royal Engineers, who was pictured in the courtyard of honour of the New Reichs Chancellery. Joseph was the youngest son of Mr and Mrs A. Warburton of 6 Moss Side Road, Cadishead. He married Jean Hesford of Winton in March 1942.

Private Edwin Hewart, serving with the Eighth Army, returned to England after 3½ years' service abroad, taking the overland route from Germany, through the Alps and then France. Of his journey through Germany, he said it was impossible to get away from the damage. *There are not many buildings that have not been touched in the towns*, he concluded. Edwin joined the Army in June 1940, went overseas in May 1942, and served with the Eighth Army from Alamein and through Italy to the Alps. Before joining the Army he was employed by Southworths Addlington, near Chorley. He resided at 35 Milton Avenue, Irlam.

Another branch of the Civil Defence was wound up on Thursday 19th July when the executive of the Irlam and Cadishead Traders' Salvage Scheme decided that the balance of funds should be equally divided between the Nursing Association and the War Comforts Fund.

Servicemen and women home on leave were invited to call on the chairman of the Council, Councillor McLean, at the Council Offices any Friday between 8pm and 9pm. When he first took office Councillor McLean announced that he would be 'at home' every Friday to ratepayers, servicemen and others, to give what help and advice he could to help them with their problems. The scheme was immediately successful, and many people participated in and benefited from the scheme.

Corporal Joseph Warburton, Royal Engineers (left)
Pictured in the courtyard of the New Reichs Chancellery

Corporal Joseph Warburton, Royal Engineers

The War Comforts Fund devised a new parcels scheme which was designed to enable them to send a few additional comforts to men serving in the South East Asia Command (SEAC) and Burma. The SEAC and Burma Parcels Scheme, which had been devised in conjunction with the Services Welfare Authorities and with the help of the Victoria League in Australia, enabled wives, relatives and friends in England to send to members of all the various services, operating in the South East Asia Command and Burma, parcels containing articles sent from Australia to service depots in India and distributed to members of the Forces with the usual air mail. The parcels consisted of an air-tight container containing the following: one tinned cake or plum pudding, half-a-pound of boiled sweets, half-a-pound of sweet biscuits, a tinned meat hot pack, one pound of vine fruits (raisins or sultanas). In the initial stages the scheme was limited to 10,000 parcels per month, but it was hoped that it would be possible to extend this considerably, if the demand was there. The cost of each parcel was seven shillings, which was paid to the Citizens Advice Bureau, Liverpool Road, Irlam. Applicants were given a label to complete and were allowed to add a short personal message (six words maximum). If a parcel was not received by the member of the Forces within ten weeks, providing the receipt was produced, another parcel would be dispatched by the Bureau without charge. It was impractical to return parcels. If for any reason the parcel could not be delivered, for example, if they were on casualty leave, the parcel was passed to one of the serviceman's friends of equal rank in his unit.

Relatives of servicemen who were expected home after a long absence were asked to inform Mary Bowker, secretary of the Comforts Fund, based at the Council Offices, so that a letter of welcome could be sent when the men arrived home.

Air Mechanic (Electrical) FX114798 John William Wright served with 804 Squadron of the Fleet Air Arm in the Far East throughout 1945. His squadron took part in air operations over Burma, Sumatra and Malaya. The following is his story:

John was born on 25th November 1924 in Cadishead, the son of Ben and Winifred May Wright (nee Dixon) of Fir Street, Cadishead. Later they moved to 18 Warwick Road, Cadishead, where they were living when war broke out. He was educated at Cadishead Senior School and then passed his 11 plus (grammar school entry) and went to Stretford Technical School.

In early 1943, 19 year old John was on an electrical apprenticeship course at Stretford Technical College, when he decided to volunteer to enlist. John joined the Fleet Air Arm as an air mechanic on 23rd February 1943, intending to use his electrical trade skills for the war effort. He was 5 feet 7½ inches tall, with brown hair, blue eyes and a fresh complexion. His friend, Bill Taylor who joined the Seaforth Highlanders, was also on the same course and would later volunteer in the same way as John. After the war, they would be best man at each other's weddings.

John did his basic training at HMS *Daedalus* (23rd February to 5th March) and then was posted to HMS *Gosling* at Risley, Warrington (6th March to 15th May), before being posted to RAF Henlow in Bedfordshire (16th May to 13th October). On 8th October he was promoted to air mechanic 2nd class. On 14th October he was posted to HMS *Godwit*, a base at Hinstock in Shropshire, and remained there until 29th July 1944. He then spent five days at HMS *Waxwing*, an overseas drafting station at Dunfermline, before being posted on 4th August to 804 Squadron, Fleet Air Arm. At the time, 804 Squadron was stationed at HMS *Malagas*, a shore based establishment at Cape Town, South Africa, and had a strength of 24 Hellcats. During his time there, John met another local man, Geoff Johnson, who was also serving with the Fleet Air Arm. John was promoted to air mechanic 1st class (electrical) on 22nd August.

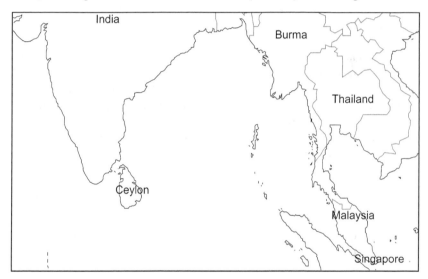

The Indian Ocean and theatre of operations

On 6th December the squadron flew aboard HMS *Ameer* to practice deck landings. Taking off and landing on aircraft carriers were dangerous tasks and there was a fair number of accidents. Sub-Lieutenant J.A. Stott mis-timed the pitching of the ship and the tail of his Hellcat JW769 hit the deck heavily on landing. A photograph of the aftermath of the crash is on the following pages. On the same day JW749 caught a wire and went into a barrier and a similar occurrence happened next day when JW736 crashed into a barrier (see photograph). On 8th December they embarked on HMS *Ameer* and sailed for Ceylon. Two aircraft, JV314 and JW723 (see photograph), were damaged on 12th December. They arrived in Ceylon seven days later, disembarking at Trincomalee, and spending six days at HMS *Bherunda* at Colombo.

On 27th December the squadron re-joined HMS *Ameer* which sailed to Chittagong to join Force 61. This was a bombardment force which was to provide support to the landings of the 3rd Commando Brigade on the Akyab peninsula on 3rd January 1945. 804 Squadron flew combat air patrols and spotting (fall of shot) for the artillery. They were assigned the same role in support of Operation Matador, the amphibious landings by 71st Brigade, 26th Division, on Ramree Island on 21st January. They next sailed on 25th January and took part in Operation Sankey, the amphibious landings on Cheduba Island. On 31st January they left the Arakan area and returned to Trincomalee, arriving there three days later. 804 Squadron disembarked to RNAS Trincomalee. The next operation for 804 Squadron was on 22nd February when they sailed as part of Force 62 to undertake Operation Stacey. This was a photographic reconnaissance of Sumatra and Kra Isthmus in preparation for future amphibious operations. 804 Squadron's role was to provide fighter cover for 888 Squadron's photograph reconnaissance Hellcats. A reduced 804 Squadron embarked on HMS *Ameer* and four further aircraft of the squadron sailed with HMS *Empress*. While cruising over the Andaman Islands, the Hellcats of 804 Squadron spotted the first Japanese aircraft on radar, but it wasn't until the 1st March when they first engaged with enemy aircraft. At 08.24, four aircraft from HMS *Ameer* attacked a Japanese aircraft which broke up and crashed into the sea. At 10.25, two Hellcats from HMS *Empress* attacked an aircraft and forced it into the sea. At 13.50 two Hellcats from HMS *Ameer* forced another enemy aircraft into the sea. These three aircraft were the first Japanese aircraft to be shot down by fighters operating from British escort carriers. After completing the reconnaissance of the Kra Isthmus, the adjacent islands and Penang, the force moved on 4th March to a position off Sumatra to fly reconnaissance missions over Sumatra. On 27th April 20 Hellcats of 804 Squadron embarked in HMS *Empress* and four in HMS *Shah* for operations against the Andaman Islands and Burma, flying coast spotting missions, providing fighter cover and carrying out bombing strikes. Four aircraft were put out of action on 28th May when Lieutenant T.H. Pemberton's Hellcat JW723 landed heavily, missed the restraining wires and struck three other aircraft. On 14th June the squadron returned to HMS *Ameer* to carry out bombing attacks on airfields in Sumatra. Runways at Binjai and Medan were put out of action, three aircraft were destroyed on the ground, seven were left burning, probably destroyed, and nine others were damaged. The airfield was strafed and afterwards, two junks were attacked and set on fire off the coast at Medan. Between 19th and 30th July the squadron provided air protection and bombing in support of minesweeping operations off Phuket Island. The squadron was preparing for assault operations on Malaya but this was cancelled when the Japanese surrendered. The squadron provided aircraft for reconnaissance in support of the occupation of Malaya. On 22nd August John was promoted to acting lead air mechanic (electrical). On 30th October 804 Squadron embarked in HMS *Ameer*, leaving their aircraft behind, and returned to England, disembarking back in the country on 18th November. John's war was over. Once he left HMS *Ameer*, he was posted to HMS *Waxwing* and then HMS *Ariel*, at Culcheth, before being demobbed on 27th March 1946. His character throughout his time with the Fleet Air Arm was described as 'very good'. John kept a fascinating photographic record of his time in the Far East and a selection of these photographs is provided on the following pages.

Suez Canal

Suez Canal
Suez Canal Defence Monument in the background

Port Said
Note the camouflaged building on the right

Port Said, Egypt

Madras, India

Fleet carrier duties - Seafires on deck
July 1944

Hellcat JW769 lands 'nose first'
South Africa, 6th December 1944

A Hellcat takes-off

Hellcats preparing for take-off

Hellcats preparing for air operations

Hellcat JW723 crashed on landing
28th May 1945

Hellcats attack an airfield
(possibly Medan or Binjai, June 1945)

Aftermath of another Hellcat crash landing

Recovering a Hellcat from the sea

John William Wright (front right) with shipmates

Hellcat landing on HMS *Ameer*

Hellcats of 804 Squadron 'Fly Past'

John William Wright, Fleet Air Arm

Another aircraft carrier serving in the Indian Ocean during this time was HMS *Arbiter*, an Arneer class escort carrier and on board was ship's medic, James 'Jim' Alban Davies. *Arbiter* was laid down in the USA and launched in September 1943, for use by the Royal Navy as part of the Lend-Lease Agreement. After sea trials, she was allocated to Western Approaches Command to serve as a ferry carrier, making several trips across the Atlantic. Jim joined the carrier at Belfast in late 1944 while she went through a tropicalisation refit. On 1st March 1945, *Arbiter* left the UK with a cargo of 24 Corsairs of 1843 Squadron, to join the Indian Ocean Fleet at Trincomalee in Ceylon (Sri Lanka), calling at Gibraltar on the way and passing through the Suez. The ship then received further orders to join the 30th Aircraft Carrier Squadron of the British Pacific Fleet at Sydney in Australia under the command of Admiral Sir Bruce Fraser, arriving in Sydney on 2nd May. The purpose of the escort carriers (Task Force 113) was to provide combat air cover for the main battle fleet in the forward area during operations against Japan, and to re-supply the larger fleet aircraft carriers with replenishment aircraft, ammunition and fuel. *Arbiter* remained in the forward battle area for quite some time, providing combat air cover and replacement aircraft and fuel to the main fleet units as and when required. The Fleet Train had its forward base at Manus in the Admiralty Islands, and after leaving Sydney to move further north, *Arbiter*'s captain decided to pull out a bit of a competitive lead over the rest of the fleet, and in doing so became the first ship ever to navigate through the Great Barrier Reef at night by the use of radar. After sailing north into the main battle area with its destroyer escort, *Arbiter* remained on combat air patrol, providing fighter cover with its Fleet Air Arm F4U Corsairs and Grumman Avenger torpedo bombers, and re-supplying the main fleet carriers with aircraft to cover the losses that they were experiencing against some very tough Japanese targets. As with HMS *Ameer*, *Arbiter* lost a small number of her aircraft during take-off and landing operations.

During these operations Jim was mentioned in despatches on account of his actions in rescuing and reviving five crew members who were trapped unconscious below deck after being overcome with fumes from aviation fuel. He took part in the rescue using breathing apparatus and succeeded in getting all five men breathing again. The incident was later reported in the medical journal *Lancet* because it was only the second time in naval history that the methods used in resuscitating the five men had been used.

During the final closing-in operations against Japan, the fleet was susceptible to kamikaze suicide aircraft attacks. Unlike their British counterparts, American built escort carriers like HMS *Arbiter*, did not have armoured flight decks and crew members joked that the escort carrier prefix CVE stood for *Combustible, Vulnerable, and Expendable.*

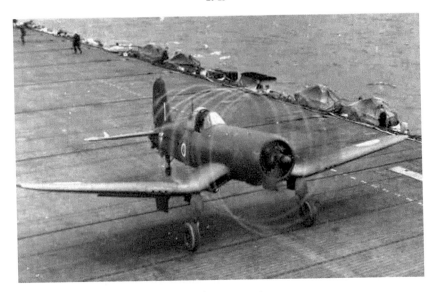

Corsair on HMS *Arbiter*

Grumman Hellcat on HMS *Arbiter*

John Beresford 'Jack' Melville, Royal Navy, served on board the Attack class escort aircraft carrier HMS *Chaser* in the British Pacific Fleet. It is believed that he had previously served on board a couple of Navy ships before joining HMS *Chaser*.

The carrier was laid down in an American shipyard in June 1941 for mercantile use. It was requisitioned by the United States Navy on 26th December 1941 for conversion as an auxiliary aircraft carrier (CVE). It later transferred to the Royal Navy under the Lend-Lease agreement and its modification, including fitting of British radar, was completed on 9th April 1943, when it was re-named HMS *Chaser*. At Norfolk, USA, on 26th June, 12 Avenger aircraft were embarked that were destined for transfer to the UK for 845 Squadron. On 30th June she joined convoy HX245 at New York for passage to the Clyde and arrived off the coast of Scotland on 6th July. During the voyage she suffered a boiler explosion, the first of several mishaps that befell HMS *Chaser*. The repairs at Rosyth took over three months to complete. On 29th October she embarked nine Swordfish and six Sea Hurricanes of 835 Squadron and was nominated for convoy defence in the Western Approaches, however, further repairs kept her out of service until February 1944, when she was directed to provide air cover for Arctic convoys. By this time 835 squadron had left and been replaced by 816 Squadron, comprising 11 Swordfish and 11 Wildcat aircraft. She sailed from Scapa Flow on 21st February, escorted by two destroyers and two frigates, to join convoy JW57. On 2nd March she joined the return convoy RA57 to provide anti-submarine cover. During the voyage her Swordfish aircraft claimed three U-boats. When she returned to UK waters, she suffered another mishap when she dragged anchor and grounded after a collision with HMS *Attacker*. She underwent repairs between April and January 1945 and then in February 1945 she embarked 20 Seafire aircraft for transport to the British Pacific Fleet, destined for 899 Squadron. In May HMS *Chaser* arrived in Sidney, Australia, where she was allocated for service with the Fleet Train (Task Force 112), which she joined at Manus in the Admiralty Islands. Her tasks involved carrying replacement aircraft to fleet carriers and collecting serviceable aircraft for refurbishment. In July she joined HMS *Arbiter*, HMS *Striker* and HMS *Speaker* for ferry carrier duties in support of air operations by British Fleet carriers. HMS *Chaser* remained in the Far East after VJ Day and was used for trooping duties.

John Beresford Melville was born in 1923 in Cadishead, the son of Frederick William and Olive Melville (nee Davenport). He worked at the Steelworks before and after the war and later at British Leyland and Gardners. He married Joan Vinton in 1947 and they settled at 12 Laburnum Road, Cadishead.

The photographs presented on the following pages are from Jack's collection from his time on board the aircraft carrier HMS *Chaser*.

Jack Melville, Royal Navy

View of HMS *Chaser* after take-off

Preparing for take-off

Seafire landing on HMS *Chaser*

Seafire crash landing

Sunset in the Pacific

Flying the Flag

Sleeping quarters

Aerial view of the aircraft carrier

HMS *Chaser* in port

Jack Melville (far right) and crew mates

Jack Melville (second from right) and crew mates

Another local man serving in the Indian Ocean was Able Seaman D/JX288776 William 'Bill' Dervin. Bill served as a torpedoman on board the destroyer HMS *Wrangler*. The destroyer had been commissioned in August 1944 and was deployed for a short time with the Mediterranean Fleet, where she supported HMS *King George V* in bombarding Milos in support of operations to retake the islands in the Aegean Sea (10th to 22nd October). On 22nd November the destroyer was transferred to the British Pacific Fleet and made passage with HMS *King George V* to Ceylon. On 17th December *Wrangler* was deployed as part of Force 67 with a fleet of destroyers, cruisers and aircraft carriers to bombard oil refineries in Sumatra. Between January and April 1945 she was under repair at Bombay dockyard. In May the destroyer sailed for Sydney, Australia, and transferred to the US Third Fleet, along with several other ships of the British Pacific Fleet, re-designated as Force 37. In July *Wrangler* and two other British destroyers escorted HMS *Indefatigable* for air operations on Tokyo and Yokohama on 23rd to 25th July. *Wrangler* was deployed as part of a defensive screen during the air attacks. Between 27th to 29th July *Wrangler* was deployed as part of an aircraft carrier screen during further attacks on airfields and shipping. On 9th August she was part of the escort for joint Royal Navy/United States Navy air attacks on targets in Honshu and Hokkaido and on 13th August for air attacks on Tokyo. On 15th August the Force continued the air attacks on Tokyo and came under Kamikaze attack. She was present, along with other ships at the formal surrender of Japan in Tokyo Bay on 2nd September 1945.

On 15th November 1944, Bill wrote a letter to his parents. To avoid the pen of the censors he used cryptic messages to identify locations to his family. At the time he was serving in the Mediterranean but it appears that the rumours in mess room no. 4

were that HMS *Wrangler* was heading east: *My dearest Mam and Dad, just a few lines to let you know that I am still keeping in the pink, and that I'm quite happy Mam and Dad. I hope this finds you both keeping the same. I sent your Christmas card last Thursday, as we were having that day from that place where I went to that camp from that last ship. Mam, I do hope you'll like it and that it arrives in good time for you, Mam. I went ashore last Wednesday on my own to have my photograph taken. Mam, I was going to have some taken just head and shoulders without any cap on Mam, as I've had none taken like that before, but I didn't bother after all for they were too dear Mam. They wanted ten shillings for only three postcard size, so I didn't bother, I went to have something to eat, then I went to the pictures to see that picture about that oil tanker which got badly damaged in the Atlantic by a German pocket battleship, the title of it was 'Direction London.' Quite a good picture, Mam. After coming out of here I went straight into the Coliseum to see 'Background to Danger' with George Raft, and Brenda Marshall. This was also quite good, Mam.*

I am now at that place where I got Sally's handbag from, and that silk cushion from Mam, so I guess it will not be very long before we get going for our own proper destination, which will most likely be where that Rogerson's lad is. Mam it may be farther on than that yet, for it might be where that fellow's son you work with Mam has been running to in that meat ship, anyway I hope I can get off here, for I will never like it Mam. I have put in for that higher course, but I haven't seen any of the officers over it yet. I am going to see the one I gave my request to tomorrow, and see if they are doing anything about it Mam. If I can't go through for it well I suppose I'll have to stick on this thing.

The weather is still keeping fine out here, but it's a lot cooler, and it is just right Mam. I hope it is keeping fine for you at home Mam. It will be more than hot when we get to that place where that Rogerson's lad is stationed, or farther on. I should have a bit of back pay to come in a bit, Mam, for what use we get in that new scheme of the Governments, it is seven shillings a week with three years' service in, and when we get to our own destination it will be another seven shillings a week, Mam, and so far we haven't received a bit of it yet, so this will come in handy towards my savings.

By the time you receive this Mam you may have heard us mentioned on the wireless. Just over a week ago I received that new suit I ordered in the first few days of June, Mam, while I was on that seven days' leave from the Nimrod, it has taken it long enough, hasn't it Mam? It will not be long from Christmas now, will it? I do hope that you have a good time, and that you enjoy yourselves Mam and Dad. I will be thinking of you all. I wish I could be home, but I suppose I can't always be luck, can I Mam. I am very tired right now Mam with working till 6pm without any tea, and it's about 8.45pm now, so I will have a wash, and then turn in early. I got paid tonight Mam but I'm not going ashore here. I will close for now Mam, sending all my fondest love to you both and I do hope that Dad and yourself are keeping in the very best of health Mam and I wish you a Very Happy Christmas Mam when it arrives. God bless you and the best of luck, give my kindest regards to all the friends at home Mam, and to your dear workmates. Cheerio and goodnight dearest Mam and Dad. I'm always thinking of you both. Your ever loving son, Bill

Able Seaman Bill Dervin, Royal Navy

Bill was born on 28th March 1921, at Liverpool Street, Salford. The family moved to 126 The Crescent, Higher Irlam, when Bill was a young child. He was educated at Irlam Central School and started work at the British Basket and Besto Company, Irlam, aged 14 and then took employment at the Steelworks as an electrician's mate. He tried to enlist as a volunteer in 1939, aged 18, but he was refused as he was in a reserved occupation. He was called up later in the war and it is believed that he served on both Arctic and Atlantic convoys before joining HMS *Wrangler*.

The *Rogerson's lad* referred to in Bill's letter was almost certainly Corporal Harold L. Rogerson of the Royal Army Service Corps, who was in Ceylon at the time. Harold was the only son of Mr and Mrs H. Rogerson of Liverpool Road, Irlam. He joined the Pioneer Corps in August 1940 and he was first stationed in London during the London Blitz of 1940. He left England in December 1941 and headed for Java. Fortunately his stay on Java was short and he had left by the time the Japanese overran the island. He transferred to Ceylon and joined the Royal Army Service Corps. He was a prominent member of Boundary Road Methodist Church, Higher Irlam, was a superintendent in the Sunday School and also a promising local preacher.

Sergeant John Wrench, East Yorkshire Regiment (attached 2nd King's African Rifles), returned to England on leave in July after having served in the Middle East, India and Burma since 1941. He had joined the Army in October 1939, went to France in January 1940, and returned to England via the Dunkirk evacuation. He was awarded the Military Medal for gallantry in Burma between August and November 1944. His brother, Tommy, had been released from a prisoner of war camp in Germany, in May 1945. They were both re-united while John was on leave. In a letter to his parents he mentioned that he had met his younger brother again. John was the eldest son of Mr and Mrs P. Wrench of 6 Ash Avenue, Cadishead. He attended Cadishead Senior School and, prior to joining the Army, he worked at Cadishead railway station.

Lieutenant Norman H. Wilson arrived home after more than four years' service in India and Italy. He was assistant scoutmaster of 1st Cadishead Scout Group and while serving overseas he had kept in close touch with the activities of the group. He visited the Scout Group and gave a short lecture on Army life, informing the scouts that most of his life in India was spent under canvas, and that in many ways his scouting had proved very useful to him. He also expressed great admiration for the Indian troops as a whole. He promised to give a more detailed talk to the wolf cubs and scouts on life in India.

Signalman Harry Smith of the Royal Navy married Dorothy Clowes, the eldest daughter of Mr and Mrs J.H. Clowes of 280 Liverpool Road, Irlam, on 21st July at St John's Church. Signalman R. Bate (possibly Roy Bate of the Royal Navy) acted as one of the groomsmen. Harry was the eldest son of Mr and Mrs H. Smith of 308 Liverpool Road, Irlam.

Another wedding took place at St John's Church on Saturday, 28th July when Private Edwin Hewart of the Eighth Army took advantage of home leave from Italy to marry Sheila Birch, the eldest daughter of Mr and Mrs S. Birch of 6 Elsinore Avenue, Irlam. Edwin was the eldest son of Mrs A. Green of 35 Milton Avenue, Irlam.

(L-R) Sapper George Robert Walker and Guardsman Ernest Walker

The flags and bunting were out in Caroline Street, Irlam, for the weekend of 28th and 29th July to welcome home Sapper George Robert Walker, the eldest son of Mrs E. Walker of 46 Caroline Street. Unfortunately his long awaited leave was delayed by a few days due to bad weather which prevented the sailing of leave ships from France. George, who was 25 years of age, joined the Army in August 1941, and went overseas in 1942, serving in the North African, Sicilian and Italian campaigns. Before joining the Forces, he was employed by the Steelworks as a fitter. His younger brother, Guardsman Ernest Walker served with the Guards Armoured Division. He went to France shortly after D-Day and took part in the Victory Parade in Brussels on Saturday, 28th July.

The British Legion continued to promote the interests of the returning servicemen and women. Peter Barrow, secretary of the local branch, wrote an open letter in the Guardian, taking the Council to task for not considering ex-servicemen for staffing the polling stations during local elections: *Sir, while the committee of this branch does not wish to thrust its views on the public, it considers the staffing of the polling stations at the recent election left much to be desired. Several of the positions could have been filled by ex-servicemen who, through disablement or age, were available and capable of carrying out the duties required. If called on we would have been pleased to submit a list of names for consideration, although we realise that the election was sudden and must have caused a lot of extra work to be done in a short time. The fact that no one appears to have had a thought for these ex-servicemen is deplorable. The committee hopes that on future occasions these men will at least be considered.*

AUGUST

Flags and bunting decorated Milton Avenue, Irlam, for the homecoming after more than four years in the Far East, of Leading Aircraftman Harry Prosser, son of Mr and Mrs Harry Prosser of 34 Milton Avenue. Harry, who joined the RAF in 1940, was sent to Singapore in 1941, and escaped when the Japanese stormed the city in February 1942. From Singapore he was moved to Rangoon and, when Burma was overrun, was transferred with his unit to India. He saw the Japanese swarm into Burma and northern India, and then witnessed the reversal of fortunes where it was the Japanese who were on the run. Before joining the RAF he was employed by the Steelworks.

Mr and Mrs G. Hodkinson of 93 Lyndhurst Avenue, Higher Irlam, received a letter from their only son, Flight Sergeant 645731 Albert Hodkinson, 10 Squadron, RAF, in which he stated that he had been awarded the Distinguished Flying Medal (Gazetted 13th July 1945). Flight Sergeant Hodkinson, who was 23 years of age at the time, joined the RAF in March 1939, and since then had taken part in 37 operational flights. Originally from the south east, he had attended the Russell Road Grammar School, Upton Park, West Ham.

The death of 28 year old Mrs Edith Hall occurred in Liverpool Maternity Hospital on Saturday, 4th August. Edith, the eldest daughter of Mr and Mrs W. Moss of Plant Cottage Farm, Astley Road, Irlam, was employed by the South British Insurance Company, Manchester. She was a regular worshipper at St John's Church, Irlam. Edith served as a corporal in the Women's Auxiliary Air Force for 2½ years and was on the RAF recruiting staff at Belfast, Leicester, Derby, Hull and Manchester. She married Flying Officer V.J.H. Hall at Belfast on 12th July 1944 and they later moved to 434 Croxteth Grove, Liverpool. Following her death Reverend Lee officiated at a funeral service held in the St John's Church, prior to interment at the Irlam New Cemetery. The mourners included Flying Officer Hall (widower), Mr and Mrs W. Moss (parents), Mr and Mrs R. Moss (brother and sister-in-law) and Mr and Mrs H. Upton (brother-in-law and sister). The RAF recruiting staffs of the Manchester and Liverpool sections were represented by Corporals E. Elliot, B. Crooks and M. Earl (WAAF).

The need for hard work, full employment and security in the post-war years was the theme chosen by Reverend Lee in August's edition of the parish magazine: *When all our men get back, life will be less fluid and uncertain, and we can only trust that what is in the crucible will take the form of employment and security for all our people. I must confess that as I look ahead and realise how vast numbers of those at present engaged on war work will no longer be so employed, and to this number will be added so many of the returned men – I feel somewhat scared. Some kind of work will have to be found for all, and the great demand appears to be for increased export trade. All the political parties have made wonderful promises and pledges. It is easy to promise, but a different thing altogether to fulfil. As a nation we must certainly get down to hard work or we shall never be able to compete with the massed production of the USA and the grim determination of the German and other peoples to restore the broken years. One of our men, writing from Hamburg, says the Germans, from 8 to 80, are working like slaves from morning till night in country and town alike. The Germans have always been a most industrious people and we must copy them at least in this respect. No nation can make such progress while engaged in war, so the more prodigious the effort to complete the great eastern task the sooner we shall get into our regular stride again. It will be a great relief when all the abnormal situations in life cease and people can settle down to normal conditions and, I hope, make up some of the lost ground in religious exercises, in cultural spheres, and find the contentment, happiness and peace which sober and diligent folk always enjoy. In this selfish age, when most foolish people magnify the material furnishings of life and seek their fleeting pleasures in a world outside themselves, except for the sight of their eyes and the hearing of their ears, usually to the decay of their personal mental and spiritual possibilities – let us remember that the home with its love, affection and loyalty is more precious than all the wealth and glamour of the Indies, and in the vital need for human happiness. One of the soul destroying forces nowadays is the 'living out' system after the American manner, by which people are attracted like moths to the gay lights, getting their wings scorched and, worse still, suffering largely in their normal and spiritual fibre and often to the neglect of their nearest and dearest. We shall not err much if we maintain first of all the responsibilities of the Kingdom of God – indeed, nothing else really matters.*

On 6th August the Americans dropped the first atomic bomb on Hiroshima and, three days later, a second bomb was dropped on Nagasaki. A local resident, Mr A.F. Horne of 32 Lyndhurst Avenue, Higher Irlam, wrote what may well be the earliest recorded protest against the bomb: *Sir, three thoughts dominate all others as we read of the truly terrifying effects of the new bomb. The first is that our country has been saved by a miracle – the miracle of the second front in Europe. From all the newspaper accounts it seems obvious that, given more time, the Germans might have perfected their own plans first. What the consequences would have been for us can be left to the imagination. We should remember with pride that it was those progressive people amongst us who were foremost in calling for a second front, believing that it was in the best interests of the British people. The others - that plans for a lasting peace must be the concern of all, and that a system of uncontrolled private enterprise is not only wasteful and inefficient but, with unrestricted power to use the products of scientific research as it pleases, can become a very menace to civilisation itself. Only a planned Socialist economy aiming for the greatest human welfare will be able to ensure that, in releasing the energy of the atom, British and American scientists have unloosed a blessing and not a curse.*

Gunner Len Wright was a prisoner of war in a Japanese camp in French Indonesia (now Vietnam) when the Atom bombs were dropped. Although the prisoners had heard rumours, the first official news of the Japanese surrender came when an American Liberator bomber dropped leaflets. As soon as they were allowed, the French civilians gave all the help they could to the prisoners. While waiting to be moved from Saigon, the native Annamese rioted against the French, and Len and his comrades were held up by rioters who were armed with spears. Apart from this the British prisoners were well-treated by the Annamese. Len described the last days of the war: *I was on the railway for 2½ years. We went back to Singapore and we loaded ships, well we unloaded coal and then we loaded up with rubber but I was on coal but I was outside tidying it up. And when it was empty they cleaned it out then they filled that one full of rubber then another coal boat come and that's how we was. And anyway then the war was practically over and we was sat there having a bit of somat to eat and three German submarines come, stopped right opposite us, and one could speak English, he said 'are you having a bit of somat to eat?' 'Aye' we said. So they threw us some fags. We said 'well where are you going now?' They talked a bit and he said 'we're going giving ourselves up to the British in the Indian Ocean, where they'll take us I don't know.' It was two weeks before the war was over. And so we went to finish, they was building a thing for aeroplanes, a landing, not an airport but a landing field and at the end was great big trees and there was two sappers with us and we hacked all these trees down and then they put explosives in and blew it out, all the bottom, the roots and that and we finished that and then they said we had two days there and then they said 'oh we're going to christen the runway' and this little aeroplane come on and they fetched tables out and chairs and some had drinks and all of a sudden we heard these American planes, they come right along it, and they waved to us, they saw us at th'end, they knew it was us, we was just going to wave to 'em then they came and bombed it. Then they fetched us back to Saigon. We were in Saigon and then they took us up a river on little boats and we come to French Indo-China then. They had tennis courts, bowling greens, lovely bowling greens, all sorts there. We slept in some bungalows and the second night a stone come through the open window, and a lad said 'who the bloody 'ell are you throwing at?' he said 'look at the paper' and it said 'the war is nearly over', then another come 'the war is definitely nearly over' and the next day it was over. I'll tell the worst day that happened to me, the aeroplanes come to Saigon, and we got in them and we flew to, no it were Vietnam and we flew to Saigon, and as I was going up for the boat I got malaria and tears ran down my eyes and I said I've gone through all that lot and now I've got malaria. I could see the damn boat and I got malaria, they wouldn't take me. And an ambulance came for me, they took me into hospital in Rangoon and I was lay there then this nurse come with a spoonful of quinine. 'Here you are. What's your name?' 'Leonard.' 'Come on get this down you.' And I'd had malaria 50 times and I took this stuff and I woke up at night and she said 'where're you from Leonard?' I said 'I'm between Cadishead and Warrington, I live at a little village called Hollins Green.' She said 'I've been through Hollins Green.' I said 'well where do you come from?' She said 'Bolton, I went down that road to Warrington.' Well she cheered me up a bit and she said 'I'll send them two lads down tomorrow only in another ward, they might know you.' So I slept and then I had some tea, nice tea and we had some bread and somat on it and a cup of tea in the hospital then who should come over, Tiny me mate, one of me mates. He said 'Len, oh I'm glad to see yer.' I said 'where did you get to?' He said 'I've been on't railroad, I've been in that camp where Fred was [Gunner Fred Thomason].' 'Oh' I said 'am I pleased to see yer.' He come talking every day and I was lay there and Friday he said 'Leonard, this nurse said you're going home.' There was about a dozen of us, we went on this ship and the Durham Light Infantry who'd just come out fighting, the Japs was still fighting when we were there and that was about three week after, they were still fighting. And we said 'let us go there with some damn guns, I'll go' and they said 'you can't, you're going home.' They were the Durham Light Infantry and they'd just come out of the Rhine and they'd put some others in because they were first there and they come on our ship.*

On Tuesday, 7th August, 19 year old Private 14715413 **Ernest Jackson** died of wounds at the EMS Hospital in Baguley. He had been wounded in the throat during the fighting in January in northern Italy.

Ernest served with the 2nd Battalion, Highland Light Infantry (City of Glasgow Regiment). He was the second son of Joseph and Martha Jackson of 77 Dixon Street, Irlam. Before joining the Forces, he was employed as an apprentice butcher by the Eccles Co-operative Society. He joined the Army in February 1944 and went overseas in September of the same year with the 51st Highland Division. The funeral took place at St John's Church, with Reverend Lee officiating at the service and at the graveside. The mourners included his parents, his brothers and other relatives. He was buried in Irlam (St John the Baptist) churchyard extension. The epitaph on his gravestone reads: *Sweet is the memory silently kept of one we loved and will never forget.*

Despite VE Day having long since passed, the Council were still debating whether to organise a formal VE celebration for children. In a meeting during August Councillor James, chairman of the General Purposes Committee, explained that the meeting was to consider a treat for schoolchildren to celebrate VE Day. The divisional officer of the Education Board had agreed to the head teachers being approached direct for their views. Mr H. Wilde, a regional representative of the National Savings Committee, attended the meeting to discuss whether the treat for children could be incorporated into the Thanksgiving Week. Mr Wilde said that matter had been considered by the local Savings Committee at an earlier meeting and he felt that the National Savings Committee could help in various ways. The chairman asked for the views of the head teachers present, from which it appeared that in their opinion the question of celebrations for Victory in Europe would best be incorporated into a combined celebration when the war with Japan was over, or peace declared, and that planning for such celebrations should start immediately, so that when hostilities ceased the arrangements would be in an advanced stage. The clerk reported that authority had been given by the Ministry of Health to spend money on celebrations, but as the sanction related specifically to VE Day celebrations, he was unable to say, without further inquiry, whether any money left over from VE Day would be able to be applied to the final celebration, which it was now considered should be the aim of the Council. After discussion it was eventually resolved that consideration of this matter be deferred, and in the meantime the clerk should find out whether it would be permissible to incur expenditure as suggested.

On Wednesday, 8th August the Scout Troop was visited while at camp at Matlock by Lieutenant Norman H. Wilson. He inspected the 'gadgets' that the scouts had created during the week and named the one he considered the best. The collection of gadgets included a camp clock, a sign-post, dressing stand and wastepaper basket.

On Friday, 10th August two Irlam brothers, Leading Aircraftman Martin Connor (right) and Leading Stoker Frank P. Connor (left) met for the first time in four years when they came home on leave together.

It was not unusual for several members of a single family to serve in the Armed Forces. Colin and Leslie Stevens served in the Army and Merchant Navy, respectively. The brothers were both born in the Irlam and Cadishead area in 1924 and 1927 respectively. They resided with their parents at 16 Bankfield Avenue, Cadishead. Leslie was a former member of the local Home Guard, which he joined on 8th September 1941, serving as Private 622 in 3 Platoon of D Company, until he joined the Merchant Navy.

Siblings Muriel (born 1923), William and Fred Salt (born 1926) all 'did their bit'. Muriel served in the Auxiliary Territorial Service and William was in the Royal Navy. Fred was a sergeant in the ATC. They were the sons and daughter of Henry George and Olive Salt (nee Henshaw) of 15 Hampton Road, Cadishead. Their father was a veteran of the First World War, having served with the Cheshire Regiment and also served as a Home Guard officer in the Second World War.

Richard, Beatrice and Brian Munslow, the children of George and Ellen Munslow (nee Blackwell) of 207 Liverpool Road, Cadishead, served in the Armed Forces. Beatrice (born 1921) served in the Auxiliary Territorial Service and Richard (1924) in the Army. Brian (possibly James B. Munslow, born 1930) was in the Army Cadets.

Colin (left) and Leslie Stevens

Fred, Muriel and William Salt

Richard, Beatrice and Brian Munslow

James Alban Davies, serving with HMS *Arbiter*, remembered the fleet being ordered to sail to a rendezvous point to the south of the Japanese home islands and await further instructions following special operations. They didn't know it at the time, but these special operations were later announced to the world as the atomic bombings of Hiroshima and Nagasaki. On 14th August the Japanese surrendered, bringing the Second World War to a close. Following the Japanese surrender, *Arbiter* was ordered to sail to Hong Kong, where the ship's captain went ashore to take charge of the British High Commission in Hong Kong, leaving command of the ship to his executive officer. The ship took on board Allied prisoners of war who had suffered at the hands of the Japanese in Hong Kong and returned them to Australia and Britain for repatriation.

Another local man in Hong Kong shortly after the Japanese surrender was Coder Joseph Edgar Dyke, who was on board HMS *Parret*. Joseph was born on 26th May 1924 in Glazebrook and he resided in Bank Street, Glazebrook. He was called up into the Royal Navy at some time around October 1942. In 1943 he sailed across the Atlantic to join HMS *Parret* (a Lend-Lease ship). *Parret* sailed to Northern Ireland, then South Africa where she was refitted in Durban and Port Elizabeth. She then sailed to Australia and undertook escort duties in the Pacific and Indian Oceans. Joseph also visited Trincomalee in Ceylon (Sri Lanka), and Hong Kong.

Though the news that Japan had capitulated was not unexpected, the timing of the announcement at midnight on Tuesday, 14th August caught many people on the wrong foot. As in the case of VE Day, the time lag between the first whispers of capitulation and the actual surrender at midnight caused a bit of an anti-climax on VJ Day itself. The extravagant midnight celebrations in the big towns and cities did not happen in Irlam and Cadishead, except on a very limited scale. However, true to the district's spirit, some bold enthusiasts, in spite of the lateness of the hour, lit previously prepared bonfires and carried on until the early hours of Wednesday. What was probably the first victory bonfire in Lancashire, if not in the whole of England, was lit in Dean Road, Cadishead, at one minute after midnight on Wednesday morning. Immediately the news was announced on the radio, residents in the street lit the previously prepared fire, had their own fireworks display, and danced to the music of a piano-accordion. The celebrations continued until 4am when it was estimated that more than 400 people, many of them hastily awoken and with scanty night attire covered by dressing gowns, took part in the festivities.

Two sailors, full of beer and the joy of life, literally rolled out the barrel as part of the VJ celebrations. Taking two empty beer barrels from the front of the Catholic Club they rolled them down Irlam Brow. The incident ended when one sailor somersaulted over his barrel and made frantic efforts to avoid being run over. Two brawny policemen intervened and ordered them to roll the barrels back up the hill to the Catholic Club.

The following photograph, taken from the deck of the aircraft carrier, HMS *Ameer,* show VJ celebrations in Trincomalee harbour, Ceylon. John William Wright, of 804 Squadron, Fleet Air Arm, was on board *Ameer* at the time of the celebrations.

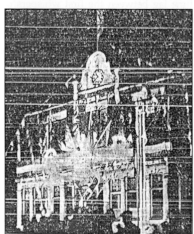

The *Guardian* reported VJ Day as follows: *The next day, officially declared VJ Day, dawned wet and miserable. The weather, however, did not dampen the victory spirit; by late morning, when the weather cleared, most streets in the district were bedecked with flags and bunting. Due to the late hour of the announcement, many workmen turned up at work only to find their workshops closed. Shops, too, were for a time in a quandary; some closed, some opened for a few hours, while a few remained open all day. Housewives went from shop to shop trying to find bread. Shortly after noon the bus service was reduced and by early evening almost all local buses had ceased to run.*

In spite of these inconveniences the public set out to enjoy themselves. Irlam Police Station was probably the first public building in the district to be decorated with flags and bunting. At night the Council Offices and British Restaurant were floodlit, the former, as on VE-Day, decorated with flags of the United Nations. Two official bonfires; one in Prince's Park, and one on the old rugby ground at Cadishead were lit and the noise of exploding fireworks reverberated over the district. Crowds of people, old, middle aged, young, parents with wide-eyed children, many of them experiencing their first night in a world at peace, surrounded the bonfires and let off their own private stock of fireworks to add to the official display. By the time the fires died down crowds of people, intent on keeping up the celebrations, made their way to the Council Offices and there, in the reflected light of the floodlit building sang, danced, threw fireworks and made general merriment until the early hours. For many people the biggest disappointment was that most of the public houses were closed. Although they had been granted an extension until 11.30pm, only four of the district's ten public houses opened, the rest displaying 'no beer' notices. The result was that residents flocked to the open houses and the clubs and quickly caused a beer 'famine'. The George Hotel, Cadishead, one of the few public houses to open on the night, went through a busy and hectic session without damage in spite of high-spirited revellers. Nature made up for this VJ immunity and on the following morning the wind flung open a top window which, in its turn, smashed a large engraved plate-glass window. The clubs in the district held celebrations for their members. Cadishead Conservative Club celebrated by providing free beer, free refreshments, free use of the billiards tables, and a concert and dance. The British Legion organised a concert which packed out the large hall and old hands avoided death from suffocation by assembling in the bar; sampling supplies and singing songs. It was inevitable that the older members of the Legion should remember other peace celebrations. An impromptu concert continued on the pavements outside the clubs until the early hours. Judging by the shortage on VJ Day, one would have thought the Japs had won, and that we the poor blooming British, were in mourning, instead of being on the eve of the biggest victory the world has known. Throughout the night, crowds of thirsty revellers - and revelling is particularly thirsty work – wandered up and down looking for liquid refreshment. The technique developed during the evening was for a scouting party to go out, find where the beer was on tap, and then send word back to the main body by the bush telegraph system known only to men with thirsts. The result was that the few public houses which opened were packed, and staff worked almost to a standstill. Incidentally, it never seems to occur to anybody that licencees and their staffs who, throughout the war, have had a pretty strenuous time, have an even harder time on occasions of this sort. For them VJ did not mean Victory of Japan, but Very Jaded when the day ended. But the thirsty hordes of Britain – who would play old Harry if they were compelled to work a 14 hour day – expect licencees to do it, and like it. Really, the human animal is nature's biggest problem. In spite of the shortage of beer and cigarettes, the public celebrated heartily, and the high spirited crowd behaved. There was no damage and very few incidents, although, at one point, some thoughtless youths threw fireworks into the middle of the crowds.

Whilst local men were vainly searching for beer on VJ Day and the succeeding days, there were places in the world where the beer flowed like water. A Cadishead sailor, whose ship was refitting at Auckland, New Zealand, on VJ Day, wrote to tell his parents how he and his shipmates fared. They had the time of their lives, and so much beer that he never wanted to see as much again (at least he had the consolation of knowing that it would be several years before he would see large quantities of beer in England). On the morning after VJ Day the Auckland cleansing department collected 20 tonnes of broken bottles from the streets.

In August Signalman Albert Edward Drum arrived in Germany from England, to serve with the British Liberation Army. He was initially posted to Hamburg where he first saw the destruction caused by Allied bombing, and from there he was posted to the Guards Armoured Divisional Signals at Aachen, a journey that took him across northern Germany. On Friday 17th August 1945 he wrote to his mother about the journey: *Our party finally left on Sunday last at 6pm from one of the Hamburg main stations. We travelled through the night and arrived at Munster at 5.30am where a truck was waiting to take us to the holding unit. We were there a day, and set off by road the next morning for Cologne.*

The journey took us through such well known RAF targets as Dortmund, Dusseldorf, Essen (where we passed the ruins of the Krupp works) and on to Cologne and it was the same story all the way, devastation, devastation and still more devastation. Never in all my travels [over 4½ years' service in North Africa, Sicily and Italy] have I seen anything to compare with it, just mile after mile of rubble and twisted ironwork and yet the amazing thing is that in some of these towns the trams are running in great style. I saw Cologne Cathedral when we were crossing the river into the town, and though it has been damaged to a certain extent, it is in marvellous condition, since the area all round is a shambles. It's either very accurate bombing or a near miracle. We passed right through Cologne and went on for about ten miles to the Guards Division transit camp which we found was in the grounds of an orphanage run by German nuns, and it was a very pleasant spot. At the time, the kiddies were gathered in from their playground and walked into the house in twos singing a German nursery rhyme which reminded me of the German kids singing on the radio in pre-war days at Christmas.

We were only a few days at this place when a truck picked us up and took us to the Guards Div Signals HQ at a place called Bad Godesburg between Bonn and Remagen in the Rhine valley. I mentioned the view in my last letter. We stayed there the night and were then split up in groups and posted to various squadrons as they call them (we called them companies in our old unit) and three of us were posted to No. 2 Squadron which is the RAHQ Signals at Aachen which is about three miles from both the Dutch and Belgian borders. We went by truck and part of the journey was along an autobahn which is the name of the super highways Hitler built, officially for easier motoring, but actually for speedy troop and supply movement to vital areas. They are wonderful roads being wide enough for at least four (and maybe five) lines of traffic [motorways did not start to be built across the UK until the 1950s]. All crossings are either under or over the road and there are side branches for traffic waiting to get off the autobahn on to one of the side roads or vice versa. These are arranged that the vehicles go off the road in the direction they are going and do not have to cut across to the wrong side thus impeding other traffic. The same applies to trucks coming on to the autobahn.

We arrived at Aachen, or at least the Squadron HQ which is at RAHQ outside Aachen and we came to the Aachen Telephone Exchange the following day and that is where we are stationed, and are we in luck. We have a good room – in the exchange building which is not badly battered, good beds plenty of reading material, a wireless in the next room and here comes the most surprising thing of all, we do not feed in the usual army manner. There is a café near the exchange which has been taken over by the army – I should imagine it is about the only café building of any use for miles around – and all we do at meal times is stroll round to the café, sit down at small café tables where the crockery and cutlery is ready laid out on the table, and a German waiter and waitress bring the food round to us and it is beautifully cooked by civvy cooks. It seems hard to believe but it is quiet true – we can hardly realise it yet but we certainly enjoy our food more than we did under the old army mess-room arrangements. They can certainly leave me here till my demob group turns up, even though there is little to do as regards entertainment in Aachen. The place is so badly battered that there are no cafés or beer houses for miles, very few civilians are there to patronise them if there were any and though there are two cinemas and a theatre run by the army they are a good walk away and there are no trams or buses. I like this life here.

Signalman Trevor Jenkins was on home leave at the time, waiting to go to the Far East: *They sent us back for further postings to the Far East, here again on my own again. Had to go and meet these..., a place called Villach in Austria, we met up there, big gang of us all from different regiments, we were going to go to the Far East, and they sent us back. An Army wagon picked us up, we sat in the back of the Army wagon all the way to Naples which took nearly two days then in an old Army truck, a ship back to Liverpool, came home. I got a disembarkation leave and an embarkation leave because I was going back to the Far East so I got about three weeks. Sarah came down to Manchester, the day I went back to go to the Far East, the day that I went back, cos you were with me, taking me to the station, crying, and me dad came with us, he said 'We'll have a drink before you go son, we'll call at that little pub,' there was a little pub under the bridges in town there where the bus stops used to be. So we went in this little pub, had a pint before I got my train back, somebody come out the back, they said 'the war's over.' So everybody sat up then, 'turn the radio up' and the war had just finished. Just announced it had finished in the Far East after they'd dropped that bloody bomb like. So even my dad says 'well you don't have to go back now, it's all over, it's finished.' I said 'I've still got to report back, I'll have to go back.' So I went back and then instead of sending me to the Far East they sent me back to Italy again, just like a policing job, that's all we were doing, doing nothing only having a good time.*

As soon as the war ended Trevor proposed to his sweetheart, Sarah Elsie Oswald. *Soon as the war finished I said 'oh we can get married now.' I wrote her a letter, I said 'we've got a four day leave for celebrating the end of the war, we can get married.' We had to get engaged first, so I come home on this leave, had to go in the pay office, see how much money you've got. Well you've been abroad, you've accumulated this, you've not been spending. Fifty odd pounds it come to, something like that. 'We owe you 50 odd pounds. How much do you want?' I said 'all of it.' He said 'I beg your pardon?' 'All of it. Can I have it all?' I spent nearly all the bloody lot on an engagement ring.'* Sarah recalled the preparations for the wedding: *What a carry on it was. I couldn't find anything, cos you were on coupons, I went to get a dress with these coupons, wedding dresses there were hardly any, know what I mean, oh it was all rush, rush, rush. Then we stopped at my nan's, my gran's didn't we.* After the wedding Trevor was posted back to Italy and remained there for almost two years.

Signalman Trevor Jenkins and Sarah Elsie Oswald

On Thursday, 16th August the district looked and felt more like a Sunday, with shops and works closed and a reduced bus service. In many streets VJ celebrations continued, however, the day was mainly dedicated to children. Dozens of street parties, made possible (as on VE Day) by the generosity of neighbours, gave pleasure to hundreds of children, many of whose fathers were away on active service.

In Lancaster Road, Cadishead, children were given an excellent meal and first class entertainment. Children in Rivington Grove also had the time of their lives. In both instances, and in all other street parties, festivities were made possible by the generosity of neighbours who sacrificed their rations. Another VJ party was held in Lyndhurst Avenue, Higher Irlam. Since VE Day, Mrs Pitchfork and Mrs Johnson had collected pennies and shillings from neighbours to provide tea and entertainment. The children thoroughly enjoyed themselves and adults enjoyed seeing the contented expressions on their faces. It was a communal effort, and Mrs Pitchfork and Johnson were assisted by Mesdames Beales, Arstall, Boyd, Russell, Spriggs, Melmore and others. Messrs Melmore, Scorah and Groom organised the bonfire and fireworks which was the high spot for the children. Mr and Mrs Spriggs threw open their garden for games and dancing to radio music which rounded off the evening.

More than 40 children from the top end of Fir Street celebrated VJ Day at a party organised by Mrs Foden and Mrs Threadgold. Neighbours had joined together to give them a good time and they sat down to a grand tea in the gaily decorated street. There were races and games and then they shared a large tub of ice cream. Then 'Tojo' went up in flames when the big bonfire was lit, and a fireworks display followed. After the children had gone to bed, tired and happy, the adults made merry, singing and dancing in the floodlit street until after midnight.

Thursday evening was a repetition on a milder scale of Wednesday's celebrations. Again the crowds assembled outside the Council Offices, and kept up the fun. And again, thirsty revellers sought liquid refreshment in vain. At midnight the revels officially ended, and the transition from war to peace was complete. But the fun and games continued until the early hours of the morning, until, finally, a tired but happy public made its way home to bed satisfied that they had saluted the return of peace in a fitting manner.

VJ parties continued throughout the month. On Saturday, 18th August several parties were held across the district. Nearly 50 children from Moss Lane, Cadishead had their VJ party in the bandroom. The party was organised by Mrs E. Taylor, who was assisted by a number of ladies from Moss Lane. The tables were loaded with cakes, jellies, tarts, and all the good things that go to make a children's party a real success. Ice cream provided by a Mrs Croft, and fruit provided by a local greengrocer, Mr Upton, added to the already generous fare. Later the children ran races and had a bonfire. The evening ended with dancing by the adults to music by Harry Hesford's band. In addition, a collection taken during the evening for the Old Folks' Treat realised £1-7s.

The children living in the area of Liverpool Road, Irlam, between Swindley's Farm and Princes Avenue, also had their VJ party celebrations on Saturday. The tea was served in Beech Avenue, and later the children were taken to Mr Swindley's field, where sports were held. These were followed by a bonfire and fireworks in Beech Avenue. The organisers were Mrs R. Scott and Mrs E. North, whilst the sports organisers were Messrs B. Brown, Warburton, R. Scott junior, and Mrs E. North. Music was provided by Mr P. Warburton (piano-accordion).

Three sittings were needed to cope with the VJ party organised for the children of Allenby and Victory Roads and Hamilton and Byng Avenues. In all, 300 people, including 135 children, had tea and later enjoyed dancing and games. Every child received ice cream and sweets, and in the evening they stood around a large bonfire. Floodlighting also lent a festive air to the party, and music was provided by piano and accordion with intervals of radio music. Games, which the children enjoyed to the full, were played, and new laid eggs were distributed as prizes.

The Victory party in Princes Avenue took place on Saturday, 19th August. The photograph includes Mr Taylor, ARP for Princes Avenue; Mr Howarth, who was on leave from the RAF; Fred Beddows, chief ARP warden; the parents of Robert Whittaker (killed in action in 1944); Mr Johnson, Home Guard; the children in front include; Edwin (left, facing away from the camera), Brian (to the right of Edwin) and Terry (to the right of Brian and seated further back) Howcroft and Arthur Wilkins (right and waving).

The Hayes Road VJ party, attended by 64 children, was held in Cadishead Co-operative Hall, on Tuesday, 21st August. Thanks to the efforts of Mrs Lunn and Mrs Baguley, and the parents of the children, there was a plentiful supply of food and ice cream was also in abundance. After tea a concert was given by adults and children. Songs were sung by Elsie Vinton, and Jennifer and Hilary Lunn. Other artists were Betty Hughes (songs), Nancy and Molly Baguley, Joan Jackson and Betty Jordan (tap dancing), Edward Johnson, Edward Davies, Mrs Lunn and Mrs Johnson (songs). Mrs Jones was the accompanist and Messrs J. and E. Hunter were in charge of the radio. Mr Johnson was responsible for the programme. The party was organised by Mrs Johnson and Mrs Brooks who were assisted by Mesdames Jackson, Blake, Thompson, Occleston, Connor, Sharkey, Baguley and Lunn. The party ended with a huge bonfire on the spare land adjoining Hayes Road, when tea and sandwiches were served.

Victory Party in Princes Avenue, Higher Irlam

Hayes Road and Green Lane VJ Party

Beech Avenue VJ Party

Allenby Road VJ Party

New Moss Road VJ Party

Boundary Road VJ Party

Wednesday, 22nd August started wet and dull, and the weather caused concern throughout the district where several VJ parties had been planned. Fortunately the weather brightened in the afternoon. One of the parties took place in New Moss Road, Cadishead, when children and adults sat down to a meal of almost pre-war proportions. Ices supplemented the children's rations and later all enjoyed the bonfire and fireworks display during which sandwiches and cakes were distributed.

Another party took place in Nelson Drive where tables were set out in the street. More than 50 children sat down to eat party food that had been provided by local residents whilst listening to music on a radio. In the evening the street was floodlit. A bonfire and fireworks provided entertainment for the youngsters who thoroughly enjoyed themselves. The arrangements were made by Mesdames Connolly, Stevens, Lawrinson and Robinson.

Victoria Road, Irlam celebrated VJ Day in the bandroom on Wednesday, 22nd August when 25 children and 14 adults had a full evening of enjoyment. In addition to the substantial and attractively served tea there was dancing in the bandroom for adults, whilst the children had a bonfire and firework display in Victoria Road, which was floodlit for the occasion. Mrs Onions and Mrs Cross were responsible for the organisation.

More than 200 people, comprising 175 adults and 70 children, celebrated VJ Day in Boundary Road on Saturday. The principal feature of a lavish tea party was a three tier victory cake made and presented by Mr H. Goodier. Later there was dancing, a bonfire and firework display and racing, and presents were given to all the children. Mrs Lea, Mrs Roberts and Mrs Lawford were the organisers of this enjoyable event. The funds remaining after the party were donated to the Old Folks' Treat.

After 3½ years in captivity, prisoners of war in the Far East were liberated. Many were in appalling condition, suffering from malnutrition and tropical diseases such as dysentery. One such man was Ron Sampson, below is his account of the liberation of the Soengei Geroeng camp, near Palembang, in Indonesia: *At the end, well we heard that the end of the war had come but the Japanese up to that time never mentioned it but it came through a Chinese source on a working party. I used to meet a Chinese chap and he was well dressed, he looked like a businessman, but I think he was intelligence department because he was asking me questions, what was the treatment from the Japanese in the prison camp, and how many men were in the prison camp, and how many died in the course of a day, well a few used to die in one day sometimes, it was a job to try and cope to get rid of the bodies. He was asking me all these sort of questions and nobody else would ask that so I ascertained, I think he's in the intelligence department, and he was gaining information on what it was like in the prison camp, and they reckon Son-je-Ron [Soengei Geroeng] Camp was one of the worst. Well the camp commander he came, lined them up, and he said 'I've got to tell you that the war is now finished, the war is over.' And then we never saw them again, they kept out of the way because I think they felt that the prisoners would take action once they knew the war was over, they'd get rid of a few of the Japs because they were wicked so and sos, they kept out of the road, you couldn't see them. And they'd taken my ring, not this one, but Elizabeth's got it now, that ring went right through the war with me and the Japs got it and I went over to the billet to look and find it, I knew what this Jap, where his billet was, and I pulled out all the belongings and he had all kinds, rings, watches, I mean all kind of jewellery and I searched through this till I found this, and do you know, you can believe it or not, I never bothered with any of the other stuff. There was all that stuff there, I could've had a handful of jewellery, watches, penknives, all kinds, all kinds of stuff was in there but I never bothered with any of that. But I got a Japanese record, I can see it now and this Japanese record, it was the tune of the three little fishes 'and they swam and they swam right over the dam' that one, but it was all in Japanese. And I brought this record in and a couple more Japanese records, they were all in Japanese but I thought it was interesting to let people hear, and it was, they could hear these records, they weren't discs, they were just little records, they were in Japanese, but it made a change, people used to listen to them, I used to let them listen to them, and they thought it sounded funny and even the three little fishes in Japanese, but that was the tune, the three little fishes. Oh and I got his uniform, he had a new hat, it was brand new you could tell, so I took that, and I was thinking at the time, I could've taken his head never mind his hat, I felt so bitter you've no idea. And twice I come to the point of strangling the Japanese for beating me, and there was nobody around them, honest to goodness. I was taught to kill, unarmed combat, special course in Rangoon, they were teaching us and we were flown from Singapore to Rangoon, special little squad, the King's Squad. And I was just going to strangle him and a Korean came up, and I don't know where he came from but if I'd have strangled that fella I'd have been handed over to the Kempeitai and that would have been the end, but that Korean saved me but I don't know where he came from because he was nowhere around, they used to go and leave the prisoners, the prisoners couldn't go anywhere but he stopped me from killing that Jap. And that happened twice, similar occasions, another time I was going to strangle a Jap and it seemed so easy, and I think I'd got as brutal as what the Japanese were, I'd no feeling when it came to them. Even now I don't want to meet Japanese.*

We were still in the prison camp long after all the camps had been relieved, we were still there. Apparently they didn't know there was a prison camp there, and I think they thought it was the Japanese camp because the British planes came over and they bombed the machine-guns on the camp and I think they thought it was a Japanese camp so we put notices up with stones and what have you, pieces of cloth, and tried to put POW, only big so as the planes could see. And it worked but one of the planes crashed, and that was sad, they'd been dropping these supplies for us and they were banking round and banking round, I can see them now, and instead of pulling out they went down like that into the ground, and it exploded because they had a load of explosives on board. Of course we went out into the jungle where it was and it was horrible, the crew were there, and with the heat of the plane they'd become roasted and where their arms and their legs had broken and the muscles had separated it looked like roast lamb, they'd been cooked. We improvised stretchers and brought them into the camp, I don't know who buried them, or how they buried them.

Well we never saw anybody for ages, but you had planes and they dropped supplies, canisters with supplies in, but some of these canisters when they hit the ground they splattered and most of the stuff inside was ruined anyway, but some landed alright. They had English cigarettes, and medicine, that baby food, presumably they knew we were undernourished, we'd need building up. And then eventually they sent troops round, British, and they said Lady Mountbatten was going to call, so we said oh dear, now we'd not spoken to an English woman for so long, we'd spoken to the Indonesians, we weren't supposed to but we used to, you weren't supposed to talk to them, but we did. Oh dear. When the British came they took away the very sick, everybody was ill, nobody well, but some were very ill, very ill, so they took those away. I didn't want to go home, I had so much hatred for the Japanese, I said 'they're going to be tried in Singapore for the atrocities. Well I don't want to go home, I want to go to Singapore, I want to explain.' And I'd written it all down, I was intending if I survived, to write a book, that was my intention, and I could tell them things people hadn't heard of, they wouldn't have believed it, the way people were treated. Singapore, and the Japanese bayoneted a lot of the Chinese, only because they were Chinese.

When I came back after I didn't want anything to do with it, I couldn't speak about it, the ordeal was too much. And the men who didn't speak, it got the better of them and they died. And they took me before a psychiatrist and they said what you've got to do is to speak about your experiences, because if you can speak about it, it's in your mind but it's halved and he said, this psychiatrist said 'go in a pub and the first couple of men that you meet go to them and tell them that you've just come out of a prison camp, and tell them one or two of the things that happened there.' We went to a pub, we saw these two chaps and we started talking to them and they were dumbfounded, they were listening intently, but it was true, when we'd finished talking to them at the end of the night we did feel better. I think when you can relieve yourself of something, but then again I have these memories, and I used to wake up and I was reliving it all again, and it was so vivid, no details seemed to be missing, it was the same thing exactly, and I asked the doctor if it was possible to have that portion of my brain removed if they could locate it, I'd like to forget it. 'Oh no, no, we don't have anything like that' he said. I couldn't have my brain removed, I had to live with it. Like today I've got so many pending operations.

When the war was over I was appointed a policeman to go into Palembang and try and keep order, because the men were going there and some were in the nuddies, they had no clothes, and they were going into the nightclubs, and the local people were buying them drinks, and they were getting sozzled and they were afraid they'd start fighting with the Japanese, and the commanding officer was really worried. And I was one of four policemen, they give us the Japanese uniform but we wouldn't wear the hat because we'd look too much like a Japanese.

The marriage of Lieutenant Norman H. Wilson to Miss Sarah E. Leighton, took place on Wednesday, 22nd August at Cadishead Wesleyan Church. Norman was the second son of Ambrose and Ethel Wilson of 27 Milton Avenue, Irlam. His father, Ambrose, was a veteran of the First World War, serving with the Royal Flying Corps. Norman was on leave from Italy, having previously served with the Royal Indian Army Service Corps in India and Burma. In civilian life Norman was employed by the Warrington Savings Bank. A guard of honour was formed by members of the 1st Cadishead Scout Troop, (Norman was the assistant scoutmaster of the troop). Sarah was the eldest daughter of Mr and Mrs G.W. Leighton of 158 Liverpool Road, Cadishead. Norman's brother, Lance Corporal Tom Wilson, Royal Army Service Corps, acted as groomsman. Earlier in the year Sarah's younger sister, Dora, had married Sergeant Richard B. Phillips (USAAF), from Lansery, Michigan, USA.

Mr and Mrs A.H. Walker of 4 Lanes End Cottage, Astley Road, Irlam, were pleasantly surprised when their eldest son, Driver Jim Walker, arrived home on Friday, 24th August. He had joined up in 1940, and went out to Africa. He was in the push from El Alamein, and later through Italy. Prior to his Army service he worked in the Steelwork's costing office, and was well-known in the district for his work at Cadishead Wesley Sunday School, and as secretary of the Rivington Football League.

A young private in the South Lancashire Regiment, who resided in Hayes Road, Cadishead, pleaded not guilty at Eccles Magistrates' Court on Friday, 24th August to a charge of driving away a motorcar in Devonshire Road, Eccles, without the consent of its owner. In court, the private expressed his regret, and said that at the time he didn't know what he was doing. He had had some beer and was not used to it and he was worried about getting back to his unit. He was trying to get to Pendleton train station. He was found guilty of the offence and fined 40 shillings.

Members of 292 (Eccles) Squadron, ATC, including cadets from the Irlam Flight, visited an airfield in the North West on Saturday, 25th August. On arrival, the cadets were split into two parties; one to go flying and the other to spend the afternoon going through a part of the Paratroop training scheme. Some of the cadets were lucky enough to go flying in a Dakota transport plane and had an excellent view of Manchester and many surrounding towns, including Irlam. Before leaving the airfield the squadron gathered in the ATA café, on the station, to discuss their experiences.

The marriage took place on Saturday, 25th August at Cadishead Congregational Church between Driver Benjamin Cartledge and Florence Poyser. Pastor Morgan, officiated. Benjamin had just returned to England after 4½ years' service overseas. He was the eldest son of the late Mr and Mrs S. Cartledge (possibly Samuel Cartledge, a veteran of the First World War) of 142 Liverpool Road, Cadishead. Florence was the second daughter of the late Mr and Mrs Poyser of 65 Liverpool Road, Cadishead.

Saturday saw another round of VJ parties. An impressive VJ celebration was staged by residents in Hollins Green. House-to-house collections by the children had produced a useful sum of money and provisions made it possible to provide enjoyment for all. At teatime in the social clubroom, more than one hundred children were seated around the tables for the feast, which included ice cream. Many parents and other adults afterwards had tea. In the evening, races were held on the recreation ground and later a giant bonfire ended the entertainment for the younger children.

Others, and many adults, continued the festivities by dancing to the accompaniment of relayed music until after midnight.

A VJ party was held in Prospect Road, Cadishead, when more than 90 people, adults and children, sat down at tables heavily laden with sandwiches, cakes, custard, jellies and fruit. Even those people in the street who were sick and unable to attend were not forgotten and tea was sent to each of them. After the meal, the flowers which had formed the table decorations were distributed among them. In the evening an effigy of the Mikado, packed with fireworks, was burnt on a large bonfire and, while he was busy burning and exploding and generally losing face, the spectators took advantage of the running buffet. Ice cream was served to all. Dancing went on until midnight in the floodlit street, and races were held for the children. The balance of the money collected was sent as gifts of five shillings to each of the residents in the street who had relatives in the Forces. Messrs Booth, Dickson, Hazlehurst and Cox were responsible for the arrangements.

Cadishead Co-operative Hall was the venue for the Victory Road party where 100 children had a thoroughly enjoyable time. Tea was provided by residents of Victory Road, and in the evening, dancing went on until 11pm. Afterwards there was a bonfire and fireworks, followed by community singing which lasted until midnight. A cake sale and collection raised over £3 for the Old Folks' Treat. Music for singing and dancing was provided at the piano by Miss Hilda Binns and Mrs Davies, while the organisers of the party were Mrs Clorley and Mrs Fairhurst.

Dean Road's VJ party, which was organised by Mrs F. Penkethman and Mrs L. Shawcross, assisted by neighbours, began early on Saturday evening and continued into the early hours of Sunday morning. The children and adults enjoyed a *real good Lancashire do*, and were entertained by Joe Tranter on his accordion and Miss A. Beard at the piano. Music included old and new songs which found a tired but happy crowd agreeing that the celebrations had been the best held in the district.

Irlam Conservative Club was the venue for the Caroline Street VJ party where about 70 children and many grown-ups attended. In addition to a lovely tea, there were games and dancing and later a bonfire. The party was organised by Mrs Lythgoe and neighbours, and the sum of £3-10s, that was left after the party, was handed to the Old Folks' Treat Fund.

Saturday was also the day chosen for the celebrations in Belgrave Road, Cadishead. Tea was served, and each child received an envelope containing half-a-crown. Afterwards the children ran races and each received a prize. Sweets, fruit and ices were provided, and later there was a bonfire, while the street was lit by coloured fairy lights. Music was provided by radio.

Although the VJ celebrations went on throughout the district, there was little formal celebrations organised by the Council. The following article appeared in the Town

Topics column of the *Guardian*: *Though the Council Offices were floodlit and decorated, and there were two bonfires and firework displays on VJ Day, little or nothing was done by the local authority to provide something in the nature of a public celebration. True, there was dancing and singing to amplified music at the Council Offices. That was not an organised affair, but a spontaneous effort by the people. In the past week I have heard plenty of sharp criticism of the Council's lack of enterprise and there is a general feeling that much more could have been done, particularly for the children. It is not as if VJ Day had caught us unawares, we had been waiting for it for several days, and in that period it should surely have been possible to make rather more elaborate arrangements than were made. It is not yet too late for the Council to do something for the children. After VE Day a suggestion was made that the children should be entertained at the cinemas, but this fell flat in the argument that it would be difficult to shepherd so many youngsters. Such an argument, in my opinion, is futile. If the cinema shows could be arranged I am prepared to bet that the services of scores of voluntary helpers would be forthcoming in a day or so. No sections of the community have been harder hit by the war than the very old and the very young. They have been deprived of many things that made life passably pleasant. It is up to the Council to see that the children, at any rate, have something that will make them remember the end of the bitterest struggle in the history of the world.*

Lancaster Road in Cadishead celebrated VJ Day in a manner that would have convinced a stranger that rationing had ended. After the children had finished tea the adults polished off the leftovers. The period between tea and supper was taken up by games. The treat of the evening was a supper of real Lancashire hotpot, followed by more games and dancing which continued late into the night.

Lancaster Road VJ Party (photograph 1)

Lancaster Road VJ Party (photograph 2)

Lancaster Road VJ Party (photograph 3)

Not all the VJ celebrations went off without incident. Mr W. Hayes of Twenty Row, Irlam, along with others, had arranged a VJ party on spare land at the back of his home. His family, like other families, helped in the preparations and were so busy that they left the doors unlocked and the house unattended. During the celebrations people were constantly entering the house, fetching and carrying food and refreshments. When Mr Hayes' daughter went in she found that more than £4 had been taken from her handbag and a further search revealed that another sum of £2 and two post office bank books were missing.

Donations for the Old Folks' Treat during late August showed a slight upward trend. VJ parties had provided an unexpected and welcome source of revenue, with organisers handing over the balance left over from the parties. Donations included £4 from the Albert Street VJ party organised by Mrs Stevens and Mrs Connolly.

More than 1,400 air cadets, including members of the Irlam detached flight of 292 (Eccles) Squadron, ATC attended a lecture by Wing Commander D.C. McKinley, DFC, AFC. Wing Commander McKinley was the skipper of the crew of the Lancaster bomber which set out from Britain on 10th May 1945 to make meteorological observations over the North Pole. He explained all the details of the trip from leaving this country to leaving Canada on the way home. After the lecture, the meeting was thrown open for questions. The cadets put forward many interesting queries, which were answered by the wing commander.

At a meeting of the Irlam and Cadishead Savings (Executive) Committee, one of the main topics for discussion was the Thanksgiving campaign, which was planned for the district in October with a target figure of £100,000. Various suggestions for publicising the campaign were discussed, and plans were made for social events throughout the week of 20th to 27th October, including a talent spotting competition. Irlam and Cadishead had a fine record for savings during the war years and even though the war was over, the need for savings remained as great as ever.

Coder Eric Graham (right) of Irlam, met Steward Walter Adams (left) of Cadishead, on board HMS *Persimmon*, a landing ship infantry (LSI) serving in the Pacific Fleet.

Eric lived at 25 Harewood Road, Irlam with his wife and young son. He worked as a clerk in the costing office of the Steelworks and was a quartermaster sergeant in the Home Guard. He joined the Royal Navy c.1943 and participated in the Battle of Malacca Strait in 1945 whilst serving on a destroyer. He was a keen bowler and sports lover.

Walter resided with his wife, Edith Joyce Adams (nee Cowburn of Shawe View, Flixton) at 5 Oak Avenue, Cadishead. He had married Edith on 21st February 1937. Walter was previously employed as a boiler minder. His father, also named Walter, had been awarded the Military Medal for gallantry while serving on the Western Front in the First World War.

Steward Walter Adams, Royal Navy

The *Guardian* carried a humorous description of an accident that occurred in Liverpool Road and dashed the district's celebrations: *Hordes of thirsty wallop-hunters who, since VJ Day, have scoured the country for the wherewithal to assuage their burning thirst, will read this paragraph and lament. They will weep, wail, rage and gnash what few teeth a war-time diet has left them. A brewer's dray loaded with delectable and desirable nourishment trundled its way through Eccles. Being a motor truck it travelled too fast for the wallop-hunters to adopt the usual stalking tactics and track it down to its destination. And while it was travelling the tragedy struck. Two large barrels slipped and fell, and oh! What a fall was there, my countrymen. Plunk in the middle of the road went the barrels and out of them poured the lovely old nut-brown, gallons and gallons of it. Strong men standing by looked on helplessly and wept. It is said that the bolder spirits obtained cups and salvaged some before it ran into the sewers, but that is only hearsay. Nor is it true that, for hours afterwards, men stood around looking woefully at the scene of the crime and savouring the odour of a beverage which, by that time, was providing the sewer rats with a VJ celebration of their own.*

Leading Aircraftman William Joseph Noakes of the Royal Canadian Air Force, of New Westminster, British Columbia, married Gladys Jean Thompson, youngest daughter of William Simpson Thompson and the late Elizabeth Thompson of 603-605 Liverpool Road, Irlam. Her old sister, Elsie Thompson, was killed in a motor accident in 1942, while serving in the Women's Royal Naval Service.

SEPTEMBER

Shortly after leaving the doctor's surgery on Thursday night, 6th September ex-ARP member, Frederick Lythgoe of 19 Caroline Street, Irlam, collapsed and died. Frederick, who was 70 years of age, had retired from the CWS Margarine Works shortly before the war. On the outbreak of hostilities he had volunteered for service with the ARP as an assistant ambulance driver. He was a keen member of the Irlam Prize Band, which he had joined at the age of 18 years. He left a widow, a son and two daughters.

On Thursday Mrs Elsie Ogden of School Lane, Hollins Green received welcome news from her brother, Gunner Len Wright, Royal Artillery, on a card written by him on 22nd August which read: *Safe and well. Hope everything is ok at home. Be home soon. Good luck and God bless!* He had been held as a prisoner of war in Japanese hands for over three years and he had not seen his family since leaving his home in School Lane on Sunday, 2nd September 1941.

A dinner was held on Friday, 7th September in the British Restaurant for members of the ARP service. Joseph Dawson MC, BA, the chief warden, explained that, during the Blitz, and the blackout, the ARP service in the district had been fully trained and prepared for any emergency and he was proud to have been the head of such a fine and efficient service. Constable Jackson of the Lancashire Constabulary, who had acted as liaison officer, was singled out for particular praise. Without his help, Joseph

Dawson said, he would not have been able to carry out his duties as chief warden. The head wardens and wardens were thanked for the part they had played in maintaining the organisation. Superintendent Garth MBE replied on behalf of the Constabulary, saying he was delighted to be present at a gathering of wardens who had given so much to the service. He knew what they had to contend with, losing rest and sleep at night, yet turning up at their work the following day. He was particularly pleased by the chief warden's reference to the work done by Constable Jackson, and closed by thanking all the wardens who had played such a big part in the service. Mr C.S. Jeffs, who proposed the toast of the ARP Committee, said they had carried a great responsibility and had been run very efficiently. He paid a particular tribute to Jack Jones, who was the first chairman of the committee and to whom it owed much of its success. In concluding, he congratulated Jack Jones on his election to Parliament as MP for Bolton.

During the evening Benjamin Neville JP, chairman of the local branch of the British Legion, took the opportunity to question the Council's post-war housing programme, when he proposed a toast to the Irlam Council. He started on a positive note by commenting that the end of the war in Europe and the Far East would allow them all to look forward with satisfaction. He then complimented the Council on the quick changeover from dim-out to normal lighting on the main road, before questioning the Council's housing policy. As a representative of local ex-servicemen he had received letters from servicemen who wanted houses when they returned and they wanted to know what the Council was doing about it. One such letter was from a man who had served abroad for over three years. He had married during the war and, in that time, he and his wife had only been able to spend seven days of married life together. He had no home to return to and neither of their parents had room.

Around this time more and more servicemen and women were returning to the district and the housing situation was causing concerning to the British Legion. Peter Barrow, secretary of the local branch wrote the following letter which appeared in the *Guardian*: *In view of the local authority stating that 75 percent of houses built would be allocated to returning servicemen, the local branch British Legion wishes to contact the Housing Committee through Mr Neville to state its views and its disappointment at the lack, on the committee's part, of considering the Legion's efforts of co-operation on housing. The Legion is receiving letters from serving members who are expecting release from the Forces, and would like to know their position when they return to civilian life.*

County Alderman McLean JP (chairman of the Council) responded by saying that the local authority was fully aware of the situation, and was trying to meet the many problems. They wanted to proceed with 50 prefabricated houses, but there was a shortage of labour. The Council had also received authorisation to start building permanent houses. Ex-servicemen would be given preference, and a points system had been established but the programme depended on finding a contractor with sufficient labour to carry out the building work.

On Saturday, 8th September Sub-Lieutenant Austin, MP for the Stretford Division, and Jack Jones, MP for Bolton, attended a victory social and dance at Cadishead. During the evening Sub-Lieutenant Austin gave a speech criticising the slowness with which men were being demobilised. The Labour Party, he said, had been blamed for the Atom bomb, the end of Lend-Lease and demobilisation. He had received more than three hundred letters on the subject of demobilisation from men in the Forces. There was a lot of justice in their criticisms and there were many in the party who felt that the Labour Government had been too slow demobilising the troops, but the new Government had inherited the existing demobilisation process introduced by the Conservative Government. He blamed the delays on high ranking officers who were determined to keep up the established strength of units in order to maintain their own jobs.

Around this time, Driver John L. Conde, who had been a prisoner of war in Japanese hands since Singapore fell in February 1942, sent a cable to his wife, Beatrice of 23 Allenby Road, Cadishead, which read: *Arrived safely in India. Hope to be home soon.* For 15 months after he had left England in October 1941 the only word that his wife had received was to say that he had arrived in India, then she received the news that he was missing at Singapore. While John had been a prisoner Beatrice had only received one card a year, around Christmastime. All the families of prisoners of war in the Far East experienced difficulties in receiving mail from their loved ones. At the time of his release John was 39 years old.

VJ celebrations continued into September. Though Fir Street and Birch Avenue were gaily decorated with flags and bunting, the actual VJ party, organised by Mrs Amos and Mrs Allison with the help of other ladies, was held at the Cadishead Co-operative Hall. One hundred and twenty adults and children attended and celebrated with a tea of, what was described as *almost pre-war abundance*. Ice cream was served to the children and those under nine years of age were given envelopes containing money. Fruit was provided by local greengrocer, Mr Upton. Games were played and people danced and then, in the evening, the party moved to floodlit Birch Avenue where a bonfire was lit. The dancing and singing continued until well after midnight. A collection raised just over £1 for the District Nursing Association.

There are a number of men who 'did their bit' but unfortunately little is known of their service history or their war experiences; men like Fred Nuttall, Gee Longbottom and Kenneth Westhead. Fred Nuttall lived opposite Cadishead Park, on Liverpool Road, Cadishead (and later Dudley Road and Ash Avenue). He was born in 1907 and he married Elizabeth Alice Sherratt in late 1932. Gee Longbottom married Margaret Howarth in 1928. Sergeant Kenneth Westhead resided in Prospect Road, Cadishead. He served in one of the battalions of the Dorsetshire Regiments.

Private Fred Nuttall

Private Gee Longbottom

Sergeant Kenneth Westhead, Dorsetshire Regiment

On Saturday, 8th September, four service weddings took place in the district. At St Mary's Church, Cadishead, the wedding took place between Signaller George W. Lawrinson, second son of Mrs Lawrinson of 16 Nelson Drive, Cadishead and Kathleen Hart of Urmston. George was on 28 days' leave from Italy.

Leading Aircraftman John K. Nelson of North Battleford, Saskatchewan, married Amelia M. Pew, only daughter of Mrs and the late Mr Pew of 37 Ferry Road, Irlam. On the same day Betty Davidson, only daughter of Mr and Mrs J. Davidson of 6 Lynthorpe Avenue, Cadishead, married Private Curtis Langhan (USAAF) of Lamesa, Texas at Cadishead Congregational Church.

Mildred Hudson married Wilfred Shoubridge of Sevenoaks, Kent at St John's Church, Irlam. Mildred, the only daughter of Mr and Mrs Hudson of 55 Baines Avenue, Irlam, had served with the ATS for over three years. She was a Sunday school teacher at St John's Church before joining up. Wilfred was serving with the Royal Electrical and Mechanical Engineers and had spent over four years in the Far East and Mediterranean theatres.

The Liverpool Road end of Victory Road celebrated VJ with an outdoor tea party, and the well-laden tables bore witness to the catering abilities, hard work and enthusiasm of the organisers, headed by Mrs Blay and Mrs Talbot. After tea, games were played and competitions were held. To add to the fun, it was decided that speed and fitness should not play a major part in the races and there were some unique and amusing events such as the kipper race, cardboard race and sack race, all organised by George Talbot. Fruit, ice cream, chocolates and sweets were distributed, followed by a concert with songs from Mrs Booth and Miss Marion Booth. At dusk, the party-goers held a torchlight procession through the floodlit and fairy-lit street and then the bonfire was set aflame. The celebrations ended just before midnight. The money left over from the VJ fund (£5) was distributed to members of the Forces who lived on the road, with each receiving a gift of four shillings.

Alexandra Grove and the surrounding area held their VJ party in Fairhills Road Methodist School (on the corner of Liverpool Road). The children were treated to sweets, cakes and ice creams and the adults enjoyed a Lancashire hotpot. The party ended late at night with a bonfire and fireworks. The event was organised by Mesdames James, Vause, Grimes, McPhee, W. Parker and N. Parker and Nurse Singleton, who were helped by a band of willing volunteers. The surplus funds amounting to £3 were handed over by Councillor R. James to the Old Folks' Treat.

Alexandra Grove VJ Party

The residents of Moss Side Road, New Moss Road, Kenmore Grove, Poplar Grove and Allotment Road, got together to celebrate VJ Day at Cadishead Conservative Club. A collection made in the weeks leading up to the party provided a splendid tea for 65 children. The tables were laid out to form the letter V and were laden with sandwiches, cakes, custards, jellies, trifles, sandwich rolls, fruit and a large victory cake. Games and dancing were held accompanied by Mrs Graham at the piano, Mr McCullen on the violin and Horace Gardner playing his banjo. Mr S. Jameson, assisted by Mrs Bannister, handed a present to each child, while refreshments were served. Later in the evening the party moved to Poplar Grove where a huge bonfire, with the emblem of Japan floating in the breeze, waited to be lit. It did not take long before the Rising Sun flag disappeared in flames to the delight of the crowd. Dancing went on until midnight. Mrs Bannister of New Moss Road and Mrs Ogden of Kenmore Grove had made all the arrangements.

The ladies of Ash Avenue held a quick 'whip round' in their neighbourhood which provided local children and adults with a meal of almost pre-war conditions to help celebrate VJ Day. After tea there was racing for the children and adults, a bonfire was lit, and the children enjoyed a sing-song to the accompaniment of a piano-accordion and a fairy godfather provided the children with ices and potato crisps. Afterwards everyone sang and danced to the accompaniment of a piano. Despite the celebratory mood, the neighbours held two minutes' silence as their thoughts turned to the men and women of the area who had sacrificed their lives. The evening was brought to a close by the singing of the National Anthem.

About two hundred children gathered together at Irlam St John's School for a grand VJ party. After a tea in the schoolroom, the children went onto the school field for sports, and later fireworks were let off. A dance was held in the evening.

Lower Irlam Co-operative Hall was the venue for a VJ party for almost 100 children from Dixon Street, Irlam. The party was made possible by collections which had been made in Dixon Street since VE Day, and the tea, served by many willing workers, quickly disappeared as the youngsters tucked in. Later the tables were re-laid, and the adults sat down for their tea. After tea there were games and dancing, the music being provided by Mr H. Broadstock, and Stanley Ralph, and Nurse Edna Richardson and Nurse Betty Jones gave a display of tap dancing. During the evening Mrs Rowbottom, who had specially saved her sweets rations for this event, gave a gift of sweets to each child. The indoor entertainment was followed by a bonfire and firework display. A draw for ¾lb of tea and a bottle of cordial realised just over a £1 for the Old Folks' Treat.

The *Guardian* carried a story about two soldiers being excluded from the celebrations at a VJ party in Cadishead: *Try, as I will, I cannot understand the mentality of some people. Take an incident at a recent Cadishead VJ party, as a case in point. The good people of the street – some of them at any rate were determined that the children should enjoy themselves. Others – and there are always others – were apparently determined to make their party really exclusive. To attain this none too laudable object they roped off the ends of the street – presumably to keep out the common herd of kids from adjoining streets. One child, however, got in, and was presented with sweets by a kindly woman, but no sooner did he get them than another woman took them from him and told him he was not entitled to them. That in itself was bad enough, but there was more to come. Two soldiers – one of them with 14 years' service – ignored the ropes and entered the reserved and adored enclosure with the object of entertaining the children and making themselves useful. They were told they were not wanted – and told in a manner which made the statement a direct insult. One of them asked if that was what they had been fighting for. Had I asked the question I should have said 'Are these the kind of people we have been fighting for?' It would be interesting to know what part the people who turned away these two lads played in the war – what sacrifices they made and what losses they suffered. Might I, in conclusion, suggest that the people of this street have such a longing for isolation and exclusiveness they should build a wall around it. Frankly, in my opinion, their VJ party, far from being a tribute and a thanksgiving, was an insult to the thousands of gallant men who made VJ possible.* One week later, the *guardian* printed a retraction: *My note last week about the barring of two soldiers from a Cadishead VJ party has brought indignant protests from several people on the other side. The two soldiers, they maintain, were at least very merry, but they were not interfered with until they became, to use the words of one of the complainants 'objectionable.' The protesters also admit that the street was roped off, but not with any intention of keeping anyone out. As regards the child and the sweets, my informants tell me that only a limited quantity of sweets could be obtained and these were to be equally divided among the children living in the street. The particular parcel of sweets was given to a child whose home is not in the street, and if one had been allowed to retain them one other child would have had to go without.*

Addison Road celebrated VJ with an outdoor tea party with heavily laden tables, including a special table which was reserved for old-age pensioners. After tea, sports were held in a field owned by Mr Swindley. Later, games were played in the road, and a bonfire was lit, while further refreshments were served. Mesdames Goulding, Ashton, Longbottom and Hodson were the organisers.

Addison Road VJ Party

More than 50 children joined in the VJ celebrations at the Fiddlers Lane (No. 2) war-time nursery, where the children had enjoyed decorating the nursery with coloured fairy lights, flags and bunting. Mr Chadwick, whose travelling fair was staying at Fiddlers Lane, devoted part of the afternoon to entertaining the children on the roundabouts and later Uncle Merrie Mac and his assistants entertained the children. The Royal Punch and Judy show, the String Marionettes, and a ventriloquist, as well as many other amusing entertainers were there for the benefit of the children. Uncle Merrie Mac presented each child with a Union Jack and the National Anthem was sung. The children then returned to the nursery to enjoy a tea which included white and blue blancmanges shaped like rabbits and tortoises, and a large cake, iced to represent the Union Jack. At the end of the tea each child was given homemade ice cream – a gift from one of the mothers.

Signalman Albert Drum, Royal Corps of Signals, and his colleagues worked on rebuilding the communications infrastructure of the German city of Aachen, such as fixing telephone lines. In a further letter home, dated 12th September, he touched on his work: *We have been working this week with a party of German linesmen from the German Post Office and they are all young chaps just demobbed from the German army. We get along with them very well and in spite of the language difficulty have had many a good laugh about Dunkirk and the 'washing on the Siegfried Line' but we had them well and truly when we mentioned Alamein and how they'd never stopped running since. They laughed till they cried at one of our boys showing them. He said 'Hey look – Germans, Alamein' and pretended he was running for all he could go and looking over his shoulder with a scared expression. He then said Tunisia and repeated the performance, and again Sicily, Italy, France, Belgium, Siegfried Line and ended triumphantly there by making a show of hanging out the washing. You could never imagine those lads who were so thoroughly enjoying a joke – against themselves too – were of the same blood as the people who have committed so many atrocities. In fact, who knows, they may have committed, but here it is. I shall say the only main difference between the Germans and ourselves is that militarism, and blind obedience to authority no matter how unscrupulous – that is the only real difference, yes, but what devils that difference can make of them. When we are out on these jobs we take our lunch with us and the driver of the truck calls at some house near where we happen to be working and asks the woman if she would mind making the tea for us. Not only do they agree readily enough but they also lay out their own crockery and cutlery for our use. We are not supposed to be entertained by Germans in their homes but when we are working we have to eat somewhere and we have gone a couple of times into the houses which are spotless, and had our meal at the table, which are always nearly white with being so well scrubbed. There is usually a crucifix or a religious picture on the wall.*

The German city of Aachen
taken from the roof of the Post Office

Another view of the bombed city of Aachen

Signalman Albert Drum (stood far left), Royal Corps of Signals at Aachen

Albert remained at Aachen, Germany, until the end of February 1946 when he was posted back to England to be demobilised from the army.

During the month Corporal Mildred Dean of the Auxiliary Territorial Service, daughter of Arthur Horace and Ellen Dean of 21 Fir Street, Cadishead, returned home on leave from Germany. Mildred, who was stationed at Kiel, with a signals unit, came home by aircraft. During her time with the ATS she had had many exciting experiences. During the London Blitz she worked on radar duties with an anti-aircraft unit and remained with it until it moved to Newcastle to combat the V1 flying-bombs on their way across the North Sea. Later, when the allied forces swept through France and Belgium, her unit was sent to Antwerp. During her service with the anti-aircraft unit in that city, flying bombs came over at the rate of one every six minutes. With the fall of Germany, she was transferred to signals and sent to Kiel with a detachment which comprised one officer and 28 other ranks. The detachment's job was to operate telephone switchboards in the Kiel area.

In August 1945 a special correspondent of *Sphinx Gazette*, an Army newspaper published in Kiel, visited the ATS detachment, and explained to his soldier readers just what sort of job they were doing. From the account, it would appear that at least 40 percent of the girls in this detachment were: *lovely, whilst the rest considered them no better than the average girl in other countries.* Fraternisation too was discussed and the general opinion among the girls was that far too much fuss had been made about it at home. Mildred's brother, Pilot Officer Arthur William 'Billy' Dean, RAF, had been held as a prisoner of war after his aircraft was shot down over German skies in 1944.

Corporal Mildred Dean, Auxiliary Territorial Service, in Kiel
(centre of photograph, wearing corporal stripes)

Corporal Mildred Dean, Auxiliary Territorial Service

A services wedding took place at St John's Church, Irlam on Saturday, 15th September when Able Seaman George L. Fisher married Edna Richmond, the only daughter of Mr and Mrs C. Richmond of 18 The Crescent, Higher Irlam. George was the only son of Mr and Mrs G. Fisher of 1 Railway Cottages, Barton Moss. He had been in the Navy three years, and had just returned from the Pacific. Edna served for three years in the Auxiliary Territorial Service with a heavy anti-aircraft battery.

On Saturday, 15th September nearly 100 children and adults from the section of the Crescent, Higher Irlam, which extended from Boundary Road to Princes Avenue, held a VJ party in the Higher Irlam Co-operative Hall. After tea, Mr S. Hobson, assisted by his daughter, entertained the audience with card and conjuring tricks, followed by dance music on the radio, and then an airman named Langley of the Royal Canadian Air Force entertained at the piano. Several of the children also provided entertainment. All present received sweets, biscuits and an apple, and later in the evening tea and further refreshments were served. The arrangements had been made by Messrs Kitchen, Lowndes, Lee and Brough and Mesdames Cheesbrough, Cook, Mason, Bleasdale, Crawford and Kitchen, ably assisted by Mesdames Harrison, Taylor, Brooks and Watson. The balance left in the fund was divided between the men from the area who were serving in the Forces.

The Crescent VJ Party

One of the unforeseen problems that demobilised servicemen had to face when they returned to the district was the difficulty of obtaining cigarettes due to rationing. During their service they had lost contact with local retailers who saved the severely rationed cigarettes for their regular customers. One local ex-serviceman commented: *I have been home for three weeks, and in that time have not been able to buy a packet of cigarettes in any of the local shops.*

Boys and girls of the Irlam and Cadishead Ambulance and Nursing Cadet Divisions celebrated VJ at a social evening at Fairhills Road School on Monday, 17th September. The celebrations were organised by Cadet Superintendents H.J. Lehrle and Miss Jackson, along with several members of the adult divisions, and were enjoyed by 45 cadets. Games and tea were followed by music and singing by Ambulance Cadets C. Jenkins, R. Bloor, Hollis, R. Dawson, N. Roberts, B. Toft, P. Hall, J. Moore, W. Ashton, Royle and Brock, and Nursing Cadets O. Collinge, M. Smith, J. Royle, B. Yates and J. Sisson. Cadet Superintendent Lehrle was the accompanist.

The marriage of Private Phyllis Young, Auxiliary Territorial Service, to Private William A. Whaites of the Canadian Army, took place at Rixton Methodist Church on Thursday, 20th September. Phyllis was the youngest daughter of Mr and Mrs R.C. Young of 40 School Lane, Hollins Green. Before joining the ATS she had attended the Methodist Church, Rixton, where she was a member of the choir. During the war she worked on radio location duties and then served with the Army Pay Corps. William was the eldest son of Mr and Mrs W. Whaites of Toronto, Canada.

A dance was held in the Irlam Conservative Club on Friday, 21st September which raised over £33 for King George's Fund for Sailors. Music was provided by Fred Broadhurst's Orchestra and Mr T. Goddard was Master of Ceremonies. A cake donated by Mary Beatrice Wiskin, realised over £19. Mary's husband, John, was a veteran of the First World War, who had served with the Royal Engineers and had been awarded the Distinguished Conduct Medal (DCM). Her brother, William Dennis, was killed in action in Belgium while serving with the Royal Scots in 1915. The Wiskin family owned a bakery in Irlam.

On the following day, Saturday, 22nd September, Sapper John Massey, Royal Electrical and Mechanical Engineers, married Gladys Dennett at St John's Church, Irlam. John had only just returned to England after four years overseas. He was born in Cadishead on 3rd December 1921. He was the adopted son of Mrs M. Whitfield of 34 Nelson Drive, Cadishead. He was educated at St Mary's School in Cadishead and Urmston Grammar School. John was called up in 1941 and after a tearful goodbye from his family at Irlam train station he had set off for military service without knowing where he would end up. Shortly afterwards, his mother answered a knock on the door and was surprised to find John on the doorstep. He had been posted to Woolden Hall on Cadishead Moss, so he borrowed a bicycle and then cycled home for a visit. He went on to serve in Palestine, Egypt, Italy, France and Belgium. One of the roles he had in the REME was as a despatch rider. During his service he was wounded by shrapnel. Earlier in 1945, while in Belgium, John had saved the life of a young child, who he had rescued from a destroyed building. As a thank you, the child's father, an optician, made him a pair of spectacles. Gladys was the elder daughter of Mr and Mrs J.H. Dennett of 70 Marlborough Road, Higher Irlam. She was employed as a crane driver on the Steelworks.

On Monday, 24th September Mrs Whitfield of 223a Liverpool Road, Cadishead, received a telegram from her husband, Gunner Frank Whitfield (pictured), in which he stated that he was safe and well in Australia. Frank had been taken prisoner at Singapore in February 1942. His wife received only four postcards from him during his four years in Japanese hands.

Mr and Mrs H. Southall of 26 Partington Avenue, Irlam, received word that their second son, Private Harry Southall, had been liberated from a Japanese prisoner of war camp. He had been taken prisoner at Singapore in 1942. Harry had moved out of the district before the war and resided with his wife at 6 Denton Grove, Kitt Green, Wigan.

All the returning Japanese prisoners of war received a letter from the King: *The Queen and I bid you a very warm welcome home. Through all the great trials and sufferings which you have undergone at the hands of the Japanese, you and your comrades have been constantly in our thoughts. We know from the accounts we have already received how heavy those sufferings have been. We know also that these have been endured by you with the highest courage. We mourn with you the deaths of so many of your gallant comrades. With all our hearts, we hope that your return from captivity will bring you and your families a full measure of happiness, which you may long enjoy together. George RI. September 1945.*

Sergeant Arthur Slater (pictured) was awarded a certificate for outstanding services rendered, signed by Lieutenant General Smith, general officer commanding, Persia and Iraq Command. Arthur, who joined the Army in December 1939, first went overseas at the beginning of 1940, and returned to England via Dunkirk. He went overseas again in July 1942, to Persia. He was the eldest son of Mr and Mrs A. Slater of 8 Marlborough Road, Higher Irlam. Before joining the Army he was employed by the Steelworks.

A meeting was held at the Council Offices on Wednesday, 26th September, between councillors and head teachers of the district, which decided that the formal VJ celebrations for the children should be held on Friday, 5th October. The deputy clerk to the Council, Fred Exley, said that the main reason the celebrations had not been earlier, was because many of the head teachers were on holiday when the news of the Japanese surrender came through, and so could not be contacted. The celebrations would be held by each school individually on the same day, and would take the form of a Victory tea, with a Punch and Judy show, and any other entertainment that could be arranged. Ice cream and fruit would also be provided. The Council granted one shilling a head for each child on the registers of the schools towards the cost of the celebrations. Local children attending grammar schools and full-time technical schools outside the district would be catered for at the district's high schools.

Arthur Robinson and Bandsman Alfred Higgs were welcomed home during the last week in September from overseas service. Both had been in action in the African and Italian campaigns. Alfred Higgs was born in 1911. He was married and resided at 17 Birch Avenue, Cadishead. He was a former member of the Home Guard which he had joined on 10th July 1940 as Private F56, 4 Platoon, D Company. He was called up in May 1941.

An all services wedding took place at St John's Church on Saturday, 29th September between Leading Aircraftman George William Hill, RAF and Private Frances Welch, Auxiliary Territorial Service. Flight Sergeant George Acton carried out the duties of groomsman. After the wedding the couple left for Blackpool, the bride wearing her ATS uniform.

Born in 1923, George was the eldest son of William and Marjory Hill of 1 Etherley Close, Higher Irlam. Before joining the RAF in November 1941, he was employed by the CWS and served as Private 188, in 2 Platoon, D Company of the local Home Guard. He was on leave from Denmark after seeing service in various European countries. Frances was the only daughter of Mr and Mrs Albert Welch of 100 Silver Street, Higher Irlam. She was previously employed by British Basket and Besto Company, Irlam.

Worried about the long waiting list at hospitals in the Manchester area, the Stretford Trades Council pressed the Lancashire County Council to open the big modern Park Hospital at Davyhulme to the public. The chairman of the Trades Council, Fred Ireland, said: *It is some time now since the American Army evacuated the hospital which is one of the finest and best equipped in the north. In the meantime the people of a wide area are deprived of its services. We are asking the county authority to get a move on with its conversion to civilian admissions.* Today this hospital is known as Trafford General Hospital and a memorial within the hospital records its role as an American military hospital during the Second World War.

OCTOBER

One hundred and twenty members of the local squad of the NFS, and their families, attended a farewell party at the Conservative Club, Irlam. After tea a concert was held at which the artists were Frank Readman (comedian), Miss M. Blundell (tap dancing), and the son of an old fireman, the late Mr F. Bradbury, who gave solos on a pair of spoons. Later in the evening there was dancing for the adults. Divisional Officer Drage, Senior Company Officer A. Royle and Company Officer Smith were all present but, Fire Chief Thomas Edgar could not attend as he was on duty. The concert was organised by Section Officer Oldham and Leading Fireman J. Eaton.

The wedding took place on Wednesday, 3rd October at St Peter's Church, Bentley, Doncaster, of Sergeant Edwin Gell, Royal Air Force and Miss Rose Mary Cannell of 31 Prospect Road, Bentley, Doncaster. Edwin was the only son of Mrs W. Leather of 97 Liverpool Road, Cadishead. In September 1940, he had been present when his stepfather's shop in Cadishead was destroyed by a German bomb (see earlier entry).

Chief Petty Officer (pilot) L/FX582317 **Thomas Bradshaw**, Royal Navy, was killed while on air operations, on Thursday, 5th October.

Thomas was serving with 802 Squadron at HMS *Wagtail*, a Royal Naval Air Station of the Fleet Air Arm, in Ayr, Scotland. He was flying a Vickers Supermarine Seafire F XV (the naval version of the Spitfire) which crashed into the sea (Firth of Clyde, off Ayr), shortly after pulling out of a dive from 34,000 to 25,000 feet after making an oxygen climb in the company of other aircraft.

Thomas was the eldest son of Arthur and Hannah Bradshaw of 31 Ferry Road, Irlam. He was educated at Irlam Central School and later Stretford Technical College, and was then employed as an apprentice bricklayer by Rich and Wrights of Warrington. He joined the Home Guard on 26th August 1941. In April 1943 he joined the Fleet Air Arm and, in February 1944, he was posted to Alma West in Canada for training. He received his wings in September 1944. Thomas has no known grave and is commemorated on the Lee-on-Solent Memorial to the missing. He was 20 years old. His name is missing from the Irlam and Cadishead War Memorial in Prince's Park. The CWGC Roll of Honour incorrectly states the year of his death as 1944 not 1945. The CWGC have been informed.

Local schools held their VJ celebrations on Friday, 5th October. During the afternoon a Punch and Judy show toured the district visiting all the schools. Until the show reached the various schools the children sang songs, danced and held plays. A tea party was arranged for the children, with food being brought from the school canteens. The children contributed jellies and cakes to the celebrations and at least one domestic science teacher had a full week's work making 300 cakes and the same number of jellies. After the tea each child received an apple and an orange. Monday, 8th October was declared a school holiday for the children.

Winston, a blue chequer cock pigeon, bred by Mr J. Thomason of 35 Lancaster Road, Cadishead, returned home again after three years of war service. Winston had been loaned to the Air Ministry and, during his time in the services, he was awarded the Meritorious Performances Certificate. Two more blue cocks from Mr Thomason's loft also received the award. Winston had made 53 operational flights and had flown thousands of miles carrying important messages from aircraft crews. After being demobilised the three pigeons returned to 'Civvy Street' for a well-earned rest, before being exhibited by Mr Thomason to raise money for the Old Folks' Treat. A letter from the Air Ministry was full of praise for the work that Winston and his two friends had done since passing out at the RAF training school at Thorney Island. Winston's record is summarised as follows: Released from the air he made the following times: 70 miles in two hours; 90 miles in one hour, 57 minutes; 145 miles in five hours, six minutes; 200 miles in five hours, 48 minutes; and 400 miles in 13 hours, 30 minutes. The Air Ministry emphasised that these times were made from flights in all directions. Winston's two loft mates who, in true Army style, were known merely as numbers, had also clocked some good times from France. NPS 42/47261 did 230 miles in six hours, 54 minutes; 130 miles in five hours, ten minutes, and 130 miles in four hours, 51 minutes; while NPS 42/7263 did 230 miles in six hours, 18 minutes, and 130 miles in five hours, ten minutes. In all Mr Thomason sent more than a hundred pigeons to the Air Ministry, but he was proudest of Winston and his two friends.

Private William S. Etherington returned home after three years in the Middle East. He had joined the Army in February 1942 and was posted overseas to North Africa and then later served in Pantelleria, Sicily and Italy. In July 1943 he was reported killed but fortunately, 13 days later, his parents received a letter from him explaining that he had been badly wounded and was in hospital. William was the second son of Mr and Mrs M.W. Etherington of 615 Liverpool Road, Irlam. Before joining the Army he was employed in the steel plant department of the Steelworks.

The wedding took place on Monday, 8th October at St Mary's Church, Cadishead, of Gunner Arthur Evans, the only son of Mr and Mrs G. Evans of 65 Fir Street, Cadishead, and Sarah M. Broom of Motherwell, Scotland. Private J. Taylor carried out the duties of groomsman. Arthur was on leave from Italy after having served all through the African and Italian campaigns.

St Peter's Church, Redcar, was the venue for the marriage of Corporal Harry Wood, eldest son of Mr and Mrs Jack Wood of 64 Harewood Road, Irlam and Beryl McLaughlin of Redcar, Yorks. Harry was born in 1922. Harry joined the Home Guard on 15th July 1940 and served as Private 388 in 2 Platoon of D Company until 6th January 1942, when he joined the Army. Beryl served as a nurse at Guisborough Hospital for over three years and Harry served as an instructor in the Army during the same period.

On Thursday, 12th October locals were treated to an unusual sight when German prisoners of war were put to work in Cadishead. A gang of about 30 prisoners were brought into the district by the Stretford Electricity Board to dig trenches for a cable from the transformer station near Hampton Road to the top end of Lords Street. The cable was for the Royal Ordnance Factory housing scheme.

Mr and Mrs Halliwell of 75 Liverpool Road, Irlam, received two letters which provided them with definite news that their son, Aircraftman Frank Halliwell, was safe. Frank had been taken prisoner in Java in 1942. The letters were written by an American soldier and an Australian nurse on behalf of Frank, who clearly was in no state to write his own letters. Though the letters were brief they hinted at the suffering of British prisoners in Japanese hands. The first letter was written by Robert E. McKillor, an American soldier, and posted from Okinawa on 17th September: *Dear Mr and Mrs Halliwell, I am an American soldier in the same hospital as Frank, and wrote the letter at his dictation. He came in last night by plane, and has the bed next to mine. He is in no pain – is as happy and cheerful a fellow as ever I saw, and may I add – the hungriest. There seems to be nothing much wrong that a little time and treatment won't cure, so do not worry about him at all. He is to start out as soon as all arrangements can be completed – wish I were going along too. There is not much more to be said, I will let him tell all. Sincerely, Robert E. McKinnor.*

Dear Mom and Dad and Spen, at last the day we have been waiting for has arrived, it sure makes us all a happy bunch of fellows. No more soup and rice for meals but good old civilised food again. I just can't get enough of it – it tastes so good. As you can see by the address I am no longer in Japan, having flown out to Okinawa to an American hospital. I am not in a very bad condition – a slight injury to my spine and a general rundown condition. Nothing serious – no need to worry – just have to be in bed for a while. I am hoping to fly home by way of the

States, and be home by Christmas. So get ready – I have quite a few to make up for. You won't recognise me. I have grown up now, and it has been so long since you have seen me. I am all in one piece and anxious to get home and see you all. Well I guess this is all for now, and I hope to see you soon.

Frank's second letter was written by an Australian nurse in an American hospital in Manila, Philippines, which stated that he was getting the best of treatment. He had met with an accident in Japan, but assured his parents that it was nothing to worry about. Frank, who was 24 years of age when he joined the RAF in 1941, went overseas in November of the same year. He was sent to the Far East to Sumatra after the fall of Singapore. He was taken prisoner in Java in February 1942.

Lance Corporal 7641037 Alfred Pattison became the first local man to return home from a Far East prisoner of war camp. He landed at Southampton, on Monday, and arrived in Cadishead on Tuesday evening, 9th October. He had been taken prisoner at the fall of Singapore in 1942. For 12 months there was no news of him until his parents received a card stating that he was a prisoner. During his 3½ years in captivity, he was forced to labour in railway construction gangs, and though he bore the signs of the hardships he had endured he was reasonably fit and well.

Lance Bombardier Fred Thomason arrived at his home, 486 Manchester Road, Hollins Green, after an arduous journey from the Far East. He had been taken prisoner by the Japanese on 7th January 1942, during fighting on the Slim River, Malaya. He was marched with others to Port Dickson, arriving there 24 days later, a distance of 200 miles. One of his friends, Gunner Aaron Taylor of Croft, was more fortunate, managing to escape capture by lying in a slimy ditch. Fred spent the next nine months in Kuala Lumpur prison, Malaya, and later he was admitted to Changi Camp hospital in Thailand suffering from dysentery. In May 1943 he was sent to another part of Thailand to drive Japanese transport wagons but when he arrived at the camp he was re-assigned to work as a cook. By the end of the year he was sent to Singapore. In this camp they had three wireless sets, one of which was hidden in a soldier's water bottle. In May 1944 he was sent to Changi gaol and while there he was put to work constructing an airfield. Fred spoke highly of the Chinese civilians who gave them food, money and other necessities. His treatment at the hands of the Japanese varied from place to place; he received good treatment in a camp near Bangkok, where he was employed on railway construction but at other places his treatment was not so good. For two years he had no boots or other footwear, and his only clothing was a sort of Japanese loin cloth, known by British troops as the G string.

His friend, Leonard Wright, was wounded during the same action and captured at Singapore over a month later. They were both put to work on railway construction work in Siam and, while not in actual contact, were able to communicate with each other by letter. The lack of news from Fred during more than three years' captivity had caused considerable anxiety at home, and the family were greatly relieved to hear of his liberation.

Gunner Len Wright arrived home in Hollins Green in the early hours of Saturday morning, 20th October, showing traces of the hardships he had endured since his capture on 15th February 1942. His main problem was an ulcerated leg, which he had suffered from for three years. After a short time at Changi gaol he was sent to No. 1 Camp, Siam where he was put to work on the Bangkok-Moulmein railway (notoriously known as the 'Death Railway' and made famous by the film *Bridge over the River Kwai*). Len worked on the railway until September 1944, and found the conditions very hard. The Siamese people that he came across during his time in Thailand treated the British prisoners with kindness. He returned to Singapore by railway cattle truck, into which 32 men were crammed, and during the five day journey they were only provided with five meals. At Singapore he was put to work at the dockyard where he found conditions to be easier although the food was bad. In March 1945 he was among 5,000 prisoners who were put aboard a 3,000 ton ship bound for Saigon, in French Indochina (modern day Vietnam). During the five day voyage the men were held in very cramped conditions and only received daily rations of three bowls of rice, and one and a half pints of water. Before reaching Saigon, the convoy was attacked by American planes, and two merchant ships and one destroyer were sunk. At Saigon, he worked on the construction of an airfield and it was there that Len experienced the worst treatment of his captivity.

Len's return to England, after more than three years in captivity, began by an air trip from Saigon to Rangoon, and ended when the liner *Orduna* berthed at Liverpool on the weekend of 13th October. He had actually put on weight during his captivity and looked surprisingly fit, even though he was suffering from malaria. The authors had the great pleasure of meeting Len in 2010, who openly shared the terrible ordeals he had experienced while in captivity; fortunately these experiences were tempered by his irrepressible sense of humour. When the ship entered the Mersey estuary, Len recognised some landmarks: *It were foggy, we were stood on the side, I said we're in Liverpool. 'How the hell do you know we're in Liverpool?' I said 'there's the lightship we've just passed it.' Because we'd been to the Isle of Man and Ireland before and we come in and there's the sun and it was beautiful, oh there was thousands. A big speaker 'nobody must come on this boat' it said, who said it I don't know. I found my brother and then they all come and Jack's there [brother-in-law] and they said 'the twelve prisoners of war, will you go to the top of the gangway.' So we had to go and get our kit bags what we had, and we went in there, side of boat, Jack's on the boat, he got hold of my kit bag and put it on his shoulder and I said 'how did you get on here?' 'I told them I was a detective,' he said, [laughter] and he came on* board, took it off me, and took me straight into the canteen. At Liverpool they said right, jump in this car, this van, four of us and we went to Maghull transit camp then they give us a lovely dinner and then after that we was examined and we had to have baths and all that and different stuff, and then they said we'll give you your back pay and everything and then it was about not far off midnight. They said you can go home if you want if you can get anything, you can go home. So I said to myself, blow it I'll ring Elsie Tonge at the Post Office at Hollins Green, it was gone midnight. And I said 150, ringing away, then I rung again and it rung away, then I rung again and then I said to myself she's coming, she said 'hello, what do you want?' 'Sorry Elsie, it's Leonard.' 'Leonard, how are you?' she said. 'Oh', I said 'I'm alright, can you tell Jack Lowe to come for me.' She said 'I will.' 'Mine's 1151, ring me back here.' Ten minutes later she said, 'he's coming straight away' and Jack and our John come. Then we went in the canteen and I said 'what do want drink Jack?' He had a glass of beer and I had a shandy and I don't know what our John had. Then she says to me after 'do you want any fags?' 'Am I entitled to some?' She says 'you're entitled to 300.' So I had Craven A, Senior Service with tabs on, so I paid for 'em. Then I got in the car and I come home and there there's a lad waiting, he said 'hello Len,' and I said 'and who are you?' He said 'I'm Jimmy Newton,' he was this tall when I went. By the heck he did seem changed. They give us cigarettes every time we stopped free from Red Cross and then our Elsie and them, I kissed 'em all, and what do think was on't table? A rice pudding [laughter]. I said 'rice pudding, I'll eat it!' Four years. And it was just a lovely homecoming.

Gunner Len Wright (centre of back row, without cap) returning home to England

A major savings event, Thanksgiving Week, took place from 20th to 27th October in Irlam and Cadishead with a target of £100,000. The purpose of the savings week was to give thanks for victory in a practical way by helping the country to meet its huge financial obligations and maintain its position among the leading nations of the world. A programme of events had been arranged, which consisted largely of social events. On Saturday, 20th October, Thanksgiving Week was officially opened by Jack Jones MP, supported by James Sinclair Kerr, the managing director of the Lancashire Steel Corporation. This was the first time that a savings week in the district had been opened by local personages, which was an acknowledgement of the work done for the town by Jack Jones and Mr Kerr as head of its largest industrial organisation.

On the same day there was a parade of Army, Navy and Air Force personnel, an ATS unit, Army cadets, St John Ambulance, scouts, girl guides, cubs and brownies, led by the Barton Hall Band. After the parade, the official opening of the savings week took place at the Council Offices. Councillor Keal, deputy chairman of the Council and chairman of the local Savings Committee, deputising for Councillor McLean, began the opening by reading telegrams from the Chancellor of the Exchequer and the Chairman of the National Savings Committee wishing the district success during the week. Declaring the week open James Sinclair Kerr said in his 18 years' association with Irlam and Cadishead he had had to make many appeals for various district charities, and the people had always given freely: *The money is now needed for reconstruction. We have finished with our victory parties, which we richly deserved and now we come to the time when we have to reconstruct. But we cannot do this if we cannot get the money. We are not demanding your money, but asking you to lend it to the Government. If, at any time, through illness or through want, you need to withdraw it you can always get it back. I am asking you to let yourselves go and contribute all you can towards this figure of £100,000. We all know the money it was costing in war for destruction; now we need that money for reconstruction. We in this country are at grips with finance. There are two alternatives to not saving, one is the Government taking the money by indirect taxation, and the other is inflation. We don't want either of these.*

The Naval detachment during the Thanksgiving parade

I do feel that the people of Irlam and Cadishead will not let us down, Jack Jones MP, said, *I have seen a lot in the Guardian about the 'Town I Want,' but you cannot get anything without paying for it. All the amenities wanted would not fall from heaven; you will have to pay for it. We want your money and I am not being nice about it either. It is your job and my job, particularly all you people who have been making good money on the works throughout the war. I am inviting you all to get your hands in your pockets and go along to the centres today. Everywhere else targets have been smashed, and we want to smash ours. We want to smash it by Wednesday, and then go on for more.* At the close of his address, Jack handed over a cheque for £3,000 to James Sinclair Kerr on behalf of the British Iron, Steel and Kindred Trades Association. The cheque represented the goodwill of the 2,000 members of the union at Irlam. A vote of thanks to James Sinclair Kerr and Jack Jones was proposed by Mr H. Wilde of the National Savings Movement, who said they had done more than anyone else to promote savings on the Steelworks. Irlam and Cadishead had set a good target, and he appealed to all to put all they could into savings and not let the district down.

Irlam Council Offices during Thanksgiving Week

In the evening a dance was held in the Steelworks canteen. Jack Jones introduced Sub-Lieutenant Austin, MP for the Stretford Division, who, in a brief speech, emphasised the need for savings which would be vital for the benefits to be enjoyed by all when peacetime conditions returned. The next day a concert was held at the Palace cinema, and on Monday there was a whist drive at Irlam Co-operative Hall. On Wednesday a dance was held at Irlam Conservative Club. A great deal of interest centred on a talent spotting competition which had been held in various works in the district, with the final of the competition being held at Irlam Junior School on Thursday evening. Six artists had been chosen and people were so keen to hear them that they crowded into the hall, stood in corridors and even in the school playground, despite the wet and windy weather. To ensure fairness, the winners were selected by judges who were not allowed to see the artists but measured their popularity by listening to the amount of applause each received. John Moore of the Steelworks won first place; W. Banks, also of the Steelworks was second and Vi and Harry of the CWS finished third. During the evening further appeals were made for increased savings and Mr H. Wilde, stressing the urgency of the situation, said that at least 9,000 people in the district had not invested during the week. He asked everyone present to do all in their power to ensure that the district achieved its target. A film show for young people and adults was organised at Irlam Council School on Thursday, the youngsters attending in the afternoon and the adults at night. A similar film show, with the same arrangements for children and adults, was held at Cadishead Council School on Friday, and the week ended with another dance at the Steelworks canteen on Saturday.

Up to Wednesday, 23rd October daily totals for savings compared favourably with those in Salute the Soldier Week which took place in June 1944. But by Thursday night it was found that the Thanksgiving Week total was £11,000 below the corresponding day in Salute Week and it appeared that the district would, for the first time, fail to reach the target of £100,000. The daily totals for Salute Week compared with Thanksgiving Week were as follows:

SALUTE		THANKSGIVING	
Saturday	£23,000	Saturday	£15,000
Wednesday	£44,000	Wednesday	£45,000
Thursday	£65,000	Thursday	£54,000

Officials of the savings movement were worried that the Thanksgiving Week target would not be achieved and we can safely assume that, as no further news was published, the district missed its target.

Edmund Potts, treasurer of the Irlam and Cadishead branch of the Royal National Lifeboat Institution, received a letter from Lieutenant Colonel Satterthwaite, OBE, secretary of the RNLI, praising the work of the branch: *I have received with very much pleasure your branch statement of accounts for the year ending September 30th. It depicts another excellent response to the appeal of the lifeboat service. It is also the last record of your branch activities in the war years, and it would be appropriate that my warmest thanks for the past year's work should be coupled with an expression of heartfelt gratitude and sincere thanks to all who have given so generously in personal service and contributions during those grim years. In spite of everything that happened or threatened, our work went on, inland as well as on the coast. The lifeboat service remained throughout a voluntary service, and it is a remarkable fact that at the end of a war, which caused such destruction and such complete disruption in the life and industry of the nation and the individual, our fleet continues to operate in that high state of efficiency demanded by the conditions under which its work had* *to be performed. Our pride in this achievement is shared by you all, and we are deeply grateful to you, to your branch officials and honorary helpers, whose grand and constant endeavour has assisted to make it possible.*

NOVEMBER

On 2nd November Leading Air Mechanic William Whalley, RAF, only son of Mr and Mrs H. Whalley of 3 Graham Crescent, Cadishead, married Audrey Negus, eldest daughter of Mr and Mrs G.W. Negus of 296 Albert Street, Marlborough, Queensland, Australia. The marriage took place at Marlborough Wesleyan Church, Queensland. One of his friends, Air Mechanic Arthur Briers was best man and the groomsman was Pilot Officer Beverley Hill. William was well-known in the district where he had been a member of Irlam Steelworks cricket team.

The annual meeting of the Irlam and Cadishead branch of the British Legion and of the British Legion Club, held at the club on Sunday, 4th November, reported a year of excellent progress. Opening the meeting, the branch's president, Mr J.A. Massie, said they met under far better circumstances than at the last annual meeting. In a reference to the Benevolent Fund, he said it had been formed to help members who needed assistance. Before the fund was established it had been the usual practice for the Sports Committee to organise events to raise money for individuals in need, however, popular members of the club benefited more than others. In addition, further calls were made on the Sports Committee and often they had several calls at the same time. The Benevolent Fund was introduced to provide a fairer system. The committee granted a loan of £100 until efforts could be started, but this was soon repaid and a further £155 was added to the fund. He, personally, felt proud of the Sports Committee, and he appealed to members to give them their full support. Concluding, Mr Massie urged the members to take an interest in the club.

Peter Barrow, DCM, called attention to the fact that at the North West Area Conference the branch brought forward a resolution regarding pensions for ex-servicemen who were suffering from psycho-neurosis. The resolution was well supported and was again brought forward at the Annual Conference in London where it had the support of Sir Ian Fraser, who had insisted that something must be done for psycho-neurosis cases. Benjamin Neville JP, the branch chairman, pointed out that the Ministry of Pensions had at least begun to realise the seriousness of this problem and in many instances men suffering from psycho-neurosis were now getting pensions.

In his annual report Benjamin Neville said vouchers had been granted to 14 members and convalescent home treatment to six members. In connection with this he had been asked to write to Mr Cox, the manager of the Byng House Convalescent Home expressing the thanks of their members who had been there. They had had a wonderful time and had been treated like Lords. Special grants had also been made to members and he had been in personal attendance at the branch to give advice on matters relating to servicemen, their pensions and to dependants. On those occasions there had sometimes been as many as 30 people seeking advice. In this he had been ably assisted by Peter Barrow who had been extremely helpful. On the pensions side they had been successful in two cases brought before the tribunal.

Mr Frier, secretary of the Stretford branch, stated that ex-servicemen in Irlam and Cadishead were getting the full support of the Legion. The demand for the services of the Legion would not lessen, but would increase and the only way to handle the problem was to have good officials and to back them up. He emphasised that the Services Committee had not been formed to serve only members, but to serve widows and dependants, and all who had been in the Forces, and the money raised on Poppy Day was for this purpose. He urged members to help educate the public to realise the value of the Legion to servicemen and ex-servicemen. Many people regarded Legion clubs as 'boozing places,' but the social side was only a small part of the Legion's work. They could convince the public that the Legion had something to offer by continuing to carry out their duty to the ex-servicemen.

After the balance sheet and statement of accounts had been read and approved, the auditor congratulated members on the sound financial position of the club. Gross turnover was £14,497, and gross profit on sales £2,375. This, added to subscriptions, donations, games and interest on bonds and other items amounted to £2,709. The total assets of the club were £7,227. A vote of thanks to the officials was proposed by Mr Massie, who congratulated them on their work. Their committees worked harmoniously, and he gave members credit for electing the right men for the right job. At the close of the meeting Mr Heyworth of Eccles branch, proposed that the two branches should get closer together. Both clubs had excellent sports committees, and he urged the respective secretaries to consider, now that transport was less difficult, renewing sports meetings. Mr Heyworth also announced that the branch had received a signal honour in the election of its chairman, Benjamin Neville, to the Area Committee.

The following officials were elected: Mr J.A. Massie, president; Mr J. Butler, vice president; Benjamin Neville, chairman; Mr J. Statham, vice-chairman; Mr G. McCallum, treasurer. Committee: Thomas Walton, Jack Newton, Henry Grindley, Archer Kell, Jack Carter, Harry Prosser, Herbert Ditchfield, Ken Taylor and Messrs J. Bickerdike, J. Crone, T. Williams and A. Hughes.

The *Guardian* carried a story about an unnamed old warrior from the district, a First World War veteran with several sons and a son-in-law who were doing their share, who was a member of the Home Guard and was responsible for the cooking. On one occasion when he and other Home Guard members were on exercises, he was detailed to get the lads something hot to eat. When he went to the butchers to draw the ration, he was met with faintly amused contempt by the butcher who ridiculed the idea of Home Guards having meat. *Meat!* he said, *Phooey! Home Guards has bones!*

And bones they got. Maybe the butcher had heard about the boys of the bulldog breed and decided to put them on a suitable diet.

Armistice Day dawned brightly on Sunday, 11th November with a crisp, cold snap in the air. At 10.15am, ex-servicemen fell in at the British Legion, while others, including members and officials of the Council, pre-service youth organisations including Army cadets and ATC, St John Ambulance Brigade Cadet and Nursing Divisions, scouts and guides, assembled at the Council Offices, where they met up with members of the British Legion, carrying the standard of the Legion. Councillor Keal (deputy chairman of the Council) and Edwin Jones led off the procession to the beat of drums. After a lapse of seven years, the melancholy notes of the *Last Post* sounded again at the War Memorial and brought back poignant memories of earlier Armistice Days to those who assembled in Prince's Park on Sunday morning. Men and women who had served in the Second World War, veterans of the First World War and relatives of both, stood silently around the memorial and listened to the simple service and, for a space, remembered those who, in two wars, had given their lives in the cause of freedom. The two minutes' silence was broken by the wail of a ship's siren, a motor horn blared and car tyres were heard along the main road. The *Guardian* commented: *These things combined, if not to totally destroy the solemnity of the occasion, at least to mar it. It was as if, in the modern atomic age, time could not be spared to remember, for two short minutes, those who, twice in half a lifetime, had gone out to battle for the things in which they believed. The silence was broken by the 'Last Post' followed by the 'Reveille'. Leslie Jones conducted a short service; the opening prayer was followed by the hymn 'Fight the Good Fight,' accompanied by the Irlam Prize Band, conducted by Mr R. Hesford. The lesson was followed by the hymn 'O God, our help in ages past,' and then the Benediction. The National Anthem brought an end to the first Armistice Day (peace-time) for seven years.*

The attendance at the Armistice service was disappointing, particularly bearing in mind that services had not been held for several years and it was the first opportunity for people to gather in remembrance of the sacrifices made by servicemen and women in the district. True to their tradition, which continues to this day, the scouts turned out in full force but other bodies including, surprisingly, the British Legion, were far from strong. The *Guardian* commented: *Can it be that, now we are more or less secure again, we are just damnably indifferent? Anyway, a word of praise for those Legion members who did turn out. Though old Anno Domini has taken a bit of spring out of some of them, they still clomped the old left, right, left, right with the precision of guardsmen. Headed by the world's youngest grandfather, who carried the Legion standard, they slogged up Irlam Brow to the Council Offices, with not more than a couple of wheezes apiece, and relatively fresh, took their places in the parade. After the service, the Legion's underground movement made it known by means of battalion runners and the bush telegraph, that every Legionnaire who paraded would get a pint when the detachment arrived back at the 'Bomb and Dagger.' That did it. The lads fell in with unwonted alacrity, sniffed the breeze like hounds on the hunt, and tore away at a rate of knots that would make a commando forced march look like a funeral procession. And, at their head, moving along at a speed which, though there was no wind, made the Legion flag stand out stiffly behind him, was the world's youngest grandfather. Believe me, there's more than a spark in the old sweats yet.*

A letter printed in the *Guardian* gave some indication of the dilapidated condition of the War Memorial at this point in time: *I, in common with many others who attended the Armistice Day service in Prince's Park, was shocked at the shabby state of the War Memorial. Huge cracks in the base and a general air of neglect make it indeed a pitiful memorial to gallant men who gave their lives. The condition is so bad that many persons present at the service – persons who lost sons and husbands and fathers in the First and Second World Wars, not only felt bitter, but expressed that bitterness in scathing terms. Something must be done, and done immediately. In its present state the memorial is an insult to the men whose memory it purports to perpetuate. I have said before – and I say again – that I am not in favour of memorials. Cold stone, no matter how artistically carved, or elaborately adorned cannot do justice to the men who died. But, as we in our wisdom decided to erect memorials after the last war, the least we can do now they are erected is to maintain them in a state of decent repair.* The old memorial was replaced in 1949.

Able Seaman D/JX516538 Robert Whittaker served on board the Submarine Depot Ship, HMS *Maidstone*. Bob was born on 6th August 1924 at 1 Ash Avenue, Cadishead. He went to Cadishead Senior School, then worked as a butcher for the Eccles Co-operative Society until he was called up into the Navy in April 1943. After training he was posted to Algiers where he joined HMS *Maidstone*, which had been stationed at Algiers. In November 1943 *Maidstone* sailed from Algiers to the Eastern Fleet, at Ceylon (now Sri Lanka) and then Freemantle, Australia. He returned to the UK, via South Africa, in late 1945. In November 1945, the *Maidstone* docked in England with 400 returning POWs from the Far East, including survivors from HMS *Exeter* which was sank off Java by the Japanese in 1942. Bob explained: *And then we sailed from there* [Freemantle], *oh we must have been there two or three months, we sailed from there round to Sydney and then from Sydney we went to, through the Malacca Straits, New Guinea, and we finished up in the Philippines. And I was in the Philippines when the war in the Pacific ended, you know Japan, surrendered. And when we were up in the Philippines there was no shore leave at all, we were on the ship all the time and NAAFI, they fetched beer, it was port watch one night and you got two tickets and you got two bottles of beer and the next night was starboard watch, that's how they went, but with luck having it with being a butcher and we had the fridges all the beer was stored in the fridges so we were never short of a bottle of beer [laughter]. And then we went from the Philippines* [Subic Bay, from May to September 1945], *we went to Hong Kong, to take the surrender of Hong Kong, and the flag that flew over Hong Kong they said was framed and hung in the mess room, in the dining room of HMS Maidstone. And then from Hong Kong we went back to Western Australia, back into Freemantle because quite a lot of the crew had got married there, but while we were in there, on our way back, we picked prisoners of war up out of the Japanese, out of a camp, oh there was naval, army, air force personnel, and then, we went back into Freemantle because all these prisoners of war were taken off to hospital to check them up, see if they were alright. I remember there were two marine butchers [among the prisoners], I was a butcher in the Navy, and there was two marine butchers, and one of them I think he was 6 feet 8 inches and he weighed seven stone something, they were in a terrible condition. And a lot of them had I think what they called beri-beri, you know if you press your leg you know it comes up but if they pressed theirs the indentation stopped there, oh they were in a terrible state. Course then we came back to Freemantle and I took a week's leave when we got back and went up to Kalgoorlie, it was a gold mining centre. Back from Kalgoorlie, back on the ship, and of all the prisoners that had been to hospital there was only one that was kept and they found out he'd got TB and he was the only one, all the others they all passed out, and we had them back on board and then we sailed from there to Durban. But we didn't go into Durban, we were outside, I think we went in for water more or less. But there was a place there in Durban called the Mayor's Parlour and all these people that were in this Mayor's Parlour they'd come out with gifts for these prisoners of war, clothing and ..., and they gave every one of the crew a bag full of mixed fruit. Then we went from there, from Durban, we went round to Simonstown which in them days was a naval base not far from Cape Town. And believe me it was the worst place I ever went to was Cape Town, apartheid was on and I thought it was disgusting the way they were treated these people. In fact the provost marshal came on board and he told us that if we were walking down the street and a black person came with a pram make sure that she got off the footpath, well you were never brought up that way, was you? If you were in England and somebody was coming with a pram you got out of the way, and I thought to myself what a place to come. Then when we got on the train to go into Cape Town we got in carriages and the blacks were in like cattle trucks at the back, and each station you went into it had a big notice 'blacks only,' full of police, and only black people could get off the train, or on. It's perhaps the wrong word but they were treated like slaves the blacks. Anyway when we left there, we went to Gibraltar and that was only a water stop and then we came back to Portsmouth. In November [1945] we docked at Portsmouth and all the people, the relations to the prisoners were all on the dockside, they all come on board the ship to meet. I went back on the ship and we went, she was going to have a big refit, and we went up to Plymouth, I don't know what happened but it wasn't done there and we sailed then to John Smith's in Greenock on the Clyde and something happened there and it wasn't there, then we went back then to Pompey, to Portsmouth and that's where I got my demob off the ship. I think it was getting on for three years that we were on board.*

And what of Bob's time in the Navy? *Perhaps enjoyable's the wrong word, but I've no regrets of being in the Navy. If I hadn't have been there I wouldn't have seen half the world the same as I did do.*

Commissioner **Rosina Battles** died in Lubbecke, Germany, as the result of an accident on 10th November (although the Commonwealth War Graves Commission records the date of death as 19th November). Rosina and three other women died of carbon monoxide poisoning due to a faulty heater in the dormitory they were sleeping in.

Commissioner Rosina Battles

Rosina served with the Allied Control Commission (British Element) for Germany, and had only been in the country for three days. After the war Germany was divided into three administration areas control by the three powers: USA, USSR and the UK and the role of the Allied Control Commission (British Element) was to support the Allied military government and to take on the role of local government. It was responsible for public safety and health, transport, intelligence (which included rooting out war criminals) and housing.

Born in 1922, Rosina (known as Rose) was the youngest daughter of Martin and Rosina Battles of 34 Francis Road, Irlam. She was formerly employed in the wages department of the Royal Ordnance Factory at Risley. She was described as one of the most popular young people in the district, with a wide circle of friends, particularly among the congregation at St Teresa's Church.

Munster Heath War Cemetery, Telgte, Germany
(Inset: Rosina Battle's CWGC headstone)

The funeral took place at Lubbecke on Tuesday, 13th November, following a Requiem Mass at the Roman Catholic Church, and service in the private chapel of the 23rd Scottish General Hospital. Six sergeants from the local administration unit carried the coffin, which was draped with the Union Jack, to the graveside in the British Military Cemetery, where the service was conducted by Reverend C.J.M. Faber. A bugler sounded the *Last Post*.

Among those present were Major Meller, representing the staff group of the Control Commission for Germany (British Element); Major Kirk, camp commandant of Lubbecke; RSM Garrett, representing warrant officers, NCOs and other ranks; Junior Commander Castle, ATS and Junior Commander Dalmer, ATS. The civilian side was represented by Mr V.G.F. Bovenizer, civilian establishments officer; Miss Shaw, civilian welfare officer; Miss Tuke, Miss Tinkler, Miss Thorogood, Miss Andrews and Miss Heaps. Rosina was later interred at Munster Heath War Cemetery, Telgte, Germany. Her name does not appear on the Irlam and Cadishead War Memorial in Prince's Park.

Flight Sergeant Hubert Jones was married at St Paul's Church, Sale, on Saturday, 10th November to Margaret Henshall, eldest daughter of Mr and Mrs N. Henshall of 46 Dane Road, Sale. Before the war they had both worked together at Hills Aircraft Factory, Trafford Park. Before joining the RAF Hubert was employed as an inspector. He was the second son of Mrs and the late Mr H. Jones of 252 Liverpool Road, Cadishead.

Warrant Officer 3652105 George Wilson received a commission to lieutenant quartermaster on 16th November. In order to take up his commission George had to be discharged from the colours. His 'Report on Leaving the Colours' described his military conduct as exemplary and gave the following reference: *An excellent type. He is energetic, alert, interested, his personal integrity is of the highest order, his sense of responsibility keen. His ability to control others is marked. He is most highly recommended for a superior position of trust.* Shortly after being commissioned he flew to India.

George was born in Birkenhead on 27th February 1914, the eldest son of George and Sarah Elizabeth Wilson (nee Green). He was a former pupil of Padgate School, Warrington. The Wilson family moved to 63 Boundary Road, Higher Irlam around 1928. By 1939 they were residing at 7 Francis Road, Irlam. George worked as a boiler maker at the Steelworks before joining the South Lancashire Regiment on 28th November 1932 and gained his first 'stripe' in the next year. He was made sergeant in 1937 and colour-sergeant on the outbreak of war. He married Hilda Vaudrey in September 1938.

George served in France with the BEF from 5th October 1939 until the evacuation of Dunkirk, arriving back in England on 1st June 1940. His promotion to warrant officer came in 1941. He went overseas with his battalion on D-Day and on that day, his brother, Benjamin, died of wounds.

George was wounded on 18th July and was returned to England two days later. By the end of his Army career he had reached the position of Captain and had served in India, Singapore and Hong Kong. He died in 1961 and was given a full military funeral.

Captain George Wilson, South Lancashire Regiment

In an open letter, Reverend Motson of St Paul's Methodist Church, Irlam, thanked members of the Forces for the services they had rendered through the long years of the war, welcomed them home and offered them an invitation to join in the Church's activities: *There is a great work to be done by all those who are anxious to see a better way of life in the world of tomorrow. We believe there is a job for every one of us in the life of the Church. In addition to the central act of worship we are engaged in the following activities; Sunday school, choir, women's fellowship, youth centre, guild fellowship, dramatic society and men's fellowship. We feel that through these channels we are performing a comprehensive ministry, and that we are providing those conditions which by their appeal to all sides of life, social, physical, cultural and spiritual, will help to promote the growth of balanced Christian personalities. We are humbled when we think of the hardships that have been endured and the sacrifices which have been made to preserve our life and to establish our freedom, especially do we honour those who have laid down their lives in the fight for liberty and peace. We ask for your cooperation in the future task of making a world worthy of their sacrifice. We pray that God will bless us all in the work to which we are called, so that under the guidance of His spirit we may help to build His kingdom here.*

An American soldier wrote a letter of thanks to the people of Irlam and Cadishead with a request that it should not be published before 17th November: *As an American soldier leaving for the United States, I wish to extend my utmost appreciation to the many friends that I have made in Irlam. Though I part sadly, I wish to thank all of you for so cheerfully filling so many of leisure hours during the past 3½ years in England. Pfc Leslie J. Cross.* On behalf of the people of the district, the *Guardian* thanked Private First Class Cross and hosts of other GIs for coming to Britain in its hour of need.

Warrant Officer Frank Dixon (pictured) returned home on leave on Saturday, 17th November. He had only recently been promoted to warrant officer at the young age of 20 years old. Only one year before, he had been promoted to flight sergeant (air gunner). He was the son of Mr and Mrs Frank Dixon of 14 Lords Street, Cadishead. Frank junior was a former pupil of Cadishead Council School and Cadishead Senior School and was apprenticed as an electric welder boilersmith at the Steelworks, before joining the RAF.

More than 130 guests, adults and children, enjoyed a fine tea at the Silver Street VJ Party, at the Higher Irlam Co-operative Hall on Saturday. Later in the evening each child was presented with a gift of a toy or game, from Mrs R. Bailey. A film show, and songs by Mr E. Whitter, and tap dancing by M. Givens and M. Stokes completed the entertainment and the evening was brought to an end by dancing. Mesdames T. Shaw, B. Ogden, J. Harris, N. Whitter, A. Grant and D. Taylor were the organising committee. The balance of the fund left over, amounting to £4, was equally divided between the Nursing Association and the Old Folks' Treat.

Silver Street VJ Party

The wedding of Sergeant Walter Hall, Corps of Military Police, and Betty Joan Wyatt of Stansted, Essex, took place at St Mary's Church, Stansted, Essex, on Saturday, 17th November. Walter was on a short leave having returned from 4½ years abroad. He was the youngest son of Mr and Mrs 'Herbie' Hall of 26 Bankfield Avenue, Cadishead. He was a regular soldier, having joined the Army c.1931 and serving in various parts of the world. When Walter had first enlisted his sister, Nancy, was a schoolgirl and they had not met since. By the time of his wedding Nancy was a sergeant serving with the WAAF. She enlisted in 1942, having previously worked at the CWS Soap Works. Nancy was born in 1918 and educated at Irlam Central School.

Gunner Joseph Sidney Hindley, the 24 year old son of Mr and Mrs Hindley of 11 Poplar Grove, Cadishead, was mentioned in dispatches for outstanding services. Joseph, who joined the Royal Artillery in February 1942, went overseas on D-Day and served continuously in the campaign in France, through Belgium and Holland and on to the Rhine. He participated in Operation Market Garden in September 1944 and the advance to Grave. He later described crossing the bridge at Nijmegen on a daily basis as: *head down and throttle open*. Before joining the Army he was employed as a bricklayer by Messrs Higgs and Hill.

Thirty-seven year old Corporal Fred Massey of the Royal Engineers returned home from Greece after 2½ years' service in the Middle East. Fred was the fifth son of Mr J. Massey and the late Mrs Massey of 9 Atherton Lane, Cadishead. He resided with his wife in Kenmore Grove, Cadishead. Before joining the Army he worked at the CWS Soap Works.

Sergeant Walter Hall, Corps of Military Police

Sergeant Nancy Hall, WAAF

Gunner Joseph Hindley, Royal Artillery
Caen 1944

Signalman Albert Drum, Royal Corps of Signals

Despite their time overseas during the war years, the district was never far from the thoughts of local soldiers, who could be very generous to their home town. For example, John M. Connelly, then serving with the 70th Field Regiment, Royal Artillery, Central Mediterranean Force, sent home a donation for the Old Folks' Treat: *Sir, please find enclosed a postal order to the value of five shillings. Not much but it might buy one of the Old Folks a pint (if he knows where to get it) or something anyway. I am sorry it is not more, but I was unable to get any other postal orders from our post clerk. I hope to be in England this Christmas and I shall certainly look out for some of the things you have 'cribbed' about in your column for the last three years.*

Signalman 2342408 Albert Edward Drum of the Royal Corps of Signals was mentioned in dispatches for distinguished service in 1945 (*London Gazette* 29th November 1945).

By the KING'S Order the name of
Signalman A.E. Drum
Royal Corps of Signals,
was published in the London Gazette on
29 November, 1945.
as mentioned in a Despatch for distinguished service.
I am charged to record
His Majesty's high appreciation.

J.J. Lawson

Secretary of State for War

Albert enlisted on 2nd May 1940 at Rhos-on-Sea and on 3rd September of the same year he was posted to HQ Company, 4th Line of Communication Signals at Rhos-on-Sea. On 5th October 1940 he embarked for North Africa with the 4th Line of Communication Signals. By the summer of 1943 he was serving with Eighth Army Signals. He served throughout North Africa (specifically Egypt, Libya and Tunisia) and he also spent a short leave in Palestine. He subsequently served in Sicily and

Italy and returned home from Italy on 13th March 1945 after 4½ years overseas. In May 1945 he met Dave McNulty, who had just arrived back from the Far East at Portsmouth. Dave went on to become a boxing and physical training instructor and was posted to Cheltenham until his discharge from the army.

Albert was stationed at Aachen with the Guards Armoured Divisional Signals. Albert served in Germany for 218 days. On 4th March 1946 Albert was posted back to England where he remained until his transfer to Class Z of the Army Reserve on 30th June 1946. His testimonial, dated 18th February 1946, on his Soldier's Release Book, completed by Commanding Officer Signals, Guards Divisional Signals stated: *This man has only been with this unit for three months but in this time has shown himself to be a good technician, a very willing and conscientious worker and always pleased to assist in work outside the normal course of duty. He is clean and tidy and in the time he has been with us has proved to be sober and honest.* On 12th December 1949 the War Office forwarded the following medals to Albert; 1939-45 Star, Africa Star with 8th Army clasp, Italy Star, Defence Medal, George VI War Medal 1939-45 and the Oak Leaf emblem signifying that he had been mentioned in dispatches.

On Sunday, 24th November Irlam Catholic Club honoured one of its younger members, Owen McCarthy, who had been awarded the Military Medal and Bar for bravery in Italy, at a concert at the club on Sunday evening. The concert, arranged by the club committee, was under the chairmanship of Martin Campbell, with Messrs J. Litler and W. Down at the piano. Servicemen on leave – many of them friends of Owen – made up a large part of the audience, and thoroughly enjoyed what was described as a first rate concert. At the close, Owen responded to many congratulations. The evening closed with the singing of *Auld Lang Syne* and the National Anthem.

Several Irlam and Cadishead men serving in the Navy, who found themselves in Sydney, Australia, during their service, owe the good time they experienced there to Mr R. Broughton of 21 Nelson Drive, Cadishead. Nearly 20 years before, Mr Broughton's brother-in-law, Warden Newclough, who was previously the manager of the Globe (later re-named the Rialto) cinema, went to Australia with his wife and became the manager of the Hoyts Bondi Road cinema. They resided at 15 Pacific Street, Bronte, Sydney. When war broke out Warden wrote to his brother-in-law and suggested that, if any local men in the Forces ever went out to Australia, he would entertain them. As a result, a number of Irlam and Cadishead servicemen enjoyed his hospitality while their ships were berthed at Sydney.

In an airmail letter from Warden to his brother-in-law, he wrote: *I was very pleased to see the boys you asked to call and am very sorry I was not able to spend more time with them, but I was always so busy in the city cinema. One boy came out to spend Sunday with me, but I forgot his name. I always think how happy poor Lizzie* [a reference to Warden's wife, who had died a few years before] *would have been to welcome them.*

DECEMBER

Well-known local families were united by the wedding, at St Teresa's Church, on Saturday, 1st December of William Adam Connor, second son of James Connor and the late Annie Connor of 30 Baines Avenue, Irlam, and Miss Renee Taylor, elder daughter of Mrs Scott, and the late James Taylor of 270 Liverpool Road, Cadishead. Father Fleming officiated and Leading Stoker Frank Connor, brother of the groom, was the best man, with Leading Aircraftman Martin Connor, and James Taylor as the groomsmen. Renee had served for over three years with the Auxiliary Territorial Service.

A wedding took place at St Joseph's RC Church, Dundee, on Saturday, 1st December between Sergeant John Robert Smith of the Queen's Own Cameron Highlanders, and Private Margaret Anderson Wiggins. John wore the full ceremonial dress of the Queen's Own Cameron Highlanders. He had been in the Army for over five years, and had spent four of them abroad. He was the elder son of Mr and Mrs J.G. Smith of 49 Marlborough Road, Higher Irlam. Margaret had served for four years in the Auxiliary Territorial Service. Sergeant David Bellamy, RAF, was best man.

News was received that an Irlam soldier, Kenneth Hankinson (pictured), serving in India, had been promoted to sergeant instructor. In April 1944, whilst still a private, he had saved the life of his officer during fighting in Burma, and was promoted to corporal. Kenneth was the only son of Mr and Mrs Hankinson, and was employed by the CWS Soap Works. He joined the Army in 1940 at the age of 18. His wife was the only daughter of Colonel Janneson of the United States Regular Army, and Lady Janneson of Boston, Massachusetts. Kenneth and his wife resided in Latham Road, Irlam.

On Tuesday, 4th December Mr H. Green, the organiser, and Mr H.H. Chesworth, secretary of the East Lancashire District Committee, addressed a meeting of servicemen and ex-servicemen, including several veterans of the 1914-18 war, in the British Legion hall. Two local men who had recently returned home from Japanese prisoner of war camps were also in attendance and they received a warm and rousing welcome from all present. The purpose of the meeting was to explain how the Legion could help ex-servicemen with advice on pensions, dependants' claims, and any other matters relating to their welfare. Benjamin Neville JP, chairman of the branch, introduced Mr Chesworth and Mr H. Green. This was the first time that a representative of the East Lancashire District Committee had visited the branch and Mr Chesworth started off by explaining that this was because the committee had always perceived that the local branch were going about their work efficiently and effectively and did not need any intervention. He went on to further explain that the Irlam and Cadishead branch was well-known and held in high regard at headquarters and the chairman of the Irlam and Cadishead branch, Mr Neville, was also chairman of the South East Lancashire District Committee and had been appointed to the North West Area Council. Moving on to the main topic of the meeting, he stated that many people only associated the British Legion with clubs and beer drinking and, as they did not advertise their activities, even some of its members did not realise what it did or what it stood for. When Earl Haig came back after the last war he realised the injustices which were being inflicted on ex-servicemen and, as a result, he instigated the establishment of the British Legion. Any man who fought in the First World War would understand the indignities, the injustices and the broken promises that they had suffered and it was largely because of the work of the Legion that those who fought in this war would not suffer the same indignities. For example, the Legion protested against the 1939 Royal Warrant, which limited a totally disabled man's pension to 32 shillings a week (it was £2 in the 1914-18 war), with the result that the pension was raised back to £2 and the Legion were demanding a further increase to £3-10s a week. In addition the Legion had fought over 7,000 successful cases before the Appeals Tribunals, including 200 cases from the First World War. He went on to explain that the Legion had convalescent homes, a rehabilitation centre fitted with modern equipment, and also had interests in housing. Since the outbreak of the war 120,000 new members had enrolled in the Legion. The organisation had also contributed £3,000 to St Dunstan's Hospice for Blind Servicemen, £150,000 to other charities, and granted business loans to 14,000 ex-servicemen. By December 1945 there were 5,000 branches, and 4,500 service committees.

Mr Green told members that if each branch in the country had set out to gain an objective as had been done at Irlam, the name of the Legion would not have been dragged through the mud. The British Legion in Irlam and Cadishead was a credit to the district. He stressed that the object of the British Legion was to help ex-servicemen whether they were members or not and that more than 80 percent of the people who received assistance were not members. The Legion was solely concerned for their welfare, and no problem was too big or too small for them to tackle. On the subject of housing for ex-servicemen, he urged the branch to contact the Council to arrange a definite priority. This was being done nationally, but it was up to each branch to get in touch with its local Council. In addition, the Legion had its own employment scheme, which tried to find suitable work for ex-servicemen. He advised those present to turn over their problems to the branch, and if they could not settle them, the area office would do their best. The Legion was also fighting for more training schemes, and there was, at that point in time, a scheme for every disabled ex-serviceman to register at the Ministry of Labour whether he was working or not. If they did that they would be given priority. He mentioned that a home for elderly ex-servicemen had been established in the south of England and there were plans for one in the north, and others throughout the country. The Legion was concerned that far too many elderly ex-servicemen were living in common lodging houses. They wanted homes for them so that, in their old age, they could mix with men of their own age, and live out their lives in comfort.

Several Welcome Home dinners were held at various points during the year to cater for over 1,600 ex-servicemen and women as they returned to the district. On Saturday, 8th December 171 discharged and demobilised men and women attended the first of a series of Welcome Home parties, organised by the Irlam and Cadishead War Comforts Fund, and held in the British Restaurant and British Legion Concert Room. As the guests arrived at the British Restaurant they were welcomed by Councillor Keal, deputy chairman of the Council and chairman of the War Comforts Fund; Edwin Jones, clerk of the Council and treasurer of the fund; Mary Bowker, secretary, and members of the committee. The guests enjoyed a three course dinner, and were then presented with gifts of money and cigarettes. Following the dinner, the party moved across the road to the British Legion concert room where they were entertained by the Nomads Concert Party.

Prior to the concert, Councillor Keal welcomed the guests, and said: *We appreciate, and are indebted to you for the dangers and privations you have endured on our behalf to save us from the horrors that have occurred on the continent. We regret to learn that some have made the supreme sacrifice, and our deepest sympathy goes out to the bereaved ones. Time alone can blunt the loss of those dear to them. To those of you who have been wounded and to those who have suffered from horrors of the concentration camps, we wish a speedy return to health. You have all been very much in our thoughts during the war years, and now you are home again we hope you will soon settle down to civilian life and take your part in solving the many problems that we have to face, both locally and nationally.*

Dealing with the work of the Comforts Fund, Councillor Keal said that 1,653 men and women from the district had served in the Forces. All local prisoners had now returned home, except two, whom he regretted to say, had died while in Japanese hands (actually three: Charles Walker, Wallace Brown and John Arthur Jacklin). The number killed, or who had died on active service, was believed at the time to be 72 men and one woman, while 11 were missing (there are 96 names on the War Memorial in Prince's Park).

Councillor Keal explained that the Comforts Fund was opened in October 1940 with the aim of co-ordinating all the funds in the district so that no one who was serving would be forgotten. During the war years the district had donated £2,960 to the fund which had been used to send out a total of 5,811 gifts to those serving in the Forces. In addition, special gifts had been made to repatriated prisoners and the wounded in hospitals. Cases of distress had also been relieved. He acknowledged that the work could not have been carried out without an enthusiastic committee, and the generous financial help which had been received from all sections of the community.

IRLAM & CADISHEAD WAR COMFORTS & WELCOME HOME FUND.

(Registered under the War Charities Act 1940)
Council Offices,
I R L A M.
8th December, 1945.

"W E L C O M E   H O M E"

At last we are able to say to you these two words which mean so much to you. For the past four years at Christmas time we have endeavoured to cheer you by sending you a message from your home town. Now we wish to express to you our heartfelt thanks for the services you have rendered, to make this home-coming worthy of the District from which you went. It is to you - the men of the Royal Navy, the Army, the Royal Air Force and the Merchant Navy - that we owe our thanks for preserving freedom for the peoples of the world. Many of you have been associated with renowned ships, famous regiments and distinguished yourselves in battle in the air. We are proud of your achievements, and to show our appreciation we have arranged this Welcome Home Dinner and Entertainment.

To the members of the WRENS, ATS, WAAFS, WLA and Nursing profession we also extend a very warm welcome home.

As a final gift from the Fund we hope you will accept the enclosed 10s/- with our good wishes, and we wish you health, happiness and joy in the future.

For and on behalf of the Committee.

A.J. KEAL.   Chairman.
EDWIN JONES.   Hon. Treasurer.
M.E. BOWKER.   Hon. Secretary.

Welcome Letter received by the returning servicemen and women

IRLAM AND CADISHEAD WAR COMFORTS
AND WELCOME HOME FUND.
(Registered under the War Charities Act, 1940).

Souvenir Programme.

The First

'WELCOME HOME' DINNER

To Demobilised Members of H.M. Forces

at the

BRITISH RESTAURANT, IRLAM,

on

SATURDAY, 8th DECEMBER, 1945.

at 4.30 p.m. and 6.0 p.m.

COMMITTEE.

Chairman: Councillor A. J. KEAL, J.P.

Councillors E. Brew, J. G. Enticott, J.P., A. C. Harrison, D. Hexford, R. James, J. McLean, J.P., C.A., W. H. J. Marshall, F. J Melville, J.P., E. Owen, C.C., R. Sutton,

and

Mrs. M. Ayres (Wesley Church, Cadishead).
Mrs. E. B. Bakker (Cadishead W.V.S.).
Mrs. M. Donnelly (St. Teresa's Church, Irlam).
Miss M. Ellis (Lancashire Tar Distillers, Ltd.).
Mrs. N. Jones (Messrs. Royles, Ltd.).
Miss I. Lofthouse (C.W.S. Soap Works).
Mrs. D. Loxley (Irlam W.V.S.).
Mrs. G. Rogerson (St. Paul's Methodist Church, Irlam).
Mrs. J. C. Seymour (British Basket & Besto Co., Ltd.).
Mrs. G. Walker (St. Mary's Church, Cadishead).
Mrs. E. M. Woodcock (Irlam W.V.S.).
Mr. J. Adams (Co-opted).
Mr. W. Armitage (L.S.C., Ltd., Workmen's Recreation Club).
Mr. E. Groome (C.W.S. Margarine Works).
Mr. W. Halliwell (Irlam & Cadishead Trades Council).
Mr. C. A. Murray, Junr. (British Tar Products, Ltd.).
Mr. B. B. Neville, J.P. (British Legion).
Mr. W. Redfern (Lancashire Steel Corporation, Ltd.).

Hon. Treasurer: Mr. EDWIN JONES.
Hon. Auditor: Mr. J. DOWSON
Hon. Secretary: Miss M. E. BOWKER.

The Welcome to our Guests and Entertainment will be given in the British Legion Hall, commencing at approximately 6.45 p.m.

Programme.

The Chairman of the War Comforts and Welcome Home Fund Committee will occupy the Chair.

Councillor A. J. KEAL, J.P.
(Chairman of the Council).

Mr. J. H. JONES, M.P.

Mr. J. A. MASSIE
(President, Irlam and Cadishead Branch British Legion)

will give a "Welcome Home" to our Guests.

Mr. FRED MILLS will present
THE LANCASHIRE NOMADS' CONCERT PARTY
in a programme of Music, Melody, Mirth and Magic.

ARTISTES:

EDITH YOUNG .... Soprano
WARWICK BROOKS .... Baritone
JACK BARRETT .... Piano Accordionist
HARRY REASON .... Comedian
FRED MILLS and PARTNER
                     Conjuror and Entertainer

OPENING CHORUS—"Here We Are Again"
                                    The Party

SOLO—"Leader of the Town Brass Band"
                                    Warwick Brooks

INSTRUMENTAL—"American Patrol"
                                    Jack Barrett

DUET—"Trot Here and There"
                     Edith Young and Warwick Brooks

COMEDY—"The Lancashire Lad" ... Harry Reason

SOLO—"The Pipes of Pan" .... Edith Young

MODERN MAGIC—Presented by
                     Fred Mills, I.B.M.-O.M. and Beatrice

INTERVAL

SOLO—"My Life is Love" .... Edith Young

COMEDY—"More Fun and Games" ... Harry Reason

DUET—"The World is Waiting for the Sunrise"
                     Edith Young and Warwick Brooks

INSTRUMENTAL—"Sing a Song and Smile"
                                    Jack Barrett

SOLO—"A Bachelor Gay Am I" ... Warwick Brooks

CLOSING CHORUS—"Goodnight to You All"
                                    The Party

Welcome Dinner Souvenir Programme

The first Welcome Home Dinner

Councillor Keal expressed his gratitude to the British Legion and the British Restaurant for their help and co-operation. He also paid a special tribute to the work of Mary Bowker, who had rendered dedicated and efficient service, displayed a keen personal interest in the welfare of the serving men and women and had not spared any time or trouble in carrying out her heavy task.

Jack Jones MP told those present that the Government was determined to see that ex-servicemen got a fair deal: *I want to see the same spirit now you have returned to civilian life that you showed in the Forces – the spirit of give and take – the comradeship which made you share a tin of 'bully' or a cigarette between four men. You have carried out the first part of the task, and now we want you to carry out the second by pledging yourselves to work for reconstruction. We have to stand together, irrespective of what we think politically, and endeavour to create a better country, and a better world. We are still the greatest nation in the world. We are still the finest people under God's sun, and this Government pledges itself, if you will help them, to give you the right to live as God intended all men should live.*

The wedding of Richard Bailey, youngest son of Mr and Mrs P. Bailey of 2 Lines Road, Irlam, and Isabelle Hamilton, only daughter of Mr and the late Mrs F. Hamilton of 64 Princes Road, Liverpool, took place at St John's Church on Saturday, 8th December. Isabelle's brother, ex-serviceman William Hamilton, acted as best man and her cousin, ex-serviceman Robert Tyer, acted as groomsman. Both Robert and

William had been prisoners of war. Richard served in the Royal Navy, and had served abroad for over two years.

In 1944 American born Dorothy Mae Moore of 40 Dean Road, Cadishead, had joined the United States Forces in the equivalent of the British ATS. Later she went overseas and served in Europe. Her sister, Mrs E.F.M. McNulty received a letter from the US War Department to say that Dorothy, who was 22 years of age at the time, had been awarded the Good Conduct Medal. The medal has been given in the words of the official citation: *For having demonstrated fidelity through faithful and exact performance of duty, efficiency through capacity to produce desired results, and because her behaviour during more than one year's continuous active Federal Military service while the United States was at war has been such as to deserve this recognition. Fine, diligent women such as Tec 5 Moore, make our Army a force that cannot be defeated. Members of this command are proud to be serving with her.*

In one of the liveliest meetings of the year the Council accepted a notice of motion tabled by Councillor Marshall and, as a result, the Housing and Town Planning Committee would consider at its next meeting whether the Council should withdraw its application for temporary houses. Councillor Marshall was pleased that the allocation of temporary houses was delayed: *I do not think they are a fit house for our servicemen to come back to. In the national Press there have been reports upon those houses. One statement says that if it rains the roofs of these temporary houses will collapse, and if a boy kicks a ball at the wall it will go through. There is only the best good enough for our boys to come back to, and I am confident that if they have patience they will have permanent houses in six months. We have the manpower. There are men coming home from the Forces who are building trade operatives living in this district and they have to be sent out of the district because there is no work for them here.*

Councillor A.C. Harrison supported Councillor Marshall: *You must take into consideration that these temporary dwellings will need roads, sewers, gas, water and electricity and also foundations will have to be laid and whilst this is being done surely the better way would be to have plans ready and get on with the job of building permanent buildings at much less cost. If this Council had been giving the matter of permanent houses serious consideration since May when we applied for temporary houses, then I contend plans would now have been passed and permanent houses would have been definitely in the course of erection. It is up to us all to resolve here and now, that the main job of our surveyor is the preparation of plans for roads and sewers for permanent houses.* The Council accepted the motion and referred it to the Housing Committee for further consideration.

A large number of WVS members and friends spent a pleasant evening on Saturday, 6th December at St Mary's School for the farewell social and dance of the Cadishead

WVS. Enid Bakker, in her farewell message as organiser, outlined the work of the WVS during the war years: *It was a record to be proud of.* She thanked Mrs Hampson for her work as deputy organiser, the committee, the rest centre leaders and all members of the WVS for their loyalty and work. Mrs Hampson replied on behalf of the committee and members, and then presented Mrs Bakker with a barometer, with a silver inscription, and a cheque, in recognition of her services. Mrs Potts, rest centre leader, and Mrs James both spoke in appreciation. During the evening, refreshments were served and Brenda Harrison entertained the crowd with music.

The first post-war Christmas was not, as far as the district were concerned, as austere as was expected. There was a shortage of many of the goods associated with Christmas but, on the whole, the local population fared as well as could be expected under the circumstances. Turkeys were almost non-existent thanks to the zoning scheme which classed Irlam and Cadishead as an 'unfortunate' area. The few which did arrive were quickly allocated. Most Christmas dinners consisted of other poultry (mostly home-reared) or pork, which had been the staple meat for many war-time Christmases. In general, there was little outward sign of Christmas, although there was plenty of goodwill. Few of the local shops or stores were decorated, and most carried on as normal. Clubs and hotels did good business, with clubs organising functions for members and friends, whilst others ran dances. But the Christmas atmosphere, perhaps because the public had been expecting hard austerity measures, was described as almost entirely lacking. There were, however, few complaints as many local people looked back to the Christmas of 1940 when the season of goodwill was heralded by the Luftwaffe's Blitz on Manchester and surrounding areas; a Christmas when fires raged in the city and rescue parties worked while more fortunate people sat down to dinner. Others recalled that only a year before, Manchester had had its last aerial attack when flying bombs were launched against the city. During the war years children's toys had largely been of poor quality but commanded high prices. The end of the war brought an end to this as, although prices remained high, the quality of goods improved as manufacturers returned to their peacetime occupations. For the children, many of them experiencing their first Christmas with a world at peace, the festival was one of real joy. Parents, maybe as a token of gratitude for perils survived, put themselves out to make it a real Christmas for the youngsters and several parties (few with any signs of austerity) gladdened the hearts of the children. Above all, however, was the thought that the war was over and done with, and that, in spite of the hardship, the first post-war Christmas would be enjoyed; if only for the fact that it heralded a new era and, perhaps, posterity.

One of the many servicemen spending their last Christmas away from home was Signalman Albert Drum. On Christmas Day he sent a Christmas card back to his family in Irlam: *On the occasion of my sixth, and last, Christmas in the Army, I want to wish you all the very best for the festive season (if I should use the word festive, considering the rations back home) and a return to more normal times in the New Year. Looking back, it*

doesn't seem long since I spent Christmas at home, but 1939 was the last I had in England.
However, 1946, will see us all together again from February onwards.

News was received that Chief Petty Officer William Alex R. Borrino, more commonly known as Alex, had been awarded the Distinguished Service Medal (DSM). Alex was the son of Lieutenant William and Eleanor Borrino of 31 Lords Street, Cadishead. His father was a veteran of the First World War and was serving with the Territorial Army when the Second World War started. Like his father, Alex had been serving with the Territorial Army in 1939, and was mobilised on the outbreak of war. However, as a skilled tradesman, he was quickly sent back to his firm for war work. Determined to serve, he left his job and joined the Royal Navy in 1941 and volunteered for the Submarine Service. His submarine had taken part in operations at Singapore and, during its time at sea, had sank 29 Japanese ships including a U-boat, a torpedo boat, a minelayer and a destroyer. Three of his brothers served in the Forces: two were serving with the Royal Navy, Midshipman Stanley Peter Borrino and Cedric Borrino; and one with the Army, Sergeant Major George Vincent Borrino, Loyal Regiment (North Lancashire). In addition to the DSM, Alex was holder of the 1939-45 Star, the Atlantic Star and Clasp, Africa Star and Clasp and the Burma Star and Pacific Clasp.

Superintendent Herbert Weston, Irlam and Cadishead Division of the St John Ambulance Brigade, received recognition from King George VI who, as sovereign head of the Venerable Order of St John, sanctioned the admission of Herbert as a serving brother of the Order. The honour was well-deserved, and long overdue, after more than 40 years' service with the St John Ambulance movement. Herbert first became associated with the brigade when, having passed the first aid examination in December 1904, he joined the Shrewsbury No. 1 Division. He obtained his medallion in 1906 and Home Nursing Certificate in 1907. In the following year he was promoted to corporal, and then advanced to sergeant and divisional secretary in 1914, serving in this position for two years. He married Edith H. Tisdale at Atcham, Shropshire, in September 1912. In 1916 he moved to Lancashire for employment but, as there was no division in the area and he was living six miles away from his place of work, his membership lapsed. When he first came to Irlam, he joined a first aid class held at the school in Lords Street, and interested some of his fellow students in the work of the brigade. With the co-operation of several of these students, the Irlam and Cadishead Division was established in May 1929 and he was appointed Divisional Superintendent on 19th November 1929. In 1933 he formed the Irlam and Cadishead Nursing Division, with the aid of Nurse G. Smith, and a Boy Cadet Division was formed in 1936. The Lancashire Steel Corporation Division was formed by James Sinclair Kerr in 1938, and in that year the Irlam and Cadishead Nursing Cadets was formed. In 1937 he visited first aid classes at Patricroft on several occasions, explaining to them the value of the brigade. This led to the formation of the Eccles Ambulance Division, with Dr Dowzer as divisional surgeon and superintendent. The Eccles Nursing Division was then established, followed by Boy and Girl Cadet Divisions. Next the Barton Corps was formed, with Dr Dowzer as corps surgeon and superintendent and Herbert as acting corps secretary. On the outbreak of war, Dr Dowzer was called up into the Army and Herbert took on full-time ARP duties and, as a result, there was not a great deal done to increase the corps during this time. During the war he attempted to form another division in Urmston and eventually one was established. In 1944 Herbert was awarded the Service Medal of the Order. On the ARP side of the brigade activities, he attended a course in anti-gas and air raid precautions in London in January 1936, and further courses in Manchester in 1936 and 1939, obtaining the LAGC certificate. He represented the brigade on the Irlam UDC and Eccles ARP Committees and gave much of his time to training personnel in ARP methods. During the four days of the Czechoslovakian Crisis (September 1938), he was loaned to the Council to help organise emergency first aid posts, and on the first day of the war (1st September 1939), he took on the role of depot superintendent of the Irlam first aid posts, until he reverted to part-time service in May 1942. He was instructor to first aid classes held by the Irlam Higher Education Committee since 1931 and during that time he trained many policemen, Home Guard members, firemen, wardens and civil defence personnel.

Sergeant Harold Boardman Neville was among the 5,000 troops and airmen from India, Burma and the Far East who arrived in Liverpool on the troopship *Georgie* in readiness for demobilisation or to enjoy long service leave. He had served in the Forces for almost six years, with the last nine months' of his service spent in the Fighting Vehicle School in India as a Royal Tank Corps instructor. Harold was born in December 1915, the son of Benjamin Brooks Neville JP and Mrs Neville who resided at 655 Liverpool Road, Irlam. He was educated at Irlam Central School, and was employed in the offices of the Steelworks, before joining the Army. He married Phyllis Marshall of Gresley in January 1943. Phyllis served with the Auxiliary Territorial Service. His father was a veteran of the First World War, having served with the Royal Army Medical Corps. He was chairman of the local branch of the British Legion.

Thomas Williamson of 19 Boundary Road, Higher Irlam, wrote a strongly worded letter to the *Guardian* to express his views on the district that he would like to come home to after several years overseas: *Sir, in the copy of the Guardian dated October 20th last, which I, now at Singapore, have just received from home, I read with interest the letters in the Readers' Forum, and one in particular attracted my attention. This one, written by 'Housewife', referring to the very sad need for places of entertainment and a general livening up of the Irlam district, has my wholehearted support. Being born and bred there, I and many others like me, have always found the district rather 'dead,' and so when the need for entertainment and relaxation is upon us, find that a trip into Manchester our nearest and only consolation. I, and many other young men, serving in the Forces, are bound to find the old town or village, as you are obliged to call it, needs more than just a better transport* service. Naturally, we are all living for the day when we shall all be settled back into 'Civvy Street,' but travelling all over the country and serving overseas, we have all seen how others find their enjoyment and spend their off duty hours. We, whom you look upon as the future fathers and possibly county councillors, will not feel inclined to carry on the old traditions and adopt the attitude that 'what is good enough for us should be good enough for our children.' We will, surely, need to find a better way to spend our evenings than sitting in a public house, so let us hope that in the near future action will be taken to make Irlam a livelier place to live in. Most definitely something must be done to make life more interesting after whole days spent at the work bench, so let us hope that in the plans for a Brighter and Better Britain, Irlam district will not be forgotten. Let there be fun as well as labour, and then we shall know that all our suffering during the years of the war will have its reward.

Signalman Roy Bate of the Royal Navy married Joan Walker on Saturday, 22nd December. Roy was the youngest son of Mr and Mrs James Bate of 12 Woodbine Avenue, Cadishead. His father was a veteran of the First World War, having served in the Royal Artillery. Roy's brother, Mr E. Bate, was the best man and his friends Messrs A. Matthews and D. Colburn (Royal Navy) were groomsmen.

Roy had enlisted in 1942 and served in minesweepers at Scapa Flow and later in South Africa. His first ship was the minesweeper M191 which had a wooden hull as protection against magnetic mines. In South Africa he served on HMS St Zeno and, after the war, he returned to England on board this ship. His bride, Joan was the youngest daughter of Mrs and the late Mr S. Walker of 16 Baines Avenue, Irlam.

Flying Officer John Hill, DFC, wrote a thank you letter to the Dean Road Welcome Home Fund for their gifts: On behalf of the servicemen and women of Dean Road, I would like to express our sincere thanks to the people of Dean Road for the kind present received by us from the Welcome Home Fund. Our sincere thanks go to Mrs Howarth, Mrs Walker and Mrs Bishop for organising the fund, and Mr Bishop, the treasurer. I am sure that we all appreciate the present, but much more than that, the expression of the thought behind it. Though we were away we were not forgotten by you who stayed behind to keep our end up at home. I'll say once again 'thank you' and wish you all a happy New Year.

Minesweeper M191 (Roy Bate)

HMS *St Zeno* (Roy Bate)

CHAPTER NINE
POST-WAR ERA

It was clear that some of the darker memories still troubled him for many years after the war

JANUARY 1946

Criticism of the War Department appeared in the *Guardian* on 5th January. This was as a result of a number of families in the district being informed, just before Christmas, that their sons, who had previously been posted as missing, were now presumed dead. The article read: *Tact and consideration for the feelings of others are certainly not officialdom's strong suits. A week before Christmas several people in Cadishead and Irlam received official news that sons and husbands, previously reported missing, must now be presumed dead. It is reasonable to assume that these instances have been common throughout the country, and that thousands of relatives, clinging pathetically to a last shred of hope, have had that hope smashed beyond repair at the one season in the year when other families are enjoying happy reunions. That can only accentuate their sense of loss. True, the truth had to be told to them at some time. But, why pick on the few days before Christmas? Many of these men have been posted as missing for several years. That being the case, it should not have been impossible to withhold the official confirmation of their deaths until a more appropriate time. To send out bald statements that 'We regret that he must now be presumed to be killed,' only a short time before the greatest religious festival of the Christian year is to add agony to already anxious minds. But, apparently, soulless machine of Bumbledom must rumble on, no matter what pain and misery it causes to the ordinary people. It will be a great day in the history of this country when Government departments are instructed by their chief to exercise a little sympathy and discretion.*

January was a special month for Charles and Eliza Vinton of 42 Hayes Road, Cadishead, as their three sons were all home on leave during the first week of the month. This was the first time they had had their sons together for five years. When George heard that Charles and Arnold were both on home leave, he managed to get a 48 hour pass. Charles Vinton was a sapper in the Royal Engineers (born 1917), and 21 year old Arnold (born 1924) and George (born 1920) were leading stokers in the Royal Navy. Charles joined the Royal Engineers in October 1940 and served in the Middle East, Italy and Greece. A former pupil of St Mary's School, Cadishead, he had worked at the Partington Coal Basin before the war. George joined the Navy in 1939 and took part in the D-Day landings. Arnold had joined the Navy in May 1942 and by 1945 had been serving in the Far East and had been to Ceylon. He was educated at Cadishead Senior School. Both Arnold and George worked at the Steelworks before the war. The three brothers were members of a large family, of eleven sisters and brothers, four of whom were still at school at the start of 1946, one sister, Eva, was living in Canada.

(L-R) Arnold, George and Charles Vinton

At the beginning of 1946 Irlam's WVS held a farewell social evening at Irlam bandroom. Mrs Loxley, the centre organiser, thanked all the members for their efforts during the war and said this would probably be the last time they would all meet together as members of the WVS. It was noted that *since 1939 when the first members enrolled they had accomplished much and had their trials and successes. They were called upon to help those who had to bear the major burdens of the war years, and responded to the best of their ability.* As this book shows the members of the local WVS were involved in a variety of activities and did much good work for the war effort.

On Saturday, 5th January the Royal Navy laid on a New Year's party for 70 children from Rixton-with-Glazebrook. This party was held at the Royal Naval Camp (Camp 4), HMS *Gosling V*, and was put on at the suggestion of Lieutenant J.M. Hay, with permission of the Captain of *Gosling V*, Captain G. Freyberg. All the servicemen at the camp contributed to the costs of the party to ensure the children had a great time.

An advert appeared in the *Guardian* on 19th January which shows the camaraderie of local ex-servicemen seeking to help each other. Glazebrook ex-serviceman, John Bailey of 14 Carlton Way, who had been a window cleaner in the district but had been unable to continue his local round since he had suffered an accident in November 1945, offered his round, which generated about £10 income per week, free to any local ex-serviceman and offered his equipment at a nominal fee.

The 1945 annual report of the Irlam and Cadishead War Comforts Fund was published in January 1946. Amongst the many facts and figures within the report were details of repatriated prisoners of war. During 1945, it reported (inaccurately) that 33 local men – 20 from Irlam and 13 from Cadishead – who had been prisoners of war returned to their homes. One prisoner (Aircraftman Jacklin) died in enemy hands, and two repatriated prisoners of war did not return to the district. The report also recorded that at the end of 1945 there were 1,126 men and 104 women from the district serving in the Forces at the time the report was compiled. The highlight of the War Comfort's Fund year was the Welcome Home Dinner and entertainment it had organised for local men and women, demobbed from the Forces on 8th December.

Signalman Trevor Jenkins was offered a field promotion to lance corporal but, as it was policy to move newly promoted men to different units and he was friends with the men in his unit, he declined. The next day he received the same offer and was told that he was being posted to the 4th Queen's Own Hussars. He went on to serve in Trieste on policing duties. Even though the war was finished, there was still work to be done. Yugoslavian partisans were disrupting radio signals and Trevor was part of a team sent out on patrol, with a radio direction finder, to locate the source of the blocking signal. They narrowed the search down to a block of flats and Trevor and his colleague 'Ginge' were ordered into the building to find the men. They worked their way through the building, from room to room and floor to floor. As they got near the top of the building, they heard the lift start to move and could see two armed men inside the steel cage of the lift. They rushed down but as they neared the bottom, the lift changed direction and went back up, followed by Trevor and his colleague. When they got to the top, they found that the door to the flat roof of the building was open. *Go on Ginge, I'll cover you*, said Trevor. Fortunately for his colleague, the two partisans already had their hands up.

FEBRUARY 1946
On Saturday, 2nd February Elsie Irene Perks, the only daughter of Mr and Mrs E.H. Perks of 10 Haig Avenue, Cadishead married Clifford Todd, Royal Air Force, youngest son of Mr and Mrs J.A. Todd of Sevenoaks, Kent. The wedding took place at Government House, Aden. The reception was held at the bungalow of Todd's Commanding Officer, Wing Commander Proctor, after which the bride and bridegroom left by aeroplane for Asmara.

During February news was received that two local servicemen; Stanley Ellis and Jack Tonge, had received awards. Flying Officer Stanley Ellis of the Royal Air Force received the Distinguished Flying Cross as a result of participating in over 60 operational flights above enemy territory. Stanley resided at 2 Dean Road, Cadishead and was educated at Urmston Grammar School. He worked at the Prudential Assurance offices at Didsbury, before joining the RAF in August 1940.

Company Sergeant Major Jack Tonge of the Royal Engineers was mentioned in dispatches. Before the war he had lived with his parents at 14 Springfield Lane, Irlam and worked for his father at Wilkinson & Tonge, Cadishead. He was called up in March 1940 and after training in England he sailed for North Africa in March 1943, on board the *Windsor Castle* which was hit by an aerial torpedo on 23rd March and sunk. He served throughout the North African campaign and was at the fall of Tunis, afterwards going through the Italian campaign. In 1945 he served in Austria, and was still serving there, at Villach, in February 1946. His wife, formerly Madge Woolley of 3 Cranbrook Road, Winton, was awaiting his return home in May 1946.

On Wednesday, 6th February Signalman 14202026 James Houghton of the Royal Signals married Bessie Corder of the Auxiliary Territorial Service at St John's Church. Bessie was the daughter of Benjamin and Ann Corder of 4 Clarendon Road, Irlam. After a reception at Cadishead Co-operative Hall the couple honeymooned in Yorkshire. Bessie was the sister of Fred Corder who was killed in action in 1944.

James William Houghton was born on 29th March 1923 and resided at 31 Liverpool Road, Irlam. He was called up into the Army on 12th February 1942 and was posted to the Highland Light Infantry. He was sent to the 91st Infantry Training Battalion at Mary Hill Barracks, Glasgow and, after three months' training, was transferred to a training barracks at Chichester for a further two months' training. Next, he transferred to the Royal Signals and was sent for training, at Putney, south west London, in wireless and telephone operator duties and qualified as an operator on wireless and line duties. He was posted to 114 Brigade, 38th (Welsh) Division and was stationed at various places including Blandford, Dorset and Ashford, Kent, where he undertook a further training course. He moved with his brigade to Great Missenden, Buckinghamshire, from where he participated in various exercises on Salisbury Plains. He was then stationed at Warkworth, Northumberland for four months, following which the brigade was moved to the Isle of Wight, around January 1944. On arrival at the Isle of Wight a message was received that A1 operators were wanted and, as a result, he was transferred to a holding regiment, at St Anne's Barracks, Blackpool, from where he was granted ten days' embarkation leave. He left England in February 1944, sailing for India, via Port Said and Suez. He disembarked at Bombay and was posted to Signal Training Battalion 1, at Mhow, India. He undertook training to acclimatise and also passed an NCO Cadre being appointed lance corporal (unpaid). Two weeks after this NCO Cadre he was posted to No. 3 Special Signals Section, at Delhi, where he reverted to signalman. On arrival at his new unit there were already enough wireless operators, so James operated the teleswitch board, and also worked in the quartermaster's stores, packaging wireless parts and radios. While at Delhi he escorted railway wagons containing wireless and radio equipment to different units in various parts of India. In 1945 he transferred to the 125th Independent Division Signals at Kurunegala, Ceylon, where he served as a wireless operator. He was posted to Singapore in September 1945, shortly after the Japanese surrender. On the morning of Christmas Day 1945 he received notification that he was going home to England for four weeks' leave. He sailed from Singapore on 4th January 1946 and arrived home at the end of the month. During his time in England he took ill with malaria and remained at home for a further 3½ weeks. He returned to Singapore in April 1946 and remained there until October 1946.

Private Bessie Corder, Auxiliary Territorial Service

Signalman James Houghton, Royal Corps of Signals

On Friday, 15th February Irlam's 'cinema pioneer', John Barnes of 44 Roscoe Road, Irlam, died in hospital, aged 76. John had settled in Irlam in the late 1880s having originally lived at Bamber Bridge. He worked on a farm on Irlam Moss until entering the cinema business in 1911. He set up a cinema in a building adjacent, and slightly to the rear, of the Ship Hotel, Irlam (to the left as you face the hotel). This was the district's first cinema (during the Second World War the building was used by the NFS - it was demolished c.1980). In 1913 John opened the Irlam Palace cinema. This building was later demolished and is now the site of Irlam Catholic Club.

On Saturday, 23rd February the second Welcome Home Dinner for around 180 local ex-servicemen and women was held at the British Restaurant. The event had been organised by the Irlam and Cadishead War Comforts Committee and the evening consisted of dinner at the British Restaurant and a concert at the British Legion Concert Hall. The chairman of the Council and the Comfort Fund (Councillor A.J. Keal) and also the Member of Parliament for Stretford (Sub-Lieutenant Herschel Lewis Austin) were present at the event. Councillor Keal outlined the work of the Comforts Fund and paid tribute to the Comforts Fund Committee. Sub-Lieutenant Austin thanked those involved in the Comforts Fund for all the work they had done for local ex-servicemen and women and in particular thanked Mary Bowker, the honorary secretary of the fund, which was loudly applauded by all present. Councillor Keal acknowledged that: *It was not all fun leaving the services and there was a process of readjustment that would need getting used to. They were coming back into a changed country and an atmosphere of struggle.* He appealed to all to meet the struggle of resettlement by recapturing the Dunkirk spirit. This second welcome home dinner and concert, like the first one, received high praise from all who were present.

Nancy Hall, youngest daughter of Mr and Mrs 'Herbie' Hall of 26 Bankfield Avenue, Cadishead, who had recently been discharged from the Women's Auxiliary Air Force, married a Belfast airman, Warrant Officer Frank Kirkpatrick Watson, Pathfinder Force, Royal Air Force, at St Mary's Church, Cadishead on Saturday, 23rd February.

MARCH 1946
On Tuesday evening, 5th March Robert Walsh of 100 Silver Street, Irlam, was knocked down by a United States Army car on Liverpool Road, near to the Nags Head Hotel and sustained serious injuries. He was taken to Eccles and Patricroft Hospital where he died the following morning.

At the beginning of the month Jack Fluck was appointed district manager of the Runcorn *Guardian*. He had been the district manager of the *Irlam and Cadishead Guardian* until 1940 when he was commissioned into the Manchester Regiment. He served in Iceland, Europe and the Middle East during his service before being demobilised after the war with the rank of major. Before working at Irlam he had previously been a journalist at Wellington, St Helen's and Batley, Yorkshire.

Welcome Home Dinner

Sub-lieutenant Austin welcoming home the troops

A member of the Women's Land Army billeted at Gungrog Hotel, Welshpool, wrote a letter to the *Guardian* complaining of the poor treatment which some Land Girls had received: *Sir, Four Land Girls, who have had their release to-day, laden with heavy cases, baggage, etc., asked their supervisor if they could have the truck to take them down to the station. The answer was 'You had better not depend on it. You can have it if you go down the same time as the girls.' Knowing that the girls were not going to work in time owing to heavy frost, the outcome was that the girls had to borrow money from friends to get a taxi. One girl was in very poor circumstances, and has been unable to save any money since joining the WLA because she has had to support her parents, who are old and unable to work. She actually went home with one shilling in her pocket. Is that the thanks we get after three years' service in the WLA? Altogether, through this war, the Land Girls have had a pretty raw deal. The Prime Minister asked on the radio last night for the girls to stay on the land. Does he expect anyone to stay after such treatment? If you are lucky you may get 20 clothing coupons to come out with providing you have turned in your full uniform. We ourselves think it is a disgusting affair altogether. I personally would like the people of Irlam, from where I come, to know.*

During the month Bessie Blay received official notification that her brother, Private Thomas Pearson Blay of 15 Atherton Lane, Cadishead, who was posted missing in April 1943 had been officially recorded as presumed killed.

Driver Ernest Austin of 4 Kitchener Avenue, Cadishead, married Kitty Taylor during the month. Although details of his war service are unknown he was stationed in Germany as part of the Army of Occupation.

In March HMS *Arbiter* returned to the UK and James Davies went ashore for the final time at Greenock, Scotland. After the war *Arbiter* had been refitted in Sydney, during which many of the crew, Jim included, spent some time ashore living with Australian families. HMS *Arbiter* and other escort carriers then sailed back across the Atlantic and returned to the custody of the US Navy (they had all been supplied to the Royal Navy under the terms of the Lend-Lease Agreement). On account of his valuable skills and experience as a war-time medic, Jim was offered a Royal Navy commission if he would be willing to sign on for a further nine years' service. However, he had always insisted that his intentions were 'hostilities only' and so he chose to leave the navy and remain at home with his wife, Margaret, and new daughter instead. Prior to leaving the Navy, Jim spent some time based at HMS *Gosling* in Risley. After demobilisation he subsequently returned to work at the Steelworks and remained there until being made redundant in 1974. After leaving the Navy, Jim returned to his voluntary work with the St John Ambulance Brigade and the Civil Defence Corps, eventually achieving the rank of area superintendent and being awarded the title of Serving Brother during a visit to Malta in 1969. He eventually retired from work and his voluntary service with the St John Ambulance Brigade at the age of 65.

APRIL 1946
Driver Albert Blundell of the Royal Electrical and Mechanical Engineers arrived home on leave on Saturday, 6th April. He resided at 6 Graham Crescent, Cadishead. He had a pleasant surprise when he met his younger brother, Private Thomas

Blundell, who was also home on leave. They had not seen each other for two years. Albert had been in the Army for six years and had served in France, Belgium and Holland and by 1946 was stationed in Germany. Thomas was serving with a unit in the 15th Scottish Division in Germany and had been in the Army for two years.

(L-R) Private Thomas Blundell and Driver Albert Blundell

Ex-serviceman, Lance Corporal Robert F. Kirkham of the Royal Engineers, wrote to the *Guardian* on 17th April to thank the ladies of Rutland Road, Cadishead for the successful Welcome Home party. Former servicemen and their families enjoyed the party which included tea, dancing and impromptu entertainments. Robert resided at 16 Rutland Road, Cadishead.

Some local war workers were feeling somewhat disgruntled over the lack of formal acknowledgement for their efforts. A letter signed by 'Five disgusted women steel workers' was sent to the *Guardian*: *Sir, we have read with much disgust that we are not having any Victory celebrations in the district, and that only arrangements are being made for the services. We admit that they have done a grand job of work, but haven't also the women, and the workers of all classes? Haven't they helped in one way or another to make a Victory possible, or don't they count as far as celebrations go? Surely it wouldn't be asking the local Council too much, for a good day say, of bands and dancing in the parks, out-door sports and a gala day for the children. In doing so, it would provide a day for all in which to celebrate a great victory.*

On Friday, 12th April an Anglo-American wedding took place with the marriage of Barbara Bullock, the youngest daughter of Mr and Mrs Bullock, 2 Hurst Fold, Higher Irlam and Corporal Raymond Hyk, US Army Air Corps, stationed in Germany, who was the eldest son of Mr and Mrs W. Hyk of Philadelphia, Pennsylvania, USA. The wedding took place at St John's Church.

On Saturday, 13th April the local Salvation Army held a Welcome Home tea for two of its members, recently demobbed from the Forces, Alan Sidney Robinson and Jack Sherratt, both of whom had served for over six years in the Forces.

Alan Sidney Robinson (pictured) served as a sapper in the Royal Engineers. He was the youngest son of Mr and Mrs C. Robinson of 649 Liverpool Road, Irlam, and was a member of the Salvation Army Band. He married Mary Catterall Ledson on 1st February 1941.

On Saturday, 13th April two sisters were married at St Mary's Church, Cadishead. Barbara Dean, youngest daughter of Arthur Horace and Ellen Dean of 21 Fir Street, Cadishead, married Private Joe Dale Herrin, eldest son of Mr and Mrs D. Herrin of Witchita Falles, Texas, USA. Her elder sister, Mildred Dean, who had been recently demobbed from the Auxiliary Territorial Service, married Trooper George Leslie Gibbon of Moss View Farm, Barton Moss. George's best man was Pilot Officer Arthur William 'Billy' Dean, RAF, brother of the bride, and Private Herrin's best man was Private G. Meade, US Army Air Corps. The reception was held at Cadishead Conservative Club and both couples honeymooned at Llandudno.

During the month the district's Home Guard Old Comrades Association opened their new club in Liverpool Road, Irlam, in a building formerly used as the principal air raid warden's guard room, chief warden's office and fire guard office. The Association had 150 members and Lieutenant Colonel Webb was the president, with Mr G. Twigg the chairman and Mr W.H. Smith and Mr Gold, secretary and treasurer.

On Saturday, 20th April recently demobilised soldier, George Anderson married Bessie Roberts, the only daughter of Mr and Mrs Roberts of Henley Avenue, Irlam, at St Mary's Church, Cadishead. The reception was held at the British Restaurant, Irlam. George had been a prisoner of war since the fall of Singapore in February 1942 and had been repatriated from the Far East in November 1945.

On Thursday, 25th April a number of huts, situated between the Old River and the Manchester Ship Canal, were severely damaged by a fire. During the war the huts housed the teams that manned the anti-aircraft guns for the defence of Irlam locks. Five men of Irlam NFS, under Company Officer Langford, tackled the blaze.

During the month, Irlam Hall was 'demobilised.' Throughout the war the hall had served as a first aid post and its finely sculptured door and windows had been bricked up and its timbers reinforced with struts. The unsightly blast protection was removed and the hall reverted to its pre-war appearance.

Irlam Hall
(This historic building, which dated back to the 17th Century, was demolished in the early 1950s)

On Saturday, 27th April another Anglo-American wedding took place when American serviceman James Francis McGuire married Dorothy Mae Moore of 40 Dean Road, Cadishead, at St Teresa's Church, Irlam. James was the youngest son of Mr and Mrs R. McGuire of Matawan, New Jersey, USA. On the same day, also at St Teresa's Church, local soldier, Lance Corporal Sydney Banks married Kathryn Lightfoot, only daughter of Mr and Mrs Lightfoot of 4 Silver Street, Irlam. Sydney served with the Royal Artillery and then the Pioneer Corps. He was the adopted son of Mr and Mrs Percy Gallamore of 19 Nelson Drive, Cadishead.

During the month two Cadishead soldiers, who had worked together at the Steelworks before joining the Army, met in India. Corporal O. Yates of the King's Own Royal Lancaster Regiment, who lived at 7 Caroline Street, Irlam, sent a letter to the editor of the *Guardian*, published on 4th May which stated: *I thought I would write to let you know the funny circumstances in which I met my old workmate out in this jewel of the Empire (I don't think), so that you might print it in the Guardian and let the folk back home know that two more local lads have met out here. It happened like this. Our battalion has got two cricket teams and I've been playing in the second XI for quite a few matches. About a month ago we had a match against the 1st Battalion Lancashire Fusiliers, and from what we had heard it was going to be a tough match. Anyhow we travelled to Lucknow where they are stationed and prepared for the game. Our team was in the nets having a knock around when the home side walked on the field and I seemed to recognise a familiar figure among them. On investigating I found to my great delight and amazement that it was my old workmate, [Fusilier] Jack Hopkinson, from [1 Dudley Road], Cadishead. You should have seen the look on his face when he saw me, and I think mine must have been the same. The rest of the team must have thought we had been touched by the sun, because we couldn't talk long then because the match started and we were put in to bat. My mate happened to be one of the opening bowlers and he took four of our wickets, mine included (score nil), but we managed to scrape up 56 all out. When the L.F.s [Lancashire Fusiliers] went in it was midday and boy, was it warm – so we were in a hurry to get things over to get out of the sun. To cut things short, we managed to win by one run, and I got my own back on Jack by catching him out. After the match, did we have a time telling what has happened to each of us since we left the 32in. Mill! I think we must have been talking for about three hours before I suddenly realised I had to catch the trucks back to Cawnpore where I am stationed, and I just made it. But I am hoping to go to Lucknow again soon for a return match and also to have another chin-wag over old times. Jack told me that there is another local lad in their battalion – a lad named Houghton, from Cadishead, but I was unable to see him. I hope to do so when I go up there again. He also used to work on the 32in. Mill, but on the opposite shift so the old place is well represented in this area.*

MAY 1946

Third Welcome Home dinner
(Seated L-R: Benjamin B. Neville JP, Mrs Briggs, Councillor Arnold Briggs, Councillor Albert Keal, Mary Bowker, Mrs Walker, Mr Redfern. Standing L-R: Edwin Jones, Councillor Edward Owen, Councillor R. James and Councillor C. Borrino)

Gunner Thomas Ryan, formerly of the Maritime Royal Artillery, was discharged medically unfit on 3rd May. He had served since July 1940, spending the first three years in the UK with light anti-aircraft batteries before transferring to the Maritime Royal Artillery, serving on defensively equipped merchant ships. On 26th September 1945 he had transferred to the British Army of the Rhine, serving in Germany until 10th February 1946. His last service was with 123 Light Anti-aircraft Battery, Royal Artillery. He was awarded the 1939-45 Star, George VI War Medal 1939-45, Atlantic Star, Italy Star and Defence Medal. He also received a certificate from the Maritime Royal Artillery. His military conduct was described as 'very good' and he received the following testimonial from his commanding officer: *A steady, hardworking type of man who has always given good service. Loyal and conscientious. Possesses good personal habits and his honesty is above suspicion.*

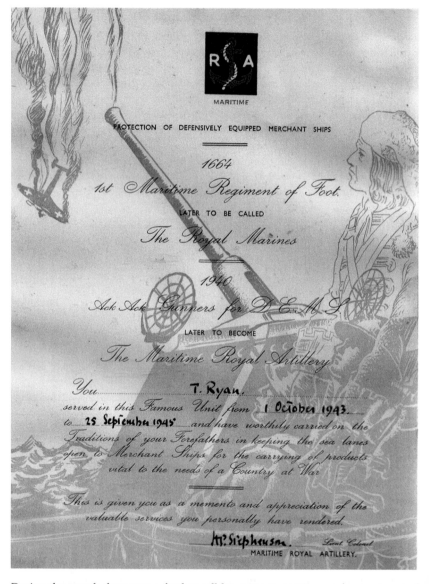

During the month there was a further call by many ex-servicemen for some sort of recognition to be bestowed on Mary Bowker of the Irlam and Cadishead War Comforts Fund for all her efforts during the war years, who as the outspoken 'town topics' columnist stated in the *Guardian*: *had done a grand job of work for the Fund and has not spared herself in the process. During the war years she was responsible for sending thousands of postal orders to local men and women in the Forces and, in addition she has maintained a personal contact with many of the men and with their families. Not the least of her voluntary duties was her membership of an area committee responsible for the welfare of prisoners of war and not a few local families can testify to the interest she took in their menfolk who were in German, Italian or Japanese hands.*

A 28 year old man, Charles George Blease (pictured) of 6 Railway Cottages, Barton Moss, Eccles was killed on Wednesday, 8th May whilst attempting to cross Barton Moss level crossing. He was hit by the Earlestown-Manchester passenger train. Charles was a former soldier (Lance Corporal 3528232) and had been demobilised from the Army having served 12 years, including over three years as a prisoner of war in a Japanese camp during the war. He was captured on 15th February 1942, probably when Singapore fell to the Japanese.

In March 1946 the Irlam and Cadishead Branch of the British Legion – which at that time had nearly 600 ex-servicemen members – applied to the Council for permission to appoint a Legion representative to the Housing and Town Planning Committee. At the beginning of May the Council refused this application. This prompted First World War veteran, and secretary of the Irlam and Cadishead branch of the British Legion, Peter Barrow DCM, to write the following letter to the *Guardian*: *All we ask for is a watching brief on behalf of the ex-servicemen in the district, we do not expect to be allowed to vote as members of the committee but simply to be present at the committee meetings in order to watch the interests of ex-servicemen. Since we made our application – which was turned down in a letter I received on Thursday – we have been informed that two out of every three vacant houses will be allocated to ex-servicemen. That is a good thing, but it does not entirely satisfy us. It is well-known that every day, between 3,000 and 4,000 people come into this district to work, if they can get houses here they will come to live in the district, and there is a danger that many of them will get houses before our own local ex-servicemen. The Council appears to regard the British Legion as a social club. It is not; it was formed to look after the interests of its members and of all ex-servicemen whether they are members or not. Because of that we feel we ought to have some sort of representation on the committee. There are hundreds of ex-servicemen in Cadishead and Irlam, quite apart from the members of the Legion, and their interests must be safeguarded. For some time now the British Legion has been fighting a 'Fit to serve; fit for pension' campaign. We in this branch also believe that if a man is fit to fight for his country he is also fit to sit as a co-opted member on a committee of such importance as the Housing and Town Planning Committee, which have to make decisions concerning the future hopes of the men who have fought for this country.*

The clerk of Irlam Council, Edwin Jones, responded that the Legion's request was *most unusual* and if granted would set a precedent, he added: *If we granted that, there is no reason why the National Union of Journalists or the Women's Guild should not be represented. The inclusion of a British Legion representative on the committee would serve no useful purpose. Out of every three houses which become vacant, two are to go to ex-servicemen. They could scarcely have a higher proportion than that. The Council has never before had a request of this kind, but the British Legion can rest assured that the interests of the ex-servicemen are being well looked after.*

During the month, Benjamin Neville, chairman of the Irlam and Cadishead Branch of the British Legion, was appointed, by the National Executive Council of the British Legion, as honorary county employment officer for the south-east Lancashire area. At that time he was already Chairman of the south-east Lancashire Committee and vice-chairman of the County Committee. He was also Cadishead and Irlam branch benevolent secretary. In June 1945 he was one of only two men in the North West area awarded a certificate for his work for the British Legion. In his post as honorary county employment officer his main role was to visit employers and promote the British Legion policy of preference for ex-servicemen and to see how the Legion could help solve the labour shortages.

On 23rd May Captain Henry Rowland John met his future wife, Helga Kühn, when he was introduced to her at his officers' club in Germany and, in his own words: *The world stood still.* Rowland had been due to leave the Army on 21st April but, fortunately for the couple, his commanding officer asked him to stay on for a further three months. On 8th July, after only knowing Helga for 46 days, he asked permission to marry her. At the time it was forbidden for an officer to marry a German citizen and he faced fierce opposition from his colonel. As a result, he extended his Army service to remain in Germany and they eventually married on 24th February 1948.

Rowland served with the Royal Army Service Corps. He had been evacuated from France in June 1940, took part in the Normandy landings in June 1944 and was involved in the advance through northern Europe. He later went on to Ostend, and then Essen in Germany and finally to Duisberg to take over a new company. As the war was coming to an end he entered Hamburg with the 4th Armoured Brigade. During his time with the Army of Occupation he visited Schleswig-Holstein, and then took a quick trip to Denmark and Lubeck before returning to Hamburg where he took over the building which had previously been the Dutch Consulate. He left the Army in April 1948, having completed eight years' service. At first Rowland and Helga settled in Flixton and then moved to Scotland. They have two sons and at the time of writing the couple are living in retirement in Dusseldorf, Germany.

On Saturday, 17th May, Russell Gordon, RAF, married Vera Rodda at St John's Church. Russell was the only son of Mrs and the late William Gordon of 2 Graham Crescent, Cadishead. After being demobilised from the RAF Russell went back to college and then took a teaching job at Urmston Council Primary School. His best man was Flying Officer Leslie Coates, RAF. Vera was the eldest daughter of Mrs and the late Mr E.D. Rodda of Rose Lea, Cutnook Lane, Higher Irlam.

Private Joseph Tighe, 2nd Battalion, Somerset Light Infantry, wrote the following letter to his parents from Bulgaria: *Dear Mam and Dad, how goes it at the ancestral home? I hope you are all feeling the May spirit and are in the best of health. I am still rather browned off after hearing the latest demob statement. I shall finish with the Army about the end of October. It was rather a blow after having built up my hopes. Still there's nothing I can do but soldier on. Tinkle went home yesterday as he is 29 group, lucky dog. He is coming up to Manchester for a week when I am on my demob leave. I have been sleeping beside him for 2½ years now and it's funny to wake up and see an empty space. He's been a good mate and I miss him a lot. Still what am I doing giving you all my troubles. I am not so badly off, it's just that I am homesick, I usually get a spell now and again. I received your postcards from Blackpool and I am glad to hear you are getting a bit of recreation for a change. It certainly looked good on the postcards. Did you go in the funhouse? I had a bit of sport myself when I went shooting wild pigs in the Bulgarian Thrace foothills two days ago. We had the natives, who are Turks, beating for us but although we saw two pigs they are still sticking to their bacon. After the hunt we were the guests of honour at a feast given by the headman of the village. It was rather complicated by the fact that they were Mohammedans and to them we were infidels. A Mohammedan will not touch food that has been touched by the hand or shadow of an infidel so we had to be very diplomatic when we squatted on the cushions to eat. We had to eat separate food to them and wasn't it a lark when they put a whole roasted sheep in front of us. There was eight of us, the colonel, four majors, including Lord Darling, a captain, a corporal and yours truly, so you can tell what a job we had to eat it all. It would be offering them a deadly insult so we got stuck in and with our fingers as we had no knives or forks. As I was the junior I got the last pick and they left me the neck. After that I had the laugh on the lots of them as the next course was about two pints of buttermilk each. Naturally enough I knocked mine back and really enjoyed it but it was the first time the others had had it and I was tickled to death to see them sitting there cross-legged with a fez on their heads trying to look as though they were enjoying it. I made it worse for them by asking for more. Well after that they fetched the local band out and I don't care what anyone says, although their idea of music is not ours, it has a sort of rhythm of its own and nearly hypnotizes you. All considered it was a great experience and I enjoyed it thoroughly although I was sick as a dog next morning. I think I have had my say for the time being so I will say cheerio for now and God Bless You Both from Your Loving Son, Joseph.*

News was received that war bride, Mrs Yvonne Peterson (nee Stewart), daughter of Mr and Mrs Stewart of 80 Marlborough Road, Higher Irlam, had arrived at Montreal, Canada. She left the district on 22nd May and travelled by train from Manchester to London. The next day she sailed on board the *Queen Mary*, arriving in Canada on 30th May where she was met by her husband and his relatives.

JUNE 1946

8th June was declared a national Victory Day (V Day), however, there were no official celebrations in the district and the only official mark of the day was decorations at the Council Offices. Most works in the district closed for the day although the Steelworks remained open and postmen, dairymen, transport drivers and policemen were out as normal. Many residents across the district had arranged tea parties for children and the licensed premises throughout Irlam and Cadishead were: *well packed to the point of discomfort and landlords and their staff worked valiantly to cope with an unprecedented situation.* There were some private Victory parties, for example a tea party, which included trifle, fruit and cream, was held for children and elderly residents of Allenby Road, Hamilton Avenue and Byng Avenue, Cadishead. Mr Toole and Mr Hunter decorated the road with bunting, fairy and tea lights and fixed up two radios. Presents for games were provided by Mr and Mrs Hunter and sweets, minerals and ice cream were distributed. The evening was rounded off with community singing. Neighbouring Rixton-with-Glazebrook organised a celebratory event with a band and tea for children.

Victory Party in The Crescent, Higher Irlam

The reasons for not preparing a special event for V Day was that 12 months had passed since Victory in Europe Day (VE Day) and Victory over Japan Day (VJ Day) had been in the previous August therefore the Council felt that the *spirit of the celebrations has gone.* The Council also held the view that due to the economic situation in the world, and the acute lack of food supplies, it would not be fitting to arrange large scale celebrations. The Council, in its defence, pointed out that on both VE Day and VJ Day thanksgiving services had been held, public buildings had been floodlit, and bonfires held throughout Irlam and Cadishead. In October 1945 schoolchildren were given a victory treat by the Council, which included oranges and ice cream, and entertainment was put on such as Punch and Judy shows. A number of Welcome Home dinners and parties had been held for discharged and demobilised ex-servicemen and women. The question had been raised about the possibility of holding a parade but the Council responded that the Civil Defence organisations and Home Guard had been disbanded and the Council believed that servicemen and women had had enough of parades. Finally the date suggested for V Day was the eve of the Whitsuntide holidays, and many residents would be away from the district at the time. All the Sunday schools in the district would also be holding their annual Whitsuntide processions and celebrations about this time.

In June 1946 all of the schoolchildren in the district, indeed all those in Great Britain, were presented with a certificate to commemorate victory over the Axis forces.

Rixton-with-Glazebrook's Victory Day celebrations started on Saturday morning with a 10.30am service at a packed St Helen's Church. The congregation included a naval party from HMS *Gosling V* and members of the Parish Council. After the service the congregation went in procession to Hollins Green War Memorial and around 350 to 400 people formed up around the War Memorial at 11.00am. After the service, Mr J. Eaves, chairman of the Parish Council laid a wreath at the memorial and said to everyone assembled: *I lay this wreath on behalf of the people of this parish, to the Glory of God and in remembrance of the gallant men who laid down their lives in the service of their country.* Behind him was a board, which had been placed next to the memorial before the service, inscribed with the words: *Lest we forget - The Empire was made by men who knew their duty, and had the courage to do it. Their glory lives, and is proclaimed forever, on every fitting occasion, both in words and in deeds.* The vicar, assisted by Mr J. Farrington, treasurer of the Victory Fund (which had raised £1,300 for distribution to local veterans), made a presentation: *During the war we all have been remembering our boys and girls in the Forces. They have done great deeds of valour all over the world. Some time ago the suggestion was made that there should be a fund created which would allow of a sum of money to be presented to all in the services, from the parish, on their return home. We have now come to the time of presenting these gifts. A few young men have given their lives for their country, and while we have all sympathy for the bereaved, we congratulate all who have come back. The village has been amazingly blessed* (a reference that only three men from the village had lost their lives), *and I trust everyone will realise the tremendous debt we owe to Almighty God.*

The vicar stated that 118 men and women who joined up from the parish would receive a cheque for £10-5s. Six local members of the services had been chosen as a representative group to receive the cheques on Victory Day. They were Corporal Jack Webster (Royal Electrical and Mechanical Engineers), Donald Hindley (Army), Marjorie Barker (ATS), Gunner Stewart Alan Sinton (Royal Navy), Flight Lieutenant Harold Burns (RAF) and Mrs James (WAAF).

T
8th June, 1946
O-DAY, AS WE CELEBRATE VICTORY, I send this personal message to you and all other boys and girls at school. For you have shared in the hardships and dangers of a total war and you have shared no less in the triumph of the Allied Nations.

I know you will always feel proud to belong to a country which was capable of such supreme effort; proud, too, of parents and elder brothers and sisters who by their courage, endurance and enterprise brought victory. May these qualities be yours as you grow up and join in the common effort to establish among the nations of the world unity and peace.

George R.I.

HYMN III.

(Selected by The Vicar)

A. & M. 165.   Tune: "S. Anne."

O GOD, our help in ages past,
Our hope for years to come,
Our shelter from the stormy blast,
And our eternal home;

Beneath the shadow of Thy Throne
Thy Saints have dwelt secure;
Sufficient is Thine Arm alone,
And our defence is sure.

Before the hills in order stood,
Or earth received her frame,
From everlasting Thou art God,
To endless years the Same.

A thousand ages in Thy sight
Are like an evening gone;
Short as the watch that ends the night
Before the rising sun.

Time, like an ever-rolling stream,
Bears all its sons away;
They fly forgotten, as a dream
Dies at the opening day.

O God, our help in ages past,
Our hope for years to come,
Be Thou our guard while troubles last,
And our eternal home. Amen.

THE BLESSING

LAYING OF WREATH ON CENOTAPH
by Chairman of the Council
(Mr. JAMES EAVES)

PRESENTATION OF VICTORY FUND CHEQUES
to Representatives of the Six Services by the
Chairman of the Committee (the Vicar,
Rev. H. FIRTH)

RIXTON-WITH-GLAZEBROOK

Peace Celebrations

United Service

in the

Parish Church of S. Helen,

on Saturday, 8th June, 1946,

at 10-30 a.m.

The Lesson will be read by
the Rev. W. W. AYRES

☩

Service continued at the
CENOTAPH
at 11-0 a.m.,
where the
BARTON HALL WORKS BAND
will play for the hymns

D545515

Order of Service

HYMN I.

(Selected by Rev. W. W. Ayres)

A. & M. 166.   Tune: "Old Hundredth."

ALL people that on earth do dwell,
Sing to the Lord with cheerful voice;
Him serve with fear, His praise forth tell,
Come ye before Him, and rejoice.

The Lord, ye know, is God indeed;
Without our aid He did us make;
We are His folk, He doth us feed,
And for His sheep He doth us take.

O enter then His gates with praise,
Approach with joy His courts unto;
Praise, laud, and bless His Name always,
For it is seemly so to do.

For why? the Lord our God is good;
His mercy is for ever sure;
His truth at all times firmly stood,
And shall from age to age endure.

To Father, Son, and Holy Ghost,
The God Whom Heav'n and earth adore,
From men and from the Angel-host
Be praise and glory evermore. Amen.

HYMN II.

(Selected by Rev. Fr. Ball)

A. & M. 172.   Tune: "Gerontius."

PRAISE to the Holiest in the height,
And in the depth be praise;
In all His words most wonderful,
Most sure in all His ways.

O loving wisdom of our God!
When all was sin and shame,
A second Adam to the fight
And to the rescue came.

O wisest love! that flesh and blood,
Which did in Adam fail,
Should strive afresh against the foe,
Should strive and should prevail;

And that a higher gift than grace
Should flesh and blood refine,
God's Presence and His very Self,
And Essence all-divine.

O generous love! that He, Who smote
In Man for man the foe,
The double agony in Man
For man should undergo;

And in the garden secretly,
And on the Cross on high,
Should teach His brethren and inspire
To suffer and to die.

Praise to the Holiest in the height,
And in the depth be praise;
In all His words most wonderful,
Most sure in all His ways. Amen.

Acting as their spokesman was Harold Burns who said: *We, in the services, realised full well that it was the 'little man in the street' who kept the spirit of freedom abroad and, bearing that in mind, I wish, on behalf of the services, to thank those who live in this parish, not only for the gifts we are receiving from them to-day, but also for the part they played during the war.*

Stewart Alan Sinton served for over four years as a Royal Naval gunner on Merchant Navy vessels. He was the eldest son of Mr and Mrs E. Sinton of 70 Glazebrook Lane, Glazebrook. He worked in the rolling mills department at the Steelworks and, in 1947, he married Ethel Muriel Eckersley of Flixton at St Michael's Church, Flixton.

During the afternoon and evening celebrations continued as 350 local children under the age of 15 were entertained on the local recreation ground. The Barton Hall Works Band played music throughout the day, a Punch and Judy show was put on and the children took part in a Sports Day. Despite rationing enough food was secured to treat all the children to a marvellous tea.

The celebrations prompted ex-Sergeant W.T. Hood of 28 Carlton Way, Glazebrook, to write to the *Guardian*: *Sir, I feel that many thanks should be tendered to all workers and subscribers who made it possible to make the gift of £10-5s to all ex-servicemen in the Rixton-with-Glazebrook area on Victory Day. This is not the only evidence of generosity, for during the war many of us, miles away in foreign countries, received a periodical gift, and a cheerful word, the latter giving great help and encouragement to face one of the heavy sacrifices, that was separation from our homes and families. I feel assured that all my comrades agree with me when I say that no village or town rendered greater service to the boys who went away to H.M. Forces, and know full well they share with me in saying many grateful thanks to everyone concerned. Your untiring efforts will live long in our memories.*

Former RAF Flight Sergeant Kenneth Browne was married on Victory Day (8th June) to Vera Flower, youngest daughter of Mr and Mrs S. Flower of 20 Baines Avenue, Irlam. The wedding took place at St John's Church. Kenneth worked in the surveyors department at Irlam Council Offices. During his RAF service he had been wounded during operations over Arnhem.

On the same day Millicent Outlaw married James William Johnson at St Mary's Church, Cadishead. Millicent had served for 4½ years with the Auxiliary Territorial Service. She was born in early 1920, the fourth daughter of John Robert and Elizabeth Outlaw (nee Briston) of 3 Moss Lane, Cadishead. Her father was a veteran of the First World War and was one of the first men of the district to arrive at the front line in 1914. Her brother, Robert Outlaw, served in the Merchant Navy and her husband, James William Johnson, was an ex-soldier who had served with the Royal Army Service Corps. He was a native of Hartlepool.

Private Millicent Outlaw, Auxiliary Territorial Service (right)

Those local men who served in Germany with the 21st Army Group, the British Army of the Rhine, received a demobilisation message from Field Marshal Montgomery.

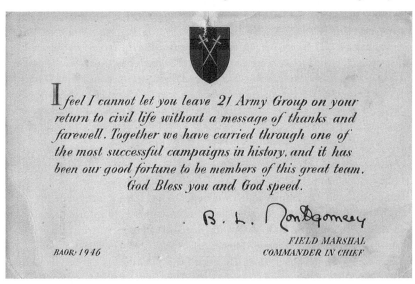

I feel I cannot let you leave 21 Army Group on your return to civil life without a message of thanks and farewell. Together we have carried through one of the most successful campaigns in history, and it has been our good fortune to be members of this great team. God Bless you and God speed.

. B . L . Montgomery

BAOR 1946

FIELD MARSHAL
COMMANDER IN CHIEF

The end of the war in Europe did not bring an end to the hazards of warfare; unexploded bombs would remain a danger for many years to come, sea mines were a hazard to shipping and were also washing up on beaches across Europe. In addition, landmines had been laid on beaches in England to guard against an invasion by the

Germans. All these mines had to be removed and safely disposed of, which was an extremely hazardous and nerve-wracking occupation. The men who carried out these tasks displayed enormous bravery.

Sergeant 2113945 Bertram 'Bert' Powell of the Royal Engineers was awarded the British Empire Medal (Military Division) in the Birthday honours list, on 13th June 1946. He received his award for carrying out hazardous disposal work on the beaches of Britain. He had enlisted into the Royal Engineers before 1942. As well as the British Empire Medal he was awarded the General Service Medal (clasp bomb and mine clearance 1945-48), the Defence Medal and George VI War Medal 1939-45. He had served in the Royal Engineers for six years until being demobilised in April 1946, five of his six years – the last three years spent in the UK – were on disposal work.

Born in 1915, he resided with his family in Dixon Street, Irlam. His brother, Joseph, had been killed in action during the Battle of Passchendaele in the First World War. Another brother, William, served as a naval gunner in the Royal Navy. After the war Bert worked at Gardners Limited, Patricroft. He married Irene Taylor in 1942 and they set up home at 3 Chestnut Avenue, Cadishead.

Acting Lance Corporal (later Sergeant) 1989908 Arthur Owen of the Corps of Royal Engineers was awarded the British Empire Medal for bomb disposal work, while stationed in London. His citation read: *Lance Corporal Owen has rendered services of exceptional merit in the disposal of defensive minefields in the United Kingdom. He was actively and directly engaged in the disposal of approximately 200 enemy bombs in the London area during the whole of the blitz period from September 1940 onwards and thereafter to the present date in the clearance of beach minefields and further enemy bombs. During the whole of this period he cheerfully and unhesitatingly accepted the special hazards of the work, continuing to do so despite the fact that on at least two occasions he was associated with bomb explosions in which members of his unit lost their lives. His general conduct and devotion to duty in circumstances of great dangers have been of the highest order.*

Arthur brought home a violin from the Blitz for his daughter, a gift from a grateful family that he had helped to rescue. Arthur was born in Openshaw in 1911 and was brought up by his grandparents in Wellington Street, Openshaw, while his father was working abroad. He moved to Irlam when his father returned from Rhodesia to work on the Steelworks railway. Arthur married Patience Pearl in 1930 and they resided at 36 Princes Avenue, Higher Irlam. He was employed by the CWS Margarine Works in Higher Irlam. The award was published in the London Gazette on 16th June 1946 which stated: *The King has been graciously pleased to approve the award of the British Empire Medal (Military Division), in recognition of gallant conduct in carrying out hazardous work in a very brave manner.*

Sergeant Bertram Powell BEM, Royal Engineers

Sergeant Arthur Owen BEM, Royal Engineers

Another local man who worked on mine disposal was Corporal Walter Dixon of the Royal Engineers. Walter had three brothers in the Armed Forces: Edward, William and Frank.

Walter was born in Irlam on 14th January 1926. He worked at the British Tar Works and acted as a signal messenger for D Company of the Home Guard (service no. 651), until in 1943, aged 17, he volunteered for the Royal Engineers. He served in Northern Ireland then Chatham on mine and bomb clearance in the south of England. While in the service, he was part of the team which disarmed the first unexploded doodlebug (V1) and this is now in the Imperial War Museum in London. During the London Blitz he was part of a team assigned to remove bodies from an underground station which had received a direct hit. Before going down they were given alcohol, which gives some idea of the trauma involved in this work. Later he was stationed at Shoreham-on-Sea, recovering and defusing sea-mines. He was sea-sick every day.

Corporal Walter Dixon, Royal Engineers, with his mother, Gertrude (WVS)

Leslie N. King, served with the Mine Clearance Service. He was born in Hastings and moved to Cadishead post-war. He married Dorothy Mills at St Mary's Church, Cadishead, in 1950.

New ration books were issued at the distribution centre, 604 Liverpool Road, Irlam, which had only been open since the end of May. By the middle of June over 10,000 new books had been issued to residents in the district.

Leslie King, Mine Clearance Service

On Sunday, 16th June, 20 year old Driver T/14902676 **Peter Albert Hill**, Royal Army Service Corps, drowned whilst trying to save a girl from drowning in a river. At the time he was serving in the Lebanon. He was the son of Mr and Mrs W. Hill of 1 Etherley Close, Irlam. The story of his death was recorded in a letter sent to Peter's parents by his Commanding Officer, Major R.V. Hutchfield, which read: *The death of your son, Peter, was the saddest incident of my Army career. The whole unit was out on a Sunday picnic that I, personally, had arranged and was attended by myself and all my officers. The boys were having a fine time, swimming, donkey rides, dancing and plenty to eat and drink. It was a beautiful day and expert local swimmers had been engaged to watch the safety of any bathers. It was at mid-day when Peter and some of his friends were out bathing and suddenly one of the girl bathers got into difficulties. Immediately Peter and some of his friends went to her rescue. The girl and the other boy swimmer managed to get ashore, but poor Peter, who was not a very good swimmer got out of his depth and was carried out to sea by the current. Many brave attempts were made by his comrades to save him but he had gone out too far. Everything humanly possible was done to save him.*

Peter was born in 1926. He worked at the Steelworks and, for a time, at Barton Grange Farm at Irlam. He enlisted into the Home Guard on 23rd July 1944, serving in 7 Platoon as Private 984 Hill. Peter was called up in 1944. He is buried at Beirut War Cemetery. He is not listed on the Irlam and Cadishead War Memorial.

Mosedale brickyards at Rixton and Flixton went back into operation during the month. Frank and Thomas Mosedale had both served in the RAF and had been shot down over enemy territory and held as prisoners of war. It later came to light that they had been held in neighbouring camps in Germany. Both men were well-known in Cadishead. After being demobilised Thomas got the Rixton brickyards back into operation and was soon producing 200,000 bricks a week. Frank was demobilised in May 1946 and he immediately started work getting the company's other brickyard at Flixton back into operation. By June it was producing 160,000 bricks a week. Frank (born 1922) and Thomas (1917) were the sons of Thomas and Hilda Mosedale (nee Willis). The Mosedale business had been founded in the 1880s by their grandfather, Thomas Mosedale.

The following letter appeared in the *Guardian*: *Sir, I have a little story of how I met Private T.B. Brown of St John Street, Irlam, which may interest readers of the Guardian. One night, as I was on guard in Poona, India, who should the duty bugler be but Private Brown. After I had done my two hours' guard duty I had quite a long talk with him about local events, and read the Guardian which he had brought on duty with him, until it was my turn to go on guard again four hours later. We arranged for a night in Poona and a good feed, so two local lads are now serving in the same battalion in India.* The letter was written by Private Gordon Lea of the 2nd Border Regiment. Gordon was born in mid-1926, the son of Thomas and Lilian Lea (nee Jones) of 22 Hamilton Avenue, Cadishead.

Private Brett Brown, Border Regiment
(centre behind drum major)

Private Brett Brown (far left)
Kalyan, India, June 1946

Private Brett Brown, Border Regiment

Lance Bombardier Jack Whitley, Royal Artillery

The other soldier referred to in the letter, Private Thomas Brett Brown (known as Brett), was born on 4th September 1922, the son of William and Sarah Brett Brown (nee Daniels) of Fir Street, Cadishead. The family later moved to 18 St John Street, Irlam, which was where Brett was living when he was called up. He served an apprenticeship with Royles Engineering as a brass finisher and was also a member of the local St John Ambulance Brigade. He was called up on his 21st birthday (1943). He was trained in Northumberland and posted to India in late 1944 or early 1945 with the 2nd Border Regiment. He was stationed at Poona, India, and his battalion were training for the invasion of Malaya when the war ended. After VJ Day he remained in India carrying out internal security duties until August 1946 when he was posted back to England and was stationed at Carlisle Castle. Brett was a good friend of Sydney Banks, who served in the North African and Italian campaigns.

Another man serving out in Poona around this time was Lance Bombardier 14755046 Jack Whitley, serving with a Royal Artillery Field Regiment, which was part of 2nd Division. He was called up in 1944 and remained in the Army until 1948. He served at Cromer in Norfolk, and Poona and Calcutta, in India. Jack resided at 21 Chapel Road, Irlam. He had been due to serve in Burma but this was cancelled when war with Japan ended in August 1945. He married Dorothy Kitt in 1946.

Dan Carradice, divisional officer of the Independent Labour Party, addressed a meeting of the Irlam and Cadishead Branch of the Independent Labour Party at the Labour Hall on Wednesday, 19th June and discussed the subject of German prisoners of war, criticising the employment of more than three quarters of a million German POWs in agriculture. He believed that this amounted to slave labour stating, that prisoners were paid four shillings a week and they were not allowed to spend it. Mr Carradice stated that: *The war is over but these men are still kept in the country. It is a peculiar thing but when questions are asked in the House of Commons whether this is in accordance with the Geneva Convention, there is no satisfactory reply. These men are being held here, are little better than slaves.*

The meeting was reported in the *Guardian* and generated a number of letters. Alf Ashcroft of Marriott's Farm, Barton Moss, wrote: *The facts are German POWs cost 1/5 ½ per hour, which is paid in camp money, and can only be spent in camp. Where Mr Carradice got his 4s per week from, or what the POWs did with it when they got it, seeing they were not allowed to spend it, I don't know? Far from POWs being the cheapest labour on the farm, they are by far the dearest, taking into account that, if a farmer wants any work done by them, he must find them some food out of his own scanty rations, which he is not supposed to do. I put it to Mr Carradice, or any of those who were listening to him: if they were British POWs on a German farm would he or any of his listeners do much work unless there was a feed before or a bayonet behind? As we are not allowed to put the bayonet behind, we do the only alternative – put what bit of food we can before them, as we don't want them on the farm either for ornament or scarecrows. Again, most of these men have never done any farming before and, as we cannot speak German, if we want a swingletree which has been left on a plough in the far field, it is much easier to go and bring it than try to explain what you want done. I can assure Mr Carradice that farmers around these parts only employ German POWs because they can get no one else. There is quite a lot of squealing now about the shortages of food. What does Mr Carradice, or anyone else, expect when farmers have to rely on POWs and school-children to harvest their crops? Does Mr Carradice think the food situation in Britain would have been improved if the 750,000 POWs had been sent back to Germany before the last harvest?* The chairman of the Irlam Branch of the National Farmers Union wrote along similar lines stating: *The only reason the farmer has for employing this so called cheap labour is in an effort to produce the maximum amount of food in these times of scarcity.*

On Sunday, 30th June, 20 year old Marjorie Norma Chapman set off from Ireland to join her fiancé in America. Marjorie was the only daughter of Mr H. Chapman, Irlam Council's sewage works manager, and Mrs Chapman of 34 Kitchener Avenue, Cadishead. She had met her future husband, Ben Hirsch, when he was serving with the United States Army Air Force, stationed at Burtonwood Air Base during the war. Ben had been discharged from the Air Force by June 1946 and had returned to his home at La Monica, Los Angeles where he worked as an engineer. Marjorie arrived at New York and was met by Ben's mother and sister. The wedding took place on Thursday, 4th July 1946.

JULY 1946

At 2.20pm on Tuesday, 2nd July local Police Sergeant Thomasson was notified that a German prisoner of war, 21 year old Hans Gunther Tannenbaum, had escaped. He was a prisoner at Garswood Park POW Camp at Ashton-in-Makerfield, but had been allowed, on day release, to work at an Irlam farm. Sergeant Thomasson made local enquiries and at 3.30pm on Thursday, 11th July he arrested Hans in the vicinity of Ox Cheek Farm, Cutnook Lane, Higher Irlam. Hans had been working at the farm for a few weeks before his escape. At the trial, Superintendent F. Waddington, stated that Hans was wearing a light grey jacket and blue raincoat: *His hair was naturally fair but at the time of his arrest had been dyed dark brown, and in his possession was found a bottle of hair dye, two one-pound notes and a ten shilling note. The officer (Sergeant Thomasson) questioned him regarding his possessions.* Sergeant Thomasson spoke with a farm worker, who said: *I gave him the raincoat a month ago. He asked me to get the hair dye when we went into Manchester. I gave him some money a month ago.* The farm worker had given Hans the blue raincoat to enable him to get back to camp as it was raining and confirmed he also gave the prisoner toothpaste, which he believed the prisoner could not get at camp. Another witness gave evidence that she had met Hans in May 1946 while he was working at her sister's farm. On Saturday, 29th June she had visited Manchester by train, leaving Irlam at 1.50pm. On the platform she met Hans and travelled to Manchester with him. On arrival at Manchester they were joined by the farm worker, who also worked at her sister's farm. On 2nd July she heard that Hans had escaped and the next day she visited her sister's farm and was told by the farm worker that Hans was hiding in woods nearby. They visited Hans in the woods where he asked for a toothbrush and toothpaste. She tried to persuade him to surrender. On 6th July she again visited the farm and was told that the prisoner was still hiding in the woods. On Wednesday, 21st August the farm worker appeared at Manchester County Magistrates Court charged with assisting an escaped enemy prisoner of war with intent to prevent his arrest or apprehension. He pleaded not guilty but was convicted of assisting an escaped prisoner and fined £5 plus six shilling in costs.

On Saturday, 6th July the following advert appeared in the *Guardian*: *Competent local ex-serviceman is prepared to do any job you don't want to do yourself. Any domestic work, decorating, repairs to car, wireless etc., gardening – Anything immediately undertaken on the spot. Old-age pensioners special consideration and rates.* The ex-serviceman, who was not named in the advert, was described as being from Cadishead and had served as a chief petty officer in the Royal Navy, being awarded the Distinguished Service Medal. This man was clearly Alex Borrino. His eagerness to work in the district ultimately did not work out as he emigrated to Australia in 1947.

A tragedy occurred on Saturday, 27th August when a 24 year old D-Day veteran, who resided at Dudley Road, Cadishead, committed suicide by jumping into the Manchester Ship Canal from Warburton Bridge. He was called up in January 1942 and served with the Royal Army Service Corps. He landed in France on D-Day and served in north west Europe and later in Palestine. During his time in northern Europe the young man was part of the force that liberated the German concentration camp at Belsen and the family believe the horror that he witnessed there was to play on his mind and lead to his death. He had only been demobilised from the Army in July 1946 and had returned to his old job as a plumber with the housing department, Irlam Council. His body was not recovered until Tuesday, 3rd September. An Inquest was held at Warrington Coroners Court on Wednesday, 4th September. His brother gave evidence of his Army service and occupation after leaving the Army. He had last seen his brother at 7.20am on 27th August at the family home getting ready to go to work and he had seemed quite content. Another witness at the inquest saw him cycling to work at 7.45am and then saw him again about an hour later at Warburton Bridge. They spoke on both occasions and he described him as appearing in quite good spirits. Another witness was the master of a tug *Hilda*; William Gilgrass of Birmingham had been travelling along the canal on that fateful day and, when about a quarter of a mile from Warburton Bridge, he heard a large splash directly under the bridge, and later, on the surface he saw a dog or a man. On the bridge was a cycle with an overcoat slung over the handlebars. Nothing further was found by the boat crew. Constable Hartley stated that Warburton Bridge was 70 feet above the level of the waterline and adequately protected by four feet rails. A pocket book was found at the scene which contained a message which read: *Please forgive give me for this. No one is responsible but myself.* The deputy coroner recorded a verdict of *Suicide, with insufficient evidence to show the state of mind.*

Cecilia Nuttall, daughter of Mrs Nuttall of 262 Liverpool Road, Cadishead, was married in America on 31st July, just 48 hours after she had left England. She boarded a plane at 7.30pm on 29th July at London and arrived at 10.00am on 31st July. The wedding arrangements had been made by her fiancé, Alcine Grillot of 50 Vine Street, Ohio. Cecilia sent a telegram home which read: *Arrived 10.00 a.m., July 31st. Married same evening. Lots of love – Mr and Mrs Grillot.* Cecilia had met her husband when he was serving as a US serviceman stationed at Glazebrook.

AUGUST 1946
For some local men the end of the war did not mean the end of hostilities. After VE Day, Sergeant Gerald Bannister of Cadishead, volunteered for service in the Far East, but the Japanese surrendered before he went. Instead, he was sent to Palestine with the 6th Airborne Division where he was involved with policing actions. During his time in Palestine he served under Major Roy Alexander Farran, who provided him with the following testimonial:

Sergeant Bannister has always been one of the best sergeants in the Regiment. He's a born leader and always stood in for the Squadron Sergeant Major when he was absent. He is a fine athletic type, who never shirks work and is completely trustworthy. He is certain to succeed in any walk of life. Major Roy Farran, Commanding C Squadron, King's Own Hussars. Dated 7th August 1946.

By a strange coincidence Roy Farran was a regular visitor to Cadishead, where his grandmother lived.

Gerald explained his time in Palestine with C Squadron, 3rd King's Own Hussars, and how he came to be there: *We were coming back to, on our way back to England, but we were staged, a staging camp at Bruges in Belgium, and there was a stadium there and this officer said 'is any of you any good at running?' and I said 'well I've been running the half mile for the 49th Division.' So he said 'well would you run for us?' I'd had some shrapnel in my leg but I said 'I'll give it a go.' And I won a cup for the medley half mile. It was a medley relay and my part was a half mile, 880 yards. And I won the half mile, 880 yards, so that was two cups I won in Bruges and they gave us the money to have them inscribed. And at that time I met the bloke who'd gone bomb happy in Normandy who was my driver, he'd been in Bruges all through the war, they'd sent him back and that was as far as he got and he was still there. That was that. From Bruges, we went to, came back to England of course, and I went to*

Larkhill on Salisbury Plain and joined the 6th Airborne Division. Larkhill was an artillery camp, a kind of barracks for artillery, opposite Stonehenge, used to run round Stonehenge in the morning, PT you know. I had the shrapnel removed from my leg there, still got the piece of shrapnel. From Larkhill, as I say I was a sergeant then, I was in charge of a party of people, we went on the Cameronia because the Palestine War, that finished you see. I went on the Cameronia to Haifa in Palestine which was about a fortnight, and on the way, the other half of the Division was on a French ship called the Champollion, it blew a boiler halfway across and had to be repaired, it passed us then we passed it going to Haifa. Went to Gaza first of all, Ianto was still with us because on the ship going to Palestine we were given a bar of Canadian chocolate and most of us ate it of course but Ianto saved his in a tin and he sent it back to Amy Herricks who was his girlfriend in England, and of course when she got it it was just a mass of paper and melted chocolate. Of course we did the same kind of things as we'd always done, you know training, that kind of thing, and policing. And by this time we had Staghound armoured cars, these were Canadian armoured cars and they were automatic. From Gaza we went to Sarafand Camp and I shared a bungalow with another sergeant who'd come from Kuala Lumpur where they'd had a little bit of a revolt in the Army in Kuala Lumpur. Yes. We were policing, or we were supposed to be, policing Palestine, the reason why we went there I suppose. And of course we had red berets. C Squadron was taken over by Roy Farran, he came as our C Squadron's CO. Don't know where he came from but I do know I spent a lot of time with Roy Farran. We had these Staghound armoured cars and we went down to the Dead Sea. And if you're going from Jerusalem down to the Dead Sea, it's about the lowest place on earth, these Staghound armoured cars, course they were automatic, they got the brakes red hot, trying to stop them, big armoured cars, Staghound. And we went down to the Dead Sea and spent some time there. Farran used to go off and say 'Bannister, look after things, I'm off to see the Mufti.' And he'd take the officers with him and they'd go on..., well they wouldn't be drinking because they were Muslims of course, but he used to go and I suppose he was a bit of an ambassador in a way. He was quite a character was Roy Farran. And we did quite a bit of firing while we were down at the Dead Sea, my particular armoured car had a different, heavier gun on than some of them and the recoil system wasn't as good as it should have been and sometimes it recoiled past you [laughter], you had to be very careful. From there I went on a course at Lake Tiberius, Sea of Galilee, with the Welsh Guards, they weren't particularly keen on having a sergeant from the Airborne with the Welsh Guards but I was there for a week, spent a week there, Lake Tiberius. Saw the fishermen catching fish. Went back to Sarafand and from there I went to Beirut. I ran in the 800 metres for the 6th Airborne in a triangular athletics meeting in Beirut, American University of Beirut, I've got a bronze medal here somewhere. Came back, you know doing the usual thing. Went over to Jordan, went to Jordan past Oman, up into the desert, on the day that they exploded the bomb in that hotel in Jerusalem. King David Hotel, we passed through before that blew up, going up to Jordan. And we were at a place called Zerka, there was nothing there really but there was a swimming pool and this is in the desert, with the sun blazing down, you think 'oh water, wonderful,' and we dived in and we could not swim the whole length of it, it was so cold, we could only swim across. Came back from there. The Jews, you know about Haganah, Irgun Zvai Leumi and the Stern Gang? Well one of them, one of those organizations, raided our, we had ammunition in a kind of marquee, and they raided it and Farran saw them and he gestured to everybody to get them. Anyway they got away. I was with Farran of course, I was more or less his squadron sergeant major because sergeant major's away, home to England. At the end of my service [August 1946] *this was a testimonial written by a man called Roy Farran. You know about Roy Farran. He had more medals than a general I can tell you that, and I was his squadron sergeant, acting squadron sergeant major in Palestine. But I came back to England, I came across the Sinai in a train with these wooden slatted seats and I came back along with a lot of other blokes. I was with a sergeant from the Queen's Irish Hussars who I made friends with coming home on the Dunnottar Castle, and we sailed from Alexandria, across the Med to Marseilles. And we stayed in Marseilles for a few days then we came on a train to Dieppe. And the train must have had the window blown out because we just had a tarpaulin, it had been fastened on and to keep it down it had bricks tied to the bottom of it, and as the train was going along it was going Bang! Bang! [laughter]. Anyhow we sailed from Dieppe to Dover, and apparently I could have been demobbed in Dover or go up to Catterick, and I wanted to go up to Catterick. I was demobbed at Catterick Camp, which was the depot for our regiment, for the Reconnaissance Corps, and that was the first time I was ever in Catterick Camp. Well I was married then, and actually the colonel really wanted me to stay in the Army and they offered me officer training but I wanted to get back to my wife of course.*

Another man serving in the Middle East was Driver T/14323168 Norman Dakers, 286 Heavy Transport Company, Royal Army Service Corps: *Next time I went out I went out to Egypt, and I needn't have gone there, they offered me a permanent job at Thetford, I thought God forsaken hole I don't want to stay there, and there was a posting going out to Egypt, I said 'well let me go with the lads, I don't want to be stuck here.' So I got posted out there with them and it was alright out there, I quite enjoyed it, I was nothing more than a glorified long-distance lorry driver, that's all, that's all I did while I was there. And do you know I had a job there for about six weeks, I used to drive 36 German prisoners 30-odd miles to a laundry where they were working from the prison camp and I was driving them back and to. I got quite pally with this sergeant there and I was going along one day and for something to say I said 'what the hell would I do now if you decided to make a run for it?' Because he was sat at the side of me with a Sten gun protecting me from the bloody Arabs, because they were like shooting at us. He said 'what do you mean run for it, where the hell would I run to? No thanks, I'll stay where I am, I'm getting well looked after in that camp, getting three meals a day.' [laughter] And I wrote to him for quite a while after I'd come out of the Army and he emigrated to America and opened a watchmaking shop, he was a watchmaker by trade, then he said don't write to me again yet I'm moving premises, and I never heard from him again after that. He emigrated to Chicago. I wasn't sorry, it was alright in Egypt. A bit naughty at times because there were one or two communist agitators there, you know, they was taking potshots at the drivers, as you were coming out of Cairo there was a big long climb with a pyramid over on your left-hand side and they were taking potshots at us, and they waited till it went dark, or dusky you know and they were taking potshots, but I don't ever remember anyone getting hit.*

Driver Norman Dakers, Royal Army Service Corps
Alamein War Cemetery

*From Cairo to Alexandria it's 187 miles and there was a place there, a marquee halfway there,
we nicknamed it the halfway house, and drivers and anybody else could go in and have a
meal, and outside it there was a telegraph pole and the telegraph like came under the ground
to there, up the pole and then across to the top at the back, this daft bugger knocked it down. I
said 'you ruddy clown, 180 miles and there's only one post stuck up and you've knocked it
down.' [laughter] Johnny went into show business he did. But the Londoners were a breed all
of their own. Do you know to be quite honest I felt more comfortable out there [northern
Europe] than I did in Egypt because you knew what you were up against and who you were
up against, but in Egypt you didn't know who the bloody hell would shake your hand or stick
a knife in your back, a treacherous lot. I didn't like them one bit. And whenever you were
travelling between, used to do a lot of long distance work and if I was ever travelling between
Cairo and Alex I always took it at night, I never went in the daytime, always went at night.
You're on your own at night and there's nobody can see you, and all it is is a white ribbon of
a road, that's all with a line down the middle, and you're staring at this, you're scared of
going to sleep while you're driving. Put a few miles in there between Cairo and Alexandria
when I was there. Travelled to the east, the south end where the Red Sea is, what's that port?
Port Tewfik, Port Said, used to get all over the place. And then I went out to Benghazi, got a
trip to Benghazi one day, taking some, there was a concert party, an Italian concert party for
them, they'd gone out there and one of our drivers had gone with them carrying some stuff for
them, scenery and whatnot they were using, and they'd left some stuff behind and I had to
take that out and it was a bloody long run from Alexandria to Benghazi, it's along the coast
most of the way and it's hot. Took a…, he sent me one day, in Alex there's a place it's where
all the, put it crudely, all the brothels were, and it was a French name, it was rue de la sœur,
it meant rue of the sisters actually, road of the sisters, and you had to get down, and go down
there to get to the docks and they had a nasty habit of if you're going down there one would
hobble out with one foot tucked under his gown to get you to slow down and if you'd
anything on the back the minute you slowed down they were on the back and taking anything
off, they were right experts at thieving. We used to have to go down there a lot to the docks
and I met a German prisoner down there and they were unloading the boat there and I saw
him go to one or two of the drivers, and I thought he's after something and he come to me, he
wanted some cigarettes and I said 'I don't smoke, I'm sorry, I can't do anything.' I said 'what
the hell are you doing, a German prisoner of war speaking with a strong Yorkshire accent.' He
said 'Yes, I had the luck of the devil didn't I, my father was German, my mother was English
and we went out there for a holiday and I got called up into the bloody German Army.' I said
'did you explain?' He said 'you must be joking, you start arguing with them they shoot you.'
[laughter] He was a rum lad he was.*

Sergeant Cliff Cole was demobbed in August and had to use all his ingenuity to
return home: *I finished up there. See when I was up at Padua, you get demobbed, and I got
papers to say report to this rail junction, get a train down to Naples where you're going to
catch a boat, and the boat's there in three days' time, so I go along and there's two or three
more with me and I'm in charge again, silly bugger. In one of the ambulances they took us to
the railway, going for the train, and there's no bloody trains, there's thousands of lads there
waiting, all waiting for transport down to Naples same as me, I said it's bloody daft, the damn*

boat's there, going in three days' time, anyway I said 'can I use your phone?' and I got on the phone back to the unit, ginger-headed RSM, I said 'hey I'm knackered here, I'm getting stuck. Do you think I can use the ambulance to get down to Naples?' 'No you can't.' I thought you bloody swine. I didn't give him my rank, anyway I slammed the phone down. Funny enough a week before, or a few days before in my unit, I had trucks as well, 3 ton Dodges, 15 cwt Dodges, and this lorry I'd given to this kid called Wiggins, Yorkshire kid and he never had, he was a poor driver, in those days there was no traffic problems or owt like that. It didn't really matter whether he messed up or what, but anyway I said 'here you can have this truck now, you're stationed up at so and so.' I think it was Ravenna where he went to, so the ambulance driver that brought us he was still there, Smithy, he was a regular bloke him and he'd been home, they called it LIAP, he'd been on leave home, if you were out there four years or more, something like that, you got a leave, he'd just come back, anyway the thing was I said 'take us up to Ravenna will you Smithy.' So he took us up to where this Wiggins had gone to, so what I did I pinched the bloody truck and off we went to Naples, I drove it all the way to Naples, pulled in for different petrols and Wiggins is still there, I don't know what happened to Wiggins but anyway when we got down to Lamy Camp it was called, in Naples, I said to the lads with him 'give him some money, treat him like,' so anyway they drop us off at this camp. Well it was full, now Vesuvius had just erupted that year and there was ash all over the place, deep in ash everywhere and this camp was smothered in it, of course everything was still, there was nobody moving and there was no boats. There were no boats, so everybody's stuck there, of course nobody knew that I'd been near Venice like.. So what happened I'm still there and I meet one or two who had left before me and they were still waiting, but what they decided upon, how they would get us home, they'd fly us home with Lancaster bombers, all these bombers are going back home there's no bombing now. There was 20 people had to go on each plane, on these bombers, and of course what happened I had two kitbags, one was packed full of cigarettes, tins of 50s, this full, I thought well I'm not throwing that off, my tin hat went off, my pack went off, and everything went off because you had to get all your weight off so I had no weight, just had just two things, anyway they stopped me like going through, 'you get shut of some of that,' so I threw whatever else, anyway to cut it short I went back after, 'okay get through now' he said and I'm on the plane, a seven hour trip that was, the time it took. It was the first time I'd flown. And we're all sat round and behind here there's like a pipe, exhaust or something, red hot it was and we'd greatcoats on an all. Anyway in the Lancaster bomber there's a lookout thing, a dome thing, and you get a ladder, a string ladder and there's a seat, you get hold of it and pull it out and sit on it and you're in the dome and when you're sat there looking at the tail and the bloody tail's going like this, I think it's gonna drop off, it was loose, I thought the bloody thing's loose, and I looked round and there's the propellers like, I was frightened to bloody death, I thought bloody thing's falling apart [laughter]. And I look down, and I thought uurgh, don't look down. Anyway I thought bugger this, I went back down and sat down.

During the month Mrs F. Dixon of 14 Lords Street, Cadishead received a letter from her daughter, Joan Gorman, stating she had arrived safely at Fort William, Ontario, Canada. She described the ship she had travelled on as being like a luxury hotel. On arrival at Canada she was met by her husband and his family and received a wholehearted welcome. She made comment on the beautifully illuminated city, a contrast to the many years of blackout or subdued lighting back in the district. Joan had married a Canadian serviceman, named Gorman, and they had a nine month old baby. Joan had worked as a packer at the CWS Soap Works.

News that two other local war brides had arrived at their new homes was received around this time. Gwendoline Green (nee Evans), daughter of Mr and Mrs Harry Evans of 44 Princes Avenue, Higher Irlam, arrived in Canada. She had married Leading Aircraftman Wesley Green of the Royal Canadian Air Force in February 1945. At that time Corporal Green was stationed at Dam Head Hall and Gwendoline was working as an operator at the Irlam telephone exchange. Gwendoline arrived at her new home at Arthur, Ontario with their seven month old daughter, Carolyn. This was the first time Corporal Green had seen his daughter. Gwendoline wrote home to her mother and was enthusiastic about Canada and its people, stating: *I know I am going to like it.*

Phyllis Clark (nee Urmston), whose family lived at 39 Princes Avenue, Higher Irlam, had married US soldier, Walter Clark of 41 Wigglesworth Street, Malden, Massachusetts, America, when he had been stationed at the US Camp at Bruche, Warrington. Walter was later stationed in Germany before returning to America. Phyllis left England on 7th August for her new home in Massachusetts, with their daughter, Doreen, who had been born on New Year's Day 1946.

SEPTEMBER 1946

After six terrible years of hate-filled war, it is a testament to the human spirit that German and Italian prisoners of war would remain and become welcome and valued members of the district. These included men such as Fritz Heinke, Heinrich W. Stephan (more commonly known as 'Bill'), Paul Schmitz and Dietrich Himmer.

Fritz Heinke
Seated centre left and his friend, John Webster, is standing behind

Bill Stephan was born on 16th October 1905. He was good friends with George Davenport, who had served in North Africa with the British Army. Bill married Olive Wilson in March 1949.

Fritz Heinke, a German paratrooper, was captured in North Africa and brought back to England, where he was put to work on Mawdsley's farm near Hollins Green. Fritz married Mary 'Polly' Mawdsley in September 1950. Fritz was born 1st June 1923. Like Bill Stephan, Fritz was good friends with a British ex-serviceman, John Webster.

Paul Schmitz was born on 3rd July 1924, at Brakel in Germany. He served as a pilot in the Luftwaffe. His Junkers 88, fitted with torpedoes and with upgraded engines to cope with the extra weight, took off from an aerodrome in Italy. It was shot down while attacking shipping in the Mediterranean. He remembered diving through a cloud of smoke and then the next thing he knew he was in the sea. Paul was pulled from the sea by an American ship that was rescuing sailors from ships that had been sunk during the attack. When the American sailors hauled Paul aboard they recognised his uniform and tried to throw him back into the sea. Fortunately an officer saved him. He was handed over to American authorities in North Africa and was then transported to America where he spent the rest of the war as a prisoner. His camp was located somewhere on the west coast of America. When the war ended, he thought he was being repatriated to Germany, but he ended up disembarking in Liverpool. Afterwards, because they had had to travel through the Panama Canal and into the Caribbean Sea, he always referred to the journey as a Caribbean Cruise. After being moved through several camps he found himself at Haydock. Bert Trautmann (later the goalkeeper for Manchester City) was in the same camp and drove a truck which transported working parties to different farms. Paul was assigned to work on a farm owned by the Bridge family on Glazebrook Lane. His future wife, Audrey Faulkner (born Cadishead, 10th April 1929), was working in Manchester as a legal secretary. On her way home from work one day she spoke to a friend on a bus. Her friend explained that she was marrying a German prisoner of war and that not many people were coming to the wedding and asked Audrey if she would attend. Audrey and Paul met at the wedding and he asked her out to the pictures. At some point in their relationship Audrey had to tell her parents, George and Edna Gladys May Faulkner, that she was marrying a German prisoner of war. George was a veteran of the First World War, having been wounded while serving with the Cambridgeshire Regiment. In the Second World War, George served the district as an air raid warden. His younger brother, John William Faulkner, was killed in action in September 1943. Audrey recounted that her father's first reaction was to threaten to fetch a gun, however, when he got to know Paul, they became very close. Paul was a great comfort to his in-laws in later life. Paul married Audrey at St John's Church, Irlam, on 11th June 1949. A large curious but benign crowd waited outside to see the married couple. When they emerged from the church, someone from the back of the crowd shouted: *That's not a German, that's Gregory Peck.*

Luftwaffe Pilot Paul Schmitz

Feldwebel Paul Schmitz, Luftwaffe

Paul Schmitz in flying gear

Paul found a job working as a motor mechanic at Bracegirdle Motors at Trafford Bar. When he was interviewed, the owner said that he could have the job as long as Max, a Jewish man who worked at the garage, agreed. Fortunately Max said yes and they became great friends. It is testament to the people of the district and to the characters of Paul and Fritz Heinke, that when they organised a reunion they chose to meet in the British Legion in Cadishead.

They would live out the rest of their lives in the district; Bill passed away in 1975, Fritz in 2001 and Paul in 2003.

During the month 'Irlam's first BAOR wife' reached Germany. Mrs Joan Pontin of 47 Boundary Road, Higher Irlam, joined her husband who was serving with the British Army of the Rhine and was stationed at Dusseldorf. She sailed from Tilbury and landed at Cuxhaven and travelled to Celle where she met her husband. They had been married for three years.

Acting Sergeant 311357 Marion Appleton of the Auxiliary Territorial Service was mentioned in dispatches (*London Gazette*, January 1949) for gallant and distinguished services in Palestine during the period between 27th September 1946 and 26th March 1947. She arrived in Palestine shortly after the Israeli terrorist group, Irgun, had bombed the King David Hotel, Jerusalem, in July 1946. Marion provided the following account: *The bombing took place just before I arrived. It damaged one end of the building, the rest was where our offices were, GHQ Palestine, and I worked in the hotel the whole time I was in Jerusalem. As to why I was mentioned in dispatches, I believe it was because on one occasion I was ordered to attend the senior officer's residence and go with a colonel and a few men, by foot, to GHQ (King David Hotel) to send a message to the War Office. We were about half way there when we were suddenly fired upon by tracer fire from nearby buildings – without any warning whatsoever. The colonel grabbed me and threw me into a ditch at the side of the road and the men who were with us returned fire. I was not hurt, just bruised a bit and had some torn clothing and was able to crawl and get back to the residence. I did not scream or complain, just followed instructions. Eventually we went to GHQ by armoured car and the message was dispatched. It was all quite scary at the time. It doesn't sound like much now but things were getting dicey at that time. Eventually the girls were not allowed out of barracks without an escort of four soldiers. Needless to say we didn't get out very often.*

Marion was born in Cadishead in 1927, the daughter of Albert and Margaret Appleton (nee Higginbottom) of Hampton Road, Cadishead. Marion enlisted in the Auxiliary Territorial Service in October 1944, at the age of 17. She was posted to Pontefract for six weeks' training; learning to drill and march and given physical and intelligence tests. She was then posted to Slough to work as a clerk in the company office. At the time V1 and V2 bombs were flying over the London area and she found it very uncomfortable. After eight months she was transferred to Longtown, near Carlisle, where she continued to work as a clerk.

Marion Appleton, Auxiliary Territorial Service

During her time in Longtown Marion was promoted to corporal. At the age of 19 she volunteered for overseas service and was posted, almost immediately, to the Middle East. She landed at Alexandria and from there she was transported by armoured vehicle to Cairo. After three weeks in Cairo, she was posted to General Officer Commanding British Troops in Jerusalem, Palestine, travelling by train across the Sinai Desert.

Marion spent Christmas 1946 in Bethlehem and visited the Dead Sea, Nazareth and Sarafand on the coast. She also spent a leave on the island of Cyprus. In December 1947 she returned to England and was demobilised in March of the following year. She married Victor Ryland in March 1948. Her brother, Arthur, served with the Royal Engineers.

OCTOBER 1946

Laura Gwyneth Penkethman, daughter of Mr F. Penkethman of 50 Dean Road, Cadishead, had met a Canadian airman, Mr Rathier, when he was serving with the Royal Canadian Air Force stationed at Dam Head Hall. They were married in February 1946 and Laura sailed for Canada on 24th August on board the *Queen Mary*. On arrival in Canada she was welcomed at a party thrown by her mother-in-law, Mrs Frances Rathier of 298 Third Avenue, Pembroke, Toronto, Ontario.

Another local woman who sailed to Canada on board the *Queen Mary* was Audrey Ludwig (nee Walker) whose mother lived at 46 Caroline Street, Irlam. On arrival in Canada she had nearly a week of rail travel before reaching her husband's home at 163 Cathedral Street, Winnipeg where she was met by her husband's family and received a typical, warm-hearted Canadian welcome. Audrey had met her husband when he was serving with the Royal Canadian Air Force stationed at Glazebrook and they were married at Torquay.

A public meeting, called by the Committee of the Higher Irlam Social Club, was held on Thursday, 24th October at the Higher Irlam Co-operative Hall, to discuss the proposed new club due to open in 1947. The committee had purchased an ex-military building that had been used as a military hospital. It was a wooden building 92 feet long and nearly 19 feet wide and it contained two wash basins, a bathroom, lavatory accommodation, gas fires and fittings. A plot of land had been acquired in Cutnook Lane where the building was to be erected which would leave room for a tennis court and bowling green.

A 'high tea' was held, at the invitation of District Officer James Sinclair Kerr, Order of St John, president of the local divisions of St John Ambulance Brigade, at the British Restaurant on Saturday, 26th October for members of the Irlam and Cadishead St John Ambulance and Nursing Divisions, the Lancashire Steel Corporation, Irlam Works Division, and the Cadet Division. Among the guests were the chairman of the Council (Councillor Arnold Briggs JP), Mrs Sinclair Kerr (president, Irlam and Cadishead Nursing Division), Miss Swan, Miss Kerr, Edwin Jones (vice-president) and Henry Nurse. This was the first social event the St John Ambulance had held since the outbreak of war in 1939. During the event Edwin Jones who had been controller of the Irlam ARP services during the war thanked the brigade for its services: *They were the first to volunteer for duty and the local ARP first aid service was built upon the St John Ambulance Brigade members. They had worked hard and, realising the possibilities of being cut off from the surrounding districts, made it possible to convert Irlam Hall into an emergency hospital.*

St John Ambulance 'high tea'

NOVEMBER 1946

On Sunday, 3rd November, the Irlam and Cadishead branch of the British Legion held its annual meeting, presided, for the final time, by the retiring branch chairman, Benjamin Neville. He had been an official in the branch for 25 years and to mark this occasion the president of the local branch, Mr J.A. Massie, presented him with a cheque, on behalf of the branch, as a tribute to the work he had done for servicemen and ex-servicemen.

During the meeting Benjamin gave an overview of the history and progress of the local branch. He explained that the branch originally began with a small wooden hut which had been presented to the National Association of Discharged Soldiers and Sailors Association by Frank W. Cooper, the managing director of the Steelworks, in 1919. It remained as such until their founder, Earl Haig, brought the British Legion into being. The United Services Fund was founded and all the National Association of Discharged Soldiers and Sailors Associations and Comrades of the Great War clubs were transferred to the British Legion. He outlined the growth of the fund and its system of grants. Benjamin stated that with one hut the accommodation was limited and it was decided to purchase another and build it at the rear of the first. He outlined the difficulties the branch went through between 1922 and 1934. It was in 1934 that the branch started developing plans for larger premises which resulted in the building of the large club premises on Liverpool Road (the building ceased to be a Legion Club in the early 2000s and is currently named the Royal Arms Club). He stated: *Little did we think at that time there would be another war but we must have had some sight of things to come and, as a result of hard work we have to-day a club really fit for heroes to come to. If we had not taken the steps we did we should never have been able to accommodate you all in the old huts.* Benjamin explained that the British Legion and United Services Fund Benevolent Department became the British Legion Services Committee and its first priority was to the branch of the Legion. That came first and the club was secondary. No ex-servicemen could be a club member without being a member of the branch but he could be a member of the branch without being a member of the club. He appealed for the returning younger generation of ex-servicemen to join the branch. He paid tribute to the work of Peter Barrow DCM who, as secretary of the branch, had a colossal task to perform due to their set up in 1946 being two committees; a Branch Committee and a Club Committee. He also welcomed Tom Walton, as the new chairman of the Irlam and Cadishead Branch. In reply Tom paid tribute to the work of Benjamin Neville during the 25 years he had been an official in the branch. The following branch and club officials and committees were elected at the meeting:

Branch: Mr J.A. Massie, president; Tom Walton, chairman; Mr J. Statham, vice-chairman; Peter Barrow DCM, secretary; Mr G. McCallum, treasurer. Committee: Archer Kell, Henry Grindley, Peter Broughton MM, Jack Newton DCM, Jack Carter and messrs J. Crone, D. Fowler, F. Lockley, A. Hughes, T. Williams and J. Butler.

Club: Mr J.A. Massie, president; Mr J. Butler, vice president; Mr G. McCallum, treasurer. Committee, Tom Walton, Archer Kell, Peter Broughton MM, Henry Grindley and Jack Newton DCM, and messrs F. Lockley, T. Williams, D. Fowler, Jack Carter, J. Crone, A. Hughes, J.E. Hampson and Herbert Ditchfield.

On Monday, 11th November the district held its annual Remembrance Day parade and service at the War Memorial. The *Guardian* reported: *Twice in a lifetime our young men have gone away to the uttermost corners of the earth to fight for what they believed to be a just cause. Twice in a lifetime they have died in the mud of European fields, the sands of African deserts, the steaming jungles of the East, the air over every theatre of war and in every sea and ocean of the earth. On Sunday, in a simple ceremony, we remembered them. Fathers who served in the First World War, and their sons, veterans of the Second World War, with their wives, mothers or sweethearts, stood side by side before the War Memorial in Prince's Park and, with bowed heads, paid silent homage to their dead of two generations. Earlier, members of the British Legion fell in at their club. Thirty years had taken the spring out of the step, stooped the shoulders and thinned or whitened the hair of many of them but, on the word of command they jumped to it, came to attention and did a smart right turn. Then, headed by Cadishead Public Band and with their blue and gold standard in the van, they moved off, heads erect, arms swinging, medals clinking, boots beating out the measured tread of men on the march, to keep the tryst with their fallen comrades.*

The ex-servicemen had gathered at the Council Offices and formed part of the procession to the memorial led by the chairman of the Council (Councillor Briggs) and Cadishead Public Band, with its conductor Mr F.V. Lloyd. Council members, officials, policemen, Home Guard Old Comrades, NFS, St John Ambulance Brigade with its Nursing and Cadet Divisions, RAOB, scouts, guides and cubs also participated in the parade. Wreaths were laid at the memorial and two minutes' silence was observed, followed by the sounding of the *Last Post*.

The Chairman of the Council (Councillor Arnold Briggs) (sixth from right) at the Remembrance Day service in Princes Park on Sunday. Also in the group are Mr. J. H. Jones, M.P. (third from right) and Mr. J. Statham, vice-chairman of the British Legion, who stands, holding a wreath, next to the chairman.

The *Guardian* wrote: *To many people – particularly those of the younger generation – it may seem strange that we who are a little older still insist on this annual solemn ceremony of remembrance. Well, it certainly is not sickly sentiment. Those who were left behind were good lads. They fought and they died for something in which they believed. And, before they died, many of them went through a hell that the last war, even in its most bitter phases, never equalled. I should be a fool to say that these men died with a smile and rousing, patriotic phrases on their lips: I should be a liar if I said they were unafraid of death: I should offend them if I called them heroes, because they never looked on themselves as such. But whether they liked it or not they were heroes. Not the death or glory heroes of the films and popular fiction, but plain, unassuming Britishers drawn from every walk of life, who had a dirty job to do and who were determined to do it. They died: and went to their deaths with fear in their hearts but with grim, bitter jests on their lips. They were heroes. Typical British heroes who would scrounge everything that could be scrounged, and yet would share the last drop of water in a canteen with a comrade; who grumbled and groused at everything, but clung doggedly to the strip of trench they were told to hold; who cursed (very quietly) everyone*

Page 1358

above the rank of acting lance corporal; who wangled all the leave and everything else they could, yet never went back on a pal; who dodged every possible parade and fatigue, but would do them for a friend; who would readily, though temporarily, change their religion if they found one padre's sermon was shorter than anothers; who would fight at the drop of the hat, no matter what the odds, and would keep on fighting until they dropped. These were our heroes – these and their sons of the last war.

The annual Poppy collection was up by £7 on the previous year with £119-11-1, collected throughout Irlam and Cadishead. Of this sum £112-5-1 was collected through poppy sales and £7-6s through the sales of wreaths. Peter Barrow DCM, secretary of the local branch of the British Legion, thanked the district for its support.

It was reported that the 20 prefabricated homes on Fairhills Road would be ready for use at the end of November. Construction had started in June but poor weather had delayed the building programme. The construction of the prefabs had been plagued with delays, due to hold-ups for materials, and more frequently for fittings. Progress was also being made at the prefabs on Moss Side Road, Cadishead. The Cadishead prefabs were made of aluminium and of a different construction to those on Fairhills Road, Irlam, which were concrete panels. They were completed in 1946 and remained in place until c.1961 when they were demolished.

On Wednesday, 20th November a well-attended public meeting took place at Fairhills Road Church, presided over by Councillor Briggs (chairman of the Council) to discuss what form the Irlam and Cadishead War Memorial should take. Councillor Briggs asked those at the meetings for suggestions and many were received, ranging from a maternity home, a cottage hospital, playing fields, a community centre and a memorial hall in the proposed new civic centre. It was the last idea which met with most approval and the view was that a new civic centre should be dedicated as a memorial, that an organ should be installed and bronze plaques bearing the names of the fallen placed in prominent positions. At this meeting it was decided to form the Irlam and Cadishead War Memorial Committee to consider the suggestions in more detail and also consider suggestions made by works, factories, guilds and other local organisations. A further public meeting would be called to hear the recommendations of the newly formed committee.

During the month the *Guardian* questioned when the district's brick built air raid shelters would be removed: *So far nothing seems to have been done in the matter and these unsightly reminders of the grim days of the war are still with us. At least one 'batch' of them – those in King's Road –should have been taken down long ago. Not only have they become a dangerous playground for children, but they create an obstruction in the road itself. With the street lighting in King's Road what is the remarkable thing is that there has not, as yet, been a serious accident. But it could happen. Still, there is always a chance that we are hanging on to our shelters so that we can have them scheduled as ancient monuments.*

DECEMBER 1946

Britain's overseas Dominions were continuing to help feed the nation. From time to time, tinned meat, fruit, jam and dried fruit was received in the district from overseas for distribution to people of 70 years of age. Since September 1946 Irlam Council had received four consignments of gifts of foodstuffs from Australia and South Africa. These gifts included 624 tins of sausage meat, 288 tins of luncheon meat, 440 tins of fruit, 240 tins of pears, 500 tins of jam, 144 boxes of candy and a small quantity of dried fruit. These goods were stored at the Citizens Advice Bureau at 604 Liverpool Road, Irlam and were distributed, under a voucher scheme, to residents aged over 70 in the district during the month.

Tinned food from South Africa and Australia

Herbert and Mabel Dugdale and their seven year old daughter, Patricia, moved from the one room they shared at Marlborough Road, Higher Irlam into the district's first completed prefabricated bungalow. On Saturday and Sunday, 7th and 8th December, the bungalow, one of twenty on Fairhills Road, was open for public viewing and people were impressed with the neat interior layout, the large cupboards, the compact bathroom with heated towel rail, the light airy bedrooms and the heating arrangements for the bedrooms (dry hot air from the living room fire flowed through vents into the rooms). They were most impressed with the kitchen, with its electric cooker, wash boiler, water heater, metal cupboards and food storage space. Herbert had been called up into the Royal Artillery in 1940 and spent four years of his service in India. He transferred to the Royal Electrical and Mechanical Engineers in 1945 and was demobbed in March 1946. Prior to joining the Army he had worked at the CWS Soap Works.

One of the prefabs on Fairhills Road, Irlam
Built in 1946 as temporary homes, one still remains in use in 2014, the other 19 were replaced with modern bungalows in the early 2000s

Prefab being constructed
New Moss Road, Cadishead

Prefabs under construction
Fairhills Road, Irlam

JANUARY 1947

Nineteen year old Gunner 14137794 **James Herbert Newton**, 51 Heavy Anti-Aircraft Regiment, Royal Artillery, was killed in a road accident at Hollins Green on Saturday, 25th January.

He had joined the Army in March 1946 and was subsequently posted to Italy after his training. In January 1947 he was home on leave in Rixton, where he lived with his parents, John Alfred and Gladys Newton (new Clarke), at 20 School Lane. Jimmy, as he was more commonly known, had been due to travel overseas back to his unit on the following Wednesday, 29th January. He was killed instantly when the motorcycle he was riding crashed into the wall of the Old Black Swan Hotel, Hollins Green. At 1.30pm Jimmy had left the family home and three hours later his father was informed that Jimmy had been involved in an accident. His father immediately made his way to the scene where he found his son lying near the building. An inquest was held by the South West Lancashire Coroner, Cornelius Bolton. One witness, John Hindley of Woodhead Lane, Rixton, gave evidence that Jimmy had asked him if he could have a ride on his motorcycle. John watched Jimmy riding towards Warrington and then head back through Hollins Green when he heard the crash. John Newton gave evidence that his son had never owned a motorcycle and John Hindley stated that, although Jimmy had said he could ride motorcycles, he had never previously seen him do so. Another witness, a bus driver John Knowsley Thompson, heard the crash whilst he was inside a shop and came out to see a man lying on the pavement. There was no other traffic on the road at the time. Constable Atkinson attended and found Jimmy lying with his feet towards the front door of the hotel. A local doctor was summoned and pronounced him dead.

The *Guardian* commented that Jimmy, a former member of the Cadishead Youth Club was: *Well liked in the village for his blithe friendliness and his death cast a shadow over the whole district.* A verdict of misadventure was recorded. Jimmy was accorded a military funeral at Hollins Green Cemetery on Thursday, 30th January a contingent of soldiers from New Brighton attended, including a bearer party of six soldiers. This was the second tragedy to hit the family. Jimmy's sister, Joyce, had died in tragic circumstances 12 years before, indirectly as a result of a cycling accident.

The recently formed Irlam and Cadishead War Memorial Committee held a public meeting on Thursday, 30th January to discuss the proposed War Memorial to commemorate those of the district lost in the Second World War. The chairman of the Committee was Councillor Briggs (chairman of Irlam Urban Council), the honorary secretary was Mary Bowker and the treasurer was Mr H.I. Jones of Martins Bank, Cadishead.

FEBRUARY 1947
On 7th February Gunner 14290431 Harry Roger Winkle, serving with the British Occupation Force in Germany, married Elgibieta Cierocka at Husum Garrison Church, Germany. Elgibieta was a Polish woman whose father and sister lived in Danzig. They had met in early 1946 at a NAAFI dance at Flensburg, northern Germany. Before the war Roger, as he was more commonly known, had worked in the laboratory at the Steelworks. He joined the Home Guard on 6th June 1940, as Private 230, 2 Platoon, D Company, until he was called up into the Royal Artillery in September 1942. During active service he was with 83rd Field Regiment, Royal Artillery, 53rd Welsh Infantry Division, and later, in 1946, he transferred to 55th Field Regiment. His wife arrived in Irlam in March 1947 and Roger was demobilised from the Army one month later. Harry Roger Winkle was born on 29th March 1916, the son of Florence and the late Harry R. Winkle of 45 Chapel Road, Irlam.

MARCH 1947

On Saturday, 1st March, after a service by Reverend Bakker at St Mary's Church, the funeral of Henry George Salt took place at Manchester Crematorium. Henry died at his home, 15 Hampton Road, Cadishead, aged 54, at the end of February. He had served as a lieutenant in the Home Guard throughout the war, He was a veteran of the First World War for 5½ years, initially with the 5th Battalion, Cheshire Regiment, and was later commissioned as a lieutenant into the Royal Welch Fusiliers.

The district's air raid shelters were demolished in the week before 15th March. An article in the *Guardian* stated: *Here's something Hitler never managed ... to knock down an air raid shelter in Cadishead and Irlam. During the past few days air raid shelters in the district have been demolished faster than they were built. The 'bone crusher' moves in, pounds them until they fall, and then the mechanical navvy scoops up the debris. The operation is speedy and effective and gives the public plenty of chance to act as 'sidewalk superintendents.'*

Gunner Harry Roger Winkle, Royal Artillery

Demolition of one of the district's brick built communal air raid shelters

By March it was clear that the War Memorial in Prince's Park, which had been unveiled in April 1923 was showing signs of wear and the *Guardian* was forthright in its views. It described the memorial as: *a pitiable affair and an insult to the memory of many gallant men. A hideous, shapeless mass of concrete surmounted by an utterly insignificant figure supposed, I imagine, to represent a Winged Victory (although it actually looks like an amateur monumental mason's conception of the Angel Gabriel), is surely not a fitting tribute to the men who sacrificed everything.* The columnist appealed to the War Memorial Committee to consider recent proposals, by the district's surveyor, Henry Nurse, to redesign and re-site the memorial.

APRIL 1947

By April 1947 it was the view of the War Memorial Committee that there *would be no cold stone monument to remind the people of Irlam and Cadishead of the local men who fell in the war.* Instead a proposal, following a public meeting, was that the memorial would take the form of an organ to be placed in the assembly room of a proposed new civic centre and by the furnishing of a specially dedicated room within this proposed building. The Committee also stated the plaques on the existing memorial at Prince's Park would be re-lettered to include the names of those who died in the 1939-45 war. A target of £5,000, to be raised by public subscription, was set. Clearly the proposals changed over the rest of 1947 and 1948, no doubt due to the deteriorating condition of the First World War Memorial at Prince's Park that necessitated the new War Memorial that stands in the park today.

 Two ex-servicemen were voted onto the district's Council: Jack Scotson of the Reconnaissance Corps (pictured) represented Irlam Central (Conservative) and ex-Flying Officer Ernest Mason of the RAF represented Cadishead Central (Labour).

At the end of April news was received that ex-Chief Petty Officer Alexander Dobson, Royal Navy, second son of Captain William and Mrs Borrino of Lords Street, Cadishead, who was living in Australia received the Distinguished Service Medal from Australia's new Governor-General, Mr W.J. McKell. Apparently Alex was the first man to be decorated by the new Governor-General.

Alex lived in Cadishead before the war and worked at Metropolitan Vickers, and like his father and brother, served with the Territorial Army and was mobilized when war broke out. Due to his specialist trade he was released from the Army but subsequently joined the Royal Navy. He spent his entire service in the Royal Navy serving in submarines and served in every theatre, receiving six campaign stars. He received the DSM for his role in the midget submarine attack on Japanese shipping at Singapore, which resulted in the sinking of a Japanese cruiser. Alex was engine room artificer on the submarine *Stygian* which towed the midget submarines. Victoria Crosses were awarded to two members of the crews of the midget submarines. In addition Alex was chief of the boarding parties which boarded and sank several Japanese supply ships. He was demobilised from the Royal Navy after the war and in January 1947 emigrated to Australia. By April he was working as a fitter in Canberra although he was *expecting an appointment in Rabaul, New Britain*. During the Second World War his father served as a captain with the Royal Army Pay Corps, his elder brother, George Vincent Borrino, was a sergeant in the Loyal Regiment (North Lancashire) who was recommended for gallantry in Italy, and two brothers, Peter and Cedric, served in the Royal Navy. Alexander's mother told the *Guardian*: *There was no special reason why her son had changed his name*, as he was no longer using the surname Borrino. Dobson was his mother's maiden name.

On Saturday, 26th April the closure of Rixton-with-Glazebrook Forces' Canteen was marked by a farewell party held at the Centenary Methodist Schoolroom. In July 1943 a decision had been taken to open a Forces canteen for the convenience of the servicemen and women stationed at the two military camps at Glazebrook. The canteen had opened in September 1943. During the 3½ years of the canteen's existence, Mr Allen (chairman of the canteen) said 30,581 members of the Forces had used the canteen, and 50,086 hot drinks and 72,468 meals had been served. Outstanding service had been rendered by a number of volunteers, particularly Mrs Stringer, Mr E. Sinton (secretary), Miss Scanes, as chief caterer, and Mr J. Baguley (treasurer). Their most generous member was Mr T. Johnson of Cadishead Moss.

MAY 1947
Local men were still serving with the Army and were demobbed piecemeal. Driver Frank McQuirk was demobbed on 5th May at York Barracks. The following is how he described the demobilisation process, from being informed in Italy to his eventual return to civilian life: *We were there* [Milan] *for quite a while, and then one day I was having my breakfast and sergeant major says 'nine o'clock outside the guard room, you're leaving us' and I said 'why?', 'don't ask questions', you know. Nine o'clock came and this lorry came and there were quite a few more blokes and I jumped in the back and nobody knew where we were going and they took us to a place called Udine, it's between Verona and Venice, and they dropped me off. The sergeant went in the guard room and they left me and I went to see the officer and he said 'well I don't know what you're doing here because we don't want you.' So they asked me one or two questions 'what can you do?' and all that sort of thing. 'I can drive', 'well we can use you.' And I didn't know at the time but they were moving men from one place to another and we were getting nearer our demob time. You know they were moving us in stages, I didn't know that at the time. It came up on our orders that they were starting demob in groups, you know number 20, 30, 40, and I can't remember the group I was, number 30 something, and they said it was so and so month, it started off like when you'd been abroad say five years, 4½ years, three. And it got down to between three years and ten months and four years, that group, and I qualified for coming home and I came home on what they called Python. I don't know what Python stands for, you know, there was two groups, there was one called LIAP, you got, I think about ten days leave before demob, it's 'leave in advance of Python', LIAP, something like that. And the other one was Python when you was on your way to be demobbed and that was it really. You gradually made your way from one place to another till you got to home.* [PYTHON was the code word for leave for servicemen who had spent over four years abroad].

We finished up at a place called Domodossola, it's near the Swiss border, and they put us on a train. They were electric trains through the tunnel to Switzerland and then we got off and on to an ordinary train and some of you got in carriages but others you had in awful wagons. We got, we volunteered for a wagon, it had a sheet on the top and it was taking mail back home and we volunteered for that because when they stopped anywhere for something to eat you got your meal first because there was only about four of you and then you'd come back and then all the rest had their meals and then we came back and we got to Calais. Calais to Dover, Dover to somewhere in Norfolk, Norfolk to Halifax, and Halifax to York. But all the way along you got these scams off sergeants. One scam, when we got to Norfolk, we got there at dinner time and when we went for our meal, queued for our meal at tea time the sergeant was there welcoming us all home and he says 'you'll be going on the passion wagon tonight?', he didn't ask me, some of the lads said 'no.' 'Well you can do a little job for me, you can peel some spuds', after being away for about four years, you know all scams. They were regular men, could go out see, lot of scams. When I finally got to Halifax, we got there about two o'clock in the morning, this place we were at it just looked like a housing estate all these, like houses, they all had little gardens, I think they must have been so that the jerries couldn't recognise it from the air, you know. And there were about 20 of us and we got to these, they called them biscuits, what we slept on, and we got them and we got our heads down and the next morning reveille, the sergeant came on and he put three of us on a charge for not reading Part 1 orders. I'd never been on a charge before but that was one of the things you were supposed to do, before you do anything else read Part 1 orders, and you were not supposed to shave in this room, you go in the ablutions to shave. And we went on parade then he marched us in to see the orderly officer and he asked us a load of questions and he said 'where've you come from?', I said 'Italy', then he just said 'dust your medals and go.' I didn't have any medals but that's what he said. So we got off, and then when we got outside this sergeant says 'you see that lorry there?' he says, a great big one 'you clean that before you get demobbed.' Scams again [laughter]. Get us all cleaning lorries that they'd been using. Frank was demobbed at York Infantry Barracks on 5th May 1947 and was finally transferred to Class Z of the Army Reserve on 14th August 1947. His military conduct was described as 'exemplary' and his officer provided the following testimonial: *He is a first class driver with much experience in both driving and vehicle recovery works. Can carry out any running repairs on heavy vehicles. Conscientious and hardworking, reliable, trustworthy, sober, honest and loyal.*

For those men who continued to serve in the Armed Forces, the end of the war had not completely removed the danger. On 6th May 1947, Flight Sergeant Harold Townend was a navigator on a Lancaster bomber (210 Squadron) which took off from St Eval in Cornwall to carry out navigation exercises and send back weather reports from the Atlantic. There were 11 crew members on board, including three trainee navigators. After take-off they climbed to 5,000 feet and at the Point of Ayr dropped to 2,000 feet. They then set course for Mizen Head, climbing to 10,000 feet. During the climb the starboard outer engine failed and the aircraft was ordered to discontinue the exercise and return to base. At about midnight they neared St Eval and the aircraft started to jettison fuel to reduce the risk of fire in the event of a crash landing. As they commenced the approach the pilot was informed of a strong cross wind on 26 runway and had to abort the landing, putting on full power on the three remaining engines to go round again. Unfortunately the port inner engine failed during the circuit. Harold takes up the story: *Oh I knew something was going to happen because we lost one engine and returned to base and it was a new pilot I'd never flown with him before, my skipper had gone on to Benson on Mosquitos. I saved the rear gunner's life actually because the skipper had a bit of a panic in his voice I'll tell you that now, I called him up on the intercom after we'd lost two engines and we're going round again, I said to him 'is it alright if I bring the rear gunner up?' 'Please yourself!' he's the skipper, 'please yourself!' So I said to the rear gunner 'better come up.' However, with two engines and the cross wind we did not get the aircraft down and with full power again on two engines, the pilot pulled away and we got to 5-600 feet when one of the remaining two engines failed and the pilot called over the intercom that we were going into the sea but that did not happen and in fact the aircraft slid sideways over St Mawgan airfield and crashed half-way between St Columb and St Dennis – and when I came to I was going through the motions of swimming but in fact I was in a ploughed field and I suddenly saw someone running and realised he was not running on water.*

Flight Sergeant Harold Townend (seated right) and the crew before the crash

The wedding of Harold Townend and Betty Dawson

The last thing I heard the skipper say was 'we're going into the sea.' How I got there, I think there was a big..., when I look back, I crawled back round and I saw this, all the tail unit and everything missing and there was this big hole, I thought it must have thrown me out of there with the force of the crash and as I say they were about an hour and half before they got to us. The second pilot had broke both his legs and other people had injuries. Nobody was killed, it was absolutely marvellous that nobody was killed when you saw the damage to that aircraft cos it was 20 past midnight when it happened. The pilot and the second pilot F'Sgt 'Chips' Causley had both pulled back on the sticks to clear a wall and the tail section and especially the rear turret was two fields away mangled up. We all escaped death but we suffered fractures. Eventually we all got back to flying.

Eighteen days later Harold married Betty Dawson at St Eval. The reception took place at the station cinema at RAF St Eval where Harold and Betty were both stationed and they went on honeymoon to Torquay. In September 1947 Harold was posted to Southern Rhodesia as an instructor at No 3 Navigation Training School. Betty joined him there and their eldest daughter, Ann Marie, was born out there.

Frances Lillian Broughton married William Bennett at St John's Church, Irlam. Frances had served with the Women's Auxiliary Air Force (WAAF) and had been demobbed in June 1946, with the equivalent rank of lance corporal. William was the third son of Mr and Mrs Bennett of 77 Ferry Road, Irlam.

JUNE and JULY 1947
During the month the officers and men of the Fleet Air Arm camp at HMS *Gosling V* at Glazebrook, which had been recently disbanded, provided a gift of a tubular steel chute with slide and steps to Cadishead County Infant Primary School.

Ex-servicewoman Jean Muriel Allan, who had served with the Women's Auxiliary Air Force for four years, married Walter Thomas Harold Kelvie of Maidstone, Kent, at St John's Church on 7th June. Jean had been demobilised in March 1947. She was the daughter of Mr and Mrs J. Allan of 53 Ferry Road, Irlam. Walter had served 5½ years with the Royal Artillery and was on demob leave at the time of the wedding.

On 28th June Irlam soldier, Cedric C. Willis, who was stationed in Germany married Fraulein Ingeburg Pawelski of Berlin at the Church of Slandesame, Germany, and, to satisfy the authorities, a second service was held at a Church of England church (presumably a Forces church near Berlin). A reception was held at the bride's home in Berlin. Ingeburg had been a leather machinist and met Cedric around 1946 at Charlottenburg, Berlin. Cedric was demobilised from the Army soon afterwards having served over 4½ years. Before the war Cedric had worked for A. Taylor, haulage contractor at Rixton. He was the eldest son of Mr and Mrs C. Willis of 50 Fiddlers Lane, Higher Irlam. The couple arrived back in the district on 28th July, to live at Fiddlers Lane.

AUGUST 1947

On 16th August Constable George Southam of Irlam retired from the Barton section of the Lancashire Constabulary after 27 years' service. George had served with the Border Regiment during the First World War and had been awarded the Military Medal for bravery at Passchendaele. He had served with the Army from 1916 until 1919 when he was demobilised. In 1920 he joined Lancashire Constabulary and trained at Lancaster Castle after which he was initially posted to Horwich and later served at Longridge, Preston, for two years. In April 1923 he was posted to the Irlam district, at that time the Police Station was at Moss Lane, Cadishead. He remained the local policeman for the rest of his service and throughout the war years. At the time of his retirement he was the longest serving and *one of the most popular* constables in the Barton section.

News was received in August that Captain William Borrino had been awarded the Territorial Efficiency Decoration for long service with the Territorial Army, reported in the *London Gazette*. William's Commanding Officer received the following notification: *I am directed to inform you that the King has been pleased to approve the award to Capt. W. Borrino, RAPC, of the Territorial Efficiency Decoration. You are requested to inform this officer accordingly.* He was a First World War veteran and was called up at the start of the Second World War. In 1947 he was stationed at the Army Pay Office, Manchester. Details of the Borrino family feature in other chapters of the book.

SEPTEMBER 1947

During the month the committee of the Irlam and Cadishead War Comforts and Welcome Home Fund decided that the Fund was to be wound up. The subscription list had closed at the end of January 1946 and in December 1946 the balance of the fund was £794-14-2. After the war ended invitations had been sent to 1,335 ex-servicemen and women to attend Welcome Home dinners and concerts; the actual numbers that attended and were attended at these events were 796. Difficulties created by shift work and personal arrangements had prevented many of the remaining local ex-service personnel attending the Welcome Home events and it was decided that instead of setting up another event, each ex-serviceman would instead receive a cash gift of £1. Since the Comforts Fund had been created £3, 271-16-4 had been raised by various efforts and subscriptions.

There was great concern that Irlam and Cadishead's War Memorial scheme was in danger of becoming a *dismal flop*. A Gift Week ran between 20th to 27th September where three local centres were open throughout the district to receive gifts. The lack of support for the scheme caused Councillor Briggs (chairman of the Council and of the War Memorial Committee) great concern and he stated: *Unless donations come in much more rapidly, I am afraid the scheme will be a failure. Our scheme includes the provision of a special room in the proposed Public Hall, the installation of an organ in the Assembly Hall and the placing of plaques, bearing the names of those who gave their lives, on the War Memorial. All this needs money and unfortunately, it is not coming in fast enough. If every man and woman in the district would contribute only the price of one 20 packet of cigarettes – and surely that is not much to ask to perpetuate the memory of the lads who gave everything – our financial difficulties would be solved.* The local columnist in the *Guardian* stated: *Do you want 'Lest we forget' to become 'Best we forget?' It's up to you and me and all of us to see that even the most absent-minded doesn't get a chance to forget.*

On 27th September the local *Guardian* published an article titled: *Begged, prayed to come back – Former POW will return to Irlam.* It told the story of Italian soldier, Michelo Prezolas, who had been captured in North Africa and was sent back to England as a prisoner of war. During the war he had worked, for 18 months, at Woodstock Farm, Astley Road, for Mr T.W. Upton, and had grown to like England. While a prisoner he had been informed that his three brothers, all serving with the Italian Army, had been killed and he later received a letter informing him that his father had died. He carried on hoping one day to return to Italy to be reunited with his mother and wife. He returned back to his home at Foggia, Italy in 1945 but soon after arriving his mother died. He decided he wanted to return to Irlam and wrote repeatedly to Mr Upton to help, which he did by contacting the authorities and organising the relevant permits. Mr Upton said: *He begged and prayed me to have him back. I have found him accommodation and obtained his permit. Now all I am waiting for is a letter to tell me when I can expect him. When he does come, he will come by air.*

During the month the British Restaurant at Cadishead was renamed the Civic Restaurant and plans for an extension had been approved, and negotiations completed with Royles Engineering, for the required land. The original building, which could accommodate 175 people, and was at the time acknowledged to be: *one of the most up-to-date and best-equipped British Restaurants in the country,* was going to continue to serve as a canteen but the planned extension would become a modern café. Councillor Briggs (chairman of the Council) said: *The café, we hope, will be one of the best of its kind, and certainly the most up to date in the district, it will have ultra-modern furniture, and there will be a staff of waitresses. The present restaurant will continue to serve midday meals and teas.*

There was criticism of the Council for the letting of houses to ex-servicemen, who it was stated were given too many privileges compared to other local people such as those who had served as miners, or with Civil Defence Services or local men who had been sent to London to repair war damage. Local people questioned the points system used by the Council to determine housing allocation. Forty of the recently built prefabs had been let to local ex-servicemen, no doubt the cause of the debate.

OCTOBER 1947

On Wednesday, 1st October former prisoner of war, ex-Corporal Leslie Shaw, who had served for 6½ years with the Royal Inniskilling Fusiliers, left Southampton with his wife and daughter and sailed for America where they would settle with Leslie's sister-in-law. On the previous weekend a reception was held at the district's civic restaurant to mark their departure where his father presented a wallet, necklace and bangle to Leslie, his daughter-in-law and granddaughter. On Sunday, a farewell concert was held at the local British Legion Hall where Mr J.A. Massie (president of the local British Legion) presented him with a silver cigarette case, a gift from the committee and local Legion members. Before the war he worked at the CWS Soap Works and played football and cricket for the works' teams. He joined the Army in 1940 and served with the First Army in North Africa from March 1943, where he was wounded and taken prisoner. He was demobilised from the Army in 1946.

On Sunday, 5th October a harvest festival was held at Rixton Methodist Church during which many chocolate bars were donated for dispatch to German children.

On Saturday, 25th October ex-Lancashire Fusilier Owen E. McCarthy MM and Bar, of 6 Baines Avenue, Irlam, was presented with a cheque by Father O'Dwyer following a collection by members of Irlam Catholic Club in appreciation of Owen's bravery during the war. Owen had received the actual Military Medal and Bar in the post in September 1947. He served in North Africa, Sicily, Italy and Austria and was demobilised in December 1946. Before the war he had worked in the cost office at the Steelworks and returned to that work after the war.

On Sunday, 26th October the first annual inspection of the Irlam and Cadishead Divisions of St John Ambulance Brigade took place in the playground of Irlam Central School. This was the first time an inspection had been held since 1938.

It was confirmed that Reverend Hendrik Bakker, vicar of St Mary's Church, Cadishead, was soon to be leaving the district after 30 years, to take up a position at Tyldesley. Hendrik was born in Cheltenham, and was educated at Ipswich Council School, London University and the Manchester University. His first curacy was at St Hilda's Church, Old Trafford in 1913 and in 1917 he was sent to Cadishead to take up an appointment at St Mary's Church. When he arrived the church was based in an old tin hut until the new church was opened in 1927.

During the month 100 families of the Admiralty housing estate, Lords Street, Cadishead, were requested by the Admiralty to find alternative accommodation. The houses had been built by the Ministry of Supply during the war to accommodate workers at the Royal Ordnance Factory (ROF) at Risley; but as few ROF workers took up the opportunity to live in the houses the Ministry of Supply let the homes to workers in the local factories. The Admiralty, who took over the housing around 1945, wanted the houses for research workers based at Risley. This caused an outcry from the tenants who believed there were other temporary housing options the

Admiralty should consider, without having to evict those living at Lords Street, such as the ex-military camp at Dam Head Hall, and the other ex-Navy and Air Force camps in the Glazebrook area. Similar questions about the camps' potential use had been asked in July 1947 and the response from the Admiralty at the time was: *The Admiralty is in possession of two camps in this area. The work of adapting one, to provide 96 flats for Admiralty civil employees at the Risley Storage Depot, was nearly complete. The second camp formed part of HMS Gosling until the beginning of June and its conversion into married quarters for Naval personnel was under consideration.*

Engineer Officer James William 'Jim' Best of the Merchant Navy married Margaret Gardner at St Peter's Church, Freshfield, Formby. Margaret, a native of Formby, was an ex-WRNS member who had worked as a cook at Glazebrook camp (HMS *Gosling V*). They resided together at Fir Street, Cadishead.

NOVEMBER 1947
The annual Poppy day collection in the district raised £150-10-2, which was an increase of over £30 on the money raised in 1946.

Remembrance Sunday was held at the Irlam and Cadishead War Memorial, Prince's Park, on Sunday, 9th November. Before the service at the Memorial: *Members of the district's British Legion paraded at their headquarters under Mr J. Butler (vice-president) with their standard whipping in a bracing wind, medals of the 1914-18 war gleaming, ribbons of the last war bringing a touch of colour to sombre suits, they stepped smartly out, and marched to the Council Offices with the Salvation Army band bringing up the rear. Here the official party assembled including the chairman of the Council (Councillor Briggs), Council members and officials, policemen, NFS, RAOB, and St John Ambulance Brigade with its Nursing and Cadet Divisions. To the accompaniment of lively marches played by Irlam Public Band and the Salvation Army the parade moved off to the Park where the formal ceremony and wreath laying took place.*

On Monday, 10th November a meeting of the Irlam and Cadishead War Memorial Committee was held and it was reported that £343 had been raised for the Memorial Fund, the target was £5,000. Another fundraising event, a music concert was held on Sunday, 16th November. This event involved local singers, a male choir and the Cadishead Public Band. Also on the same day the Irlam and Cadishead branch of the British Legion held its annual meeting and reported on the efforts it had made to provide temporary financial support to local veterans and also to the children of servicemen who had died in the war. The committee secretary reported how the branch had successfully obtained an increased war pension for one local disabled serviceman and had also provided grants to send three ex-servicemen to convalescent homes. Other achievements were outlined that clearly demonstrated that the district's British Legion branch was actively supporting local ex-servicemen and women. As of November 1947 the local branch of the British Legion consisted of:

Committee of the local British Legion Club: Mr J.A. Massie, president; Mr J. Butler, vice-president. Committee Members: Messrs Jack Newton DCM, E. Hampson, L. Conde, James N. Howes, Herbert Ditchfield, Henry Grindley, Jack Carter, Peter Broughton MM, T. Williams, A. Hughes, J. Crone, J. Statham, Jack Cox. District branch officials and committee members: Mr J.A. Massie, president; Mr J. Butler, vice-president; Jack Newton DCM, chairman; Mr J. Statham, vice-chairman; Mr G. McCallum, treasurer and Peter Barrow DCM, secretary. Committee: Messrs Peter Broughton MM, Jack Carter, Jack Cox, James N. Howes, L. Conde, J.E. Hampson, T. Williams, A. Hughes, G. Heaton, Henry Grindley, J. Crone, D. Fowler.

On Sunday, 30th November a large gathering of the district's ex-servicemen assembled at the weekly concert held at the local British Legion Hall to pay tribute to Mary Bowker. At the event Jimmy Howes, who had served in India and other places during the war, on behalf of all ex-servicemen and women in the district, presented Mary with a writing bureau and cheque. This was in recognition of all her work during the war for the Comforts Fund which, through the gifts sent to local men and women who were serving with HM Forces in the UK and throughout the world, had brought home a little closer for them. A local ex-serviceman recalled the work of Mary Bowker and the War Comforts Fund: *What a thrill those letters with the Irlam or Cadishead postmark used to give us! Not so much for the postal orders as for the news they contained of our home town when we were so far away from anywhere that mattered. I hope we shall not forget what fine work Miss Bowker did.* Jack Carter spoke at the event stating that the idea of the presentation was first suggested by Jack Cox and Jimmy Howes who had both worked hard developing the idea and gaining support of veterans throughout the district. From October 1947 collection boxes had been placed at the British Restaurant, the Palace and Rialto cinemas, Cadishead Conservative Club, Irlam Steel Works Club, the British Legion, Old Comrades Club and the Catholic Club. Mr J. Butler (vice-president of the British Legion), spoke of the grand work Mary Bowker had done for the Comforts Fund. In the 1914-1918 war he said, there were no local organisations for the dispatch of parcels and gifts to serving soldiers and sailors and, many times, the men abroad thought they were forgotten. In this war, every serving man and woman had received gifts thanks to the work of Mary Bowker and the War Comforts Fund Committee. In presenting her with their gifts, ex-servicemen of the 1939-45 war were merely trying to show their gratitude for what she had done for them.

An overview of the War Comforts Fund was given by Councillor Ernest Mason (ex-flying officer, RAF) who reported that the first meeting of the committee had been held in October 1940, and the first list of local service personnel contained 390 names. In June 1941 the first gifts of 2s 6d were sent to 701 servicemen, and the fund grew as more men were called up resulting in more gifts being sent. In January 1942 there were 982 names on the books and in December 1945 the number had grown to 1,694. Gifts had also been sent to 39 local men who were prisoners of war. During its existence £3,271-16s had been raised by the committee and, following the end of the war, Welcome Home dinners and concerts had been given to 796 ex-servicemen and women who each received ten shillings. The 687 men and women unable to attend each received a gift of £1. Councillor Ernest Mason concluded by saying the facts were evidence of the tremendous amount of work undertaken by Mary Bowker and that all local veterans passed on a very deep and heartfelt thank you. Mary said she was touched by the gifts, which she would always treasure but stated that without the unfailing help of Councillor Keal (chairman of the Comforts Fund) and the enthusiasm of the committee they would have never achieved success.

DECEMBER 1947

On Tuesday, 16th December Curt and Betty Lanagan (nee Davidson) of 6 Lynthorpe Avenue, Cadishead, left the district bound for London and a flight to America, where they intended to settle at Amarillo, Texas. Curt was an American who had served as a technician with the US Army Air Force during the war, stationed at Bruche, Warrington. He was a native of Lamesa, Texas, where his parents owned a ranch. Posted to England in 1942, Curt met Betty the following year and they married in 1945 at Cadishead Congregational Church.

On Tuesday, 23rd December Bill Horne, brother of Mr A.F. Horne of Lyndhurst Avenue, Higher Irlam, featured on a BBC radio programme, 'Window on the World,' describing his experiences in Europe. Bill had left England in July and hitchhiked across eight European countries. He left Paris on 14th July and headed to Prague to attend a Festival of Youth. Whilst there, together with hundreds of others, he assisted in the rebuilding of Lidice, a village destroyed by the Germans during the war. He then worked on other Government building projects before travelling to Belgrade, capital of Yugoslavia, where together with many volunteers, he helped to build a 300 mile railway. It was reported that he was: *Commandant of the International Brigade, formed during the railway's construction.*

CHAPTER TEN
REMEMBRANCE

*They were not merely names. They are persons, people we knew and loved; brothers, sons,
husbands, fathers. We remember them with thankfulness*

On 4th July 1948 a memorial plaque was unveiled in Cadishead Wesleyan
schoolroom in Lords Street which commemorated the church's two Sunday School
teachers, Leslie Arstall and William Porter, who lost their lives during the war.
According to the *Guardian*: *Mr J.H. Barnes, who performed the unveiling ceremony, paid
tribute to the faithful service of the two men and said that wherever they went, whatever they
were called upon to do, they did it in such as manner as would bring credit to the church,
school and especially upon their parents and their homes. If any son or daughter could bring
credit to his or her home it was something of which they could be proud. 'It is in the home that
men and heroes are made; in fact, it is from the home all virtues come,' he added. A service
was conducted by the Minister, Reverend Welbourne, who also gave a short address.*

Unveiling of the Memorial Plaque to Leslie Arstall and William Porter

Shown on the photograph are (L-R): Reverend T.S. Welbourne, Miss I. Andrews (primary
superintendent), Mr J. Ashton (Sunday school secretary), Mr J.H. Barnes, Miss Shephard
(superintendent), Mr F. Pincham (superintendent) and Miss D. Johnson (primary superintendent).

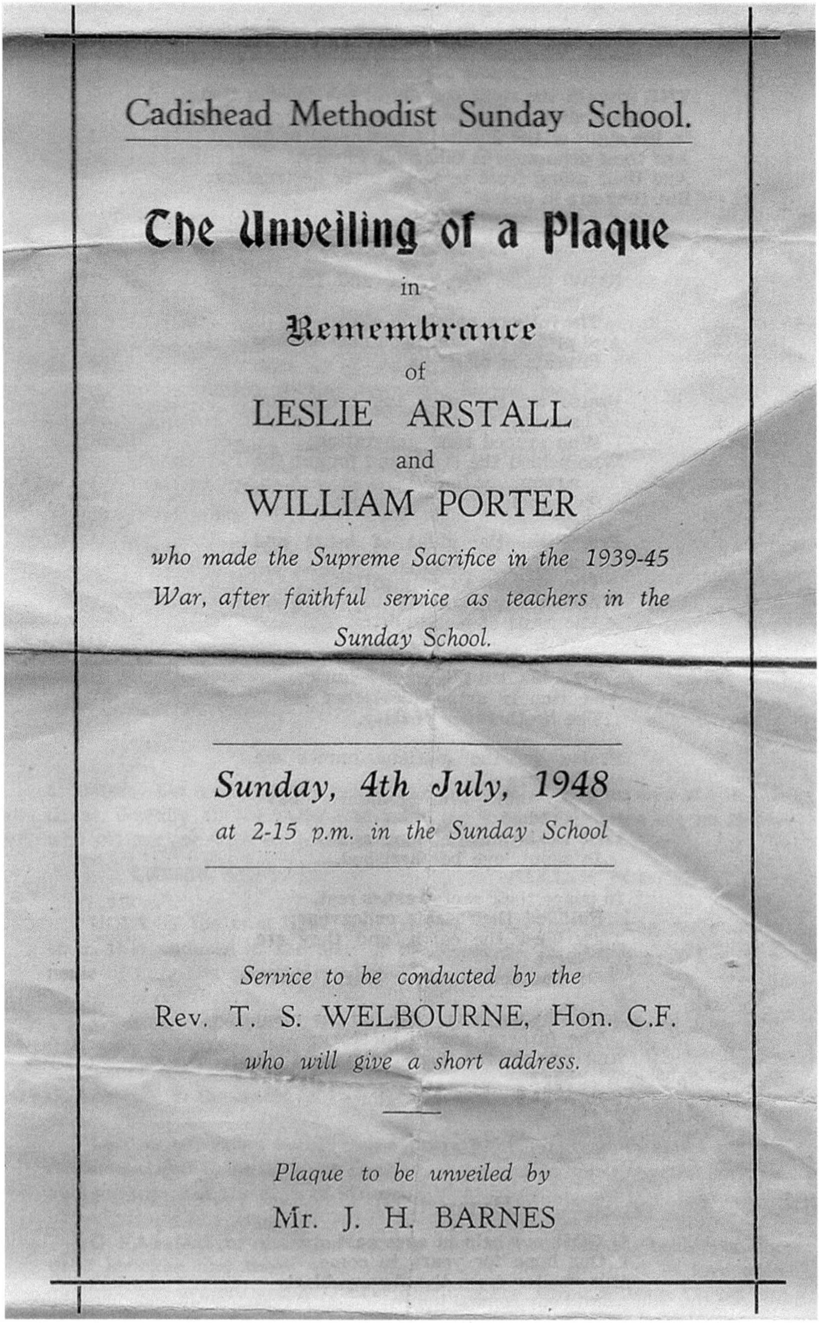

Cadishead Methodist Sunday School.

The Unveiling of a Plaque

in

Remembrance

of

LESLIE ARSTALL

and

WILLIAM PORTER

who made the Supreme Sacrifice in the 1939-45 War, after faithful service as teachers in the Sunday School.

Sunday, 4th July, 1948

at 2-15 p.m. in the Sunday School

Service to be conducted by the

Rev. T. S. WELBOURNE, Hon. C.F.

who will give a short address.

Plaque to be unveiled by

Mr. J. H. BARNES

The sacrifices of Leslie Arstall and William Porter continue to be remembered in the Cadishead Wesleyan Church on Lords Street

On Sunday, 9th October 1949, the original First World War Memorial in Prince's Park, Irlam, was demolished. A detachment of the 123rd Field Regiment, Royal Engineers (a Territorial Army unit based at Manchester) led by a Captain G. Clarke, was detailed to carry out the work. On arrival, they surveyed the memorial which was standing forlornly in its grass circle surround, its base weather stained with cracks across its face. The two bronze plaques and the figure of peace had already been removed. Captain Clarke decided that the first part of the job would be to remove the granite plinth from the top of the base. A team of NCOs and sappers carried tools and  equipment from their vehicle to the memorial, and a working platform was built. Two men climbed on the platform and used a pneumatic drill to bore a hole 3 feet below the plinth. When the captain was satisfied with the drilling, he gave a no smoking order. Two cartridges of gelignite (1lb) were placed in the hole and a length of Cordex fuse wire was attached. The hole was then sealed with wet soil and a safety fuse was attached to the fuse wire. The captain casually advised onlookers: *I don't think it will come this way but if anything does, duck.* The explosion tore a large hole in the side of the base but the plinth remained in place. A rope was tied to it and a truck tried to pull the plinth over, but without success.

The original First World War Memorial

Three further holes were drilled and 2lb of gelignite were used on each hole which were then sealed with wet clay. The explosion toppled the plinth and exposed the core of the base which consisted of clinker, bricks, wood, gas piping, a roll of barbed wire and rubble. Five explosions in all were required to reduce the base sufficiently for it to be broken up by pick and shovel.

The new memorial was designed by the former surveyor to the Council, Henry Nurse, and the work was supervised by Edwin Shaw, surveyor to the Council. It was built from York stone and re-used the figure of peace from the original memorial as its centre-piece. The two bronze plaques bearing the names of the fallen from the First World War were placed on the left and two new bronze plaques, bearing the names of the 94 men and one woman from the district who died in the Second World War, were placed on the right. The figure of peace was mounted on a plinth bearing the words *Their Names Liveth for Evermore*. The War Memorial was unveiled on Saturday, 5th November 1949. Members of the Council, representatives of the War Memorial Committee, ex-servicemen and relatives of the fallen gathered in the rose garden in front of the flag-draped memorial.

The sun shone behind the clouds as the chairman of the Council, Councillor Owen, explained that the new memorial had been built because they were concerned about the dangerous condition of the old one. The hymn *O God our Help in Ages Past* was sung, accompanied by the Salvation Army Band. Reverend G.A. Johnson, minister of the Congregational Church, offered a prayer and Lieutenant J. Reed of the Salvation Army read the lesson.

Irlam & Cadishead War Memorial, Prince's Park, Irlam

Unveiling and Dedication

. of .

War Memorial

IN

PRINCES PARK, IRLAM

Saturday, 5th November, 1949

AT 3-0 P.M.

Foreword

The new War Memorial is to commemorate those from Irlam and Cadishead who gave their lives in the Country's service in the 1914-18 and the 1939-45 Wars.

The fabric of the old War Memorial, which stood on another site in Princes Park for 26 years, was in a dangerous condition, and it has been deemed advisable to remove it; the bronze figure of Peace and the two plaques containing the names of those who fell in the 1914-18 War have been incorporated in the new structure.

The new Memorial is of simple rectilinear design, constructed of fine York stone upon which are mounted the plaques recording the names of those of our citizens who paid the supreme sacrifice in the two wars.

The setting of the new War Memorial, facing nearly due East, in the Rose Garden in Princes Park, is appropriate for a Garden of Remembrance and will help to perpetuate the memory of those whose name liveth for evermore.

The Irlam and Cadishead War Memorial Committee have made a substantial contribution towards the cost of the provision of the Memorial and the sincere thanks of the Urban District are due to them for their willing co-operation and practical help.

The District is also grateful to the Irlam and Cadishead Branch of the British Legion who have generously presented the two bronze plaques containing the names of those who fell in the 1939-45 Wars.

▨ ▨ ▨

May this Memorial and the Garden of Remembrance be a
perpetual reminder in the years to come that
" They died that we might live."

Programme

The Chairman of the Irlam Urban District Council (COUNCILLOR E. OWEN, J.P., C.C.) will preside over the proceedings.

The Service will be conducted by Rev. G. A. Johnson, Rev. W. Lee,   Lieut. Joan Reed (Salvation Army) Rev. T. S. Welbourne, Hon C.F.

Hymn
O God, our help in ages past.

Prayer

Reading

Unveiling of War Memorial

by
Mr. J. NEWTON, D.C.M.

Last Post and Reveille

Prayer of Dedication

Laying of Wreaths

SHORT ADDRESS

Hymn
Thy Kingdom come, O God

Blessing

NATIONAL ANTHEM

Rain fell as Jack Newton DCM, chairman of the British Legion, stepped forward and pulled the tapes attached to the flags which dropped to the ground to reveal the memorial. Edwin Jones, clerk to the Council, read the names of the 137 men from the First World War and Councillor Arnold Briggs, chairman of the War Memorial Committee, announced the names of the fallen from the Second World War. Councillor Briggs placed the first wreath and many residents placed bunches of flowers at the foot of the memorial. Reverend Lee read the dedication prayer. He later said that he wondered what visitors to the park would think when they read the names on the memorial. When they read their history they would recall how those people fought to stem the wave of aggression which rolled across Europe in the two wars. Perhaps they would thank God for the service and sacrifice those men had given: *They were not merely names. They are persons, people we knew and loved; brothers, sons, husbands, fathers. We remember them with thankfulness. We can remember them as happy boys who grew to man's estate, answered the call of their country and went to defend the loved ones they knew were praying for them in their homes.* He added that seven of the fallen were buried in the local graveyard, others in sunlit North Africa and Europe, and some in the oceans. They were all waiting for the last reveille: *We can only pray the spirits of those men are resting in peace under the shadow of the mighty cross of Jesus. Perhaps someday through the love of God and the sacrifices of those who gave their lives, we may emerge into the golden sunlight of the era of peace. It can only come when all the children of mankind have become the children of God.* He also asked the gathering to bear in mind those who had been blinded or maimed during the wars. The hymn, *Thy Kingdom Come, O God* was sung and, after a blessing by Reverend P.W. Wills, vicar of Cadishead, the National Anthem was sung.

Over the years many people have attended the Remembrance Day parades and each has their own reason. Carol Johnson (nee Wilson) is one such person. Every year, with few exceptions, she has attended the Remembrance Parade in Irlam and Cadishead in honour of her father, Ben Wilson, who was killed on D-Day. She first attended with her grandparents in the early 1950s.

In a similar way to the First World War, when men and women returned to civilian life, most did not want to talk about their experiences in the war. When they did talk it was often about camaraderie and humorous times rather than the horrors of war. One such man was James Alban Davies, who had served as a ship's medic in the Royal Navy. His son Andy remembered that: *Jim was reluctant to dwell too much on his war-time experiences - he would often talk about the lighter side of navy life and could relate countless comical war-time stories. But like so many others who took part in the war, he would have that serious far away look in his eye if questioned too closely about the horrors that he witnessed on the Normandy beaches and in the Pacific. It was clear that some of the darker memories still troubled him for many years after the war.*

The parents of Ben Wilson and his daughter, Carol

In the 64 years since the new War Memorial was dedicated, Remembrance Parades have taken place annually. Attendances have fluctuated over the years but were particularly strong during the 1950s, 60s and 70s when large numbers of veterans from both wars and families of the fallen were still living in the district. Nowadays many people still turn out to remember.

Early Remembrance Day Service

Ex-Signalman Trevor Jenkins on Remembrance Sunday 2009

THEIR
NAME
LIVETH
FOR
EVERMORE

Cliff Cole at Prince's Park Memorial 2011

In 1967 the *Guardian* interviewed five local men who had taken part in the Battle of El Alamein in Egypt; Clifford Cole, Joseph Thorpe, Eddie Williams, Tom Brown and Harry Walton. When questioned about whether the years spent fighting the Germans were unhappy and wasted, the five men shared their views: *No,* said Joe Thorpe, *but if only the same effort could be put into peacetime, this country would be able to pay its way.* Cliff said: *I wish I could have put the same effort into something else. But it is nice to know that you have done it. Certainly you only remember the good times.* Tom Brown did not exactly enjoy his time in the desert but at the same time he would not have wanted to have been in 'civvy street' during the war: *we never got the same comradeship in civvy street,* he added. Harry Walton also believed the good times outweighed the bad, and he did not hold anything against the German people. *They were only doing their job,* he said. Eddie Williams looked back with great regret at the death-toll. He also regretted that too few people cared about the relatives of the fallen and those who returned home badly injured. *Out there the lads said they would do anything if they could get out alive. But today there are only a few of us helping the Legion to do things that Governments should have been doing years ago.* They were also asked what they thought of the future and the young people. *If the test came the youth of today* [1967] *possibly would measure up to the youth of 1939 and answer the call,* said Eddie. Harry agreed but Cliff felt that it would be his age group walking around with banners proclaiming peace and not the youngsters: *But, in the same way, they don't want to know what we did. I can remember not taking any notice of World War One veterans,* he said.

Some families, supported by the British Legion, travelled to Normandy after the war to visit the graves of their sons. Harold Longbottom, a veteran of the First World War who was wounded at the Battle of Passchendaele in 1917, lost his son, John Kenneth Longbottom in Normandy, July 1944. He visited La Delivrande War Cemetery, Normandy, France, twice during the post-war era.

Many veterans of the war made pilgrimages to the scenes of their actions; for example, Sydney Brooks returned to Normandy in the 1990s and Harry Bannister returned to the same area in 2004 (the 60th anniversary of the D-Day landings). Stanley Wilkinson formed an Association for the survivors of HMS *Capel* and attended the HMS *Capel* and HMS *Affleck* Reunion and Memorial service on 26th May 1994 at Cherbourg.

Other men kept in touch with colleagues they had served with, either through formal associations or through personal contact. For example, Harold Townend is a member of the RAF Coastal Command Association and still attends events and Walter McArthur was a member of HMS *Renown's* Association and attended reunions until recent years. Robert McLean attended 44 Royal Marine Commando Reunions for many years. When he died in 2002 Captain Hedley J. Phillips had this to say about him: *'Big Mac' – he will always be remembered by us with that name – was big in every way, and his lugubrious sense of humour accompanied by an irresistible twinkle in his eye made him many friends. As a marine and non-commissioned officer he was highly respected, and you will know of course how he has regularly attended the Commando's Reunion for many years; indeed in the last 37 years he has hardly missed one, and on the few occasions when he did it was due to unavoidable illness. His pride in the corps and in particular in the commando was well known, and for this and for his many attributes both as a man, a soldier and a comrade he will be remembered by us; we shall all miss him very much indeed.*

Post war reunion 3 Bulk Petrol Company, including two local men, Cliff Cole centre rear row, Wilfred Hilton front row right

In 2005 the National Lottery paid for veterans and relatives to return to the former battlefields; Cliff Cole and Trevor Jenkins were two men who took this opportunity to return to Italy.

Former Royal Marine Commando Harry Bannister
RM41 Commando Memorial (2004)

Sydney Brooks in Normandy

Stanley Wilkinson (front, second from left)
HMS *Capel* Memorial service, May 1994

Another local man who remained a member of his regiment's old comrades association was Bill Taylor. He was particularly proud to have served with the Seaforth Highlanders and as an infantryman who participated in some of the toughest fighting in North West Europe. Bill later returned to the former battlefields a number of times in the years following the war, including Normandy, France and Best and Tilburg in Holland, where he took part in a number of commemorative events proudly wearing his glengarry, kilt and medals.

Bill Taylor (facing the camera)
Seaforth Highlanders' reunion in Tilburg

Bill was an avid collector of all things relating to the Seaforth Highlanders, particularly badges, and was widely known in collecting circles as an expert in such. He was also instrumental in collecting, during the 1960s and 1970s, a large amount of photographs and material relating to men from the district who served in the armed forces during the First World War, and many of these photographs featured in the authors' first book, District at War. Bill passed away on 12th February 2002, aged 76.

Remembrance Day services have taken place in the district annually, with a parade commencing at the former Royal British Legion Club, now the Royal Arms Club, on Liverpool Road and marching to the Prince's Park War Memorial, where a short service takes place at the eleventh hour. In 2013 in a break with tradition the venue changed, with the parade beginning at Irlam Catholic Club and marching a shorter distance to the War Memorial.

In researching the book the authors have enjoyed several meetings with veterans from the war. The following photographs were taken at the book launch for 'A District at War' in 2010 and after presentations given in October 2011 and June 2013.

1939-45 and 2010
From L-R: Roy Taylor, Harold Townend, Trevor Jenkins, Mary McArthur, Walter McArthur and Cliff Cole at the launch of 'A District At War'

St Helen's Church, Hollins Green (October 2011)

From L-R: Pete Thomas, Roy Taylor, Walter McArthur, Harold Townend, Len Wright, Harry Bannister, Cliff Cole, Bob Whittaker, Neil Drum

St Paul's Church, Irlam (June 2013)

From L-R (front row): Neil Drum, Mary McArthur (nee Smart), Nancy Taylor (nee Hazlehurst), Roy Taylor, Trevor Jenkins, Norman Dakers (back row): Pete Thomas, Walter McArthur, Roy Brotherton, Harry Bannister, Gerald Bannister

Cliff Cole 1940 and 2010

Remembrance

The below poem was written by an unknown local and was printed in the *Cadishead and Irlam Guardian* on 25th August 1945. It feels like the most apt way to bring the story of the district's involvement in the Second World War to a close:

They paced the decks when all was black
Through U-boat haunts they made their track
Through all the forces that prevailed they brought supplies, and never failed

They swept the skies and daring flew, dauntless as the mighty Few
Who kept the flag of freedom high when clouds loomed darkest in the sky
They made hazardous trips by day and night, fair weather or foul, they made their flight
They sounded the prelude o'er land and sea, to the glorious march of Victory

We on the outside will never know
What hardships our men had to undergo
There is many a hero, unnamed, unsung
Whose very soul into battle was flung

Remember those who were maimed for life
In those long years of weary strife
They ask no pity, but prove must we
Our need of them for years to be

Remember, too, the prisoners of war
Who knows what their proud spirits bore
How much they suffered, east and west
The despair of waiting, they know it best

They fought as their fathers, years before
For the same cause fought in the last Great War
May we preserve this peace, so dearly earned
That Britain's face to war no more be turned

May we be mindful, war is no jest
That it demands and takes the best
The gallant men who paid the price
Who made, for us, the sacrifice
They died that we may live in peace
That freedom might remain
May they never be forgotten
Nor their dying be in vain
Tis a mighty debt we owe them

God help us – everyone
To make the children's world
A brighter, better one!

CHAPTER ELEVEN
TRIBUTE TO SIMON
ANNIS

The final chapter of our book is dedicated to another young local soldier who was killed on active service, not in the Second World War but in more recent times: Fusilier Simon Annis of the 2nd Battalion of the Royal Regiment of Fusiliers. His story is told in a marvellous book entitled *Butterflies and Feathers* written by his mother, Ann Annis. It is hoped that Simon will be the last of the district's heroes to make the supreme sacrifice.

Simon was born on 9th August 1987, the son of Peter and Ann Annis of Allotment Road, Cadishead. He was educated at Hollins Green Junior School and Culcheth High School and, after leaving school, he worked as an apprentice joiner for a local building firm. He was a keen rugby player with Cadishead Rhinos. In his family's words: *He was always comical, so laid back and totally hilarious at times with his off the cuff remarks. He was a good natured lad with a heart of gold who would genuinely do anything for anybody.*

One day he announced to the family that he intended to enlist in the Army. His brother, Stuart, was already serving in the Royal Marines. Simon enlisted on 12th August 2006, three days after his 19th Birthday, and was sent to the Infantry Training Centre Catterick where he undertook the Combat Infantryman's Course. His proud parents attended the passing out parade on 9th February 2007. Simon was now Fusilier 25225641 Simon Annis of 2nd Battalion, The Royal Regiment of Fusiliers.

His first overseas posting was to Cyprus a few weeks after his passing out parade and then he went to Jordan on a six week training exercise. In 2008 he returned to the UK (Hounslow Barracks) and his duties included sentry duty outside London's Royal Palaces. In July he was posted to Belize in South America, where he celebrated his 21st Birthday. In January 2009 he returned to Hounslow Barracks to prepare for a tour on Afghanistan, which started on 24th March 2009. In one of his letters home Simon wrote: *People out here actually want help, the way people live and survive here is so different to home you wouldn't imagine.* In June 2009 he spent two weeks on home leave, followed by three days at Hounslow Barracks, then back to Afghanistan for the last three months of his tour.

Sangin, Afghanistan, Sunday, 16th August 2009: At around 5am, Lance Corporal James Fullarton, section commander of a British foot patrol, was seriously wounded when he accidentally triggered a plate activated Improvised Explosive Device (IED).

His colleagues, including Fusilier Simon Annis, raced to provide first aid. Shortly afterwards he was lifted gently onto a stretcher with Simon at the front and Fusilier Louis Carter at the rear and carried towards the designated helicopter landing site. Within a few metres, a second explosion took the lives of the three friends; Lance Corporal James Fullarton, Fusilier Louis Carter and Fusilier Simon Annis.

Simon was repatriated to RAF Lyneham, England on 21st August 2009. He was the 201st British soldier to die in the Afghanistan conflict. He was accorded a full military funeral on Thursday, 3rd September, with a service at St John's Church, Irlam, followed by interment at Hollins Green Cemetery. Hundreds of people lined the route to the church including uniformed members of the police and fire brigade who saluted as the hearse passed them. His Union Jack bedecked coffin was carried into the church by fellow soldiers, and fusiliers from his regiment formed a guard of honour.

His mother wrote the following moving words: *A community normally buzzing with town life stood still as if time itself had stood still, sad faces filled the pavements, heads bowed, silently, Simon passed each and every one of them, the silence broken by sobs. People sobbed for a hero, they sobbed for the loss of a boy too young to bear the burden of war on his innocent shoulders, strangers sobbed for this sacrifice, all to ensure a better and safer life for them. But most of all they sobbed because they knew Simon and all the town sobbed because he was their local boy, it was all too close to home for them as for most, the reality of this bloody brutal war was now a reality and all too plain to see.*

His commanding officer, Lieutenant Colonel Charlie Calder, wrote: *Fusilier Simon Annis was a larger than life character and a dedicated soldier. Always at the heart of whatever was going on, it was no surprise to me that he died whilst trying to save his mortally wounded section commander. He should be seen as a shining example to the nation of what selfless commitment really means.*

Fusilier Simon Annis
Passing Out Parade in 2007

Tribute to Simon Annis

Fusilier Simon Annis
Photographed during a training exercise in Scotland

Fusilier Simon Annis, 2nd Royal Regiment of Fusiliers
Afghanistan

Page 1400

Fusilier Simon Annis, 2nd Royal Regiment of Fusiliers
Afghanistan

Afghanistan War Memorial in Prince's Park

Afghanistan Memorial in Prince's Park

25225641 FUSILIER

SIMON ANNIS

2ND BATTALION THE
ROYAL REGIMENT OF FUSILIERS
16TH AUGUST 2009 · AGE 22

"ARTE ET MARTE"
THE DAY YOU LEFT
LITTLE BIT OF U
WITH YO

Hollinfare Cemetery

APPENDIX I
CASUALTIES

The Commonwealth War Graves Commission (CWGC) classifies any serviceman or woman who died between 3rd September 1939 and 31st December 1947 as official war casualties. The Commission commemorates, with either a marked grave or by name on a memorial, those who died between these dates regardless of cause of death. It is irrelevant whether the person was killed in action, died of wounds, died during training or road accidents, of natural causes, sickness, suicide or other reasons, they are all commemorated.

The CWGC also commemorates discharged service personnel but only in specific circumstances: the individual has to have died between the qualifying period and the cause of death has to be proven to be directly linked to their military service, such as the result of wounds, sickness or injury sustained during service.

The following table lists all the casualties from or associated with the Irlam and Cadishead district:

1939

None

1940

HEYWOOD, Frederick Noel	19th – 29th May	France (Dunkirk evacuations)
WHITFIELD, Cyril	21st – 30th May	France (Dunkirk evacuations)
JOPSON, Arthur	31st May	Belgium (Dunkirk evacuations)
CLAXTON, Ernest George	31st May	Belgium (Dunkirk evacuations)
MORRIS, William	4th June	England (Dunkirk evacuations)
SHERRATT, Joseph Arthur	8th June	Lost at sea
GRINDLEY, Robert Henry	8th June	Lost at sea
PICKERSGILL, Robert Whitfield	28th July	Buried at sea
BUNTING, Robert	23rd December	England (Manchester Blitz)

1941

PARKER, William	5th January	England (London Blitz)
PARKER, Harriet	6th January	England (London Blitz)
BOARDMAN, Stanley	24th May	Lost at sea
BARENSCHE, Joseph Frederick	18th June	Died at sea
JOHNSON, Samuel Lawrence	16th September	Scotland
WHITTLE, Samuel Anderson	20th September	Lost at sea
SUNTER, John Edward	24th November	Lost at sea
EAVES, Joseph Raymond	10th December	Lost at sea
HANLEY, Bernard Harry	19th December	Lost at sea
STAINSBY, Thomas Frederick	19th December	Lost at sea

1942

WHITFIELD, Harry Cromwell	10th February	Lost at sea
BLACKBURN, John Eric	22nd February	Air operations England
DARBYSHIRE, Walter	4th March	Lost at sea
EAVES, Harold	4th March	Lost at sea
FOWLER, John Douglas	7th March	Burma
PROCTOR, William	17th March	Lost at sea
WALTON, John Percy	1st April	England
LOWE, Richard William	3rd April	Lost at sea
SADLER, Alexander Igil	8th May	Kenya
EDMONDS, Kenneth	2nd June	Air operations Holland
TINSLEY, Robert Moss	27th July	England
KERSHAW, Eric Gilbert	7th August	Air operations Germany
BIRCHALL, William	13th August	Iraq
THOMPSON, Elsie	17th August	Scotland
GREEN, William	24th August	Air operations England
BEDDOWS, Edward	14th September	India
CAWLEY, William	16th November	Lost at sea
HARTLEY, Horatio	3rd December	Libya
WALKER, Charles	20th December	Thailand (prisoner of war)
THORNLEY, Alfred George	27th December	Burma

1943

NEWMAN, Joseph Philip	17th January	Air operations Germany
BOOKER, Charles Henry	21st January	Tunisia
LLOYD, William Henry	13th February	Canada
MENZIES, Charles James	24th February	Lost at sea
SMITH, Cyril Victor	1st March	Tunisia
BLAY, Thomas Pearson	15th March	Burma
WHITTAKER, Leslie	28th March	Tunisia
FAIRHURST, John	6th April	Tunisia
PORTER, John William	10th April	Tunisia
WALSH, Edward	28th May	Tunisia
CLAYTON, Harold	8th June	Algeria
DONKIN, Dixon David	7th August	Air operations France
TIGHE, John Gerard	8th September	Italy
FAULKNER, John William	10th September	Italy
STOKES, Frederick Raymond	20th September	Lost at sea
BRETT, William	23rd September	Lost at sea
DARBY, John	11th October	Lost at sea
BROWN, Wallace	14th October	Thailand (prisoner of war)
ARSTALL, Leslie	23rd October	Lost at sea
MUSKETT, Harry	7th November	Italy
SIMPSON, Harry	7th December	England
KILLEN, John	17th December	Air operations England
THOMAS, Harold Parry	20th December	Air operations Germany

1944

DICKINSON, George	26th/27th January	Burma
DUNN, John Roland	28th January	Italy

Appendix I

ADAMS, Eric	7th February	Italy
BREWER, Reginald	8th February	Italy
WALTON, Cyril	8th February	Burma
ALLCOCK, Albert Edward	12th February	Lost at sea
CHAPPELL, Albert	21st February	Air operations Germany
WENHAM, Roy	25th February	Lost at sea
SMITH, James	1st March	Lost at sea
MACE, William Henry	20th March	Burma
WHITTLE, Cyril	23rd April	Air operations England
DALE, Henry	9th May	Air operations Belgium
SWEENEY, James	6th June	France (D-Day)
BELL, Kenneth Sydney	6th June	France (D-Day)
HILTON, Arthur	6th June	France (D-Day)
WILSON, Benjamin	6th June	France (D-Day)
HILLYARD, Clifton	8th June	Lost at sea (Normandy campaign)
THOMPSON, Ernest	21st June	Italy
HILTON, Leslie Herbert	26th June	England
PORTER, William	28th June	Died at sea
LONGBOTTOM, John Kenneth	8th July	France (Normandy campaign)
ARSTALL, Herbert	9th July	France (Normandy campaign)
GRATRIX Thomas	17th July	France (Normandy campaign)
SOUTHERN, Robert Driscoll	17th July	France (Normandy campaign)
ACKERLEY, Joseph Thomas	18th July	France (Normandy campaign)
JONES, Henry	23rd July	Egypt
HALL, Sydney Ernest	6th August	France (Normandy campaign)
BEIRNE, John Patrick	6th August	France (Normandy campaign)
WHITTAKER, Robert	9th August	France (Normandy campaign)
MORGAN, Kenneth Irvin	11th August	Lost at sea (Normandy campaign)
WARD, Albert	12th August	France (Normandy campaign)
CORDER, Fred	27th August	France (Normandy campaign)
MORT, Charles	19th September	Italy
JIBSON, James Henry Prince	14th October	Air operations Hungary
TAYLOR, William	7th November	Lost at sea
ALLEN, Frederick Roberts	21st November	Burma
PALIN, William	11th December	England

1945

HARRIS, Henry	2nd February	Burma
AINSCOUGH, Jack	5th February	England
BOWEN, Horace	9th February	Holland
SHAW, Frank	18th February	Germany
THOMAS, John Victor	18th February	Germany
HANCOCK, James Henry	13th March	Burma
DARBYSHIRE, Herbert	16th March	Air operations France
TALBOT, Joseph Eric	10th April	England
JAQUES, Ronald Thornley	18th April	Air operations North Sea
TALBOT, Frederick	22nd April	Germany
SOUTHERN, Harold	30th May	Germany
JACKLIN, John Arthur	2nd July	Java (prisoner of war)
HOLLEY, Alfred Hunt	9th July	Died at sea

JACKSON, Ernest	7th August	England
BRADSHAW, Thomas	5th October	Air operations Scotland
BATTLES, Rosina	10th November	Germany

1946

| HILL, Peter Albert | 16th June | Palestine |

1947

| NEWTON, James Herbert, | 25th January | England |

Unknown

FELL, H.
GARDINER, D.
GARDNER, A.

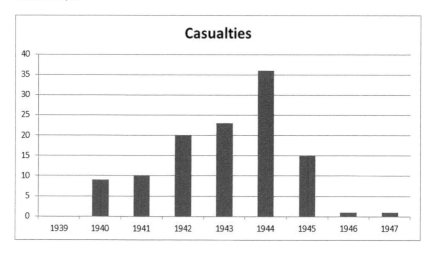

Casualties

Commonwealth War Graves Commission (CWGC)

A search of the CWGC database identified the following casualty whose wife was living in the district, however, it seems almost certain that he had no connection with the area while still alive. It appears that his wife moved into the district after the end of the war. He is not commemorated on the Irlam and Cadishead War Memorial however his family may still be part of the local community and descendants may still live in the district:

On Tuesday, 13th July 1943 Flight Lieutenant 106519 **George Hood**, who was serving with 296 Squadron (Glider Towing Squadron), Royal Air Force Volunteer Reserve, was killed on air operations during Operation Fustian.

Operation Husky, the Allied invasion of enemy-held Sicily, commenced on the night of 9th/10th July. During Husky a British airborne assault (Operation Fustian) was launched on the night of 13th/14th July to seize and hold the Primosole Bridge, over the River Simeto, south of Mount Etna. 296 Squadron, operating Armstrong Whitworth Albermarle planes, were involved in the operation towing troop carrying Hadrian gliders. A number of the Squadron's aircraft, including George's, were lost.

George was the son of George William and Rose Hood and the husband of Honora T. Hood of Higher Irlam. He has no known grave and is therefore commemorated on the Malta Memorial to Missing Commonwealth Air Forces, located at Floriana, Malta. This memorial commemorates almost 2,300 Commonwealth airmen who died whilst serving from bases in Austria, Italy, Sicily, the islands of the Adriatic and Mediterranean, Malta, Tunisia, Algeria, Morocco, West Africa, Yugoslavia and Gibraltar, and who have no known graves. He was 28 years old.

APPENDIX II
ROLL OF HONOUR

The A-Z roll is collated from the names we found during our research in contemporary local newspapers, military records and other sources of service men and women who were born, resided, worked or were otherwise closely connected to the district and immediate surrounding areas during the period covered by the book (1938-1949). Every effort has been made to add service details to all those listed where they could be ascertained. The soldiers whose names are listed in **Bold** denote those who died as a result of the war. Where we have been unable to identify a specific battalion or regiment we have stated 'Army' to differentiate from the other two Forces. Unfortunately space does not permit a similar roll to be compiled for the thousands of men and women who served in the district's Civil Defence Services, albeit many are mentioned by name throughout the book.

ACKERLEY, Joseph Thomas. Fusilier 3461589, 2nd/5th Lancashire Fusiliers. Pages 917, 1407, 1463.
ADAIR, James. Royal Navy (rating unknown). Only son of Mr and Mrs James Adair of 25 Moss Side Rd, Cadishead. Married Gwendolene Thomas of Cadishead, 31.10.42. Sergeant James Dam, Royal Army Medical Corps, was the best man.
ADAMS, Eric. Leading Seaman D/JX141656, Royal Navy, HMS *Hannibal*. Pages 547, 718, 1407.
ADAMS, Walter. Steward, Royal Navy, HMS *Persimman*. Pages 1249, 1250.
AINSCOUGH, Ernest. Sergeant (regiment unknown). Page 1463.
AINSCOUGH, Jack. Able Seaman D/JX176309, Royal Navy, HMS LST415. Pages 156, 818, 1028, 1040, 1407, 1456, 1504.
AINSWORTH, Gerald. RAF (rank unknown).
AINSWORTH, Kenneth. Lance Corporal 7346234, Royal Army Medical Corps, Royal Army Ordnance Corps and then Royal Electrical and Mechanical Engineers. Pages 465, 467.
AINSWORTH, Thomas Lee. Lance Corporal, Corps of Military Police. Page 664.
ALLAN, Jean Muriel. Women's Auxiliary Air Force (rank unknown). Daughter of Mr and Mrs J. Allan of 53 Ferry Road, Irlam. Enlisted c.1943. Pages 550, 1370.
ALLCOCK, Albert Edward. Stoker 2nd Class, D/KX524747. Royal Navy. Pages 731, 1407, 1456.
ALLCOCK, Jack. Driver, Royal Army Service Corps. Pages 582, 731, 1439.
ALLCOCK, Ronnie. Driver, Royal Army Service Corps. Pages 582, 731, 1104.
ALLEN, Frederick Roberts. Lance Corporal 3659994 2nd Green Howards (Yorkshire Regiment). Pages 11, 993, 1407, 1458.
ALLEN, James (Jim). Royal Navy (rating unknown). Son of First World War casualty Thomas Allen. Resided Caroline Street, Irlam.
ALLEN, J. Service details unknown (possibly ALLEN, James above)
ALLEN, Thomas (Tom). Army (rank and regiment unknown). Son of First World War casualty Thomas Allen. Resided Caroline Street, Irlam.
ALLSEY, Herbert Eric (Eric). Able Seaman D/JX399961, Royal Navy. Pages 874, 875, 876.
AMBROSE, John. Private, South Lancashire Regiment. Resided Hayes Rd, Cadishead.
AMOS, Victor. Private (regiment unknown). Pages 145, 146, 1459.
ANDERSON, George. Corporal, Loyal Regiment. Passed away in 1983, aged 69. Pages 357, 361, 882, 1073, 1317, 1459.
ANKERS, Richard. Air Sea Rescue Service, RAF (rank unknown). Lyndhurst Ave, Higher Irlam.
APPLETON, Arthur. Sapper, Royal Engineers. Pages 983, 985.
APPLETON, Marion. Sergeant (acting) 311357, Auxiliary Territorial Service. Pages 1353, 1354, 1439.
APPLETON, Ralph. Service details unknown.
APTED, Frederick. Sergeant (navigator/observer), RAF. Served on Liberators with USAAF in North Africa. Survived aircrash. Resided Liverpool Rd, Irlam (between Chapel Rd and Woodbine Terrace).
ARMSTRONG (Christian name and rank unknown). Auxiliary Military Pioneer Corps.

Appendix II

ARSTALL, Charles Whitfield. Able Seaman, Royal Navy. Pages 733, 1463.

ARSTALL, Cyril. Service details unknown. Page 1463.

ARSTALL, Frank. Royal Marines. Resided Nelson Dr, Cadishead. Page 631.

ARSTALL, George R. Artificer, Royal Navy, HMS *Basilisk*. Page 158.

ARSTALL, Herbert. Private 3455758, 2nd Battalion, Essex Regiment. Pages 905, 1407, 1456.

ARSTALL, Jack Hesford. Seaman, Royal Navy, HMS *Ark Royal*. Discharged medically unfit c.1941 and immediately joined the Army. Driver, Royal Army Service Corps. Pages 320, 321, 322, 733, 745.

ARSTALL, James E. Sapper, Royal Engineers. Pages 820, 1464.

ARSTALL, Leslie. Marine PLY/X103609, Royal Marines, HMS *Charybdis*. Pages 655, 656, 657, 658, 1140.

ARSTALL, Walter. Sergeant 1090391, Royal Engineers. Rixton Roll of Honour. Pages 845, 847, 1454.

ASHLEY, Gladys May. Lance Corporal, Auxiliary Territorial Service. Page 912.

ASHLEY, Tom. Major, regiment unknown. Page 691.

ASHTON, Albert. Army (rank and regiment unknown). Resided Irlam. Son of First World War veteran Albert Ashton.

ASHTON, Clifford RAF (rank unknown). Pages 331, 332, 452.

ASHTON, Douglas. Royal Tank Regiment (rank unknown). Pages 154, 834.

ASHTON, Harold (rank and regiment unknown). Believed to have been at Dunkirk and took part in D-Day landings. Born Weaste. Resided Hayes Rd, Cadishead.

ASHTON, T. 923 Squadron, RAF (rank unknown). Enlisted as an auxiliary in RAF, May 1939. Called up in August 1939, aged 39. Previous military experience, seven years in the Royal Marines. Home service only. Page 1065.

ASHTON, William. Leading Aircraftman, RAF. Page 424.

AUSTEN, Arthur. Lieutenant, Army (regiment unknown). Page 70.

AUSTIN, Ernest. Driver, Army (regiment unknown). Served in Germany. His father, Henry Austin, resided at 4 Kitchener Ave, Cadishead. Page 1315.

AUTY, Harry. Stoker, Royal Navy, HMS *Renown*. Page 628.

AUTY, Joseph. Service details unknown.

BAGSHAW, Cyril Arthur. Flight Sergeant (wireless operator, mechanic, air gunner) 3011897, RAF. Pages 123, 994, 995.

BAILEY, Frank. Royal Navy (rating unknown).

BAILEY, John Edwin. Service details unknown. Resided Glazebrook. Rixton Roll of Honour. Pages 1308, 1454.

BAILEY, Oswald. Service details unknown. Rixton Roll of Honour. Page 1454.

BAILEY, Richard. Royal Navy (rating unknown). Page 1300.

BAKER, Charles E. Fifth Army (rank and regiment unknown). Resided Irlam.

BANKS, Sydney. Gunner, Royal Artillery and later Lance Corporal, Pioneer Corps. Pages 558, 559, 560, 1318, 1339, 1464.

BANNISTER, Gerald Edward. Sergeant 1062503, 49th Reconnaissance Regiment. Later C Squadron, 3rd King's Own Hussars. Pages 3, 347, 759, 859, 861, 864, 873, 909, 1166, 1342, 1343, 1394, 1464.

BANNISTER, Harry. Marine POX121855, No. 41 (Royal Marine) Commando. Pages 3, 196, 216, 653, 830, 831, 873, 933, 1389, 1391, 1394.

BANNISTER, William Ernest. Lance Bombardier, Royal Artillery. Pages 170, 172.

BARBER, Cyril. Service details unknown. Resided 39 Caroline St, Irlam. By 1946 he was a patient at a military hospital in Malta where he met Cadishead soldier Aubrey Davies.

BARENSCHE, Joseph. Merchant Seaman, Merchant Navy, SS *Marconi*. Pages 268, 788, 1405, 1451.

BARKER, Marjorie. Private, Auxiliary Territorial Service. Resided Rixton-with-Glazebrook. Rixton Roll of Honour. Pages 1325, 1454.

BARLOW, Thomas Spencer. Sick Bay Attendant, Royal Navy. Page 506.

BARNABY, Kenneth. LX28759. Royal Navy, HMS *Starling*. Passed away October 2009. Pages 3, 532, 533, 534, 813, 1465.

BARNES, George Edward. Petty Officer, Royal Navy. Page 1106.

BARROW, Frank. Leading Aircraftman (wireless operator), RAF. Pages 564, 761, 762, 763, 764.

BARROW, Frank. Trooper (regiment unknown). Pages 1020, 1020.

BARROW, Fred. Private, Royal Army Service Corps. Page 780, 1020, 1141, 1459.

BARROW, Herbert. Guardsman (regiment unknown). Page 1020.

BARTHOLOMEW, Florence A. Service details unknown. Rixton Roll of Honour. Page 1454.

BASSETT, Ernest. Bombardier, Royal Artillery. Pages 752, 983.

BATE, H.R. South Atlantic Command (rank and service unknown). Page 987.

BATE, John. Lance Corporal, Royal Corps of Signals. Resided Prospect Ave, Cadishead.

BATE, Roy. Royal Navy (rating unknown). Pages 1221, 1305, 1306.

BATES, Jack. Royal Navy (rating unknown). Page 488.

BATES, John Littler. Service details unknown. Page 1465.

BATTLES, Rosina. Commissioner, Allied Control Commission. Pages 1282, 1284, 1283, 1408, 1458.

BAXTER, Ellis Thomas. RAF (rank unknown). Pages 551, 869, 1465.

BAXTER, Thomas W. Service details unknown. Page 1465.

BEARD, George. Service details unknown. Page 1465.

BEBBINGTON, Jack. Royal Navy (rating unknown).

BEBBINGTON, Wilfred. Service details unknown. Page 1465.

BEDDOWS, Edward. Private 3600754, 4th Battalion, Border Regiment. Pages 454, 1406, 1457.

BEHENNA, James Henry (Harry). Sergeant (rear gunner), 115 Squadron, No. 3 Bomber Group, RAFVR. Pages 761, 766, 1466.

BEIRNE, John Patrick. Private 4204985 2nd Argyll and Sutherland Highlanders. Pages 926, 1407, 1458.

BEISLY, William. Sergeant, RAF. Page 1192.

BELL, George William. Engine Room Artificer, Royal Navy. Pages 866, 1466.

BELL, Kenneth Sydney. Gunner 2082283, Royal Artillery (Commando attached to No. 3 Commando, Army Commandos). Pages 804, 820, 823.

BELL, Ronald. Able Seaman, Royal Navy. Pages 803, 823, 1190.

BELL, Stanley. Signalman, Royal Corps of Signals. Pages 864, 1407.

BELL, Sydney. Service details unknown. Pages 866, 1466.

BENNETT, George. Service details unknown. Page 1466.

BENTHAM, Fred. Sergeant 3657233, 2nd South Lancashire Regiment. Pages 809, 810, 811.

BEST, James William. Engineer Officer, Merchant Navy. Pages 788, 792.

BICKERTON, Clarence (Clarry). Service details unknown. Employed at CWS Soap Works.

BICKERTON, Ernie. Service details unknown.

BICKERTON, Frank. Gunner/Driver 1822643, 21 Battery, 8th (Belfast) Heavy Anti-Aircraft Regiment, Royal Artillery. Pages 919, 921.

BICKERTON, William. Service details unknown.

BILLAM, Frank Barron. Signalman, Royal Corps of Signals. Son of Mr and Mrs H.T. Billam of 22 Ashfield Grove, Irlam. Married Edith Doris Weston, daughter of Herbert and Edith Weston of 8 Lines Rd, Irlam.

BILSBORROW, Thomas Hatcher. Army (rank and regiment unknown). Page 1038.

BIRCH, Derek. Driver, Royal Electrical and Mechanical Engineers. Page 997.

BIRCH, Frank K. Royal Navy (rating unknown). Son of Mr and Mrs Birch of 6 Elsinore Avenue, Irlam. Page 998.

BIRCHALL, William. Private 1493936, Royal Ordnance Corps. Pages 450, 1406.

BIRD, Frank. Corporal, RAF. Page 662.

BLACKBURN, John Eric. Sergeant (air observer) 1051863, RAF. Pages 363, 365, 366, 367, 1154, 1406, 1456, 1504.

BLAY, Kenneth. Service details unknown. Page 1466.

BLAY, Sidney. Canadian Army (rank and regiment unknown). Page 535.

BLAY, Thomas Pearson. Private 3780055, 13th King's (Liverpool Regiment). Pages 534, 1315, 1406, 1456.

BLEASE, Charles George. Lance Corporal 3528232, Army (regiment unknown). Pages 357, 360, 1321, 1459.

BLOOR, Roland (Roly). Royal Engineers (rank unknown).

BLOWER, (Christian name unknown). Able Seaman, Royal Navy. Page 628.

BLUNDELL, Albert. Driver, Royal Electrical and Mechanical Engineers. Page 1315.

BLUNDELL, Joseph. Leading Hand, Royal Navy. Eldest son of Mr and Mrs Blundell of Moss Side Lane, Rixton. Married Edith Roberts, youngest daughter of the late Mr W. Roberts and Mrs Roberts of 6 Hayes Rd, Cadishead, in July 1943.

BLUNDELL, Thomas A. Private, Army (regiment unknown). 15th Scottish Division. Pages 1069, 1315.

Appendix II

BOARDMAN, Stanley. Acting Petty Officer P/JX 140291, Royal Navy, HMS *Hood*. Pages 258, 259, 1405.

BOLTON, Eric. Royal Engineers (rank unknown). Page 998.

BOLTON, Frank Edward. Service details unknown. Page 1467.

BOOKER, Charles Henry. Lance Corporal 7018526, 2nd London Irish Rifles, attached to the Royal Ulster Rifles. Pages 509, 1406.

BORRINO, Cedric Arthur. Royal Navy (rating unknown). Pages 548, 807, 1303.

BORRINO, George Vincent. Sergeant Major, Loyal Regiment. Pages 548, 779, 1303, 1366

BORRINO, Stanley Peter. Midshipman (later sub-lieutenant), Royal Navy. Pages 779, 868, 1303, 1366.

BORRINO, William. Captain. Royal Army Pay Corps. Pages 548, 1303, 1366, 1371.

BORRINO, William Alex R. Chief Petty Officer, Royal Navy. Pages 548, 779, 807, 1303, 1341, 1366, 1438.

BOWEN, Horace. Lance Corporal, 3536857, 10th Battalion, Highland Light Infantry (City of Glasgow Regiment). Pages 1045, 1407, 1456.

BOWEN, Harold. Army (rank and regiment unknown). Served Belgium. Brother of Horace. Page 1046.

BOYDELL, Frederick Walter. Private 14358422, 350 Company, Pioneer Corps. Pages 1103, 1099.

BOYLE, Francis (Frank). Corporal 7687604, Royal Military Police. He passed away in January 1997, aged 82. Pages 424, 426.

BRACEGIRDLE, Alan. Royal Navy (rating unknown).

BRACEGIRDLE, Ernest. Service details unknown. Page 1467.

BRADBURY, Bert. Able Seaman, Royal Navy. Page 661.

BRADSHAW, Thomas. Chief Petty Officer (Pilot) L/FX582317 Royal Navy. Pages 11, 1269, 1408, 1458, 1467.

BRADY, William (Billy). Stoker KX159279, Royal Navy. Page 584.

BRAILSFORD, Kenneth. Private, Royal Army Service Corps. Page 169.

BRENNAN, Frank. Merchant Navy (rating unknown). Page 790.

BRENNAN, Joseph. Stoker, Merchant Navy. Pages 3, 217, 788, 790, 794.

BRENNAN, Mabel (See EGERTON, Mabel).

BRENNAN, Patrick. Merchant Navy (rating unknown). Page 790.

BRETT, Samuel E. Royal Electrical and Mechanical Engineers (rank unknown). Page 641.

BRETT, William. Signalman D/JX357031, Royal Navy, HMS *Itchen*. Pages 639, 640, 1406, 1456.

BREWER, Reginald. Private 14203159, 2nd North Staffordshire Regiment. Pages 718, 719, 891, 1407, 1457.

BRIDGE, John. Lieutenant, Royal Navy. Page 1066.

BRIDGE, John William. Service details unknown. Page 1468.

BRIGGS, Arnold. Sergeant, RAF. Pages 16, 41, 63, 64, 79, 98, 129, 190, 1319, 1355, 1358, 1359, 1363, 1371, 1372, 1374, 1385.

BRIGGS, Ernest. Private, Eighth Army (regiment unknown). Pages 565, 571, 938.

BRIGGS, Harry. Army (rank and regiment unknown). Pages 565, 938.

BRIGGS, Maurice. Royal Navy (rating unknown). Pages 565, 938, 940, 1468.

BRITTON, Edith. Private, Auxiliary Territorial Service (rank unknown).

BRITTON, John Raymond. Merchant Navy. Page 790.

BROAD, Francis Reginald. Captain, Merchant Navy. Pages 182, 430, 605.

BROAD, Francis W. Third Officer, Merchant Navy. Page 430.

BROAD, Jack. Bandsman, Royal Marines. Page 430.

BROADHURST, Bessie. Corporal, Women's Auxiliary Air Force. Pages 550, 554.

BROADHURST, Harold. Service details unknown.

BROCK, David. 1st Class Stoker, Royal Navy. Page 1468

BROOK, Joseph (Joe). Driver, Royal Artillery. Page 662.

BROOKS, Colin. Royal Tank Regiment (rank unknown).

BROOKS, Hubert. RAF (rank unknown).

BROOKS, James. Sergeant, RAF. Pages 587, 1439.

BROOKS, Sydney. Private, Loyal Regiment (North Lancashire), then Bombardier, Royal Artillery. Pages 906, 907, 1389, 1391.

Appendix II

BROTHERTON, Norman Roy (Roy). Ordinary Seaman MX100697 then Leading Seaman JX370666, Royal Navy. Pages 3, 380, 382, 465, 482, 714, 1128, 1394.

BROUGHTON, Frances Lillian. Lance Corporal, Women's Auxiliary Air Force. Pages 550, 551, 555, 1370.

BROWN, Frank. Private, Army (regiment unknown). Pages 1149, 1459.

BROWN, Gwendoline. Auxiliary Territorial Service (rank unknown). Graham Crescent, Cadishead. Married John George Close, Royal Army Service Corps, while stationed at Middridge, County Durham (August 1942).

BROWN, Gwilym. Leading Stoker, Royal Navy. Page 992.

BROWN, James Edward. Royal Navy (rating unknown). Page 1468.

BROWN, Robert. Service details unknown. Page 1468.

BROWN, Thomas Brett. Private, 2nd Border Regiment. Pages 1336, 1337, 1339.

BROWN, Thomas (Tom). Trooper, Royal Tank Regiment, 8th Armoured Brigade. Pages 472, 543, 759, 1389.

BROWN, Wallace. Gunner 893872, 135th (The Hertfordshire Yeomanry) Field Regiment, Royal Artillery. Pages 357, 360, 654, 1297, 1406, 1459.

BROWNE, Kenneth. Flight Sergeant, RAF. Pages 257, 620, 954, 957, 1328.

BRYAN, Tom. Private, Army (regiment unknown). Page 807.

BUCKLEY, George. Royal Navy (rating unknown).

BUDWORTH, George Joseph. Service details unknown. Page 1469.

BURGESS. W. Leading Aircraftwoman, Women's Auxiliary Air Force. Page 1032.

BURGESS, Ernest. Anti-Aircraft Battery (rank unknown). Page 1469.

BURKE, James. Royal Navy (rating unknown). Pages 433, 780.

BURKE, Martin. Guardsman, Irish Guards. Page 780.

BURKE, Patrick. Guardsman 2719971, Irish Guards. Pages 780, 1459.

BURNS, Harold. Flight Lieutenant, RAF. Resided Rixton-with-Glazebrook. Pages 139, 1325.

BURNS (or BURNES), Jack. Believed to have served in the Black Watch (rank unknown). Dean Rd, Cadishead and later, Fir St, Cadishead.

BURROWS, Henry. Royal Corps of Signals (rank unknown). Pages 380, 863, 864, 1469.

BURROWS, Katherine. Auxiliary Territorial Service (rank unknown). Page 864.

BURROWS, Sidney. Driver 4042147, Royal Army Service Corps. Pages 862, 864, 1469.

BURY, John. Fleet Air Arm (rank unknown).

BUSHELL, Eric. Royal Navy (rating unknown). Page 1469.

BUTLER, Sidney. Gunner, Royal Navy. Page 545.

CAIRNS, Ron. Service details not known.

CALDERBANK, H. Private, Army (regiment unknown). Page 1024.

CALLAGHAN, Jack. Private, Royal Artillery. Page 1074.

CAMERON, Charles. 2nd Manchester Regiment (rank unknown). Served in India and Burma (after the battles of Imphal and Kohima).

CAMPBELL, Colin. Leading Aircraftman, RAF. Page 1000.

CAMPBELL, Frank. Sergeant Major, Army (regiment unknown). Page 1000.

CAMPBELL, Leo. Sergeant Major, Royal Artillery. Page 1000.

CAMPBELL, Miles. Dispatch rider, Army (rank and regiment unknown). Page 1000.

CARTER, Reginald. Service details unknown. Page 1470.

CARTLEDGE, Benjamin. Driver, Army (regiment unknown).

CASSIDY, John. Gunner, Royal Artillery. Pages 1126, 1459.

CASTLE, Ernie. Fourth Engineer, Merchant Navy. Pages 788, 793.

CAUFIELD, William. Gunner, Maritime Royal Artillery. Pages 745, 742.

CAWLEY, William. Able Seaman C/SSX32316, Royal Navy, HMS *Arethusa*. Pages 485, 1406.

CHADWICK, Kenneth. Sergeant, Royal Engineers. Pages 724, 723.

CHANNON, Noel. Sergeant, Royal Corps of Signals. Best man at wedding of John Bate, Royal Corps of Signals in February 1944. Page 175.

CHAPPELL, Albert. Sergeant 1591968, Bomber Command, RAFVR. Pages 732, 1407, 1451, 1504.

CHILTON, Gilbert. Gunner, Royal Artillery. Pages 547, 584, 685.

CLAGUE, Frederick L. Driver, Royal Army Service Corps. Page 603.

CLARE, Albert E. Private, 1st South Lancashire Regiment. Pages 905, 912, 914, 915, 916.

Appendix II

CLARE, Thomas. Leading Aircraftman, RAF. Son of Mr and Mrs W. Clare of 9 Charles St, Cadishead. Married Marion Needham, only daughter of Mr and Mrs G. Needham of 75 Dixon St, Irlam, at St John's Church in July 1946. Page 1470.

CLARKE, Fred. Flight Sergeant, RAF. One of two brothers who served in Forces. Son of Henry Clarke of 5 Leader Williams Rd, Irlam. Page 806.

CLARKE (Christian name, rank and regiment unknown). One of two brothers who served in Forces. Son of Henry Clarke of 5 Leader Williams Rd, Irlam.

CLARKE, Harold. Service details unknown. Page 1470.

CLARKE, V. Women's Auxiliary Air Force. Daughter of Henry Clarke of 5 Leader Williams Rd, Irlam. Page 550.

CLAXTON, Ernest George. Private 3655469 1st Lancashire Fusiliers. Pages 150, 1405.

CLAYTON, Harold. Guardsman 2661000, 2nd Coldstream Guards. Pages 582, 587, 1406.

CLEWORTH, Edward. Sergeant, Royal Army Service Corps. Enlisted 1940, served Europe and North Africa. Demobbed 1946. Born 1918. Resided 60 Bank St, Glazebrook. Worked at Metropolitan Vickers, Trafford Park (pattern shop).

CLOSE, Gwen. Auxiliary Territorial Service (rank unknown).

COATES, Richard Thomas. Signalman 2389304, Royal Corps of Signals. Demobilised 15.03.47. Pages 580, 724.

COLE, Clifford. Corporal 121957, Royal Army Service Corps. Demobbed 1946. Pages 3, 100, 139, 140, 191, 269, 270, 272, 273, 279, 292, 434, 439, 436, 471, 475, 603, 616, 1065, 1066, 1346, 1388, 1389, 1390, 1394.

COLLINSON, Jack. Lancashire Fusiliers (rank unknown). Wounded (no further details available).

CONDE, John Leslie. Acting Lance Corporal T/240083, Royal Army Service Corps. Passed away in 1949, aged 42. Pages 357, 360, 546, 1253, 1459, 1470.

CONNELLY, John M. 70th Field Regiment, Royal Artillery, Central Mediterranean Force. Page 1293.

CONNOR, Frank P. Leading Stoker D/KX136468, Royal Navy. Pages 277, 1106, 1227, 1295.

CONNOR, Hugh. Service details unknown.

CONNOR, James Edward. Private, 2nd South Lancashire Regiment. Pages 476, 1107.

CONNOR, Martin. Leading Aircraftman, RAF. Pages 303, 564, 565, 1107, 1227, 1295, 1471.

COOK, Raymond. Stoker, Royal Navy. Page 745.

COOKE, Douglas. Royal Navy, Ordinary Seaman. Page 1091.

COOKE, Raymond (Ray). Royal Navy (rating unknown). Page 627.

COOKE, Thomas (Tom). Air Training Corps and then Army (rank and regiment unknown). Page 445.

COOKSON, Gwendoline. Aircraftwoman, Women's Auxiliary Air Force. Pages 556, 557.

COOKSON, Raymond. Gunner 14337244, 439 Battery, 55th Field Regiment, Royal Artillery. Attached 3rd Battalion, Irish Guards. Guards Armoured Division. Pages 3, 557, 890, 891, 892, 906, 952, 953, 955, 1160.

CORDER, Benjamin. Service details unknown. Pages 685, 687.

CORDER, Bessie. Private, Auxiliary Territorial Service. Pages 1310, 1311.

CORDER, Fred. Private 1607306. 2nd Essex Regiment. Pages 941, 943, 1310, 1407.

CORDER, Ronald. Service details unknown. Page 944.

CORDWELL, George. Signalman, Army. Pages 582, 1038.

COTTAM, Lawrence. Seaman, Royal Navy. Pages 35, 499, 500, 596, 621, 623, 707, 708, 769, 808, 812, 818, 1471, 1505.

COTTAM, John. Gunner 3663859, Royal Artillery. Discharged 21st May 1946. Pages 537, 535, 808.

COTTAM, Reginald. Sapper, Royal Engineers. Pages 807, 808.

COX, Edward (Ted). Private, Royal Electrical and Mechanical Engineers, First Army. Pages 563, 569.

CRABTREE, Joseph. Service details unknown. Page 1471.

CRAWFORD, Harry. Radio Officer, Merchant Navy. Page 659.

CROFT, Alf. Captain, Royal Artillery. Page 225.

CROWCROFT, Hector. Quarter Master Sergeant (regiment unknown). Page 158.

CROZIER, Edgar. Bombardier, Royal Artillery. Pages 582, 980, 1438.

CUBBIN, William. Fusilier (regiment unknown). Pages 1155, 1438.

DAKERS, Margaret. NAAFI. Page 993.

DAKERS, Norman. Driver, T/14323168, Royal Army Service Corps. Pages 3, 196, 218, 499, 848, 849, 851, 993, 1087, 1344, 1345, 1394.

DALE, Eric. Ordinary Seaman FX105552, Fleet Air Arm. Pages 3, 631, 632, 904, 905.

DALE, Henry. Sergeant (air gunner) 2210202. 35 Squadron, No. 8 Group, Bomber Command. RAFVR. Pages 797, 1407, 1457, 1504.

DAM, James. Sergeant, Royal Army Medical Corps. Page 1410.

DANIELS, Arthur. Royal Navy (rating unknown).

DANIELS, Gladys Mona. Auxiliary Territorial Service (rank unknown). Page 778.

DANIELS, Roy. Sergeant, Royal Artillery. Born 1921. Resided 34 Baines Ave, Irlam. Married Annie Ward, only daughter of Mr and Mrs Ward of 7 Haig Ave, Cadishead, at St John's Church in June 1946. Page 1472.

DARBY, John. Ordinary Seaman P/JX428200, Royal Navy, Minesweeper HMS *Hythe*. Pages 646, 1406, 1456, 1504.

DARBYSHIRE, Herbert. Sergeant 1481728, 49 Squadron, No. 5 Group, Bomber Command, RAFVR. Pages 1081, 1082, 1083, 1407, 1451, 1504.

DARBYSHIRE, Joseph. Service details unknown. Page 1472.

DARBYSHIRE, Walter. Leading Stoker 1st Class D/KX96164, Royal Navy. Pages 326, 374, 375, 1083, 1406, 1451, 1504.

DARNTON, Arthur. Gunner, Royal Artillery. Page 806.

DARNTON, James (Jimmy). Signalman, Royal Corps of Signals. Pages 582, 799, 801, 1038.

DAVENPORT, Alice. Private, Auxiliary Territorial Service. Served 7 years including service in Italy and Austria and was demobilised Christmas 1946. Second daughter of Mr and Mrs Davenport of Ash Farm, Davenport. Married 6th September 1947, at St Mary's, Cadishead, to Henry Jones of Rowen, Conway, Wales, who had served in HM Forces including four years at Malta.

DAVENPORT, George Haslam. Lance Corporal, Royal Army Service Corps. Pages 406, 407, 408, 1349.

DAVENPORT, Gladys. Private, Auxiliary Territorial Service. Page 1422.

DAVENPORT, Joseph. Lance Bombardier, Royal Artillery. Pages 269, 584, 685.

DAVIES, Aubrey. Army (rank and regiment unknown). 12 Prospect Rd, Cadishead. In 1946 he was serving in Malta where he met Irlam serviceman, Cyril Barber. Married Dorothy Elliot, WAAF. Pages 1411, 1417.

DAVIES, James. Service details unknown. Born 1925. Resided 1 Allotment Rd, Cadishead. Joined Home Guard 17.08.42 (no. 719), served in HQ of D Company. Joined HM Forces 26.01.44. Next of kin: Mrs M. Davies.

DAVIES, James Alban. Leading Sick Berth Attendant D/MX 555965, Royal Navy, HMS *Arbiter*. Passed away in November 1994. Pages 839, 990, 993, 991, 993, 1209, 1231, 1315, 1385, 1439.

DAVIES, Kenneth H. Captain, Royal Electrical and Mechanical Engineers. Pages 1109, 1110, 1438.

DAVIES, Thomas Stanley. Service details unknown. Page 1472.

DAVIES, Vera. Private, Auxiliary Territorial Service. Stationed at barrage balloon post at Edinburgh.

DAVIS, George. Service details not known.

DAWES, Thomas. Royal Electrical and Mechanical Engineers (rank unknown). Stationed in Gibraltar. Born Cadishead. Employed Steelworks. Resided Victory Rd, Cadishead, and then 12 Kenmore Rd, Cadishead. Medically discharged. Son of Stanley and Dora Dawes.

DAWSON, Ann Elizabeth (Betty). Leading Aircraftwoman, Women's Auxiliary Air Force. Pages 550, 970, 972, 1370.

DEAN, Arthur William (Billy). Pilot Officer 1096163, 102 Squadron, RAFVR. Passed away at Salford Royal Hospital on 9th March 2010, aged 87. Pages 3, 551, 705, 706, 758, 1146, 1317, 1459, 1472.

DEAN, Horace (Dixie). Service details unknown. Page 707.

DEAN, Mildred. Sergeant, Auxiliary Territorial Service. Pages 1263, 1264, 1317.

DENTON, Thomas. Gunner, Royal Artillery. Pages 276, 468, 489, 586, 614, 1074, 1091, 1124, 1473.

DERVIN, William. Able Seaman D/JX288776, Royal Navy. Pages 1218, 1220.

DICKINSON, Eric. Highland Light Infantry (rank unknown).

DICKINSON, George. Lance Corporal 5119046, 1st Somerset Light Infantry. Pages 709, 710, 719, 1406.

DICKINSON, Robert Bernard. RAF (rank unknown). Pages 710, 805, 1473.

DICKSON, Donald. Pilot Officer, RAF. Pages 621, 895.

DITCHFIELD, Alma. Auxiliary Territorial Service (rank unknown).

DITCHFIELD, Walter. Corporal, Royal Engineers. Pages 730, 1438.

DIXON, Edward. Royal Corps of Signals (rank unknown). Pages 829, 1473.

DIXON, Frank. Corporal 2358748, Royal Corps of Signals. Pages 825, 826, 829, 1473.

DIXON, Frank. Warrant Officer, RAF. Pages 1018, 1287.

DIXON, J. Private, Airborne Forces. Pages 952, 953.

DIXON, Jessie (see WILMOT, Jessie).

DIXON, Walter. Corporal, Royal Engineers. Pages 830, 1333.

DIXON, William Seymour. Signalman W/2371018, Royal Corps of Signals. Pages 564, 829, 830.

DOBSON, Noel. Private, Army (regiment unknown). Passed away 1953. Page 784.

DODD, Eric James. Chief Electrical Artificer, Royal Navy. Born 1914. Enlisted 1941, demobbed 1946. 79 Devon Rd, Cadishead. Worked at Metropolitan Vickers, Trafford Park (inspector, mechanical inspection dept; tester, dynamo test dept, later inspecting engineer, headquarters, CEA, 1949).

DODD, Harold. RAF (rank unknown).

DODD, John. Gunner, Royal Artillery. Pages 603, 709, 1085, 1086.

DODD, Joseph. Sergeant, Royal Artillery. Page 709.

DONKIN, Dixon David. Pilot Officer (navigator), 138397, 620 Squadron, RAFVR. Pages 182, 430, 605, 606, 1066, 1406.

DONNELLY, Hugh. Gunner, Heavy Anti-Aircraft Battery, Royal Artillery. Trained at Kinmel Park, Wales then home service based in Norfolk. Page 1473.

DONNELLY, Joseph. Private, Royal Army Service Corps. Served Normandy, northern Europe, Germany and Austria. Brother of Hugh.

DOOLEY, Frederick Joseph. Service details unknown. Page 1474.

DOWSON, Ron. Service details unknown.

DOYLE, 'Louey'. Possibly Royal Army Medical Corps (rank unknown). Called up 05.11.42.

DRAFFIN, Joseph. Royal Navy (rating unknown). Pages 432, 433.

DRUM, Albert Edward. Signalman 2342408, Royal Corps of Signals. Passed away at Salford Royal Hospital, 6th January 1992, aged 76. Pages 1, 209, 210, 291, 402, 404, 424, 692, 895, 1234, 1261, 1262, 1292, 1293, 1302, 1439.

DRUMMOND, Jack. Corporal, RAF. Pages 584, 999.

DRUMMOND, Patrick. Service details unknown.

DUGDALE, Hubert Harry. Sergeant, Royal Artillery, then Royal Electrical and Mechanical Engineers. Pages 919, 1360.

DUNN, Alfred W. Lance Corporal, Army (regiment unknown). Page 151.

DUNN, John Roland. Lance Corporal 4206117, 2nd Cameronians (Scottish Rifles). Pages 712, 1406, 1456, 1474.

DUNN, Percy. Service details unknown. Resided 54 Harewood Rd, Irlam.

DUNN, Stephen Edward. Service details unknown. Page 1474.

DUPREE, George. RAF (rank unknown).

DUTTON, Winifred. Private, Auxiliary Territorial Service (Corps of Signals). Page 1106.

DYKE, Joseph Edgar. Coder, Royal Navy, HMS *Parret*. Page 1231.

EATON, John Douglas. Second Lieutenant P/289769, 270 Field Company, Royal Engineers. Pages 170, 705, 1438.

EAVES, Harold. Able Seaman D/J196797, Royal Navy. Pages 258, 260, 326, 374, 377, 1406.

EAVES, James Henry. Flight Lieutenant (bomb aimer/navigator), Bomber Command, RAFVR. Rixton Roll of Honour. Pages 410, 1171, 1172, 1454.

EAVES, Joseph Raymond. Engine Room Artificer 4th Class P/MX67992, Royal Navy, HMS *Prince of Wales*. Pages 325, 377, 1405.

EDEN, James. Royal Navy (rank unknown). Believed to have served in the Pacific. Resided Chestnut Ave, Cadishead.

EDMONDS, Kenneth. Sergeant, 1288523, RAFVR. Pages 418, 419, 420, 1171, 1406.

EDWARDS, Cyril. Gunner, 136th (1st West Lancashire) Field Regiment, Royal Artillery. Page 719.

EDWARDS, Fred. Sergeant, Army (regiment unknown). Pages 159, 1143.

EGERTON, Charles. Stoker, Royal Navy. Pages 478, 1089.

EGERTON, Mabel. Corporal, Auxiliary Territorial Service. Married Stoker Joe Brennan of the Merchant Navy 1950. Pages 3, 1089, 1090.

ELLIOTT, Dorothy. Leading Aircraftwoman 2102263, Women's Auxiliary Air Force. Married Aubrey Davies. Pages 550, 553, 557, 1416.

ELLIOTT, Harry. Air Training Corps and Army (rank and regiment unknown). Page 445.

ELLIOTT, Molly. Women's Auxiliary Air Force. Married T.H. (Harry) Johnson. Pages 550, 553, 557.

ELLIS, Robert. RAF (rank unknown).
ELLIS, Stanley. Flying Officer, RAF. Page 1309.
ELLISON, Clarence Mervyn. Royal Navy (rating unknown). Employed CWS Soap Works. Page 1474.
ERTHINGTON, John. Merchant Navy.
ETHERINGTON, William S. Private, Army (regiment unknown) (probably Eighth Army). Page 1309.
EVANS, Arthur. Lance Bombardier, Royal Artillery. Pages 558, 1270.
EVANS, Evan. Private, Pioneer Corps. Pages 558, 559, 560.
EVANS, Frank. Corporal, 49th Reconnaissance Regiment, 49th West Riding Division. Pages 347, 348, 1167, 1343.
EVANS, George. Craftsman 14823464, Royal Electrical and Mechanical Engineers. Pages 3, 216, 867, 868.
EVANS, Harry. Chief Petty Officer, Royal Navy. Page 1057.
EVANS, Johnny. Long Range Desert Group (rank unknown). Married Olwyn Williams, sister of John L. Williams (RAF). Resided Lines Road, Irlam.
EVE, Harry. Service details unknown. Page 1475.
EVE, William. Dentist, RAF.
EVERETT, Sydney. Artificer, Royal Navy. Resided Oak Avenue, Cadishead.
FAIRCLOUGH, Joseph N. Captain, Royal Army Service Corps. Page 878.
FAIRHURST, John. Private 2934672, 5th Queen's Own Cameron Highlanders. Pages 500, 528, 542, 675, 1406, 1475.
FAIRHURST, William Leslie. Bombardier, Royal Artillery. Pages 528, 675.
FARRAND, Ernie. Gunner, Maritime Royal Artillery.
FARRELL, Charles Edward. Royal Army Medical Corps (rank unknown). Brief Army service in 1939-40. Resided Cadishead. Passed away February 1946, aged 24.
FAULKNER, John William. Lance Corporal PO/X 105886, No. 41 (Royal Marine) Commando. Pages 510, 622, 624, 1349, 1406, 1456.
FEGAN, Nicholas Ephraim. Sergeant, RAF. Pages 74, 75, 841.
FELL, H. Service details unknown. Pages 1408, 1453.
FIELD, Joan. Private, Auxiliary Territorial Service. Pages 368, 1091.
FINDLATER, Colin. Service details unknown.
FIRTH, John. Service details unknown. Page 1475.
FISHER, George L. Able Seaman, Royal Navy. Page 1265.
FLEMING, Henry. Merchant Navy. Page 790.
FLETCHER, Jack. Driver, Royal Army Service Corps. Page 561.
FLETCHER, J. Gordon. Private (regiment unknown).
FLUCK, Jack. Major, Manchester Regiment. Pages 689, 947, 1313.
FORD, Ronnie. Royal Navy (rating unknown).
FOWLER, Frank. RAF (rank unknown). Married Emily Joan Spooner of Cadishead on 18th April 1942. Pages 377, 1086.
FOWLER, John Douglas. Private 4539857, 1st West Yorkshire Regiment. Pages 377, 379, 1086, 1406, 1456.
FOWLES, John James. Royal Navy (rating unknown). Page 1475.
FRAME, Andrew Skilling. Lance Corporal, Cameronians. Page 598.
FRENCH, Gladys. Private, Auxiliary Territorial Service. Page 368.
FREW, Robert William. Service details unknown. Medically discharged from Army. Born 20.05.19 at Lymm. Resided 2 Tramway Rd, Irlam. Father, Robert Frew, First World War veteran. Mother Nellie (Taylor).
FRITH, Arthur. Sergeant, Army Commandos. Page 659.
FRITH, Dennis. Service details unknown. Pages 659, 1476.
FRYER, Harry. Bombardier, Royal Artillery. Pages 582, 595.
FRYER, John. Royal Artillery (rank unknown). Page 596.
FRYER, William. Guardsman, Scots Guards. Pages 582, 595.
GALLAGHER, John J. Able Seaman, Royal Navy. Pages 200, 507.
GALLAGHER, Thomas. Stoker 1st Class C/KX143180, Royal Navy. Demobilised 29.09.46. Pages 200, 507, 508.
GALLICHAN, James (Jimmy). Lance Corporal, 1st Gordon Highlanders. Pages 1184, 1438

Appendix II

GARDINER, D. Service details unknown. Pages 1408, 1453.

GARDNER, A. Service details unknown. Pages 1408, 1451.

GARDNER, Alan. Royal Navy (rating unknown). Attended Irlam Central School. Resided Addison Rd, Higher Irlam.

GARDNER, Ernest. Private, Royal Marine Commandos. Page 980.

GARDNER, George. Private, Army (regiment unknown). Page 980.

GARLICK, Charles Ratcliffe. Lance Corporal, Corps of Military Police (CMP). Page 481.

GARLICK, Ray. Driver, Royal Army Service Corps. Page 481.

GELL, Edwin. Sergeant, RAF. Rixton Roll of Honour. Pages 194, 1269, 1454.

GEORGE, Lionel. Merchant Navy (rating unknown).

GIBBON, George Leslie. Trooper, Tank Corps. Pages 1032, 1034, 1317, 1476.

GILLESPIE, Joseph. Service details unknown.

GILLIBRAND, Geoffrey. Sergeant, Army (regiment unknown). Pages 264, 1152, 1459.

GILLIGAN, John. RAF (rank unknown).

GIVENS, James Richard, Royal Navy (rank unknown). Pages 1032, 1063, 1476.

GIVENS, Veronica C. Leading Aircraftwoman, Women's Auxiliary Air Force. Enlisted 1941. Daughter of Mrs S. Givens of 28 Ferryhill Road, Irlam. Pages 550, 1032.

GLOVER, Albert. Sapper, Royal Engineers. Pages 421, 662, 1476.

GLOVER, George. Gunner, Royal Artillery. Pages 421, 661, 1148, 1459.

GODDARD, Edward. RAF (rank unknown).

GOODIER, Brian G. Officer Cadet, Royal Bombay Sappers and Miners, later Lieutenant, regiment unknown. Pages 276, 494, 691.

GOODIER, Joyce. Officer, Women's Royal Naval Service.

GORDON, Russell. RAF (rank unknown). Page 1322.

GRAHAM, Eric. Coder, Royal Navy. Page 1249.

GRATRIX, Thomas. Lance Corporal 4202357, 7th Battalion, Royal Welch Fusiliers. Pages 911, 1407, 1457.

GRAYSON, Herbert. Army (rank and regiment unknown). Pages 260, 1476.

GREEN, Catherine (Kitty). Leading Aircraftwoman 464590, Women's Auxiliary Air Force. Passed away 2012. Pages 3, 549, 552, 583, 869, 983.

GREEN, Harry. Gunner, Maritime Royal Artillery. Resided Liverpool Rd, Irlam.

GREEN, James. Royal Navy (rating unknown). Served Malta. Page 584.

GREEN, Marjorie. Teleprinter operator, Women's Auxiliary Air Force. Pages 550, 557.

GREEN, Ronald. Able Seaman, Royal Navy, HMS *Fame*. Page 872.

GREEN, William. Sergeant 1129659, RAFVR. Pages 424, 425, 452, 1406, 1504.

GREEN, William Lawrence. Air Mechanic, Fleet Air Arm. Pages 631, 633, 636, 1477.

GREEN, Winifred (See SANDERCOCK, Winifred).

GRILLS, William. Corporal, RAF. Page 1108.

GRINDLEY, John (Jack). Engine Room Artificer, Royal Navy. Page 168.

GRINDLEY, Robert Henry. Leading Stoker D/KX 81169, Royal Navy, HMS *Glorious*. Pages 166, 168, 169, 1405, 1456.

GROVES, Eric. Leading Stoker, Royal Navy. Page 471.

GROVES, Roy. Royal Navy (rating unknown). Pages 471, 1477.

HALL, Edith. Corporal, Women's Auxiliary Air Force. Pages 551, 1223.

HALL, Nancy. Sergeant, Women's Auxiliary Air Force. Pages 550, 1288, 1290, 1313.

HALL, Sydney Ernest. Lance Corporal 2617483, 4th Grenadier Guards. Pages 356, 923, 924, 925, 1407.

HALL, Thomas William. Private, Royal Army Service Corps. Passed away at Rotherham in 1987. Pages 728, 729.

HALL, Victor John. Flight Sergeant, RAF.

HALL, Walter. Sergeant, Corps of Military Police. Pages 1288, 1289.

HALLIWAY, Bernard. Service details unknown.

HALLIWELL, Frank. Corporal, Royal Army Service Corps. Elder son of Mr and Mrs Halliwell of 9 Victory Rd, Irlam.

HALLIWELL, Frank Charles. Aircraftman 1st Class 1235358, RAF. Born 3rd December 1921. Passed away in 1992, aged 71. Pages 389, 545, 546, 1271, 1459.

HALLMARK, Norman. Sergeant, Royal Army Ordnance (or Service) Corps.

HAMBLETT, Robert Norman. Royal Navy (rating unknown). Page 1478.

HAMER, William Albert. Service details unknown. Page 1478.

HAMILTON, J. Army (rank and regiment unknown). Served Greece. Page 1065.

HAMILTON, William. Gunner 850821, Royal Artillery. Passed away 1980, aged 61. Pages 338, 339, 607, 1300.

HAMPSON, Charles Raymond (Ray). Gunner, Royal Artillery. Pages 649, 1075.

HAMPSON, Eric. Corporal, Royal Army Medical Corps. Pages 649, 1075.

HAMPSON, James E. (Eddie). Corporal, Royal Corps of Signals. Pages 649, 1075, 1124.

HAMPSON, W.H. Sapper, Royal Engineers. Page 947.

HANCOCK, James Henry. Private 3663060, 2ⁿᵈ Green Howards (Yorkshire Regiment). Pages 1078, 1407.

HANCOCK, Leslie. RAF (rank unknown). Page 551.

HANDSLEY, Clarence (Clarry). Royal Navy (rating unknown). Pages 842, 844, 842.

HANDSLEY, Kenneth. Army (rank and regiment unknown). Pages 842, 845.

HANDSLEY, John William. Army (rank and regiment unknown). Page 842.

HANKINSON, Arthur. Service details unknown. Born 1902 in Rixton. Lied about age to serve in the First World War and re-enlisted in the Second World War. Resided 84 Lords St, Cadishead.

HANKINSON, Cyril Frederick (Fred). Lance Corporal 1887407, Royal Engineers, (Heavy Mechanical Equipment (3a Sec RE), serving with 21ˢᵗ Army Group. Pages 1038, 1039.

HANKINSON, Kenneth. Sergeant Instructor, Army (regiment unknown). Page 1295.

HANLEY, Bernard Harry. Boy 1ˢᵗ Class D/JX162179, Royal Navy, HMS *Neptune*. Pages 103, 333, 334, 335, 1405, 1451.

HARPER, Annie. Private, Auxiliary Territorial Service. Parents resided at 13 Haig Ave, Cadishead. Married Allan Archibald Sim in November 1943. Allan was a native of Kelloholme, Kirkconnel, Scotland, and served in the RAF.

HARRIS, Henry. Lance Corporal 3651387, 2ⁿᵈ Border Regiment, Pages 1037, 1407, 1456.

HARRIS, Henry L. Service details unknown. Rixton Roll of Honour. Page 1454.

HARTLEY, Horatio. Sapper 2148333, 1 Field Squadron, Royal Engineers, Pages 486, 1406.

HASLAM, George. Private, Army (regiment unknown). Page 935.

HASLAM, Mildred. Leading Aircraftwoman, Women's Auxiliary Air Force. Pages 680, 683.

HAYES, Jeff. Craftsman, Royal Electrical and Mechanical Engineers. Page 738.

HAYMAN, Albert Edward George. Fusilier 3655544, 2ⁿᵈ/8ᵗʰ Lancashire Fusiliers. Passed away 11ᵗʰ July 1998. Pages 154, 488, 952, 954, 956.

HAYMAN, Clifford William. Private, Royal Army Service Corps then Royal Electrical and Mechanical Corps. Passed away 5ᵗʰ June 1995. Pages 154, 155, 488.

HAYMAN, Henry John. Private, Royal Army Service Corps. Passed away 27ᵗʰ August 1946. Pages 154, 834, 835, 836.

HAYWARD, Edwin Randall (also known as Edwin Randall Hayward-Lumber). Private, Royal Army Ordnance Corps. Page 780.

HAYWARD, Stephen (also known as Stephen Hayward-Lumber). Royal Navy (Submarine Service) (rating unknown). Pages 780, 781.

HEAP, Norman. Chief Petty Officer (Engine Room Artificer), Royal Navy. Only son of William Gaskell Heap (a local First World War veteran) of 2 Victoria Rd, Irlam. Married Barbara Sherratt, elder daughter of Mr and Mrs Ernest Sherratt of 31 Nelson Dr, Cadishead, in July 1942.

HEATON, John. Service details unknown. Page 1479.

HEWART, Edwin. Private, Eighth Army (regiment unknown). Pages 1193, 1222.

HEWART, James. Sergeant, 1ˢᵗ Loyal Regiment (North Lancashire). Pages 558, 561.

HEYWOOD, Frederick Noel. Corporal 3449057, 1ˢᵗ/8ᵗʰ Lancashire Fusiliers. Pages 10, 142, 143, 144, 1405.

HIGGINBOTTOM, Herbert. Royal Artillery. 23 Green Lane, Cadishead. He had served for 22 years with the Army, 16 years of which were with the Royal Artillery. It is believed he served during WW2. He worked at the blast furnace at the Steelworks and had been a member of the British Legion and the Haydock Labour Club. He was married with a son.

HIGGS, Alfred. Service details unknown. Pages 1268, 1479.

HIGSON, Sidney. Sherwood Rangers (rank unknown). Page 716, 931.

Appendix II

HILL, Charles. Gunner, L Battery, S/L Unit, Motor Transport Section, Royal Artillery. Pages 1033, 1036.

HILL, Eddie. Royal Artillery (rank unknown).

HILL, George Alcuin. Chief Petty Officer P/XK75723, Royal Navy. Pages 649, 650, 651, 652.

HILL, George William. Leading Aircraftman, RAF. Pages 1268, 1480.

HILL, Gordon. Service details unknown. Page 1480.

HILL, John. Pilot Officer, RAF. Pages 1033, 1305, 1035, 1438.

HILL, Peter Albert. Driver T/14902676, Royal Army Service Corps. Pages 1335, 1408, 1458, 1480.

HILLYARD, Annie. Driver, Auxiliary Territorial Service. Pages 551, 854.

HILLYARD, Clifton. Stoker 1st Class, D/KX136480, Royal Navy, HM Landing Craft Tank 390, 4th Flotilla. Pages 551, 853, 1407, 1456, 1480, 1504.

HILLYARD, Herbert. Royal Navy (rating unknown). Pages 551, 853.

HILLYARD, Irene. Corporal, Women's Auxiliary Air Force. Pages 550, 551, 853.

HILTON, Arthur. Corporal PLY/X120196, No. 48 (Royal Marines) Commandos. Pages 680, 820, 823, 824, 825, 1407, 1456.

HILTON, Fred. Guardsman, Irish Guards. Pages 1074, 1076.

HILTON, John (Jack). Corporal, 9th Royal Tank Regiment. Pages 859, 1480.

HILTON, Leslie H. Captain, Royal Army Dental Corps. Pages 877, 1407.

HILTON, Roy. Guardsman, Irish Guards (Armoured). Pages 1073, 1074, 1076, 1077.

HILTON, Wilfred. Private, Royal Army Service Corps. Pages 100, 225, 434, 472, 603, 604, 1074, 1077.

HINDLEY, Donald. Private, Army (regiment unknown). Resided Rixton-with-Glazebrook. Page 1325.

HINDLEY, Harry. Private, Royal Army Medical Corps. Married Elizabeth Emma Rogers of 646 Liverpool Rd, Irlam, at St Mary's Church, Cadishead, 27.02.43. Page 158.

HINDLEY, J.A. Service details unknown. Page 1480.

HINDLEY, Joseph Sidney. Gunner, Royal Artillery. Pages 952, 1288, 1291, 1439.

HINDLEY, Joseph S. Service details unknown. Married Muriel Harrison on 05.06.43. Resided 107 Fir St, Cadishead. Possibly the same man as above.

HODGE, Nancy. Leading Aircraftwoman, Women's Auxiliary Air Force. Pages 550, 551.

HODGES, Thomas Reginald. Trooper, Royal Armoured Corps. Pages 864, 865, 1480.

HODGSON, Charles Roy. Telegraphist, Royal Navy (rating unknown). Served Indian Ocean. Addison Rd, Higher Irlam.

HODGSON, Herbert. Service details unknown. Page 1480.

HODKINSON, Albert. Flight Sergeant, 645731, 10 Squadron, RAF. Pages 1223, 1438.

HODKINSON, Eric. Royal Navy (rating unknown). Resided Irlam.

HODSON, Bert. Royal Navy (rating unknown).

HODSON, L. Army (rank and regiment unknown). Page 948.

HOLLAND, Arthur. Gunner, Royal Navy. Page 675.

HOLLAND, Harry. Service details unknown.

HOLLAND, Joan Mary. See JOHNSON, Joan Mary.

HOLLEY, Alfred Hunt. Stoker 1st Class, Royal Navy, HMS *Barricade.* Pages 1191, 1407, 1456, 1480, 1504.

HOLLIS (Christian name and service details unknown). Resided Moss Side Rd, Cadishead.

HOLT, Frederick (Eric). Private 14221286, Royal Army Service Corps. Pages, 854, 580, 581, 895.

HOOD, WT. Sergeant (service/regiment unknown). Page 1328.

HOPKINSON, Jack. Fusilier, 1st Lancashire Fusiliers. Page 1319.

HORNBLOW, Frank. Corporal, RAF. Enlisted 1939. Served home and overseas. Demobbed 1945. Born 1920. Resided 66 Dudley Rd, Cadishead. Worked at Metropolitan Vickers, Trafford Park (production engineer, K Rheo Production Dept, then sales correspondent, Industrial Controls Sales Dept from 1951).

HOUGHTON, Albert. Private, Army (regiment unknown). Passed away 20th July 1986. Pages 1158, 1163, 1164.

HOUGHTON, Frederick. Service details unknown.

HOUGHTON, James William. Signalman 14202026, Royal Corps of Signals. Passed away 24th May 1989, aged 67. Pages 3, 1310, 1312.

HOUGHTON, James. Service details unknown. Page 1480.

HOUGHTON, Sydney. Fusilier, Army (regiment unknown). Page 671.

Appendix II

HOUGHTON, (Christian name unknown). Fusilier, 1st Lancashire Fusiliers. Page 1319.

HOWARD, J.R. Service details unknown. Mediterranean Expeditionary Force.

HOWARTH, Fred. Royal Marines (or Royal Navy) (rank unknown).

HOWARTH, Harold. Private, Royal Army Service Corps. Page 661.

HOWARTH (Christian name unknown). RAF. Page 1238.

HOWES, James N. Corporal, Army (regiment unknown). Pages 685, 736, 753, 767, 783, 893, 920, 976, 987, 1375.

HUDSON, Derek. Private 3533604, Manchester Regiment, later Loyal Regiment (North Lancashire), King's Regiment, Corps of Military Police and Royal Army Ordnance Corps. Page 152.

HUDSON, Mildred. Auxiliary Territorial Service (rank unknown). Page 1257.

HUGHES, Albert. Service details unknown. Page 1481.

HUGHES, Clifford. Private, Army (regiment unknown). Pages 926, 1149, 1459.

HUGHES, Jack. Private, King's Own Yorkshire Light Infantry. Son of Mr and Mrs J. Hughes of 11 Preston Ave, Irlam. Married Kathleen Smith Winrow of Hamilton Avenue, Cadishead, in September 1942. His sister, Gladys Florence Hughes, married a Warrington serviceman, Driver Charles William Mallett, RAF (Transport) in February 1940 at St John's Church.

HUGHES, Jack. Sergeant, Army (regiment unknown). Served in Belgium. Possibly the same man as above.

HUGHES, Robert William. Sergeant 4196489, 10th Royal Welch Fusiliers. Pages 338, 336.

HUGHES, William. Sergeant Royal Welch Fusiliers. Page 338, 337.

HUMPHREYS, Eric. Service details unknown. Page 1481.

HUMPHREYS, Thomas William. Gunner, Royal Artillery. Page 962.

HUNT, Kenneth Edward. Chief Petty Officer, Royal Navy. Married Gladys Davenport, Auxiliary Territorial Service (of Cadishead) in 1943. Page 1481.

HUNT, Samuel Baden Powell. Service details unknown. Page 1481.

HURST, Charles. RAF Regiment (rank unknown). Served in Burma. Resided Prospect Avenue, Cadishead and then moved to Higher Irlam.

HUTCHINSON, Harry E. Fusilier, Lancashire Fusiliers. Pages 145, 427, 808, 1050, 1051, 1459.

HUTCHINSON, Raymond. Private, Loyal Regiment (North Lancashire).

HUTCHINSON, Raymond. Private, Royal Army Medical Corps. Only son of Mr and Mrs T. Hutchinson of 8 Springfield Lane, Irlam. Married Renee Blinkthorn of Irlam, January 1943. Possibly the same man as above. Page 158.

ILLINGWORTH, Norman. Service details unknown.

IMESON, Arthur. Service details unknown. Page 1482.

INGAMELL, Mary. Private, Auxiliary Territorial Service. Page 545.

INGROUILLE, Henry. Royal Navy (rating unknown).

INTIN, Sydney. Service details unknown. Page 1482.

JACKLIN, John Arthur. Aircraftman 1st Class 1116011, RAFVR. Pages 378, 589, 698, 1189, 1309, 1407, 1459.

JACKMAN, Harry. Service details unknown. Page 1482.

JACKMAN, Henry. Sapper, Royal Engineers. Pages 759, 760, 1482.

JACKMAN, John. Private 13086706, Pioneer Corps. Pages 1099, 1102.

JACKMAN, Robert. Lance Bombardier 1077016, Royal Artillery. Passed away 1961. Pages 1099, 1101.

JACKSON, Ernest. Private 14715413, 2nd Highland Light Infantry (City of Glasgow Regiment). Pages 1226, 1408, 1457.

JACKSON, Frank. Royal Tank Regiment (rank unknown). Pages 441, 500, 1482.

JACKSON, Leonard. Driver 4462093, Durham Light Infantry then Queen's Royal Regiment. Pages 662, 737.

JACKSON, R.T. Royal Artillery (rank unknown). Page 997.

JACKSON, Robert. Service details unknown. Page 1482.

JAMES, Harold Albert. Lance Corporal 14722432, 1st East Yorkshire Regiment. Pages 1095, 1097, 1098.

JAMES, Harold K. Leading Aircraftman, RAF. Page 561.

JAMES (Mrs). First name unknown. Women's Auxiliary Air Force (rank unknown). Page 1325.

JAMES, Wilfred. Service details unknown. Page 1482.

JAQUES, Ronald Thornley. Flight Sergeant 1522705, 640 Squadron, RAF. Pages 380, 804, 1111, 1407, 1456, 1482, 1504.

Appendix II

JAQUES, Roy. Royal Navy (rating unknown).

JENKINS, Clifford. RAF (rank unknown).

JENKINS, Ivor. RAF (rank unknown).

JENKINS, John Trevor (Trevor). Lance Corporal, Royal Corps of Signals then 4th Queen's Own Hussars. Pages 3, 216, 335, 698, 700, 701, 816, 866, 959, 1032, 1123, 1135, 1160, 1234, 1235, 1236, 1309, 1387, 1390, 1394, 1482.

JENKINS, William. Royal Navy (rating unknown).

JIBSON, James Henry Prince. Sergeant (air gunner) 545369, 178 Squadron, Mediterranean Allied Air Force Command, RAFVR. Pages 974, 1407, 1504.

JOHN, Henry Rowland. Captain 159735S, Royal Army Service Corps. Pages 3, 159, 319, 845, 846, 1322.

JOHNSON, Andrew. Royal Navy (rating unknown).

JOHNSON, Charles H. Service details unknown. Rixton Roll of Honour. Page 1454.

JOHNSON, Frank. Sapper, Royal Engineers. Rixton Roll of Honour. Pages 257, 1155, 1454, 1459.

JOHNSON, Frank. Anti-Aircraft Battery (rank and regiment unknown). Page 1482.

JOHNSON, Geoff. Fleet Air Arm (rank unknown). Military trade: engine fitter. Pages 631, 634, 669, 730, 1197, 1482.

JOHNSON, Gilbert Denis. Service details unknown. Page 1482.

JOHNSON, Harry H. Fusilier, 1st/8th Battalion, Lancashire Fusiliers. Passed away at St Ann's Hospice 02.09.04. Pages 145, 146.

JOHNSON, Herbert H. Lieutenant, Army (regiment unknown). Pages 187, 669, 912.

JOHNSON, Hubert [Hughie]. Private, Parachute Regiment.

JOHNSON, Hugh Charles. Private 4202425, Army Air Corps. Pages 600, 1459.

JOHNSON, James. Corporal, 627th Field Squadron, Armoured Engineers, 1st Armoured Division. Pages 131, 551, 582, 669.

JOHNSON, James William. Private, Royal Army Service Corps. Page 1328.

JOHNSON, J. Douglas. Private, Army (regiment unknown). Page 113.

JOHNSON, Joan Mary. Leading Aircraftwoman, Women's Auxiliary Air Force. Page 675.

JOHNSON, Raymond. Private, Army (regiment unknown). Page 1048.

JOHNSON, Samuel Lawrence. Gunner 1610167, 443 Battery, 130th Heavy Anti-Aircraft Regiment, Royal Artillery. Pages 294, 1405.

JOHNSON, Thomas. Army (rank and regiment unknown). Page 669.

JOHNSTON, Richard. Service details unknown.

JOHNSTONE, Robert. Royal Artillery (rank unknown)

JONAS, Richard (Dick). Service details unknown.

JONES, Dai. Loyal Regiment, then Merchant Navy (rating unknown). Page 1050.

JONES, Derek. Service details unknown.

JONES, Eric. Flight Sergeant (navigator/air gunner) 1580403, RAF. Pages 393, 394.

JONES, Florence Gwendoline (Gwen). Radio Operator 2081591, Women's Auxiliary Air Force. Page 393.

JONES, Frank. Leading Signalman P/JX162963, Royal Navy. Page 260.

JONES, George Arnold. Private, Welch Regiment. Pages 393, 394.

JONES, Henry (Harry). Leading Aircraftman 1014423, RAFVR. Pages 918, 1407, 1456.

JONES, Hubert. Private, Army (regiment unknown). Pages 145, 146, 427, 808, 1152, 1459.

JONES, Hubert. Flight RAF. Page 1285.

JONES, Hugh. RAF Bomber Command (rank unknown). Lancaster bombers.

JONES, Norman. Sergeant 2045586, 39 (7th Lancashire Fusiliers) Anti-Aircraft Battalion, Royal Artillery. Pages 816, 963, 964, 965, 1144.

JONES, Owen M. Sapper, Royal Engineers. Resided at 34 Dean Rd, Cadishead. Married Bessie Rushton of 21 Baines Ave, Irlam in November 1940.

JONES, Peter. Royal Navy (rating unknown). Page 394.

JONES, Ron. Royal Navy (rating unknown).

JONES, Thomas (Tommy). Able Seaman, Royal Navy, HMS *Cossack*. Pages 114, 115.

JONES, William. Royal Navy (rating unknown). Page 225.

JOPSON, Arthur. Private (Drummer) 3647464, 1st South Lancashire Regiment. Pages 149, 1405.

JORDAN, Albert. Service details unknown. Page 1483.

JORDAN, George. RAF (rank unknown). Page 77.

Appendix II

JORDAN, Vera. Women's Auxiliary Air Force (rank unknown). Page 550.
KEAVENEY, Frank. RAF (rank unknown). Page 1483.
KEAVENEY, John. Service details unknown. Born 1918. Served in Egypt in 1941.
KELLY, Jack. Company Quartermaster Sergeant, Army (regiment unknown). Pages 582, 800.
KERSHAW, Eric Gilbert. Sergeant (wireless operator/air gunner) 1360538, 7 Squadron, RAFVR. Pages 443, 444, 1406, 1458.
KERSLAKE, William. Lancashire Fusiliers (rank unknown).
KILLEN, John. Flight Sergeant (air gunner) 1055997, 97 Squadron, No. 8 Group, Bomber Command, RAFVR. Pages 680, 682, 683, 1406, 1504.
KILLON, Harry. Fusilier, Royal Scots Fusiliers (probably 6th Battalion, 15th Scottish Division). Pages 1086, 1088, 1483.
KILNER, Arthur. Royal Navy (rating unknown). Employed CWS Soap Works.
KING, Leslie N. Mine Clearance Service (rank unknown). Pages 1333, 1334.
KINSEY, Arthur. 2nd Manchester Regiment (rank unknown). Page 433.
KINSEY, J. Lance Corporal (other service details unknown). Page 547.
KIRKHAM, Annie. Service details unknown. Rixton Roll of Honour. Page 1454.
KIRKHAM, Robert F. Lance Corporal, Royal Engineers. Page 1316.
KITCHING, Wilfred Harold. Carpenter R293082, Merchant Navy. Pages 787, 788, 791.
KNIGHT, James. Lance Corporal, Royal Army Service Corps. Pages 176, 730.
KNOWLES. Harold. Private, Army (regiment unknown). Pages 582, 880.
KNOWLES, Joseph. Trooper, Royal Tank Regiment. Pages 582, 880.
KREIBICH, Julius Leonard. Lieutenant, King's African Rifles and REME. Pages 1023, 1026, 1484.
KRGUSH, Frederick. Gunner, 39 (7th Lancashire Fusiliers) Anti-Aircraft Battalion, Royal Artillery. Page 70.
LATHAM, Joseph. Army. Other service details unknown. Resided Cadishead. Parents Samuel Latham and Mrs Latham of 43 Lancaster Rd, Cadishead. Married Annie Booth of Culcheth 12.05.43.
LAVERTY, Dorothy. Auxiliary Territorial Service. Page 1183.
LAWRENCE, John Henry. Private, Worcester Regiment. Youngest son of late Mr and Mrs Lawrence. Married Alice Brooks of 7 Lines Rd, Irlam, 07.11.42.
LAWRINSON, George William. Signaller, Royal Corps of Signals. Pages 347, 557, 557, 1257, 1484.
LEA, Gordon. Private, 2nd Border Regiment. Page 1336.
LEARY, Kenneth John. Leading Aircraftman 651816, 84 Squadron, RAF. Pages 389, 1459.
LEECH, Kenneth. Naval Gunner D/JX266040, Royal Navy. Passed away 28th September 2009. Pages 309, 311, 319, 745, 1505.
LEIGH, Sarah Winifred. See ROBERTS, Sarah Winifred.
LENNELL, K. Sapper, Royal Engineers. Page 820.
LENNIE, Francis Norman. Private, Royal Army Service Corps. Pages 582, 732, 767, 769, 1484.
LEWIS, David Eric. Service details unknown. Married Irene Bolton in Warrington 1937. Page 1484.
LILLEY, Jack. Leading Aircraftman (electrical artificer) 3012777, RAF. Pages 445, 965, 967.
LITCHFIELD, Albert. Service details not known
LITCHFIELD, Arthur. Service details not known.
LLOYD, Daisy. Lance Corporal, Auxiliary Territorial Service (attached Royal Signals). Page 805.
LLOYD, Gwen. Private, Auxiliary Territorial Service. Page 805.
LLOYD, Marjorie. Private, Auxiliary Territorial Service. Page 805.
LLOYD, Mary. Private, Auxiliary Territorial Service (attached Royal Artillery). Page 805.
LLOYD, Samuel. Private 3651318, 2nd South Lancashire Regiment. Later served in the Pioneer Corps. Pages 153, 154.
LLOYD, William Henry. Leading Aircraftman 1528351, RAFVR. Pages 520, 1406, 1457, 1485.
LOCKLEY, Frederick. Lance Bombardier, 39 (7th Lancashire Fusiliers) Anti-Aircraft Battalion, Royal Artillery. Page 70.
LOFTUS, Ernest. Flight Sergeant, RAF. Page 1078.
LOFTUS, Thomas. Royal Navy, HMS *Berwick* (rating unknown). Pages 3, 733.
LOMAS, Cyril. Service details unknown. Page 1485.
LONGBOTTOM, Bernard. Merchant Navy (rating unknown).
LONGBOTTOM, Gee. Army. Other service details unknown. Pages 1253, 1255.

LONGBOTTOM, John Kenneth. Private 14206410, 2nd East Yorkshire Regiment. Pages 902, 903, 904, 1389, 1407, 1457.

LOWE, Eric. Royal Navy (rating unknown). Pages 400, 1485.

LOWE, Harold. Private T/14649965, Royal Army Service Corps. Pages 400, 397, 1173, 1174, 1485.

LOWE, Richard William. Able Seaman D/JX154121, Royal Navy, HMS *Newmarket*. Pages 103, 395, 396, 397, 398, 399, 1406.

LOWE, Thomas. Service details unknown. Page 1124.

LOWNDES, Archibald (Archie). Army (probably Royal Electrical and Mechanical Engineers, rank unknown). Page 563.

LOWNDES, Harry. Able Seaman, Royal Navy. Pages 665, 855.

LOWNDES, James. Service details unknown. Page 1485.

LOWNDES, Thomas. RAF (rank unknown).

LUKE, Albert. Sapper, 5 Assault Regiment, Royal Engineers, 79 Armoured Divn. Pages 833, 837, 838.

LYNCH, John. Private, Army (regiment unknown). Page 1104.

LYNCH, Michael. Driver, Royal Army Service Corps. Pages 558, 1104.

LYTHGOE, Amy Ruth. Women's Auxiliary Air Force (rank unknown). Resided Parrs Farm. Married Robert Willis Millar, Royal Navy.

LYTHGOE, Ruth. Auxiliary Territorial Service (rank unknown).

MACE, Amy. Auxiliary Territorial Service (rank unknown). Sister of William Mace.

MACE, Edward. Private, Army (regiment unknown). Served on the Chindit expeditions. Pages 582, 1021, 1023.

MACE, Frederick. Corporal (regiment unknown). Believed to have served in an Intelligence unit. Page 1485.

MACE, William Henry. Fusilier 3655932, 1st Battalion, Lancashire Fusiliers. Pages 269, 754, 755, 756, 1022, 1407, 1456.

MADDICK, Harold William. RAF (rank unknown). Served over four years including service at India, Malaya and Singapore. Demobilised May 1947. Youngest son of Mr and Mrs T.S. Maddick of 15 Henley Ave, Irlam.

MADDOCKS, Ted. Service details unknown.

MAHON, Edward. Sapper, Royal Engineers (Parachute). Pages 952, 953.

MAHON, Hugh. Service details unknown. Pages 952, 953.

MALIN, Joseph. Petty Officer, Royal Navy. Pages 1108, 1486.

MARCHANT, Joseph. Leading Stoker, Royal Navy. HMS *Trinidad*. Pages 414, 415, 416.

MARK, Norman Hall. Sergeant, Royal Army Ordnance Corps.

MARSHALL, Herbert James. Able Seaman, Royal Navy. Pages 280, 281, 282, 974.

MARSHALL, John Robert (Jack). Sapper, Royal Engineers. Pages 1121, 1123, 1486.

MARSHALL, Roy. Able Seaman, Royal Navy. Pages 280, 281, 974, 1486.

MARSHALL, Thomas. Able Seaman JX294746, Royal Navy. Pages 280, 281, 282, 974, 1486.

MARSLAND, John R. RAF (rank unknown). Page 947.

MARTON, Harold William. Petty Officer, Royal Navy. Youngest son of Mr and Mrs Oswald Marton of 10 Lynthorpe Ave, Cadishead. Married Olga Mather of Lowton St Mary's, in April 1943.

MASON, Ernest Flying Officer, RAF. Pages 693, 1070, 1366, 1375.

MASON, Norman. Royal Navy (rating unknown). Eldest son of Mr and Mrs J. Mason of Cadishead. Married Norah Owen, at Ironbridge Parish Church, Shropshire, 24.07.43. Page 1063.

MASSEY, Arthur. Gunner, Royal Artillery. Pages 603, 961.

MASSEY, Fred. Sapper, Royal Engineers. Pages 582, 961, 1288.

MASSEY, Horace. Sapper, Royal Engineers. Pages 947.

MASSEY, John. Sapper, Royal Electrical and Mechanical Engineers. Page 1266.

MASTERS, Harold. RAF (rank unknown).

MATTHEWS, William. Staff Sergeant (regiment unknown). Eldest son of Mrs Whiting of 92 Lords St, Cadishead, and the late Mr J.T. Matthews. Married Margaret Leyland, the youngest daughter of Mr and Mrs Leyland of Shipley 25.05.42.

MATTOCK, Arthur. Service details unknown.

MATTOCKS, Edwin William. Ordinary Seaman, Royal Navy. Eldest son of Mr and the late Mrs Mattocks of 30 Fiddlers Lane, Higher Irlam. Married Margaret Roberts of Cadishead, on 18th April 1942.

Appendix II

McARTHUR, Mary. See SMART, Mary.

McARTHUR, Leslie. Corporal, Durham Light Infantry. Pages 622, 625.

McARTHUR, Walter. Leading Stoker D/KX165162 (or D/KX165126), Royal Navy, HMS *Renown*. Pages 3, 331, 622, 626, 628, 630, 672, 1004, 1007, 1126, 1389, 1394, 1486.

McCARTHY, Owen Eugene. Corporal 3663241, Lancashire Fusiliers. Worked at Steelworks until aged 55, then British Tar Works, Cadishead until retirement. Moved to Flixton in 1950s. An active member of the Lancashire Fusiliers Association. Passed away 31st December 2008. Pages 3, 803, 868, 1104, 1294, 1373, 1438, 1486.

McDONAGH, John. Private, King's Royal Rifle Corps. Pages 410, 671, 1153, 1459.

McGLYNN, James. Corporal 1000657, RAF. Served Aden (1941), Rhodesia, Kenya, North Africa, Italy and Sardinia.

McLEAN, James Campbell. Leading Aircraftman, RAF. Page 804.

McLEAN, John Pollock. Leading Aircraftman, RAF. Page 805.

McLEAN, Robert. Sergeant PO/X113812, 44 Royal Marine Commando. Pages 751, 805, 1390, 1486.

McNULTY, Bernard. Royal Artillery (rank unknown). Brother of David. Joined Territorials and saw service in Orkneys and then landed in Normandy on D+2.

McNULTY, David Reginald. Sergeant 3972057, Royal Signals. Demobbed at Cheltenham in 1945. Passed away at Salford, December 1998, aged 82. Pages 3, 269, 270, 492, 493, 719, 1294.

McQUIRK, Frank. Driver T/14320285, Royal Army Service Corps. Pages 3, 478, 480, 615, 617, 724, 1367, 1486.

McQUIRK, Henry. Private, Army (regiment unknown). Page 480.

McVEY, H.G. Sapper, Royal Engineers. Page 878.

MEEHAN, Patrick Joseph. Sergeant, Royal Army Medical Corps. Pages 3, 438, 439.

MELLING, Norman Edward. RAFVR (rank unknown). Page 1486.

MELLING, Thomas. Corporal, Lancashire Fusiliers and then Royal Electrical and Mechanical Engineers. Page 920, 922.

MELLOR, Alan. Royal Navy (rating unknown). Page 1487.

MELLOR, Silvia. Radio Operator, Auxiliary Territorial Service. Page 812.

MELLOR, Walter. Army (rank and regiment unknown).

MELTON, Charles. Private, Devonshire Regiment and later Gunner, Royal Artillery. Pages 582, 961, 1474.

MELTON, George. Private, Coldstream Guards. Pages 587, 588.

MELVILLE, Donald. Pilot Officer, RAF. Pages 540, 698, 1439.

MELVILLE, John Beresford (Jack). Royal Navy (rating unknown). Pages 1211, 1212, 1217, 1218.

MENZIES, Charles James. Able Seaman D/JX 305275, Royal Navy. Pages 500, 521, 522, 523, 524, 526, 1406, 1487.

MENZIES, David. Royal Engineers (rank unknown). Page 526.

MENZIES, Douglas Stewart. Sapper 14812244, Royal Engineers. Pages 3, 1092, 1093, 1144.

MEREDITH, George. Royal Navy (rating unknown).

MICKLEWRIGHT, Norman. Fusilier, Army (regiment unknown). Page 1145.

MICKLEWRIGHT, William Ernest. Fusilier, Army (regiment unknown). Pages 114, 421, 942.

MILLAR, James. Anti-Aircraft Battery, Royal Artillery (rank unknown). Page 207.

MILLAR, Robert Willis. Royal Navy (rating unknown), HMS *Sheffield*. Family originated from Scotland. Brother James. Robert married Amy Ruth Lythgoe (WAAF). Resided 129 Liverpool Road, Irlam.

MILLER, Lillian. Women's Auxiliary Air Force. Demobilised October 1945. Employed General Post Office, Manchester (post-war). Passed away at Manchester Northern Hospital, 10th June 1946, aged 25. Buried 15th June at Hollins Green Cemetery. Page 550.

MILLER, William Harry. Engine Room Artificer, Royal Navy. Son of Mr and Mrs W. Miller of 75 Marlborough Rd, Higher Irlam. Married Miss Annie Harrop of Cadishead, 13.09.41.

MILNER, Robert Joseph. RAF (rank unknown). Elder son of Mr and Mrs H. Milner of 2 Fiddlers Lane, Higher Irlam. Page 1054.

MILLS, Alice. Women's Auxiliary Air Force (rank unknown).

MILLS, Harry. Corps of Military Police (rank unknown).

MITCHELL, Harry. Sapper, Royal Engineers. Page 558.

MITCHELL, Kenneth S. Service details unknown. Page 1487.

Appendix II

MOLLOY, George. Corporal 4131044, Cheshire Regiment then 1st Battalion, Manchester Regiment. Passed away 20th November 2007. Pages 129, 130.

MOORE, Basil. Royal Navy (rating unknown), HMS *Eagle*. Page 446.

MOORE, Dorothy Mae. Private, American Women's Army Corps. Pages 1033, 1301, 1318.

MORGAN, Kenneth Irvin. Engine Room Mechanic P/MX502273, Royal Navy, HMS *Albatross*. Pages 931, 1407.

MORRIS, Stanley. Private (regiment unknown). Pages 150, 923, 1438, 1439.

MORRIS, William. Sergeant 1066984, 88 Battery, 14 Anti-Tank Regiment, Royal Artillery. Pages 11, 160, 1405, 1458.

MORT, Charles. Trooper 3458870, 51st Royal Tank Regiment, Royal Armoured Corps. Pages 959, 1407.

MORT, Stanley F. Highland Light Infantry (rank unknown). Page 997, 1487.

MOSEDALE, Frank. Flying Officer, Fighter Command, RAFVR. Pages 596, 994, 1045, 1145, 1335, 1459.

MOSEDALE, Thomas. Warrant Officer, RAFVR. Pages 596, 994, 1145, 1335, 1459.

MOSS, Winifred. Women's Auxiliary Air Force (rank unknown). Page 550.

MOSS, Edith. See HALL, Edith.

MOULDER, Arthur. Service details unknown.

MUCKLEY, Thomas. Royal Marines (rank unknown). Resided Dudley Rd, Cadishead.

MUNDAY, Roy. Service details unknown. Page 1488.

MUNSLOW, Beatrice. Private, Auxiliary Territorial Service. Sister of Brian and Richard. Resided 207 Liverpool Rd, Cadishead. Pages 1227, 1230.

MUNSLOW, Brian. Private, Army (regiment unknown). Resided 207 Liverpool Rd, Cadishead. Pages 1227, 1230.

MUNSLOW, Richard. Private, Army (regiment unknown). Resided 207 Liverpool Rd, Cadishead. Pages 1227, 1230.

MURRAY, Vincent. Leading Aircraftman, RAF. Married Theresa Ann Lindley 01.01.44. Eldest son of Mr and Mrs Patrick Murray of 32 Milton Ave, Irlam.

MUSKETT, Harry. Guardsman 2919278, 6th Grenadier Guards. Pages 670, 1406, 1457.

MUSKETT, James. Private, 2nd Argyll & Sutherland Highlanders. Passed away at Salford in 1986. Pages 670, 906, 908.

MUSKETT, Thomas. Royal Navy (rating unknown). Page 670.

NEEDHAM, Lin. Royal Electrical and Mechanical Engineers (rank unknown). Served Italy 1944. Resided 75 Dixon St, Irlam.

NEEDHAM, William. Sapper 2092952, Royal Engineers. Resided 75 Dixon St, Irlam. By March 1943 was serving with 255th Army Field Company RE, Eighth Army, in Algiers. Cousin of Henry, John and Robert Jackman.

NELSON, Clifford. RAF (rank unknown).

NELSON, Noel. Sapper, Royal Engineers. Passed away 31st January 1984. Pages 1122, 1488.

NELSON, Reginald. Service details unknown.

NELSON, Robert. Gunner, Royal Navy. Page 439.

NEVILLE, Harold Boardman. Sergeant, Royal Tank Corps. Pages 661, 1304.

NEWMAN, Joseph Philip. Sergeant (air gunner) 1146100, 1654 Conversion Unit, 5 Group, Bomber Command, RAFVR. Pages 159, 507, 1406, 1488.

NEWTON, James Herbert. Gunner 14137794, 51 Heavy Anti-Aircraft Regiment, Royal Artillery. Pages 1274, 1362, 1408, 1458.

NEWTON, Wilfred Charles. Pilot, RAFVR and 71 Air Sea Rescue Marine Craft Unit, Gibraltar. Pages 512, 514, 515, 516, 517, 518, 519.

NEYLAN, Andrew. Service details unknown. Page 1488.

NEYLAN (Christian name unknown). Royal Navy (rating unknown). Possibly NEYLAN, Andrew.

NICHOLS, Herbert. 71 Lancashire Anti-Aircraft Battalion (rank unknown). Page 1488.

NICKLIN, William. RAFVR (rank unknown). Military trade: air gunner. Pages 1141, 1460.

NOCK, John. Sergeant Pilot, RAFVR. Page 734.

NORMAN, Cyril. Acting Leading Seaman, Royal Navy. Page 476.

NORTON, Thomas Leslie. Private, North Staffordshire Regiment. Page 878.

NUTTALL, Fred. Private, Army (regiment unknown). Passed away 1956. Pages 1253, 1254.

NUTTALL, John. Royal Navy (rating unknown). Pages 466.

Appendix II

OCCLESTON, Frederick. Service details unknown. Page 1489.
OCCLESTON, Harold. Private, Queen's Own Cameron Highlanders.
OCCLESTON, William. Service details unknown. Pages 547, 685, 686.
O'DONNELL, Edward (Teddy). Private, Army (regiment unknown).
O'DONNELL, James. Driver, Royal Army Service Corps. Page 680.
OGDEN, Albert Edward. Service details unknown. Page 1489.
OGDEN, Arthur. Heavy Anti-Aircraft Battery, Royal Artillery (rank unknown). Rixton Roll of Honour. Page 1454.
OGDEN, Clifford. Guards Unit (rank and regiment unknown).
OGDEN, David. Private, 13th King's (Liverpool Regiment). Page 535.
OGDEN, Robert. Captain, Royal Artillery. Page 596.
O'REILLY, Anthony. Royal Navy (rating unknown).
OUTLAW, Millicent. Auxiliary Territorial Service (rank unknown). Pages 1328, 1329.
OUTLAW, Robert. Merchant Navy (rating unknown). Pages 788, 795.
OWEN, Alfred. Service details unknown. Page 1489.
OWEN, Arthur. Sergeant, Royal Engineers. Pages 1330, 1332, 1438.
OWEN, Arthur. Service details unknown. Page 1489.
OWEN, Harold. Private, South Lancashires. Escorted German POWs to USA on Atlantic convoys. Resided Boundary Rd, Higher Irlam.
OWEN, James Edward (Eddie). Corporal 1546348, RAF (Air Sea Rescue). Pages 512, 513.
PALIN, William. Sapper 1941239, No. 4 Bomb Disposal Company, Royal Engineers. Pages 998, 1407.
PALING, Charles Royse. Corporal, Royal Army Medical Corps. Born 1919, Warrington. Resided 362 Liverpool Rd, Irlam. Educated at Urmston Grammar School and the College of Technology. Joined the sanitary department of Irlam Council in September 1936 and later became assistant to Lawrence Atherton. He left Irlam in November 1941 to take up a similar position with Shrewsbury Corporation. Married Ivy Margaret Wright, 28.03.42.
PARRY, Frank. Able Seaman, Royal Navy. Pages 456, 457, 1489, 1505.
PARRY, Roy. Royal Navy (rating unknown).
PATTISON, Alfred H. Lance Corporal 7641037, Royal Army Ordnance Corps. Passed away in 1950, aged 40. Pages 357, 360, 600, 1272.
PEACOCK, George E. Driver, Royal Electrical and Mechanical Engineers. Pages 912, 914.
PEERS, William. Private, Royal Electrical and Mechanical Engineers. Pages 563, 572, 578, 579.
PERKS, Elsie Irene. Service details unknown. Page 1309.
PERRIN, Douglas. Chief Petty Officer, Royal Navy. Pages 400, 713.
PERRIN, Osborne Peter. RAF (rank unknown). Pages 528, 631, 1018, 1490.
PERRIN, William Sidney. Leading Aircraftman 1540731, 2873 Squadron, RAF Regiment. Pages 528, 631, 1016, 1017, 1490.
PERRYMAN, Ernest. Royal Engineers and then Royal Army Medical Corps (rank unknown). Page 1158, 1163, 1165.
PETERS, William. Private, Army (regiment unknown). Married Hilda Hughes in October 1943. Youngest son of Mrs and the late Mr W. Peters of 14 George St, Higher Irlam. Served in Gibraltar from 1939 to June 1943.
PIMBLEY, Harold. Royal Navy (rating unknown). Resided Addison Rd, Higher Irlam. Brother of Norman.
PIMBLEY, Norman. Royal Navy (rating unknown). Resided Addison Rd, Higher Irlam. Brother of Harold.
PLATT, Wilfred. Leading Aircraftman, RAF. Military trade: electrician. Served at a staging post in central Africa. Resided Liverpool Rd, Irlam.
PONTIN (Christian name, rank and regiment unknown). Army. Page 1353.
POOLE, M. Driver. Service details unknown. Believed to have served with British Forces in Greece in June 1946.
POOLE, Richard. Diver, Royal Navy. Pages 232, 1438.
PORTER, John William. Private 10562280, Royal Army Ordnance Corps. Pages 542, 1406.
PORTER, William. Private 3657072, 2nd Border Regiment. Pages 655, 893, 894, 1379, 1407, 1456.
POTTS, George. Private, Army (regiment unknown). Page 584.
POTTS, Liam. Fleet Air Arm (rating unknown). Resided Allotment Rd, Cadishead.

Page 1428

POTTS, Raymond. Lance Corporal, Royal Corps of Signals. Pages 188, 547, 728.

POVEY, Robert. Private, York and Lancaster Regiment. Page 565.

POWELL, Bertram. Sergeant 2113945, Royal Engineers. Passed away 1986. Pages 807, 1330, 1331, 1438.

POWELL, Roland. Sergeant, RAF. Pages 1021, 1061, 1063.

POWELL, William. Naval Gunner, Royal Navy. Page 807.

PRENDERGAST, Anne. Women's Auxiliary Air Force (rank unknown). Enlisted 1939. Daughter of Mr T. Prendergast of 63 Baines Avenue, Irlam. Pages 550, 1158.

PRESTON, Leonard. Private, Royal Army Ordnance Corps.

PRICE, E. Private, Royal Army Medical Corps. Page 1115.

PRICE, W. Gunner, Light Anti-Aircraft Regiment. Page 1015.

PRIDDING, Ken. Royal Navy (rating unknown).

PROCTOR, William. Senior 3rd Engineer Officer, MV *Athelqueen*, Merchant Navy. Pages 387, 388, 389, 390, 788, 1406.

PROSSER, Harry. Leading Aircraftman, RAF. Page 1223.

RAVENSCROFT, Mona. Auxiliary Territorial Service (rank unknown).

RAYNER, R. Sergeant. Other service details unknown.

REDFERN, Douglas. Service details unknown. Page 1491.

REID, Joyce. Auxiliary Territorial Service (rank unknown). Later married Robert Whittaker, RN. Page 607.

RENNIE, Ernie. Royal Navy (rating unknown).

RICHARDSON, Richard. Lance Corporal, Northumberland Fusiliers. Pages 349, 1459.

RICHARDSON, Stephen. Guardsman, Scots Guards. Pages 432, 895, 946, 1459.

RICHMOND, Edna. Anti-Aircraft Battery, Auxiliary Territorial Service (rank unknown). Page 1265.

RICKETTS, George Harold. Gunner 1121278, Royal Artillery. Served with 5th Field Training Regiment. Died 7th November 2006. Husband of Hilda Ricketts (died 1984). Page 409.

RIORDAN, Denis. Corporal, Royal Army Medical Corps. Page 520.

RIORDAN, Gerard. Fusilier later Lieutenant, Lancashire Fusiliers. Pages 520, 1123, 1459.

ROBERTS, Arthur. Able Seaman JX2727064, Royal Navy. Pages 529, 812.

ROBERTS, Charles. RAF (rank unknown). Passed away 1981. Pages 973, 974.

ROBERTS, Harold. Private, Manchester Regiment. Page 169.

ROBERTS, J. Service details unknown.

ROBERTS, Kenneth. Service details unknown. Page 1492.

ROBERTS, Reginald. Irish Guards (rank unknown). Page 923.

ROBERTS, Sarah Winifred. Leading Aircraftwoman 2081118, Women's Auxiliary Air Force. Demobbed 30th October 1945 at RAF Padgate. Pages 550, 553, 637

ROBERTS, Vera. Women's Auxiliary Air Force (or Women's Royal Naval Service) (rank unknown). Page 551.

ROBINSON, Alan Sidney. Sapper, Royal Engineers. Page 1317.

ROBINSON, Arthur. Royal Army Service Corps (rank unknown). Pages 582, 786, 1268.

ROBINSON, Ernest K. Captain, Salvation Army (Red Shield Canteen). Page 1108.

ROBINSON, Frank. Service details unknown. Page 1492.

ROBINSON, John Joseph. Private, 1st Battalion, Manchester Regiment. Passed away in 1999, aged 83 (death registered in Oldham in June 1999). Pages 357, 358, 620, 942.

ROBINSON, Ken. RAF (rank unknown).

ROBINSON, Marjorie. Women's Auxiliary Air Force (rank unknown). Daughter of Mr and Mrs J.H. Robinson of 20 Nelson Drive, Cadishead. Page 550.

ROBINSON, Philip. Petty Officer, Royal Navy. Worked in the cost office at Steelworks. Married Helena Cameron of Glasgow, at the Congregational Church, Cadishead in September 1947. Page 1492.

ROGERS, Harry. Sergeant (mechanic), RAF. Resided Lords St, Cadishead.

ROGERS, Wilfred. Lance Corporal, Royal Army Medical Corps. Passed away 1967. Pages 543, 544.

ROGERSON, Eric. Engineer, Merchant Navy. Elder son of Mr and Mrs T. Rogerson of Devon Rd, Cadishead.

ROGERSON, Harold L. Corporal, Pioneer Corps and Royal Army Service Corps. Pages 547, 1221.

ROGERSON, James. Service details unknown. Page 976.

ROGERSON, Ken. Royal Artillery (rank unknown).

Appendix II

ROSBOTTOM, Harold. Leading Aircraftman, RAF Regiment. Pages 642, 643, 644, 897, 1069, 1153, 1459.

ROSBOTTOM, James (Jack). Army (rank and regiment unknown). Page 642.

ROSBOTTOM, William (Bill). Fusilier, Lancashire Fusiliers. Pages 642, 645.

ROURKE, Clifford. Sapper, Field Park Company, Royal Engineers and later Merchant Navy. Born c.1904.Resided 62 Silver St, Higher Irlam.

ROWE, Andrew McKenzie. Able Seaman, Royal Navy, HMS *Rodney*. Page 260.

ROWE, Ernest. Royal Engineers (rank unknown). Served France and Flanders before Dunkirk evacuation. Later served in Africa.

ROY, Cecil. Petty Officer, Royal Navy. Pages 253, 1438.

ROYLE, Alfred. Gunner, 39 (7th Lancashire Fusiliers) Anti-Aircraft Battalion, Royal Artillery. Page 70.

ROYLE, Basil J. Army (rank and regiment). Born in the district 1920.

ROYLE, Herbert. Royal Artillery (rank unknown).

RUSHTON, John T. Sub Lieutenant, Royal Navy. Pages 5, 770, 772.

RYAN, John. Leading Aircraftman 1487651, 2844 Squadron, RAF Regiment. Pages 740, 1130, 1134, 1135, 1493.

RYAN, Thomas. Lance Bombardier1624870, 4th Regiment, Maritime Royal Artillery. Pages 2, 739, 741, 1135, 1319.

SADLER, Alexander Igil. Stoker 1st Class D/KX112549, Royal Navy, HMS *Caledon*. Pages 409, 1406.

SALT, Muriel. Auxiliary Territorial Service (rank unknown). Pages 1227, 1229.

SALT, William. Royal Navy (rating unknown). Pages 1227, 1229.

SAMPSON, Ronald. Corporal P/LX2755, 381 King's Squad, Royal Marines. Passed away 2012. Pages 3, 326, 329, 330, 347, 352, 882, 884, 885, 1242, 1459.

SANDERCOCK, Ernest Victor George. Private, Devonshire Regiment and then Fusilier, Army (regiment unknown). Page 784.

SANDERCOCK, Winifred (nee Green). Auxiliary Territorial Service (rank unknown). Page 784.

SAUNDERS, Fred. Lancashire Fusiliers (rank unknown).

SAUNDERS, James (Jim). Service details unknown (possibly 10th Lancashire Fusiliers). Page 492.

SAVAGE, George W. Service details unknown. Page 1493.

SAVAGE, Robert Taylor. Aircraftman, RAF. Robert was born in the district (birth registered Barton I., March 1921), the second son of the late Thomas and Hilda Ellen Savage of 35 Hayes Rd, Cadishead. Married Muriel Winifred Weston, youngest daughter of Herbert and Edith Weston of 8 Lines Rd, Irlam on 27th December 1941. Muriel's father was Divisional Superintendent of Irlam and Cadishead Division of the St John Ambulance Brigade.

SCOTSON, Jack. Reconnaissance Regiment. Page 1366.

SCOTT, Harry. Driver, Royal Army Service Corps. Page 665.

SCOTT, John. Private 7617953, Royal Army Ordnance Corps. Pages 291, 570, 580.

SECOMBE, Sid. Service details unknown.

SENIOR, Irvin. Private, Sherwood Foresters. Page 880.

SENIOR, John (Jack). Private, Staffordshire and later served with the Cheshire Regiments. Pages 879, 880.

SENIOR, Jeff (or Geoff). RAF (rank unknown). Post-war address: Brookfield Rd, Culcheth. Believed to be Aircraftman 1099753 Geoffrey Senior, RAF. Passed away January 2006. Pages 378, 1459.

SHAKESHAFT, Walter Harry. Private, Cheshire Regiment. Page 564.

SHANNON, Ernie. Service details unknown.

SHARP, Joseph. Royal Marines, HMS *Renown*. Page 628.

SHARP, Thomas. Leading Aircraftman, RAF. Pages 303, 469, 946, 1115, 1493.

SHARP, William Henry. Fusilier, 2nd Lancashire Fusiliers. Pages 671, 946 1493.

SHAW, Frank. Private 14246188, 2nd Seaforth Highlanders. Pages 1054, 1407, 1456.

SHAW, J. 2nd Lieutenant, Pioneer Corps. Page 1062.

SHAW, Joseph. Private (regiment unknown). Born 13.02.10. Served in India and then stationed in England in POW camps.

SHAW, Joseph. Service details unknown. Resided 2 Oak Ave, Cadishead. Married Mary Eileen Wilkinson, elder daughter of Mr and Mrs A.H.C. Wilkinson of 5 Kings Rd, Irlam at Cadishead Congregational Church in December 1944 (possibly the same man as above).

SHAW, J.L. Sapper, Royal Engineers. Pages 145, 146, 660, 1459.

Appendix II

SHAW, Leslie. Corporal, Royal Inniskilling Fusiliers. Pages 582, 878, 1373, 1459.
SHAWCROSS, Harry. Service details unknown. Page 1494.
SHAWCROSS, Thomas. Service details unknown. Page 1494.
SHEPHERD, Percy. Service details unknown. Married Violet Howey 1929. Page 1494.
SHERBURN, Frank. Naval Ordnance Mechanic, Royal Navy. Demobbed in December 1945. Passed away 14th December 1999. Pages 718, 744, 746, 1494.
SHERLOCK, Robert (Bert). Royal Navy. Page 512.
SHERLOCK, Thomas (Tom). Service details unknown. Page 512.
SHERRATT, Jack. Driver (regiment unknown). Served North Africa with Eighth Army. Page 1128, 1317
SHERRATT, Joseph Arthur. Able Seaman D/JX1517108, Royal Navy, HMS *Glorious*. Pages 166, 167, 168, 588, 1128, 1405.
SIMPSON, Elizabeth. Officer's Batwoman, Women's Auxiliary Air Force. Pages 761, 765.
SIMPSON, Eric. RAF (rank unknown). Page 676.
SIMPSON, Harry. Signalman 3533663, Royal Corps of Signals, serving with 6th (Airborne) Division Signals. Pages 675, 677, 1406, 1456.
SIMPSON, Jesse. Private, West African Field Forces (regiment unknown). eldest son of the late Mrs Simpson and Mr H. Simpson of 31 The Crescent, Higher Irlam. Married Elsie Kitson at St Helen's Church, Hollinfare, 04.03.44, while on home leave from West Africa. Elsie was the eldest daughter of Mr and Mrs Kitson of 10 Carlton Way, Glazebrook. She worked as a nurse at Irlam war-time nursery.
SINTON, Stewart Alan. Gunner, Royal Navy. Page 1328.
SLATER, Arthur. Sergeant (regiment unknown). Pages 1267, 1439.
SMALLSHAW, John. Army (other service details unknown. Resided 15 Hartford Grove, Cadishead.
SMART, Mary. Wren (air mechanic) 74009, Women's Royal Naval Service. Pages 3, 220, 672, 673, 1126, 1125, 1394.
SMITH. General Service Corps (Christian name and rank unknown).
SMITH, A. Sergeant (regiment unknown).
SMITH, Cecil. Sergeant (rear gunner), RAF. Pages 432, 433.
SMITH, Clifford. Service details unknown. Page 1494.
SMITH, Cyril Victor. Trooper 3460099, 56th Regiment, Reconnaissance Corps. Pages 527, 1406, 1457.
SMITH, Gordon Ernest. Marine, Royal Marines. Page 607.
SMITH, Harold. Guardsman (regiment unknown). Pages 1050, 1494.
SMITH, Harry. Signalman, Royal Navy. Pages 986, 988, 1221.
SMITH, James. Ordinary Seaman D/JX561470, Royal Navy, HMS *Gould*. Pages 735, 736, 1407, 1458.
SMITH, John Robert. Sergeant, Queen's Own Cameron Highlanders. Pages 558, 1049, 1295.
SMITH, Kenneth. Private, Army (regiment unknown). Page 1494.
SMITH, Les. Service details unknown.
SMITH, Norman. Electrical Mechanic, Royal Navy. Brother of John. Page 1049.
SMITH, Robert Henry. Private, Army (regiment unknown). Page 1085.
SMITH, Wilfred Harold. Corporal, RAF. Married Marie Hall, at St John's Church 11.03.44. Page 685.
SOUTHALL, Harry. Private 7653018, Army (other service details unknown). Pages 357, 360, 1267, 1459.
SOUTHERN, Ellis. RAF (rank unknown). Pages 649, 1160.
SOUTHERN, Harold. Leading Aircraftman 612874, 2750 Squadron RAF Regiment. Pages 649, 1160, 1162, 1407.
SOUTHERN, Ronald Driscoll. Private 3389328, 1st Battalion, East Lancashire Regiment. Pages 911, 912, 913, 1407, 1457.
SOUTHERN, Thomas Edwin (Eddie). Sergeant (flight mechanic and air gunner), 210 Squadron, RAF. Pages 647, 648, 773, 1160.
STAINSBY, Thomas F. Stoker 1st Class D/KX105126, Royal Navy, HMS *Neptune*. Pages 103, 335, 1405, 1456.
STAINTHORPE, John William. Corporal, RAF. Page 411.
STEEL, Arthur Anderson. Service details unknown. Pages 279, 1495.
STEEL, W. Royal Navy (rating unknown).
STEPHENS, Donald Bramwell Muir. Royal Navy (rating unknown). Served on destroyers. Page 500.
STEVENS, Colin. Army (other service details unknown). Pages 1227, 1228.

STEVENS, Leslie. Merchant Navy (rating unknown). Pages 1227, 1228.

STEWART, John (Jack). Private, Manchester Regiment and later Sergeant 3534062, Royal Electrical and Mechanical Engineers. Pages 389, 391, 392.

STOKES, Frederick Raymond. Third Radio Officer, SS *Fort Longueuil*, Merchant Navy. Pages 639, 1406.

STRINGER, Stanley. Corporal 644189, 43 Squadron, RAF. Pages 360, 897, 898, 899, 900.

STRUTHERS, James 'Jim'. Royal Welch Fusiliers (rank unknown). Son of James Osborne Pye and Mary A. Struthers (nee Walton). Page 1496.

SUNTER, John Edward. Corporal PO/X1412 Royal Marines, serve on board HMS *Dunedin*. Pages 323, 324, 1405, 1451.

SUTOR, Eric. Private, Somerset Light Infantry. Pages 710, 711, 719, 724, 1496.

SUTTON, James. Corporal 984644, RAF. Passed away February 1983 aged 68. Page 548.

SWEENEY, James. Corporal 3658740, 1st South Lancashire Regiment. Pages 11, 820, 821, 1407, 1458.

SWIFT, George Edward. Service details unknown. Page 1496.

SWINDELLS, Thomas. (rank and regiment unknown). South East Asia Command. Pages 776, 949.

SYKES, Ernest William Ronald. Sergeant, RAF. Pages 265, 1459.

TALBOT, Frederick. Fusilier 14775385, 6th Royal Welch Fusiliers. Pages 1115, 1407, 1456.

TALBOT, George. Able Seaman, Royal Navy. Pages 607, 1496.

TALBOT, Joseph Eric. 4th Engineer Officer, Merchant Navy. Pages 788, 1104, 1105, 1407.

TALBOT, Robert. Lancashire Fusiliers and later Royal Artillery (rank unknown).

TARRY, Francis. Service details unknown. Page 1496.

TATHAM, Walter Frederick. Service details unknown. Page 1496.

TAYLOR, Albert. Sapper, Royal Engineers. Native of Irlam.

TAYLOR, Charles. Sergeant, Glider Pilot Regiment. Pages 200, 952, 1112, 1496.

TAYLOR, Charles. Pilot Officer, RAF.

TAYLOR, Donald. Service details unknown. Native of Winton. Married Loretta Mason of Cadishead. Resided 25 Kitchener Ave, Cadishead, Victory Rd then Dam Lane, Rixton.

TAYLOR, Edward James. Gunner 1522931, Royal Artillery. Born 07.08.14 at 28 Lynthorpe Ave, Cadishead. Residing in Chorlton-on-Medlock in 1940s.

TAYLOR, Edwin Roy (Roy). Sergeant 2151337, Royal Engineers. Rixton Roll of Honour. Pages 3, 541, 562, 566, 1116, 1119, 1120, 1394, 1454.

TAYLOR, Eileen. Auxiliary Territorial Service (rank unknown). Pages 368, 370.

TAYLOR, Francis (Frank). Stoker 1st Class KX133391, Royal Navy, HMS *Roberts*. Pages 510, 511, 839, 840, 988, 1497.

TAYLOR, Hindley. RAF (rank unknown).

TAYLOR, Kenneth Cyril. Sapper, Royal Engineers. Page 914.

TAYLOR, John Leslie. Leading Aircraftman, RAF. Born 1914. Only son of Mr and Mrs John Taylor of Inglenook Poultry Farm, Cutnook Lane, Higher Irlam. Joined Home Guard 07.06.40. Joined RAF April 1941. Married Lily Wilkinson of Heather Brae, Cutnook Lane, Higher Irlam 04.01.42. Page 1497.

TAYLOR, Renee. Private, Auxiliary Territorial Service. Page 1295.

TAYLOR, Robert. Driver, Royal Army Service Corps.

TAYLOR, R. (possibly Robert above). Service details unknown. Page 895.

TAYLOR, S. (rank and regiment unknown). Central Mediterranean Force.

TAYLOR, Tom. Royal Army Service Corps (rank unknown).

TAYLOR, Vernon. Gunner, Royal Artillery. Resided 222 Liverpool Rd, Cadishead. Married Ruby Houlding of Darcy, in December 1942.

TAYLOR, William. Able Seaman D/JX237857, HM Landing Ship Tank 420, Royal Navy. Pages 988, 989, 1407, 1456.

TAYLOR, William Arthur (Bill). Private 14414250, Highland Regiment, Cameron Highlanders and 7th Seaforth Highlanders. Pages 855, 856, 857, 858, 1052, 1053, 1392.

THOMAS, Arthur. Army (rank and regiment unknown). Born c.1909. Rent collector for Irlam UDC. Called up Thursday, 26th November 1941. Two brothers served in HM Forces.

THOMAS, Harold Parry. Sergeant (air gunner) 2216159, 44 Squadron, No.5 Group, Bomber Command, RAFVR. Pages 688, 1406, 1456, 1497, 1504.

THOMAS, John Victor. Private 14762696, 6th King's Own Scottish Borderers. Pages 1055, 1056, 1407.

THOMAS, William 'Bill'. Royal Army Pay Corps (rank unknown).

THOMASON, Frederick. Lance Bombardier, Royal Artillery. Rixton Roll of Honour. Born 1919. Pages 345, 1226, 1272, 1454, 1459.

THOMPSON, A. Private, Royal Army Medical Corps. Page 753.

THOMPSON, A. Royal Army Service Corps (rank unknown).

THOMPSON, Elsie. WREN 34666, Women's Royal Naval Service (WRNS). Pages 11, 450, 451, 453, 1406.

THOMPSON, Ernest. Fusilier 4460264, 1st Royal Fusiliers (City of London Regiment). Pages 877, 1407, 1451, 1457.

THOMPSON, George Hanson. Chief Petty Officer, Royal Navy. Passed away in 1987. Pages 743, 745, 1497.

THOMPSON, Joyce. Private, Auxiliary Territorial Service. Page 1073.

THOMPSON, 'Rowley.' Driver. Army (regiment unknown). Page 986.

THOMPSON, W.R.T. Driver, Army (regiment unknown).

THOMPSON, William. Royal Artillery (rank unknown).

THORNE, William. Corporal, Army (regiment unknown). Pages 558, 562.

THORNLEY, Alfred George. Fusilier 3458893, 10th Lancashire Fusiliers, Pages 492, 1406, 1458.

THORPE, Joseph Richard. Gunner, Royal Artillery. Pages 472, 474, 852, 1389.

THWAITES, Edward. Aircraftman 2nd Class, RAF. Page 994.

TIGHE, James. Sergeant (navigator), Royal Air Force. Pages 621, 1498.

TIGHE, John Gerard. Marine PO/X106270, HM Landing Craft Tank 4, Royal Marine Commandos, Pages 621, 1406, 1456, 1498.

TIGHE, Joseph. Private 14206732, 2nd Somerset Light Infantry. Pages 621, 719, 720, 721, 995, 1323, 1498.

TINSLEY, Arnold. RAF (rank unknown).

TINSLEY, Frederick. Private. Other service details unknown. Third son of Mr and Mrs Tinsley of 111 Eldon Rd West, Irlam. Married Elsie Eyers of Liverpool in May 1944.

TINSLEY, Heywood. Service details unknown.

TINSLEY, Irene. Women's Auxiliary Air Force (rank unknown).

TINSLEY, Robert Moss. Private T/121987, Royal Army Service Corps. Pages 434, 603, 1406, 1451, 1457.

TOAL, Harry. Sapper 1901343, Royal Engineers. Passed away at Salford, March 1998, aged 79. Pages 3, 435, 437, 1123.

TOFT, Joseph. Service details unknown. Page 1498.

TOMLINSON, W. Royal Artillery (rank unknown). Page 200.

TONGE, Charles. Service details unknown. Rixton Roll of Honour. Page 1454.

TONGE, George. Service details unknown. Rixton Roll of Honour. Page 1454.

TONGE, Jack. Company Sergeant Major, Royal Engineers. Pages 539, 1309, 1439.

TONGE, Ronald. Sergeant (pilot), RAFVR. Rixton Roll of Honour. Pages 3, 67, 68, 69, 243, 419, 1167, 1168, 1169, 1454.

TOPPING, Eric. Sub Lieutenant, Royal Navy.

TOWNEND, Harold. Flight Sergeant 1235933 (navigator), RAFVR. Pages 3, 968, 971, 1057, 1058, 1136, 1368, 1369, 1389.

TOWNSEND, Denis Charles. Leading Supply Assistant D/MX580335, Royal Navy. Pages 935, 936, 938.

TOWNSEND, Kenneth John. Petty Officer FX609373, Fleet Air Arm, Royal Navy. Pages 937, 938.

TRAYNOR, William. Service details unknown. Page 1498.

TYER, George Alfred. RAF (rank unknown). Discharged medically unfit. 5 Haig Ave, Cadishead.

TYER, George A. Service details unknown. Page 1498.

TYER, Robert. Driver, Royal Army Service Corps. Pages 188, 264, 660, 1300, 1459.

UPTON, David. Black Watch (rank unknown).

VALENTINE, Roy. Signaller, Royal Marines. Pages 812, 1499.

VANN, Thomas E. Sergeant 3781418, King's (Liverpool Regiment). Pages 535, 536, 981, 999.

VAUDREY, Herbert. 8th Indian Division, Army (rank and regiment unknown). Pages 410, 412, 938.

VAUDREY, John. Private 3659903, 2nd Battalion, Green Howards. Pages 1093, 1096.

VAUDREY, Thomas. Gunner 1109637, Royal Artillery (brother of John). Pages 411, 851, 852, 902, 1000, 1001, 1045, 1086, 1128.

VAUDREY, Thomas. Gunner. Royal Artillery. Pages 1063, 1064.
VINTON, Arnold. Leading Stoker, Royal Navy. Pages 1307, 1308.
VINTON, Charles. Sapper, Royal Engineers. Pages 1307, 1308.
VINTON, George, Leading Stoker, Royal Navy. Pages 1307, 1308.
WAKEFIELD, Joseph. Service details unknown. Page 469.
WALKER, Charles. Private 3529183, 1st Battalion, Manchester Regiment. Pages 357, 358, 490, 1406, 1459.
WALKER, Ernest. Guardsman, Coldstream Guards, Guards Armoured Division. Page 1222.
WALKER, George Robert. Sapper, Royal Engineers. Page 1222.
WALKER, James 'Jim'. Driver, Army (regiment unknown). Page 1245.
WALSH, Edward. Private 4042280. 1st Battalion, King's Shropshire Light Infantry. Pages 582, 585, 586, 1099, 1406, 1456, 1499.
WALSH, Elias. Marine CH/106061, Royal Navy. Page 598.
WALSH, Peter. Sergeant, Royal Army Service Corps. Brother of Edward. Pages 586, 1099, 1439.
WALTON, Cyril. Private 3864509, 2nd West Yorkshire Regiment. Pages 719, 722, 1407, 1458.
WALTON, Harry. Gunner, Royal Artillery. Pages 475, 1389.
WALTON, John Percy. Lieutenant 120146, Royal Engineers. Pages 303, 304, 394, 1406, 1438, 1458.
WANSTALL, Robert. Service details unknown. Page 1499.
WARBURTON, Joseph James. Corporal, Royal Engineers. Pages 1193, 1194, 1195.
WARD, Albert. Corporal 3454498, 9th Durham Light Infantry. Pages 931, 1407.
WARD, Ray. Lance Corporal/Signaller (regiment unknown). East Africa Command. Page 782.
WARING, John. Radio Officer, Merchant Navy. Page 693.
WARREN, William. Service details unknown. Page 1500.
WARRIOR, George. Major, Royal Army Ordnance Corps. Military Identity Card No A439874, Personal Number 242666. Passed away 20th November 1977 in Irlam. Pages 1024, 1027, 1500.
WATERMAN, James. Leading Cook, Royal Navy. Page 488.
WEBSTER, John. Corporal 1575115, Royal Electrical and Mechanical Engineers. Pages 120, 562, 567, 568, 1325, 1349.
WELCH, Frances. Private, Auxiliary Territorial Service. Page 1268.
WENHAM, George. Green Howards (rank unknown).
WENHAM, Roy. Able Seaman D/JX396031, Royal Navy, HMS *Mahratta*. Pages 733, 1407, 1456.
WESTALL, Dennis. Fusilier. Page 806.
WESTALL, Norman. Royal Navy (brother of Thomas).
WESTALL, Thomas (Tom). Captain, Army (regiment unknown). Resided 1 New Moss Rd, Cadishead.
WESTHEAD, Kenneth. Sergeant, Dorsetshire Regiment. Pages 1253, 1256.
WHALLEY, William. Leading Air Mechanic, RAF. Pages 200, 1278, 1500.
WHEATON, Charlotte. Auxiliary Territorial Service. Only daughter of Mrs Wheaton of 7 Oak Ave, Cadishead. Married Sapper Jack Edward Kirby, Royal Engineers (native of Knowl Hill, Reading) 26.12.42. The wedding took place at St Peter's Church, Knowl Hill, and both the bride and bridegroom wore their uniforms for the wedding.
WHITE, Oscar Henry. Gunner, Royal Artillery then Sapper, Royal Engineers. Pages 616, 618, 619, 1500.
WHITFIELD, Albert. Marine, Royal Marines. Page 730.
WHITFIELD, Ambrose. Private (regiment unknown). Wounded Malta 1940. Brother of Cyril. Page 147.
WHITFIELD, Arthur. Fleet Air Arm (rank unknown). Page 461.
WHITFIELD, Cyril. Private 3651479 1st South Lancashire Regiment. Pages 147, 1405.
WHITFIELD, Ernie. RAF (rank unknown).
WHITFIELD, Frank. Gunner 1809045, Royal Artillery. Passed away in 1982, aged 74. Pages 378, 599, 1267, 1459.
WHITFIELD, Fred. RAF (rank unknown). Military trade: rear gunner, Page 461.
WHITFIELD, Harry. Stoker KX107313, Royal Navy. Demobilised in 1946 and married Margaret Stringer on 21.12.46 at St John's Church, Irlam. Passed away 29th December 1981, Cadishead. Pages 461, 462.
WHITFIELD, Harry Cromwell. Able Seaman C/SSX17514, Royal Navy, HMS *Tempest*. Pages 355, 356, 1406.

Appendix II

WHITFIELD, Norman. RAF (rank unknown). Page 461.

WHITFIELD, Walter. Leading Seaman, Royal Navy. Page 938, 939.

WHITLEY, Jack. Lance Bombardier 14755046, 10th (or 16th) Field Regiment, Royal Artillery. Pages 1338, 1339.

WHITTAKER, Alfred. Fusilier, Lancashire Fusiliers. Pages 926, 929, 1022.

WHITTAKER, Jim. Private, Royal Army Service Corps. Pages 926, 930.

WHITTAKER, Leslie. Lance Bombardier 946721, 146th (Pembroke Yeomanry) Field Regiment, Royal Artillery. Pages 538, 539, 665, 1406, 1456.

WHITTAKER, Norman. Gunner, Royal Artillery. Pages 70, 926, 928.

WHITTAKER, Robert Gallagher. Able Seaman D/JX516538, Royal Navy. Pages 3, 665, 666, 667, 1281, 1394, 1429.

WHITTAKER, Robert. Lance Corporal 2720865. 3rd Battalion, Irish Guards. Pages 926, 927, 1238, 1407, 1456.

WHITTLE, Cyril. Sergeant (Flight Engineer) 1106196, 103 Squadron, No. 1 Group, Bomber Command, RAFVR. Pages 782, 1407, 1456.

WHITTLE, Samuel Anderson. Junior Engineer Officer, *Cingalese Prince*, Merchant Navy. Pages 295, 361, 788, 882, 1073, 1405.

WILCOX, Eric. RAF (rank unknown). Resided 18 Dean Rd, Cadishead.

WILDE, Harold. Private (regiment unknown). Page 981.

WILDE, Vernon. Service details unknown. Page 1501.

WILKINS, Arthur. Gunner, 39 (7th Lancashire Fusiliers) Anti-Aircraft Battalion, Royal Artillery. Pages 70, 1010.

WILKINSON, Ernest H. Service details unknown. Son of Mr and Mrs Henry Wilkinson of 61 Cutnook Lane, Higher Irlam. Brother of James and Henry.

WILKINSON, George. Private, serving in either the East or West Yorkshire Regiment. Pages 784, 785.

WILKINSON, Henry William. Engine Room Artificer, Royal Navy. Son of Mr and Mrs Henry Wilkinson of 61 Cutnook Lane, Higher Irlam. Married Constance Armitage of 57 Cutnook Lane in January 1943. Henry's brother, Sapper James Wilkinson, was best man. Also brother of Ernest. Joined Royal Navy in 1940, prior to which he was an engineer at the Steelworks.

WILKINSON, James. Sapper, Royal Engineers. Son of Mr and Mrs Henry Wilkinson of 61 Cutnook Lane, Higher Irlam. Brother of Ernest and Henry. Married Dorothy Lea of Irlam in October 1940.

WILKINSON, Stanley. Able Seaman JX296940, Royal Navy. Pages 1010, 1011, 1012, 1013, 1389

WILKINSON (Christian name unknown). Driver, Royal Army Service Corps. Son of Mr and Mrs G. Wilkinson of 667 Liverpool Rd, Higher Irlam.

WILLIAMS, Douglas. Army (rank and regiment unknown). Page 1019.

WILLIAMS, Eddie. Royal Navy (rank unknown), Combined Ops (possibly Edward or Edwin Williams below).

WILLIAMS, Edward. Service details unknown. Rixton Roll of Honour. Pages 1454, 1501.

WILLIAMS, Edwin. Marine, Royal Marines. Page 918, 1501.

WILLIAMS, Eric. Flying Officer, RAF. Pages 931, 1159.

WILLIAMS, Glynn. Auxiliary Military Pioneer Corps (rank unknown).

WILLIAMS, Hubert. Lance Corporal (regiment unknown). Pages 263, 923, 1148, 1149.

WILLIAMS, J.J. Alan. Royal Navy (rank unknown), HMS *Dido*.

WILLIAMS, John Edward. RAF (rank unknown). Son of Mr and Mrs Williams, 74 Caroline St, Irlam.

WILLIAMS, John Llewellyn. Leading Aircraftman (armourer) 1326402, RAF. Demobbed 15.01.46. Passed away in 1979 aged 68. Pages 814, 815, 1019.

WILLIAMS, R. Army (rank and regiment unknown). Page 154.

WILLIAMSON, Thomas E. Marine, Royal Marines. Pages 1091, 1304, 1501.

WILLIS, Cedric Charles. Service details unknown. Page 1501.

WILMOT, Jessie. Private 235149, Auxiliary Territorial Service (Royal Artillery). Pages 828, 829.

WILSON, Alfred. Service details unknown. Page 1501.

WILSON, Benjamin. Private 3655928 1st South Lancashire Regiment. Pages 172, 264, 368, 607, 820, 820, 822, 1385, 1386, 1407, 1456.

WILSON, George. Sergeant, later Major, 1st South Lancashire Regiment. Pages 172, 188, 607, 1285, 1286.

Appendix II

Appendix II

The following Second World War veterans have resided in the district for most of their lives, although their association with the area began some years after the war, they became valued members of the local community. The authors are proud to include their stories within the book:

BATE, Harold. Corporal 2601840, Royal Corps of Signals. Pages 3, 410, 413, 812, 958, 982, 1086.
CORDWELL, Arthur. Coder C/JX572640, Royal Navy. Page 841.
HILTON, William. Leading Stoker KX134286, Royal Navy. Pages 446, 448.
MOODY, Gladys. Aircraftwoman 2nd Class 2114619, Women's Auxiliary Air Force. Pages 3, 244, 949, 950, 951.
ROSCOE, Nancy Laura. Women's Land Army. Page 449.
WORSLEY, Frank. Air crew, Bomber Command, RAF (rank unknown). Pages 372, 373.

Women's Land Army
ATTENBOROUGH, Dorothy. Women's Land Army. Page 607.
IZZARD, Doris. Women's Land Army. Pages 607, 608.
LAVERTY, Joan E. Women's Land Army. Page 1183.
MARSLAND, Maureen. Women's Land Army. Page 607.
REID, Lillian. Women's Land Army. Pages 607, 610, 612.
WILSON, Edna. Women's Land Army. Pages 368, 607, 609.

APPENDIX III
MILITARY HONOURS &
AWARDS

Order of the British Empire
Captain Francis Reginald Broad, Merchant Navy

Member of the British Empire
Diver Richard Poole, Royal Navy

Military Cross
Captain Kenneth H. Davies, Royal Electrical and Mechanical Engineers
Second Lieutenant John Douglas Eaton, Royal Engineers

Distinguished Flying Cross
Flying Officer Stanley Ellis, Royal Air Force
Pilot Officer John Hill, Royal Air Force

George Medal
Second Lieutenant John Percy Walton, Royal Engineers

Distinguished Service Medal
Chief Petty Officer William Alex Borrino, Royal Navy
Petty Officer (telegraphist) Cecil Roy, Royal Navy

Military Medal
Corporal Owen McCarthy, Lancashire Fusiliers (Military Medal and Bar)
Private Stanley Morris (regiment unknown)
Lance Corporal H. Williams (regiment unknown)
Sergeant John Wrench, East Yorkshire Regiment

Distinguished Flying Medal
Flight Sergeant Albert Hodkinson, Royal Air Force

British Empire Medal
Sergeant Arthur Owen, Royal Engineers
Chief Petty Officer Douglas Perrin, Royal Navy
Sergeant Bertram Powell, Royal Engineers

Certificate of Merit
Bombardier Edgar Crozier, Royal Artillery
Fusilier William Cubbin (regiment unknown)
Corporal Walter Ditchfield, Royal Engineers
Lance Corporal James Gallichan, Gordon Highlanders
Lance Corporal Cyril Frederick Hankinson, Royal Engineers

Certificate of Merit cont'd.
Sergeant Arthur Slater (regiment unknown)
Corporal Sidney J.J. Yates, Royal Electrical and Mechanical Engineers

Mentioned in Dispatches
Driver Jack Allcock, Royal Army Service Corps
Sergeant Marion Appleton, Auxiliary Territorial Service
Ship's Medic James Alban Davies, Royal Navy
Sergeant James Brooks, Royal Air Force
Signalman Albert Edward Drum, Royal Signals
Gunner Joseph Sidney Hindley, Royal Artillery
Flying Officer Donald Melville, Royal Air Force
Private Stanley Morris (regiment not known)
Company Sergeant Major Jack Tonge, Royal Engineers
Sergeant Peter Walsh, Royal Army Service Corps

APPENDIX IV
MEDAL ENTITLEMENTS

This section provides information on the various campaign and general service medals issued to British servicemen and women, and in some cases those who served with civilian organisations, for their service during the Second World War. Unfortunately, unlike the medals awarded to British personnel in the First World War, the campaign medals and stars issued to servicemen and women did not contain the individuals name, rank, number or unit, although an individual could have these details added at their own expense.

It should be noted that no individual was awarded more than five campaign stars and the two medals (Defence Medal and 1939-45 War Medal) but could wear a bar to their medals to indicate campaign service when they were not entitled to a campaign medal. Thus an individual could be awarded a combination of:

1939-45 Star
Atlantic (or Air Crew Europe or France and Germany) Star
Africa Star
Arctic Star
Pacific (or Burma) Star
Italy Star
Defence Medal
King George VI War Medal 1939-45

The subject of medal entitlements is a complex area and this appendix is only intended to give the briefest information to enable the reader to at least identify medals that they may have tucked away in drawers and cupboards at home. There are many books available that provide detailed information on British medals, one recommendation is the Medal Year Book published annually by Token Publishing and the monthly magazine, Medal News, also published by Token Publishing. Another very detailed source of information recommended is British Battles and Medals by J. Hayward, D. Birch and R. Bishop, published by Spink in 2006. There are also a number of websites that provide information on medals.

Second World War Medals

The Defence Medal 1939-1945
This medal was awarded for non-operational service between 3rd September 1939 to 2nd September 1945. As well as those serving with the Armed Forces, this medal was also awarded to civil organisations such as the Police, Fire Services, Civil Defence Services and Home Guard. The qualifying time required to be awarded this medal was 1,080 days service in the UK, 360 days in non-operational roles overseas or 180 days overseas service in a non-operational role in an area deemed to be closely threatened or subject to air attack. The medal is made from cupro-nickel and the ribbon has a flame coloured stripe in the centre, with green edges symbolic of enemy attacks on the UK and black stripes down the centre of the green edges symbolising the black out.

King George VI War Medal 1939-45

This medal was awarded to all full-time personnel in the Armed Forces wherever they served, either in operational or non-operational roles, as long as it was for more than 28 days between 3rd September 1939 and 2nd September 1945. This medal was also awarded to Merchant Navy personnel as long as the individual had served at least 28 days at sea. The ribbon consists of a narrow red stripe in the centre flanked by a narrow white stripe on either side, a broad stripe of blue each side of the white stripe and then broad stripes on both edges of the ribbon.

Second World War Campaign Stars

1939-45 Star

The Star was awarded for service between 3rd September 1939 and 2nd September 1945. For Army personnel to qualify for the medal they had to serve for at least six months in an operational command and for Royal Navy personnel it was six months service in areas of active operations. There were slightly different criteria for Airborne troops, Merchant Navy, Royal Air Force and Fleet Air Arm. The ribbon has three vertical stripes, from left to right, equal bands of dark blue, red and light blue. These colours represent the equal contributions to victory made by the Royal Navy, Army and Royal Air Force respectively.

Atlantic Star

The Atlantic Star was awarded to those who participated in the Battle of the Atlantic, between 3rd September 1939 and 8th May 1945. It was issued to Royal Navy and Merchant Navy personnel. The individual had to qualify for the 1939-45 Star before the qualifying period for the Atlantic Star could begin. This qualifying period was six months service at sea, or in the case of air crews, two months' service in air operations. Individuals who were awarded the Atlantic Star and then qualified for the Air Crew Europe Star and/or the France and Germany Star did not receive these medals but were instead awarded the 'Air Crew Europe' clasp and/or 'France and Germany' clasp worn on the ribbon of the Atlantic Star. The ribbon is shaded and watered, from left to right when facing the wearer, dark blue, white and sea green to represent the colours of the Atlantic Ocean.

Air Crew Europe Star

This medal was awarded to air crew who participated in operational flights over Europe flying from bases in the United Kingdom between 3rd September 1939 and 5th June 1944. The qualifying period for this medal, two months service as air crew, would only begin once the 1939-45 Star had been earned. Those individuals who were awarded the Air Crew Europe Star and subsequently qualified for the Atlantic Star and/or France and Germany Star were entitled to wear one clasp denoting service for which the second Star would have been awarded. The ribbon is light blue with black edges and two yellow stripes, representing continuous service day and night, the sky being represented by pale blue, night operations by the black stripes and the yellow stripes representing enemy searchlights.

Africa Star

This Star was awarded for one or more days' service in North Africa between 10th June 1940 and 12th May 1943. This medal was awarded to all branches of the Armed Forces and the Merchant Navy. It was also awarded to recipients who served in the Mediterranean Sea and those who served in Abyssinia, Somaliland, Eritrea, Sudan and Malta. Personnel who served inshore or on escort duty off the North African coast between 23rd October 1942 and 12th May 1943 were entitled to wear the clasp 'North Africa 1942-43', a rosette denoted this award if only ribbons were worn. Those who served with the 8th Army between 23rd October 1942 and 12th May 1943 were entitled to wear the clasp '8th Army' on the ribbon when the Star was worn, or a numeral '8' on the ribbon when the actual medal was not worn. Those who served with the 1st Army between 8th November 1942 and 12th May 1943 were entitled to wear the clasp '1st Army' on the ribbon when the Star was worn and a numeral '1' on the ribbon when the medal was not worn. If the recipient was entitled to more than one clasp only one was allowed to be worn and that would be the first one the individual became entitled to. The ribbon is a pale buff colour with a central red stripe and two narrow stripes, one of which is dark blue and the other light blue. This is representative of the desert, the Royal Navy, the Army and the Royal Air Force.

Pacific Star

This Star was awarded for service in the Pacific theatre of operations between 8th December 1941 and 2nd September 1945 inclusive. Royal Navy and Merchant Navy personnel had to have earned the 1939-45 Star by six months' service before the qualifying period for Pacific Star could begin, unless they served in the Pacific zone for less than six months after 2nd March 1945. The Star was awarded for service in the Pacific Ocean, South China Sea and the Indian Ocean, east of a line running approximately south of Singapore. For the Army the Star was awarded for service in territories that had been subject to enemy or allied invasions. This included service in China and Malaya during the period 8th December 1941 to 15th February 1942, Hong Kong 8th December 1941 to 15th February 1942 and Sumatra 8th December 1941 to 23rd March 1942. Service in Burma was excluded. Members of the Royal Air Force had to complete at least one operational flight over the relevant theatres. Those who qualified for both the Pacific and Burma Stars were only entitled to wear the Star they earned first and a clasp to denote the second. The ribbon is dark green with red edges and central yellow stripe, with a thin dark blue stripe and a thin light blue stripe. The green represented the jungle, the yellow the beaches. The Navy (including Merchant Navy), Army and Royal Air Force were represented by stripes of dark blue, red and light blue respectively.

Burma Star

This Star was awarded in recognition of service in the Burma campaign between 11th December 1941 and 2nd September 1945. It was also awarded for certain specified service in Hong Kong between 26th December 1941 and 2nd September 1945, China and Malaya between 16th February 1942 and 2nd September 1945 and Sumatra between 24th March 1942 and 2nd September 1945. Personnel who served in these areas prior to the stated dates were awarded the Pacific Star. If the recipient was subsequently entitled to receive the Pacific Star but already had the Burma Star they were awarded the clasp 'Burma' which is worn on the ribbon of the Pacific Star. It was also awarded to Royal Navy and Merchant Navy personnel who had qualified for the 1939-45 Star, who served in the area of the Bay of Bengal. Army personnel qualified through service in any part of Burma or service in the Indian Provinces of

Bengal and Assam during the period 1st May 1942 to 2nd September 1942. Royal Air Force aircrew had to make one operational flight and ground crew qualified in the same way as the Army. The ribbon consists of a broad dark blue stripe and red stripe representing British Commonwealth forces and bright orange stripes representing the sun.

Italy Star

This was issued for operational service, on land, in Italy, Greece, Yugoslavia, Pantelleria, the Aegean area and Dodecanese Islands, and Elba at any time between 11th June 1943 and 8th May 1945. Other areas included Sicily 11th June 1943 to 17th August 1943, Sardinia 11th June 1943 to 19th September 1943 and Corsica 11th June 1943 to 4th October 1943. Those who served with the Royal Navy and Merchant Navy had to qualify for the 1939-45 Star before qualifying time for the Italy Star could commence. Personnel who served in the Mediterranean Sea, the Aegean Sea and operations in and around the Dodecanese Islands, Corsica, Greece, Sardinia, Yugoslavia and Southern France from 11th June 1943 qualified for the Italy Star. For Army and Royal Air Force personnel there was no prior time requirement and air crew qualified for the Star if they undertook air crew service within the Mediterranean theatre, which included sorties conducted from bases in the Mediterranean area over Europe. Entry into Austrian territory during the last few days of the war qualified for this Star and not the France and Germany Star. The ribbon has equal stripes of red, white and green which represent the Italian flag.

France and Germany Star

This Star was awarded for service in France, Belgium, Holland or Germany between 6th June 1944 (D-Day) and 8th May 1945. Members of the Royal Navy or Merchant Navy qualified for sea service in direct support of land operations in France, Belgium, Holland and some other defined areas. The only qualification for the Army was participation in any operation on land in the above stated countries. Royal Air Force personnel received the Star if they participated in any air operations over Europe between the above dates (unless they were air crew who undertook operations over Europe from bases in the Mediterranean in which case they received the Italy Star instead). Royal Air Force ground crew were eligible under the same qualification as the Army. Service in the South of France did not entitle an individual to this Star. Personnel who qualified for the Atlantic, Air Crew Europe or France and Germany Stars, or two of them, were only awarded the Star for which they first qualified and a clasp for the second. A second clasp was not issued to those who qualified for all three Stars. The ribbon was equal stripes of Blue, White, Red, Blue which represented the Union flag and those of France and the Netherlands.

Arctic Star

All the above mentioned Campaign Stars were issued in the immediate period following the Second World War, this Star, however, is a retrospective award approved by Her Majesty The Queen to recognise the service of those who served in the Armed Forces or Merchant Navy above the Arctic Circle, which included those participating in or undertaking duties in support of convoys to North Russia, commonly known as the Arctic Convoys. The Star was first issued in 2013 to surviving veterans; it will also be issued to the widows and families of those who have passed away. The ribbon is edged in black, with colours representing the Armed Forces and red for the Merchant Navy, with a central white stripe representing the Arctic.

Appendix IV

Clasps (also known as bars) that can be seen on Campaign Stars
Battle of Britain
Air Crew Europe
France and Germany
Atlantic
8th Army
1st Army
North Africa 1942-43
Burma
Pacific
Bomber Command*

*In 2013 a further clasp was awarded, 'Bomber Command' to surviving air crew veterans who served for at least sixty days, or completed a tour of operations, on a Bomber Command operational unit and flew at least one operational sortie on a Bomber Command operational unit from 3rd September 1939 to 8th May 1945 inclusive. The clasp is worn on the 1939-45 Star and is denoted by a silver rose emblem when the ribbon alone is worn. This clasp, approved by Her Majesty The Queen, was introduced to recognise the bravery of Bomber Command air crew. It is also being awarded to widows and the families of those who died during the war, or who have since passed away.

Ephemera

Many veterans of the Second World War kept various items of ephemera generated during their time in the forces, amongst the items frequently seen are pay books, discharge documents, letters home, leave passes and photographs.

All of this material provides important information regarding a serviceman or woman's service during the war, such as rank, service number, units in which the recipient served or, in the case of letters and photographs, fascinating insights into daily life.

These items are often found tucked away in drawers, boxes and old family albums and should be treasured and preserved as well as the recipient's medals and other items often kept as souvenirs, such as regimental insignia.

APPENDIX V
MEMORIALS

Prince's Park War Memorial

The Prince's Park War Memorial contains four plaques. The two plaques on the left hand wing commemorate the men who lost their lives in the First World War. These two plaques were on the original War Memorial which was demolished on 9th October 1949 and replaced by the current memorial on 5th November 1949. The two wings on the right hand side commemorate the names of the men and one woman of the district who made the ultimate sacrifice. One plaque is dedicated to Irlam and the other to Cadishead. Each plaque contains 48 names.

The Irlam Plaque (Prince's Park)

The Cadishead Plaque (Prince's Park)

St John's Church War Memorial, Irlam

St John's Church 1939 – 1945 Plaque

British Legion Memorial, St Mary's Church, Cadishead

IN PROUD REMEMBRANCE OF
THE TEACHERS OF THIS SUNDAY SCHOOL
WILLIAM PORTER & LESLIE ARSTALL,
WHO GAVE THEIR LIVES IN THE
WORLD WAR 1939 ~ 1945.
"Their Sun went down while it was yet Day"

Cadishead Wesleyan Church Sunday School Memorial

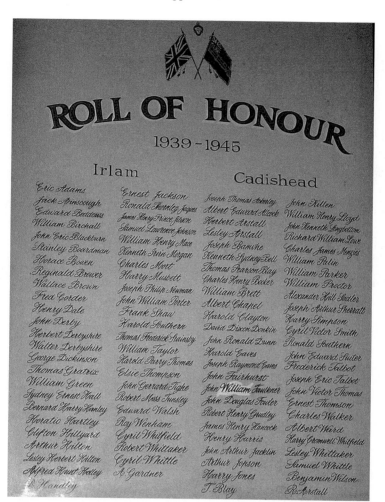

Irlam and Cadishead 1939 – 1945 Roll of Honour
St Mary's Church, Cadishead

The Roll of honour, which was formerly on display at the Royal British Legion Club, Liverpool Road, was moved to St Mary's Church following the closure of the club. It contains some discrepancies when compared with the Prince's Park Memorial. Additional names include B. Handley (assumed to be a duplication of Bernard Harry Hanley who is listed in the same column), A. Gardner, R. Arstall and W. Parker (possibly William Parker, killed in the London Blitz). In addition there are several spelling errors: the names of the Darbyshire brothers, Robert Moss Tinsley, Joseph Barensche, Albert Chappell, John Edward Sunter and Ernest Thompson are all spelt incorrectly.

St Mary's Church, Cadishead

IN GRATEFUL MEMORY
OF MEMBERS OF THIS
SCHOOL WHO FELL IN THE
WORLD WAR 1939-1945

J.AINSCOUGH	B.H.HANLEY
A.E.ALCOCK	C.HILLYARD
W.BIRCHALL	E.JACKSON
J.E.BLACKBURN	R.T.JAQUES
S.BOARDMAN	J.K.LONGBOTTON
R.BREWER	W.H.MACE
E.CLAXTON	F.SHAW
F.CORDER	J.A.SHERRATT
H.DARBYSHIRE	J.E.TALBOT
W.DARBYSHIRE	H.P.THOMAS
H.EAVES	ELSIE THOMPSON
J.D.FOWLER	R.M.TINSLEY
D.GARDINER	R.WENHAM
W.GREEN	H.C.WHITFIELD
H.SIMPSON	L.WHITTAKER
R.D.SOUTHERN	H.FELL

Irlam Central School War Memorial

This memorial contains two unknown names: D. Gardiner and H. Fell (the latter's name appears to have been added at a later date). It is on display in the entrance foyer to Irlam and Cadishead College.

Rixton Roll of Honour

The Roll of Honour records the names of members of the Rixton Methodist Church who served in the Armed Forces during the Second World War.

Hollins Green War Memorial

ROLL OF HONOUR LIST

Each of the major employers in the area maintained a Roll of Honour listing out the men who died while serving with the Forces. Unfortunately the locations of all these rolls of honour are unknown. The Rolls of Honour contained the names of the following:

Lancashire Steel Corporation Ltd
Jack Ainscough, 143 Eldon Rd, Irlam
Albert E. Allcock, 2 Oak Ave, Cadishead
John Eric Blackburn, 9 Chapel Rd, Irlam
William Brett, 36 Nelson Drive, Cadishead
Walter Derbyshire, 33 Devon Rd, Cadishead
John R. Dunn, 5 Haig Ave, Cadishead
John Darby, 51 Mond Rd, Higher Irlam
John Douglas Fowler, 30 Milton Ave, Irlam
Robert Henry Grindley, 17 Haig Ave, Cadishead
Harry Harris, 12 Kenmore Grove, Cadishead
Clifton Hillyard, 2 Addison Rd, Higher Irlam
Arthur Hilton, 45 Marlborough Rd, Higher Irlam
Alfred Hunt Holley, 64 Fiddlers Lane, Higher Irlam
Ronald I. Jaques, 6 Silver St, Irlam
Harry Jones, 4 Devon Rd, Cadishead
William Henry Mace, 77 Ferry Rd, Irlam
Frank Shaw, 41 Baines Ave, Irlam
Thomas Stainsby, 75 Baines Ave, Irlam
Frederick Talbot, 39 Lancaster Rd, Cadishead
William Taylor, 2 Liverpool Rd, Higher Irlam
Harold Parry Thomas, 17 Boundary Rd, Irlam
John Tighe, 1 Bradburn Rd, Irlam
Edward Walsh, 7 Annable Rd, Irlam
Leslie Whittaker, 22 Nelson Drive, Cadishead
Benjamin Wilson, 16 Partington Ave, Irlam

Irlam Urban District Council
Henry John Hayman, The Bungalow, Dudley Rd, Cadishead
William Porter, 35 Victory Rd, Cadishead

Royles Engineering Ltd
Harry Simpson, 4 Allenby Rd, Cadishead
Robert Whittaker, 37 Princes Ave, Irlam
Cyril Whittle, 7 The Crescent, Higher Irlam

Irlam CWS Soap Works
Herbert Arstall, 134 Lords St, Cadishead
Horace Bowen, 18 Caroline St, Irlam
T. Pearson Blay, 15 Atherton Lane, Cadishead
Harold Clayton, 15 Lytherton Ave, Cadishead
John William Faulkner, 8 Poplar Grove, Cadishead
Roy Wenham, Hope Cottage, Irlam Moss

Appendix V

CWS Margarine Works
Harry Muskett, 4 St John St, Irlam

Wilkinson & Tonge
Reginald Brewer, 15 Boundary Rd, Higher Irlam

Brew Brothers
Edward Beddows, 91 Eldon Rd, West, Irlam
William Henry Lloyd, 9 The Vista, Cadishead
John Kenneth Longbottom, 11 Green Lane, Cadishead

Eccles & District Co-operative Society Ltd.
Henry Dale, 78 Ferry Rd, Irlam
Thomas Gratrix, 108 The Crescent, Higher Irlam (grocery department)
Ernest Jackson, 77 Dixon St, Irlam (butchering department)
Cyril Victor Smith, 16 Fir St, Cadishead (grocery department)
Ronald Southern, 24 Lytherton Ave, Cadishead (butchering department)
Ernest Thompson, 29 Fir St, Cadishead (milk department, Urmston)
Robert Moss Tinsley, 6 Victoria Rd, Irlam (coal department)

APPENDIX VI
MISSING FROM THE
WAR MEMORIAL

When the lists were produced for the War Memorial in the post-war era, the committee would have used a number of sources, including the various Rolls of Honour which had been kept by the various firms in the district, the *Cadishead and Irlam Guardian* and lists maintained by the War Comforts Fund and the British Legion. They would also have relied on people coming forward and proposing the names of relatives and friends who had died in the war. However, there are a number of people who were either born in the district but had moved away or were born elsewhere but living or working in the area at the time of the war. Hopefully these men are commemorated on the War Memorials in other towns. Others are inexplicably missing from the Prince's Park War Memorial. The names of all the missing are listed below:

- ❖ Frederick Roberts Allen
- ❖ Rosina Battles
- ❖ John Patrick Beirne*
- ❖ Thomas Bradshaw
- ❖ Robert Bunting
- ❖ Ernest Claxton
- ❖ Peter Albert Hill
- ❖ Eric Gilbert Kershaw
- ❖ William Morris

- ❖ James Herbert Newton**
- ❖ Harriet Parker
- ❖ William Parker
- ❖ Robert Whitfield Pickersgill
- ❖ James Smith
- ❖ James Sweeney
- ❖ Alfred George Thornley
- ❖ Cyril Walton
- ❖ John Percy Walton

* Rixton
** Hollins Green

APPENDIX VII
PRISONERS OF WAR

Bold denotes died in captivity.
* denotes assumed date

Surname	Christian Name	Captured	Country Held	Year
Amos	Victor	France	Germany	1940
Hutchinson	Harry	France	Poland & Germany	1940
Jones	Hubert	France	Germany	1940
Shaw	J.L.	France	Germany	1940
Winstanley	Norman	France (Bethune)	Poland & Germany	1940
Gillibrand	Geoffrey	Crete, Greece	Germany	1941
Johnson	Frank	Greece	Greece & Austria	1941
Sykes	Ernest William R	Germany	Germany	1941
Tyer	Robert	Crete, Greece	Germany	1941
Williams	Hubert	Crete, Greece	Crete, Czech & Germany	1941
Anderson	George	Singapore	Korea	1942
Barrow	Fred	Libya (Tobruk)	Italy & Germany	1942
Blease	Charles George	Far East	Far East	1942
Brown	**Wallace**	**Singapore**	**Thailand**	**1942**
Cassidy	John	Libya	Italy & Germany	1942
Conde	John Leslie	Singapore		1942
Glover	George	Middle East	Italy & Germany	1942
Halliwell	Frank Charles	Java	Java, Singapore & Japan	1942
Hamilton	William	Hong Kong	Burma & Japan	1942
Jacklin	**John Arthur**	**Java**	**Indonesia**	**1942**
Leary	Kenneth John	Java	Singapore & Japan	1942
Pattison	Alfred H	Singapore		1942
Richardson	Richard	Tobruk, Libya	Italy	1942
Richardson	Stephen	Libya	Italy	1942
Robinson	John J.	Singapore		1942
Sampson	Ron	Indonesia	Indonesia	1942
Senior	Jeff	Java	Java, Moluccas, Singapore	1942
Southall	Harry	Singapore		1942
Thomason	Frederick	Malaya	Thailand	1942
Walker	**Charles**	**Singapore**	**Thailand**	**1942**
Whitfield	Frank	Java		1942
Wright	Leonard	Singapore	Thailand	1942
Brown	Frank	Western Desert	Italy & Germany	*1943
Burke	Patrick	Italy	Germany	1943
Houghton	Albert	North Africa	Italy & Germany	1943
Johnson	Hugh Charles	Italy (Sicily)	Germany	1943
McDonagh	John	Leros, Greece	Germany	1943
Mosedale	Thomas	Germany	Germany	1943
Riordan	Gerard	Leros, Greece	Germany	1943
Rosbottom	Harold	Cos, Greece	Germany	1943
Shaw	Leslie	North Africa	North Africa	1943
Dean	Arthur William	Germany	Germany	1944
Hughes	Clifford	France	Germany	1944
Mosedale	Frank	Italy	Germany	1944

Surname	Christian Name	Captured	Country Held	Year
Williams	Eric	Germany	Poland & Germany	1944
Wrench	Thomas	France	Germany	1944
Wright	Alfred	Italy	Italy & Germany	1944
Wrigley	Ernest	Italy	Germany	1944
Wright	William Norman	Germany	Germany	1945
Nicklin	William	Germany	Germany	Unknown

In all there were at least 49 prisoners of war from or connected with the district. The largest group (17 men) were captured in 1942 when the Japanese overran the Far East.

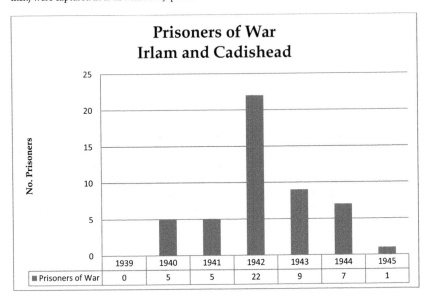

Prisoners of War
Irlam and Cadishead

	1939	1940	1941	1942	1943	1944	1945
■ Prisoners of War	0	5	5	22	9	7	1

APPENDIX VIII
HOME GUARD RECORDS

This roll has been compiled by merging information found in the following records, held at the Lancashire Record Office, Preston:

- D Company nominal roll 1940 to 1944, noting address, next of kin, year of birth and date of enrolment, annotated with details of transfers, resignations etc. Record Group HG 4/3
- D Company nominal roll of all ranks serving on 3rd December 1944, by company structure. Record Group HG 4/4
- D Company nominal roll June 1942, including rank by detachment. Record Group HG 4/5

HG4/4 and HG4/5 are nominal rolls broken down by platoon and, in the case of HG 4/5 down to section level and provided a good snap shot of the Company structure in 1942 and 1944. These records also included the National Registration number of each man, these have not been included the below roll. However, for ease of reference and the fact that many men changed platoons during the war, and in some cases no platoon is recorded, all men have been listed in alphabetical order irrespective also of whether they were officers or other ranks. It should be noted that some of the entries have been difficult to read in the original records and whilst every effort has been made to ensure the information in this roll is accurate, the authors apologise for any errors that may have occurred.

The format of each entry consists of:

Surname,
First name or initials,
Rank, where known and this will be final rank achieved.
Regimental number,
B: year of birth,
Home address and subsequent wartime addresses,
Next of kin recorded as W: Wife, M: Mother, F: Father, SF: Stepfather, B: Brother, S: Sister, G: Guardian, GR: Grandmother, Da: Daughter.
E: Date of enlistment.

Reason and date for leaving is recorded as D: Deceased, DMU: Discharged on medically grounds, R: Resigned, SD: Stand Down (see note 1 below), So: Struck off strength, T: Transfer, HMF: joined His Majesty's Forces (see note 2 below)

Note 1: 03.12.44: Where this date is recorded this means the man was still serving at Stand Down, if a platoon follows the date then this is his final platoon which may differ from the platoon he was recorded with earlier in the war.

Note 2: HMF: there may be a difference between the date in these records to the actual start date with HMF but it is reasonable to believe it would have been on or about the date listed.

The structure of the 42nd Battalion, Home Guard c.1944, with their areas of responsibility is as follows:

A Company – Eccles
B Company – Swinton
C Company – Swinton
D Company – Irlam & Cadishead
E Company – Eccles
F Company – Swinton
G Company – Irlam & Cadishead
H Company – This is possibly the mobile force and is believed to have contained men from across the battalion area.

It is important to note that this roll only relates to D Company, many hundreds more local men served in G Company, and some others served in other companies of the battalion as well as other Home Guard units. Unfortunately no rolls have been located regarding local men serving in the other companies of 42nd Battalion. The authors have, however, compiled a list of local men known to have served in G Company through articles published in the *Guardian*. This list is appended at the end of the D Company roll of honour below.

The D Company roll, which cannot be confirmed to be 100% complete, is an example of the scale of contribution by the men of Irlam and Cadishead and surrounding areas who were often too young or too old to serve in the Armed Forces and/or retained at home in reserved occupations, which were jobs deemed important to the war effort.

In June 1942 D Company was composed of seven platoons, numbered 1 to 7 platoon. Each platoon had three sections and a platoon headquarters. No. 7 Platoon was the Headquarters platoon. Local works also had Home Guard detachments, for example 1 Section of 4 Platoon was the CWS Margarine Works section and 2 Section, also part of 4 Platoon, covered the CWS Soap Works.

At the Stand Down of the Home Guard on 3rd December 1944 D Company appears by then to have consisted of a small Company Headquarters which included the Officer Commanding D Company, Major Gold, and other key officers and other ranks, for example the company sergeant major and company quartermaster sergeant. There was also a HQ Platoon and 7 Platoons. Many men serving with D Company have 'H', 'H/4', 'H/5' etc noted against their entries, the authors have interpreted this to mean the individual later served with H Company, the number being the platoon.

Reviewing the roll of honour it will be apparent that there was a regular turnover of men throughout the war. There are many reasons for this, some of the more elderly members, many of whom were First World War veterans, who joined the Local Defence Volunteers during the dark days of the summer of 1940 when it was an amateur organisation left when the Home Guard, as it was later renamed, began to be shaped into a professional organisation particularly from the winter of 1941 onwards. The required fitness and duties on top of their normal day jobs or their age took their toll and caused many to resign.

Many others left to join His Majesties Forces (HMF) during the war, which included the Army, Navy and Air Force and others would have joined the Merchant Navy. Other reasons why men left the company included medical reasons, transfers to other Home Guard units or due to moving from the district. The majority of the men who served with D Company came from Irlam and Cadishead although there was a few men from surrounding areas such as Rixton, Glazebrook, Hollins Green, Patricroft, Carrington and Flixton, presumably they worked locally and it was preferable, due to going to Home Guard duties after work or due to close friends serving, for them to serve with D Company rather than Home Guard units covering their own districts. Finally later in the war a number of Home Guardsmen were transferred to Anti-Aircraft duties manning gun batteries in the Salford, Manchester and surrounding areas. Those Home Guardsmen that served at least three years with the Home Guard were entitled to the Defence Medal.

Note 3: All references to 'Company' in the below roll of honour relate to 42nd Battalion, Home Guard, unless stated otherwise.

ABBOTT, Thomas William. 470. B: 1902. 127 Eldon Rd, Irlam. W: Mrs Abbott. E: 23.09.40. 2 Platoon. R: 11.02.41.
ACKERLEY, Joseph Thomas. 120. B: 1909. 91 New Moss Rd, Cadishead. W: Betsy Ackerley. E: 05.06.40. 4 Platoon, later with 3 Platoon. HMF: 19.03.42.
ACTON, William. 187. B: 1921. 60 Lyndhurst Ave, Higher Irlam. F: George H. Acton. E: 06.06.40. 2 Platoon. R: 23.07.41.
ADAIR, Alexander Hay. Sergeant 196. B: 1901. 8 Lyndon Rd, Irlam. W: Mary Adair. E: 06.06.40. In June 1942 he was a Private in 1 Section, 2 Platoon. SD: 03.12.44.
ADAMS, William. Private B83. B: 1898. 9 Devon Rd, Cadishead. W: Florence May Adams. E: 08.07.40. 1 Section, 6 Platoon. R: 19.06.44.
AINSCOUGH, Ernest. 309. B: 1922. 127 Liverpool Rd, Higher Irlam. M: Harriett A. Ainscough. E: 05.06.40. 2 Platoon. HMF: 02.12.41.
AINSCOUGH, James. 645. B: 1924. 143 Eldon Rd West, Irlam. F: James Ainscough. E: 30.10.41. 8 Platoon and later HQ Platoon.
AIREY, R. Private. 77 Fiddlers Lane, Higher Irlam. 4 Platoon. SD: 03.12.44.
ALDRED, Thomas. Corporal 151. B: 1905. 36 Harewood Rd, Irlam. W: Mrs Aldred. E: 05.06.40. In June 1942 was serving with 1 Section, 2 Platoon. SD: 03.12.44.
ALLAN, Roy. 690. B: 1925. 96 Lord St, Cadishead. M: Mrs E. Allan. 8 Platoon and later HQ Platoon.
ALLCROFT, George. Lance Corporal 568. B: 1907. 179A Liverpool Rd, Cadishead. S: Mrs Ellen Rawding, 185 Cleveland St, Higher Crumpsall. E: 27.05.41. June 1942 serving with 1 Section, 7 Platoon (HQ). Served Transport Platoon. SD: 03.12.44, HQ Platoon.
ALLDRED, T. Private. 1 Section, 2 Platoon (June 1942).
ALLEN, Richard. 626. B: 1916. 382 Liverpool Rd, Irlam. M: Mrs B. Allen, Brooklands Park, Hatfield. E: 20.10.41. 4 Platoon and later HQ Platoon.
ALLMAND, George Henry. B25. B: 1906. 7 Moss Lane, Partington. M: Sarah Allmand. E: 07.01.40. 6 Platoon. R: 13.02.42.
ARDERN, William. B1. B: 1889. 13 Chapel Rd, Irlam. W: Annie Ardern. E: 06.07.40. 6 Platoon. R: 12.02.42.
ARNISON, Harold Edwin. 239. B: 1899. 75 Baines Ave, Irlam. W: Anne Arnison. E: 06.06.40. Initially served 3 Platoon and later believed to have served with H Company. R: 26.12.40.
ARNOLD, T. Private. 12 Mond Rd, Higher Irlam. 7 Platoon. SD: 03.12.44.
ARSTALL, Albert Edward. B26. B: 1922. 19 Haig Ave, Cadishead. F: Jason Arstall. E: 06.07.40. 6 Platoon. R: 20.02.42.
ARSTALL, Charles Whitfield. 495. B: 1922. 13 Ash Ave, Cadishead. Son of Harry Arstall. E: 04.12.40. 4 Platoon, later 3 Platoon. HMF: date unknown.
ARSTALL, Cyril. 483. B: 1922. 8 The Crescent, Irlam. F: Ernest Arstall. E: 02.10.40. 2 Platoon. HMF: 31.10.41.

Appendix VIII

ARSTALL, Harry. Sergeant 925. B: 1891. 13 Ash Ave, Cadishead. W: Rose Arstall. E: 28.08.40. In June 1942 serving with 2 (Soap Works) Section, 4 Platoon. Later 5 Platoon. SD: 03.12.44.
ARSTALL, J. Private. 14 Bankfield Ave, Cadishead. 3 Platoon. SD: 03.12.44.
ARSTALL, James. B100. B: 1911. 94 Lords St, Cadishead. W: Hilda Arstall. E: 19.07.40. 6 Platoon. HMF: 22.11.42.
ARSTALL, Roland. 246. B: 1922. 8 Lord St, Cadishead. M: Alice Arstall. E: 06.06.40. 3 Platoon, later with 4 Platoon. R: 21.05.41.
ARSTALL, Wilfred. Private 206. B: 1903. 7 Lytherton Ave, Cadishead. W: Hilda Arstall. E: 06.06.40. Platoon. SD: 03.12.44.
ASHBROOKE, E. Private. 276 Liverpool Rd, Irlam. 4 Platoon. SD: 03.12.44.
ASHLEY, Frederick George. Lieutenant 139. B: 1911. 65 Cutnook Lane, Higher Irlam, later 136 Liverpool Rd, Irlam. W: Dorothy Ashley. E: 05.06.40. 6 Platoon and later Transport Platoon. SD: 03.12.44, 6 Platoon.
ASHLEY, Robert Henry. 439. B: 1914. 91 Fir St, Cadishead. M: Mrs H.A. Ashley. E: 30.07.40. 4 Platoon. R: 03.11.40.
ASHTON, A. 30 Liverpool Rd, Higher Irlam. Private in HQ Platoon. SD: 03.12.44.
ASHTON, Albert. 955. B: 1896. 10 Kenmore Grove, Cadishead. W: Mrs Ashton. E: 28.08.40. 4 Platoon. R: 16.02.42.
ASHTON, George. 349. B: 1910. Moss Side, Belgrave Rd, Cadishead. W: Hilda Ashton. E: 20.08.40. Initially served 5 and later believed to have served with H Company.
ASHTON, Harold. Corporal B27. B: 1905. 29 Bradburn Rd, Irlam. W: Annie Ashton. E: 06.07.40. 2 Section, 6 Platoon. SD: 03.12.44.
ASHTON, J. Private. 48 Addison Rd, Higher Irlam. 4 Platoon. SD: 03.12.44.
ASHTON, John James. Sergeant 504. B: 1908. 14 Hampton Rd, Cadishead. W: Nellie Ashton. E: 22.08.40. Corporal serving with 1 Section, 7 Platoon (HQ) in June 1942. SD: 03.12.44.
ASHURST, Stanley. Lance Corporal B58. B: 1913. 24 Moss Lane, Cadishead. W: Mary A. Ashurst. E: 04.07.40. 1 Section, 6 Platoon, later Home Guard Cadets. SD: 03.12.44, Private, HQ Platoon.
ATKINSON, Allan. 61 Marlborough Rd, Higher Irlam. Cycle orderly attached HQ Platoon.
ATKINSON, Eric A. Private F650. B: 1903. 38 Marlborough Rd, Irlam. W: Annie Atkinson. E: 24.11.41. in 2 Platoon. SD: 03.12.44.
ATKINSON, John. Private 616.B: 1896. 24 Liverpool Rd, Higher Irlam. W: Louisa Ellen Atkinson. E: 26.08.41. 1 Section, 7 Platoon (June 1942) and some time with Transport Platoon. SD: 03.12.44, HQ Platoon.
ATKINSON, William Heywood. 464. B: 1923. 66 Bank St, Glazebrook. M: Mary Atkinson. E: 19.09.40. 5 Platoon and later believed to have served with H Company.
AUSTIN, Fred. Private 78. B: 1914. 98 Ferry Rd, Irlam. W: Elizabeth Austin. E: 05.06.40. 3 Section, 2 Platoon. SD: 03.12.44.
AUTY, Harry. 548. 8 Platoon and later HQ Platoon.
BAGNALL, Wilfred. B: 1905. 84 The Crescent, Higher Irlam. E: 25.05.43. R: 10.08.44.
BAILEY, Bertram. 506. B: 1921. 41 Victory Rd, Cadishead. M: Elsie Bailey. E: 06.08.40. 5 Platoon and later believed to have served with H Company.
BAILEY, George Henry. 230. B: 1895. 65 Princes Ave, Higher Irlam. W: Mrs Bailey. E: 07.06.40. 1 Platoon. R: 06.11.40.
BAILEY, John Frank. Private B118. B: 1898. Resided Patricroft. W: Edith Bailey. E: 05.07.40. 2 Section, 6 Platoon and later Company HQ. T: July 1943 to A Company, 42nd Battalion.
BAKER, George Edward. B: 1923. 77 New Moss Rd, Cadishead. F: Sydney Baker. E: 12.11.40. 4 Platoon.
BALDERSON, Thomas. Private. B: 1898. 18 Silver St, Higher Irlam. W: Mrs M. Balderson. E: 18.07.43. 4 Platoon. SD: 03.12.44.
BALL, Jack A. 492. B: 1921. 2 Cornwall Rd, Cadishead. F: William Ball. E: 07.11.40. 5 Platoon and later believed to have served with H Company.
BANKS, Ernest. Lance Corporal 922. B: 1911. 68 Liverpool Rd, Cadishead. W: Mrs M. Banks. E: 25.05.43. 4 Platoon. SD: 03.12.44.
BANKS, Sydney. 485. B: 1920. 19 Nelson Dr, Cadishead. Aunt, Maud Gallamore. E: 21.09.40. 4 Platoon and later 3 Platoon. HMF: 21.05.41.
BANNISTER, Gerald Edward. B: 1922. Rosebank, New Moss Rd, Cadishead. E: 04.06.41. 3 Platoon. HMF: 15.01.42.
BANNON, Arthur. 970. 65 Dixon St, Irlam. W: Mrs F. Bannon. E: 24.09.43. R: 18.10.43.

BARBER, John. Private 640. B: 1898. 39 Caroline St, Irlam. B: Cyril Barber. E: 22.10.41. Royles and in June 1942 with 2 Section, 5 Platoon. R: 28.07.44.

BARKER, Geoffrey. Sergeant 642. B: 1920. 27 Chapel Rd, Irlam. E: 20.10.41. June 1942, private with 1 Section, 2 Platoon. SD: 03.12.44.

BARKER, James. Private 41. B: 1898. 18 Sandy Lane, Irlam. W: Mrs Barker. E: 24.07.40. 2 Section, 2 Platoon. SD: 03.12.44.

BARKER, James. 479. B: 1890s. 32 Addison Rd, Irlam. W: Mrs Barker. E: 25.10.40 (another record states 24.07.40). 2 Platoon.

BARLOW, Harry. 695. 44 Liverpool Rd, Higher Irlam. 1 Platoon.

BARLOW, William. B: 1924. 11 Rutland Rd, Cadishead. F: W.A. Barlow. E: 27.05.41. Later believed to have served with 8, Platoon, H Company.

BARMORE, Harry. Private. 75 Eldon Rd East, Irlam. W: Mrs B.M. Barmore. E: 25.05.43. 4 Platoon. SD: 03.12.44.

BARNABY, C.W. Private. B: 1901. 5 Hamilton Ave, Cadishead. W: Mrs Barnaby. E: 25.05.43. 4 Platoon. SD: 03.12.44.

BARNABY, Kenneth. 524. B: 1924. 5 Hamilton Ave, Cadishead. E: 16.02.41. Later believed to have served with 8 Platoon, H Company.

BARNABY, Roy. 675. B: 1925. 5, Hamilton Ave, Cadishead. F: C.W. Barnaby. Later believed to have served with 8 Platoon, H Company.

BARNES, Lawrence. B: 1903. 108 Ferry Rd, Irlam. M: Mary Barnes. E: 04.07.40. 2 Platoon and later with 6 Platoon.

BARNES, Leonard. B: 1909. 10 Gleaves Rd, Eccles. W: Annie Barnes. E: 10.07.40. 4 Platoon. R: 31.12.41.

BARNES, Sydney. B: 1901. 6 Marlborough Rd, Higher Irlam. E: 10.07.40. June 1942, sergeant with 1(Margarine) Section, 4 Platoon. Later commissioned Lieutenant. SD: 03.12.44, Company HQ.

BARNES, William R.Y. 523. B: 1916. 61 Victory Rd, Cadishead. M: Mrs Barnes. E: 16.02.41. Later believed to have served with 8 Platoon, H Company.

BARNETT, Harold. 720. B: 1921. 4 Rose Crescent, Irlam. F: E. Bennett. E: 20.04.42. Later believed to have served with 4 Platoon, H Company.

BARNFATHER, Leonard. Private 976. 28 Partington Ave, Irlam. E: 14.01.44. 4 Platoon. SD: 03.12.44.

BARNSHAW, Arthur. Corporal 672. B: 1910. 110 Liverpool Rd, Higher Irlam. E: 18.03.42. June 1942, private with 2 Section, 1 Platoon. SD: 03.12.44.

BARR, John A.C. 710. B: 1922. 43 Harewood Rd, Irlam. F: R. Ball. E: 17.04.42. Later believed to have served with 4 Platoon, H Company.

BARROW, Frank. 13 Melville Rd, Cadishead. 4 Platoon. DMU: 12.12.43.

BARRY, Leo. B: 1901. 33 Dean Rd, Cadishead. W: Evelyn Barry. E: 03.07.40. 5 Platoon. R: 16.02.42.

BARWICK, George Thomas. 16. B: 1891. 18 Haig Ave, Cadishead. E: 09.07.40. 5 Platoon and later believed to have served with H Company.

BATE, Henry Roy. 508. B: 1923. 12 Woodbine Ave, Cadishead. F: J. Bate. E: 02.02.41. 5 Platoon and later believed to have served with H Company.

BATE, James. 300 (later 551). B: 1891. 12 Woodbine Ave, Cadishead. W: Ellen Bate. E: 14.06.40. 5 Platoon and later believed to have served with H Company. R: date unknown. Re-enlisted: 28.02.41. 3 Platoon and later Company HQ. R: 31.08.42.

BATE, William. B: 1896. 19 Addison Rd, Higher Irlam. W: Mrs E.E. Bate. E: 30.07.43. DMU: 26.04.44.

BATES, John Littler. B: 1920. 23 Haig Ave, Cadishead. F: J. Bates. E: 30.07.40. 6 Platoon and later Company HQ. HMF: 07.10.40.

BATTLES, Michael. B: 1915. 34 Francis Rd, Irlam. E: 18.09.40. 4 Platoon. T: date unknown to H Company.

BAXTER, Ellis Thomas J. 216 B: 1922. 87 Eldon Rd, Irlam. F: Ellis Baxter. E: 06.06.40. 05.11.41.

BAXTER, Thomas W. Private B: 1905. 138 The Crescent, Irlam. W: Mrs Baxter. E: 02.11.40. 2 Platoon and also later believed to have served with 4 Platoon, H Company. Platoon. HMF: 03.02.44.

BEALES, J. William. B: 1887. 10 Princes Ave, Higher Irlam and later 30 Robert St, Patricroft. W: Beatrice Beales. E: 07.07.40. 1 (Margarine Works) Section, 4 Platoon. R: 25.03.43.

BEARD, Charles Henry. Private. B: 1907. 43 Dean Rd, Cadishead. W: Mrs A. Beard. E: 12.09.42. 7 Platoon and later with 3 Platoon. SD: 03.12.44.

BEARD, George. 46. B: 1911. 77 Fir St, Cadishead. W: Mrs Beard. 4 Platoon and later 3 Platoon. HMF: 26.11.40.

BEBBINGTON, Harry. 252. B: 1892. 12 Ash Ave, Cadishead. W: Nellie Bebbington. E: 06.06.40. 4 Platoon and later with 3 Platoon. R: 16.02.42.

Appendix VIII

BEBBINGTON, Wilfred. B: 1907. Sunset View, Liverpool Rd, Irlam. W: Margaret Bebbington. E: 10.07.40. 4 Platoon. HMF: 15.04.41.
BEHENNA, James Henry. 76. B: 1906. 94 Liverpool Rd, Cadishead. M: Clara Behenna of 1 Sycamore St, Gorton. E: 05.06.40. 5 Platoon and later believed to have served with H Company. HMF: date unknown.
BELL, George William. 237. B: 1922. 12 Laburnum Rd, Cadishead. F: Lance Bell. E: 06.06.40. 4 Platoon and later with 3 Platoon. HMF: 30.11.42.
BELL, Isaac. B28. B: 1900. 3 Station Rd, Padgate. W: Mrs Bell. E: 02.07.40. 6 Platoon. R: 23.02.42.
BELL, Percy. Private 516. B: 1893. 75 Fir St, Cadishead. W: Mrs E. Bell. E: 12.02.41. 4 Platoon and in June 1942 with 2 Section, 3 Platoon. SD: 03.12.44.
BELL, Sydney. 496. B: 1924. 12 Laburnum Rd, Cadishead. F: Lance Bell. E: 18.02.41. 4 Platoon and later 3 Platoon. HMF: 26.02.41.
BELL, Thomas. 450. B: 1921. 13 Lytherton Ave, Cadishead. M: Frances Margaret Bell. E: 03.09.40. 5 Platoon later believed to have served with H Company.
BENN, Henry. Private B79. B: 1912. 8 Bankfield Ave, Cadishead. W: Mary Benn. E: 29.07.40. 1 Section, 6 Platoon. D: 16.12.43.
BENNETT, George. 841. B: August 1906. 21 Birch Ave, Cadishead. W: Mrs J. Bennett. E: 04.08.42. 5 Platoon. HMF: 02.03.44.
BENNETT, Thomas. Private 823. B: 1904. 31 Henley Ave, Irlam. W: Mrs M. Bennett. E: 22.07.42. 7 Platoon and later 5 Platoon. SD: 03.12.44.
BENT, Arthur Gregory. 855. B: 1904. 2 Cutnook Lane, Irlam. F: E. Bent. E: 05.08.42. R: 10.12.42.
BENT, William Henry. B: 1912. 3 Eldon Rd East, Irlam. F: Sam Bent of Langworthy Rd, Pendleton. E: 05.06.40. 2 Platoon. R: 1941.
BERRY, John William. Private 874. B: 1904. 99 New Moss Rd, Cadishead and later 658 Liverpool Rd, Irlam. W: Mrs M. Berry. E: 11.08.42. 3 Platoon. SD: 03.12.44.
BERRY, William Nelson. 342. B: 1901. 14 Ferryhill Rd, Irlam. W: Edna Berry. E: 01.07.40. 2 Section, 2 Platoon. T: 17.06.43 to 24 (Lancashire) Battalion, Home Guard.
BESWICK, Allan. 632. B: 1924. 562 Liverpool Rd, Irlam. F: H.E. Beswick. E: 20.10.41. Later believed to have served with 4 Platoon, H Company.
BICKERDIKE, Leslie. Private 733. B: 1924. 28 Kitchener Ave, Cadishead. M: Mrs B. Bickerdike. G Company 42nd Battalion. T: early in the war to D Company, 1 Section 6 Platoon. SD: 03.12.44.
BICKERTON, George. Private 339. B: 1914. 35 Mond Rd, Higher Irlam, then 7 Beech Ave and then 25 Nelson Dr, Cadishead. F: Charles Bickerton. E: 01.07.40. 2 Section, 1 Platoon. SD: 03.12.44.
BILLAM, Henry Tom. Private. B: 1887. 22 Ashfield Grove, Irlam. W: Emily Billam. E: 16.09.40. 1 Section, 6 Platoon. R: 31.05.43.
BILLINGSBY, J. B: 1901. 11 Warwick Rd, Cadishead. W: Mrs Billingsby. E: 25.10.40. 4 Platoon. R: 05.07.41.
BILLINGTON, James. B2. B: 1902. 87 Liverpool Rd, Irlam. W: Miriam Billington. E: 24.07.40. 6 Platoon. R: 09.02.42.
BIRCHALL, James . Private. B: 1906. 61 Lyndhurst Ave, Irlam. W: Beatrice Birchall. E: 11.07.40. 1 (Margarine Works) Section, 4 Platoon. SD: 03.12.44, HQ Platoon.
BIRCHALL, Joseph. 824. B: 1903. 77 Lyndhurst Ave, Irlam. W: Mrs E. Birchall. E: 22.07.42. 5 Platoon. Transferred from 13th (East Norfolk) Battalion, Home Guard. SD: 03.12.44, 1 Platoon.
BIRD, Frank. 444. B: 1917. 45 Lord St, Cadishead. F: John Bird. E: 26.08.40. 5 Platoon and later believed to have served with H Company.
BIRD, J.H. Collins. Private B55. B: 1905. 631 Liverpool Rd, Peel Green. W: Letitia Bird. E: 04.07.40. 2 Section, 6 Platoon. SD: 03.12.44.
BIRD, John. Private. B: 1915. 45 Lords St, Cadishead. F: John Bird. E: 21.07.42. 3 Platoon. SD: 03.12.44.
BITHELL, Harry. Lance Corporal 794. B: 1923. 46 Ferryhill Rd, Irlam. F: A. Bithell. E: 21.07.42. 5 Platoon and later with 7 Platoon. SD: 03.12.44.
BLAY, Clifford. Private 714. B: 1911. 24 Francis Rd, Irlam. F: George Blay. E: 20.04.42.
BLAY, George. B3. B: 1886. 1 Dean Rd, Cadishead. W: Annie Blay. E: 06.07.40. R: April 1942.
BLAY, George J. B55. B: 1907. 24 Francis Rd, Irlam. W: Elizabeth Ann Blay. E: 29.07.40. 09.02.42. Re-enlisted 07.09.42. 7 Platoon. SD: 03.12.44.
BLAY, Horace. Private B29. B: 1919. 6Victory Rd, Cadishead and later 61 Belgrave Rd, Cadishead. F: Herbert Blay. E: 06.07.40. 2 Section, 6 Platoon. SD: 03.12.44.
BLAY, Kenneth. Private 598. B: 24.11.23. 1 Dean Rd, Cadishead. F: George Blay. E: 06.08.41. 1 Section, 6 Platoon. HMF: 31.01.43.

BLOOR, Herbert. 63. B: 1922. 12 Vista, Cadishead. F: James Bloor. E: 06.06.40. 5 Platoon and later believed to have served with H Company.

BLOOR, Horace. B: 1914. 12 Vista, Cadishead. F: James Bloor. E: 20.08.40. 5 Platoon and later believed to have served with H Company.

BLUNDELL, Gilbert James. Private. B: 1923. Woolden View Farm, Cadishead. E: 29.06.43. 4 Platoon. SD: 03.12.44.

BLUNDELL, Henry. B60. B: 1900. 54 Silver St, Irlam. E: 04.07.42. 6 Platoon. R: 17.02.42.

BLUNDELL, Thomas Fairhurst. Private 461. B: 1915. Mill Drain Farm, Chat Moss. F: Thomas Blundell. E: 05.06.40. June 1942 serving with 1 Section, 7 Platoon (HQ). Transport Platoon and 4 Platoon. SD: 03.12.44, HQ Platoon.

BODEN, Harry M. Lance Corporal 406. B: 1911. Arnymede, Woolden Rd, Cadishead. Another wartime address recorded was Millbrook Farm, Cadishead Moss. W: Bessie Boden. E: 16.07.40 (a further entry in HG records states enlisted 16.09.40). Transport Platoon. 27.08.41. Re-enlisted 20.04.43. HQ Platoon. SD: 03.12.44.

BOLAND, Robert J. Private. B: 1902. Birch Ave, Cadishead and later 8 Melville Rd, off Lords St, Cadishead. W: Mrs Boland. E: 28.08.40. 2 (Soap Works) Section, 4 Platoon and later 6 Platoon. SD: 03.12.44.

BOLTON, Frank Edward. Private 668. B: 1910. 59 Ferry Rd, Irlam. W: Mrs M. Bolton. E: 13.02.42. 2 Section, 2 Platoon and later with 3 Platoon. HMF: 04.04.44.

BOLTON, Joseph. Lance Corporal 277. B: 1896. 18 Mond Rd, Higher Irlam. W: Emma Bolton. E: 06.06.40. Transport Platoon. In June 1942 serving with 7 Platoon (HQ). SD: 03.12.44.

BOND, Thomas. Private 98. B: 1918. Ring Pitt Farm, Cadishead. F: Thomas Bond. E: 06.06.40. 4 Platoon, 3 Platoon and in June 1942 with 2 Section, 7 Platoon (HQ) and with Home Guard Guides. SD: 03.12.44, HQ Platoon.

BOOTH, James Bennett. Private. B: 1914. 129 Liverpool Rd, Irlam. W: Mrs Booth. E: 29.06.43. 4 Platoon. SD: 03.12.44.

BOOTH, John. Private 811. B: 1907. 37 Baines Ave, Irlam. W: Mrs A. Booth. E: 22.07.42. 5 Platoon. SD: 03.12.44.

BOOTH, John. Private B86. B: 1910. 12 Rutland Ave, Cadishead and later 23 Victory Rd, Cadishead. W: Mrs M. Booth. E: 24.09.40. 6 Platoon. R: 18.02.42. Later re-enlisted 14.09.42 and served 7 Platoon and later with 5 Platoon. SD: 03.12.44.

BOOTH, John Quarrell. B: 1898. 37 Boothfield, Winton. W: Doris Booth. E: 10.07.40. 4 Platoon. R: 25.04.41.

BOWDEN, Richard. Corporal 928. B: 1904. 40 Victory Rd, Cadishead. W: Mrs L. Bowden. E: 25.05.43. 7 Platoon and later with 4 Platoon. SD: 03.12.44.

BRACEGIRDLE, Clifford. Private. B: 1907. 518 Liverpool Rd, Hollins Green. E: 03.07.40. 6 Platoon and in June 1942 was in 1 Section, 5 Platoon. R: 20.02.43.

BRACEGIRDLE, Ernest. 408. 6 Lyndon Rd, Irlam. E: 18.07.40. 2 Platoon. HMF: 06.01.44.

BRACEGIRDLE, Herbert. B4. B: 1915. 4 Bradburn Rd, Irlam. F: J. Bracegirdle. E: 03.07.40. 6 Platoon. R: 14.02.42.

BRACEGIRDLE, James. B32. 47 Baines Ave, Irlam. W: Florence Bracegirdle. E: 03.07.40. 6 Platoon. R: 13.02.42.

BRACEGIRDLE, John Albert. Private 790. B: 1914. 2 Rose Crescent, Irlam. W: Mrs M. Bracegirdle. E: 17.07.42. 7 Platoon and later with 5 Platoon. SD: 03.12.44.

BRADLEY, Leonard. B: 1910. Tetlens, Eastway, Flixton. W: Mrs H. Bradley. E: 27.05.41. June 1942 served with 1 Section, 7 Platoon (HQ). SD: 03.12.44.

BRADSHAW, Arthur. 25. B: 1914. 31 Ferry Rd, Irlam. E: 30.06.40. 2 Platoon. R: 1941.

BRADSHAW, Thomas. 31 Ferry Rd, Irlam. E: 26.08.41.

BRADY, William. 522. B: 1923. 40 Caroline St, Irlam. M: Mrs Annie Brady. E: 14.02.41. 5 Platoon and later believed to have served with H Company.

BRATT, James. Lance Corporal. B: 1898. Princes Ave, Higher Irlam and later 26 Liverpool Rd, Higher Irlam. W: Mrs Bratt. E: 22.08.40. 7 Platoon, 2 (Soap Works) 4 Platoon and later 2 Platoon. SD: 03.12.44.

BRAYTON, William Morrison. 864. B: 1902. 240 Manchester Rd, Rixton. W: Mrs M.A.J. Brayton. E: 05.08.42. 7 Platoon. So: 27.04.44 (left district).

BRECKNELL, Charles Frederick. 396. B: 1904. 13 Silverdale Ave, Higher Irlam. W: Gertrude S. Brecknell. E: 15.07.40. T: 17.10.42to 45th (Lancashire) Battalion, Home Guard.

BREW, Donovan J. 445. B: 1911. The Bungalow, Victory Rd, Cadishead. F: W. Brew. E: 27.08.40. 5 Platoon and later believed to have served with H Company.

BREW, Edwin. 365. B: 1914. 304 Liverpool Rd, Cadishead. F: Herbert Brew. E: 06.07.40. 5 Platoon and later believed to have served with H Company.

BREWER, Samuel. Private 738. B: 1900. 15 Boundary Rd, Higher Irlam. W: Elizabeth Brewer. E: 28.05.42. 1 Platoon. SD: 03.12.44, HQ Platoon.

BRICKHILL, James Henry. Private 866. B: 1901. Partington Ave, Irlam and later at 25 Allenby Road, Cadishead. W: Mrs H. Brickhill. E: 10.08.42. 6 Platoon. SD: 03.12.44.

BRIDGE, John William. 888. B: 1906. 1 The Parade, Fiddlers Lane, Higher Irlam. W: Mrs M. Bridge. E: 04.09.42. 4 Platoon. HMF: 09.05.44.

BRIGGS, Alfred.14 Lancaster Rd, Cadishead. W: Mrs M.E. Briggs. E: 25.05.43. R: 17.07.44.

BRIGGS, Maurice. 723. 2 Marlborough Rd, Higher Irlam. F: George Briggs. E: 22.04.42. 3 Section, 1 Platoon. HMF: 22.04.42.

BRITTAIN, Alfred. Private. B: 1921. 70 Ferry Rd, Irlam. F: A. Brittain. E: 14.07.42. 7 Platoon. SD: 03.12.44.

BRITTAIN, Arthur. Private. 70 Ferry Rd, Irlam. W: Emma Brittain. 2 Section, 6 Platoon. DMU: 21.04.13.

BROAD, Jack. 455. B: 1922. 17 Graham Crescent, Cadishead. M: Mrs Broad. E: 14.09.40. 5 Platoon and later believed to have served with H Company.

BROADHURST, Richard. 290 Liverpool Rd, Cadishead. E: 28.08.40. 2 (Soap Works) Section, 4 Platoon and later 6 Platoon. DMU: 07.03.44.

BROADY, John. Private B31. 9 Bucklow Ave, Partington. W: Mrs Broady. E: 06.07.40. 1 Section, 6 Platoon. SD: 03.12.44.

BROCK, Alexander. B: 1886. 9 Ferryhill Rd, Irlam. E: 26.06.40. 2 Platoon. R: 14.02.42.

BROCK, David. 630. B: 07.06.24. 52 Addison Rd, Higher Irlam. M: Margaret Brock. E: 20.10.41. 1 Section, 2 Platoon. HMF: date unknown.

BROCK, Gordon. Lance Corporal 310. B: 1920. 9 Ferryhill Rd, Irlam. F: Alexander Brock. E: 06.06.40. 2 Section, 2 Platoon. SD: 03.12.44.

BRODIE, John. Private 792. B: 1903. 13 The Vista, Cadishead. W: Mrs E.M. Brodie. E: 23.07.42. 5 Platoon. SD: 03.12.44.

BROOKES, Daniel. B: 1923. Brook House, Cutnook Lane, Irlam. F: J.W. Brookes. E: 27.08.40. 25.04.41.

BROOKES, Norman. 459. B: 1921. Brook House, Cutnook Lane, Irlam. F: J. William Brookes. E: 14.09.40. 2 Platoon. R: 16.09.41.

BROOKS, Cyril. 415. B: 1912. 11 Lytherton Ave, Cadishead. W: Ethel May Brooks. B: 06.07.40. 5 Platoon and later believed to have served with H Company.

BROOKS, George. Private 842. B: 1905. 39 Hayes Rd, Cadishead. W: Mrs L. Brooks. E: 04.08.42. 5 Platoon. SD: 03.12.44.

BROUGHTON, Peter. 147. Lieutenant. B: 1896. 27 Lancaster Rd, Cadishead. W: Mrs Broughton. E: 06.06.40. Platoon Commander of 4 Platoon but reverted to section commander at his own request 12.01.41. Later served with 3 Platoon until he transferred to G Company, 42nd Battalion.

BROUGHTON, Richard Henry. Sergeant 197. B: 1903. 22 Nelson Dr, Cadishead. W: Mrs L. Broughton. E: 06.06.40. 4 Platoon and later with 1 Section, 3 Platoon. SD: 03.12.44.

BROWN, Alfred Edward. Sergeant. B: 1899. 13 Hartington Rd, Winton. W: Mrs Brown. E: 13.09.40. 1 (Margarine) Section, 4 Platoon. SD: 03.12.44, HQ Platoon.

BROWN, G.S. 661. B: 1921. 43 Baines Ave, Irlam. F: F. Brown. E: 15.01.42. Later believed to have served with 4 Platoon, H Company.

BROWN, Harry. 40. B: 1899. 15 Warwick Rd, Cadishead. W: Edith Brown. E: 06.06.40. 5 Platoon and later believed to have served with H Company.

BROWN, James. 131. B: 1903. 1 Warwick Rd, Cadishead. W: Mrs M. Brown. E: 06.06.40. 5 Platoon and later believed to have served with H Company.

BROWN, James. Private. 8 Lytherton Ave, Cadishead. W: Gladys Brown. E: 02.11.40. 2 (Soap Works) Section, 4 Platoon and later 6 Platoon. SD: 03.12.44.

BROWN, J. Arthur. Private. B: 1914. 40 Harewood Rd, Irlam. W: Ethel Brown. E: 03.07.40. R: 11.01.42. Re-enlisted at some point SD: 03.12.44, HQ Platoon.

BROWN, James Edward. B: 03.07.11. 13 Moss Side Rd, Cadishead. W: Mrs A. Brown. E: 07.09.42. 7 Platoon. HMF: 16.01.44.

BROWN, Reginald George. 73. B: 1912. 15 Milton Ave, Irlam. F: Bernard Brown. E: 04.06.40. 3 Platoon. Later believed to have served with H Company.

BROWN, Robert. 424. B: 1922. 4 Beech Ave, Higher Irlam. M: Agnes Brown. E: 21.07.40. 1 Platoon. HMF: 11.08.41.

BROWN, William. 831. B: 1903. 80 Liverpool Rd, Irlam. W: Mrs A. Brown. E: 23.07.42. 7 Platoon. So: 27.06.44.

BUCKLEY, George. 500. B: 1923. 46 Silver St, Higher Irlam. M: Martha Buckley. E: 12.01.41. 1 Platoon. R: 16.01.42.

BUCKLEY, John. B: 1897. 6, Fairfield Rd, Cadishead. W: Edith Buckley. E: 24.07.40. R: 30.06.43.

BUDWORTH, George Joseph. Private 625. B: 1916. 6 Nelson Dr, Cadishead. F: G. Budworth of Over Hulton, Bolton. E: 16.09.41. 1 Section, 3 Platoon. HMF: 31.03.43.

BUNN, Frank Frederick William. Private. B: 1899. 17 Fiddlers Lane, Irlam. W: Mary Hannah Bunn. E: 03.10.40. 6 Platoon and later with 2 Section, 1 Platoon. SD: 03.12.44.

BUNN, Horace Leslie. Private. B: 1913. 82 Ferry Rd, Irlam. W: Alice Bunn. E: 13.08.41. 2 (Soap Works) Section, 4 Platoon. DMU: 17.01.44.

BUNTING, George. Private 973. B: 1913. 23 Leyland Ave, Higher Irlam. W: Mrs L. Bunting. Transferred to D Company from 3rd (Lancaster City) Battalion, Home Guard on 07.03.43. 1 Platoon. SD: 03.12.44.

BURGESS, Ernest. 963. Officer in Home Guard. B: 25.12.94. 21 Silverdale Ave, Higher Irlam. W: Mrs M. Burgess. E: 23.07.43. T: 07.02.44 to 71st Heavy Anti-Aircraft, Home Guard.

BURGESS, Thomas. Private. B: 1921. 3 Lynton Ave, Cadishead. W: Mrs M. Burgess. E: 1943. 3 Platoon. SD: 03.12.44.

BURGESS, William. Private. B: 1913. 49,Ferry Rd, Irlam. E: 21.07.42. 2 Platoon. SD: 03.12.44.

BURGESS, William. Private. B: 1923. 3 Lynton Ave, Cadishead. F: George Burgess. E: 06.08.40. 2 Section, 6 Platoon. SD: 03.12.44.

BURKE, James. 520. B: 1922. 38 Caroline St, Irlam. M: Mrs M. Burke. E: 14.02.41. 3 Platoon and later believed to have served with H Company.

BURNES, L. 2nd Lieutenant. 108 Ferry Rd, Irlam. 6 Platoon. SD: 03.12.44.

BURNS, L. Private. Serving with 2 Section, 2 Platoon in June 1942. Possibly same man as above before being commissioned, slight difference in surname spelling.

BURROWS, Henry. 484. B: 1920. 17 Marlborough Rd, Irlam. M: Selina Elizabeth Burrows. E: 23.12.40. 2 Platoon and later Transport Platoon. R: 22.11.41.

BURROWS, Joseph. 971. 4 Barton Terrace, Irlam. W: Mrs Burrows. 2 Platoon. Also served some time with 71st Heavy Anti-Aircraft, Home Guard. R: 12.07.44.

BURROWS, Joseph. B: 1918. 17 Marlborough Rd, Irlam. M: Mrs Burrows. E: 28.03.41. 2 Platoon. T: date unknown to A Company. R: 30.04.41.

BURROWS, Sidney. 261. B: 1922. 17 Marlborough Rd, Irlam. M: Elizabeth Burrows. E: 06.06.40. HMF: 11.01.42.

BUSHELL, Eric. 852. B: February 1920. 5 The Crescent, Higher Irlam. M: Mrs E.M. Bushell. E: 05.08.42. 7 Platoon. HMF: 14.12.43.

BUTLER, Jack. 696. B: 1925. 93 Fir St, Cadishead. F: H. Butler. E: 13.04.42. Later believed to have served with 8 Platoon, H Company.

BUTLER, James. Sergeant 128. B: 1890. 1 Charles St, Cadishead. W: Gertrude E. Butler. E: 06.06.40. 4 Platoon and later 2 Section, 3 Platoon. SD: 03.12.44.

BUTLER, Sydney. 333. B: 1921. 93 Fir St, Cadishead. F: Walter Henry Butler. E: 01.07.40. 4 Platoon and later with 3 Platoon. R: 21.05.41.

BYROM, George J. Lance Corporal B: 1909. 2 St John's St, Irlam. W: Mrs E. Byrom. E: 07.09.42. 7 Platoon. SD: 03.12.44.

CALDICUTT, Robert. F561. B: 1904. 17 King Edward St, Patricroft. W: Doris Caldicutt. E: 23.04.41. 4 Platoon. R: 21.02.42.

CALLAGHAN, John. 262. B: 1901. 15 Victory Rd, Cadishead. W: Mrs K. Callaghan. E: 06.06.40. 5 Platoon and later believed to have served with H Company.

CALLAGHAN, William Ronald. Private 800. B: 1913. 65 Fiddlers Lane, Higher Irlam and later 160 Lords St, Cadishead. W: Mrs M. Callaghan. E: 21.07.42. 3 Platoon. SD: 03.12.44.

CALLAND, William. 153. 94 Fir St, Cadishead. 4 Platoon. R: 07.07.40.

CANDALL, John. 355. B: 1916. 67 Fir St, Cadishead. M: Mrs Candall. E: 02.07.40. 4 Platoon and later Transport Platoon.

CARBERRY, Joseph. Lance Corporal 878. B: 1914. 123 Eldon Rd, West. W: Mrs E. Carberry. E: 17.08.42. 7 Platoon. SD: 03.12.44.

CARBERRY, Patrick. Captain 600. B: 1896. Welwyn, Boat Lane, Irlam. In June 1942 he was a lieutenant serving with 1 Platoon. SD: 03.12.44, captain, Company HQ.

CARDING, Harry. Corporal 959. B: 1902. 9 Prospect Ave, Cadishead. W: Mrs Carding. E: 18.09.40. 2 (Soap Works) Section, 4 Platoon and later with 7 Platoon. SD: 03.12.44, HQ Platoon.

CARROLL, Richard Leighton. Private 381. B: 1906. 9 Fir St, Cadishead. W: Louie Carroll. E: 30.07.40. 6 Platoon. April 1942. He also served with 7 Platoon and 5 Platoon. SD: 03.12.44.

CARSON, Robert Lloyd. 95.B: 1903. 1 Stuart Ave, Irlam. W: Mrs Carson. E: 22.08.40. 4 Platoon. R: 27.02.42.

CARTER, Reginald. 322. B: 1921. 26 Lynthorpe Ave, Cadishead. G: Lillian Edge. E: 22.06.40. 4 Platoon. June 1942 with 2 Section, 3 Platoon. HMF: 15.06.42.

CARTLEDGE, Roland. 655. B: 1924. 573 Liverpool Rd, Irlam. B: Samuel Cartledge. E: 29.02.42. Later believed to have served with 4 Platoon, H Company.

CASE, William Henry. Private 59. B: 1904. 14 Leyland Ave, Higher Irlam. W: Catherine Case. E: 30.09.40. 4 Platoon. R: 25.04.41. Re-enlisted 17.05.42 into 3 Section, 2 Platoon. T: 16.08.43 to 21st (Cheshire) Battalion, Home Guard.

CASSIDY, Robert. Private 788. B: 1907. 46 Ferry Rd, Irlam. W: Mrs Cassidy. E: 14.07.42. 5 Platoon and later 7 Platoon. SD: 03.12.44.

CHALKLEY, William Ronald. 244. B: 1910. 27 Allenby Rd, Cadishead. F: William J. Chalkley. E: 06.06.40. 5 Platoon and later believed to have served with H Company.

CHARLTON, Frank. B98. Resided Flixton. W: Ada Charlton. E: 30.07.40. 6 Platoon. T: date unknown to 44th Battalion, Home Guard.

CHENEY, Albert Cecil. Private 758. B: 1914. 5 Moss Lane, Cadishead. W: Mrs Cheney. E: 10.07.42. 5 Platoon. SD: 03.12.44.

CHILD, David. 539. E: 11.03.41. Later believed to have served with 8 Platoon, H Company.

CHISNALL, Edward. 157. B: 1905. 42 Francis Rd, Irlam. W: Mrs Chisnall. E: 06.06.40. HQ Platoon. R: 12.07.44.

CHRISTIAN, Charles. Private 601. 31 Harewood Rd, Irlam. E: 18.07.40. 1 Section, 2 Platoon.

CLARE, John L. 918. B: 1916. 12 Rose Crescent, Irlam. W: Mrs Clare. E: 25.05.43.

CLARE, Norman. B: 1925. 36 Milton Ave, F: Arthur Clare. E: 28.05.42. Later believed to have served with 4 Platoon, H Company.

CLARE, Thomas. 157. B: 1922. 9 Charles St, Cadishead. M: Ada Clare. E: 06.06.40. 4 Platoon and later with 3 Platoon. R: 12.11.41. HMF: 30.11.42.

CLARKE, Harold. B82. B: 1911. 4 Bobs Lane, Cadishead. 6 Platoon. W: Florence Clarke. E: 29.07.40. HMF: 18.11.40.

CLARKE, Thomas. Private 77. B: 1910. 102 Ferry Rd, Irlam. W: Edith A. Clarke. E: 05.07.40. 3 Section, 2 Platoon. SD: 03.12.44.

CLAYTON, James. Lance Corporal 398. B: 1922. 20 Bankfield Ave, Cadishead. F: Mr Clayton. E: 16.07.40. 4 Platoon. June 1942, 2 Section, 3 Platoon. SD: 03.12.44.

CLAYTON, Josiah. 263. B: 1880. 22 Lytherton Ave, Cadishead. W: Mrs Clayton. E: 07.06.40. 5 Platoon and later believed to have served with H Company.

CLEWORTH, Harold. Private B75. B: 1907. 80 Bank St, Glazebrook. F: Mr Cleworth. E: 04.07.40. 1 Section, 6 Platoon. SD: 03.12.44.

CLORLEY, John. 341. B: 1899. 63 Victory Rd, Cadishead. W: Mrs Clorley. E: 01.07.40. 5 Platoon and later believed to have served with H Company.

CLORLEY, John Leonard. 22. B: 1921. 63 Victory Rd, Cadishead. F: J. Clorley. E: 30.06.40. 5 Platoon and later believed to have served with H Company.

CLOWES, Harold. 340. B: 1896. 219 Liverpool Rd, Cadishead. W: Mrs Clowes. E: 01.07.40. 5 Platoon and later believed to have served with H Company.

CLUTTERBUCK, Harry. Private 354. B: 1908. 38 Ferryhill Rd, Irlam. W: Mrs A. Clutterbuck. E: 02.07.40. 2 Platoon. R: 17.11.42.

COATES, Leslie. 662. B: 1924. 3 Kitchener Ave, Cadishead. F: Mr Coates. E: 15.01.42. Later believed to have served with 4 Platoon, H Company.

COLLINSON, George Alfred. Private 399. B: 1915. 46 Princes Ave, Higher Irlam and later 52 The Crescent, Higher Irlam. M: Mrs A. Collinson. 1 Section, 1 Platoon. SD: 03.12.44.

COLTON, Stanley. 209. B: 1910. 601 Liverpool Rd, Irlam. M: Mrs Colton. E: 07.06.40. 3 Platoon and later believed to have served with H Company. R: 14.05.41.

CONDE, John Leslie. 61. B: 1906. 23 Allenby Rd, Cadishead. W: Mrs Beatrice Conde. E: 05.06.40. 5 Platoon later believed to have served with H Company.

CONNELLY, John. 433. B: 1922. 10 Marlborough Rd, Higher Irlam. M: Mrs Margaret Connolly. E: 25.07.40. 1 Platoon.

CONNELLY, Thomas. Private. 10 Marlborough Rd, Higher Irlam. SD: 03.12.44, 4 Platoon.

CONNOR, Francis Michael. 868. 4 Nelson Dr, Cadishead. W: Mrs Connor. E: 10.08.42. 5 Platoon. R: 22.10.43.

Appendix VIII

CONNOR, Martin. 103. B: 1920. 30 Baines Ave, Irlam. F: J. Connor. E: 05.06.40. 4 Platoon and later believed to have served with H Company. HMF: date unknown.

COOKE, Frederick. B51. B: 1886. 129 Peel Green Rd, Barton. W: Alice Cooke. E: 03.07.40. R: 27.02.42.

COOKSON, Herbert. Private 889. B: 1901. 45 Cutnook Lane, Higher Irlam. W: Mrs E. Cookson. E: 07.09.42. 7 Platoon. SD: 03.12.44.

COOPER, Arthur. Private B33. 19 Palatine Close, Irlam. F: Arthur Cooper. E: 01.07.42. 1 Section, 6 Platoon. R: 22.03.42.

COOPER, Clifford. Private E4. B: 1904. 8 Laburnum Rd, Cadishead. W: Marie Cooper. E: 03.07.40. 5 Platoon. June 1942 with 1 Section, 7 Platoon (HQ). SD: 03.12.44, corporal, HQ Platoon. Notes on the rolls state serving under armourer sergeant with Company HQ.

COOPER, George Douglas. 457. B: 1921. 6 Holcroft Lane, Culcheth. M: Mrs L. Cooper. E: 14.09.40. 5 Platoon and later believed to have served with H Company.

COOPER, Herbert G. Private 592. B: 1891. 6 Holcroft Cottage, Culcheth. W: Mrs Cooper. E: 11 or 20.06.41. 2 (Soap Works) Section, 4 Platoon.

COPE, Frederick. 292. B: 1898. 56, Caroline St, Irlam. W: Amy Cole. E: 10.06.40. 3 Platoon and later believed to have served with H Company.

CORDELL, Norman. F41. B: 1899. 39 Boothfield, Winton. E: 10.07.40. R: 25.04.44.

COSTELLO, Francis. 681. 23 Francis Rd, Irlam. Later believed to have served with 4 Platoon, H Company.

COTTAM, Lawrence. 577. B: 1924. 61 Lord St, Cadishead. E: 27.05.41. Later believed to have served with 8 Platoon, H Company. HMF: date unknown.

COWARD, Frank. 126. B: 1910. 77 Baines Ave, Irlam. W: Lily Coward. E: 05.06.40. 1 Platoon. R: 07.11.40.

CRABTREE, Joseph. 634. B: 1906. 94 Fir St, Cadishead. W: Sarah H. Crabtree. E: 20.10.41. 3 Platoon. HMF: 31.12.41.

CRASHLEY, Richard. 135. B: 1891. 41 Devon Rd, Cadishead. W: Edith Crashley. E: 05.06.40. 5 Platoon and later believed to have served with H Company.

CRAVEN, Frank. 471. B: 1923. 66 Baines Ave, Irlam. E: 22.09.40. 1 Platoon. R: 21.05.41.

CRAWFORD, John. 961. B: 1895. 112 Silver St, Higher Irlam. W: Mrs M. Crawford. E: 30.07.43. R: 21.12.43.

CRIBBS, John R. Private 69. B: 1905. 10 Nelson Dr, Cadishead. W: Emily Cribbs. E: 23.08.40. 4 Platoon and later 1 Section, 3 Platoon. SD: 03.12.44.

CRIPPIN, William. Private 581. B: 1878. 186 Liverpool Rd, Cadishead. W: Annie Crippin. E: 20.06.41. 1 Section, 2 Platoon. R: 16.08.43.

CROMWELL, Edward. 375. B: 1896. 28 Warwick Rd, Cadishead. W: Eva Cromwell. E: 13.07.40. 4 Platoon and later believed to have served with 5 Platoon, H Company.

CROPLEY, Oliver Charles. 859. B: 1903. 11 Oak Ave, Cadishead. W: Mrs M.J. Cropley. E: 05.08.42. DMU: 14.08.42.

CROTTY, Ambrose. 378. B: 1884. 4 Baines Ave, Irlam. W: Kathleen Crotty. E: 06.07.40. 3 Platoon and later believed to have served with H Company. R: 12.02.41.

CROTTY, Patrick Francis. 610. B: 1914. 4 Baines Ave, Irlam. F: Ambrose Crotty. E: 13.08.41. Later believed to have served with 4 Platoon, H Company.

CULLEY, Frederick. 282. B: 1881. 42 Bradburn Rd, Irlam. W: Mary Culley. 4 Platoon and later believed to have served with H Company.

CUNDALL, J. Private (later Sergeant). 67 Fir St, Cadishead. E: June 1942. 1 Section, 7 Platoon (HQ). SD: 03.12.44, HQ Platoon.

CUNNINGHAM, Albert. 404. B: 1899. 22 Moss Lane, Cadishead. W: Caroline Cunningham. E: 16.07.40. 5 Platoon. R: 16.02.42.

DAINTITH, David Arthur. 207. B: 1889. 21 Victoria Rd, Irlam. W: Doris Hilton Daintith. E: 06.06.40. 2 Platoon and later with Company HQ.

DAINTITH, Harold. 215. B: 1922. 21 Victoria Rd, Irlam. M: Doris Hilton Daintith. E: 06.06.40. 2 Platoon. R: 11.09.40.

DAKERS, Adam. B70. B: 1907. 5 Peel Green Rd, Barton. W: Emily Dakers. E: 06.07.40. 6 Platoon. T: date unknown to A Company, 42nd Battalion.

DAKERS, William. Private. B: 1879. 4 Brereton Grove, Cadishead, W: Mrs S. Dakers. E: 06.09.41. 1 Section, 7 Platoon. R: 10.11.42.

DAKERS, William. 377. B: 1911. 4 Brereton Grove, Cadishead. M: Mrs S. Dakers. E: 13.07.40. 4 Platoon and later 3 Platoon. R: 21.05.41.

DALE, James E. 182. B: 1882. 157 Liverpool Rd, Cadishead. W: Mrs Elsie Dale. E: 06.06.40. 5 Platoon and later believed to have served with H Company.

DALE, John Frederick. Private 762. B: 1913. 37 Atherton Lane, Cadishead. W: Mrs H. Dale. E: 10.07.42. 7 Platoon and later 4 Platoon. SD: 03.12.44.

DALE, R. Private. In June 1942 serving with 1 (Margarine Works) Section, 4 Platoon.

DALE, Robert Lythgoe. Private F620. B: 1902. 66 The Crescent, Irlam. W: Mrs B. Dale. E: 06.09.41. 1 Platoon and later 2 Platoon. SD: 03.12.44.

DALE,T. 980. 5 Platoon.

DALE, Thomas Frederick. Private 172. B: 1918. 5 Bradburn Rd, Irlam. M: Lilian Dale. E: 06.06.40. 4 Platoon and later served with 5 Platoon. SD: 03.12.44.

DANIELS, Harold. 886. B: 1902. 155A Liverpool Rd, Cadishead. F: R. Daniels. E: 02.09.42. 5 Platoon. SD: 03.12.44. (Stand Down roll records address as 154 Liverpool Rd, Cadishead).

DANIELS, Joseph. B575. B: 1909. 8 Barsbank, Lymm. W: Doris M. Daniels. E: 27.05.41. 6 Platoon. R: 31.12.41.

DANIELS, Roland. Private 808. B: 1913. 143 Fir St, Cadishead. W: Mrs E. Daniels. E: 21.07.42. 5 Platoon. SD: 03.12.44.

DANIELS, Roy. 409. B: 1921. 34 Baines Ave, Irlam. E: 23.07.40. 3 Platoon and later believed to have served with H Company. HMF: 01.02.41.

DARBY, Joseph. 407 (409). B: 1899. 51 Mond Rd, Higher Irlam. W: Emily Darby. E: 17.07.40. 1 Platoon. R: 18.04.41. Re-enlisted (date unknown). SD: 03.12.44, 1 Platoon.

DARBYSHIRE, Joseph. B64. B: 1915. 20 St James St, Eccles. W: Lillian Darbyshire. E: 04.07.40. HMF: 09.09.41.

DARLEY, J. Lance Corporal. June 1942 serving with 2 Section, 1 Platoon.

DARLEY, Neal. Corporal B120. B: 1914. 2 Kitchener Ave, Cadishead, W: Rose Darley. E: 17.02.40. 1 Section, 6 Platoon. SD: 03.12.44.

DARNTON, Ernest. 312. B: 1888. Helena House, Cadishead Moss. Son, Jason Darnton. E: 17.06.40. Transport Platoon. R: 24.02.42.

DARNTON, James Edward. 327. B: 1915. Rose Bank Farm, Cadishead Moss. W: A. Darnton. E: 01.07.40. 4 Platoon and later with Transport Platoon. In June 1942 served with 1 Section, 7 Platoon (HQ). SD: 03.12.44, HQ Platoon.

DAVENPORT, Edward P. Corporal 217. B: 1917. Ash Farm, Irlam, then 537 Liverpool Rd, Irlam and later at 182 Liverpool Road, Cadishead. M: Emily Davenport. E: 06.06.40. 1 Section, 3 Platoon. SD: 03.12.44.

DAVENPORT, Ernest. Corporal 221. B: 1913. 28 Nelson Dr, Cadishead. W: Mrs Davenport. E: 06.06.40. 4 Platoon and later with 3 Platoon. SD: 03.12.44.

DAVENPORT, Fred. Private 751. B: 1919. Ash Farm, Cadishead. F: F. Davenport. E: 11.06.42. 3 Platoon. SD: 03.12.44, HQ Platoon.

DAVENPORT, T. Home Guard Guides. June 1942 serving with 1 Section, 3 Platoon.

DAVIDSON, William Edward. 849. B: 1909. 18 Partington Ave, Irlam. W: Mrs H. Davidson. E: 04.08.42. T: 01.10.42 to 79th Battalion, Home Guard.

DAVIES, Arthur. B17. B: 1893. 88 Woodsend Rd, Flixton. W: Mrs Davies. E: 03.07.40. R: 25.02.42.

DAVIES, Frederick. 706. B: 1920. 1 Graham Crescent, Cadishead. F: A. Davies. E: 15.04.42. Later believed to have served with 8 Platoon, H Company.

DAVIES, James. Private 719. B: 1925. 1 Allotment Rd, Cadishead. E: 20.04.42. 3 Section, 3 Platoon. Later served HQ Platoon.

DAVIES, T. Corporal. 11 Allenby Rd, Cadishead. 6 Platoon. SD: 03.12.44.

DAVIES, Thomas. Corporal B78. B: 1903. 9 Ash Grove, Cadishead. W: Janet Davies. E: 29.07.40. 1 Section, 6 Platoon.

DAVIES, Thomas Stanley. 313. B: 1918. 12 Kenmore Grove, Cadishead. M: Mrs Davies. E: 17.06.40. 4 Platoon and later 3 Platoon. HMF: 31.05.41.

DAVIS, Wilfred L. 701. B: 1922. 66 Lords St, Cadishead. M: Mrs Davis. E: 15.04.42. Later believed to have served with 8 Platoon, H Company.

DAWSON, Donald. 36 Silverdale Ave, Higher Irlam. Attached to HQ, D Company as cycle orderly.

DAY, Harry. 290. B: 1912. 63 Liverpool Rd, Cadishead. W: Sylvia Day. E: 10.06.40. R: 30.01.41.

DEAN, Albert. E45. B: 1915. 10 Elm Rd, Hollins Green. W: Georgina Mary Dean. E: 14.10.40. 5 Platoon.

DEAN, Arthur. 769. B: 1907. 9 Leyland Ave, Higher Irlam. W: Winifred Dean. E: 13.07.42. 5 Platoon and later with 7 Platoon. R: 29.09.44.

DEAN, Arthur William. 38. B: 1922. 21 Fir St, Cadishead. F: Arthur H. Dean. E: 05.06.1940. 4 Platoon and later 3 Platoon. HMF: 09.11.41.

DELVE, John. Private 775. B: 1907. 31 Dixon St, Irlam. W: Mrs Delve. E: 13.07.42. 3 Platoon. SD: 03.12.44.

DENNEHY, Thomas. 602. B: 1915. 4 Baines Ave, Irlam. F: Mr Dennehy. E: 06.08.41. Later believed to have served with 4 Platoon, H Company.

DENT, Robert. 212. B: 1891. 24 Mond Rd, Higher Irlam. W: Mrs Dent. E: 07.06.40. 1 Platoon. R: 27.04.41.

DENTON, Thomas. 480. B: 1908. 24 Harewood Rd, Irlam. W: Mary Ellen Denton. E: 30.09.40. 2 Platoon. HMF: 12.07.41.

DESMOND, George. Private 834. B: 1901. 33 Moss Side Rd, Cadishead. E: 23.07.42. 7 Platoon and later 6 Platoon. SD: 03.12.44.

DICKENSON, Nathaniel. Private F7. B: 1898. 30 Marlborough Rd, Higher Irlam. W: Emma Jane Dickenson. E: 15.07.40. 1 (Margarine Works) Section, 4 Platoon and later 2 Platoon. SD: 03.12.44.

DICKINSON, Robert Bernard. 97. B: 1907. 88 Caroline St, Irlam. W: Mrs A. Dickinson. E: 28.08.40. HMF: 06.06.41.

DICKINSON, Samuel. 963. 23 Partington Ave, Irlam. W: Mrs E. Dickinson. E: 06.09.43. 4 Platoon. R: 25.05.44.

DITCHFIELD, Herbert. Private 210. B: 1898. 17 Dean Rd, Cadishead. W: Jane Ditchfield. E: 06.06.40. 4 Platoon and later with 1 Section, 3 Platoon. SD: 03.12.44.

DIXON (Christian name unknown). Acting Sgt. (Instructor) D Company, Home Guard Guides.

DIXON, Denis. Private 505. B: 1924. 133 Liverpool Rd, Irlam. F: Joseph Dixon. E: 24.01.41. 2 Platoon. SD: 03.12.44, HQ Platoon.

DIXON, Edward. 550. B: 1922. 133 Liverpool Rd, Irlam. F: Joseph Dixon. E: 27.04.41. 2 Platoon and later 2 Section, 7 Platoon (HQ). HMF: 22.06.42.

DIXON, Frank. 137. B: 1919. 133 Liverpool Rd, Irlam. F: Joseph Dixon. E: July 1940. HMF: 03.01.41.

DIXON, George. B119. B: 1905. 25 The Crescent, Irlam. W: Ethel Dixon. E: 21.01.41. R: 14.02.42.

DIXON, Harry. Private 953. 2 Lynthorpe Ave, Cadishead and later 18 Warwick Rd, Cadishead. E: 30.08.43. 4 Platoon. SD: 03.12.44.

DIXON, Henry. 92. B: 1922. 37 Bradburn Rd, Irlam. F: Mr Dixon. E: 05.06.40. 3 Platoon and later believed to have served with H Company.

DIXON, John. Private F587. B: 1903. 2 Lynthorpe Rd, Cadishead. F: John Dixon. E: 20.06.41. 1 (Margarine Works) Section, 4 Platoon and later 2 Section, 6 Platoon. SD: 03.12.44.

DIXON, Joseph. B72. B: 1879. 133 Liverpool Rd, Irlam. W: Gertrude Dixon. E: 29.07.40. R: 01.10.42.

DIXON, Robert John. 401. B: 1889. 19 Boundary Rd, Higher Irlam. E: 16.07.40. 1 Platoon.

DIXON, Roy. 670. B: 1925. 68 Marlborough Rd, Higher Irlam. F: J.A. Dixon. E: 09.03.42. Later believed to have served with 8 Platoon, H Company.

DIXON, Walter. 651. 133 Liverpool Rd, Irlam. F: Joseph Dixon. Signals messenger.

DIXON, William. Sergeant 142. B: 1892. Keeper's Cottage, Irlam Moss. W: Miriam Dixon. E: 05.06.40. D Company Home Guard guides. Sergeant with 1, Section 7 Platoon (HQ). SD: 03.12.44.

DIXON, William. 611. B: 1924. 15 Baines Ave, Irlam. F: John Dixon. E: 13.08.41. Later believed to have served with 4 Platoon, H Company.

DODD, Eric James. 90. B: 1914. Sunnyside, Bobs Lane, Cadishead. F: J. Dodd. E: 05.06.40. 5 Platoon and later believed to have served with H Company.

DODD, Frank E. 911. B: 1912. 34 Dixon St, Irlam. 5 Platoon. T: 17.01.44 to 19 Cheshire Home Guard Battalion.

DODD, Frederick. Assistant Transport Officer 33. B: 1906. 15 Chapel Rd, Irlam. W: Ivy Dodd. E: 03.06.40. Transport Platoon and later believed to have transferred to G Company.

DODD, Harold. 873. B: 1911. 58 Marlborough Rd, Higher Irlam. W: Mrs Dodd. E: 10.08.42. 5 Platoon and later 7 Platoon. R: 06.06.44.

DODD, Samuel. Private 820. B: 1904. 31 Bradburn Rd, Irlam. E: 15.07.40. 3 Platoon and later believed to have served with H Company. R: 23.04.41. Re-enlisted 22.07.42. 5 Platoon. SD: 03.12.44.

DONNELLY, Hugh. 286. B: 1921. 26 Boundary Rd, Higher Irlam. M: Mary Donnelly. E: 07.06.40. 1 Platoon. HMF: 29.11.40.

DONNELLY, J. Private 652. B: 1924. 98 Ferry Rd, Irlam. 2 Section, 2 Platoon. Discharged 17.02.43.

DONNELLY, James. 8. B: 1919. 26 Boundary Rd, Higher Irlam. F: J. Donnelly. E: 27.06.40. 1 Platoon. R: 19.02.40.

DONNELLY, Joseph. 251. B: 1922. 26 Boundary Rd, Higher Irlam. E: 06.06.40. 1 Platoon. M: Mary Donnelly. T: 11.11.40 to Eccles.

DONOVAN, Leonard. 565. B: 1919. 10 Baines Ave, Irlam. F: Richard Thomas Donovan. E: 30.04.41. Later believed to have served with 4 Platoon, H Company.

DOOLEY, Frederick Joseph. 245. B: 1923. 70 Liverpool Rd, Irlam. E: 07.06.40. 3 Section, 1 Platoon. Joined HMF: 16.05.44. Next of kin: Mrs Cromwell (mother).

DOUGLAS, James. 778. B: 1907. 119 Liverpool Rd, Irlam. B: Mr A. Douglas. E: 13.07.42. R: 16.11.42.

DOWSON, Joseph. Private 213. Lyndhurst, New Moss Rd, Cadishead. W: Mrs Mildred Dowson. E: 06.06.40. 4 Platoon and later with 3 Section, 3 Platoon. SD: 03.12.44.

DOYLE, William. F17. B: 1907. 56 The Crescent, Irlam. W: Ida Doyle. E: 10.07.40. 4 Platoon. R: April 1941.

DRIVER, Charles Hugh. 13. B: 1902. 46 Marlborough Rd, Irlam. W: Mary Ann Driver. E: 07.06.40. 1 Platoon. R: 16.07.41.

DRUM, Wilfred. 113. B: 1910. 3 Alexandra Grove, Irlam. M: Mary Elizabeth Drum. E: 09.07.40. 3 Platoon and later believed to have served with H Company. T: date unknown to Heavy AA Battery near Eccles. Passed away 27th January 1992 at Bridgewater, Somerset. Brother of Albert (Royal Signals), John (Home Guard) and Robert (Home Guard).

DUFFICEY, Jack. Private 755. B: 1920. 15 Hamilton Ave, Cadishead. F: D. Dufficey. E: 08.07.42. HQ Platoon. SD: 03.12.44.

DULSON, William. Private 782. B: 1905. 49, Princes Ave, Higher Irlam. W: Mrs A. Dulson. E: 13.07.42. 2 Platoon. SD: 03.12.44.

DUNN, Albert. Private 766. B: 1912. 117, Liverpool Rd, Cadishead. W: Mrs Dunn. E: 10.07.42. 5 Platoon. SD: 03.12.44.

DUNN, Charles Thomas. 358. B: 1906. 5 Green Lane, Cadishead. W: May Dunn. E: 02.07.40. 5 Platoon and later believed to have served with H Company.

DUNN, John Roland. 247. 5 Haig Ave, Cadishead. 5 Platoon and later believed to have served with H Company. HMF: 16.03.42.

DUNN, Stephen Edward. 368. B: 1920. 56 Harewood Rd, Irlam. W: Alice Dunn. E: 10.07.40. 3 Section, 2 Platoon. HMF: 28.02.42.

DUTTON, Kenneth Maddock. 161. B: 1921. 9 Holcroft Lane, Culcheth. M: Ethel Dutton. E: 06.06.40.

DUTTON, Thomas. Private 754. B: 1915. 73 Eldon Rd, Irlam. W: Ethel Dutton. E: 03.07.42. 2 Platoon. SD: 03.12.44.

DUTTON, Thomas. F6. B: 1887. 34 Hayes Rd, Cadishead. W: Mary Dutton. E: July 1940. 4 Platoon. R: 25.04.41.

EDEN, James H. B: 1925. 7 Chestnut Ave, Cadishead. F: H. Eden. E: 18.05.42.

EDWARDS, Arthur. Private 160. B: 1922. 23 Nelson Dr, Cadishead. F: Arthur Edwards. E: 06.06.40. 4 Platoon and later with 1 Section, 3 Platoon. SD: 03.12.44.

EDWARDS, Herbert Joseph. 26. B: 1910. 679 Liverpool Rd, Irlam. W: Mrs Edwards. E: 24.07.40. 3 Platoon and later believed to have served with H Company.

EDWARDS, William. Sergeant 256. B: 1892. 18 Marlborough Rd, Irlam. W: Georgina Griffiths. E: 06.06.40. 1 Section, 1 Platoon. SD: 03.12.44, HQ Platoon.

EDWARDS, Wynn. 266. B: 1919. 48 Marlborough Rd, Irlam. F: Mr Edwards. E: 06.06.40. June 1942 with 1 Section, 1 Platoon. So: 17.01.44.

EGAN, Joseph. B588. B: 1890. 13 Hayes Rd, Cadishead. W: Mrs Egan. E: 03.07.40. 6 Platoon. R: 13.02.42.

EGERTON, Charles. 18. B: 1922. 5 Eldon Rd, Irlam. F: Harry Egerton. E: 30.06.40. 2 Platoon. R: 16.07.41. HMF: date unknown.

EGERTON, Kenneth. 20. B: 1923. 5 Eldon Rd, Irlam. F: Harry Egerton. E: 30.06.40. 2 Platoon. R: 16.07.41.

ELLAMS, J. George. Private. B: 1903. Bowden House, MacDonald Rd, Irlam. W: Dorothy Ellams. E: 13.07.40. 5 Platoon and later with 3 Section, 3 Platoon. SD: 03.12.44.

ELLERAY, James Stanley. 148. B: 1891. 40, Ferryhill Rd, Irlam. W: Lily Elleray. E: 05.06.40. 2 Platoon. R: 03.11.40.

ELLIOTT, Leslie. Private B5. B: 1903. 13 New Moss Rd, Cadishead, then 7 Poplar Grove and finally 19 Kitchener Ave, Cadishead. W: Lily Elliott. E: 16.09.40. 2 Section, 6 Platoon. SD: 03.12.44.

ELLISON, Clarence Mervyn, 979. B: 1922. 9 Drake Ave, Cadishead. F: Jonathan Ellison. E: 06.01.41. 4 Platoon. HMF: 20.10.41.

ELLISON, Henry. Private 383. B: 1900. 36 Ferryhill Rd, Irlam. W: Mrs E. Ellison. E: 04.07.40. 2 Section, 2 Platoon. SD: 03.12.44.

ELMS, Bernard. 628. B: 1924. 22 Lords St, Cadishead. E: 20.10.40. Later believed to have served with 8 Platoon, H Company.

ETCHELLS, G. Platoon Commander, 6 Platoon. Second in command, D Company. Later believed to have served with G Company, 42nd Battalion.

ETCHELLS, George Albert. Captain B18. B: 1897. 29 Boundary Rd, Irlam. W: Dorothy Etchells. E: 09.07.40. 6 Platoon. June 1942 with 1 Section, 7 Platoon (HQ). R: 17.04.44.

ETCHELLS, Herbert. B34. B: 1895. 2 Ashley Ave, Flixton. W: Annie Etchells. E: 05.07.40. 6 Platoon. T: 25.02.42 to C Company.

ETCHELLS, Walter. Private 908. B: 1926. 29 Boundary Rd, Irlam. F: G.A. Etchells. E: 20.02.43. Cycle orderly (Home Guard messenger) at Company HQ and later served 2 Platoon. SD: 03.12.44.

ETHERINGTON, George. 205. B: 1920. 615 Liverpool Rd, Irlam. F: George William Etherington. E: 06.06.40. 3 Platoon and later believed to have served with H Company.

ETHERINGTON, William. 97. B: 1923. 615 Liverpool Rd, Irlam. F: George William Etherington. E: 05.06.40. 3 Platoon and later believed to have served with H Company.

EVANS, Edward. 195. B: 1883. 169 Liverpool Rd, Cadishead. B: William Evans. E: 06.06.40. 5 Platoon and later believed to have served with H Company.

EVANS, F.A. 538. E: 16.03.41. Later believed to have served with 8 Platoon, H Company.

EVANS, Frank. Private 165. B: 1923. 11 Prospect Rd, Cadishead. M: Annie Evans. E: 23.08.40. 4 Platoon and later 3 Platoon. SD: 03.12.44.

EVANS, Frank W. 965. B: 1902. 85 Liverpool Rd, Irlam. W: Mrs S. Evans. E: 18.08.43. 4 Platoon. R: 07.09.43.

EVANS, Gwilym. 960. B: 1892. 65 Fir St, Cadishead. E: 18.09.43. 4 Platoon. R: 29.09.43.

EVE, Harry. 697. B: 14.10.07. 8 Penry Ave, Cadishead and later at 9 The Vista, Cadishead. W: M. Eve. E: 13.04.42. 2 Section, 3 Platoon. HMF: 31.10.42.

FAIRHURST, John. 490. B: 1919. 27 Moss Lane, Cadishead. M: Mrs O. Whistlecroft. E: 26.12.40. 5 Platoon later believed to have served with H Company. HMF: date unknown.

FAIRHURST, Lewis. 482. B: 1923. 60 Victory Rd, Cadishead. F: William Henry Fairhurst. E: 10.09.40. 5 Platoon. Later believed to have served with H Company.

FARDON, James. Private 947. B: 1893. 9 Green Lane, Cadishead. W: Mrs Fardon. E: 28.08.40. 2 (Soap Works) Section, 4 Platoon and later 6 Platoon. SD: 03.12.44.

FARNWORTH, Dennis A. Private 983. 28 Boundary Rd, Higher Irlam. E: 03.07.44. 2 Platoon. SD: 03.12.44.

FARNWORTH, John L. Private 812. B: 1905. 28 Boundary Rd, Higher Irlam. W: Mrs C.M. Farnworth. E: 22.07.42. 7 Platoon. SD: 03.12.44.

FARRAND, Henry. Private 816. B: 1901. 46 Fir St, Cadishead. W: Mrs E. Farrand. E: 22.07.42. 5 Platoon. SD: 03.12.44.

FARRELL, Joseph. 269. B: 1909. 32 Silverdale Ave, Higher Irlam. W: Florence Farrell. E: 06.06.40. as Platoon Commander, 1 Platoon. R: 07.08.41.

FENNER, Walter. 948. B: 26.11.97. 298 Liverpool Rd, Cadishead. W: Mrs Fenner. E: 16.07.43. DMU: 17.01.44.

FENNEY, Arthur. F557. B: 1896. 25 Eldon Rd, Irlam. B: Harry Fenney. E: 23.04.41. 4 Platoon. R: 15.08.41.

FENTON, Arthur. Private B35. B: 1919. 16 Mersey Ave, Irlam. W: Charlotte Fenton. E: 05.07.40. 2 Section, 6 Platoon. R: 04.06.43.

FERGUSON, James. Lieutenant 260. B: 1899. 21 Ferryhill Rd, Irlam. W: Beatrice Ferguson. E: 06.06.40. 2 Platoon and later 7 Platoon. SD: 03.12.44.

FIELD, Arthur. B30. B: 1885. 41 Marlborough Rd, Higher Irlam. W: Mrs Field. E: 26.09.40. 6 Platoon. R: 18.02.42.

FIRTH, John. Private B36. B: 1922. 9 Moss Lane, Partington. F: Jonas Firth. E: 05.07.40. 2 Section, 6 Platoon. HMF: 15.01.43.

FISHER, Edward. Sergeant 167. B: 1909. 16 Lynthorpe Ave, Cadishead. E: 05.06.40. 2 Section, 3 Platoon and later 4 Platoon. SD: 03.12.44.

FLETCHER, John Braid. Private 715. B: 1911. 69 Fiddlers Lane, Higher Irlam. W: Mrs Fletcher. E: 19.04.42. 1 Section, 1 Platoon. SD: 03.12.44.

FLOWERS, Samuel. Lance Corporal B68. B: 1896. 20 Baines Ave, Irlam. W: Sarah Flowers. E: 03.07.40. 2 Section, 6 Platoon. SD: 03.12.44.

FLYNN, John. 248. B: 1913. 23 Marlborough Rd, Higher Irlam. W: Selina Flynn. E: 06.06.40. 1 Platoon. R: 20.04.41. Re-enlisted 11.08.42, re-numbered 875. R: 02.09.42.

FORDE, William. 448. B: 1900. 68 Dixon St, Irlam. W: Mrs Forde. E: 26.08.40. 3 Platoon and later believed to have served with H Company.

FOWLER, J. Private. June 1942 with 3 Section, 3 Platoon.

FOWLES, John James. 623. B: 1924. 19 Partington Ave, Irlam and later 25 Ash Ave, Cadishead. F: R. Fowles. E: 13.09.41. 2 Platoon and later HQ Platoon. HMF: 28.06.44.

FRENCH, Frederick. Sergeant 716. B: 1891. 9 Eldon Rd, Irlam. W: Mrs French. E: 20.04.42. June 1942, private with 3 Section, 2 Platoon. SD: 03.12.44, HQ Platoon.

FRENCH, Frederick John. Private 374. B: 1916. 2 Mond Rd, Higher Irlam. E: 12.07.40. 2 Section, 1 Platoon. SD: 03.12.44.

FRITH, Dennis. Private 547. B: 1923. 48 Nelson Dr, Cadishead. M: Mrs Frith. E: 28.03.41. 3 Section, 3 Platoon. HMF: 16.05.44.

GALBRAITH, John. 654. B: 1924. 46 Dixon St, Irlam. E: 29.01.41. Later believed to have served with 4 Platoon, H Company.

GANLEY, James. F48. B: 1900. 63 Princes Ave, Higher Irlam. W: Mary Ganley. E: 10.07.40. 4 Platoon. R: 25.04.41.

GARDNER, Charles Horace. Lieutenant 420. B: 1908. Lynvale, Boat Lane, Irlam. W: Doris Gardner. E: 22.07.40. June 1942 with 2 Section, 2 Platoon and later served 4 Platoon. SD: 03.12.44.

GASKELL, John. B7. B: 1899. 26 Marlborough Rd, Higher Irlam. W: Edith Gaskell. E: 03.07.40. 6 Platoon and later with 2 Section, 1 Platoon. SD: 03.12.44.

GATER, Harry. 372. 38 Victory Rd, Cadishead. 5 Platoon and later believed to have served with H Company.

GAVIN, John. 943. B: 1908. 70 Hampden Grove, Patricroft. W: Mrs L. Gavin. E: 28.08.40. 4 Platoon. R: 25.08.41.

GEDDES, Francis. 21. B: 1892. 50 Baines Ave, Irlam. W: Mrs Geddes. E: 30.06.40. 3 Platoon and later believed to have served with H Company. R: 16.07.41.

GIBBON, George Leslie. 11. B: 1922. Moss View Farm, Barton Moss. F: George William Gibbon MM. E: 26.06.40. 1 Platoon. HMF: 08.12.41.

GILFEDDE, Isaac. 334. B: 1912. 37 Hayes Rd, Cadishead. S: Mrs Johnson. E: 18.08.40. 5 Platoon and later believed to have served with H Company.

GILLBODY, John Arthur. 231. B: 1891. 76 Caroline St, Irlam. W: Mary Gillbody. E: 07.06.40. 3 Platoon and later believed to have served with H Company. T: 09.04.41 to G Company, 42nd Battalion.

GILLESPIE, Joseph O'Reilly. Private 367. B: 1916. 7 Victoria Rd, Irlam. F: J. Gillespie. E: 10.07.40. 7 Platoon. SD: 03.12.44.

GILLIGAN, William. Lieutenant 641. Platoon Commander. B: 1889. Liverpool Rd, Irlam. W: Mrs M. Gilligan. E: 05.06.40. R: 12.02.41. Re-enlisted 30.10.41. June 1942, private with 2 (Soap Works) Section, 4 Platoon. Later commissioned and commanded 3 Platoon. Joined Police 20.05.43.

GIVENS, James Richard. 466. B: 1922. 28 Ferryhill Rd, Irlam. GR: Sarah Givens. E: 19.02.42. 2 Section, 1 Platoon. HMF: 30.06.43.

GIVENS, John W. Corporal 163. B: 1903. 3 York Rd, Cadishead. W: Mrs Givens. E: 06.06.40. 4 Platoon and later 3 Section, 3 Platoon. SD: 03.12.44.

GIVENS, Stanley. Corporal 267. B: 1910. 16 Gerrards Close, Irlam. W: Mrs Edna Givens. E: 06.06.40. 2 Section, 2 Platoon. SD: 03.12.44.

GLOVER, Albert. Private B97. B: 1913. 6 The Vista, Cadishead. F: Albert Glover. E: 06.07.40. 1 Section, 6 Platoon. HMF: 30.04.43.

GLOVER, William Edward. Private 803. B: 1916. 6 The Vista, Cadishead. F: Albert Glover. E: 21.07.42. 3 Platoon. SD: 03.12.44.

GOLD, Francis G. Service no. 1. B: 1886. Irlam Hall. W: Mrs Gold. E: 05.06.40. 3 Platoon and then 7 Platoon (HQ) before joining Company HQ. SD: 03.12.44, major, officer commanding D Company.

GOLDSTEIN, Benson. 857. B: 1911. 531 Liverpool Rd, Irlam. W: S. Goldstein. E: 05.08.42. T: 22.11.42 to B Company, Rutland Battalion.

GOOCH, Alfred Sydney. Private 837. B: 1906. 25 Lytherton Ave, Cadishead. W: Mrs D.E. Gooch. E: 04.08.42. 3 Platoon. SD: 03.12.44.

GOODIER, Harry. Lieutenant 92. B: 1909. 16 Boundary Rd, Higher Irlam. W: Lilian Goodier. E: 05.06.40. 1942, sergeant with 2 Section, 1 Platoon and later commissioned. SD: 03.12.44.

GOSTRIDGE, Thomas. 944. B: 1898. 63 Lancaster Rd, Cadishead. W: Mrs Gostridge. E: 16.07.43. R: 25.09.43.

GOULDING, William George. Private 728. B: 1908. 46 Addison Rd, Higher Irlam. W: Mrs Goulding. E: 07.04.42. 3 Section, 2 Platoon.

GRANT, Donald J. Private 913. B: 925. Rose Ave, Irlam and later at Larkhill Farm, Astley Rd, Irlam. M: Mary J. Grant. E: 24.05.43. 4 Platoon. SD: 03.12.44.

GRAYSON, Herbert. 486. B: 1922. 121 Eldon Rd West, Irlam. F: Wilfred Grayson. E: 23.10.40. 2 Platoon. HMF: 31.07.41.

GREEN, J. Private. 71 Liverpool Rd, Irlam. SD: 03.12.44, 4 Platoon. Possibly Pte 979 Green.

GREEN, Jack. 979. T: date unknown from H Company to D Company.

GREEN, James. 563. B: 1924. 8 Alexandra Grove, Irlam. F: Joseph Green. E: 27.05.41. Later believed to have served with 4 Platoon, H Company.

GREEN, Joseph Wilson. Corporal 125. B: 1913. 56 Ferry Rd, Irlam. W: Mrs Green. E: 05.06.40. 4 Platoon and 1 Section 7 Platoon (HQ). SD: 03.12.44.

GREEN, Osborne. 373. B: 1904. 14 Kitchener Ave, Cadishead. E: 12.07.40. 5 Platoon and later believed to have served with H Company.

GREEN, Samuel. 384. B: 1917. 6 Annable Rd, Irlam. W: Mrs S. Green. E: 14.07.40. 3 Platoon and later believed to have served with H Company. R: 09.11.40.

GREEN, Thomas. Private 967. B: 1922. 29 Ferryhill Rd, Irlam. M: Mrs Green. T: date unknown from 49th Lancashire Battalion, Home Guard to D Company, 42nd Battalion, Home Guard. 1 Platoon. SD: 03.12.44.

GREEN, William Lawrence. 66. B: 1922. 21 Warwick Rd, Cadishead. F: Walter Green. E: 05.06.40. 4 Platoon and later 3 Platoon. HMF: 21.05.41.

GREGORY, Edwin. 443. B: 1917. 11 Vicarage Rd, Irlam. S: Annie Gregory. E: 24.08.40. 3 Platoon and later believed to have served with H Company.

GREGORY, Ronald. Private F60. B: 1906. 67 Lords St, Cadishead. W: Maud Elizabeth Gregory. E: 02.11.40. 1 (Margarine Works) Section, 4 Platoon. SD: 03.12.44, HQ Platoon.

GREGORY, Thomas. 37. B: 1914. 32 Francis Rd, Irlam. W: Edith Gregory. E: 05.06.40. 3 Platoon and later believed to have served with H Company.

GRIFFITHS, Edward. B109. B: 1901. 26 Barsbank Lane, Lymm. W: Mary Elizabeth Griffiths. E: 06.07.40. 6 Platoon. R: 09.09.41.

GRIFFITHS, James William. Private 850. B: 1911. Silver St, Higher Irlam and later at 378 Liverpool Rd, Patricroft. S: Mrs Royle. E: 08.08.42. 7 Platoon. SD: 03.12.44.

GRINDLEY, Albert. 236. B: 1913. 17 Haig Ave, Cadishead, later 6 Rose Crescent, Irlam. W: Nellie Grindley. E: 06.06.40. 5 Platoon and later believed to have served with H Company. R: date unknown. Re-enlisted 10.07.42 and re-numbered Lance Corporal 764. 7 Platoon and later 5 Platoon.

GRINDLEY, Eric. B: 1926. 37 Addison Rd, Higher Irlam. 5 Platoon, cycle orderly (Home Guard messenger).

GRINDLEY, Henry. 143. B: 1884. 17 Haig Ave, Cadishead. W: Sarah Grindley. E: 05.06.40. 5 Platoon and later believed to have served with H Company.

GROVES, Alfred. Private 689. 53 Silver St, Higher Irlam. W: Mrs Groves. E: 07.04.42. 2 Section, 6 Platoon. R: 20.09.43.

GROVES, Roy. Private 569. B: 1923. 53 Silver St, Higher Irlam. F: Alfred Groves. E: 27.05.41. 1 Section, 1 Platoon. HMF: at some point between 1941 and 1944.

GRUNDY, Allan. 214. B: 1909. 27 Dixon St, Irlam. W: Mrs Grundy. E: 06.06.40. 3 Platoon and later believed to have served with H Company.

GRUNDY, T. Corporal (Orderly). Serving with 1 Platoon in June 1942. Possibly Thomas Arthur Grundy (see below).

GRUNDY, Thomas Arthur. Lieutenant 475. B: 1905. 2 Beech Ave, Higher Irlam. W: Vera Grundy. E: 28.08.40. HQ Platoon. SD: 03.12.44, Company HQ.

GRUNDY, Thomas Laurence. 12. B: 1900. 22 Liverpool Rd, Higher Irlam. W: Alice Ann Grundy. E: 28.06.40. 1 Platoon. R: 16.07.41.

HADDOCK, Leonard. Private 702. B: 1900. 6 Princes Ave, Higher Irlam. W: Mrs J. Haddock. E: 15.04.42. 1 Section, 1 Platoon. SD: 03.12.44.

HADFIELD, George. Lance Corporal 101. B: 1906. 34 The Crescent, Higher Irlam. W: Alice Hadfield. E: 05.06.40. 1 Section, 1 Platoon. SD: 03.12.44.

HAGUE, John. Private 757. B: 1919. 47 Ferry Rd, Irlam. F: M. Hayes. E: 09.07.42. 2 Platoon. SD: 03.12.44.

HAINES, G.R. Officer. M 115 396. Later believed to have served with G Company.

HALFPENNY, Jack. Private 507. B: 1913. 94 Silver St, Higher Irlam. W: Elsie Halfpenny. E: 19.12.40. 1 Section, 1 Platoon. SD: 03.12.44.

HALL, Bertram. 117. B: 1921. Lower Stanley Bank Farm, Cadishead Moss. F: Ernest Hall. E: 05.06.40. 4 Platoon and later with 3 Platoon. R: 16.07.41. Brother of Lance Corporal Sydney Ernest Hall, Grenadier Guards who was killed on 6th August 1944.

HALL, Harold. Private B37. Kenstone, New Moss Rd, Cadishead and later at 3 Brereton Grove, Cadishead. F: Thomas W. Hall. E: 05.07.40. 2 Section, 6 Platoon. SD: 03.12.44.

HALLIWELL, Harry. Private 108. B: 1897. 55 Mond Rd, Higher Irlam. W: Mrs H. Halliwell. E: 05.06.40. 1 Platoon. SD: 03.12.44.

HALLIWELL, John Thomas. F54. B: 1893. 75 Liverpool Rd, Higher Irlam. W: Miriam Halliwell. E: 21.04.41 (alternative date, 03.04.41 is also recorded). 1 (Margarine Works) Section, 4 Platoon. R: 02.09.42.

HALSTEAD, James. Private 637. B: 1909. 94 Fir St, Cadishead. W: Mrs Halstead. E: 30.10.41. 3 Section, 3 Platoon. R: 01.07.42.

HAMBLETT, Robert Norman. 227. B: 1923. Drake Ave, Cadishead and later 9 Nelson Dr, Cadishead. M: Margaret Ellison. E: 06.06.40. 1 Section, 3 Platoon. HMF: 31.07.43.

HAMER, R.A. 972. B: 1915. 18 Gerrards Close, Irlam. W: Mrs Hamer. R: 26.04.44.

HAMER, William Albert. 219. B: 1914. 51 Lyndhurst Ave, Higher Irlam. W: Edith May Hamer. E: 06.06.40. 2 Platoon. HMF: 11.08.41.

HAMILTON, Donald. 93. B: 1922. 46 Bradburn Rd, Irlam. F: Robert Hamilton. E: 05.06.40. 3 Platoon and later believed to have served with H Company.

HAMILTON, Robert. 281. B: 1895. 46 Bradburn Rd, Irlam. W: Mrs Hamilton. E: 06.06.40. 3 Platoon and later believed to have served with H Company.

HAMILTON, Thomas M. 454. B: 1919. 18 Graham Crescent, Cadishead. M: Mrs Hamilton. E: 14.09.40. 5 Platoon and later believed to have served with H Company.

HAMPSON, Charles. Private B38. B: 1925. 7 Kenmore Grove, Cadishead and later 243 Liverpool Rd, Cadishead. E: 01.07.40. 2 Section, 6 Platoon.

HAMPSON, Cyril. 359. B: 1918. Cadishead. E: 03.07.40. 4 Platoon and later with 1 Section, 3 Platoon. T: 08.03.43 to E Company.

HAMPSON, Harry. 442. B: 1905. 6 Bankfield Ave, Cadishead. W: Marion Hampson. E: 19.08.40. 5 Platoon and later believed to have served with H Company.

HAMPSON, Sidney. Lance Corporal 862. B: 1921. 7 Drake Ave, Cadishead. F: S. Hampson. E: 05.08.42. 3 Platoon. SD: 03.12.44.

HAMPSON, William Oliver. Private B15. B: 1916. The Gables, Warburton Lane, Partington. F: Oliver Hampson. E: 09.07.40. 6 Platoon. R: 26.02.42. Re-enlisted 25.08.42, re-numbered 883. 7 Platoon and later 6 Platoon. SD: 03.12.44.

HANCOCK, John Leslie. 317. B: 1921. 2 Warwick Rd, Cadishead. M: Mrs Hancock. E: 22.06.40. 5 Platoon and later believed to have served with H Company.

HANKINSON, Kenneth. G10. B: 1922. 2 Latham Rd, Irlam. E: 20.08.40. 4 Platoon. R: 25.04.41.

HANKINSON, William. 86. B: 1889. 91 Lord St, Cadishead. W: Mary Hankinson. E: 05.06.40. 5 Platoon and later believed to have served with H Company.

HANKINSON, William Edmund. Private E9. Tayfield, Belgrave Rd, Cadishead. W: Mrs Hankinson. E: 18.07.40. 2 Section, 5 Platoon and later 2 Platoon. SD: 03.12.44.

HANLEY, Harry Newall. Private 41. B: 1888. 149 Liverpool Rd, Irlam. W: Amy Hanley. E: 05.06.40. 3 Section, 2 Platoon. R: 26.01.42.

HANNON, Charles. 512. B: 1922. 23 Victoria Rd, Irlam. F: John Hannon. E: 10.02.41. 3 Platoon and later believed to have served with H Company.

HARFORD, Thomas. 545. E: 07.03.41. Believed to have served with 4 Platoon, H Company.

HARGREAVES, Cyril. Private 417. B: 1914. 25 Hayes Rd, Cadishead. W: Maud Hargreaves. E: 22.07.40. Transport Platoon. June 1942, 1 Section, 7 Platoon. R: 28.06.43.

HARPER, David. Private 785. B: 1907. Liverpool Rd, Irlam and later 21 Bradburn Rd, Irlam. W: Mrs E.A. Harper. E: 13.07.42. 3 Platoon. SD: 03.12.44.

HARRIS, Emanuel. Lieutenant (Platoon Commander) 288. B: 1897. 29 Victory Rd, Cadishead. W: Hilda Harris. E: June 1940. 5 Platoon and later believed to have served with H Company.

HARRIS, Sydney. 371. B: 1917. 29 Nelson Dr, Cadishead. M: Mrs F. Harris. E: 18.07.40. 4 Platoon and later with Transport Platoon. R: 13.11.41.

HARRIS, Sydney J. G11. B: 1900. 40 Princes Ave, Higher Irlam. W: Mrs E. Harris. E: 28.08.40. 4 Platoon. R: 25.04.42.

HARRISON, Fred. 955. B: 1896. Fir St, Cadishead. W: Mrs E. Harrison. E: 30.07.43. R: 25.07.44.

HARRISON, Herbert. Private B39. B: 1922. 22 Poplar Grove, Cadishead. F: J.H. Harrison. E: 03.07.40. 2 Section, 6 Platoon. SD: 03.12.44.

HARRISON, Thomas Claude. B112. B: 1897. 33 Roseneath Rd, Urmston. W: Marion Harrison. E: 27.09.40. 6 Platoon. R: 27.02.42.

HARRISON, Wilfred. Private F22. B: 1898. 65 The Crescent, Higher Irlam. W: Barbara Harrison. E: 10.07.40. 1 (Margarine Works) Section, 4 Platoon and later 2 Platoon. SD: 03.12.44.

HART, Frederick. 224. B: 1917. Hope Cottage, Astley Rd, Irlam. F: Mr Hart. E: 07.06.40. 3 Platoon and later believed to have served with H Company.

HARTLEY, Cyril Frank. Private 839. B: 1912. 60 Harewood Rd, Irlam. W: Mrs A.P. Hartley. E: 31.07.42. 5 Platoon. SD: 03.12.44, HQ Platoon.

HARTLEY, Ronald Johnson. 28 Buckingham Rd, Cadishead. E: 04.02.43. 6 Platoon. T: 04.12.43 to 45th Battalion, Home Guard.

HARTLEY, Wallace. E45. B: 1875. 8 Boundary Rd, Higher Irlam. W: Edith Hartley. E: 26.09.40. 2 Section, 5 Platoon. R: 01.07.42.

HARVEY, Francis Harold. 51. B: 1887. 10 Eldon Rd, Irlam. W: Mrs Harvey. E: 05.06.40. 2 Platoon. R: 21.05.41.

HASLAM, Fred. 366. B: 1911. 14 Kitchener Ave, Cadishead. F: Fred C. Haslam. E: 05.07.40. 5 Platoon and later believed to have served with H Company.

HASLAM, James. Corporal. B: 1881. 175 Glazebrook Lane, Glazebrook. W: Elizabeth Hudson. E: 29.07.40. 2 Section, 6 Platoon. R: 12.02.43.

HAUGHTON, James. 6. B: 1909. 97 New Moss Rd, Cadishead. W: Edna Haughton. E: 25.06.40. 4 Platoon and later believed to have served with H Company.

HAYES, Edmund. 360. B: 1902. 7 Lynton Ave, Cadishead. W: Daisy Hayes. E: July 1940. 4 Platoon. R: 26.11.40.

HAYES, Wilfred. Private. 155. B: 1898. 4 Lynton Ave, Cadishead. W: Florence Hayes. E: 05.06.40. 4 Platoon and later 3 Platoon. R: 08.06.41. Re-enlisted 28.05.42, re-numbered 698, Company HQ. SD: 03.12.44.

HAZELDINE, George. 746. B: 1925. 77 Lord St, Cadishead. F: H. Hazeldine. E: 31.05.42. Later believed to have served with 8 Platoon, H Company.

HAZLEHURST, Brian. B: 1926. 6 Boundary Rd, Higher Irlam. Home Guard messenger (cycle orderly duty), attached Company HQ.

HEATH, Douglas. Private 781. B: 1905. 249 Liverpool Rd, Cadishead. W: Mrs D.M. Heath. E: 13.07.42. 3 Platoon. SD: 03.12.44.

HEATH, Edward James. Lance Corporal 946. B: 1899. 1 Dorset Rd, Cadishead. W: Mrs Heath. E: 29.06.43. 1 Platoon. SD: 03.12.44, 4 Platoon.

HEATON, John. B96. B: 1912. 18 Dean Rd, Cadishead. W: Bertha Heaton. E: 10.08.40. 1 Platoon. HMF: 09.04.41.

HERRICKS, Frank Hubert. Lance Corporal 835. B: 1917. 19 Preston Ave, Irlam. W: Mrs M.A. Herricks. E: 23.07.42. 7 Platoon. SD: 03.12.44.

HERRIDGE, Robert Shaw. 717. B: 1925. 3 Allenby Rd, Cadishead. F: Amos Herridge. E: 20.04.42. Later believed to have served with 8 Platoon, H Company.

HESFORD, Clarence. 39. B: 1901. 19 Lytherton Ave, Cadishead. W: Emily Hesford. E: 05.06.40. 5 Platoon and later believed to have served with H Company. R: date unknown. Re-enlisted 29.06.43, re-numbered 929. R: 05.08.43.

HESFORD, George. F644. B: 1910. 64 The Crescent, Higher Irlam. M: Jane Hesford. E: 30.10.41. 4 Platoon. R: 13.02.42.

HESFORD, Henry. 747. B: 1924. 21 Allotment Rd, Cadishead. M: Mrs Hesford. E: 18.05.42. Believed to have served with 8 Platoon, H Company.

HESFORD, James. Corporal 518. B: 1910. 67 Belgrave Rd, Cadishead and later 1 Boundary Rd, Higher Irlam. W: Annie Hesford. E: 13.02.41. 4 Platoon. SD: 03.12.44, 1 Platoon.

HESFORD, Joseph. E7. B: 1893. 3 Nelson Dr, Cadishead. W: Martha Hesford. E: 03.07.40. 3 Platoon. R: 30.03.43.

HEYES, Austin. Private 925. B: 1900. 43 Silver St, Higher Irlam. S: Miss. K. Heyes of Southport. E: 29.06.43. 4 Platoon. SD: 03.12.44.

HIGGINSON, William Harold. B87. B: 1887. 4 Worthington Ave, Partington. W: Mary Higginson. E: 18.07.40. DMU: 27.08.43.

HIGGS, Alfred. F56. B: 1911. 17 Birch Ave, Cadishead. W: Mrs Higgs. E: 10.07.40. 4 Platoon. HMF: 15.05.41.

HIGHAM, Ernest. Private H4. B: 1913. 31 Allenby Rd, Cadishead. F: J.T. Higham. E: 29.07.40. 2 Section, 6 Platoon. SD: 03.12.44.

HIGSON, Andsel. Private 68. B: 1911. Woodbarn Farm, Irlam. F: Peter Higson. E: 21.09.40. 1 Platoon and later 7 Platoon (HQ) (recorded as Home Guard guides). SD: 03.12.44, HQ Platoon.

HIGSON, Henry. 436. B: 1914. Woodbarn Farm, Irlam. F: Peter Higson. E: 27.07.40. Company HQ (Home Guard Guide). D: 13.01.44.

HILL, Charles. 700. B: 1916. Lords St, Cadishead. W: Mrs E. Hill. E: 14.04.42. Later believed to have served with 8 Platoon, H Company.

Appendix VIII

HILL, George. 121. B: 1908. 12 Liverpool Rd, Cadishead. W: Edna Hill. E: 05.06.40. 5 Platoon and later believed to have served with H Company.
HILL, George William. 188. B: 1923. 1 Etherley Close, Irlam. M: Mrs M. Hill. E: 06.06.40. 2 Platoon. HMF: 30.11.41.
HILL, Gordon. 904. HMF: 31.05.43.
HILL, J.T. Officer. Later believed to have served with G Company.
HILL, John. 543. E: 11.03.43. Later believed to have served with 8 Platoon, H Company.
HILL, Peter Albert. 984. B: 1926. 1 Etherley Close, Irlam. F: W. Hill. E: 23.07.44. 7 Platoon. HMF: 1944.
HILL, Raymond. 635. B: 1907. 19 Marlborough Rd, Higher Irlam. W: Mrs D. Hill. E: 20.10.41. 3 Section, 1 Platoon. T: 12.04.43 to E Company.
HILLYARD, Clifton. 534. B: 1921. 2 Addison Rd, Higher Irlam. F: Walter Hillyard. E: 08.04.41. 2 Platoon. HMF: 24.08.41.
HILTON, John. 416. B: 1914. 45 Marlborough Rd, Higher Irlam. E: 22.07.14. 2 Section, 1 Platoon. HMF: 31.03.43.
HINDLEY, J.A. 975. B: 02.06.26. 4 Lancaster Rd, Cadishead. M: Mrs A. Hindley. E: 22.11.43. 4 Platoon. HMF: 18.04.44.
HINDLEY, Joseph. 264. B: 1921. 7 Poplar Grove, Cadishead. F: J.A. Hindley. E: 06.06.40. 4 Platoon and later 3 Platoon.
HINDLEY, William. Private 770. B: 1908. 12 Tramway Rd, Irlam. W: Margaret Hindley. E: 13.07.42. 5 Platoon. SD: 03.12.44.
HODGES, Thomas Reginald. 618. B: 1924. 8 Hamilton Ave, Cadishead. F: Robert Hodges. E: 06.09.41. Later believed to have served with 8 Platoon, H Company. HMF: date unknown.
HODGSON, Charles. 241. B: 1889. 57 Addison Rd, Higher Irlam. E: 07.06.40. 4 Platoon. R: 16.02.42.
HODGSON, Herbert. 118. B: 1922. 64 Liverpool Rd, Higher Irlam. F: J.J. Hodgson. E: 05.06.40. 2 Platoon. HMF: 14.03.41.
HODGSON, William. Private 863. B: 1914. 5 Windsor Ave, Higher Irlam. W: Mrs L. Hodgson. E: 05.08.42. 7 Platoon. SD: 03.12.44.
HOLLEY, Alfred Hunt. B: 1908. 64 Fiddlers Lane, Higher Irlam. W: Mrs Holley. E: 01.07.40. 3 Platoon later believed to have served with H Company. HMF: date unknown.
HOLMES, Edward John. Corporal 877. B: 1923. 116 Lords St, Cadishead. F: E.J. Holmes. E: 17.08.42. 5 Platoon. SD: 03.12.44.
HOLT, Albert. B101. B: 1884. 15 Prospect Rd, Cadishead. W: Isabella Holt. E: 16.07.40. 6 Platoon. R: 14.02.42.
HOLT, Albert. G48. B: 1889. 222 Liverpool Rd, Irlam. W: Mrs Holt. E: 28.08.40. 4 Platoon.
HOLT, Jack Haydn. 350. B: 1921. 97 New Moss Rd, Cadishead (Further address recorded 75 Belgrave Rd, Cadishead). F: John Holt. E: 02.07.40. Company HQ. R: March 1941.
HOPKINSON, James. Private 983. B: 1893. 56 Nelson Dr, Cadishead. W: Edith May Hopkinson. E: 18.07.40. 3 Section, 3 Platoon in 1942. SD: 03.12.44.
HOPKINSON, John. 541. B: 1924. 1 Dudley Rd, Cadishead. F: J. Hopkinson. E: 04.03.41. Later believed to have served with 8 Platoon, H Company.
HORNBY, John Richard. Private 838. B: 1901. 123 Liverpool Rd, Irlam. W: Mrs A. Hornby. E: 05.08.42. 7 Platoon. SD: 03.12.44.
HOTCHKISS, Harold. Lance Corporal 191. B: 1908. 10 Rivington Grove, Cadishead. W: Phyllis Hotchkiss. E: 06.06.40. 4 Platoon and later 3 Section, 3 Platoon. SD: 03.12.44, HQ Platoon.
HOTCHKISS, John Nelson. Private 799. B: 1905. 9 Rivington Grove, Cadishead. W: Mrs E. Hotchkiss. E: 21.07.42. 3 Platoon. SD: 03.12.44.
HOUGHTON, James. Service no. 6. Lynton Lodge, Cadishead. W: Edna Houghton. E: 25.06.40. HMF: 07.05.41.
HOUGHTON, James. Sergeant 895. 10 Kitchener Ave, Cadishead. W: Mrs E. Houghton. E: 11.09.42. HQ Platoon. SD: 03.12.44.
HOUGHTON, Norman. Private E28. B: 1913. Marlborough Rd, Higher Irlam and later 15 Victoria Rd, Irlam. E: 03.07.40. 2 Section, 5 Platoon in June 1942 and later 2 Platoon. SD: 03.12.44.
HOUGHTON, Robert Mawdsley. Private 945. B: 1900. 5 Boundary Rd, Higher Irlam. M: Mrs A. Houghton. E: 16.07.43. 4 Platoon. SD: 03.12.44.
HOVER, David Norman. 110. B: 1911. 104 Silver St, Higher Irlam. F: Mr Hover. E: 05.06.40. 1 Platoon. R: 14.10.41.
HOWARTH, George. Private 830. B: 1902. 23 Allotment Rd, Cadishead. W: Mrs L. Howarth. E: 23.07.42. 5 Platoon. SD: 03.12.44, Company HQ.

Page 1480

HOWARTH, John. Lance Corporal 584. 11 Dean Rd, Cadishead. W: Josephine Howarth. E: 20.06.41. 3 Platoon. SD: 03.12.44.

HOWARTH, Percy. Private 503. B: 1910. 71 Ferry Rd, Irlam. W: Lily Howarth. E: 16.01.41. 3 Section, 2 Platoon. SD: 03.12.44.

HOWARTH, Ronald. 441. B: 1903. 15 Moss Lane, Cadishead. E: 06.08.40. 4 Platoon and later 3 Platoon. R: 19.11.40.

HOYES, Harry. Private F19. B: 1894. 34 Elsinore Ave, Irlam. W: Beatrice Mary Hoyes. E: 10.07.40. 1 (Margarine Works) Section, 4 Platoon and later 7 Platoon. SD: 03.12.44.

HUDSON, Arthur. Private 472. B: 1898. 3 Dixon St, Irlam. W: Letitia W. Hudson. E: 27.09.40. June 1942 with 1 Section, 7 Platoon (HQ). Transport Platoon. SD: 03.12.44, HQ Platoon.

HUDSON, George. B52. 24 Lawrence Rd, Flixton. W: Clara Hudson. E: 03.07.40. 6 Platoon. Missing believed drowned.

HUDSON, Leslie. E8. B: 1913. 20 Allenby Rd, Cadishead. W: Mary Hudson. E: 03.07.40. 5 Platoon. R: 12.10.41.

HUGHES, Albert. Sergeant 177. B: 1923. 45A Hayes Rd, Cadishead. F: Frederick K. Hughes. E: 06.06.40. 1 (Margarine) Section, 4 Platoon and later 3 Platoon. HMF: 17.07.41.

HUGHES, Albert. Lieutenant F50. B: 1897. 9 Oak Ave, Cadishead. W: Martha Hughes. E: 10.07.40. 4 Platoon. SD: 03.12.44, Company HQ.

HUGHES, Ernest. Private 772. B: 1904. 38 Lords St, Cadishead. W: Agnus Hughes. E: 13.07.42. 5 Platoon. SD: 03.12.44.

HUGHES, Frank William. 774. B: 1907. 1 Lyndhurst Ave, Higher Irlam. W: Mrs E. Hughes. E: 13.07.42. 2 Platoon. R: 12.06.44.

HUGHES, Herbert. Private 703. B: 1901. 46 Princes Ave, Higher Irlam. W: Mrs E. Hughes. E: 15.04.42. 1 Section, 1 Platoon. SD: 03.12.44.

HUGHES, John Hamer. Lieutenant 403. B: 1896. Fairfield, 141 Fir St, Cadishead and later 139 Fir St, Cadishead. W: Winifred Ethel Hughes. E: 16.07.40. 4 Platoon. June 1942, with 3 Platoon. SD: 03.12.44.

HUGHES, Roy. Lieutenant B10. B: 1917. 6 Lytherton Ave, Cadishead. F: Clarence Hughes. E: 26.09.40. 1 Section, 6 Platoon. SD: 03.12.44.

HUGHES, William. Sergeant 272. B: 1911. 11 Moss Lane, Cadishead. W: Mrs Hughes. E: 08.06.40. 4 Platoon. June 1942, with 3 Platoon. SD: 03.12.44.

HULMES, Herbert. Lance Corporal 175. B: 1907. 71 Princes Ave, Higher Irlam. W: Mrs D. Hulmes. E: 06.06.40. 1 Section, 1 Platoon. SD: 03.12.44.

HUMPHREYS, Eric. B49. B: 1914. 17 Moss Lane, Cadishead. W: Matilda Humphreys. E: 01.07.40. 6 Platoon. HMF: 28.02.41.

HUNT, B. Private. In June 1942 he was serving with 1 (Soap Works) Section, 4 Platoon.

HUNT, Charles Edward. Private F28. B: 1886. 28 Silver St, Higher Irlam. W: Amy Hunt. E: 10.07.40. 1 (Margarine Works), 4 Platoon. R: 18.12.42.

HUNT, Kenneth Edward. 235. B: 1921. Only son of Mr and Mrs Hunt of 28 Silver St, Higher Irlam. E: 07.06.40. 1 Platoon. HMF: 19.01.41.

HUNT, Samuel Baden Powell. F49. B: 1900 (registered at Prescott). 38 Lyndhurst Ave, Higher Irlam. B: Walter Hunt. E: 23.07.40. 1 (Margarine Works) Section, 4 Platoon. HMF: 31.10.42.

HUNTER, Joseph. E596. B: 1891. 477 Warrington Rd, Glazebury. W: Mary Hunter. E: 06.08.41. T: 03.10.41 to 79th (Newton-le-Willows) Battalion, Home Guard.

HURST, David Henry. Private F21. B: 1898. 6 Charles St, Cadishead. W: Mrs M. Hurst. E: 10.07.40. 4 Platoon. R: 25.04.41. Re-enlisted 24.09.43, re-numbered 966. 4 Platoon. SD: 03.12.44.

HURST, Roger. Private B67. B: 1884. 19 Leyland Ave, Higher Irlam. W: Mabel Christina Hurst. E: 04.07.40. 1 Section, 6 Platoon. R: 28.03.43.

HURST, Sydney. Sergeant 780. B: 1906. 370 Liverpool Rd, Irlam. W: Mrs Hurst. E: 13.07.40. 5 Platoon. SD: 03.12.44.

HURST, Thomas J. B76. B: 1888. 125 Parrin Lane, Monton. W: Patience Hurst. E: 02.07.40. 6 Platoon. R: 18.02.42.

HUSSEY, Harry. Private B88. B: 1898. Resided in Carrington and later 387 Washway Rd, Sale. W: Margaret Hussey. E: 18.07.40. 1 Section, 6 Platoon. SD: 03.12.44.

HUSSEY, James. F53. B: 1897. 69 Goldsworthy Rd, Flixton. W: Mrs J. Hussey. E: 23.07.40. 4 Platoon.

HUTCHINGS, George. Private 768. B: 1911. Delamere, Kenmore Grove, Cadishead. E: 10.07.40. 7 Platoon and later 5 Platoon. SD: 03.12.44.

HUTCHINGS, Victor James. 463. B: 1920. Rosebank, New Moss Rd, Cadishead. E: 19.09.40. 5 Platoon and later believed to have served with H Company.

HYLAND, John. 801. B: 1920. 14 Vicarage Rd, Irlam. W: Mrs R. Hyland. E: 09.07.42. 7 Platoon. T: 05.08.43 to E Company. Roll also records transferred to ROF [Royal Ordnance Factory] Home Guard.

IMESON, Arthur. 894. 8 Prospect Ave, Cadishead. G: Mrs Trownson of 19 Fir St, Cadishead. E: 08.09.42. 7 Platoon. HMF: 31.03.43.

INTIN, Sydney. B24. B: 1922. 3 Dean Rd, Cadishead. W: Mary Powel Intin. E: 16.09.40. 6 Platoon. HMF: 1941.

IZZARD, George. Private 284. B: 1918. 20 Princes Ave, Higher Irlam. M: Mrs Izzard. E: 06.06.40. 1 Platoon, later with 2 Section, 7 Platoon (HQ). Recorded as part of the Home Guard guides. R: 19.08.42.

JACKMAN, Harry. 624. B: 1922. 90 Dover St, Crumpsall. F: J.H. Jackman. E: 07.07.40. HMF: 06.11.41.

JACKMAN, Henry. Private 504. B: 1918. 5 Dixon St, Irlam. M: Mrs E. Jackman. E: 22.01.41. 3 Section, 1 Platoon. SD: 03.12.44.

JACKSON, Frank. 578. B: 1923. 27 Carlton Way, Glazebrook. M: Mrs Jackson. E: 27.05.41. 8 Platoon and later believed to have served with H Company. HMF: date unknown.

JACKSON, James. 43. B: 1889. The Hut, Lord St, Cadishead. E: 05.06.40. 5 Platoon and later believed to have served with H Company.

JACKSON, Joseph. 947. B: 1898. 77 Dixon St, Irlam. W: Mrs Jackson. E: 16.07.43. R: 27.08.43.

JACKSON, Robert. 344. 34 Silverdale Ave, Higher Irlam. E: 1940. R: 03.11.40. 1 Platoon.

JACKSON, Robert. 380. B: 1920. 366 Liverpool Rd, Irlam. F: Thomas Jackson. E: 22.08.40. 2 Platoon. HMF: 01.04.41.

JACKSON, Sydney. F30. B: 1894. 37 Fiddlers Lane, Higher Irlam. W: Mrs Jackson. E: 11.07.40. 4 Platoon. R: 25.05.41.

JACKSON, Thomas. 144. B: 1890. 366 Liverpool Rd, Irlam. W: Mrs A. Jackson. E: 27.06.40. 2 Platoon. R: 24.03.42.

JACKSON, Walter Charles. 447. B: 1915. 1 Ferryhill Rd, Irlam. W: Edna Jackson. E: 28.08.40. 2 Platoon. Discharged 31.03.42.

JAMES, Ernest James. 299. B: 1912. 12 Haig Ave, Cadishead. E: 14.06.40. 5 Platoon and later believed to have served with H Company.

JAMES, Wilfred. 2nd Lieutenant 80. 24 Moss Side Rd, Cadishead. W: Mrs A.I. James. E: 05.06.40. 4 Platoon. June 1942, with 1 Section, 7 Platoon (HQ). HMF: 31.08.42.

JAQUES, James Thornley. Private 819. B: 1902. 54 Marlborough Rd, Higher Irlam. W: Mrs A. Jaques. E: 22.07.42. 7 Platoon. SD: 03.12.44.

JAQUES, Ronald Thornley. 473. B: 1923. 6 Silver St, Higher Irlam. E: 25.09.40. 2 Platoon. HMF: 06.01.42.

JEFFREY, Horace. 240. B: 1898. 16 Kenmore Grove, Cadishead. W: Millicent Jeffrey. E: 06.06.40. 4 Platoon and later 3 Platoon. R: 14.10.41.

JEFFS, Victor. 556. B: 1923. 16 Lytherton Ave, Cadishead. F: G. Jeffs. E: 30.04.41. 8 Platoon and HQ Platoon.

JENKINS, John Trevor. 536. B: 1924. 12 Francis Rd, Irlam. E: 07.04.41. 4 Platoon and HQ Platoon. HMF: date unknown.

JOHNSON, Andrew. 927. B: 1924. 52 Liverpool Rd, Higher Irlam. F: A. Johnson. E: 29.06.43. Discharged 03.08.43.

JOHNSON, Eric. Private 853. B: 1922. 175 Liverpool Rd, Cadishead. F: B. Johnson. E: 05.08.42. 7 Platoon and later HG Cadets. SD: 03.12.44, HQ Platoon.

JOHNSON, Ernest. 821. B: 1904. 6 Eldon Rd East, Irlam. W: Mrs A. Johnson. 2 Platoon.

JOHNSON, Ernest. Private 385. B: 1904. 6 Eldon Rd, Irlam. E: 15.07.40. 2 Platoon. R: 09.09.41. Re-enlisted, date unknown, into D Company. SD: 03.12.44, 2 Platoon.

JOHNSON, Frank. 597. B: 06.02.14. 5 Gerrards Close, Irlam. W: Sarah Johnson. E: 06.08.41. 2 Section, 2 Platoon. T: 21.02.44 to Home Guard Anti-Aircraft.

JOHNSON, Geoffrey. 671. B: 1924. 175 Liverpool Rd, Cadishead. F: Mr Johnson. 8 Platoon and later HQ Platoon.

JOHNSON, Gilbert Denis. 104. B: 1922. 557 Liverpool Rd, Irlam. F: Isaac Johnson. E: 05.06.40. 3 Platoon and later believed to have served with H Company. HMF: 29.11.40.

JOHNSON, James. 476. B: 1913. 37 Lyndhurst Ave, Higher Irlam. M: Mrs Johnson. E: 07.10.40. 1 Section, 1 Platoon. T: 29.11.41 to Risley Royal Ordnance Factory.

JOHNSON, James. Private 880. 10 Vicarage Rd, Irlam. B: 1910. W: Mrs E. Johnson. E: 10.10.42. 5 Platoon, and later 7 Platoon. SD: 03.12.44.

JOHNSON, John. Private 429. B: 1906. 27 Princes Ave, Higher Irlam. W: Isabella Johnson. E: 26.07.40. 1 Platoon. SD: 03.12.44.

JOHNSON, John. B54. B: 1902. 16 Lytherton Ave, Cadishead. W: Mrs Johnson. E: 30.09.40. 6 Platoon. R: 14.02.42.

JOHNSON, Joseph R. 220. B: 1910. 12 Vicarage Rd, Irlam later 4 Mond Rd, Higher Irlam. W: Annie Johnson. E: 06.06.40. 3 Section, 2 Platoon. SD: 03.12.44. May have later served with HMF.

JOHNSON, Norman. Sergeant 428. B: 1923. 28 Fiddlers Lane, Higher Irlam. M: Mrs Johnson. E: 25.07.40. June 1942, private with 3 Section, 1 Platoon. SD: 03.12.44, HQ Platoon.

JOHNSON, Sam Charles. 962. B: 1893. 23 Windsor Ave, Flixton. W: Mrs A. Johnson. E: 02.11.40. 4 Platoon. T: 15.12.41 to 44th Battalion, Home Guard.

JONES, Eric. 166. B: 1922. 336 Liverpool Rd, Irlam. E: 18.07.40. 3 Platoon and later believed to have served with H Company.

JONES, Fred. 375. B: 1892. 26 Lord St, Cadishead. W: Mrs E.K. Jones. E: 15.07.40. 5 Platoon and later believed to have served with H Company.

JONES, George. 924. B: 1902. 23 Milton Ave, Irlam. W: Mrs E. Jones. E: 25.05.43. 3 Platoon. R: 25.05.44.

JONES, George William. Private F42. B: 1884. 30 Cannon St, Patricroft. E: 10.07.40. 1 (Margarine Works) Section, 4 Platoon and later 1 Platoon. R: 22.08.43.

JONES, Herbert Ivor. Sergeant 242. B: 1893. 51 Boundary Rd, Higher Irlam. W: Gertrude Jones. E: 06.06.40. 1 Section, 7 Platoon (HQ) in June 1942. R: 12.06.44.

JONES, John William. Corporal 203. B: 1921. 336 Liverpool Rd, Irlam. F: John Henry Jones. E: 06.06.40. 3 Platoon and later 5 Platoon. SD: 03.12.44.

JONES, Joseph. 687. B: 1925. 55 Dean Rd, Cadishead. F: Joseph Jones. 8, and later HQ Platoon.

JONES, Norman. 938. B: 1922. 3 Gladstone Rd, Urmston. E: 22.08.40. R: 1941 (albeit there is a N. Jones serving with 2 Section, 2 Platoon in June 1942).

JONES, William. 929. 6 Devon Rd, Cadishead. 4 Platoon. R: 02.03.42.

JONES, William Herbert. 885. B: 1900. 54 Allotment Rd, Cadishead. B: Edward Jones. S: Ethel H. Jones. E: 31.08.42. 7 Platoon. R: 08.06.43.

JONES, William Norman. 351. B: 1922. 60 Marlborough Rd, Higher Irlam. W: Mrs H. Jones. E: 02.07.40. 1 Platoon. T: 04.12.43 to 44th Battalion, Home Guard.

JONES, William Trevor. Private 940. 63 Boundary Rd, Higher Irlam. W: Mrs E.J. Jones. E: 16.07.43. 4 Platoon. SD: 03.12.44.

JORDAN, Albert. 498. B: 1922. 12 Hampton Rd, Cadishead. M: Mrs A. Jordan. E: 29.12.40. 4 Platoon and later 3 Section, 3 Platoon. HMF: 01.12.43.

JORDAN, Julian. Private F607. B: 22.06.95. 67 Princes Ave, Higher Irlam. W: Bertha Jordan. E: 13.08.41. 1 (Margarine Works) Section, 4 Platoon and later 1 Platoon. DMU: 1944.

JORDAN, Royal James. Corporal 287. B: 1901. 23 Laburnum Rd, Cadishead. W: Emily Jordan. E: 10.06.40. 4 Platoon in 1942 and later 3 Section, 3 Platoon. SD: 03.12.44.

JOSH, Bernard. 430. B: 1892. 26 Addison Rd, Higher Irlam. W: Beatrice A. Josh. E: 26.07.40. 1 Platoon. R: 19.12.43.

KEAVENEY, Frank. 529. B: 1921. 5 Baines Ave, Irlam. F: P. Keaveney. E: 27.02.41. 3 Platoon and later believed to have served with H Company. HMF: 20.08.41.

KEIGHLEY, Harold. 318. B: 1903. 1 Annable Rd, Irlam. W: Mrs L. Keighley. E: 22.06.40. 3 Platoon and later believed to have served with H Company.

KELL, Archer Holmes. Private 381. B: 1895. 13 Poplar Grove, Cadishead. E: 10.07.40. 4 Platoon and later 2 Section, 3 Platoon. SD: 03.12.44.

KENNEDY, Edgar. B20. B: 1910. 32 Cliftonville Rd, Woolston. E: 01.07.40. 6 Platoon. R: 28.08.41.

KENNEDY, John. Private 633. B: 1912. 44 Lyndhurst Ave, Higher Irlam. W: Elsie M. Kennedy. E: 20.10.41. 1 Section, 2 Platoon. T: 17.06.43 to A Company, 42nd Battalion.

KENNEDY, Norman. 27. B: 1920. 44 Lyndhurst Ave, Higher Irlam. E: 30.06.40. 2 Platoon. R: 11.12.40.

KENNEDY, Robert William. Private. B: 1902. 71 Marlborough Rd, Higher Irlam. W: Mrs M. Kennedy. E: 09.07.42. 7 Platoon. SD: 03.12.44.

KENYON, Maurice. Private 879. B: 1915. 8 Woodbine Ave, Cadishead and later 28 Caroline St, Irlam. E: 17.08.42. 7 Platoon and later 5 Platoon. SD: 03.12.44.

KERSHAW, Daniel Robert. Private 949. B: 1898. 2 Leyland Ave, Higher Irlam. F: R. Kershaw. E: 28.08.40. 2 (Soap Works) Section, 4 Platoon later served 2 Platoon. SD: 03.12.44.

KEWSTEAD, John. 343. B: 1911. 259 Liverpool Rd, Cadishead. M: Ann Kewstead. E: 01.07.40. Company HQ.

KILLON, Harry. 542. B: 1924. 14 Hamilton Ave, Cadishead. E: 04.03.41. Believed to have served with 8 Platoon, H Company. HMF: date unknown.

KILNER, James. B13. B: 1890. 159 Walkden Rd, Worsley. B: Albert Edward Kilner. E: 26.09.40. 6 Platoon. T: 31.08.41 to 44th Battalion, Home Guard.

KING, George. Private 743. B: 1914. 34 Princes Ave, Higher Irlam, later 40 Buckingham Rd, Cadishead. M: Mrs E. King. 3 Section, 1 Platoon. T: date unknown to G Company. T: date unknown to D Company. SD: 03.12.44, 1 Platoon, D Company.

KING, Harry. Lance Corporal 410. B: 1919. 72 Fir St, Cadishead. E: 19.07.40. 4 Platoon and later 3 Section, 3 Platoon. SD: 03.12.44.

KING, Herbert Leslie. Private E10. B: 1902. 72 Lords St, Cadishead. W: Lily King. E: 03.07.40. 6 Platoon. June 1942, with 1 Section, 5 Platoon. DMU: 15.06.43.

KIRK, Frank. Private 752. B: 1909. 62 Marlborough Rd, Higher Irlam. W: Mrs Kirk. E: 16.06.42. 1 Platoon. SD: 03.12.44.

KIRKHAM, Joseph P. Lance Corporal 777. B: 1905. 8 Francis Rd, Irlam. W: Mrs E.D. Kirkham. E: 13.07.42. 5 Platoon. SD: 03.12.44.

KITCHEN, Harry. B: 1904. 23 Harewood Rd, Irlam. M: Mrs F.E. Kitchen of Wythenshawe. E: 23.07.42. R: 15.08.44.

KITCHEN, William. 826. B: 1904. 5 Bradburn Rd, Irlam. B: A. Kitchen of 5 Lewis St, Patricroft. E: 22.07.42. 5 Platoon. SD: 03.12.44.

KNIBBS, Harry. 954. B: 1895. 22 Dean Rd, Cadishead. E: 30.07.42. DMU: 19.01.44.

KREIBICH, Julius L. 47. B: 1923. 11 Victory Rd, Cadishead. 3 Platoon. F: Julius W. Kreibich. E: 04.10.40. R: 08.10.41. HMF: date unknown.

KREIBICH, Julius Wilfred. Lieutenant 509. B: 1891. 11 Victory Rd, Cadishead. W: Gladys May Kreibich. E: 22.07.40. 4 Platoon and later platoon commander, 3 Platoon. SD: 03.12.44.

LACEY, E. Corporal. 201 Liverpool Rd, Irlam. 2 Section, 6 Platoon. SD: 03.12.44.

LAMB, J. William. B16. B: 1894. Resided Partington. E: 05.07.40. 6 Platoon.

LARGE, Harold. Private 971. B: 1914. 18 Lytherton Ave, Cadishead and later 17 Caroline St, Irlam. W: Marie Large. E: 02.11.40. 2 (Soap Works) Section, 4 Platoon and later 6 Platoon. SD: 03.12.44.

LATHAM, J. Winstanley. E30. B: 1881. 2 Bradburn Rd, Irlam. W: Bertha Latham. E: 03.07.40. 2 Section, 5 Platoon in June 1942. Discharged 05.08.42.

LAVERTY, Kenneth. 603. B: 1923. 24 Addison Rd, Higher Irlam. F: Mr Laverty. E: 06.08.41. Later believed to have served with 4 Platoon, H Company.

LAWFORD, John Walters. Private 232. B: 1897. 41 Princes Ave, Higher Irlam. W: Mrs Lawford. E: 07.06.40. 1 Section, 1 Platoon. SD: 03.12.44.

LAWFORD, Norman. Private B605. 34 Lynthorpe Ave, Cadishead. F: Frank Lawford. E: 06.08.41. 2 Section, 6 Platoon.

LAWFORD, Reginald. Private 176. B: 1911. 20 Boundary Rd, Higher Irlam. W: Harriet Lawford. E: 06.06.40. 1 Platoon. SD: 03.12.44.

LAWRINSON, George William. 585. B: 1922. 16 Nelson Dr, Cadishead. F: E. Lawrinson. E: 04.06.41. 3 Platoon. HMF: 05.08.41.

LAWSON, Hugh. Private 867. B: 1903. 222 Liverpool Rd, Cadishead. W: Mrs D. Lawson. E: 10.08.42. 3 Platoon. SD: 03.12.44.

LAWTON, Arnold. Private 938. B: 11.04.12. 1 Hartley Grove, Higher Irlam. W: Mrs Lawton. E: 16.07.43. 4 Platoon. SD: 03.12.44.

LAWTON, N. Private. 34 Lynthorpe Ave, Cadishead. 6 Platoon. SD: 03.12.44.

LAWTON, Tom. Sergeant 426. B: 1910. 11 Hartley Grove, Higher Irlam. W: Mary Lawton. E: 25.07.40. 3 Section, 1 Platoon. SD: 03.12.44.

LEA, Norman. 32. B: 1902. 5 Beech Ave, Higher Irlam. W: Catherine Lea. E: 05.06.40. 3 Section, 2 Platoon. T: 20.07.44 to G Company.

LEACH, Henry. B89. B: 1898. 7 Bucklow Ave, Partington. W: Florence M. Leach. E: 18.07.40. 6 Platoon. R: 14.02.42.

LEATHER, Thomas. Corporal F2. 147 Rush Green, Lymm. W: Marjorie Leather. E: 13.08.40. 1 (Margarine Works) Section 4 Platoon and later 5 Platoon.

LEE, George. Private 776. B: 1907. 40 Francis Rd, Irlam. E: 13.07.42. 3 Platoon. SD: 03.12.44.

LEE, William. Reverend. Private 745. B: 1887. The Vicarage, Irlam. W: Mrs Pearson Lee (address given as Avondale, Manchester Rd, Thornham). E: 30.05.42. 7 Platoon. SD: 03.12.44, HQ Platoon.

LEGGETT, Charles W. 606. B: 1924. 47 Silverdale Ave, Higher Irlam. F: William Leggett. E: 07.08.41. 1 Platoon. R: 11.02.42.

LENNIE, Francis Norman. 306. B: 1918. 82 Liverpool Rd, Cadishead. F: Albert E. Lennie. E: 06.06.40. 4 Platoon and later 3 Platoon. HMF: 05.03.41.

LEVER, John. 437. B: 1914. 6 Leyland Ave, Higher Irlam. W: Isabella Lever. E: 23.07.40. Transport Platoon. R: 24.08.41. Re-enlisted 23.11.41, re-numbered Lance Corporal 649. 1 Platoon, Transport Platoon and in June 1942 with 1 Section, 7 Platoon (HQ). SD: 03.12.44, 1 Platoon.

LEWIS, David Eric. Lance Corporal B8. B: 1912. 192A Liverpool Rd, Cadishead. W: Irene Lewis. E: 09.07.40. June 1942, with 1 Section, 6 Platoon. HMF: 30.12.42.

LEWIS, Francis. 765. B: 1913. 679 Liverpool Rd, Irlam. F: John Lewis. E: 10.07.42. 7 Platoon and later 5 Platoon. DMU: 20.04.44.

LEWIS, Thomas. 387. B: 1916. 679 Liverpool Rd, Irlam. F: John Lewis. E: 15.07.40. 3 Platoon and later believed to have served with H Company.

LIFE, Edward William Norman. Corporal 704. B: 1914. 11 Lyndhurst Ave, Higher Irlam. W: Mrs Life. E: 15.04.42. 1 Section, 1 Platoon. SD: 03.12.44.

LILLEY, Gracchus Peter. Sergeant 88. B: 1904. 86 Eldon Rd, Irlam. W: Annie Lilley. E: 05.06.40. 2 Section, 2 Platoon. SD: 03.12.44, company sergeant major, Company HQ.

LISTER, Frank. Private 688. B: 1896. 6 Stuart Ave, Irlam. W: Mrs Lister. E: 09.04.12. 1 Section, 2 Platoon. SD: 03.12.44.

LITCHFIELD, Albert Edward. 119. B: 915. 88 Fir St, Cadishead. M: Maud Litchfield. E: 05.06.40. 5 Platoon and later believed to have served with H Company.

LITTLER, Joseph. 487. B: 1923. 28 Caroline St, Irlam. F: J. Littler. E: 29.10.40. 3 Platoon and later believed to have served with H Company.

LLOYD, J. Edward. B59. B: 1894. 13 Allotment Rd, Cadishead. W: Mrs J.E. Lloyd. E: 04.07.40. R: 23.02.42.

LLOYD, Joseph. Private B21. B: 1905. 4 Hastings Ave, Flixton. W: Eveline Lloyd. E: 03.07.40. 2 Section, 6 Platoon. SD: 03.12.44.

LLOYD, William H. 370. B: 1921. 9 The Vista, Cadishead. F: William H. Lloyd. E: 07.07.40. 5 Platoon and later believed to have served with H Company. HMF: date unknown.

LOFTUS, Kenneth. 572. B: 1923. 239 Liverpool Rd, Irlam. F: H.J. Loftus. E: 27.07.41. Later believed to have served with 4 Platoon, H Company.

LOMAS, Cyril. 36. B: 1921. 85 Lyndhurst Ave, Higher Irlam. F: Arthur Lomas. E: 05.06.40. 2 Platoon. HMF: 24.08.41.

LONGBOTTOM, William Alan. 357. B: 1915. 74 Baines Ave, Irlam and later 22 Chestnut Ave, Cadishead. W: Mrs Longbottom. E: July 1940. 4 Platoon and later with Transport Platoon. R: 24.08.41.

LORD, Herbert. Private E11. B: 1885. 5 Allotment Rd, Cadishead. W: Phoebe Emma Lord. E: 03.07.40. June 1942, with 1 Section, 5 Platoon and later served 7 Platoon. R: 04.06.43.

LOVELL, Ernest W. 257. B: 1891. Springfield, Springfield Lane, Irlam. W: Alice Lovell. E: 06.06.40. 2 Platoon. T: 04.11.40 to G Company.

LOWE, Eric. 676. B: 1924. 28 Allenby Rd, Cadishead. F: William Lowe. Later believed to have served with 8 Platoon, H Company.

LOWE, Harold. 186. B: 1923. 28 Allenby Rd, Cadishead. M: Mrs Lowe. E: 12.08.40. 5 Platoon and later believed to have served with H Company.

LOWE, J. James. Private B90. B: 1916. 28 Allenby Rd, Cadishead and later 6 Green Lane, Cadishead. F: William Lowe. E: 19.07.40. 1 Section, 6 Platoon. SD: 03.12.44, HQ Platoon.

LOWE, Thomas (Junior). 253. B: 1918. 16 Kitchener Ave, Cadishead. F: Thomas Lowe. E: 06.06.40. 5 Platoon and later believed to have served with H Company.

LOWE, William. Sergeant 423. B: 1887. 28 Allenby Rd, Cadishead. E: 24.07.40. in 5 Platoon, 1 Section, 7 Platoon and with HG Cadets. R: 04.09.44.

LOWNDES, David Arthur. 326. B: 1905. 19 Mond Rd, Higher Irlam. W: Gladys Lowndes. E: 01.07.40. 1 Platoon. R: 16.07.41.

LOWNDES, James. Private 531. B: 1923. 42 Fiddlers Lane, Higher Irlam. E: 22.03.41. 1 Section, 1 Platoon. HMF: 04.11.43.

LOWNDES, Samuel. 324. B: 1911. Birch View Farm, Irlam. W: Mrs Lowndes. E: 22.06.40. 2 Section, 2 Platoon. DMU: 18.06.43.

LUCY, Ernest. B53. B: 1908. 201 Liverpool Rd, Irlam. W: Winifred Edith Lucy. E: 03.07.40. 6 Platoon.

LYNCH, William. Private 178. B: 1922. 23 Birch Ave, Cadishead. B: Michael Lynch. E: 06.06.40. 4 Platoon and in June 1942 with 2 Section, 3 Platoon. SD: 03.12.44.

MACE, Arthur N. 713. 20 Lords St, Cadishead. F: George Mace. E: 17.04.42. Later believed to have served with 8 Platoon, H Company.

MACE, Frederick. 515. B: 1924. 23 Liverpool Rd, Cadishead. F: William H. Mace. E: 11.02.41. Transport Platoon. HMF: 17.09.41.

MAHONEY, J. Private F9. B: 1904. 59 Princes Ave, Higher Irlam. E: 11.07.40. W: Mrs H. Mahoney. 1 (Margarine Works) Section, 4 Platoon and later with 2 Platoon. SD: 03.12.44.

MAKINSON, Robert Wilkinson. B74. B: 1905. 1 Wilding St, Barton. W: Lilian Makinson. E: 09.07.40. T: 04.02.42 to A Company, 42nd Battalion.

MALIN, Joseph. 328. B: 1922. 2 Rose Ave, Irlam. F: Joseph Malin. E: 13.06.40. 3 Platoon and later believed to have served with H Company. HMF: date unknown.

MALONE, James. 307. B: 1888. 4 Lynthorpe Ave, Cadishead. W: Mrs P. Malone. E: 07.06.40. 4 Platoon and later 3 Platoon. R: 07.11.42.

MALONEY, H. Private. 1 Section, 2 Platoon (June 1942).

MANN, Sydney. Private 369. B: 1915. 72 The Crescent, Higher Irlam. M: Mrs L. Mann. E: 08.07.40. 1 Section, 1 Platoon. SD: 03.12.44.

MARSHALL, Edward. B574. B: 1924. 488 Manchester Rd, Hollins Green. F: Clarence Marshall. E: 27.05.42. 6 Platoon. T: 24.02.42 to 79th (County of Lancaster) Battalion, Home Guard.

MARSHALL, John Robert. 64. B: 1920. 25 Poplar Grove, Cadishead. F: William Marshall. E: 05.06.40. 4 Platoon and later with 3 Platoon. HMF: 31.05.41.

MARSHALL, Roy. 497. B: 1923. 290 Liverpool Rd, Irlam. F: William H.J. Marshall. E: 31.12.41. 1 Platoon. R: 02.03.42. HMF: date unknown.

MARSHALL, Thomas. 183. B: 1921. 9 Princes Ave, Higher Irlam. F: William H.J. Marshall. E: 06.06.40. 1 Platoon. HMF: 24.08.41.

MARTON, Harold W. 469. B: 1917. 70 Lynthorpe Ave, Cadishead. F: Oswald Marton. E: 22.07.40. 4 Platoon and later with 3 Platoon. R: 04.12.41.

MASSEY, David. Private 265. B: 1908. 90 Lord St, Cadishead. W: Elizabeth Massey. E: 06.06.40. 5 Platoon. SD: 03.12.44.

MASSEY, Nicholas. 452. B: 1902. 3 The Vista, Cadishead. W: Edith M. Massey. E: 05.09.40. 5 Platoon and later believed to have served with H Company.

MASSEY, Richard. Private B102. B: 1905. 76 Lord St, Cadishead. W: Amelia Massey. E: 01.10.40. 1 Section, 6 Platoon. SD: 03.12.44.

MASSEY, Thomas George. B71. B: 1898. 30 Tootal Rd, Weaste. E: 05.07.40. 6 Platoon. R: 18.02.42.

MASSEY, Willam Hampson. 162. B: 1907. 9 Lytherton Ave, Cadishead. W: Mrs Massey. E: 06.06.40. 5 Platoon and later believed to have served with H Company.

MATTHEWS, Arnold. Private 274. B: 1920. 44 The Crescent, Irlam. F: Frank Matthews. E: 06.06.40. 1 Section, 1 Platoon. Discharged 05.08.42.

MATTOCK, William. Private 427. B: 1893. 30 Fiddlers Lane, Higher Irlam. B: J. Mattock. E: 27.07.40. 2 Section, 1 Platoon. SD: 03.12.44.

McARTHUR, David. 379. B: 1882. 20 Marlborough Rd, Irlam. W: Phoebe McArthur. E: 14.07.40. 1 Platoon. R: 16.07.41.

McARTHUR, Walter. HMF: date unknown.

McCARTHY, Owen. 521. B: 1922. 6 Baines Ave, Irlam. M: Mary McCarthy. E: 14.02.41. 3 Platoon and later believed to have served with H Company. HMF: date unknown.

McCARTNEY, Leslie. 646. B: 1924. 44, Ferryhill Rd, Irlam. F: Peter McCartney. E: 30.10.40. Later believed to have served with 4 Platoon, H Company.

McCAUGHAY, Archibald. 181. B: 1872. 56 New Moss Rd, Cadishead. E: 06.06.40. 4 Platoon and later 3 Platoon. R: 07.11.40.

McCLOUGHRIE, E. Private. 23 Addison Rd, Higher Irlam. SD: 03.12.44.

McGUIRE, P. Private. 33 Milton Ave, Irlam. 5 Platoon. SD: 03.12.44.

McKAY, Joseph. Private 60. B: 1920. 647 Liverpool Rd, Irlam. F: J. McKay. E: 16.09.40. 3 Platoon and later 2 Section, 6 Platoon. SD: 03.12.44.

McKAY, Joseph. B9. B: 1895. 647 Liverpool Rd, Irlam. W: Ethel McKay. E: 28.06.40. 6 Platoon.

McLEAN, James. 255. B: 1879. 16 Oak Ave, Cadishead. Da: Caroline McLean. E: 06.06.40. 4 Platoon and later with 3 Platoon. R: 07.11.40.

McLEAN, Robert. Private B95. B: 1923. 16 Oak Ave, Cadishead and later Caroline St, Irlam. F: James McLean. E: 31.07.40. 2 Section, 6 Platoon. HMF: 13.06.42.

McMURTRIE, Robert. 140. B: 1908. 18 Graham Crescent, Cadishead. W: Florence McMurtrie (nee Shawcross). E: 05.06.40. 5 Platoon and later believed to have served with H Company.

McNEILL, C. Private. 4 The Vista, Cadishead. 4 Platoon. SD: 03.12.44.

McNULTY, William Sydney. Private 264. B: 1908. 35 Harewood Rd, Irlam. W: Mrs McNulty. 1 Section, 7 Platoon (HQ). R: 21.11.42.

McQUIRK, Frank. 494. B: 1923. 67 Eldon Rd East, Irlam. E: 03.12.40. 2 Platoon. R: 29.09.41. HMF: date unknown.

MELIA, J.J. E48. B: 1917. 67, Langworthy Estate, Salford. F: Alfred Melia. E: 14.10.40. 5 Platoon. R: 30.04.41.

MELLING, Norman Edward. 56. B: 1907. 320 Liverpool Rd, Irlam. F: Edward Melling. E: 05.06.40. HQ Platoon. HMF: 25.09.41.

MELLOR, Alan. 465. B: 1923. 41 Ferry Rd, Irlam. E: 19.09.40. 1 Section, 1 Platoon and later with HQ Platoon. M: Margaret Mellor. HMF: 07.12.43.

MELLOR, Alfred William. Private. B: 1881. 56 Dixon St, Irlam. E: 24.07.40. 5 Platoon and later with 3 Section, 3 Platoon. R: 30.06.43.

MELLOR, Harold. B: 1927. 40 Ferryhill Rd, Irlam. Home Guard messenger.

MELTON, Arthur. 17. B: 1901. 88 Lords St, Cadishead. W: Mrs Melton. E: 30.06.40. 5 Platoon and later believed to have served with H Company.

MELTON, E. Private. 17 Ash Ave, Cadishead. 5 Platoon. SD: 03.12.44.

MELTON, G. Private. 110 Lords St, Cadishead. 6 Platoon. SD: 03.12.44.

MELVILLE, J. E36. B: 1897. 16 Addison Rd, Higher Irlam. E: 03.07.40. 1 Platoon. DMU: date unknown.

MENZIES, Charles. 564. B: 1923. 9 Byng Ave, Cadishead. F: David Menzies. E: 29.05.41. Later believed to have served with 8 Platoon, H Company. HMF: date unknown.

MERRICK, W. Lance Corporal. 230 Liverpool Rd, Cadishead. 5 Platoon. SD: 03.12.44.

MILFORD, Frederick James. 478. B: 1903. 50 Victory Rd, Cadishead. W: Ruth Milford. E: 05.07.40. 5 Platoon and later believed to have served with H Company.

MILLAR, James Hill. 211. B: 1913. 18 Moorfield Rd, Higher Irlam and later 1 Nelson Dr, Cadishead. M: Margaret Millar. E: 02.06.40. 2 Section, 2 Platoon. T: 27.05.43 to 71st Lancashire Home Guard Heavy Artillery Battery.

MILLINGTON, James Albert. 95. B: 1916. 49 Baines Ave, Irlam. F: J. Millington. E: 05.06.40. 3 Platoon and later believed to have served with H Company.

MILLINGTON, Robert. 614. B: 1910. 69 Caroline St, Irlam. W: Mrs R. Millington. E: 26.08.41. Later believed to have served with 4 Platoon, H Company.

MILLINGTON, Thomas. 79. B: 1922. 49 Baines Ave, Irlam. F: J. Millington. E: 05.06.40. 3 Platoon and later believed to have served with H Company.

MILTON, M.J. Private. 33 Fiddlers Lane, Higher Irlam. 7 Platoon. SD: 03.12.44.

MINSHULL, Ernest. 50. Born: 1897. 31 Marlborough Rd, Higher Irlam. W: Alice Minshull. E: 05.06.40. 3 Platoon and later believed to have served with H Company.

MITCHELL, Kenneth S. B.599. B: 10.01.24. 27 Bradburn Rd, Irlam. F: K. Mitchell. E: 06.08.41. 6 Platoon. HMF: 06.04.44.

MITCHELL, K.S. Private. 5 Bradburn Rd, Irlam. 2 Section, 6 Platoon (June 1942). SD: 03.12.44.

MOFFATT, Charles. Captain 636. B: 1894. 590 Liverpool Rd, Irlam. W: Amy Moffatt. E: 20.10.41. June 1942, with 2 Section, 7 Platoon (HQ). SD: 03.12.44, captain, Company HQ.

MOFFATT, J. Lance Corporal. 288 Liverpool Rd, Cadishead. 5 Platoon. SD: 03.12.44.

MOORE, Daniel. 228. B: 1877. 4 Mersey Ave, Irlam. W: Elizabeth Ellen Moore. E: 06.06.40. 3 Platoon and later believed to have served with H Company.

MOORE, Daniel. Lieutenant 34. B: 1897. 11 Gerrards Close, Irlam. W: Mrs S.A. Moore. E: 05.06.40. Platoon Commander, 2 Platoon. SD: 03.12.44.

MOORE, F. Private. Lanes Cottage, Carrington. 4 Platoon. SD: 03.12.44.

MORGAN, Alan. Private 316. B: 1921. Ryefield Farm, New Moss Rd, Cadishead. F: Joseph Morgan. E: 21.06.40. 4 Platoon. June 1942, with 2 Section, 7 Platoon (HQ). SD: 03.12.44, HQ Platoon.

MORGAN, J. Private. 17 Leyland Ave, Higher Irlam. 7 Platoon. SD: 03.12.44.

MORGAN, P.H. Private. The Fallows Farm, Higher Irlam. SD: 03.12.44, HQ Platoon.

MORRIS, C. Private. 67 Fiddlers Lane, Higher Irlam. SD: 03.12.44, HQ Platoon.

MORRIS, David. 106. B: 1915. 26 Caroline St, Irlam. W: Violet Morris. E: 05.06.40. 3 Platoon and later believed to have served with H Company.

MORRIS, Harry. Private 311. Born c.1886. 28 Addison Rd, Higher Irlam. W: Ellen Morris. E: 17.06.40. 1 (Margarine Works) Section, 4 Platoon. R: 24.01.41. Re-enlisted 27.05.41 into D Company, re-numbered F567, 1 Platoon. SD: 03.12.44.

MORRIS, Leslie. Private 320. B: 1909. 27 Silverdale Ave, Higher Irlam. E: 22.06.40. 1 Platoon. R: 31.07.41. Re-enlisted later in the war, 7 Platoon. SD: 03.12.44.

MORRIS, Norman Leslie. Private 174. B: 1911. 73 The Crescent, Higher Irlam. W: Mrs Morris. E: 06.06.40. 2 Section, 1 Platoon. SD: 03.12.44.

MORRIS, Ronald. Private 552. B: 1923. 67 Fiddlers Lane, Higher Irlam. F: Joseph Morris. E: 23.04.41. 3 Section, 1 Platoon. SD: 03.12.44.

MORT, Robert. Private 259. B: 1895. 29 The Crescent, Higher Irlam. W: Mrs D. Mort. E: 07.06.40. 2 Section, 1 Platoon. SD: 03.12.44.

MORT, Stanley. 658. B: 1924. 29 The Crescent, Higher Irlam. F: Robert Mort. E: 15.01.42. Transport Platoon. HMF: 31.03.43.

MORTON, Leonard. B63. B: 1903. 3 Roslyn Ave, Flixton. W: Jessie Morton. E: 04.07.40. 1 Platoon. T: 22.04.42 to 44th (County of Lancaster) Battalion.

MORTON, William Mitchell. 2nd Lieutenant M. 141. B: 1909. Westholme, Astley Rd, Irlam. W: Doris A. Morton. E: 05.06.40. 3 Platoon. June 1942, with 1 Section, 7 Platoon (HQ) and later with Company HQ. Acting platoon commander whilst acting as company collator.

MOSS, Robert. 449. B: 1919. Plant Cottage, Astley Rd, Irlam. M: Rose Plant. E: 30.08.40. 3 Platoon and later believed to have served with H Company.

MOUNFIELD, Thomas. G.593. B: 1897. 6 Mond Rd, Higher Irlam. W: Mrs Mounfield. E: 20.06.41. R: 24.02.42.

MULLINEUX, A.J. Lance Corporal. 27 Chapel Rd, Irlam. 6 Platoon. SD: 03.12.44.

MUNDAY, Roy. B116. B: 1924. 5 Atherton Lane, Cadishead. F: Walter Munday. E: 06.10.40. 6 Platoon. HMF: 05.05.42.

MURPHY, Thomas Herbert. 930. B: 1889. 30 Allenby Rd, Cadishead. W: Mrs Murphy. E: 28.08.40. 4 Platoon.

MURRAY, Patrick. 146. B: 1902. 32 Milton Ave, Irlam. W: Alice Murray. E: 05.06.40. 3 Platoon and later believed to have served with H Company. Discharge accepted 22.04.41.

MURRAY, Vincent. 302. B: 1922. 32 Milton Ave, Irlam. M: A. Murray. E: 05.06.40. 3 Platoon and later believed to have served with H Company. R: 13.02.41.

MUSGRAVE, Christopher. 169. B: 1923. 81 Eldon Rd, Irlam. E: 06.06.40. 2 Platoon. T: 14.05.41 to G Company, 42nd Battalion.

MUSGRAVE, Stanley. Private 431. B: 1907. 103 Eldon Rd West, Irlam. E: 27.07.40. 1 Section, 2 Platoon (June 1942). SD: 03.12.44.

MYLCHREEST, Harry. B110. B: 1888. 10 Pleasant St, Barton. F: Harry Mylchreest. E: 27.09.40. 6 Platoon.

NASH, Ellis George. Private 29. B: 1900. 47 Fiddlers Lane, Higher Irlam, later 10 Princes Ave, Higher Irlam. W: Mrs E.A. Nash. E: 01.07.40. 3 Section, 1 Platoon. SD: 03.12.44.

NELSON, Joseph William. 617. B: 1920. 16 Hamilton Ave, Cadishead. E: 06.09.41. Later believed to have served with 8 Platoon, H Company.

NELSON, Noel. 535. B: 1919. 2 The Crescent, Higher Irlam. E: 28.03.41. 1 Platoon. R: 19.02.42. HMF: date unknown.

NELSON, Robert. 501. B: 1922. 17 Kitchener Ave, Cadishead. F: Mr Nelson. E: 09.11.41. 5 Platoon and later believed to have served with H Company.

NELSON, William. Private B594. B: 1896. 12 Moss Lane, Partington. W: Edith Nelson. E: 20.06.41. 1 Section, 6 Platoon. R: 28.12.42.

NEWMAN, Joseph Philip. 85. B: 1920. 629 Liverpool Rd, Irlam. M: Mary Newman. E: 05.06.40. 3 Platoon and later believed to have served with H Company. HMF: 17.09.41.

NEWSTEAD, John Leslie. Lieutenant 343. B: 1911. 259 Liverpool Rd, Cadishead. E: 01.07.40. 5 Platoon and later a sergeant with 1 Section, 7 Platoon (HQ). SD: 03.12.44, 2 Platoon.

NEWTON, Jack. 573. B: 1923. 20 Fir St, Cadishead. E: 27.05.41. Later believed to have served with 8 Platoon, H Company.

NEYLAN, Andrew. F558. B: 1908. 16 Caroline St, Irlam. W: Ivy Neylan. E: 23.04.41. 4 Platoon. HMF: 06.01.42.

NICHOLS, Herbert. Private 612. B: 1921. 4 Hurst Fold, Higher Irlam. M: Mrs E. Nichols. E: 14.08.41. 1 Section, 1 Platoon. T: 12.01.44 to 71 Lancashire Anti-Aircraft Battalion.

NOLAN, John. Private 986. B: 1915. Ackers Lane, Carrington. B: Wilfred Nolan. E: 16.08.44. 4 Platoon. SD: 03.12.44.

NORCOTT, Leslie W. Private 987. B: 1924. Asphadel Farm, Carrington. F: W. Norcott. E: 29.08.44. 4 Platoon. SD: 03.12.44.

NORFOLK, Robert. Private 802. B: 1914. 39 Moss Lane, Cadishead. W: Mrs V.J. Norfolk. E: 21.07.42. 7 Platoon and later 6 Platoon. SD: 03.12.44.

NORMAN, Eric. Private 694. B: 1910. 21 Springfield Lane, Irlam. E: 22.04.42. 1 Section, 2 Platoon. SD: 03.12.44.

NORTH, Bertie. B40. B: 1900. 60 Caroline St, Irlam. W: Mrs North. E: 05.07.40. 6 Platoon. R: 15.02.42.

NORTH, Ellis. Private E38. B: 1900. 14 Liverpool Rd, Higher Irlam. W: Hilda North. E: 25.07.40. 2 Section, 5 Platoon (June 1942), then 4 Platoon and finally 2 Platoon. SD: 03.12.44.

NORTON, Charles. 338. B: 1906. 8 Haig Ave, Cadishead. W: Mrs Norton. E: 01.07.40. with 5 Platoon and later believed to have served with H Company.

NORTON, Walter. B99. B: 1911. 28 Hayes Rd, Cadishead. W: Mary Norton. E: 03.10.40. 6 Platoon. R: 14.02.42.

Appendix VIII

O'BRIEN, John. F40. B: 1893. 38 Peel St, Eccles. W: Mary O'Brien. E: 10.07.40. 4 Platoon. T: 21.01.42 to E Company, 42nd Battalion, Home Guard.

O'DONNELL, Edward J. B106. B: 1896. 43 Fiddlers Lane, Higher Irlam. W: Florence O'Donnell. E: 03.10.40. 6 Platoon. R: 25.02.42.

O'HARE, Francis. 519. B: 1922. 45 Dean Rd, Cadishead. F: J. O'Hare. E: 14.02.41. 3 Platoon and later believed to have served with H Company.

O'MARA, John. 138. B: 1915. 657A Liverpool Rd, Irlam. W: Maud O'Mara. E: 05.06.40. R: 12.11.40. Re-enlisted 20.11.40. 3 Platoon, 5 Platoon and later believed to have served with H Company.

O'NEILL, William. Private F8. B: 1903. 53 Boundary Rd, Higher Irlam. W: Bertha O'Neill. E: 11.07.40. 4 Platoon. R: 25.04.41. Re-enlisted 10.08.42, re-numbered 872, 7 Platoon. SD: 03.12.44.

O'REILLY, Anthony. 604. B: 1921. 5 Latham Rd, Irlam. F: Anthony O'Reilly. E: 06.08.41. 4 Platoon and later believed to have served with H Company.

OATES, John E. 493. B: 1923. 68 Ferry Rd, Irlam. M: Mrs K. Oates. E: 1940. Transport Platoon. R: 16.07.44.

OCCLESTON, Frederick. 931. B: 1910. 50 Hayes Rd, Cadishead. M: Mrs A. Occleston. E: 28.08.40. 4 Platoon. HMF: 22.11.41.

OCCLESTON, Harry. B41. B: 1897. 31 Hayes Rd, Cadishead. W: Matilda Occleston. E: 05.07.40. 6 Platoon. R: 11.02.42.

OCCLESTON, John. 746. B: 1924. 31 Hayes Rd, Cadishead. F: H. Occleston. E: 18.05.42. Later believed to have served with 8 Platoon, H Company.

OGDEN, Albert Edward. 331. B: 1904. 9 Silver St, Higher Irlam. E: 01.07.40. 1 Platoon. HMF: 17.03.41. Next of kin: William Odgen (father).

OGDEN, Francis. F11. 242 Liverpool Rd, Irlam. W: Mrs Ogden. E: 1940. 4 Platoon. R: 18.04.41.

OGDEN, George. Company Sergeant Major 301. B: 1896. 65 Lancaster Rd, Cadishead. W: Eliza A. Ogden. E: 15.06.40. June 1942, with 7 Platoon (HQ). R: 12.06.44.

OGDEN, Kenneth. 665. B: 1924. 3 Poplar Grove, Cadishead. F: Fred Owen. Later believed to have served with 8 Platoon, H Company.

ONIONS, Charles John. 72. B: 1907. 12 Lyndhurst Ave, Higher Irlam. W: Elizabeth Ann Onions. E: 05.06.40. 1 Platoon. R: 16.07.41.

OWEN, Alfred. 814. B: 02.03.12. 27 Nelson Dr, Cadishead. B: Mr W. Owen. E: 21.07.42. 3 Platoon. HMF: 06.01.44.

OWEN, Arthur. 190 (later M 115.398). B: 1906. 21 Fir St, Cadishead. W: Dorothy Owen. E: 06.06.40. 4 Platoon and later Company HQ as Liaison Officer. HMF: 09.01.42.

OWEN, Bertie. Private 836. B: 1902. 45 Boundary Rd, Higher Irlam. W: Mrs F.M. Owen. E: July 1942. 7 Platoon. SD: 03.12.44.

OWEN, Ernest. 28. B: 1911. 47 Harewood Rd, Irlam. W: Mrs E. Owen. E: 30.06.40. 2 Platoon and later Transport Platoon. June 1942, with 2 Section, 7 Platoon (HQ). SD: 03.12.44, HQ Platoon.

OWEN, Henry. 871. B: 1904. 10 Silver St, Higher Irlam. E: 10.08.42. R: 23.12.42.

OWEN, John. B6. B: 1902. 17 Harewood Rd, Irlam. W: Anne Owen. E: 16.09.40. R: 17.02.42.

PACKER, Lewis. 109. B: 1897. 24 Milton Ave, Irlam. W: Lilian Parker. E: 05.06.40. 3 Platoon and later believed to have served with H Company.

PARKER, Fred. 208. B: 1912. 555 Liverpool Rd, Irlam. F: J. Parker. E: 07.06.40. 3 Platoon and later believed to have served with H Company.

PARKER, Robert. 445. B: 1910. 555 Liverpool Rd, Irlam. E: 26.08.40. 3 Platoon and later believed to have served with H Company. R: 11.12.42.

PARKINSON, Joseph William. Private 185. B: 1910. 38 The Crescent, Higher Irlam and later 6 Liverpool Rd, Higher Irlam. M: Mrs Parkinson. E: 28.06.40. 2 Section, 1 Platoon. SD: 03.12.44.

PARNCUTT, Charles Henry. Lance Corporal 84. B: 1912. 36 Boundary Rd, Higher Irlam. W: Ivy Parncutt. E: 05.06.40. 1 Section, 1 Platoon. SD: 03.12.44.

PARRY, Frank. 916. B: 1922. 39 Marlborough Rd, Higher Irlam. F: Mr Parry. E: 28.08.40. 4 Platoon. HMF: 20.10.41.

PARRY, Harold. Private 809.B: 1911. 49 Francis Rd, Irlam. W: Mrs Parry. E: 21.07.42. 3 Platoon. SD: 03.12.44.

PAYNE, William Ernest. B12. B: 1915. 21 Dixon St, Irlam. W: Amy Payne. E: 03.07.40. 6 Platoon. R: 14.02.42.

PEARL, James. B22. B: 1906. 26 Tindale St, Peel Green. E: 03.07.40. 6 Platoon. T: 04.02.42 to A Company, 42nd Battalion, Home Guard.

PEARS, Robert. Lieutenant 271. B: 1905. 73 Lyndhurst Ave, Higher Irlam. W: Annie Pears. E: 06.06.40. 1 Platoon and later Transport Platoon and back to 1 Platoon on 12.06.41. SD: 03.12.44.

PEARSON, Reuban. Private F30. B: 1898. 69 The Crescent, Higher Irlam. W: Mrs Pearson. E: 01.07.40. June 1942, with 1 (Margarine Works) Section, 4 Platoon and later with 1 platoon. SD: 03.12.44.

PEASE, Norman. Private 96. B: 1908. 34 Allotment Rd, Cadishead. F: Mr Pease. E: 05.06.40. 4 Platoon and later 3 Section, 3 Platoon. SD: 03.12.44.

PELL, H. Private. June 1942, with 1 (Margarine Works) Section, 4 Platoon.

PERBERDY, George. B: 1889. 3 Carden Ave, Flixton. W: Mrs Perberdy. E: 30.09.40. Believed to have served with 2 (Soap Works) Section, 4 Platoon. T: date unknown to Flixton Home Guard.

PERKINS, Henry. Lance Corporal 933. B: 1896. 69 Lancaster Rd, Cadishead. W: Mrs Perkins. E: 28.08.40. 2 (Soap Works), 4 Platoon and later with 6 Platoon. SD: 03.12.44.

PERKS, Edgar Harry. 35. B:1894. 10 Haig Ave, Cadishead. W: Lily Perks. T: 03.07.40 to Royles (Factory Home Guard). Re-enlisted 24.02.41 into D Company, re-numbered E50, corporal in 1 Section, 5 Platoon. T: 10.03.43 to 5 Platoon, re-numbered 934. R: 15.07.43.

PERRIN, Osborne Peter. 458. B: 1920. 68 Bank St, Glazebrook. F: Peter Perrin. E: 13.09.40. 5 Platoon and later believed to have served with H Company. R: 22.11.40. Re-enlisted 20.10.41, H8 Platoon.

PERRIN, William Sidney. 293. B: 1923. 68 Bank St, Glazebrook. F: Peter Perrin. E: 12.06.40. 5 Platoon and later believed to have served with H Company.

PHILLIPS, A. Corporal. June 1942, with 1 Section, 2 Platoon.

PHILLIPS, Arthur. Sergeant 303. B: 1901. 95 Eldon Rd West, Irlam. W: Mrs E. Phillips. E: 07.06.43. 7 Platoon. SD: 03.12.44.

PHILLIPS, John. Lance Corporal 869. B: 1904. 3 Devon Rd, Cadishead and later 12 Rutland Rd, Cadishead. W: Mrs M. Phillips. E: 10.08.42. 5 Platoon. SD: 03.12.44.

PHILLIPS, William Lewis. 982. B: 1890. 56 Whitelake Ave, Flixton. E: 12.02.41. 4 Platoon. T: date unknown to 44th Battalion, Home Guard.

PICKERING, Thomas. Corporal 31. B: 1908. 13 Charles St, Cadishead. W: Hannah Pickering. E: 07.08.40. 4 Platoon and later 1 Section, 3 Platoon. SD: 03.12.44.

PICKWICK, Bertram George. B23. B: 1894. 195 Flixton Rd, Flixton. W: Edith Emily Pickwick. E: 04.07.40. 6 Platoon. R: 16.02.42.

PILLING, Jordan. Private F16. B: 1906. 78 The Crescent, Higher Irlam. W: Mary Pilling. E: 10.07.40. 1 (Margarine Works) Section, 4 Platoon. R: 27.11.42.

PINCHES, John Wesley. 54. B: 1909. 9 Palatine Close, Irlam. F: Edwin Pinches. E: 05.06.40. 3 Platoon and later believed to have served with H Company.

PINCHES, Stanley. Private 294. B: 1913. 9 Palatine Close, Irlam. W: Doris Pinches. E: 06.06.40. 3 Platoon and later believed to have served with H Company. R: 23.04.41. Re-enlisted, 10.07.42, re-numbered 767, 5 Platoon. By 1942 he was residing at 545 Liverpool Rd, Irlam. SD: 03.12.44.

PITCHER, William George. Lance Corporal F1. B: 1895. 62 Marlborough Rd, Higher Irlam. W: Louisa Pitcher. E: 08.07.40. 1 (Margarine Works) Section, 4 Platoon and later with 2 Platoon. SD: 03.12.44.

PLATER, John Edward. E12. B: 1904. 3 Allotment Rd, Cadishead. W: Gertrude Plater. E: 04.07.40. June 1942, with 1 Section, 5 Platoon and later 6 Platoon. R: 18.05.43.

POLE (POLL), Herbert. Private F12. B: 1905. 1 Devon Rd, Cadishead. W: Mary E. Pole. E: 11.07.40. 4 Platoon and later 6 Platoon. SD: 03.12.44.

POLLARD, Alfred. B91. B: 1896. Westside, Warburton Rd, Partington. W: Mary Hannah Pollard. E: 18.07.40. 6 Platoon. R: 26.02.42.

POLLARD, Arthur Geoffrey. 810. B: 1921. Lynwood, Station Rd, Partington. E: 21.07.42. 3 Platoon. T: 04.12.42 to 23 (Cheshire) Battalion, Home Guard.

POLLARD, Leslie. 881. B: 1920. Broom Cottage, Station Rd, Partington. F: H. Pollard. E: 17.08.42. T: 17.11.42 to 23 (Cheshire) Battalion, Home Guard.

POOLE, David A. Private. B: 1901. 87 New Moss Rd, Cadishead. W: Mona Poole. E: 28.04.42. 3 Section, 3 Platoon. SD: 03.12.44.

POOLE, Vincent J. Private 907. B: 1925. 87 New Moss Rd, Cadishead. E: 20.01.43. 7 Platoon and later 5 Platoon. SD: 03.12.44.

PORTER, George. Private 517. B: 1921. 8 Kitchener Ave, Cadishead. F: W. Porter. E: 17.10.40. 1 Section, 5 Platoon and later believed to have served with H Company. T: 18.04.41 to Royles No. 5 (Factory Home Guard). T: 18.02.44 to G Company, 42nd Battalion.

PORTER, Henry. Private 773. B: 1908. 9 Poplar Grove, Cadishead. W: Mrs E. Porter. E: 13.07.42. 3 Platoon. SD: 03.12.44.

POTTS, John. 571. B: 1923. 102 The Crescent, Higher Irlam. E: 27.05.41. 3 Section, 2 Platoon. R: 27.11.42.

POWELL, Charles William. 649. B: 1922. 72 Allotment Rd, Cadishead. M: Mrs Powell. E: 31.03.42. Later believed to have served with 8 Platoon, H Company.

POWELL, Henry. 527. B: 1880. 19 Carlton Way, Glazebrook. W: Mrs Powell. E: 17.02.41. 5 Platoon and later believed to have served with H Company.

POWELL, John Charles. B591. B: 1902. 15 School Lane, Hollinfare. W: Annie Powell. E: 20.06.41. 6 Platoon. T: date unknown to 79th Battalion, Home Guard. R: 04.02.42.

PRESTON, Arthur. B: 1921. 1 Walker Rd, Irlam. F: Joseph Preston. E: 08.01.41. Later believed to have served with 4 Platoon, H Company.

PRICE, Gordon J. 691. B: 1925. 19 Birch Ave, Cadishead. F: Mr Price. Later believed to have served with 8 Platoon, H Company.

PRICE, Richard Thomas. 422. B: 1895. 38 Milton Ave, Irlam. W: Sarah Ellen Price. E: 23.07.40. 4 Platoon and later 1 Section, 3 Platoon. D: 27.09.43.

PRIDDING, Thomas. 60. B: 1882. 69 Liverpool Rd, Higher Irlam. W: Edith Pridding. E: 05.06.40. 2 Platoon. R: 21.05.41.

PRINCE, Alfred. 275. B: 1904. 29 Fir St, Cadishead. E: 06.06.40. 4 Platoon and later 3 Platoon.

PROCTOR, William. Private 967. B: 1896. 64 Lyndhurst Ave, Higher Irlam. W: Mrs O. Proctor. E: 20.08.43. 4 Platoon. SD: 03.12.44.

PYATT, James. 905. B: 1919. 35 Partington Ave, Irlam. W: Mrs E. Pyatt. E: 13.10.42. 7 Platoon and later 4 Platoon. T: 07.08.44 to 16th (Cheshire) Battalion, Home Guard.

QUAYNE, John. Private F16. B: 1883. 63 Cutnook Lane, Higher Irlam. W: Jeannie Quayne. E: 10.07.40. 1 (Margarine Works) Section, 4 Platoon and later 2 Platoon. SD: 03.12.44.

RATCLIFFE, Frank. 669. B: 1925. 15 Francis Rd, Irlam. F: W.H. Ratcliffe. E: 18.03.42. Later believed to have served with 4 Platoon, H Company.

READMAN, Frank. Corporal 680. B: 1911. 60 Silver St, Higher Irlam. W: Edna Readman. E: 31.03.42. 1 Section, 1 Platoon. SD: 03.12.44.

REDFERN, Anthony C. 579. B: 1922. 4 Station Rd, Irlam. F: W. Redfern. E: 29.05.41. Later believed to have served with 4 Platoon, H Company.

REDFERN, Douglas. Lieutenant 4. B: 1900. 186A Liverpool Rd, Cadishead. W: Doris Redfern (nee Harper). E: 11.06.40. 2 Section, 6 Platoon and later Platoon Commander, 5 Platoon. HMF: 31.08.42.

REID, Sydney. 513. B: 1923. 44 Lord St, Cadishead. F: Harold Reid. E: 10.02.41. 5 Platoon and later believed to have served with H Company.

RENFREW, Kenneth. Messenger. B: 1925. 125 Liverpool Rd, Irlam. Messenger attached to Company HQ.

RENNEY, James Henry. Private 753. B: 1914. 46 Dean Rd, Cadishead. W: Mrs Renney. E: 18.06.42. 5 Platoon. SD: 03.12.44.

RENNEY, Raymond. Private 481. B: 1920. 35 Dean Rd, Cadishead. W: Lily Renney. E: 30.09.40. 4 Platoon and later 1 Section, 3 Platoon. SD: 03.12.44.

RENSHAW, Albert. Private F3. B: 1895. 9 Kenmore Grove, Cadishead. W: Annie Renshaw. E: 10.06.40. 1 (Margarine Works) Section, 4 Platoon and later with 6 Platoon. DMU: 25.02.44.

REYNOLDS, Clifford. 815. B: 1905. 10 Chapel Rd, Irlam. W: Mrs R. Reynolds. E: 22.07.42. 2 Platoon. SD: 03.12.44.

RICHARDS, Allan. 549. B: 1922. 4 Keswick Ave, Flixton. M: Florence Richards. E: 23.04.41. Later believed to have served with 4 Platoon, H Company.

RIGBY, Ernest. F31. B: 1893. 15 Moss Side Rd, Cadishead. W: Ailleen Rigby. E: 10.07.40. DMU: 25.03.41.

RIGBY, E. Private. June 1942, with 1 (Margarine Works) Section, 4 Platoon.

RIGBY, Harold. Private 962. B: 1902. 15 Kitchener Ave, Cadishead. W: Mrs K. Rigby. E: 06.09.43. 4 Platoon. SD: 03.12.44.

RIGBY, Harry. B61. B: 1885. 32 Fiddlers Lane, Higher Irlam. W: Florence H. Rigby. E: 04.07.40. 6 Platoon. R: 28.02.42.

RIGBY, Thomas. 976. B: 1899. 13 Marlborough Rd, Higher Irlam. W: Mrs B. Rigby. E: 12.11.40. 2 (Soap Works) Section, 4 Platoon. R: 29.11.42.

RILEY, William John. Lance Corporal 412. B: 1908. 84 Ferry Rd, Irlam. W: Mrs M. Riley. E: 19.07.40. June 1942, with 1 Section, 2 Platoon. SD: 03.12.44.

RIMMER, James. Private 786. B: 1905. 21 Lancaster Rd, Cadishead. W: Mrs A. Rimmer. E: 14.07.42. 3 Platoon. SD: 03.12.44.

RIMMER, John Edmund. 65. B: 1913. Moss Hall Farm, Cadishead. F: John Rimmer. E: 05.06.40. 1 Section, 3 Platoon. Home Guard guides. R: 13.09.43.

RIMMER, J. Oliver. Private H553. B: 1900. Station Cottage, Glazebrook. W: Mrs Rimmer. E: 22.10.40. June 1942, with 2 Section, 6 Platoon. SD: 03.12.44, HQ Platoon.

RISPIN, James Arthur. Corporal 289. B: 1900. 35 Lyndhurst Ave, Higher Irlam. W: Lily Rispin. E: 10.06.40. 3 Section, 1 Platoon. SD: 03.12.44.

RISPIN, Kenneth. Private 887. B: 1925. 125 Liverpool Rd, Irlam. F: Robert William Rispin. E: 03.09.42. as Home Guard messenger with Company HQ and later 3 Section, 2 Platoon. SD: 03.12.44.

RISPIN, Robert William. Private 234. B: 1899. 125 Liverpool Rd, Irlam. W: Mrs Rispin. E: 07.06.40. 3 Section, 2 Platoon. SD: 03.12.44.

ROACH, John. Private F13. B: 1908. 16 Dean Rd, Cadishead. W: Elizabeth Ann Roach. E: 08.01.41. June 1942, with 1 Section, 5 Platoon and later 6 Platoon. SD: 03.12.44.

ROBERTS, Alan. 1 Windsor Terrace, Fiddlers Lane, Higher Irlam. Home Guard messenger.

ROBERTS, George. 488. B: 1882. 50 Dixon St, Irlam. E: 27.11.40. 5 Platoon, also noted as Royles (Factory Home Guard).

ROBERTS, George W. Private 737. B: 1921. 28 Ferryhill Rd, Irlam. E: 04.06.42. 2 Platoon. SD: 03.12.44.

ROBERTS, Humphrey. Private 941. B: 1899. 6 Byng Ave, Cadishead. E: 16.09.43. 6 Platoon. SD: 03.12.44.

ROBERTS, John Richard. Private 348. B: 1909. 22 Boundary Rd, Higher Irlam. W: Nellie Roberts. E: 01.07.40. 1 Section, 1 Platoon. SD: 03.12.44.

ROBERTS, John Richard. 466. B: 1922. 28 Ferryhill Rd, Irlam. G: Mrs Givens. E: 1940. 1 Platoon. Changed name to Givens 21.02.41.

ROBERTS, Kenneth. 425. B: 1921. 8 Alfred St, Cadishead. F: William Edward Roberts. E: 24.07.40. 4 Platoon and later with 3 Platoon. HMF: date unknown.

ROBERTS, Thomas. Senior Sergeant B19. B: 1901. 38 Lancaster Rd, Cadishead. E: 15.08.40. 6 Platoon. R: 02.03.42.

ROBERTS, Thomas. B42. B: 1895. 38 Prospect Rd, Cadishead. W: Hilda Roberts. E: 01.07.40. 6 Platoon. R: 07.10.42.

ROBINSON, Frank. 843. B: 17.08.07. 19 Allenby Rd, Cadishead. W: Mrs M.A. Robinson. E: 04.08.42. 7 Platoon and later 5 Platoon. HMF: 06.04.44.

ROBINSON, James. B: 1893. B108. 128 Irlam Rd, Flixton. 6 Platoon. W: Elizabeth Robinson. E: 27.09.40. 6 Platoon. R: 28.02.42.

ROBINSON, Philip. 94. B: 1921. 20 Nelson Dr, Cadishead. F: J.H. Robinson. E: 05.06.40. 6 Platoon. HMF: 20.12.41.

ROBINSON, Phillip. 570. B: 1908. 95 Fir St, Cadishead. F: W. Robinson. E: 27.05.41. Later believed to have served with 8 Platoon, H Company.

ROBSON, Alfred William J. Private 653. B: 1911. 274 Liverpool Rd, Cadishead. W: Marjorie Robson. E: 30.12.41. 1 Section, 7 Platoon (HQ). SD: 03.12.44, lieutenant with Company HQ.

ROGERSON, Alfred. B85. B: 1896. 11 Haig Ave, Cadishead. W: Bessie Rogerson. E: 27.09.40. 6 Platoon.

ROGERSON, Eric. Private 532. B: 1923. 97 Fir St, Cadishead. E: 27.02.41. 3 Section, 3 Platoon. T: 10.05.42 to G Company.

ROGERSON, James. 613. B: 1924. 11 Haig Ave, Cadishead. E: 26.08.41. Later believed to have served with 8 Platoon, H Company.

ROOK, William. 325. B: 1905. 19 Caroline St, Irlam. W: Millie Rook. E: 01.07.40. 3 Platoon and later believed to have served with H Company.

ROSBOTTOM, John. 510. B: 1923. 284 Liverpool Rd, Cadishead. F: John Rosbottom. E: 08.02.41. 4 Platoon and later 3 Platoon. R: 24.10.41.

ROSE, George. 291. B: 1904. 12 Devon Rd, Cadishead. W: Mrs Rose. E: 06.06.40. 5 Platoon and later believed to have served with H Company.

ROWE, Frank. Sergeant 440. B: 1904. 22 The Crescent, Higher Irlam. W: Mary Anna Rowe. E: 31.07.40. June 1942, lance corporal with 3 Section, 1 Platoon. SD: 03.12.44, address then recorded as 2 Boundary Rd, Higher Irlam.

ROWEN, Joseph. F27. B: 1915. 84 Silver St, Higher Irlam. E: 03.07.40. 5 Platoon. R: 25.04.41.

ROYLE, Albert. Private 958. B: 1918. 42 Boundary Rd, Higher Irlam. E: 18.09.40. 2 (Soap Works) Section, 4 Platoon and later 1 Platoon. SD: 03.12.44.

ROYLE, Ernest. Private 555. B: 1922. 35, Princes Ave, Higher Irlam and later 25 The Crescent, Higher Irlam. F: J. Royle. E: 23.04.41. 2 Section, 1 Platoon. SD: 03.12.44.

ROYLE, George. Private 827. B: 1923. 13 Caroline St, Irlam. M: Mrs G. Royle. E: 22.07.42. 3 Platoon. SD: 03.12.44.

ROYLE, Harold. F47. B: 1903. Tan House Farm Cottage, Woodsend Rd, Flixton. W: Bessie Royle. E: 27.07.40. 4 Platoon. R: 25.04.41.

ROYLE, Jack. F559. 12 Riverside Dr, Flixton. E: 23.04.41. 4 Platoon.

ROYLE, Noah. Private B43. B: 1917. 16 Haig Ave, Cadishead. F: Jack Royle. E: 09.07.40. 1 Section, 6 Platoon. SD: 03.12.44.

RUBERY, Herbert Arthur. F560. B: 1906. 29 Gilbert St, Peel Green. W: Mrs B. Rubery. E: 27.07.41. 4 Platoon. T: 04.02.42 to H Company.

RUSSELL, Charles Stanley. 678. B: 1918. 23 Francis Rd, Irlam. F: William Russell. E: 31.03.42. Later believed to have served with 4 Platoon, H Company.

RUSSELL, William Mills. F23. B: 1882. 31 Lyndhurst Ave, Higher Irlam. E: 10.07.40. 4 Platoon. R: 04.04.41.

RYAN, John. 533. B: 1922. 34 Addison Rd, Higher Irlam. F: Michael Ryan. E: 08.04.41. 2 Platoon. HMF: 31.07.41.

RYCROFT, John. Private 685. B: 1913. 7 Moss Lane, Cadishead. E: 06.04.42. 2 Section, 7 Platoon (HQ). R: 16.09.42.

RYCROFT, William. Lance Corporal. B: 1913. 72 Liverpool Rd, Higher Irlam. W: Hilda Rycroft. 2 Section, 5 Platoon. T: 08.07.42 to 18th Cheshire Battalion, Home Guard.

RYLES, Horace. Corporal 771. B: 1907. 112 The Crescent, Higher Irlam. W: Mrs H. Ryles. E: 13.07.42. 5 Platoon and later 7 Platoon. SD: 03.12.44.

SALMON, Robert. 74. B: 1913. 10 Lytherton Ave, Cadishead. W: Eva Salmon. E: 05.06.40. 5 Platoon and later believed to have served with H Company.

SALT, Henry George. Lieutenant 400. B: 1892. 15 Hampton Rd, Cadishead. W: Olive Salt. E: 16.07.40. Platoon Commander 4 Platoon. R: 31.12.43.

SALT, Stanley. Private 739. B: 1911. 22 Partington Ave, Irlam. W: Rose Salt. E: 28.05.42. 3 Platoon. SD: 03.12.44.

SAUNDERS, J. Herbert. Private 918. B: 1891. 3 Addison Rd, Higher Irlam. W: Mrs Saunders. E: 28.08.40. 1 Platoon and by June 1942 with 2 (Soap Works) Section, 4 Platoon. SD: 03.12.44.

SAVAGE, George W. B104. B: 1920. 23 Hayes Rd, Cadishead. E: 26.08.40. 6 Platoon. HMF: 02.10.41.

SAVAGE, James. 647. 35A Hayes Rd, Cadishead. M: Mrs Savage. E: 30.10.41. Later believed to have served with 8 Platoon, H Company.

SAVERY, John. Private 352. B: 1924. 12 Princes Ave, Higher Irlam. F: J. Savery. E: 02.07.40. 3 Section, 1 Platoon. SD: 03.12.44.

SAXON, Gilbert. Private 952. B: 1894. 1 Warwick Rd, Cadishead. W: Mrs S.E. Saxon. E: 30.07.43. 4 Platoon. SD: 03.12.44.

SCOTT, Harry. Private F20. B: 1904. 52 Boundary Rd, Higher Irlam. E: 10.07.40. 1 (Margarine Works) Section, 4 Platoon and later with 1 Platoon. T: 13.12.43 to unknown unit.

SCOTT, J.M. Corporal. 3 Drake Ave, Cadishead. June 1942, with 2 Section, 6 Platoon. SD: 03.12.44.

SCOTT, Robert W. 222. B: 1916. 3 St John St, Irlam. W: Elsie Scott. E: 06.06.40. 2 Platoon. R: 16.07.41.

SCOTT, Ronald. 83. B: 1911. 9 Allotment Rd, Cadishead. SF: J.W. Hayman. E: 05.06.40. 4 Platoon and later with 3 Platoon. R: 25.04.41.

SCOTT, William Charles. 968. B: 1902. 581 Liverpool Rd, Irlam. W: Mrs M.A. Scott. E: 24.09.43. DMU: 12.10.43.

SEAL, Leonard. Sergeant 53. B: 1912. 74 Silver St, Higher Irlam. M: Mrs E.J. Seal of 76 Athol St, Winton. E: 05.06.40. 1 Platoon and also some time with Transport Platoon. June 1942, corporal serving with 1 Section, 7 Platoon (HQ). SD: 03.12.44, 1 Platoon.

SEDDON, Albert. 184. 16 Princes Ave, Higher Irlam. W: Betsy Seddon. E: 06.06.40. 1 Platoon. R: 27.11.40.

SEDDON, Thomas. Sergeant 59. B: 1906. 7 Hampton Rd, Cadishead. W: Mary Seddon. E: 05.06.40. 4 Platoon. June 1942, with 1 Section, 7 Platoon (HQ). SD: 03.12.44.

SEDGWICK, William. Private 699. B: 1911. 64 Eldon Rd West, Irlam. W: Nora Sedgwick. E: 14.04.42. 1 Section, 1 Platoon. SD: 03.12.44.

SELBY, Joseph Luke. B: 1910. F55. B: 1910. 129 Eldon Rd West, Irlam. W: Irene Selby. E: 10.07.40. 4 Platoon. R: 25.04.41.

SHADE, Harold. 791. B: 1914. 57 Marlborough Rd, Higher Irlam. W: Mrs M. Shade. E: 21.07.42. 7 Platoon. T: 16.04.44 to 10th (Cheshire) Battalion, Home Guard.

SHARP, Robert. 919. B: 1916. 65 Baines Ave, Irlam. M: Mrs Sharp. E: 28.08.40. 4 Platoon. R: 22.12.42.

SHARP, Robert Nelson. 156. B: 1897. Irlam. W: Lena Sharp. E: 06.06.40. 2 Platoon. R: 08.01.42.

SHARP, Thomas. 65 Baines Ave, Irlam. F: Richard Sharp. E: July 1940. 3 Platoon and later believed to have served with H Company. HMF: date unknown.

SHARP, William Henry. 462. B: 1910. 6 Lines Rd, Irlam. W: Mary Sharp. E: 18.09.40. 3 Platoon and later believed to have served with H Company. R: 23.04.41. Re-enlisted 26.10.42 and re-numbered 902. 7 Platoon. HMF: 17.02.43.

SHAW, Frederick. Lance Corporal 233. B: 1899. 7 Ferryhill Rd, Irlam. W: Mrs W. Shaw. E: 07.06.40. 1 Section, 2 Platoon. SD: 03.12.44.

SHAW, John. 304. B: 1876. 34 Princes Ave, Higher Irlam. E: 08.06.40. 1 Platoon. R: 21.05.41.

SHAW, Joseph. 453. B: 1910. 50 Fir St, Cadishead. W: Mrs H. Shaw. E: 08.09.40. 5 Platoon and later believed to have served with H Company.

SHAW, Walter. Lance Corporal 932. B: 1903. 22 Haig Ave, Cadishead. W: Mrs Shaw. E: 08.07.43. 4 Platoon. SD: 03.12.44.

SHAWCROSS, Fred. Private 795. B: 1911. 92 Eldon Rd West, Irlam. W: Mrs E. Shawcross. E: 21.07.42. 5 Platoon and later 7 Platoon. SD: 03.12.44.

SHAWCROSS, Harry. 297. B: 1902. 7 Warwick Rd, Cadishead. W: Mrs Shawcross. E: 14.06.40. 5 Platoon and later believed to have served with H Company.

SHAWCROSS, Harry. Private B69. B: 1923. 52 Nelson Dr, Cadishead. F: Thomas Shawcross. E: 28.09.40. 2 Section, 6 Platoon. HMF: 19.06.42.

SHAWCROSS, Thomas. 276. B: 1914. 11 Nelson Dr, Cadishead. M: Mary Shawcross. E: 22.08.40. 4 Platoon and later with 3 Platoon. HMF: 21.05.41.

SHEPHERD, Percy. G21. B: 1903. 6 Etherley Close, Irlam. W: Violet Shepherd (nee Howey). E: 28.08.40. 2 (Soap Works) Section, 4 Platoon. HMF: date unknown.

SHEPPARD, Fred Hall. Sergeant B44. B: 1891. 43 Devon Rd, Cadishead. W: Emma Sheppard. E: 05.07.40. 2 Section, 6 Platoon. R: 13.07.44.

SHERBURN, Frank. 202. B: 1913. 22 Laburnum Rd, Cadishead. F: Harry Sherburn. E: 06.06.40. 4 Platoon and later with 3 Platoon. HMF: 14.02.41.

SHERLOCK, Douglas. 851. B: 1915. 5 Ash Ave, Cadishead. F: Tom Sherlock. E: 05.08.41. 7 Platoon and later 6 Platoon. DMU: 20.01.44.

SHERLOCK, Tom. 194. B: 1892. 5 Ash Ave, Cadishead. W: Ethel Sherlock. E: 06.06.40. 4 Platoon and in June 1942 with 2 Section, 3 Platoon. DMU: 12.01.44.

SIMMS, Thomas. Sergeant 116. B: 1920. 166 Liverpool Rd, Irlam. M: Ann Simms. E: 05.06.40. June 1942, lance corporal with 3 Section, 2 Platoon. SD: 03.12.44.

SIMMS, William. Lance Corporal 684. B: 1917. 166 Liverpool Rd, Irlam and later 90 Ferry Rd, Irlam. B: Thomas Simms. E: 02.04.42. Believed to have later served 4 Platoon, H Company. There are two entries for this Home Guardsman and one stated enlisted 28.05.42 and his platoon as 2 Platoon. SD: 03.12.44, lance corporal, 2 Platoon.

SLAVEN, John. 609. B: 1910. 34 Francis Rd, Irlam. W: Winifred Slaven. E: 13.08.41. Believed to have later served 4 Platoon, H Company.

SLAVEN, Thomas. Private 822. B: 1913. 7 Annable Rd, Irlam. W: Mrs K. Slaven. E: 04.08.42. 5 Platoon. SD: 03.12.44.

SMITH, Clifford. B107. B: 1907. 146 The Crescent, Higher Irlam. W: Evelyn Smith. E: 02.12.40. 6 Platoon. HMF: 24.06.41.

SMITH, Gerald. 712. B: 1924. 27 Bradburn Rd, Irlam. F: H. Smith. E: 17.04.42. Believed to have later served 4 Platoon, H Company.

SMITH, Gordon Ernest. 71. B: 1923. 26 Harewood Rd, Irlam. F: Fred Smith. E: 05.06.40. 2 Platoon. R: 21.05.41.

SMITH, H. Private. 86 Eldon Rd West, Irlam. SD: 03.12.44.

SMITH, Harold. 595. B: 1924. 26 Harewood Rd, Irlam. M: Clara Smith. E: 06.08.41. 3 Section, 1 Platoon. HMF: 31.08.43.

SMITH, Horace L. Corporal 315. B: 1907. 16 Fir St, Cadishead. F: Jesse Smith. E: 21.06.40. 4 Platoon and later with 3 Platoon. SD: 03.12.44.

SMITH, John Wilkinson. 860. B: 1921. 28 Lynthorpe Ave, Cadishead. F: J. Smith. E: 05.08.42. T: 24.02.43 to E Company (ROF).

SMITH, John William. B113. B: 1889. 26 Alexandra Rd, Peel Green. W: Emily Smith. E: 23.08.40. 6 Platoon. R: 18.02.42.

SMITH, Jubal. 934. B: 1896. 4 Enticott Rd, Cadishead. W: Mrs E. Smith. E: 09.07.43. Enrolment cancelled.

SMITH, Kenneth. Private 170. B: 1922. 12 Dorset Rd, Cadishead. F: James Smith. M: Edith Smith (nee Gibbins). E: 06.06.40. 4 Platoon and later 2 Section, 3 Platoon. R: 21.05.41.

SMITH, Leonard. B: 1927. 56 Boundary Rd, Higher Irlam. Home Guard messenger

SMITH, Norman. 49 Marlborough Rd, Higher Irlam. Company HQ as a cycle orderly.

SMITH, Norman. 26 Harewood Rd, Irlam. Home Guard messenger (possibly SMITH, Norman above).

SMITH, Richard. 136. B: 1891. 16 Lancaster Rd, Cadishead. W: Miriam Smith. E: 05.06.40. 5 Platoon and later believed to have served with H Company. D: 25.12.44.

SMITH, Sidney. 73 Eldon Rd, Irlam. Home Guard messenger.

SMITH, William Douglas. 2nd Lieutenant 736. B: 1909. 1 Chestnut Ave, Cadishead. W: Margaret Smith. E: 05.05.42. June 1942, private with 2 Section, 7 Platoon (HQ). SD: 03.12.44, 4 Platoon.

SMITH, William Henry. Private F14. B: 1904. 53 Lancaster Rd, Cadishead. W: Elizabeth Smith. E: 10.07.40. 1 (Margarine Works) Section, 4 Platoon and later 6 Platoon. SD: 03.12.44.

SMYTH, Gerald. 105. B: 1917. 15 Bradburn Rd, Irlam. F: J. Smith. E: 05.06.40. 3 Platoon and later believed to have served with H Company.

SOUTHERN, Ernest. Corporal 964. B: 1894. 675 Liverpool Rd, Irlam. W: Mrs A. Southern. E:13.08.43. 4 Platoon. SD: 03.12.44.

SOUTHERN, James Edward. 254. B: 1892. 27 Warwick Rd, Cadishead. W: Edith Southern. E: 06.06.40. 3 Platoon and later believed to have served with H Company.

SOUTHERN, Herbert Wright. 337. B: 1890. 152 Liverpool Rd, Irlam. W: Mrs Southern. E: 01.07.40. 2 Platoon. R: 16.07.41.

SOUTHERN, John. 974. B: 1926. 27 Warwick Rd, Cadishead. E: 22.11.43. 4 Platoon. T: 04.05.44 to H Company.

STANDISH, Edwin. Corporal 666. B: 1898. 36 Dean Rd, Cadishead. W: Mrs L. Standish. E: 13.02.42. 6 Platoon. SD: 03.12.44.

STANDISH, Harold. Private B45. B: 1896. 15 Bucklow Ave, Partington. W: Sarah A. Standish. E: 05.07.40. 1 Section, 6 Platoon. SD: 03.12.44.

STANIER, George William. 179. B: 1904. 5 Bradburn Rd, Irlam. E: 06.06.40. 3 Platoon and later believed to have served with H Company.

STANLEY, Brian. 402. B: 1900. 63 The Crescent, Higher Irlam. E: 16.07.40. 2 Platoon. R: 14.02.42.

STANLEY, Daniel. Private E1. B: 1894. 3 Ash Ave, Cadishead. W: Mary Jane Stanley. E: 17.07.40. 3 Platoon. June 1942, with 1 Section, 5 Platoon. SD: 03.12.44.

STANLEY, J. E16. B: 1907. 34 Moss Lane, Cadishead. W: Jessie Stanley. E: 03.07.40. 1 Section, 5 Platoon. R: 31.08.42.

STANLEY, J. Pritchard. Lieutenant E38. B: 1898. 4 Hartley Grove, Irlam and later 26 Moss Lane, Cadishead. W: Sarah Stanley. E: 03.07.40, 5 Platoon. June 1942, sergeant, 1 Section, 5 Platoon. SD: 03.12.44, 5 Platoon.

STANSFIELD, Walter. F44. B: 1883. 54 Tindall St, Peel Green. W: Mary Alice Stansfield. E: 10.07.40. 4 Platoon. R: 25.04.41.

STEEL, Arthur Anderson. 627. B: 1917. 9 Charles St, Cadishead. W: Mrs H. Steel. E: 20.10.41. 3 Platoon. HMF: 08.01.42.

STEEL, John H. Private 910. B: 1919. 11 Leyland Ave, Higher Irlam and later at 9 Gaskell Rd, Eccles. F: H. Steel. E: 31.03.43. 7 Platoon. SD: 03.12.44.

STEPHENS, Henry Private G. 961. B: 1914. 27 Allenby Rd, Cadishead and later 58 Eldon Rd West, Irlam. W: Mrs Stephens (at the time, residing in Ruislip, Middlesex). SD: 03.12.44, HQ Platoon.

STEPHENSON, J. Jeffrey. Private 693. B: 1910. 14 Lyndhurst Ave, Higher Irlam. E: 10.04.42. 1 Section, 2 Platoon. So: 25.11.42.

STEPHENSON, John. 438. B: 1914. 13 Boundary Rd, Higher Irlam. E: 29.07.40. 1 Platoon. R: 03.01.41. Re-enlisted later in 1941, re-numbered 514, 1 3 Section, Platoon. DMU: 07.09.43.

STEVENS, Donald. 619. B: 1924. 18 Nelson Dr, Cadishead. F: Frederick Stevens. E: 06.06.41. Later believed to have served with 8 Platoon, H Company.

STEVENS, Frederick William. 336. 10 Rutland Rd, Cadishead. 5 Platoon and later believed to have served with H Company. R: 03.11.40.

STEVENS, Frederick William. 833. B: 1901. 18 Nelson Dr, Cadishead. W: Mrs A. Stevens. E: 23.07.42. 7 Platoon and later with 5 Platoon. DMU: 19.06.44.

STEVENS, Leslie. Private 622. B: 1924. 16 Bankfield Ave, Cadishead. M: Mrs Stevens. E: 08.09.41. 2 Section, 3 Platoon. SD: 03.12.44.

STEVENS, Wilfred. 114. B: 1915. 12 Hampton Rd, Cadishead. E: 05.06.40. 5 Platoon and later believed to have served with H Company.

STEWART, Arthur. 660. B: 1916. 38 Baines Ave, Irlam. F: William Stewart. E: 08.01.42. Later believed to have served with 4 Platoon, H Company.

STOREY, C.W. 7. B: 1879. 3 Bradburn Rd, Irlam. W: Mrs Storey. E: 08.06.40. First officer to command local LDV. 4 Platoon and later Company HQ. R: April 1941.

STOTT, Stanley. 421. B: 1911. 55 Harewood Rd, Irlam. W: Ellen Stott. E: 23.07.40. 2 Platoon. R: 21.05.41.

STREET, Frank. 223. B: 1921. 22 Fir St, Cadishead. F: Harry Street. E: 06.06.40. 4 Platoon and later 3 Platoon. R: 16.07.41.

STRUTHERS, James. 57. B: 1922. 2 Victoria Rd, Irlam. F: Osborne Pye Struthers. E: 05.06.40. 2 Platoon. HMF: 04.06.41.

STRUTHERS, Thomas. 150. B: 1898. 203 Liverpool Rd, Irlam. W: Ruth Struthers. E: 05.06.40. 3 Platoon and later believed to have served with H Company. R: 02.09.41.

STUART, Charles. Lance Corporal 818. B: 1905. 13 Victoria Rd, Irlam. W: Mrs E. Stuart. E: 22.07.40. 5 Platoon. SD: 03.12.44.

STUBBS, John. 250. B: 1903. 10 Lancaster Rd, Cadishead. W: Mrs B. Stubbs. E: 06.06.40. 5 Platoon and later believed to have served with H Company.

STUBBS, Kenneth Albert. 528. B: 1885. 19 Carlton Way, Glazebrook. W: Mrs E. Stubbs. E: 17.02.41. 5 Platoon and later believed to have served with H Company.

SUMMONS, Arthur. F37. B: 1895. 2 Vaughan St, Winton. W: Emma Summons. E: 11.07.40. 4 Platoon. R: 25.04.41.

SUTCLIFFE, Ralph Bates. Corporal 394. B: 1910. 93 (or 95) Eldon Rd, Irlam and later 22 The Crescent, Higher Irlam. W: Doris Sutcliffe. E: 15.07.40. 2 Section, 2 Platoon. SD: 03.12.44.

SUTOR, Eric. 590. B: 1922. 38 Harewood Rd, Irlam. F: Harold Suter. 2 Platoon. HMF: 09.06.42.

SWALWELL, Moses. Private 761. B: 1913. 24 Rose Ave, Irlam. W: Mrs M. Swalwell. E: 10.07.42. 3 Platoon. SD: 03.12.44.

SWIFT, George Edward. E34. B: 1921. 2 Rose Crescent, Irlam. F: James Swift. E: 03.07.40. 5 Platoon. HMF: 03.10.41.

SWIFT, George Edward. 981. B: 1921. 10 Rose Ave, Irlam and later 89 Lord St, Cadishead. W: Mrs Swift. E: 11.05.44.

SWIFT, G.E. 37 Lords St, Cadishead. 6 Platoon. SD: 03.12.44. Possibly Private 981 G.E. Swift, above.

SWINDELL, Norman. 249. B: 1913. Olive Mount Cottage, Astley Rd, Irlam. W: Mrs A. Swindell. E: 07.06.40. 3 Platoon and later believed to have served with H Company.

SWINDELL, William. 413. B: 1903. 25 Ash Ave, Cadishead. W: Alice Swindell. E: 06.07.40. 5 Platoon and later believed to have served with H Company.

SWINDELLS, Edward. Private 935. B: 1897. 5 Charles St, Cadishead. W: Ethel Swindells. E: 28.08.40. 2 (Soap Works) Section, 4 Platoon and later with 3 Platoon. SD: 03.12.44.

TALBOT, Frederick. Private E39. B: 1898. 39 Lancaster Rd, Cadishead. W: Hilda Talbot. E: 25.07.40. 6 Platoon. June 1942, with 1 Section, 5 Platoon. SD: 03.12.44.

TALBOT, George. 525. B: 1924. 39 Lancaster Rd, Cadishead. F: Fred Talbot. E: 16.02.41. Later believed to have served with 8 Platoon, H Company. HMF: date unknown.

TARRINGTON, C.W. Private. 5 Harewood Rd, Irlam. 2 (Soap Works) Section, 4 Platoon and later 7 Platoon. SD: 03.12.44.

TARRY, Alfred. 392. B: 1909. 68 Eldon Rd, Irlam. W: Kathleen Tarry. E: 14.07.40. 4 Platoon and later 3 Platoon. R: 17.10.42.

TARRY, Francis. Private 70. B: 1923. 113 Eldon Rd, Irlam. M: Emma Tarry (of Middlesbrough). E: 05.06.40. 2 Platoon. HMF: 30.10.41.

TARRY, Herbert A. Private 686. B: 1910. 105 Eldon Rd West, Irlam. E: 06.04.42. 2 Section, 2 Platoon. SD: 03.12.44.

TARRY, James William. 544. B: 1914. 8 Etherley Rd, Irlam. W: Mrs E. Tarry. E: 10.03.41. R: date unknown. E: 10.04.42, re-numbered 692. Later believed to have served with 4 Platoon, H Company.

TATHAM, Walter Frederick. 298. B: 1914. 599 Liverpool Rd, Irlam. M: Hannah E. Tatham. E: 14.06.41. Transport Platoon. June 1942, 1 Section, 7 Platoon (HQ). HMF: date unknown.

TAYLOR, Alfred. 330. B: 1891. 30 Lord St, Cadishead. W: Mrs Taylor. E: 01.07.40. 5 Platoon and later believed to have served with H Company.

TAYLOR, Charles. 285. B: 1888. 100 Liverpool Rd, Cadishead. W: Mrs W. Taylor. E: 06.06.40. 5 Platoon and later believed to have served with H Company.

TAYLOR, Clifford Henry. 705. B: 1920. 20 Lancaster Rd, Cadishead. F: F. Taylor. E: 15.04.42. Later believed to have served with 8 Platoon, H Company.

TAYLOR, Edward. 731. B: 1914. 2 Liverpool Rd, Cadishead and later 46 Fiddlers Lane, Higher Irlam. E: 28.04.42. 3 Section, 2 Platoon. SD: 03.12.44.

TAYLOR, Eric. 111. B: 1905. 55 Addison Rd, Higher Irlam. W: Alice Taylor. E: 05.06.40. 3 Section, 1 Platoon. R: 16.07.41. Re-enlisted (date unknown) and re-numbered 674. Later believed to have served with 4 Platoon, H Company.

TAYLOR, Ernest. 442. B: 1896. 67 Cutnook Lane, Higher Irlam. W: Doris Taylor. E: 10.08.40. 1 Platoon. R: date unknown. Re-enlisted (date unknown), re-numbered 674. Later believed to have served with 4 Platoon, H Company. SD: 03.12.44, 1 Platoon.

Appendix VIII

TAYLOR, Francis. 451. B: 1920. 2 Liverpool Rd, Higher Irlam. B: George Taylor. E: 03.09.40. 2 Platoon. HMF: 1941.

TAYLOR, Frank. 499. B: 1913. 30 Boundary Rd, Higher Irlam. E: 31.08.41. 2 Platoon. T: date unknown to E Company, 44th Battalion, Home Guard.

TAYLOR, Harry. 474. B: 1922. 41 Eldon Rd East, Irlam. B: Harold Taylor. E: 25.09.40. 2 Platoon. R: 15.09.41.

TAYLOR, James Maurice. Private 926. 253 Liverpool Rd, Cadishead. W: Mrs T. Taylor. E: 29.06.43. 4 Platoon. SD: 03.12.44.

TAYLOR, John Leslie. 218. B: 1914. Inglenook, Cutnook Lane, Higher Irlam. F: J. Taylor. E: 07.06.40. 1 Platoon. HMF: 06.04.41.

TAYLOR, Maurice. 956. B: 1896. 14 Milton Ave, Irlam. W: Mrs A.P. Taylor. E: 30.07.43. R: 25.05.44.

TAYLOR, Maurice. Sergeant 391. B: 1919. 14 Sandy Lane, Irlam. E: 15.07.40. Transport Platoon. In June 1942 served 1 Section, 7 Platoon (HQ). T: 11.02.43 to 75th Battalion, Home Guard (St. Helens).

TAYLOR, Sandie. G639. B: 1894. 33 Victory Rd, Cadishead. W: Mrs E. Taylor. E: 30.10.40. 2 (Soap Works) Section, 4 Platoon. R: 31.12.41.

TAYLOR, Thomas. Private 23. B: 1916. 9 Rose Crescent, Irlam. W: Mrs S. Taylor. E: 30.06.40. 4 Platoon and later Transport Platoon. June 1942, 2 Section, 7 Platoon (HQ). SD: 03.12.44, 4 Platoon.

TAYLOR, William. 107. B: 1912. Woodside Farm, Woolden Moss, Cadishead. F: William Taylor. E: 05.06.40. 4 Platoon and later 3 Platoon. R: 03.11.40.

THOMAS, Francis Herbert. Private B94. B: 1907. 19 Moss Lane, Cadishead. W: Florence Thomas. E: 09.08.40. 6 Platoon. SD: 03.12.44.

THOMAS, Frank. Private 364. B: 1909. 1 Drake Ave, Cadishead. F: George Thomas. E: 04.07.40. 4 Platoon and later 1 Section, 3 Platoon. SD: 03.12.44.

THOMAS, Frederick George H. Sergeant 362. B: 1900. 26 Lyndhurst Ave, Higher Irlam. W: Ethel Thomas. E: 02.07.40. 3 Section, 2 Platoon. SD: 03.12.44.

THOMAS, Granville. 89. B: 1910. 5 Chestnut Ave, Cadishead. W: Beatrice Thomas. E: 05.06.40. 4 Platoon and later 2 Section, 3 Platoon. R: 09.11.41. Re-enlisted 01.04.42, re-numbered 683, HQ Platoon. SD: 03.12.44.

THOMAS, Harold Parry. Private 268. B: 1917. 17 Boundary Rd, Higher Irlam. E: 06.06.40. Transport Platoon. June 1942, with 2 Section, 7 Platoon (HQ). HMF: 31.01.43.

THOMAS, William. 709. B: 1913. 29 Allenby Rd, Cadishead. W: Alice Thomas. E: 17.04.42. Later believed to have served with 8 Platoon, H Company.

THOMAS, William. Private 759. B: 1914. 22 Victory Rd, Cadishead and later at 19 Marlborough Rd, Higher Irlam. E: 10.07.42. 5 Platoon, later 7 Platoon. SD: 03.12.44.

THOMASON, Edward. Private 844. B: 1906. 116 The Crescent, Higher Irlam. W: Mrs M. Thomason. E: 04.08.42. HQ Platoon. SD: 03.12.44.

THOMASON, Frank. Private 806. B: 1902. 68 Addison Rd, Higher Irlam. E: 22.07.42. 5 Platoon. SD: 03.12.44.

THOMPSON, Alfred. 511. B: 1918. 25 Bradburn Rd, Irlam. E: 10.02.41. 3 Platoon and later believed to have served with H Company.

THOMPSON, Arthur. Lance Corporal 435. B: 1907. 45 Silverdale Ave, Higher Irlam. W: Mary Thompson. E: 27.07.40. 1 Section, 1 Platoon. SD: 03.12.44.

THOMPSON, Eric. 200. B: 1915. 246 Liverpool Rd, Cadishead. B: Arthur Thompson. E: 06.06.40. 5 Platoon and later believed to have served with H Company.

THOMPSON, George. 10. B: 1911. 5 Nelson Dr, Cadishead. E: 26.06.40. 4 Platoon and later 1 Section, 3 Platoon. HMF: 31.05.43.

THOMSON, Alvin Vivien. Sergeant 152. B: 1896. 57 Lyndhurst Ave, Higher Irlam. W: Elsie Thompson. E: 05.06.40. June 1942, sergeant, 1 Section, 2 Platoon. SD: 03.12.44.

THOMSON, Roy. 389. B: 1920. 57 Lyndhurst Ave, Higher Irlam. E: 15.07.40. 2 Platoon. R: 16.07.41.

THORNE, Harry. Corporal 390. B: 1904. 38 Allotment Rd, Cadishead. W: Mrs M. Thorne. E: 15.07.40. 4 Platoon and later 2 Section, 3 Platoon. SD: 03.12.44.

THORNLEY, James. B111. B: 1883. 14 Bridgewater St, Little Hulton. W: Agnes Thornley. E: 27.09.40. 6 Platoon. R: 18.02.42.

THORNLEY, James William. 347. B: 1915. 85 Baines Ave, Irlam. M: Elizabeth Thornley. E: 24.07.40. 3 Platoon and later believed to have served with H Company. R: 23.04.41.

THORNTON, Frederick W. Private 763. B: 1903. 24 Allenby Rd, Cadishead. W: Mrs Amy Thornton. E: 10.07.42. 3 Platoon. SD: 03.12.44.

THORNTON, John J. Private 953. B: 1898. Squire Lea, Glazebrook. E: 28.08.40. 2 (Soap Works) Section, 4 Platoon and later 6 Platoon. SD: 03.12.44.

THORPE, William H. Private 789. B: 1905. 29 Windsor Ave, Flixton. W: Mrs M. Thorpe. E: 22.07.42. 5 Platoon. SD: 03.12.44.

TIGHE, Hugh Maurice. 81. B: 1921. 1 Bradburn Rd, Irlam. F: John Tighe. E: 05.06.40. 3 Platoon and later believed to have served with H Company.

TIGHE, James. 489. 1 Bradburn Rd, Irlam. F: John Tighe. E: 02.09.40. 3 Platoon and later believed to have served with H Company. HMF: date unknown.

TIGHE, John Gerard. 397. B: 1919. 1 Bradburn Rd, Irlam. M: Margaret Tighe. E: 15.07.40. 3 Platoon and later believed to have served with H Company. HMF: date unknown.

TIGHE, Joseph. 346. B: 1922. 1 Bradburn Rd, Irlam. F: John Tighe. E: 30.06.40. 3 Platoon and later believed to have served with H Company. HMF: date unknown.

TINSLEY, Harry. Sergeant B46. B: 1897. 36 Victory Rd, Cadishead. W: Gertrude Mary Tinsley. E: 05.07.40. 1 Section, 6 Platoon. SD: 03.12.44.

TITMARSH, Reginald James. Private 638. B: 1914. 4 Hartley Grove, Higher Irlam. F: F. Titmarsh. E: 07.06.40. 3 Section, 1 Platoon. SD: 03.12.44.

TOFT, John. Private 845. B: 1904. 89 Lords St, Cadishead. W: Mrs D.W. Toft. E: 04.08.42. 5 Platoon. SD: 03.12.44.

TOFT, Joseph. B: 20.11.15. 17 Atherton Lane, Cadishead. E: 22.07.42. 5 Platoon. F: Joseph Toft. M: Maggie Toft. HMF: 31.08.43.

TONGE, Ernest William. 727. B: 1923. 13 Oak Ave, Cadishead. F: William Tonge. E: 25.04.42. Later believed to have served with 8 Platoon, H Company.

TONGE, John. B47. B: 1900. 53 Ackers Lane, Partington. W: Ethel Tonge. E: 05.07.40. 6 Platoon. R: 17.02.42.

TONGE, William. 726. B: 1899. 13 Oak Ave, Cadishead. E: 25.04.42. June 1942, 2 Section, 5 Platoon.

TOOTELL, Henry. Private 173. B: 1913. 29 Marlborough Rd, Higher Irlam. W: Florence Tootell. E: 22.08.40. Transport Platoon. June 1942, 2 Section, 7 Platoon (HQ). SD: 03.12.44, HQ Platoon.

TOWNSEND, Kenneth J. 663. B: 1924. 35 Addison Rd, Higher Irlam. E: 15.01.42. Later believed to have served with 4 Platoon, H Company.

TRAYNOR, William. 361. B: 1919. 10 Prospect Ave, Cadishead. F: William Traynor. E: 04.07.40. 4 Platoon and later served 3 Platoon. HMF: 11.09.41.

TROWNSON, Harry. Private 978. B: 1927. 19 Fir St, Cadishead. M: Mrs M. Trownson. E: 03.01.43. 4 Platoon. SD: 03.12.44.

TUCKER, George Goss. 201. B: 1905. 71 Belgrave Rd, Cadishead. W: Gladys Tucker. E: 06.06.40. 4 Platoon and later with 3 Platoon. R: 17.08.42.

TUPLING, Ernest. 2nd Lieutenant 908. B: 1913. 25 Chapel St, Irlam. W: Mrs N. Tupling. E: 31.05.40 into 44th (Lancashire) Battalion, Home Guard. T: 13.10.42 to 2 Platoon, D Company. SD: 03.12.44, 6 Platoon.

TUPLING, George. Private 491. B: 1923. 19 Ash Ave, Cadishead. F: W. Tupling. E: 12.11.40. 5 Platoon. SD: 03.12.44.

TUPLING, George Norman. Private 813. B: 1903. 61 Lancaster Rd, Cadishead. W: Mrs Tupling. E: 22.07.42. 3 Platoon. June 1942, with 1 Section, 7 Platoon (HQ). SD: 03.12.44, HQ Platoon.

TUPLING, Leonard. Sergeant 99. B: 1909. 82 Eldon Rd West, Irlam. W: Lilian Tupling. E: 05.06.40. June 1942, corporal 3 Section, 2 Platoon. Later 7 Platoon. SD: 03.12.44.

TUPLING, William Robert. 225. B: 1896. 19 Ash Ave, Cadishead. W: Imogene Tupling. E: 06.06.40. 1942 company quartermaster sergeant, 1 Section, 7 Platoon (HQ). SD: 03.12.44, Company HQ.

TUPPIER, Hugh C. F39. B: 1902. Monton, Eccles. W: Ethel Tuppier. E: 10.07.40. 4 Platoon. R: 31.12.41.

TURRINGTON, Charles William. 964. B: 1908. 5 Harewood Rd, Irlam. W: Mary Turrington. E: 16.10.40. 4 Platoon and later 7 Platoon.

TWIGG, George. Private 270. B: 1915. Orchard Farm, Cutnook Lane, Higher Irlam and later 42 Silver St, Higher Irlam. F: Jack Twigg. E: 07.06.40. Transport Platoon. June 1942, 2 Section, 7 Platoon (HQ). SD: 03.12.44, HQ Platoon.

TWINNING, Freeman. Private 936. B: 1903. 52 Princes Ave, Higher Irlam. W: Mrs S.E. Twinning. E: 12.07.43. 4 Platoon. SD: 03.12.44.

TYER, George A. 530. B: 1921. 13 The Crescent, Higher Irlam. F: Robert Tyer. E: 12.02.41. 1 Platoon. HMF: 27.08.41.

TYNAN, Herbert. Private E44. B: 1923. 115 Liverpool Rd, Cadishead. F: John Tynan. E: 27.08.40. 3 Platoon. June 1942, with 1 Section, 5 Platoon. SD: 03.12.44, HQ Platoon.

TYNAN, William Johnson. Corporal F51. B: 1907. 48 Boundary Rd, Higher Irlam. S: Mrs J. Parker, Ebenezer Farm, Higher Irlam. E: 10.07.40. 1 (Margarine Works) Section, 4 Platoon. SD: 03.12.44.

UNSWORTH, Frank Oswald. 798. B: 1920. Enderley, Ferry Rd, Irlam. F: F. Unsworth. E: 21.07.42. 5 Platoon. T: 18.01.44 to G Company.

UPTON, James. 198. B: 1922. Rose Farm, Astley Rd, Irlam. M: Mrs Upton. E: 08.07.40. 3 Platoon and later HQ Platoon.

URMSTON, William. B50. B: 1908. 10 Bobs Lane, Cadishead. W: Katherine Urmston. E: 29.07.40. 6 Platoon. R: 14.02.42.

VALENTINE, Kenneth. B: 1927. 24 Ash Ave, Cadishead. F: William Valentine. E: 30.09.41. Home Guard messenger and orderly duties at D Company HQ.

VALENTINE, Roy. 419. B: 1922. 24 Ash Ave, Cadishead. F: William Valentine. E: 22.07.40. 4 Platoon and later 3 Platoon. HMF: 17.09.41.

VALENTINE, William. 149. B: 1887. 24 Ash Ave, Cadishead. W: Lucy Valentine. E: 05.06.40. 4 Platoon and later 2 Section, 3 Platoon. R: 03.10.42.

VALLANTYNE, Peter. Private 848. B: 1908. 28 Eldon Rd, East, Irlam. W: Mrs Vallantyne. E: 05.08.42. 5 Platoon and later 7 Platoon. SD: 03.12.44.

VAUDREY, J. Private. 41 Harewood Rd, Irlam. E: June 1942, 2 Section, 5 Platoon and later 7 Platoon SD: 03.12.44.

VAUDREY, Joseph. E35. B: 1906. 18 Milton Ave, Irlam. W: Emma C. Vaudrey. E: 03.07.40. 5, 3 and 7 Platoons in succession.

VAUGHAN, Kenneth. 91. B: 1922. 2 Rutland Rd, Cadishead. F: J. Johnson. E: 05.06.40. 4 Platoon and later 3 Platoon. R: 12.11.41.

VICKERS, George. 405. B: 1904. 101 Fir St, Cadishead. W: Florence Vickers. E: 06.07.40. 4 Platoon and later 3 Platoon. D: 27.01.42.

VINTON, Walter. 817. B: 1902. 4 Ash Ave, Cadishead. W: Mrs E. Vinton. E: 22.07.42. 3 Platoon. DMU: 22.06.44.

WADSWORTH, Harry. Private 796. B: 1915. 45 Lancaster Rd, Cadishead. F: P. Wadsworth. E: 21.07.42. 5 Platoon. SD: 03.12.44.

WALHER, Arthur. 554. B: 1924. 32 Hayes Rd, Cadishead. M: Ethel Walher. E: 27.04.41. 3 Platoon. R: 17.09.41.

WALKER, Herbert. 969. B: 1897. Hazeldine, Hampton Rd, Cadishead. W: Mrs C.R. Walker. E: 24.09.43. DMU: 12.12.43.

WALKER, Herbert. 159. B: 1921. 32 Ferryhill Rd, Irlam. F: George Walker. E: 06.06.40. 3 Section, 2 Platoon. R: 09.03.44.

WALKER, Walter junior. Private 102. B: 1916. 17 Nelson Dr, Cadishead. F: Walter Walker. E: 05.06.40. 4 Platoon then Transport Platoon. June 1942, 2 Section, 7 Platoon (HQ). SD: 03.12.44, HQ Platoon.

WALKER, William. 308. B: 1913. 50 Caroline St, Irlam. M: Catherine Walker. E: 06.06.40. 3 Platoon and later believed to have served with H Company.

WALKER, William Henry. Private 629. B: 1915. 57 Harewood Rd, Irlam. W: Mrs Walker. E: 20.10.41. 2 Section, 1 Platoon. SD: 03.12.44.

WALSH, Edward. 469. B: 1923. 617 Liverpool Rd, Irlam. S: Kathleen Walsh. E: 23.09.40. 3 Platoon and later believed to have served with H Company. HMF: date unknown.

WALSH, William. Private 667. B: 1912. 32 Harewood Rd, Irlam. W: Mrs H.A. Walsh. E: 04.04.42. Transport Platoon. June 1942, 2 Section, 7 Platoon (HQ). SD: 03.12.44, HQ Platoon.

WALTON, Frank. Sergeant 356. B: 1902. 69 Belgrave Rd, Cadishead and later 9 Ash Ave, Cadishead. W: Emily Walton. E: 02.07.40. SD: 03.12.44, HQ Platoon.

WALTON, James. 783. B: 1905. 57 Princes Ave, Higher Irlam. W: Mrs A. Walton. E: 13.07.42. DMU: 14.08.42.

WALTON, Joseph. 468. B: 1904. Ellesmere Farm, Cadishead. M: Eleanor Walton. E: 21.09.40. 4 Platoon and later Transport Platoon. R: 22.12.41.

WANSTALL, Robert. 847. B: 07.01.04. 32 Eldon Rd East, Irlam. W: Mrs E.R. Wanstall. E: 04.08.42. HMF: 30.11.42.

WARD, William. 42. B: 1900. 39 Victory Rd, Cadishead. W: Mrs Ward. E: 05.06.40. 5 Platoon and later believed to have served with H Company. R: 29.11.43.

WARDLE, Fred. 314. B: 1907. 5 Graham Crescent, Cadishead. W: Eileen Wardle. E: 21.06.40. 5 Platoon and later believed to have served with H Company.

WAREING, James. Private 784. B: 1905. 48 Ferry Rd, Irlam. W: Mrs E. Wareing. 1 Platoon. E: 13.07.42. SD: 03.12.44.

WARREN, Arthur. F18. B: 1907. 12 Elsinore Ave, Irlam. W: Mrs Warren. E: 10.07.40. 4 Platoon. R: 25.04.41.

WARREN, Frederick Henry. 975. B: 1923. 50 Whitelake Ave, Flixton. F: H. Warren. E: 02.08.40. 4 Platoon. R: 12.04.41.

WARREN, William. F37. B: 27.02.08. 40 Elsinore Ave, Irlam. W: Beatrice Warren (nee Liptrott). E: 27.07.40. 4 Platoon. R: 25.04.41. (Possibly related to Arthur Warren, same street and resignation date). Re-enlisted 10.08.42, re-numbered 870. HMF: 31.10.44.

WARRIOR, George. 192. B: 1918. 2 Drake Ave, Cadishead. F: George Warrior. E: 06.06.40. 4 Platoon later HQ Platoon. HMF: 02.04.42.

WARRIOR, Thomas. Lance Corporal 48. B: 1920. 2 Drake Ave, Cadishead. F: George Warrior. E: 23.08.40. 4 Platoon and later 1 Section, 3 Platoon. SD: 03.12.44, HQ Platoon.

WARSOP, Arthur Leonard. 283. B: 1897. 6 Haig Ave, Cadishead. W: Mrs Warsop. E: 06.06.40. 5 Platoon and later believed to have served with H Company.

WARSOP, Leslie. 319. B: 1906. 296 Liverpool Rd, Cadishead. W: Mrs Warsop. E: 22.06.40.

WATKINSON, John. 944. B: 1889. 2 Greenbank Rd, Ashton-on-Mersey. W: Mrs V.A. Watkinson. E: 28.08.40. 4 Platoon. R: 19.02.42.

WATSON, David. 580. B: 1923. 6 Dixon St, Irlam. F: Mr Watson. E: 20.06.41. Later believed to have served with 4 Platoon, H Company.

WATSON, John Henry. 332. B: 1909. 50 Lyndhurst Ave, Higher Irlam. W: Edith Watson. 1 Platoon. T: date unknown to H Company. R: 22.04.42.

WATTS, Arthur. Private 87. B: 1905. 6 Lyndhurst Ave, Higher Irlam. W: Alice Louisa Watts. E: 05.06.40. 3 Section, 1 Platoon. SD: 03.12.44.

WEALE, Frederick Thomas. 414. B: 1880. 71 New Moss Rd, Cadishead. W: Jane Weale. E: 11.07.40. 4 Platoon and later 3 Platoon. R: 21.05.41.

WEBSTER, William Duckworth. 100. B: 1905. 199 Liverpool Rd, Irlam. M: Mrs A. Webster. E: 05.06.40. 3 Platoon and later believed to have served with H Company.

WELCH, Albert. 258. B: 1897. 100 Silver St, Higher Irlam. W: Mary Welch. E: 06.06.40. 3 Section, 1 Platoon. SD: 03.12.44.

WENHAM, Kenneth. 189. B: 1922. Hope Cottage, Chat Moss, Irlam. M: Mary Wenham. E: 06.06.40. R: 16.07.41.

WENHAM, Ralph Hope. Lance Corporal 58. B: 1918. Hope Cottage, Chat Moss, Irlam and later 56 Caroline St, Irlam. M: Mary Wenham. E: 05.06.40. Home Guard guides. June 1942, 3 Section, 2 Platoon. SD: 03.12.44, HQ Platoon.

WESTLEY, Boyed. B77. B: 1888. 44 Kingsway Park, Davyhulme. W: Margaret Westley. E: 02.07.40. 6 Platoon. R: 26.02.42.

WHALLEY, Harold. Private 942. B: 1899. 4 Gerrards Close, Irlam. W: Mrs M.A. Whalley. E: 16.07.43. 4 Platoon. SD: 03.12.44.

WHALLEY, William. 199. B: 1917. 3 Graham Crescent, Cadishead. M: Mrs Whalley. E: 06.06.40. 5 Platoon and later believed to have served with H Company.

WHEATON, William Arthur. 345. B: 1906. 27 Lytherton Ave, Cadishead. W: Bridget Wheaton. E: 02.07.40. 5 Platoon and later believed to have served with H Company.

WHISTLECROFT, Thomas. 229. B: 1881. 27 Moss Lane, Cadishead. W: Olive Whistlecroft. E: 06.06.40. 4 Platoon. R: 06.06.42.

WHITE, Albert. Private 957. B: 1919. 27 Moss Side Rd, Cadishead. W: Mrs M. White. E: 30.07.43. Serving with 4 Platoon. SD: 03.12.44.

WHITE, Harry. 456. B: 1923. 68 Victory Rd, Cadishead. M: Mrs White. E: 14.09.40. 5 Platoon and later believed to have served with H Company.

WHITE, Oscar Henry. B84. B: 1915. 97 New Moss Rd, Cadishead. W: Leticia White (nee Outlaw). E: 29.09.40. 6 Platoon. HMF: 07.12.40.

WHITEHOUSE, Reginald Stephen. Private 393. B: 1903. 14 Gerrards Close, Irlam. W: Louisa Whitehouse. E: 15.07.40. 2 Section, 2 Platoon. SD: 03.12.44.

WHITFIELD, John W. Private 950. 40 Lynthorpe Ave, Cadishead. W: Mrs E. Whitfield. E: 23.07.43. HQ Platoon. SD: 03.12.44.

WHITTAKER, Robert. 958. B: 1895. 3 Rutland Rd, Cadishead. W: Mrs M. Whittaker. E: 30.07.43. DMU: 26.08.43.

WHITTER, James. B: 1918. 150 Liverpool Rd, Irlam. F: Robert Whitter of Atherton. E: 04.07.40. 2 Platoon. R: 21.05.41.

WHITTLE, John William. 15. B: 1891. 7 The Crescent, Higher Irlam. W: Elizabeth Whittle. E: 29.06.40. 4 Platoon. R: 18.02.42.

WIGGLESWORTH, George. Private 75. B: 1903. 32 Princes Ave, Higher Irlam. W: Gladys Wigglesworth. E: 05.06.40. HG Cadets. June 1942, with 2 Section, 1 Platoon. SD: 03.12.44, HQ Platoon.

WIGNALL, George. 937. 83 Dixon St, Irlam. W: Mrs Wignall. E: 13.07.43. DMU: 26.04.44.

WIGNALL, Joseph Edward. 936. B: 1905. 17 Devon Rd, Cadishead. W: Mrs A. Wignall. E: 28.08.40. 4 Platoon. T: 13.05.42 to H Company.

WILCOCK, Alfred. B80. B: 1879. 268 Liverpool Rd, Irlam. W: Mary Wilcock. E: 28.09.40. 6 Platoon. R: 11.11.41.

WILCOX, Eric. Private 722. B: 1921. 10 Dean Rd, Cadishead. F: William W. Wilcox. E: 21.04.42. 2 Section, 7 Platoon (HQ). T: 12.07.43 to 41ˢᵗ Battalion, Home Guard.

WILDE, Vernon. Private 729.B: 1924. 3 Mond Rd, Higher Irlam. E: 27.04.42. 3 Section, 2 Platoon. HMF: date unknown.

WILES, Christopher Henry. Sergeant B103. B: 1906. 33 Warwick Rd, Cadishead. M: Alice Wiles. E: 25.08.40. 1 Section, 6 Platoon. SD: 03.12.44.

WILKES, Samuel. 193. B: 1879. 7 Palatine Close, Irlam. E: 06.06.40. 3 Platoon and later believed to have served with H Company.

WILKINSON, Peter. Lance Corporal B66. B: 1901. 26 Ferryhill Rd, Irlam. W: Mabel Wilkinson. E: 04.07.40. 2 Section, 6 Platoon. SD: 03.12.44.

WILKINSON, William. B65. B: 1876. 7 Vicarage Rd, Irlam. W: Charlotte Wilkinson. E: 04.07.40. 6 Platoon. R: 18.02.42.

WILLIAMS, Charles Robert. B48. B: 1897. 42 Higher Croft, Barton. W: Mary Williams. E: 05.07.40. 6 Platoon. R: 24.01.42.

WILLIAMS, Edward. 477. B: 1923. 22 Milton Ave, Irlam. 3 Platoon and later believed to have served with H Company.

WILLIAMS, Edward. H10. B: 1907. 2 Chapel Lane, Rixton. W: Mrs Williams. E: 14.02.41. 5 Platoon. HMF: 30.12.41.

WILLIAMS, Edwin. 67. B: 1922. 47 Eldon Rd East, Irlam. F: J. Williams. E: 05.06.40. 2 Platoon. HMF: date unknown.

WILLIAMS, James J.A. 540. E: 04.03.41. Later believed to have served with H Company.

WILLIAMS, James. Sergeant F5. B: 1903. 38 Fiddlers Lane, Higher Irlam. W: Mary Williams. E: 15.07.40. June 1942, lance corporal, 1 (Margarine Works) Section, 4 Platoon. Later served HQ Platoon. SD: 03.12.44.

WILLIAMS, John Llewellyn. 353. B: 1912. 5 Silverdale Ave, Higher Irlam. W: Gladys Williams. HMF: 01.07.41.

WILLIAMS, John Price. Lance Corporal 708. B: 1913. 12 Beech Ave, Higher Irlam. W: Mrs M. Williams. E: 16.04.42. 1 Platoon. SD: 03.12.44.

WILLIAMSON, Gilbert. Private F52. B: 1895. 19 Boundary Rd, Higher Irlam. W: Evelyn Williamson. E: 23.07.40. 4 Platoon and later 1 Platoon. DMU: 21.02.44.

WILLIAMSON, Thomas E. 724. 19 Boundary Rd, Higher Irlam. F: Albert W. Williamson. B: 1924. E: 22.04.42. 3 Section, 1 Platoon. HMF: 31.03.43.

WILLIS, Cedric Charles. Private 707. B: 1925. 54 Fiddlers Lane, Higher Irlam. E: 16.04.42. 1 Section, 1 Platoon. HMF: 31.05.43.

WILLIS, Henry (Harry) Garner . B: 1926. 50 Fiddlers Lane, Higher Irlam. Attached to D Company HQ as cycle orderly, Home Guard messenger.

WILSON, Alfred. 321. B: 1909. 37 Silverdale Ave, Higher Irlam. W: Edna Wilson. E: 22.06.40. 1 Platoon. HMF: 17.03.41.

WILSON, Alfred. Sergeant 145. B: 1893. 15 Fiddlers Lane, Higher Irlam. W: Mrs J. Wilson. E: 06.06.40. 3 Section, 1 Platoon. SD: 03.12.44.

WILSON, Harold. 132. Lieutenant. B: 1899. 137 Liverpool Rd, Irlam. W: Gladys Wilson. E: 05.06.40. 2 Platoon. SD: 03.12.44.

WILSON, Solomon. 44. B: 1882. 12 Mersey Ave, Irlam. W: Maria Wilson. E: 05.06.40. 3 Platoon and later believed to have served with H Company.

WILSON, William Henry. Private 171. B: 1915. 40 Silverdale Ave, Higher Irlam. W: Jesse Wilson. E: 06.06.40. 2 Platoon and later 3 Section, 1 Platoon. SD: 03.12.44.

WINKLE, Harry Roger. 130. B: 1916. 45 Chapel Rd, Irlam. E: 06.06.40. 2 Section, 2 Platoon. HMF: 30.09.42.

WINTER, Edward. 711. B: 1913. 108 Liverpool Rd, Higher Irlam. F: E. Winter. E: 17.04.42. Later believed to have served with 8 Platoon, H Company.

WITHERS, Ernest. Lance Corporal E37. B: 1899. 9 Silverdale Ave, Higher Irlam. W: Mrs K. Withers. E: 02.07.40. 5, 3 and 7 Platoons. June 1942, 2 Section, 5 Platoon. SD: 03.12.44, 7 Platoon.

WOODS, Ernest. Lieutenant 3. B: 1888. 190 Liverpool Rd, Irlam. W: Dorothy Woods. E: 05.06.40. Transport officer with Transport Platoon. SD: 03.12.44, Company HQ.

WOOD, Harry. 388. B: 1922. 61 Harewood Rd, Irlam. F: Jack Wood. E: 15.07.40. R: 06.01.42.

WOOD, Jack. Private 943. B: 1898. 61 Harewood Rd, Irlam. W: Mrs M. Wood. E: 16.07.43. SD: 03.12.44, 4 Platoon.

WOOD, Norman. F566. B: 1897. Mayfield, Boat Lane, Irlam. W: Mary Wood. E: 27.05.41. 4 Platoon. R: 17.09.41.

WOOD, Ralph. 280. B: 1892. 386 Liverpool Rd, Irlam. W: Rose Wood. E: 06.06.40. 3 Platoon and later believed to have served with H Company. R: 13.02.41.

WOODNETT, Joseph. F33. B: 1909. 9 Grosvenor Rd, Urmston. W: Elsie Woodnett. E: 10.07.40. 4 Platoon. HMF: 15.04.41.

WORNER, Harry. 949. B: 20.08.10. 35 Boundary Rd, Higher Irlam and later 6 Mond Rd, Higher Irlam. W: Mrs M. Worner. E: 23.07.43. HQ Platoon. SD: 03.12.44.

WRENCH, Thomas Levi. 418. B: 1923. 6 Ash Ave, Cadishead. F: Percy Wrench. E: 22.07.40. 4 Platoon and later 3 Platoon. R: 13.01.41. HMF: date unknown.

WRIGHT, Austin. Platoon Commander. 5. B: 1885. 27 Prospect Rd, Cadishead. W: Annie Wright. E: 04.06.40. June 1942, with 1 Section, 7 Platoon (HQ). Also known to have been Platoon Commander, 2 Platoon. R: 05.08.43.

WRIGHT, Benjamin. Private. B: 1899. 18 Warwick Rd, Cadishead. W: Winifred Wright. E: 23.07.40. 5 Platoon and later 2 Section, 6 Platoon. DMU: 12.12.43.

WRIGHT, Eric. B: 1915. 583. 9 Prospect Rd, Cadishead. F: Mr Wright. E: 30.05.41. Later believed to have served with 8 Platoon, H Company.

WRIGHT, Joseph Samuel. Private 941. B: 1902. 40 Dam Lane, Rixton and later 39 Carlton Way, Glazebrook. W: Lucy Wright. E: 28.08.40. 2 (Soap Works) Section, 4 Platoon and later with 6 Platoon. DMU: 25.02.44.

WRIGHT, Robert Arthur. 386. B: 1906. 55 New Moss Rd, Cadishead. W: Ann Wright. E: 14.06.40. 4 Platoon and later served 3 Platoon. R: 11.09.41.

WRIGHT, Thomas Henry. Private E49. B: 1903. 9 Prospect Rd, Cadishead and later 93 Eldon Rd, Irlam. E: 06.06.40. 5, 3 and 2 Platoons. June 1942, 1 Section, 5 Platoon. T: 21.11.40 to E Company. Later served 3 Platoon, D Company. SD: 03.12.44.

WRIGLEY, Joseph. Corporal 278. 17 Ash Ave, Cadishead and later 20 Victory Rd, Cadishead. E: 30.05.41. 3 Platoon. R: 12.07.44.

WRIGLEY, William. B57. B: 887. 40 Lord St, Cadishead. W: Edith Wrigley. E: 04.07.40. 6 Platoon. R: 17.02.42.

YATES, Fred. Private B92. 1 Jellicoe Ave, Cadishead. B: 1923. F: Jack Yates. E: 18.07.40. 2 Section, 6 Platoon. SD: 03.12.44.

YATES, Joseph. Lance Corporal 14. B: 1889. 29 Devon Rd, Cadishead. W: Mrs F. Yates. E: 29.06.40. 4 Platoon and later 3 Section, 3 Platoon. T: 09.04.41 to E Company.

YATES, Wilfred. 846. B: 21.08.06. 48 Partington Ave, Irlam. W: Mrs Amy Yates (nee Newton). E: 04.08.42. 5 Platoon. HMF: 02.03.44.

G Company, 42nd Battalion

The below named are only a few of the many hundreds of local men known to have served with G Company and these names have been extracted from various *Guardian* articles published during the war:

BLEASDALE. Corporal.
BOWER, Charles Durand Elcote.
BRACEGIRDLE, G. Private.
BRADY, Francis.
BREWERTON, T.F. Corporal.
BROADSTOCK, E. Private.
BROOKS, R. Lance Corporal.
BROWN, H. Private.
BUCHAN, W.H. Private.
CAVANAGH, L. Private.
CHADWICK. Lance Corporal.
CLARE, A. Lance Corporal.
CRAVEN, G.T. Corporal.
DONNELLY, J. Private.
EANTLEY. Corporal.

EARLAM. Corporal.
EDWARDS, J. Corporal.
ELLIS, J. Corporal.
GLOVER, J. Private.
GOLDEN, H. Lance Corporal.
HAINES, G.R. Captain, Second in Command, G Company.
HARTLEY, A. Lance Corporal.
HASSALL, F.T. Captain.
HEYES, E. Private.
HILL, J.T. Major, Officer Commanding G Company
HUGILL, H. Private.
HULME, N. Corporal.
HUMPHRIES, J. Private.
HUMPHRIES, M. Private.
JENKINS, D. Private.
JOHNSON, J. Corporal.
JONES, J.A. Lance Corporal.
JONES, S. Private.
KING, T. Private.
LEA, G. Lance Corporal.
LEA, H. Private.
LEDSON, G.C. Private.
OCKERBY. Company Sergeant Major.
OVERTON, A. Private.
PAIN. Company Sergeant Major.
PARKIN, G. Sergeant.
PARRY, A. Private.
PARRY, J.R. Private.
PEMBERTON, A. Lance Corporal.
PRICE, J. Private.
SARGESSON, P. Private.
SMITH, D. Private.
STEWART, C.E. Lance Corporal.
TAYLOR, G. Lance Corporal.
TAYLOR, T. Corporal.
WALTON, F. Private.
WATERMAN, A. Corporal.
WATERMAN, W.G. Private.
WHITFIELD, N. Lance Corporal.
WILSON, A. Private.
YARWOOD, J. Sgt.
YOUNG, C.H. Lance Corporal.
YOUNG, J.R. Sergeant.

Other known Home Guardsmen:

DRUM, John. B: 23.11.07 in Irlam. Served with a Home Guard unit at Kingsbury, near London. Passed away 14th April 1994. Brother of Albert (Royal Signals), Robert (Home Guard) and Wilfred (Home Guard).

DRUM, Robert Patrick. 2nd Lieutenant. B: 27.06.12 at Alexandra Grove, Irlam. Moved to Davyhulme in 1937. W: Ellen Drum (nee Davies). E: 03.06.41. 45th Battalion, Home Guard. Promoted to lance corporal 13.10.41, corporal 06.02.42, sergeant 10.08.42. Commissioned, 2nd lieutenant, 28.09.43. SD: 31.12.45. Passed away at Davyhulme, 31st August 2004. Brother of Albert (Royal Signals), John (Home Guard) and Wilfred (Home Guard).

REED, John H. Born in Sunderland. Served in Hollins Green Home Guard. Resided 21 Victory Rd, Cadishead. Died 21st January 1945.

APPENDIX IX
BIBLIOGRAPHY

Ministry of Defence:

MOD	*The Drive on Caen, Northern France 7th June – 9th July 1944* (2004).
MOD	*The Battle of Kohima, North East India 4 April – 22 June 1944* (2005).
Air Historical Branch	*RAF Form 1180 (Accident Record Card)*. Information on RAF casualties: Blackburn, Dale, Green, Killen, Thomas, Jibson, Chappell, Darbyshire and Jaques.
Naval Historical Branch	*S.6833 HMS Ameer, Summary of Service* (August 1965).
Naval Historical Branch	Information on Naval casualties: Ainscough, Darby, Darbyshire, Hillyard, Holley and Morgan.

The National Archives:

HO/198/197	*Air Raid Summary of Occurrences: Raid Summary 3548*, File No. TM/5/2/4 (30), Irlam, 10.09.40.
WO /199 / 3347	*42nd County of Lancaster (Irlam) Battalion HG 4.*
WO /373	*Recommendations for Honours and Awards (Army) 1935-1990.*
War Office	Various battalion war diaries.

Lancashire Records Office (Lancashire Archives):

HG 4/1	*Administrative history: B Company nominal roll, giving members organised by platoon and section, annotated with amendments showing movements, transfers and discharges Jun. 1942 - Mar. 1943.*
HG 4/2	*B Company nominal roll, giving members organised by platoon and section, annotated with amendments showing movements, transfers and discharges Mar. 1943 - Apr. 1944.*
HG 4/3	*D Company nominal roll, noting address, next of kin, year of birth and date of enrolment, annotated with details of transfers, resignations etc 1940-44.*
HG 4/4	*D Company nominal roll of all ranks serving on 3 Dec. 1944, by company structure. Undated 1944.*
HG 4/5	*Archival history: Found in HG 4/3. D Company nominal roll, including rank by detachment and with a letter of reprimand from the East Lancashire Territorial Army and Air Force Association for its incorrect format, Jun. 1942.*
HG 4/6	*Archival history: Found in HG 10/3. E Company Part II Orders, listing postings, transfers, promotions, deaths, discharges, changes of address and other personnel information 2 Jan. 1943 - 21 Nov. 1944*

Newspapers:
Cadishead and Irlam Guardian (1938 to 1949)
Manchester Guardian (1938 to 1945)
Irlam and Cadishead Advertiser (1989)

Publications:

Annis, A.	*Butterflies and Feathers* (Manchester: Ann Annis, 2011).
Beale, P.	*Tank Tracks – 9th Battalion Royal Tank Regiment at War 1940-1945* (Stroud: Sutton Publishing, 1995).
Beeston, M & Culpin, R.	*Irlam and Cadishead in the Past* (Worsley: Duffy, 1986).
Beevor, A.	*D-Day, The Battle for Normandy* (London: Penguin, 2009).
Bell, A.C	*History of the Manchester Regiment : First and Second Battalions 1922-1948* (Altrincham: John Sherratt & Sons, 1954).
Bishop, P.	*Target Tirpitz* (London: Harper Press, 2012).
Churchill, W.	*The Second World War* (London: Pimlico, 1959).

Appendix IX

Clay, E. *The Path of the 50th: The Story of the 50th (Northumbrian) Division in the Second World War 1939-1945* (Aldershot: Gale & Polden, 1950).

Cottam, L. *Farmer, Sailor, Preacher – an autobiography*

Doyle, P. *ARP and Civil Defence in the Second World War* (Oxford: Shire Publications, 2010).

Duckers, P. *British Campaign Medals 1914-2000* (Shire Publications, 2001)

Durnford-Slater, J. *Commando: Memoirs of a Fighting Commando in World War Two* (London: Greenhill Books, 2002).

Evans, A.S. *Beneath the waves: A History of HM Submarine Losses 1904-1971* (London: William Kimber & Co. Ltd., 1986).

Farran, R. *Winged Dagger* (London: Cassell, 1948).

Ford, K. *D-Day Commando – From Normandy to the Maas with 48 Royal Marine Commando* (Stroud: Sutton Publishing, 2005).

Gordon, L. *British Battles and Medals.* Revised by Hayward, J., Birch, D. & Bishop, R. (Spink, 7th Edition, 2006).

Halley, D. *With Wingate in Burma* (London: William Hodge & Co. Ltd., 1945).

Knight, P. *The 59th Division: Its War Story* (59th (Staffordshire) Infantry Division Reunion Organisation, 1954).

Longden, S. *Dunkirk: The Men They Left Behind* (Constable & Robinson Ltd., 2009)

Martin, H.G. *The History of the Fifteenth Scottish Division 1939-1945* (Edinburgh and London: William Blackwood & Sons, 1948).

McLynn, F. *The Burma Campaign: Disaster into Triumph 1942-45* (London: Vintage Books, 2011).

Mackay, J. & Mussell, J.W. *Medal Yearbook* (Token Publishing Ltd, 2004).

Mitchell, R. *They Did What Was Asked of Them: 41 (Royal Marines) Commando 1942-1946* (Poole: Firebird Books, 1996).

Neillands, R. *Eighth Army: From the Western Desert to the Alps 1939-1945* (John Murray (Publishers), 2004).

Norman, W. *Halifax Squadron: the Wartime Bombing Operations of No. 640 Squadron, Leconfield.* Preston, Lancashire: Compaid Graphics/Bill Norman Publications, 2005.

Rossiter, M. *Bomber Flights Berlin* (London: Corgi Books, 2011).

Smith, P.J.C. *Luftwaffe over Manchester: The Blitz Years 1940-1944* (Manchester: Neil Richardson Publication, 2003).

Robertson, G.W. *The Rose and the Arrow: A Life Story of 136th (1st West Lancashire) Field Regiment, Royal Artillery 1939-46* (England: 136 Field Regiment Old Comrades Association).

Rushton, J. *The Whirligig of Time.* (BBC WW2 People's War, Article ID: A2901124)

Molesworth, G. *History of the Somerset Light Infantry (Prince Albert's): 1919-1945* (Naval & Military Press, 2003).

Sebag-Montefiore, H. *Dunkirk: Fight to the Last Man* (London: Penguin Books, 2007).

Spencer, W. *Medals: The Researcher's Guide* (Kew: The National Archives, 2006).

Storey, N.R. *The Home Guard* (Oxford: Shire Publications, 2009).

Woodman, R. *Arctic Convoys 1941-1945* (Barnsley: Pen and Sword Maritime, 2007).

Other Sources:
Irlam, Cadishead and District Local History Society. *Wartime Memories.*
Diary of Naval Gunner Kenneth Leech (unpublished)
Diary of Naval Gunner Frank Parry (unpublished)

Websites:
53rdmediumregtra.webs.com
www.53rdwelshdiv.webs.com
www.ancestry.co.uk
bbc.co.uk/ww2peopleswar
www.britishmedalforum.com
www.cofepowdb.org.uk
www.convoyweb.org.uk
www.cwgc.org

www.deepimage.co.uk
www.hansonclan.co.uk
www.historylearningsite.co.uk
hmsmahratta.50megs.com/index.html
www.kenthistoryforum.co.uk
www.naval-history.net
oldirlamvillage.atfreeforum.com
www.ordersofbattle.com
www.pegasusarchive.org
www.rafweb.org
www.royalnavyresearcharchive.org.uk
royalartilleryunitsnetherlands1944-1945.com
www.royalengineersbombdisposal-eod.org.uk
salfordwarmemorials.proboards.com
www.ww2talk.com